Java Programming

Complete Concepts and Techniques

Java Programming

Complete Concepts and Techniques

Gary B. Shelly

Thomas J. Cashman

Joy L. Starks

COURSE
TECHNOLOGY
™
THOMSON LEARNING

COURSE TECHNOLOGY
25 THOMSON PLACE
BOSTON MA 02210

SHELLY
CASHMAN
SERIES®

Australia • Canada • Denmark • Japan • Mexico • New Zealand • Philippines • Puerto Rico • Singapore
South Africa • Spain • United Kingdom • United States

**COURSE
TECHNOLOGY**

™

THOMSON LEARNING

COPYRIGHT © 2001 Course Technology, a division of Thomson Learning.
Printed in the United States of America

Asia (excluding Japan)
Thomson Learning
60 Albert Street, #15-01
Albert Complex
Singapore 189969

Japan
Thomson Learning
Palaceside Building 5F
1-1-1 Hitotsubashi, Chiyoda-ku
Tokyo 100 0003 Japan

Australia/New Zealand
Nelson/Thomson Learning
102 Dodds Street
South Melbourne, Victoria 3205
Australia

Latin America
Thomson Learning
Seneca, 53
Colonia Polanco
11560 Mexico D.F. Mexico

South Africa
Thomson Learning
Zonnebloem Building,
Constantia Square
526 Sixteenth Road
P.O. Box 2459
Halfway House, 1685
South Africa

Canada
Nelson/Thomson Learning
1120 Birchmount Road
Scarborough, Ontario
Canada M1K 5G4

UK/Europe/Middle East
Thomson Learning
Berkshire House
168-173 High Holborn
London, WC1V 7AA United Kingdom

Spain
Thomson Learning
Calle Magallanes, 25
28015-MADRID
ESPANA

PHOTO CREDITS: *Project 1, pages J 1.2-3* Scott McNealy, Bill Joy and Sun server photos, Courtesy of Sun Microsystems, Inc.; *Project 2, pages J 2.2-3* Car, couple at computer, ticket, Courtesy of PhotoDisc, Inc.; *Project 3, pages J 3.2-3* Plant leaves, butterflies, Courtesty of PhotoDisc, Inc.; *Project 4, pages J 4.2-3* Map, Courtesy of PhotoDisc, Inc.; *Project 5, pages J 5.2-3* American flag, Courtesy of PhotoDisc, Inc., Background, Courtesy of Corbis; *Project 6, pages J 6.2-3* Hubble's look at Mars, Courtesy of NASA and STScI, laptop with Java code, Courtesy of PhotoDisc, Inc.; *Project 7, pages J 7.2-3* Space views, astronaut, Space Shuttle, satellite, Courtesy of Digital Stock.

ISBN 0-7895-6099-2

1 2 3 4 5 6 7 8 9 10   BC   05 04 03 02 01

Java Programming

Complete Concepts and Techniques

C O N T E N T S

● PROJECT 2

MANIPULATING DATA USING METHODS

● PROJECT 3

DECISION, REPETITION, AND COMPONENTS IN JAVA

Preface

The Shelly Cashman Series® offers the finest books in computer education. In our Java books, you will find an educationally sound and easy-to-follow pedagogy that combines a step-by-step approach with corresponding screens. An Introduction to Java Programming section at the beginning of the book emphasizes good programming practices and gives students the foundation to produce well-written applications and applets. The Other Ways and More About features offer in-depth knowledge of Java. The project openers provide a fascinating perspective on the subject covered in the project. The Shelly Cashman Series Java books will make your programming class exciting and dynamic and one that your students will remember as one of their better educational experiences.

Objectives of This Textbook

Java Programming: Complete Concepts and Techniques is intended for a three-credit course on Java programming. No experience with a computer is assumed, and no mathematics beyond the high school freshman level is required. The objectives of this book are:

- To teach the basic concepts and methods of object-oriented programming
- To teach the fundamentals of Java programming
- To use practical problems to illustrate application-building techniques
- To use applets for Web publishing and interactivity
- To encourage independent study and help those who are working alone in a distance education environment
- To use Java's Abstract Windows Toolkit (AWT) to build applications and applets with a graphical user interface
- To teach the efficiency of using Java as a programming language
- To teach the advantages of using IDE software over JDK

When students complete the course using this book, they will have a firm knowledge and understanding of beginning Java and will be able to develop a wide variety of applications.

Obtaining a Copy of Borland JBuilder 3.0 University Edition

A copy of Borland JBuilder 3.0 University Edition as well as a 60 day trial edition of the Borland JBuilder Enterprise Edition is included at no additional cost with this text, so your students will have their own copy of JBuilder University Edition. Bundling the textbook and software is ideal for those schools without an IDE version of Java or for students working at home at their own personal computers. Because Borland's JBuilder 3.0 University Edition does not contain all of the standard features of the Enterprise Edition, some projects in this book may be limited, depending on which version of Java you use.

Other Ways

1. To add project, click Add to Project button in Navigation Pane toolbar
2. To add project, press ALT+INSERT
3. To compile, press CTRL+F9
4. To execute, press F9

More About

Array Data

If you want to store data of different types in a single structure, or if you need a structure whose size can change dynamically, use a Collection implementation, such as a Vector, instead of an array.

The Shelly Cashman Approach

Features of the Shelly Cashman Series Java books include:

- **Project Orientation:** Each project in the book builds a complete application using the three-step process: designing the application, writing structured code, and converting to an applet.

- **Screen-by-Screen, Step-by-Step Instructions:** Each of the tasks required to complete a project is identified throughout the development of the project. Then, steps to accomplish the task are specified. The steps are accompanied by screens.

- **Thoroughly Tested Projects:** Every screen in the book is correct because it is produced by the author only after performing a step, resulting in unprecedented quality.

- **Other Ways Boxes for Reference:** When the Java environment provides a variety of ways to carry out a given task, the steps are followed by an Other Ways box. Displayed at the end of many of the step-by-step sequences, the Other Ways boxes specify alternate methods to accomplish the task completed in the steps. Thus, the steps and the Other Ways box make a comprehensive reference unit.

- **More About Feature:** These marginal annotations provide background information that complement the topics covered, adding interest and depth to learning.

Organization of This Textbook

JavaProgramming: Complete Concepts and Techniques provides detailed instruction on how to use Java. The material is divided into an introductory section and seven projects as follows:

Introduction to Java Programming This section provides an overview of Java, program development methodology, structured programming, control structures, and object-oriented programming.

Project 1 – Creating a Java Program Project 1 introduces students to the basic elements of Java. Students develop a splash screen for Anita's Antiques, an e-commerce Web site. The process of building the application consists of three steps: designing the application, writing source code, and testing the applicaton. Topics include starting NotePad; writing a simple Java output program; inserting block and line comments as documentation; compiling and executing a Java program; editing and saving source code; and converting the application to an applet.

Project 2 – Manipulating Data Using Methods Project 2 teaches students how to create a program that stores and retrieves data. Variables, operators, formulas and a variety of Java methods are used to create an application for Bert's Loan Kiosk. Topics include entering sample data; using proper naming conventions; using constructors to add labels, text fields and buttons; adding interactive components into an applet; and identifying Java source code files and Java class files on a storage device.

Project 3 – Decision, Repetition, and Componets in Java Project 3 extends the basics of building applications. The CandleLine Shipping Charges application in this project consists of components and decision structures. Topics include coding structures and events; designing a program using components; writing decision structures; testing individual components; and using addItemListener to add components to an applet.

Project 4 – External Classes, Arrays, and Choices Project 4 discusses how to use arrays and manipulate large amounts of data. Topics include reviewing code behind a sorting algorithm and using it to sort an array of names and data; referencing array elements and subscript numbers; employing various operators; and adding Choice components to applets.

Project 5 – Using Java's Abstract Windows Toolkit Project 5 teaches students how to use AWT components in a stand-alone application and in an applet by creating a Calculator Program. Topics include placing objects in containers; converting values; performing sequential searches; writing code to implement methods; and setting frame attributes.

Project 6 – Using External Data Project 6 teaches students how to create a GUI-based application which creates a data file and will operate on any computer platform. Topics covered include volatile and non-volatile data; sequential and random access files; using super keywords to override a class; an explanation of client/server architecture; and identification of the parts of a two-tier, three-tier, and multi-tier system.

Project 7 – Using the JBuilder IDE Project 7 uses the Calculator Program created in Project 5 to teach students how to use an Integrated Development Environment to increase productivity. Topics include working with the JBuilder interface, wizards, and properties; editing tools; compiling a program using JBuilder; creating an Applet Project using JBuilder; and using Help.

Appendices

Appendix A describes how to download the Java 2 Standard Development Kit (SDK) from the Sun Microsystems Web site. Instructions for installing both the SDK and JBuilder 3.0 University Edition are also included. Appendix B provides a list of reserved keywords in Java. Appendix C describes the types of certification available for Java programmers and developers and information on certification exams. Appendix D describes the compile and runtime options you may include at the command prompt and some programming exceptions for input and output errors.

End-of-Project Student Activities

A notable strength of the Shelly Cashman Series Java books is the extensive student activities at the end of each project. Well-structured student activities can make the difference between students merely participating in a class and students retaining the information they learn. The end-of-project activities in the Shelly Cashman Series Java books follows.

- **What You Should Know** This section includes a listing of the tasks completed within a project together with the pages where the step-by-step, screen-by-screen explanations appear. This section provides a perfect study review for students.
- **Test Your Knowledge** Four pencil-and-paper activities designed to determine the students' understanding of the material in the project are included in this section. Included are true/false questions, multiple-choice questions, and two short-answer activities.

- **Apply Your Knowledge** This exercise requires students to open and manipulate a file on the Java Data Disk that accompanies the Java book. Students may obtain a copy of the Java Data Disk by following the instructions on the inside back cover of this book.

- **In the Lab** Three in-depth assignments per project require students to apply the knowledge gained in the project to solve problems on a computer.

- **Cases and Places** These six unique case studies require students to apply their knowledge to real-world situations.

Shelly Cashman Series Teaching Tools

A comprehensive set of Teaching Tools accompanies this book in the form of a CD-ROM. The CD-ROM includes an electronic Instructor's Manual and teaching and testing aids. The CD-ROM (ISBN 0-7895-5967-6) is available through your Course Technology representative or by calling one of the following telephone numbers: Colleges and Universities, 1-800-648-7450; High Schools, 1-800-824-5179; and Career Colleges, 1-800-477-3692. The contents of the CD-ROM follow.

- **Instructor's Manual** The Instructor's Manual is composed of Microsoft Word files. The files include lecture notes, solutions to laboratory assignments, and a large test bank. The files allow you to modify the lecture notes or generate quizzes and exams from the test bank using your own word processor. Where appropriate, solutions to laboratory assignments are embedded as icons in the files.

- **Figures in the Book** Illustrations for most of the figures in the textbook are available. Use this ancillary to create a slide show from the illustrations for lecture or to print transparencies for use in lecture with an overhead projector.

- **Course Test Manager** Course Test Manager is a powerful testing and assessment package that enables instructors to create and print tests from the large test bank. Instructors with access to a networked computer lab (LAN) can administer, grade, and track tests online. Students also can take online practice tests, which generate customized study guides that indicate where in the book students can find more information for each question.

- **Lecture Success System** Lecture Success System files are for use with the application software, a personal computer, and projection device to explain and illustrate the step-by-step, screen-by-screen development of a project in the book without entering large amounts of data.

- **Instructor's Lab Solutions** Solutions and required files for all the In the Lab assignments at the end of each project are available.

- **Student Files** All the files that are required by the student to complete the Apply Your Knowledge exercises are included.

- **Interactive Labs** Eighteen hands-on interactive labs, which take the student from 10 to 15 minutes each to complete, help solidify and reinforce mouse and keyboard usage and computer concepts. Student assessment is available in each interactive lab by means of a Print button. The assessment requires students to answer questions.

Distance Learning

Various distance learning options are available for your Java programming course:

MyCourse.com

MyCourse.com is an online syllabus builder and course enhancement tool. Hosted by Course Technology, MyCourse.com adds value to your course by providing additional content that reinforces student learning.

Most importantly, MyCourse.com is flexible. You can choose how you want to organize the material — by date, by class session, or by using the default organization, which organizes content by chapter. MyCourse.com allows you to add your own materials, including hyperlinks, school logos, assignments, announcements, and other course content. If you are using more than one book, you even can build a course that includes all of your Course Technology texts in one easy-to-use site!

Start building your own course today! Just go to www.mycourse.com/instructor

WebCT and Blackboard

For an additional charge, you can create a distance learning course in either WebCT or Blackboard. Course Technology has partnered with WebCT and Blackboard to offer state of the art Course Management tools and high quality content so you can add an online component to your course or offer a full course online. Course Technology provides robust content in addition to the content from your textbook — in essence, a pre-assembled course. You can select one of the following options: hosting courses at your school, WebCT, or Blackboard. Visit www.course.com/distancelearning for more information.

Data Disk for Java Programming

The Java Data Disk is required for some of the exercises and projects. Students can obtain a copy of the Java Data Disk by following the instructions on the inside back cover of this book. The Shelly Cashman Series Teaching Tools CD-ROM contains a copy of the files that comprise the Java Data Disk.

Shelly Cashman Online

Shelly Cashman Online is a World Wide Web service available to instructors and students of computer education. Visit Shelly Cashman Online at www.scseries.com

- **Series Information** This site contains information on the Shelly Cashman Series products.
- **Teaching Resources** This area includes password-protected instructor materials.
- **Student Center** The Student Center is dedicated to students learning about computers with Shelly Cashman Series books and software. This area includes cool links, data that can be downloaded, and much more.
- **Community** The Shelly Cashman Series team provides opportunities to discuss your course and your ideas with instructors in your field and with the Series team.
- **Java Programming Web Site** More information on various Java topics, as described in the More About sidebars in each project, is available at www.scsite.com/java/more.htm

Acknowledgments

The Shelly Cashman Series would not be the leading computer education series without the contributions of outstanding publishing professionals. First, and foremost, among them is Becky Herrington, director of production and designer. She is the heart and soul of the Shelly Cashman Series, and it is only through her leadership, dedication, and tireless efforts that superior products are made possible. Becky created and produced the award-winning Windows series of books.

Under Becky's direction, the following individuals made significant contributions to these books: Doug Cowley, production manager; Ginny Harvey, series specialist; Ken Russo, senior Web designer; Mike Bodnar, associate production manager; Mark Norton, Web designer; Meena Moest, production editor; Michelle French, Christy Pardini, Chris Schneider, and Kenny Tran, graphic artists; Jeanne Black, Quark expert; Lyn Markowicz, copyeditor; Kim Kosmatka, proofreader; Cristina Haley, indexer; and Sarah Evertson of Image Quest, photo researcher.

Special thanks go to Richard Keaveny, associate publisher; Lora Wade, product manager; Francis Schurgot Web product manager, Erin Bennett, associate product manager; Marc Ouellette, associate Web product manager; Erin Runyon, editorial assistant; and Samantha Smith Cooper, developmental editor. Particular thanks go to the the reviewers of this book, Jean Curtin, Bill Dorin, Kristen Enders, Laurel Helm (Projects Introductory-2), Mark Jaeger, Deborah LaBelle, Neil Mercer, and Michael Mick.

Gary B. Shelly
Thomas J. Cashman
Joy L. Starks

Shelly Cashman Series – Traditionally Bound Textbooks

The Shelly Cashman Series presents the following computer subjects in a variety of traditionally bound textbooks. For more information, see your Course Technology representative or call 1-800-648-7450. For Shelly Cashman Series information, visit Shelly Cashman Online at **www.scseries.com**

COMPUTERS	
Computers	Discovering Computers 2002: Concepts for a Digital World, Web Enhanced, Complete Edition
	Discovering Computers 2002: Concepts for a Digital World, Web Enhanced, Introductory Edition
	Discovering Computers 2002: Concepts for a Digital World, Web Enhanced, Brief Edition
	Discovering Computers 2001: Concepts for a Connected World, Web and CNN Enhanced
	Discovering Computers 2001: Concepts for a Connected World, Web and CNN Enhanced, Brief Edition
	Teachers Discovering Computers: Integrating Technology in the Classroom
	Exploring Computers: A Record of Discovery 4e
	Study Guide for Discovering Computers 2002: Concepts for a Digital World, Web Enhanced
	Essential Introduction to Computers 4e (32-page)

WINDOWS APPLICATIONS	
Microsoft Office	Microsoft Office 2000: Essential Concepts and Techniques (5 projects)
	Microsoft Office 2000: Brief Concepts and Techniques (9 projects)
	Microsoft Office 2000: Introductory Concepts and Techniques, Enhanced Edition (15 projects)
	Microsoft Office 2000: Advanced Concepts and Techniques (11 projects)
	Microsoft Office 2000: Post Advanced Concepts and Techniques (11 projects)
	Microsoft Office 97: Introductory Concepts and Techniques, Brief Edition (6 projects)
	Microsoft Office 97: Introductory Concepts and Techniques, Essentials Edition (10 projects)
	Microsoft Office 97: Introductory Concepts and Techniques, Enhanced Edition (15 projects)
	Microsoft Office 97: Advanced Concepts and Techniques
Microsoft Works	Microsoft Works 6: Complete Concepts and Techniques[1] • Microsoft Works 2000: Complete Concepts and Techniques[1] • Microsoft Works 4.5[1]
Microsoft Windows	Microsoft Windows 2000: Complete Concepts and Techniques (6 projects)
	Microsoft Windows 2000: Introductory Concepts and Techniques (3 projects)
	Microsoft Windows 2000: Brief Concepts and Techniques (2 projects)
	Microsoft Windows 98: Essential Concepts and Techniques (2 projects)
	Microsoft Windows 98: Complete Concepts and Techniques (6 projects)[2]
	Introduction to Microsoft Windows NT Workstation 4
	Microsoft Windows 95: Complete Concepts and Techniques[1]
Word Processing	Microsoft Word 2000[2] • Microsoft Word 97[1] • Microsoft Word 7[1]
Spreadsheets	Microsoft Excel 2000[2] • Microsoft Excel 97[1] • Microsoft Excel 7[1] • Microsoft Excel 5[1] • Lotus 1-2-3 97[1]
Database	Microsoft Access 2000[2] • Microsoft Access 97[1] • Microsoft Access 7[1]
Presentation Graphics	Microsoft PowerPoint 2000[2] • Microsoft PowerPoint 97[1] • Microsoft PowerPoint 7[1]
Desktop Publishing	Microsoft Publisher 2000[1]

PROGRAMMING	
Programming	Microsoft Visual Basic 6: Complete Concepts and Techniques[1]
	Microsoft Visual Basic 5: Complete Concepts and Techniques[1]
	QBasic • QBasic: An Introduction to Programming • Microsoft BASIC
	Java Programming: Complete Concepts and Techniques[1] • Structured COBOL Programming 2e

INTERNET	
Browser	Microsoft Internet Explorer 5: An Introduction • Microsoft Internet Explorer 4: An Introduction
	Netscape Navigator 6: An Introduction • Netscape Navigator 4: An Introduction
Web Page Creation and Design	HTML: Complete Concepts and Techniques[1] • Microsoft FrontPage 2000: Complete Concepts and Techniques[1] • Web Page Design: Introductory Concepts and Techniques • Netscape Composer 6
	JavaScript: Complete Concepts and Techniques[1]

SYSTEMS ANALYSIS	
Systems Analysis	Systems Analysis and Design 4e

DATA COMMUNICATIONS	
Data Communications	Business Data Communications: Introductory Concepts and Techniques 3e

[1]Also available as an Introductory Edition, which is a shortened version of the complete book
[2]Also available as an Introductory Edition, which is a shortened version of the complete book and also as a Comprehensive Edition, which is an extended version of the complete book

Shelly Cashman Series – Custom Edition® Program

If you do not find a Shelly Cashman Series traditionally bound textbook to fit your needs, the Shelly Cashman Series unique **Custom Edition** program allows you to choose from a number of options and create a textbook perfectly suited to your course. Features of the **Custom Edition** program are:

- Textbooks that match the content of your course
- Educational materials for the latest versions of personal computer applications software
- Shelly Cashman Series quality, with the same full-color materials and Shelly Cashman Series pedagogy found in the traditionally bound books
- Affordable pricing so your students receive the **Custom Edition** at a cost similar to that of traditionally bound books

The table on the right summarizes the available materials.

For more information, see your Course Technology representative or call one of the following telephone numbers: Colleges and Universities, 1-800-648-7450; High Schools, 1-800-824-5179; and Career Colleges, 1-800-477-3692; Canada, 1-800-268-2222; and Corporations and Government Agencies, 1-800-340-7450.

For Shelly Cashman Series information, visit Shelly Cashman Online at **www.scseries.com**

COMPUTERS	
Computers	Discovering Computers 2002: Concepts for a Digital World, Web Enhanced, Complete Edition
	Discovering Computers 2002: Concepts for a Digital World, Web Enhanced, Introductory Edition
	Discovering Computers 2002: Concepts for a Digital World, Web Enhanced, Brief Edition
	Discovering Computers 2001: Concepts for a Connected World, Web and CNN Enhanced
	Discovering Computers 2001: Concepts for a Connected World, Web and CNN Enhanced, Brief Edition
	Study Guide for Discovering Computers 2002: Concepts for a Digital World, Web Enhanced
	Essential Introduction to Computers 4e (32-page)

OPERATING SYSTEMS	
Microsoft Windows	Microsoft Windows 2000: Complete Concepts and Techniques (6 projects)
	Microsoft Windows 2000: Introductory Concepts and Techniques (3 projects)
	Microsoft Windows 2000: Brief Concepts and Techniques (2 projects)
	Microsoft Windows 98: Essential Concepts and Techniques (2 projects)
	Microsoft Windows 98: Introductory Concepts and Techniques (3 projects)
	Microsoft Windows 98: Complete Concepts and Techniques (6 projects)
	Microsoft Windows 98: Comprehensive Concepts and Techniques (9 projects)
	Microsoft Windows 95: Introductory Concepts and Techniques (2 projects)
	Introduction to Microsoft Windows NT Workstation 4
	Introduction to Microsoft Windows 95 (3 projects)
	Microsoft Windows 95: Complete Concepts and Techniques

WINDOWS APPLICATIONS	
Microsoft Office	Microsoft Office 2000: Brief Concepts and Techniques (5 projects)
	Microsoft Office 97: Introductory Concepts and Techniques, Brief Edition (396-pages)
	Microsoft Office 97: Introductory Concepts and Techniques, Essentials Edition (672-pages)
	Object Linking and Embedding (OLE) (32-page)
	Microsoft Outlook 97 • Microsoft Schedule+ 7
	Using Microsoft Office 97 (16-page)
	Using Microsoft Office 95 (16-page)
	Introduction to Integrating Office 97 Applications (48-page)
	Introduction to Integrating Office 95 Applications (80-page)
Word Processing	Microsoft Word 2000* • Microsoft Word 97* • Microsoft Word 7*
Spreadsheets	Microsoft Excel 2000* • Microsoft Excel 97* • Microsoft Excel 7*
	Lotus 1-2-3 97* • Quattro Pro 6
Database	Microsoft Access 2000* • Microsoft Access 97* • Microsoft Access 7*
Presentation Graphics	Microsoft PowerPoint 2000* • Microsoft PowerPoint 97*
	Microsoft PowerPoint 7*

INTERNET	
Internet	The Internet: Introductory Concepts and Techniques (UNIX)
Browser	Netscape Navigator 4 • Netscape Navigator 3
	Microsoft Internet Explorer 5 • Microsoft Internet Explorer 4
	Microsoft Internet Explorer 3
Web Page Creation	Netscape Composer

*Also available as a mini-module

Java Programming

Java Programming

Java First, an Introduction to Java Programming

You will have mastered the material in this project when you can:

OBJECTIVES

- Describe why Java is a good tool to learn computer programming
- Relate Java's history to the history of other programming languages
- Describe each of the steps in the program development life cycle
- Define structured programming
- Read and explain a flowchart
- Read and explain a hierarchical input process output (HIPO) chart
- Explain sequence, selection, and repetition control structures
- Describe object-oriented programming (OOP)
- Define the terms: objects, attributes, methods, and events
- Compare object-speak terminology to parts of speech
- Read, explain, and create a generalization hierarchy
- Read, explain, and create an object structure diagram
- Read, explain, and create an event diagram
- Define and explain encapsulation, inheritance, and polymorphism
- Describe rapid application development (RAD) and prototyping
- List the benefits of object-oriented programming (OOP)

Java Programming

Java First, an Introduction to Java Programming

CASE PERSPECTIVE

Over the years, the Computer Technology Department at Central College has tried a variety of different programming languages in its Introduction to Programming Concepts course. The course attracts a wide array of students — both computer majors and minors, as well as students from other disciplines who know how vital computer skills have become. While many students have been successful in the course, instructors report that some students come to advanced courses focused on screens, graphics, and buttons of the user interface, but know little about the underlying structures of good programs.

The Computer Technology Department has asked students to enroll in a special trial section of this first programming course, taught with the Java programming language. The department hopes that the structure of Java, along with its object-oriented features and Web application, will facilitate the learning of programming constructs and help students to develop good beginning programming skills. If successful, next semester all sections of Introduction to Programming Concepts will use Java. You decide to enroll in the course.

INTRODUCTION

I

Introduction

Why Java? Why first?

▶ Beginning programmers need to learn the basic concepts of computer programming and the elementary structures that create good programs. *Java is a structured language.*

▶ Beginning programmers are more likely to improve when they see that their work is applicable to the real world. *Java is the language of choice for applications on the Web.*

▶ Beginning programmers who persevere tend to do so in direct relationship to accessibility to hardware and software. *Java is platform-independent.*

▶ Beginning programmers want to learn what is marketable. *Java is object-oriented.*

Java is a good general-purpose programming language. Schools, companies, and software houses are realizing that Java is extremely marketable, and that it provides the structured basis necessary to write good computer programs. Most industries that write computer programs also are coming to realize that object-oriented approaches create programs that are easier to develop, debug, and maintain. Beginning students, who are sometimes overwhelmed by the complexity of programming languages or those who become carried away with the bells and whistles of graphical user interfaces, need the structure — with the interactivity — of a language like Java to develop good programming habits.

What Is Java?

Java is a computer programming language. Before a computer can start to produce desired results, it must have a step-by-step or systematic description of the task to be accomplished. A computer **program** is a set of instructions that tells a computer what to do. Java is a newcomer to the more than 2,000 programming languages and tools used to write computer programs. A **programming language** is a set of words, symbols, and codes used to create instructions a computer can understand or recognize. **High-level languages**, like Java, use commands and words instead of cryptic numeric codes or memory location addresses to process data into information. Each instruction in a high-level language corresponds to many instructions in the computer's machine language. The particular set of grammar or rules that specify how the instructions are to be written is called the **syntax** of the language.

History of Java

Java was designed in the early 1990s by a team from Sun Microsystems lead by James Gosling. Java designers began with the basic syntax of languages like C, C++, and Smalltalk. The Java team wanted to develop a compact object-oriented language. Java first was used for information appliances such as cellular phones; however, within a few years, Sun Microsystems was using Java to provide animation and interactivity on the World Wide Web. IBM has adopted Java as its major application development language.

Web browsers have provided the opportunity to run Java **applets**, which are mini-programs that can be downloaded and executed as part of a displayed Web page. This has made Java the language of choice for applications on the Web. **JavaScript** is not the same as Java. It is a scripting tool created by Netscape and Sun to insert code statements directly into the **hypertext markup language (HTML)** of a Web page, adding functionality and improving the appearance of the Web page. Unlike a JavaScript statement, which is embedded in the HTML document, an applet is sent to the browser as a separate file alongside an HTML document. Examples of applets might include adding an interactive animation or game to a Web page.

Java is the fastest growing programming language in the world due in part to the design team's successful effort to make the language parsimonious, robust, secure, and portable. Computer professionals use the word **parsimonious** to mean that a language has a compact set of commands without numerous versions or adaptations of the same command. **Robust** means that Java supports the development of programs that do not accidentally overwrite memory and corrupt data, making Java suitable for network and distributed applications. Access to arrays of data, for example, is checked at run time to ensure that such access is within bounds. Java is a **strongly typed language**, which means that its compiler provides extensive compile-time checking for potential problems with data types — a big plus for beginning programmers. Java is **secure** because its programs are easy to protect from viruses and tampering.

Portability is attributed to a computer program if it can be used in an operating system other than the one in which it was created, without requiring major rework. Java is **platform-independent,** which means that it is architecturally neutral. You can use Java to write a program on any platform with any operating system, whether it is a PC, Macintosh, Unix, or mainframe machine. The Java **compiler,** which comes with Sun's Java Development Kit (JDK), converts the Java source code into computer-readable object code called **bytecode.** The same object bytecode can be run on any computer, as long as the computer has an **interpreter** to execute the Java byte-code. The interpreter for the Java programming language is called the **Java Virtual Machine (JVM).** The JVM, which also comes with the JDK, contains the interpreter and the run-time system. The **run-time system** includes all the files and packages necessary to run Java programs. Other programming languages need system-specific interpreters and compilers.

In this text, the Java Development Kit will be used to develop **stand-alone** programs, which means that the programs can run independent of any other software. The programs will be executed by typing commands at the command prompt of the operating system, without an external user interface. Programs that run from the command line of an operating system are said to run in **console mode.** Many user interfaces and **Integrated Development Environments (IDEs)** have been developed to assist with the writing of Java programs. However, because schools and businesses may use a wide variety of different user interfaces and IDEs, running your programs in the console mode will make this text portable. It also will employ only true Java commands and classes, rather than those created by the interface. In each project, you will run your program in console mode and then you will modify the code to execute your program with the Java Applet Viewer. You also can run the modified version with a Web browser. You will learn more about Java's Web capabilities and IDEs as you progress through the projects.

Sun Microsystems released the Java 2 SDK Platform in 1999. The SDK includes the development tools such as the compiler, and the Java 2 Runtime Environment, Standard Edition, ver. 1.2. For more information on downloading the software from the Sun Microsystems Web site, see Appendix A. Inprise's J-Builder 3 University Edition, which may be included on a CD-ROM in the back of the book, also installs the Java 2 SDK.

Programming a Computer

Most computer users do not write their own programs. Programs required for common business and personal applications such as word processing or spreadsheets can be purchased from software vendors or stores that sell computer products. These purchased programs are referred to as application software packages. **Applications** are programs that tell a computer how to accept instructions from the end user and how to produce information in response to those instructions.

Even though good application programs can be purchased inexpensively, people still need to learn programming. Learning a programming language improves logical and critical thinking skills for computer-related careers, and teaches why applications perform as they do. Large companies need industry-specific software not available in the retail market due to its limited use. Programs need constant maintenance and monitoring. Smaller companies want programs that can be adjusted and tailored to fit their needs. The software houses that produce application software always are looking for more programmers. As hardware, networking, and the Internet progress and change, people will be needed to meet the challenge of creating new applications. Programming, a combination of engineering and art, is a marketable skill.

The Program Development Life Cycle

Programmers do not sit down and start writing code right away. Instead, they follow an organized plan, or **methodology**, that breaks the process into a series of tasks. Just as there are many programming languages, there are many application development methodologies. These different methodologies, however, tend to be variations of what is called the **program development life cycle (PDLC)**. The PDLC follows these six steps: (1) analyze the problem, (2) design the program, (3) code the program, (4) test the program, (5) formalize the solution, and (6) maintain the program. Table I-1 describes each step that a programmer goes through to arrive at a computer application. Figure I-1 portrays the PDLC as a continuing process or loop. When the maintenance phase identifies change, the cycle begins again.

Table I-1	Steps in the Program Development Life Cycle	
STEP	PROCEDURE	DESCRIPTION
1	Analyze the problem	Precisely define the problem to be solved, and write program specifications — descriptions of the program's inputs, processing, outputs, and user interface.
2	Design the program	Use algorithmic thinking to develop a detailed logic plan using tools such as pseudocode, flowcharts, object structure diagrams, or event diagrams to group the program's activities into modules; devise a method of solution or algorithm for each module; and test the solution algorithms.
3	Code the program	Translate the design into an application using a programming language or application development tool or IDE, by creating the user interface and writing code; including internal documentation (comments and remarks) within the code that explains the purpose of the code statements.
4	Test the program	Test the program, finding and correcting errors (debugging) until it is error-free and contains enough safeguards to ensure the desired results.
5	Formalize the solution	Review and, if necessary, revise internal documentation; formalize and complete end-user (external) documentation. Implement the solution at the user level.
6	Maintain the program	Provide education and support to end-users; correct any unanticipated errors that emerge and identify user-requested modifications (enhancements).

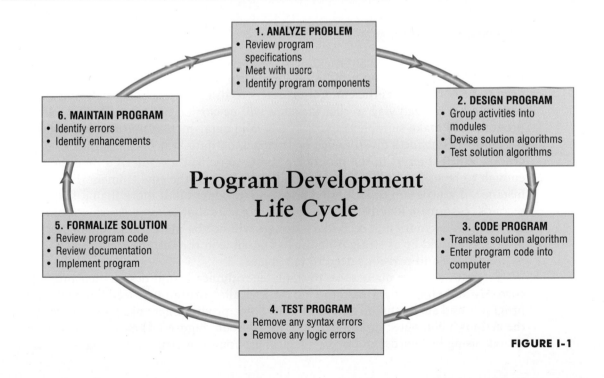

FIGURE I-1

Structured Programming

Java is a structured language. The concepts of a structured programming language are based on its ability to break down a large programming task into smaller, modular activities. Designing programs by following the steps of the PDLC, which is modular in nature, will lead to structured programs. Each phase of the PDLC will contain modules as well. For instance, in the design phase of the PDLC, the modular process of zooming in from the big picture to the lowest level of instruction is called top-down design. Figure I-2 illustrates a **hierarchy chart**, also called a **top-down chart** or **hierarchical input process output (HIPO) chart**. Java supports the modularity of taking the original set of program specifications and breaking it down into smaller, more manageable components, each of which is easier to solve than the original.

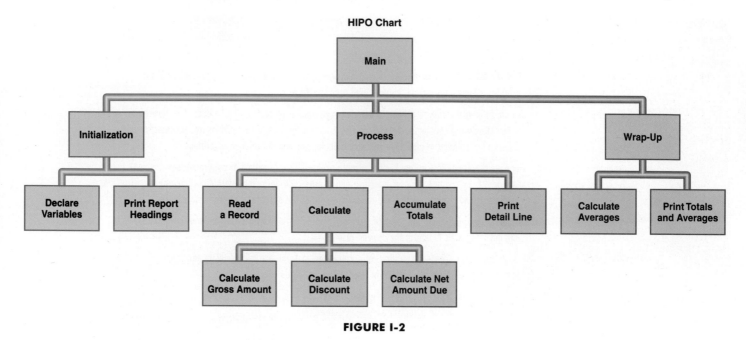

FIGURE I-2

Algorithmic Thinking

The goal of computer programming is to create an **algorithm**, a clear and unambiguous specification of the steps needed to solve a problem. Algorithms also need to be correct and efficient. **Correct** refers to using logical constructs and valid data in an organized way so that the steps will be carried out correctly and the program will make suitable responses to invalid data, such as warning messages for numbers outside a given range, or feedback on data that does not match certain criteria. **Efficient** refers to the program's ability to deliver a result in a time short enough to be useful, and in a space small enough to fit the environment. For instance, if a program to look up a price on a product takes more than a few seconds, customers may be lost; or computer games that take an enormous amount of computer memory and secondary storage will not be marketable. Computer programs should be as straightforward as possible in the certain event that modifications and revisions need to take place.

Programmers use many tools to think algorithmically and design their programs correctly and efficiently. Diagramming the logical algorithm first leads to well-written programs and successful applications later. Some programmers use pseudocode to list the actions a computer should perform. **Pseudocode** (Figure I-3) expresses computer actions using keywords, and depicts logical groupings or structures using indentation.

Other programmers use a diagram or picture of the logic called a flowchart. A **flowchart** is a design tool used to graphically represent the logic in a solution algorithm. Table I-2 shows a standard set of symbols used to represent various operations in a program's logic. Figure I-10 on page J I-11 shows a complete flowchart.

When you draw a complete flowchart, you must begin with a terminal symbol connected by a flowline to the first logical step in solving the problem. Most of the time, each step in solving a problem is represented by a separate symbol. Most of the flowcharting symbols, except the decision diamond, have one entering flowline and one exiting flowline. Inside the symbol, you write words describing the logical step. Flowcharts typically do not display programming language commands. Rather, they state the concept in English, pseudocode, or mathematical notation. After the last step, you end a flowchart with a final flowline connected to another terminal symbol.

Pseudocode

```
MAIN MODULE:

      Call Initialization
      Call Process
      Call Output

END

PROCESS MODULE:
      Do While not End of File
            Read a record
            Call Calculate
            Call Accumulate
            Print detail line
      End Do

RETURN

CALCULATE MODULE:

      If Hours > 40 then
            Call Overtime
      Else
            Call Regular time
      End If

RETURN
```

FIGURE I-3

Table I-2 Flowcharting Symbols and Their Meanings

SYMBOL	NAME	MEANING
 ▭	Process Symbol	Represents the process of executing a defined operation or group of operations that results in a change in value, form, or location of information. Also functions as the default symbol when no other symbol is available.
 ▱	Input/Output (I/O) Symbol	Represents an I/O function, which makes data available for processing (input) or displaying (output) of processed information.
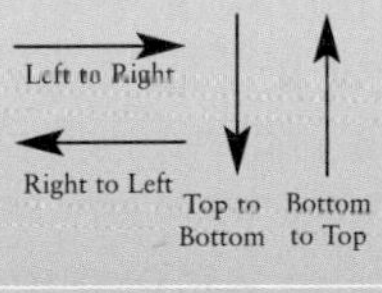 Left to Right → / Right to Left ← / Top to Bottom ↓ / Bottom to Top ↑	Flowline Symbol	Represents the sequence of available information and executable operations. The lines connect other symbols, and the arrowheads are mandatory only for right-to-left and bottom-to-top flow.
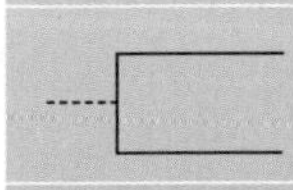 ⌐	Annotation Symbol	Represents the addition of descriptive information, comments, or explanatory notes as clarification. The vertical line and the broken line may be placed on the left, as shown, or on the right.
 ◇	Decision Symbol	Represents a decision that determines which of a number of alternative paths is to be followed.
 ⬭	Terminal Symbol	Represents the beginning, the end, or a point of interruption or delay in a program.
○	Connector Symbol	Represents any entry from, or exit to, another part of the flowchart. Also serves as an off-page connector.
 ▣	Predefined Process Symbol	Represents a named process consisting of one or more operations or program steps that are specified elsewhere.

Because Java is used in designing Web pages and graphical user interfaces (GUIs), programmers may create a **storyboard** or hand-drawn sketch of how the screen will look and where the controls or objects will be placed on the screen. A storyboard also can serve as a reference for the logical names of these controls as you code your program (Figure I-4).

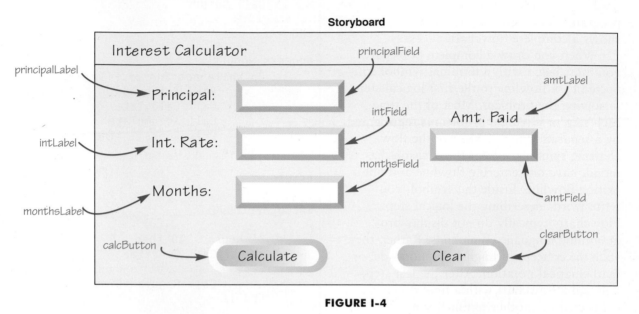

FIGURE I-4

Many programmers use combinations and variations of the algorithmic tools. Your instructor or supervisor may prefer one type of algorithmic tool to another, and you will probably find one or two more useful in your own programming style. As you will see later in this project, there are some additional types of diagrams to help you think logically about the objects that Java code will manipulate.

Control Structures

No matter what **procedures,** or progression of logical actions, that you wish the computer to perform, all program logic can be broken down into one of three control structures or constructs. A **control structure** is a standard progression of logical steps to control the sequence of statement execution. The logic controls the order in which the program instructions are executed. The three basic control structures used in structured design are sequence, selection, and repetition. Each module in a program usually contains more than one control structure. Boxes, diamonds, and arrows are used to graphically depict or diagram the structures for design purposes. A rule of structures dictates that structures must demonstrate **single-entry, single-exit**, which means that a structure stays intact. You should not draw a line going into the middle of a structure; nor should you arbitrarily exit a control structure. Rather, the logic should flow into a structure at only one spot and out of the structure at only one spot.

Sequence Control Structure

When a series of instructions is performed one after another, the logic order is called a **sequence control structure.** One action followed in order sequentially by another is executed as shown in Figure I-5. Actions can be inputs, processes, or outputs. For example, if you want the computer to retrieve a number, perform a calculation on that number, and then print the result exactly in that order, you would use a logical sequence of instructions. Flowcharting symbols representing the type of operation are used with flowlines connecting the sequential steps.

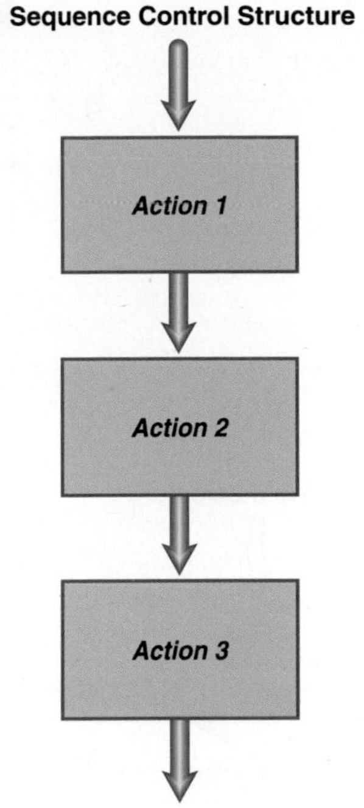

Selection Control Structure

The **selection control structure** is used to tell the program which action to take based on a certain condition (Figure I-6). When the condition is evaluated, its result is either true or false — only these two choices are allowed. If the result of the condition is true, one action is performed; if the result is false, a different action is performed. The selection control structure is also called the **If...Then...Else structure**. For example, you decide that if a value is greater than zero, then you perform a calculation, otherwise you decide to print the value on an exception report. The computer has to evaluate the number to determine whether or not to perform the calculation. The action performed as a result of testing the condition may be a single instruction, or the action itself could be another control structure.

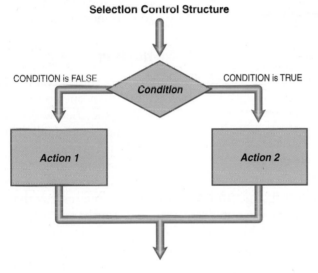

FIGURE I-6

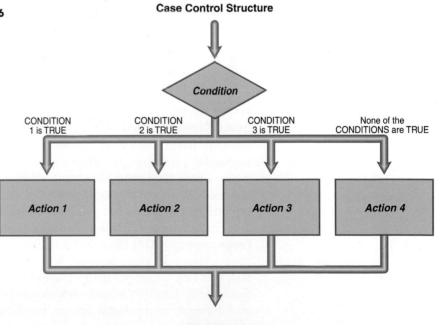

Sequence Control Structure

FIGURE I-5

The **case control structure** is a special kind of selection control structure that allows for more than two choices when the condition is evaluated (Figure I-7). For example, if a user can pick from several choices on a menu, the logic of the code behind that menu evaluates the choice. If a match is found, then the appropriate action is performed. Alternatively, if no match is found, the case control structure can provide that feedback to the user or store the result of no match for later use in the program.

Case Control Structure

FIGURE I-7

Repetition Control Structure

The **repetition control structure** is a logical way to write code that instructs the computer to perform a set of actions over and over again. This structure, sometimes called **looping** or **iteration**, is extremely useful in computer programming.

The key step of the repetition control structure is that a condition must be met to terminate the repetition. Two variations exist. The **Do...While loop** evaluates a condition and then repeats as long as a condition is true (Figure I-8). The **Do...Until loop** is similar, but it evaluates the condition at the end of the loop (Figure I-9). This means that the action(s) in the Do...Until loop always executes at least once, as opposed to the action in a Do...While loop, which may never execute if the condition is false.

A classic example of the repetition control structure involves data file processing. A condition says to continue executing commands while there are more records to process (or do the processing while the end-of-file marker is not hit). When the condition no longer is true, logic says to exit the structure (do no more processing on the data).

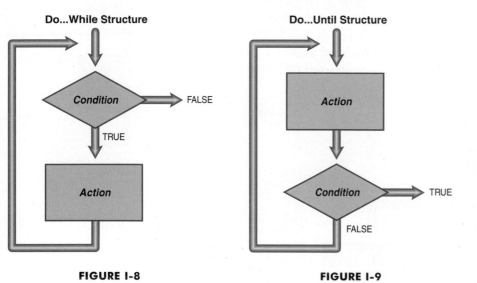

FIGURE I-8

FIGURE I-9

Nesting

Procedures commonly contain more than one control structure. The action specified within a control structure may be a single instruction, multiple instructions, or the procedure may activate other procedures. **Nested** control structures are completely contained within other control structures. One rule of nesting logic is that a nested structure must finish before the outer structure may finish.

Figure I-10 shows a flowchart that illustrates the processing required to compute the average commission paid to a company's sales personnel and to determine the number of male and female salespeople. The flowchart contains sequence, selection, and repetition control structures. Notice that the selection control structure is nested entirely within the repetition control structure.

The Object-Oriented Approach

Java is **object-oriented**, meaning that it packages the data and procedures together using elements called objects. Older programs that are not object-oriented are more linear in nature and must define precisely how the data will be used in each particular program. Traditionally, when the structure of the data changed, such as when a new field was added to a table in a database, the program had to be changed. With the dynamic nature of data in this information age, traditionally structured programs have limited use-time and high maintenance costs.

The concepts of **Object-Oriented Analysis and Design (OOAD)** and **Object-Oriented Programming (OOP)** represent a relatively recent methodology of application development. About 30 years ago, Dr. Kristen Nygaard of Norway and a design team had the task of using a computer to simulate boat movement through the fjords. When traditional programming became hopelessly bogged down due to the ever-changing data about speed, water displacement, fjord configuration, etc., Dr. Nygaard came up with the idea of keeping the boat (object) and the size, weight, and speed (data) packaged

Flowchart

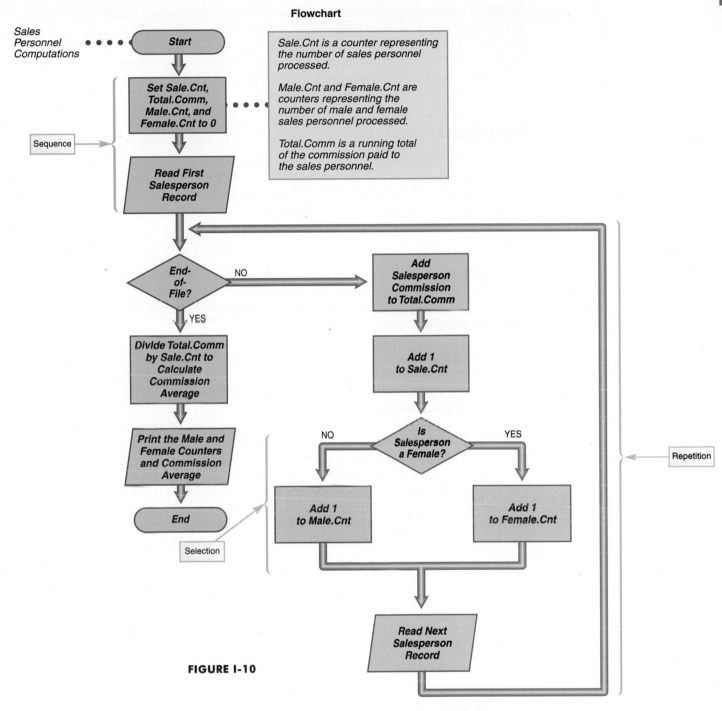

FIGURE I-10

together to make appropriate responses to the fjord configuration. The resulting programming language, **Simula**, was the first language to use objects and methods.

OOP languages now are widely used in industry. Companies such as, General Motors, now program their assembly line cars (objects) to send messages to paint booths asking for an available slot and color (data).

However, even after 30 years, the object-oriented methodology still is not well-defined. Each book you read uses slightly different terminology. A number of Internet newsgroups exist in which the definitions, constructs, and implementations of OOP are debated hotly. Some managers still do not know how to parcel OOP modules to programmers in an efficient manner, nor do they estimate cost and time correctly. However, as the market requires these types of applications more and more, the concepts will become more stable.

Object-oriented programming has evolved as a better way to isolate logically related portions of an application than is possible in traditionally structured design. The benefit is that it is easier to develop, debug, and maintain applications that are becoming tremendously more complex than those created even a few years ago. Object-oriented design represents the logical plan of a program as a set of interactions among objects and operations.

Object-Speak

The use of an object-oriented programming language such as Java requires some new terminology, as well as some old terms with new definitions. The following sections describe the nouns, verbs, and adjectives of object-speak, along with the grammatical rules or constructs of object-oriented languages.

Nouns

An **object** is anything real or abstract about which you store both data and operations that manipulate the data. You can think of an object as any noun. Examples of objects are an invoice, a file or record, a computer screen used to interact with a computer program, or a check box. An object may be composed of other objects, which in turn may contain other objects. A **class** is an object or a set of objects that share a common structure and a common behavior. A class is created when objects are used repeatedly. A class also can be thought of as a general category of object types, sometimes called an implementation, which can be used to create multiple objects with the same attributes and behavior.

Each class may have one or more lower levels called **subclasses** or one or more higher levels called **superclasses**. For example, Java supports the creation of interactive toolbars in application development. A menu bar is a type of subclass of toolbar on a screen. On the other hand, the menu bar is a superclass to drop-down menus. The relationship among the classes, subclasses, and superclasses form a hierarchy. A **generalization hierarchy** (Figure I-11) is an object-oriented design tool used to show the relationships among classes of objects. **Data abstraction** is the process of creating new high-level data structures based on a defined object, through a set of interface operations instead of by directly manipulating the object. You will learn more about data abstraction in a later project.

A unique object or a specific occurrence of a class of objects is called an **instance**. Think of an instance as a proper noun. For example, options buttons are used on computer screens to allow users to choose from a list of options. Option buttons are a class of objects with the same attributes and the same method of displaying selected or not. The accompanying label, defining the purpose of the option button, has a unique value, signifying a particular instance. Specifically, an option button to set an electronic game for two players is a unique instance of the general class of option button objects. Each instance has a unique object name.

You can think of an object as a **black box** — a box that you cannot see inside. This is because an object is packaged with everything it needs to work in a computer program. The box receives and sends messages. The box also contains code and data. Users should never need to peek inside the box because the object package is self-sufficient. Programmers, however, need to know *how* the object works so they will be able to send messages to the object and use it effectively.

Generalization Hierarchy

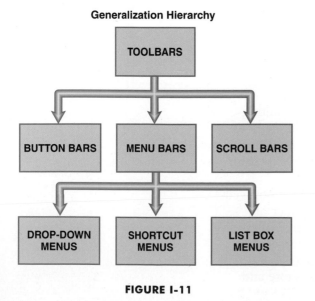

FIGURE I-11

Verbs

An **operation,** or service, is an activity that reads or manipulates the data of an object. You can think of an operation as an active verb. Examples of operations include the standard mathematical, statistical, and logical operations as well as the input, output, and storage operations associated with computer data. A **method** is the code used to perform the operation or service.

For an object to do something, it must receive a message. The **message** defines the interaction of the object. Everything an object can do is represented by the message. The message has two parts — the name of the object to which the message is being sent, and the name of the method that will be performed. The impetus, or **trigger,** that causes the message to be sent may come from another object or an external user. The entire process of a trigger sending a message that causes an operation to occur is called an **event.** For example, if you click a button to save data, that action is the trigger. A message is sent to the disk to prepare for input. Writing the data to the disk is the operation. Saving is the event.

Programmers draw **event diagrams** to visually plan their programming of events and show relationships among events and operations. Event diagrams display the **trigger** as a shadowed button. When you draw an event diagram, you list the external trigger that causes this event to happen in the shadowed rectangle at the upper-left corner of the diagram (Figure I-12). Then you begin the next part of the diagram on an independent line, to show that the trigger is external.

On the independent line, you list the internal processing that describes the event. Many students find it helpful to describe what the computer senses at this point, or imagine themselves thinking from the CPU's point of view.

Operations are shown in rounded rectangles as results of the event. Here you should list any visual or procedural inputs and outputs. Some operations are an end to themselves. In contrast to flowcharts that must include terminal symbols, notice that these operations are dead ends because they cause no other events to occur. Other operations, however, may send additional messages or be triggers for other events. When possible, event diagrams are drawn left to right to represent what happens over time.

As shown in Figure I-12, nothing happens unless the trigger sends a message and causes the event to occur. At the conclusion of the operation, the system again will do nothing until another trigger causes an event to occur. This relationship is a key feature of OOP, and programs that are constructed in this way are said to be **event-driven.**

Event Diagram

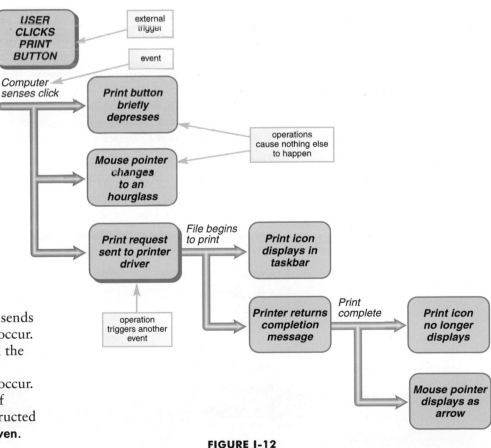

FIGURE I-12

Adjectives

In object-oriented terminology, the data stored about an object is referenced by an attribute, or property. **Attributes** are identifying characteristics of individual objects such as name, size, or color. You can think of attributes as adjectives that describe an object. The attributes of a hyperlink on a Web page might include the font, the color, the font size, and the underline. Attributes should not be confused with the data itself. Color is an attribute; red is the data.

An **object structure diagram** provides a visual representation of an object, its attributes, and its methods (Figure I-13 and Figure I-14). The operations are described in terms of what they do, not how they do it.

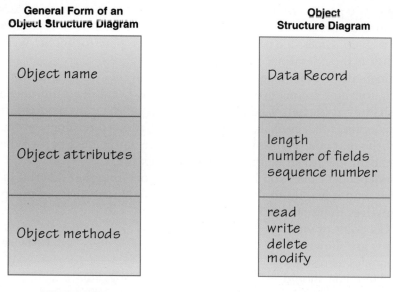

General Form of an Object Structure Diagram

Object name

Object attributes

Object methods

FIGURE I-13

Object Structure Diagram

Data Record

length
number of fields
sequence number

read
write
delete
modify

FIGURE I-14

Table I-3 lists the ten steps to object-speak in a quick reference format.

Table I-3   Ten Steps to Object-Speak
1.   An **object** is the basic unit of organization, a combination of a data element and a set of procedures.
2.   A **method** is the code to perform a service or operation, including tasks such as performing calculations, storing values, and presenting results.
3.   A **class** is an object or a set of objects that share a common structure and a common behavior. A class is created when objects are used repeatedly. A specific occurrence of an object class is called an **instance**.
4.   A **subclass** is a lower-level category of a class with at least one unique attribute or method of its own, although it can make use of the same methods as its **superclass**. The resulting tree-like structure is called a **class hierarchy**.
5.   A subclass **inherits** the **attributes,** methods, and variables from its superclass.
6.   A **message** requests objects to perform their method. A message is comprised of the object name together with the method.
7.   An **event** occurs when a **trigger** causes an object to send a message.
8.   **Encapsulation** is the process of hiding the implementation details of an object from its user by combining attributes and methods.
9.   **Polymorphism** allows instructions to be given to an object in a generalized rather than specific detailed command.
10.   **Data abstraction** is the process of creating new high-level data structures based on a defined object.

Object-Oriented Synonyms

As the concepts of Object-Oriented Technology (OT), Object-Oriented Analysis and Design, and Object-Oriented Programming become more ingrained into computer curriculums and applications, the terminologies will solidify. Currently, many people use the terms class and object interchangeably. Table I-4 lists some of the synonyms used by different object-oriented philosophers, programmers, and reference books.

Table I-4 Object-Oriented Terminology Synonyms

QT TERM	OAD TERM	OOP TERM
Object	Object Type Object Class	Class Package Module
Operation	Service	Method
Message		Request Event
Attribute		Variable

The Philosophy of Object-Oriented Programming (OOP)

OOP is not just a different set of tools and methods from traditionally structured programming. It represents a different philosophy about the nature of computer programs and how they are assembled. The following case scenario about two students enrolled in the Java programming course is designed to help illustrate these differences and provide an analogy for discussing OOP constructs.

Paul Randall is a student of traditionally structured programming. He wants to create a work and study area in his room where he can write and draw and be able to store his work. He wants to sit at the work area, write, and then store his papers. Paul views the system as a set of functions — sitting, writing, and storing.

After a great deal of effort in drawing up blueprints, Paul has designed a one-piece, integrated study unit consisting of a writing surface with rolltop cover, a bench, and two drawers. By designing an integrated unit, the functions of sitting, writing, and storing will be compatible with each other and he will save on material costs and construction time. Paul travels to several lumber and hardware stores and purchases all the materials.

After considerable construction time, Paul is finished and satisfied with the result. He can work comfortably and does not need to reach too far to lift up the desktop or pull open the file drawers. Several weeks pass and Paul begins to think about making enhancements to his system. His bench is not as comfortable as he would like, his writing area feels cramped, and his two drawers are full. Paul decides to live with his system's shortcomings, however, because any change would require a substantial effort to dismantle and rebuild the entire system.

Mary Carter is a student of object-oriented programming. She would like to have a study area with the same functionality as Paul's study area. Mary, however, views the system as a set of objects — a sitting object, a writing surface object, and a storage object. Even though they are separate objects, Mary is confident she can make them interoperate with each other for an effective study area. Mary travels to a furniture factory warehouse and begins evaluating the hundreds of different chairs, desks, and file cabinets for their suitability to her needs and their compatibility with each other.

Mary returns to her room after purchasing a matching chair, two-drawer file cabinet, and rolltop desk. When the desk handle is pulled, it activates a hardware mechanism that raises the rolltop. With little effort, Mary's study area is complete.

Although Mary's furniture cost more than Paul's materials, the savings on her labor costs have more than made up for the difference. After several weeks, Mary's file cabinet is full. She returns to the furniture store, buys a three-drawer cabinet of the same style, and replaces the one in her study area.

Encapsulation, Inheritance, and Polymorphism

Just as sequence, selection, and repetition are building constructs of logical procedural code, encapsulation, inheritance, and polymorphism are the conceptual building blocks of object-oriented design.

Encapsulation

Encapsulation is the capability of an object to have data (properties) and functionality (methods) available to the user, without the user having to understand the implementation within the object. In other words, encapsulation implements data abstraction. Traditionally structured programming separates data from procedures. In the object-oriented world, an object contains functional methods as well as that method's associated data. Encapsulation is the process of hiding the implementation details of an object from its user, making those details transparent. **Transparent** refers to the ability to see through something that appears not to exist when in fact it really does. This process of making the implementation and programming details transparent to the user also is called **information hiding**. Providing access to an object only through its messages, while keeping the details private, is an example of information hiding. Users know what operations may be requested of an object, but do not know the specifics of how the operations are performed. Encapsulation allows objects to be modified without requiring the applications that use them also to be modified.

In the case scenarios, both Paul and Mary want drawers that cannot be pulled all the way out accidentally. In constructing his system, Paul had to attend to the details of how drawer stops work, which ones to use, and how to build them into the system. This is not to say that Paul understands his system better than Mary does. Mary, as an object-oriented programmer, does need to understand how her system is constructed. However, from a user's point of view, Mary did not need to concern herself with how the safety stops on her drawers work; only that they *do* work. For Mary, the safety stop functionality and behavior is encapsulated within the file cabinet object.

Inheritance

Inheritance is the concept that a programmer can use a class, along with its functions and data, to create a descendent class or subclass — a capability of object-oriented programming that saves time and coding. A subclass usually differs from its superclass in at least one way, containing just the code or data necessary to explain the difference. Its status as a subclass is enough to give it access to all the superclass's functions and data. This is a very efficient way of reusing code. Also known as **subclassing**, this provides a way for programmers to define a class as an extension of another class, without copying the definition. If you let a class inherit from another class, it automatically will have all the data and methods of the parent class.

Mary's desk, chair, and cabinet all have similar wood grain, color, and style. If you think of the furniture as a superclass, then Mary's individual pieces are subclasses of that furniture line. Because they are subclasses of the same superclass, they *inherited* the same wood grain, color, and style attributes from the superclass.

Polymorphism

Polymorphism allows an instruction to be given to an object using a generalized, rather than a specifically detailed, command. The same command will get different, but somewhat predictable, results depending on the object that receives the command. While the specific actions (internal to the object) are different, the results would be the same. In this way, one OOP function can replace several traditional procedures.

Paul must lift up his desktop when he wants to open it. You could say he must perform a lifting operation. To open his desk or file drawers, he must perform a pulling operation. Recall that Mary's rolltop desk has a pull handle with hardware encapsulated within the desk that translates the pull of the handle into the raising of the desktop. Mary's desk and file cabinet objects are polymorphic with respect to opening. Mary applies the same method, pulling, to open either object. She knows that the pull method will result in the object opening. As a user, how the object opens, or even that the object does open differently, is not a concern to Mary.

Many OOP languages, like Java, provide libraries, classes, and objects that already have been programmed to work in certain ways. Therefore, object-oriented programmers can employ these tools without knowing the intricacies of the programming behind them. From a programming point of view, you still need to understand how the drawer handle hardware is connected to the desk and what happens when you pull it.

Rapid Application Development (RAD) and the Benefits of Object-Oriented Programming

Rapid application development (RAD) refers to the use of pre-built objects to make program development much faster. Using pre-built objects is faster because you use existing objects rather than writing everything yourself. The result is shorter development life cycles, easier maintenance, and the capability to reuse components in other projects. One of the major premises on which industry implementation of OOP is built is greater reusability of code.

Sun Microsystems uses an approach to RAD called the Java Factory. When a client company approaches Sun with a programming problem, Sun brings together Sun programmers, client programmers, and client users, for four to six weeks of intensive program development. The result is a **prototype,** or scaled-down working model, of a desired application. The client programmers return to their company understanding the classes, methods, and approach to the problem, and then are able to complete the full application in-house.

The adoption of object-orientation means that not all members of a development team need to be proficient in an object-oriented programming language such as Java. A practical and economical approach is to separate the task of creating objects from the task of assembling objects into applications. Some programmers, such as the client programmers that attend a Java Factory session, are called class providers.

Class providers can focus on creating classes and objects while other developers, called **class users,** leverage their knowledge of business processes to assemble applications using OOP methods and tools. An **end user** is the person who takes the Java program and executes it, either as an application or as an applet accessed over the Web. An end-user interacts with the program, and may be prompted to provide feedback or data.

Table I-5 summarizes the benefits of OOP.

Table I-5	The Benefits of Object-Oriented Programming
BENEFIT	EXPLANATION
Reusability	The classes are designed so they can be reused in many systems, or modified classes can be created using inheritance.
Stability	The classes are designed for repeated use and become stable over time.
Easier design	The designer looks at each object as a black box and is not as concerned with the detail inside.
Faster design	The applications can be created from existing components.

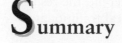

Summary

This introduction provided an overview of computer programming and the history of the Java programming language. The steps of the program development life cycle are essential to object-oriented programs as well as traditionally structured programs. Object-oriented programs use objects, methods, attributes, and events to package data and procedures together for rapid application development. Building block control structures, as well as the concepts of encapsulation, inheritance, and polymorphism, create reusable, stable programs that are easier and faster to design. This overview has provided a basic introduction to the concepts and technologies involved in the projects within this book. Java is a powerful and complex object-oriented programming language that is platform-independent, highly structured, and enormously marketable for applications on the Web.

Test Your Knowledge

1 True/False

Instructions: Circle **T** if the statement is true or **F** is the statement is false.

T F 1. The program development life cycle is an outline of steps used to build **software applications.**

T F 2. The selection control structure also is called looping.

T F 3. A flowchart is used to show the relationships among classes of objects.

T F 4. In object-speak, when a trigger sends a message to an object, it is called **an event.**

T F 5. Inheritance also is called information hiding.

T F 6. Pseudocode is the object-oriented version of traditional code.

T F 7. Event diagrams show the relationship among events and operations.

T F 8. Do...While loops always are performed at least once.

T F 9. A prototype is a scaled-down working model.

T F 10. Data abstraction refers to reading data from a disk.

2 Multiple Choice

Instructions: Circle the correct response.

1. A method is another word for the code to perform a(n) _____ .
   a. service
   b. iteration
   c. event
   d. property change

2. Which of the following is a diagramming tool associated specifically with object-oriented concepts?
   a. flowchart
   b. event diagram
   c. HIPO chart
   d. pseudocode

3. A Java _____ is a mini-program that can be downloaded and executed as part of a displayed Web page.
   a. instance
   b. applet
   c. JavaScript
   d. method

4. The If...Then...Else structure is an example of _____ .
   a. sequence
   b. subclassing
   c. selection
   d. iteration

Test Your Knowledge

5. _____ allows objects to be modified without requiring the applications that use them to be modified.
   a. Inheritance
   b. Polymorphism
   c. Encapsulation
   d. Data Abstraction

6. A(n) _____ is a unique occurrence of an object.
   a. instance
   b. attribute
   c. property
   d. event

7. Of the following, which is <u>not</u> a benefit of OOP?
   a. reusability
   b. disposability
   c. stability
   d. faster development

8. _____ refers to the use of pre-built objects to make application development faster.
   a. OOAD
   b. PDLC
   c. RAID
   d. RAD

9. Which of the following is <u>not</u> a reason to choose Java as a beginning programming language?
   a. Java is a structured language
   b. Java is used to develop applications on the Web
   c. Java is object-oriented
   d. Java is easier to learn than other programming languages

10. The compiled version of a Java program that can run on any platform is called _____ .
    a. J++
    b. JVM
    c. JDK
    d. bytecode

Test Your Knowledge

3 Understanding Flowcharts

Instructions: A flowchart representation of part of a cardiovascular disease risk assessment is shown in Figure I-15. The higher the point total, the greater the risk. In the spaces provided, write the point total for the following persons.

1. A 33-year-old non-smoker with normal blood pressure who eats a low fat diet.

   _____

   _____

2. A 50-year-old non-smoker with high blood pressure who eats a high fat diet.

   _____

   _____

3. A 19-year-old non-smoker with high blood pressure who eats a high fat diet.

   _____

   _____

4. A 27-year-old smoker with high blood pressure who eats a low fat diet.

   _____

   _____

5. A 17-year-old non-smoker with normal blood pressure who eats a high fat diet.

   _____

   _____

6. A 43-year-old smoker with high blood pressure who eats a high fat diet.

   _____

   _____

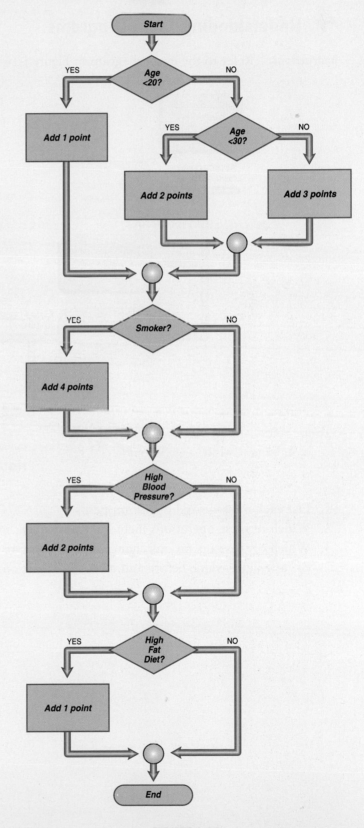

FIGURE I-15

Test Your Knowledge

4 Understanding Event Diagrams

Instructions: Refer to the event diagram in Figure I-16 to answer the following questions:

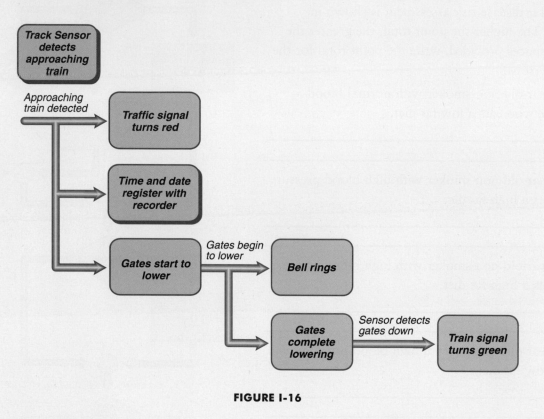

FIGURE I-16

1. List each message and operation pair.
2. Which of these operations includes a subsequent message? List any pairs of operations and their message.
3. Which of these operations changes the value of an attribute of an object? List the operation, attribute, and the attribute's value before and after the operation.

Apply Your Knowledge

1 Creating a Generalization Hierarchy

Instructions: Pick any class of objects that interests you (for example, books, clothes, musical instruments, physical fitness equipment, etc.). Create a generalization hierarchy showing at least four levels of subclasses and superclasses. For each subclass, identify several attributes inherited from each of its superclasses.

2 Creating Object Structure Diagrams

Instructions: Draw an object structure diagram for each object in Figure I-16.

3 Creating an Event Diagram

Instructions: Using Figure I-16 as an example, draw an event diagram to raise the gates when the track sensor has detected the train is clear of the intersection. The trigger is the lack of weight on the tracks. The events that happen include the sensor detecting the loss of weight and the gates raising. Possible operations include traffic signal changing, time and date recording, and gate movement.

4 Thinking Algorithmically

Instructions: Take one of the following tasks and write a set of instructions, sufficiently complete so that another person could perform the task without asking questions. Test your solution by giving it to another class member and have him or her perform the steps. Notate selection structures with the words if, then, and else — if a step in your task is dependent upon two conditions. Notate repetition structures with the words do while, do until, or do a certain number of times.

1. light a candle
2. make a cup of tea
3. sharpen a pencil
4. walk from the classroom to the bookstore
5. logon to your school's network or intranet

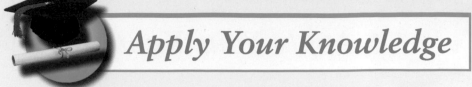

Apply Your Knowledge

5 Understanding a Flowchart

Instructions: Using a drawing template or a drawing program on your computer system, re-create the flowchart shown in Figure I-17. Then, referring to the control structure examples and figures in the project, use colored pencils or markers to indicate the following on your flowchart. (Alternately, circle and label each structure or see your instructor about ways to turn in this assignment.)

1. Circle all selection structures in red.
2. Circle all repetition structures in green.
3. Highlight in yellow all flowlines indicating a sequential step.

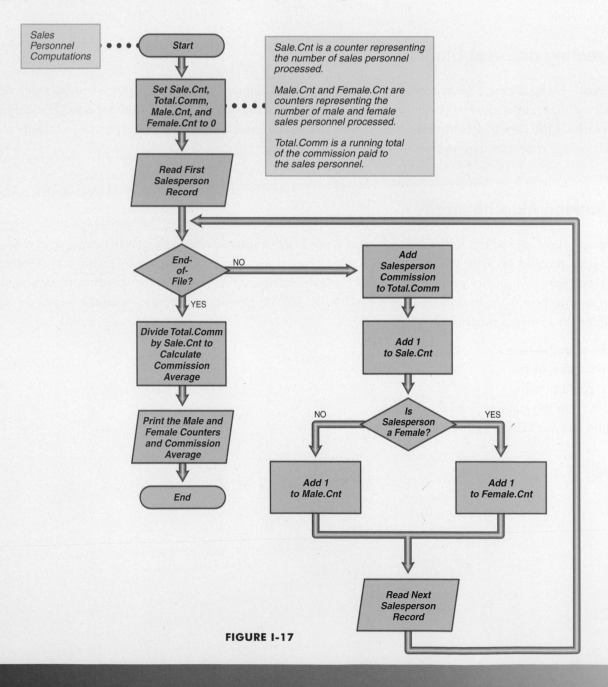

FIGURE I-17

Java Programming

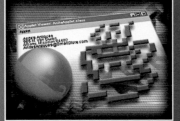

Java Programming

Creating a
Java Program

You will have mastered the material in this project
when you can:

- Start Notepad to insert Java source code
- Open and format an MS-DOS Prompt window
- Arrange the desktop to facilitate Java program
  editing and compiling
- Define a Java program
- Write a simple Java output program
- Insert block and line comments as
  documentation
- Use proper naming conventions for classes
  and files
- Identify the parts of a method header
- Compile a Java program
- Execute a Java program
- Save Java source code
- Edit Java source code
- Differentiate between an application
  and an applet
- Create an applet from Java source code
- View an applet using Applet Viewer
- Create an HTML host document
- Use escape code sequences

The Network Is The Computer™

Bright Days Ahead for Sun Microsystems

I magine this job description: "Chat on the telephone, read lots of e-mail and trade rags, ride airplanes, and give speeches."

Sound like the ideal job? That is how Sun Microsystems' Scott McNealy describes his position as chairman and CEO. Despite these humble words, CBS-TV's 60 Minutes calls him "one of the most influential businessmen in America," and The New Yorker magazine says this amiable network industry leader is "one of the industry's budding celebrities."

From a meager beginning in 1982 with only four employees, McNealy has helped Sun Microsystems (www.sun.com) grow to a multi-billion dollar global entity with more than 29,000 employees in 150 countries.

McNealy graduated from Harvard University with a Bachelor of Arts degree in economics. He then earned a master's degree in business administration from Stanford, which he fondly describes as "the farm." Soon afterwards he co-founded SUN, an acronym for Stanford University Network, with Bill Joy.

Part of Sun's success is due to Java, the programming language and environment you will use throughout this book. Sun software engineers coined the name Java during a brainstorming session to "come up with a name that evoked the essence of the technology liveliness, animation, speed, interactivity,

1982

2001

995

and more. The name is not an acronym, but rather a reminder of that hot, aromatic stuff that many programmers like to drink lots of."

The leader behind the Java technology development is James Gosling. On his home page (java.sun.com/people/jag/), he portrays himself as "do[ing] odd jobs like helping out with the system architecture and wandering around the country giving talks like why Java is the greatest thing since sliced bread."

When Java was introduced 1995, he described it as "A simple, object oriented, distributed, interpreted, robust, secure, architecture neutral, portable, high performance, multithreaded, dynamic language." Originally named Oak, Java's inception was part of Sun's Green project, which began in 1990 as part of the company's efforts to shape the "next wave" of

computing. The Java engineers disassembled and reassembled a variety of products with the goal of developing digitally controlled devices for consumers and computers that are simple to manufacture, easy to use, and communicate with each other irregardless of who built them. This platform took off when Java migrated to the World Wide Web and made Web pages come alive.

Sun's slogan, "The Network Is The Computer™," depicts the company's vision of connecting computers seamlessly in a wide variety of applications. Today more than 900,000 programmers are using this technology in a majority of the world's medium-to large-sized corporations.

For example, more than 120 Sun servers and 4.5 terabytes (trillion bytes) of storage were used to create Disney's Toy Story 2 at the Pixar Animation Studios. Sun's technology powers e-commerce systems at Egghead.com, CDNOW, and the GO Network, and it supports telecommunications giants AT&T and Ericsson Mobile Communications.

With this marketplace presence, certainly McNealy, Gosling, and the rest of the software engineers can chat on the phone and read their e-mail while enjoying a hot cup of java.

Java Programming

Creating a Java Program

P R O J E C T

1

CASE PERSPECTIVE

Anita's Antiques is a small antique store in Albany, Missouri. The store sells antique craft creations including quilts, doilies, homemade toys, artwork, antique china, and collectibles.

Anita Louks, the owner, has asked you to help her get started with the Java programming language. She plans to set up a Web site to help sell her products. Anita recently downloaded the Java Development Kit from the Web and is ready to get started.

You both agree that creating a small program in Java to print the store's name and address on the screen will give you experience in programming and be something that the store can use in the future as it moves to e-commerce on the Web. Because you are studying the Java programming language, you volunteer to write the Java program.

Introduction

The way in which you give instructions to a computer and receive feedback from the computer is called a **user interface**. Java's user interface may take on many forms. In its simplest state, the user interface is a command line that displays input and output on a blank screen, which is called **console mode** or **stand-alone mode**. Java programmers may view the output of applet programs using a Java tool called Applet Viewer. The **Applet Viewer**, which comes with the JDK and Java 2 platform, is like a mini-browser that can display the applet on the desktop. It loads and executes applets, but does not contain the menus and buttons that display in a full version of a browser. Recall that applets are mini-programs that may be executed as part of a displayed Web page.

In order for programmers to use Applet Viewer, or a browser to view their applets, they must create an accompanying **hypertext markup language** (**HTML**) program that directs the applet to the appropriate Java code. A growing number of third-party products, generally referred to as **Interface Development Environments** (**IDEs**), can be purchased and used to facilitate the creation of **graphical user interfaces** (**GUI**). IDEs, such as JBuilder and J++, provide programmers with a set of development tools which may include color coded editors, menus for compiling programs, and pre-written Java classes.

The first few projects in this text use the console mode and a text editor to write, compile, and execute Java programs. Even though communicating with a computer by typing at a command line may seem a tedious task in today's interactive, mouse-clicking world, typing commands is a common, easy place to start without having to purchase additional software. In this project, you will learn the basic parts of a Java program and the use of proper syntax. A programming language's **syntax** is the spelling of its commands, the order in which they are entered, and the required symbols that are a part of the language. After you analyze, design, and code the program, you will test for compile errors, and then run or execute the program. Finally, you will edit your program to make it run as an applet and create the HTML file to execute it.

In the Introduction Project, you learned that the **program development life cycle** (**PDLC**) is a good outline of steps to follow when creating a new computer program. The six steps are: (1) analyze the problem, (2) design the program, (3) code the program, (4) test the program, (5) formalize the solution, and (6) maintain the program.

Project One — Anita's Antiques

ANALYZING THE PROBLEM A computer program that will display the name and address of Anita's Antiques on the screen is required as a first step in preparing an e-commerce Web site. It is a modest task, but it is a good starting point in creating a user interface. In this program, the user will read the name and address on the screen. You will use Java to create the user interface.

DESIGNING THE PROGRAM The structure of the program will be sequential in nature. The three lines will print one after another on the screen. Running the program from the command line of a computer, you will use code to send a message to an object — the default display device of your system (Figure 1-1a). You will add a line to display the company's e-mail address and then modify the program to run on the Web. The four lines will display in a window of their own (Figure 1-1b). The program should contain appropriate documentation and be saved for future use.

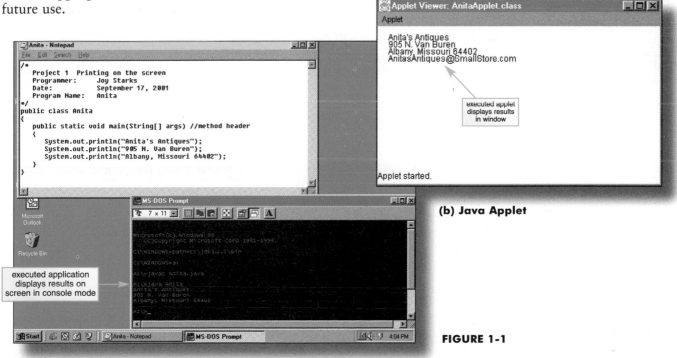

(a) Java Application

(b) Java Applet

FIGURE 1-1

Figure 1-2a displays a flowchart of the sequence of steps. Figure 1-2b displays an event diagram illustrating the execution of the program as a trigger to the display event.

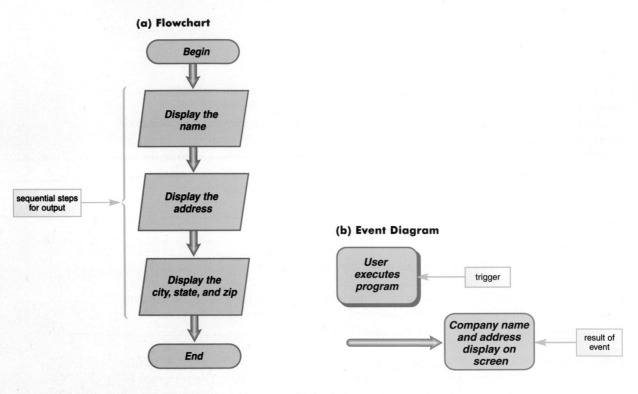

FIGURE 1-2

CODING THE PROGRAM   You will create Java source code using the syntax and commands of the Java programming language. This project presents a series of step-by-step instructions to write the code, explaining its parts.

TESTING THE PROGRAM   You will test the program by compiling it using the javac compiler and then by executing it in console mode using the Java interpreter. In the Introduction Project, you learned that compiling a Java program means using Sun's javac program to convert the Java source code into computer-readable bytecode — a necessary step in order to execute the program. The interpreter then runs the byte-code. You also will test the applet version of the program by viewing it, using Applet Viewer.

FORMALIZING THE SOLUTION   You will review the source code, use proper documentation, edit, recompile, and print a copy.

MAINTAINING THE PROGRAM   You will modify the program to move the output farther right on the screen and to include the e-mail address of the company.

Setting Up the Desktop

Figure 1-3 shows a typical desktop with two open windows. In the upper-left portion of the screen, the Notepad application displays. You will use Notepad to edit Java source code. In the lower-right portion of the screen, the MS-DOS Prompt window displays. You will use the MS-DOS Prompt window to compile and execute your Java programs. Keeping both of these applications open on the desktop facilitates moving back and forth while editing and executing Java programs.

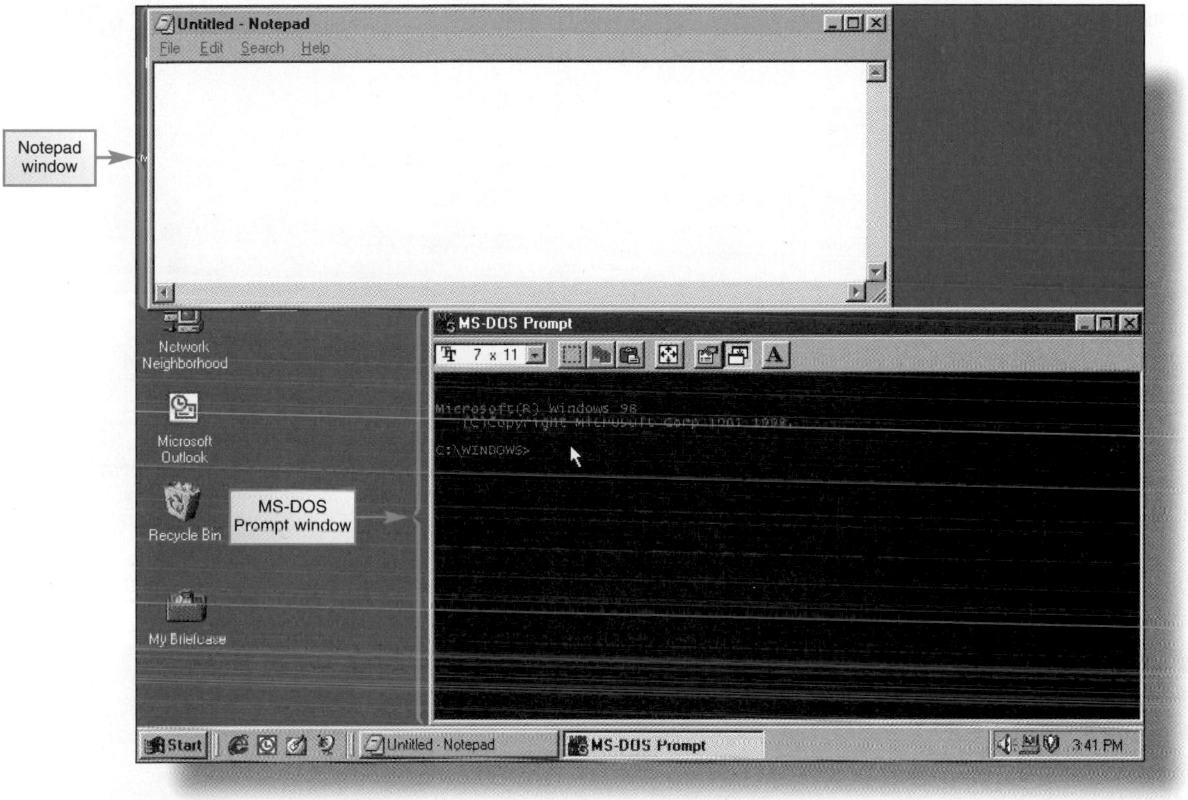

FIGURE 1-3

Starting Notepad

Any text-editing program capable of creating a text file can be used to write Java programs. Text files are files without any special formatting. The examples in this book use Notepad, which is a common application on many desktop computers. You may use other programs to create text files, such as WordPad, Microsoft Works, WordPerfect, or Microsoft Word.

In order to start Notepad, Windows must be running. Perform the steps on the next page to start Notepad.

More About

Using Microsoft Word to Write Code

You may use any text-editing program to enter Java code. Features in Microsoft Word such as setting tabs and spell checking make Word a desirable Java editor. If you decide to use Microsoft Word, be sure to save your code as a text file. On Word's File menu, click Save As. Then, in the Save As dialog box, click the Save as type box arrow. Choose Text Only (*.txt) in the list. You must still enclose the name of the file and its .java extension in quotation marks.

Steps **To Start Notepad**

1 **With the Windows desktop displayed, click the Start button on the taskbar and then point to Programs on the Start menu. Point to Accessories on the Programs submenu and then point to Notepad.**

The Programs submenu and Accessories submenu display (Figure 1-4). This desktop is Windows 98. Your system may have a different set of menus.

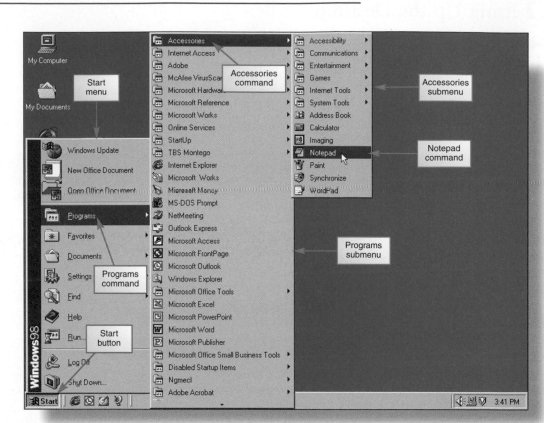

FIGURE 1-4

2 **Click Notepad. When the Notepad window opens, drag the title bar to move the window to the upper-left corner of the desktop. Drag the lower-right corner to resize the window as shown in Figure 1-5.**

Notepad displays on approximately one-third of the desktop (Figure 1-5).

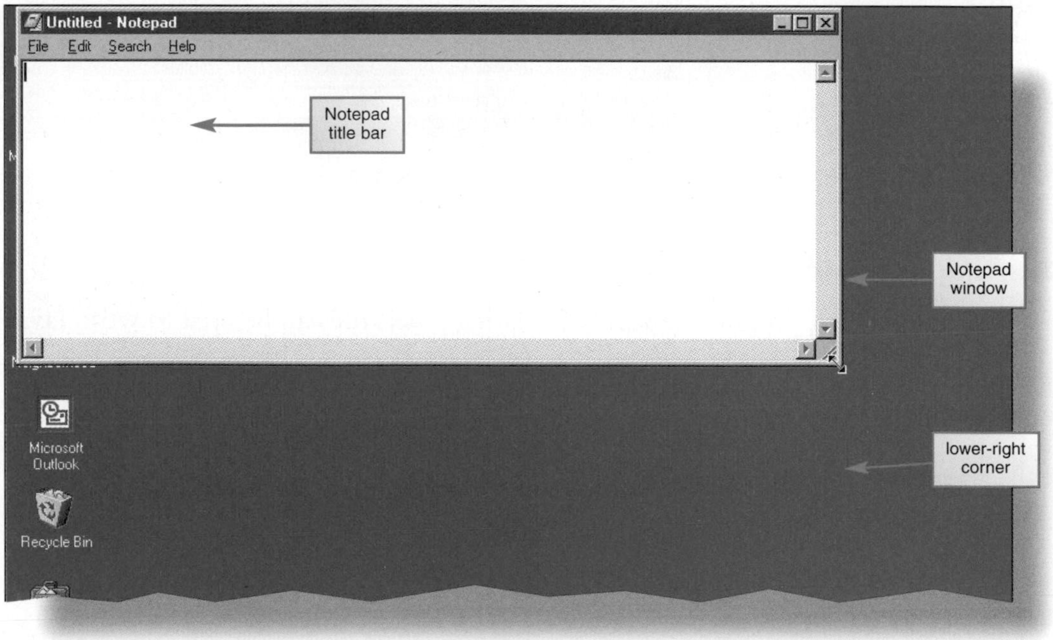

FIGURE 1-5

Other **Ways**

1. Right-click desktop, point to New, click Text Document, double-click the New Text Document icon that displays on the desktop

You will use this Notepad window to type and save lines of Java code that will occur during execution. Also referred to as a **list**, these lines of code will be entered and edited later in the project.

Opening the Command Prompt Window

Accessing the command prompt allows you to **execute**, or **run**, Java programs that you have created. The **command prompt** is a way to communicate with the operating system without using any specific application. The command prompt normally displays as white text on a black screen. The Windows operating system displays the command prompt as a disk drive location, followed by a subdirectory location (if any), followed by a greater-than sign (>), and finally a flashing insertion point. You can access the command prompt by restarting the machine in its operating system mode, by temporarily exiting the Windows interface, or by opening a command prompt window on the desktop. However, opening a command prompt window on the desktop facilitates moving between editing the program and running it.

Perform the following steps to open and format the command prompt window.

<table>
<tr><td>

More About

Running Java Programs

Java applications can be run using the Run command on the Start menu if your path is set automatically at start-up. Simply click the Start button, click Run, and then, in the Run dialog box, type `java` followed by the name of the compiled program.

</td></tr>
</table>

Steps **To Open and Format the Command Prompt Window**

---

1 **With the Notepad window still open, click the Start button on the taskbar. Point to Programs on the Start menu and then point to MS-DOS Prompt or Command Prompt for Windows NT on the Programs submenu.**

The Programs submenu displays (Figure 1-6).

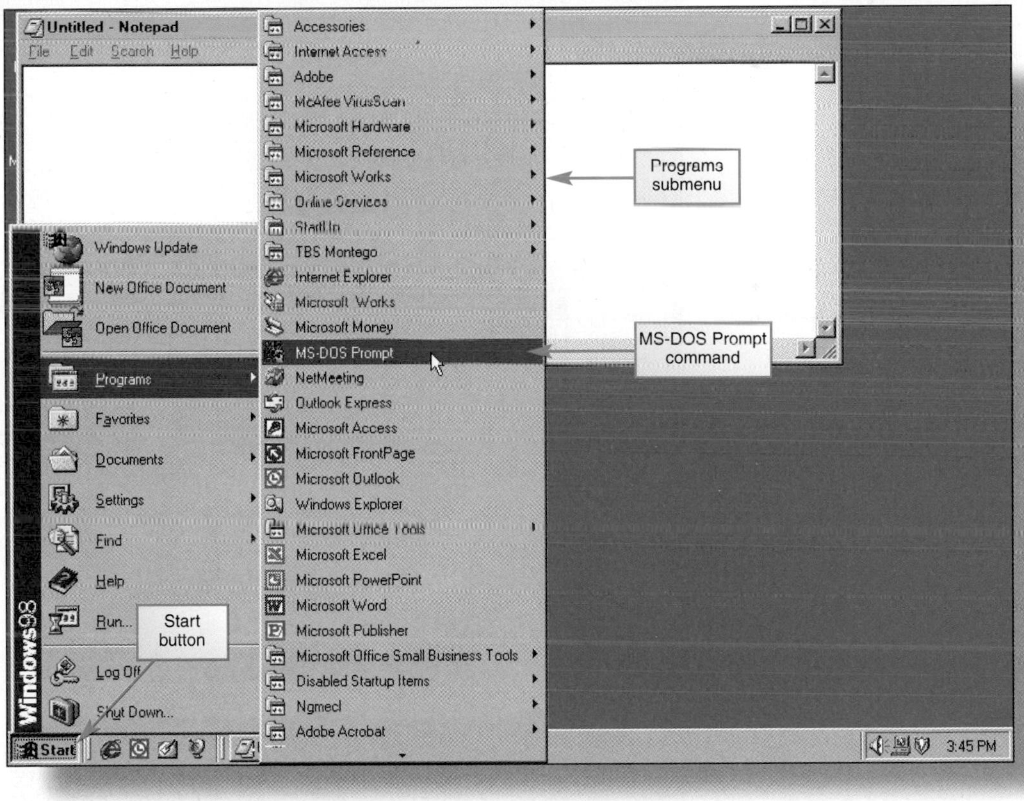

FIGURE 1-6

Click MS-DOS Prompt.

If the MS-DOS Prompt window displays full screen, it will cover the entire desktop as shown in Figure 1-7a. Otherwise, it displays with a title bar as shown in Figure 1-7b.

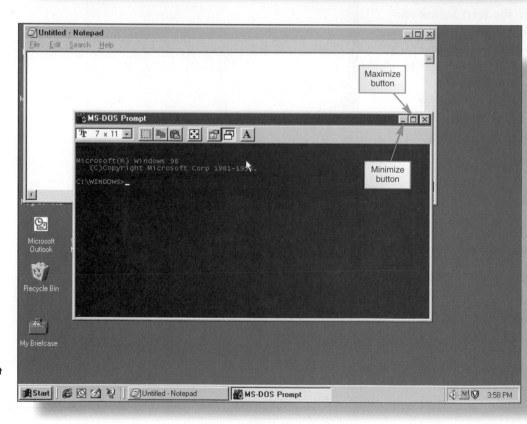

(a) MS-DOS Prompt Window, Full Screen

(b) MS-DOS Prompt Window, Run On Desktop

FIGURE 1-7

3 If your system displays the MS-DOS Prompt window as a black, full screen, press and hold the ALT key while pressing the TAB key to minimize the window. Otherwise, minimize the MS-DOS Prompt window by clicking the Minimize button on the title bar. After minimizing, point to the MS-DOS Prompt button on the taskbar.

The MS-DOS Prompt button displays on the taskbar (Figure 1-8).

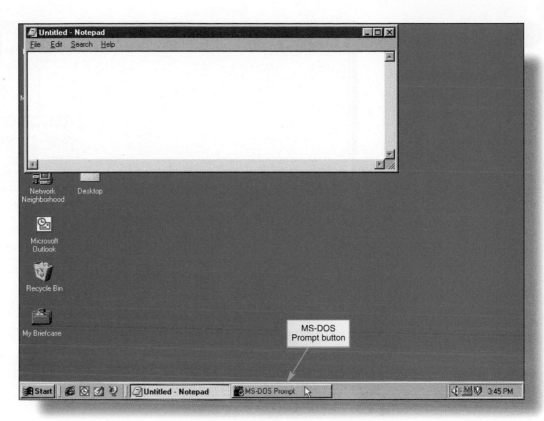

FIGURE 1-8

4 Right-click the MS-DOS Prompt button and then point to Properties on the shortcut menu.

The shortcut menu displays (Figure 1-9).

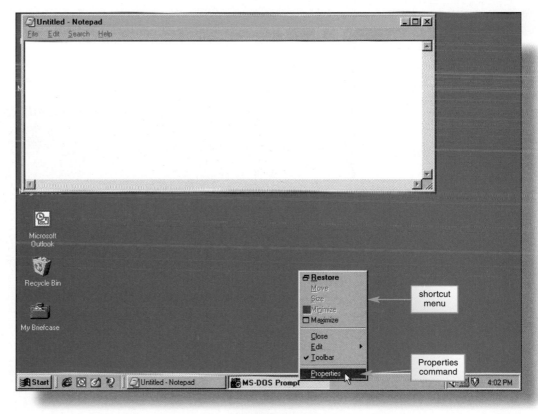

FIGURE 1-9

5 Click Properties. When the MS-DOS Prompt Properties dialog box displays, point to the Font tab.

The MS-DOS Prompt Properties dialog box contains options to configure how the window will display (Figure 1-10). The options on your system may differ.

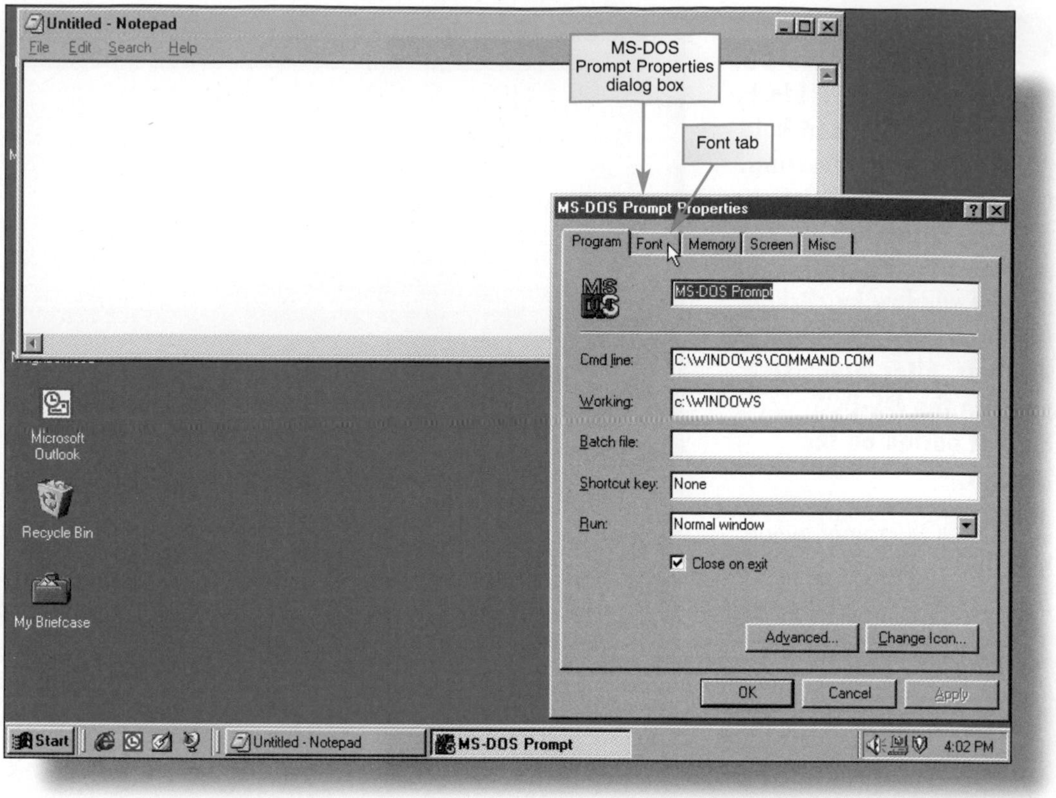

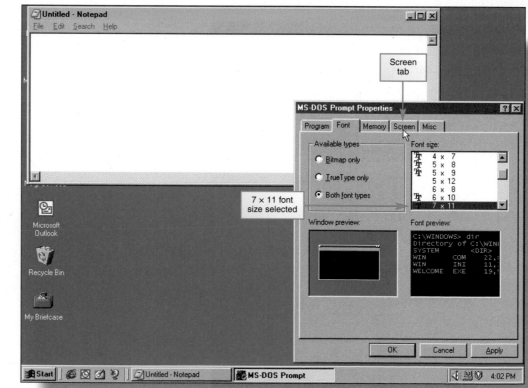

FIGURE 1-10

6 Click the Font tab. In the Font size box, scroll to and then click the 7 × 11 font size or a similar size font. Point to the Screen tab.

The 7 × 11 font size is selected (Figure 1-11).j

FIGURE 1-11

7 Click the Screen tab. If necessary, click the Window option button in the Usage area to select it. If necessary, click the Display toolbar check box in the Window area so that it displays a check mark. All other settings should match those in Figure 1-12. Point to the OK button.

The dialog box displays the selected options (Figure 1-12). The Window option button causes the MS-DOS Prompt window to display in a less than full screen view. The toolbar also will display. Windows NT may display these options on an Options tab.

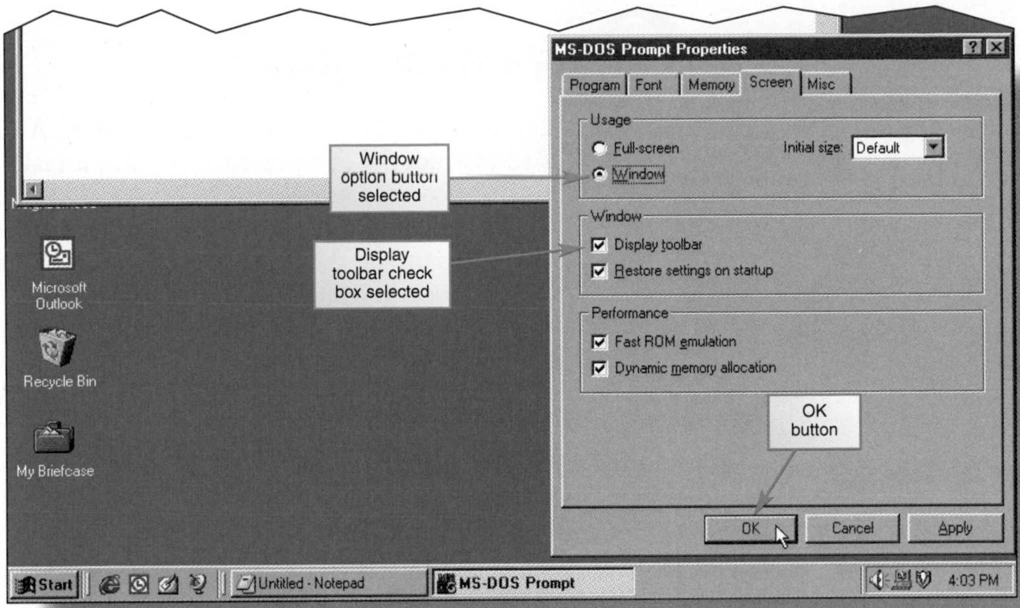

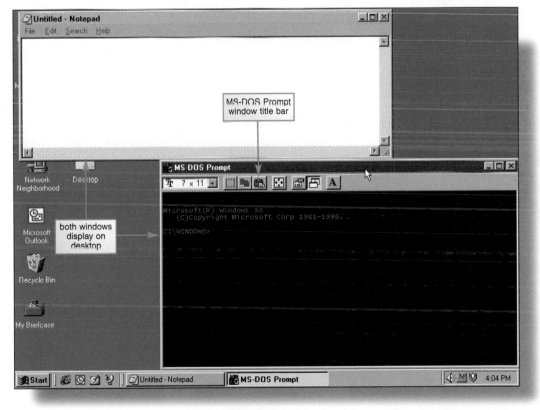

FIGURE 1-12

8 Click the OK button. If necessary, click the MS-DOS Prompt button on the taskbar to display the MS-DOS Prompt window. When the MS-DOS Prompt window displays, drag its title bar so that the window displays in the lower-right corner of the screen as shown in Figure 1-13.

FIGURE 1-13

Java programmers set up their desktops in a variety of ways. Some like to maximize the Notepad window. Others use different text editors such as WordPad or Microsoft Word. Your instructor may suggest other ways to setup the desktop.

Other Ways

1. Click Start button, click Run, type command.com, click OK button

Coding the Program

The third step of the PDLC is to code the program. A **program** is a set of detailed instructions to instruct the computer to perform a task. Figure 1-14 displays the lines of instructions, called **source code**, in the Java programming language to perform the given task. The task to be performed by the first program is to display the name and address of the company on the screen. Instructing the computer to save a set of instructions to perform the task, and then learning how to execute those instructions on any computer platform or the Web, is a stepping stone to creating larger, more intricate, and more useful programs. You may want to refer to Figure 1-14 as you read through the explanation of the code and commands on the following pages.

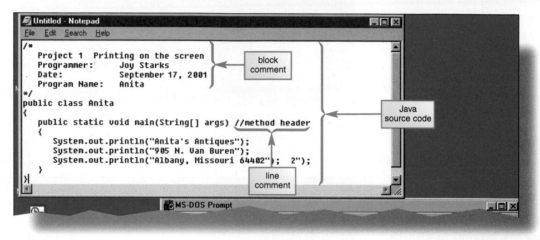

FIGURE 1-14

Documentation

It is a good programming practice to include in Java programs remarks that are documentary in nature, providing comments about the program and programmer. Even though documentation sometimes is a means of formalizing the solution to a computer programming problem, including remark lines from the beginning is a good habit to form. When it is necessary to look at source code, comments placed at the beginning of the program provide an immediate description of what the program is going to do. Comments also help the programmer to think clearly about the purpose of the upcoming code.

The following lines of code are typical of documentation at the beginning of a Java program:

```
/*
    Project 1  Printing on the screen
    Programmer:    Joy Starks
    Date:          September 17, 2001
    Program Name: Anita
*/
```

These **comments** remind the programmer and other users of the purpose of the program, the name of the programmer, the date, and other pieces of important documentation. The comments are not executed when the program runs. Comment lines display in the coding itself and on printouts of the source code, but they do not cause the computer to perform any given task.

In Java, comments can take two different forms. A **block comment** begins with a forward slash followed by an asterisk (/*) and ends with the symbols reversed, an asterisk followed by a forward slash (*/). Block comments must stay together in a block; they cannot be interrupted or separated by commands or other lines of code. However, block comments can be placed before or after other lines of codes. Block comments may span as many lines as necessary within the beginning and ending marks. Typically, each line within a block comment is indented for ease in reading. Programmers may use a block comment at the beginning of a program to describe the entire program, or in the body of a program to describe the function of a specific method or routine.

A **line comment** is a comment that spans only a single line or part of a line. Sometimes called a traditional comment, a line comment commonly is used to describe the purpose of a single command and is placed at the end of the same line as that command. Line comments begin with two forward slashes (//). During execution, the two forward slashes cause the rest of that line to be ignored. Line comments have no ending symbol. A line comment is useful especially when describing the intended meaning of the current line of code, whereas the block comment generally is more useful in describing larger sections of code.

In Figure 1-14, the first six lines are a block comment. Line 9 contains a line comment describing that line.

The Access Modifier and Class Name

After the comments, the first active line of code identifies how your code will be accessed and specifies the class name.

```
public class Anita
```

As you read in the Introduction Project, a class is an object or a set of objects that shares a common structure and a common behavior. The entire program in Java is considered a class. The keyword, public, is called an access modifier. Java code must begin with an **access modifier**, which specifies the circumstances in which the class can be accessed. In this program, public, indicates that this code can be accessed by all objects and can be extended, or used, as a basis for another class. If you omit the keyword, public, you limit the access to this class. Other access modifiers are discussed in a later project.

The access modifier is followed by the word, class, and the class name, which in this case is Anita. The **class name** or class identifier is assigned by you. It should be a user-friendly word that is not on the list of reserved words (see Appendix B). Java sets forth certain rules about class names; a class name may contain no spaces, and must not begin with a number. It is customary to begin a class name with a capital letter. Table 1-1 displays the naming rules and examples of legal class names as well as illegal names.

Table 1-1 Java Class Naming Rules		
RULE	LEGAL EXAMPLES	ILLEGAL EXAMPLES
Class names must begin with a letter (preferred because it is more user-friendly), an underscore, or a dollar sign.	Employee	123Data
Class names may contain only letters (preferred), digits, underscores, or dollar signs.	Record Record123	Record#123 Record 123
Class names may not use reserved words. Refer to Appendix B for a list of reserved words.	MyClass	Class

When you save your file, the Java compiler expects the file name to match the same class name that you assigned at the beginning of your program. Java is **case-sensitive**, which means that if you use a class name beginning with a capital letter, you must name the file with a capital letter, too. The Java compiler considers uppercase and lowercase as two different characters. Conventionally, Java programmers use capital letters to distinguish words in the class names, such as MyAddressProgram or MarchPayroll.

Everything after the class name is considered the contents of the class and must be enclosed in **braces { }**.

```
public class Anita
{
 . . .
}
```

It does not matter if you place the first brace on the same line as the access modifier and class name or place it on the line below. Also, some Java programmers indent the braces; others do not. In any case, consistency makes for a more legible program, and each opening brace must be paired with a closing brace.

Methods and the Method Header

The first line of code inside the class is the **method header**.

```
public static void main(String[ ] args)
```

As discussed in the Introductory Project, a method is the code to perform a service or operation, including tasks such as performing calculations, storing values, and presenting results. The **main method** is the usual starting point for all stand-alone Java applications.

In the above line of code, the word, public, is the access modifier. It declares or establishes the method as accessible to all classes. The word, static, is a method modifier. **Method modifiers** enable you to set properties for the method, such as where it will be visible and how subclasses of the current class will interact with the method. Static, as a modifier, means that this method is for a class, not an instance. An **instance** is a unique object or a specific occurrence of a class of objects or a method.

After the modifiers, a typical method has three parts: the return value, the method name, and the arguments list. In the program for this project, the method is written as follows:

```
void main(String[ ] args)
```

Void means that this method does not return a value when it is called. Methods can result in an **answer**, similar to the return value of a function in a spreadsheet application; or they can return nothing — as is the case in this method. The name of the method, main, comes next followed by parentheses. Inside the parentheses is any number of arguments. An **argument** is a piece of data, or a data location, sent along with the method to help it perform its operation. For example, a method to calculate sales tax would need to know the amount of the sale and the tax rate in order to return an answer. The sales amount and the tax rate would be arguments. In this example, args is an identifier for any string or character argument that the method, main, may need. An **identifier** is like a variable storage location to hold information.

Naming it args is traditional, but you can give it other names. The word, String, refers to a **data type**, or the type of data you expect the identifier to be. In this case, it must be capitalized.

Programmers and language documentation would say Java's main method accepts a String argument identified as args, and returns void.

Code

You must enclose the lines of code, or **body**, of the method in pairs of braces just as you did with the class. The body of the method usually is indented to facilitate reading and editing. These lines of code in braces, following the main method header, actually perform the tasks.

```
{
    System.out.println("Anita's Antiques");
    System.out.println("905 N. Van Buren");
    System.out.println("Albany, Missouri 64402");
}
```

Classes, objects, methods, and arguments are used in this code. System is the name of the class. Out is the object that represents the default display, which is the monitor. Println is the name of a method that takes a string argument. Println returns its value to the System.out device. The method's argument, in this case, is a string of characters enclosed in quotation marks. The string of characters is called a **literal**, which means the data inside the quotes literally will display on the monitor.

These lines of code in Java must end with a semicolon (;). During execution, these command lines tell the default output device, the monitor, to print the literal text on the screen. Figure 1-14 on page J 1.14 displays the entire source code.

After entering the code, you will save the program. To prevent Notepad from assigning its standard .txt extension during the save process, you will enclose the file name in quotation marks.

Perform the following steps to enter the Java source code and save it on a floppy disk.

More About

System.out

The out object can accept methods related to things other than printing text. Methods such as writing data to a stream of characters, flushing data from that stream and checking for errors, and closing the stream each have their own method name and arguments.

More About

Displaying Blank Lines

If you want to display a blank line as part of your screen output, enter the Java statement, `System.out.println("")`, at the appropriate location in your code. The null string, `""` will display nothing on the screen, but println will force a carriage return and line feed creating the blank line.

Steps To Enter and Save Java Source Code

1 **Click the Notepad window.**

The insertion point displays in the Notepad window (Figure 1-15).

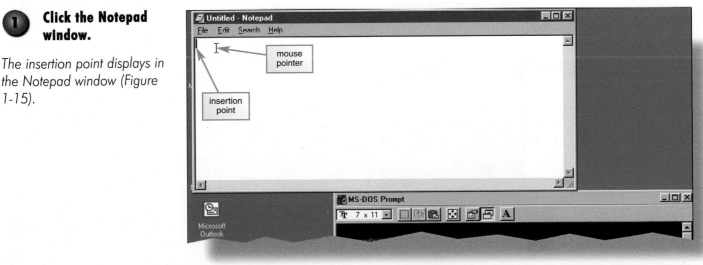

FIGURE 1-15

2 Type the code as shown in Figure 1-16. Be sure to indent as shown using either the SPACEBAR key or the TAB key, and remember that Java is case-sensitive.

The Notepad window displays the Java source code (Figure 1-16).

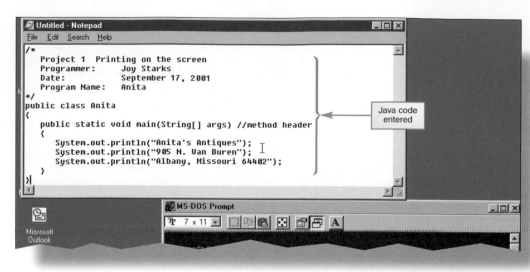

FIGURE 1-16

3 With a floppy disk in drive A, click File on the menu bar, and then point to Save As.

The File menu displays (Figure 1-17).

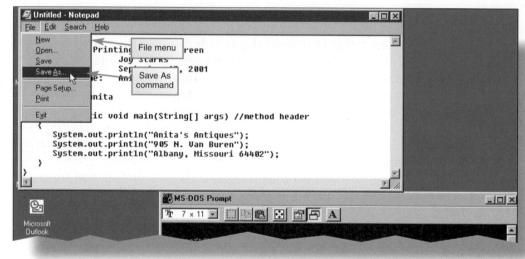

FIGURE 1-17

4 Click Save As. When the Save As dialog box displays, type "Anita.java" in the File name text box. Point to the Save in box arrow.

The Save As dialog box displays options for saving the code (Figure 1-18). Remember that Java is case-sensitive.

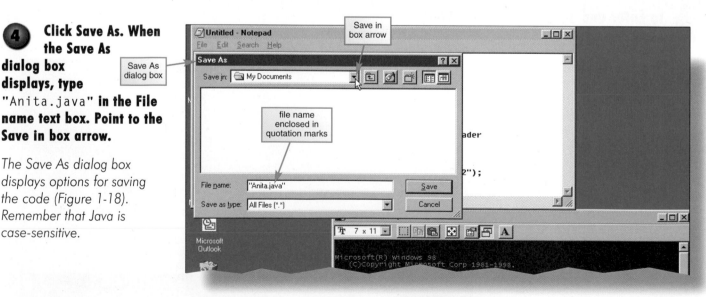

FIGURE 1-18

5 **Click the Save in box arrow and then click 3½ Floppy (A:) in the list. Point to the Save button.**

Drive A is selected (Figure 1-19).

6 **Click the Save button.**

The file is saved on drive A.

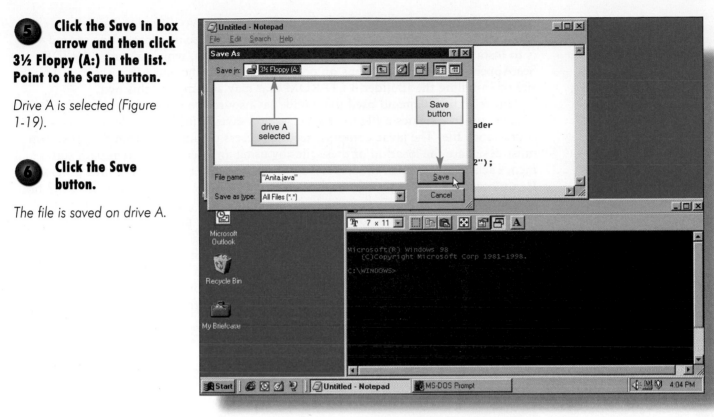

FIGURE 1-19

Other Ways

1. Type code, press ALT+F, press A

Notepad usually saves files with the extension .txt. Enclosing the file name in quotation marks in the File name text box forces Notepad to save the file as typed; that is, with the extension .java so that the compiler will recognize the file. If you decide to use another application to create the Java program, make sure you remember to save the file in a plain text format with the extension .java.

Testing the Program

The fourth step of the PDLC is to test the program. Once you have written the program you must execute it in order to make sure it runs properly. In the Java programming language, executing the program is a two step process. First, you must compile the source code, and then you must run the resulting bytecode.

Compiling the Source Code

Source code provides the keywords, commands, and language syntax that become the source the Java compiler can understand. Java source code must be compiled before it can be executed. A **compiler** is a programming language tool that translates source code that is closer to English, to executable code that is closer to machine language. Recall that Sun provides a Java compiler, javac, which translates the source code into bytecode. **Bytecode** is the code that can be interpreted on any machine. The name of the interpreter is called the Java Virtual Machine (JVM).

A Java programmer needs all of these tools in order to write, compile, interpret, and execute a Java program. The **Java 2 Software Development Kit (SDK)**, containing

More About

Setting the DOS Path

If you do a lot of programming in Java, you might want to consider changing the path statement in your autoexec.bat file which eliminates the need to set the path each time you open the MS-DOS Prompt window. For more information on adding the JDK path to your system, visit the Java Programming Web page (www.scsite.com/java/more.htm) and click Path Statements.

the JDK and accompanying tools, may be obtained in two different ways. First, programmers may download the SDK from the Web, free of charge. The second way is to install an IDE, such as Inprise's JBuilder 3 program, which includes the JDK. See Appendix A for instructions on downloading from the Sun Microsystems Web site or installing the JBuilder 3 CD-ROM that may accompany this text.

Javac is the command used to compile Java source code into bytecode. The compilation process creates a file for each class and saves it in the same directory as the source code file. The javac compiler needs to access certain files from the JDK. You must designate the location of these files by using an operating system path statement each time you open the MS-DOS Prompt window to compile a Java program. If you downloaded the JDK from the Sun Web site, your path will be c:\jdk1.2.2\bin. If you installed JBuilder 3, your path will be c:\jbuilder3\java\bin. Alternately, ask your instructor for ways to permanently add the correct path statement to your system's start up process.

In this project, however, you will use a path command at the command prompt to change the path for this session. The **path command** is an operating system command that sets the search path for executable files. Perform the following steps to designate the correct path and then compile the Anita program.

 To Set the Path and Compile the Program

1 **Click the MS-DOS Prompt window.**

The insertion point displays in the MS-DOS Prompt window (Figure 1-20).

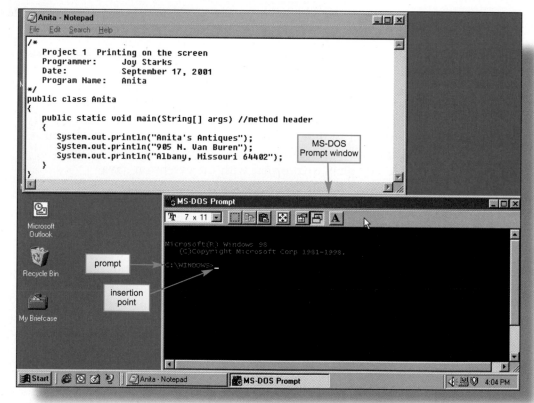

FIGURE 1-20

2 **If you downloaded Java from the Sun Microsystems Web site, type** path=c:\jdk1.2.2\bin **at the prompt and then press the ENTER key. If you installed the Java compiler from the JBuilder 3 CD-ROM that may accompany this text, type** path=c:\jbuilder3\ java\bin **and then press the ENTER key.**

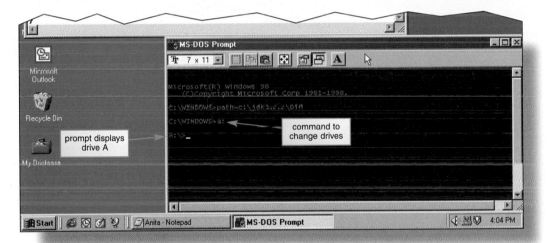

FIGURE 1-21

The command prompt redisplays (Figure 1-21). If no error messages display, the system accepted the command. See your instructor for the exact path of your JDK installation. The path statement is not case-sensitive.

 3 **Type** a: **and press the ENTER key to change to drive A.**

The command prompt now displays an A:\> indicating communication with drive A (Figure 1-22).

FIGURE 1-22

4 **Type** javac Anita.java **at the prompt and then press the ENTER key.**

The system compiles the program on drive A (Figure 1-23). After a few moments, the command prompt redisplays on a new line. If no errors occur, only the command prompt will display.

FIGURE 1-23

During compilation, javac adds a file to the disk called Anita.class, which is the actual bytecode.

Errors

If the JDK is not properly installed or the path is incorrect, your program will not compile. The path command, as explained on page J 1.20, must direct the operating system to the location of the javac Java compiler in order for your program to compile. Additionally, you must reference the correct location, in this case on the floppy disk, by either changing to drive A or including an A: before the file name when compiling, as explained on page J 1.21. Javac also needs to find a valid Java file name, spelled correctly and with the correct capitalization.

If your program compiles but displays error messages, you may have a syntax, semantic, run-time, or other logic error.

The process of fixing errors is called **debugging**. Finding the bugs in your code and in your logic is a skill that will improve as you learn to program. It can be a time-consuming and frustrating process, which is why a thorough test of the code is done while formalizing the solution.

Syntax Errors

Syntax errors usually are typing errors. Java attempts to isolate the error by displaying a line of code and pointing to the first incorrect character in that line. However, the problem may not be at that exact point. For instance, if you omit a necessary semicolon at the end of a line, you will see a message similar to Figure 1-24. The first error message says, Invalid type expression, and generates a second error, Invalid declaration. Both errors are due to the same missing semicolon and will not display once the syntax of the code is corrected. When the compiler cannot find the end of the first line, it generates a message with the file name, the line number, and suspected type of error. The compiler then tries to compile the two lines together, which results in a second error. A rule of thumb is to correct the first mistake in a long list. Doing so may reduce the total number of errors dramatically.

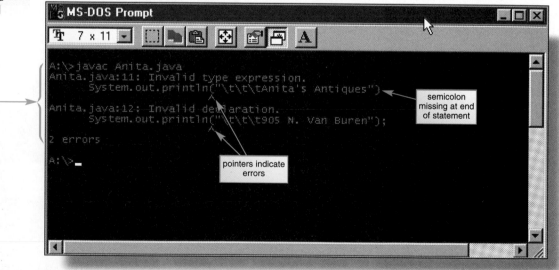

FIGURE 1-24

The most common mistakes are in capitalization, spelling, the use of incorrect special characters, and omission of correct punctuation. Table 1-2 lists some common syntactical errors, the messages you may see on the screen, and the method of correction.

Semantic Errors

Whereas syntax refers to code structure or grammar, a **semantic error** is one dealing with the meaning of the code. These types of errors display themselves as unrecognizable code to the Java compiler. For example, if you misspell a method like println, the compiler will return an error that says the method was not found. If you use a variable name that has not been declared properly, the compiler will return an error that says the variable is undefined.

TABLE 1-2 Typical Syntax Errors		
SYNTAX ERROR	SAMPLE ERROR MESSAGE	METHOD OF CORRECTION
missing semicolon	invalid type expression invalid declaration ';' expected	Add a semicolon at the end of the line
missing punctuation	')' expected	Insert missing) or }
incorrect file name	public class must be defined in a file	Make sure your class name and file name match exactly, both in spelling and capitalization
incorrect number of arguments	invalid argument	Add a comma between arguments in an argument list
incorrect use of mathematical operators	missing term	Correct operand error

Most semantic errors can be fixed by correcting the spelling of the keyword or by properly defining the codes and methods you wish to use.

If errors occur when you try to compile your program, correct the errors in the Notepad window, save the file again, and then compile the program again using javac. If Java still displays error messages after correcting all typing errors, consult your instructor.

Run-time Errors

Run-time errors will not display until you run or execute the program. Even programs that compile successfully may display wrong answers if the programmer has not thought through the logical processes and structures of the program. Your goal should be to have error-free programs, and by implementing the PDLC correctly, you will achieve that goal.

Occasionally, a logic error will surface during execution of the program because of an action the user performs, something that the programmer did not plan for ahead of time. During execution, users who input numbers outside of valid ranges, or those who enter the wrong types of data, can cause programs to stop executing. In future projects, you will learn how to look for data entry errors involving validity, range, and reasonableness. In this project, the user inputs no information, so you should not experience any abrupt termination of your program.

Other run-time errors may occur as you run a program. For instance, if you, as the programmer, entered the wrong address in a link or used an incorrect operator, the program still would compile and run correctly, but the wrong output would display. No run-time error message would occur. It is these kinds of errors that sometime appear in the final solutions to programs, even after the code has been released to the users.

A run-time error message also will display if you misspell the Java command, misspell the name of the bytecode file, or add an extension by mistake.

Run Errors

If you receive this error, "Exception in thread "main" java.lang.-NoClassDefFoundError:" Java cannot find your compiled bytecode file. One of the places in which Java tries to find your bytecode file is your current directory. If you do not store your files on drive A, you should change your current directory to that folder. Alternately, you can change the classpath permanently. For more information on changing the classpath, visit the Java Programming Web page (www.scsite.com/java/more.htm) and click Classpath Statements.

Running the Program

Once the program is compiled, programmers use the Java interpreter to run the program. An **interpreter** executes instructions line by line. Once the program is compiled, you simply type the command, java, followed by the name of the program to begin execution, as shown in the following step.

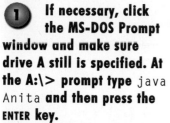

To Run the Java Program

1 **If necessary, click the MS-DOS Prompt window and make sure drive A still is specified. At the A:\> prompt type** java Anita **and then press the** ENTER **key.**

Java runs the program and displays the name and address of the company on the screen (Figure 1-25).

output displays

command to execute compiled program

FIGURE 1-25

In addition to the println method, Java supports a method called print. The **print** method does not send a carriage return/line feed message to the monitor like println. The print method is useful when you want the insertion point to stay on the same line.

Editing the Source Code and Recompiling

When you edit or modify the source code in any way, you must go through the steps of saving, compiling, and re-executing the program. Even something as simple as changing the spacing between characters necessitates these steps if you want the program to run properly.

Formatting Output Using Escape Characters

In the Anita program, you will insert some special codes to move the output from the left side of the screen so it is positioned more toward the middle. Java uses **escape characters** inside the string arguments of the println method to move the insertion point, which thereby moves the text output. Escape characters, also called escape codes or escape sequences, are non-printing control codes. Table 1-3 displays some of the Java escape code characters related to the monitor.

TABLE 1-3	Java Escape Codes	
CODE	CONCEPT	RESULT
\t	horizontal tab	moves insertion point eight spaces to the right
\b	Backspace	moves insertion point one space to the left
\n	new line	moves insertion point down one line and to the left margin
\r	carriage return	moves insertion point to the left margin

In the following steps, you will edit the Anita program by adding escape characters to the string argument of the println method. You also will add an e-mail address to the output. Perform the following steps to edit the program.

Steps: To Edit a Java Program and Save It with the Same File Name

1 **Click the Notepad window,** immediately to the left of the word, Anita's, on line 11.

The insertion point displays between the quotation mark and the A of Anita (Figure 1-26).

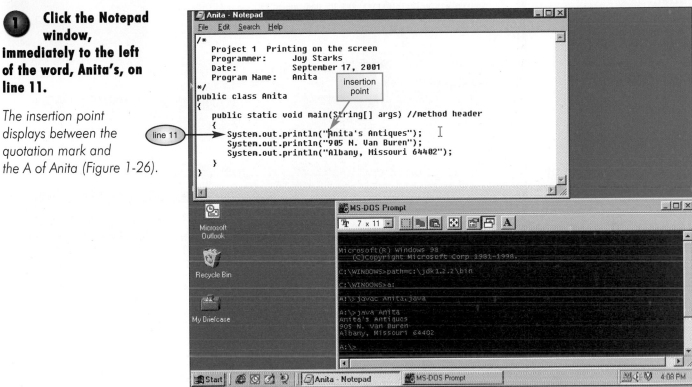

FIGURE 1-26

2 **Type \t\t\t after the quotation mark in line 11.**

The escape code characters display as part of the string argument (Figure 1-27). They will cause the insertion point to move 24 spaces to the right — eight spaces for each escape code — before printing the string on the monitor.

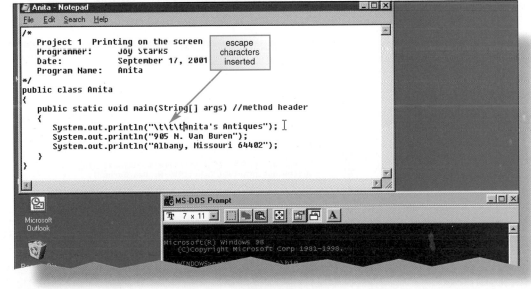

FIGURE 1-27

3 Repeat Step 2 for the address line, and the city/state/zip line of code, making certain you position the insertion point between the quotation mark and the first character.

The three println methods display escape code characters in their string arguments (Figure 1-28).

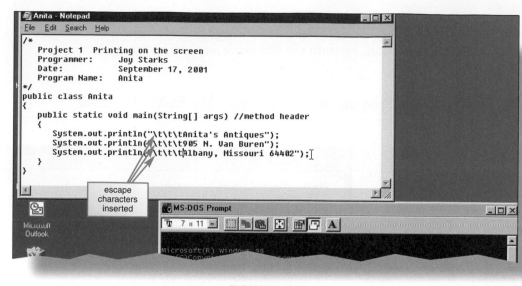

FIGURE 1-28

4 Click at the end of line 13. Press the ENTER key. Press the SPACEBAR or TAB key so the insertion point is positioned under the S in System on the previous line.

A new line displays with the flashing insertion point (Figure 1-29).

FIGURE 1-29

5 Type System.out. println("\t\t\ tAnitasAntiques@Small Store.com"); **to add an e-mail address line to the program.**

The new line of code displays (Figure 1-30).

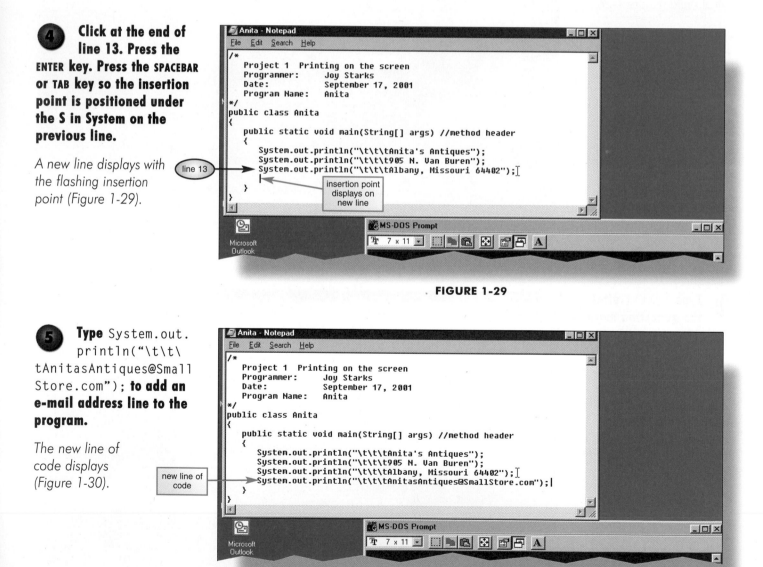

FIGURE 1-30

6 **Click File on the menu bar and then point to Save.**

The File menu displays (Figure 1-31).

7 **Click Save.**

The file saves in the same location as specified in the previous Save As command, on drive A with the same file name, "Anita.java". The old version of the file is replaced with the new, edited file.

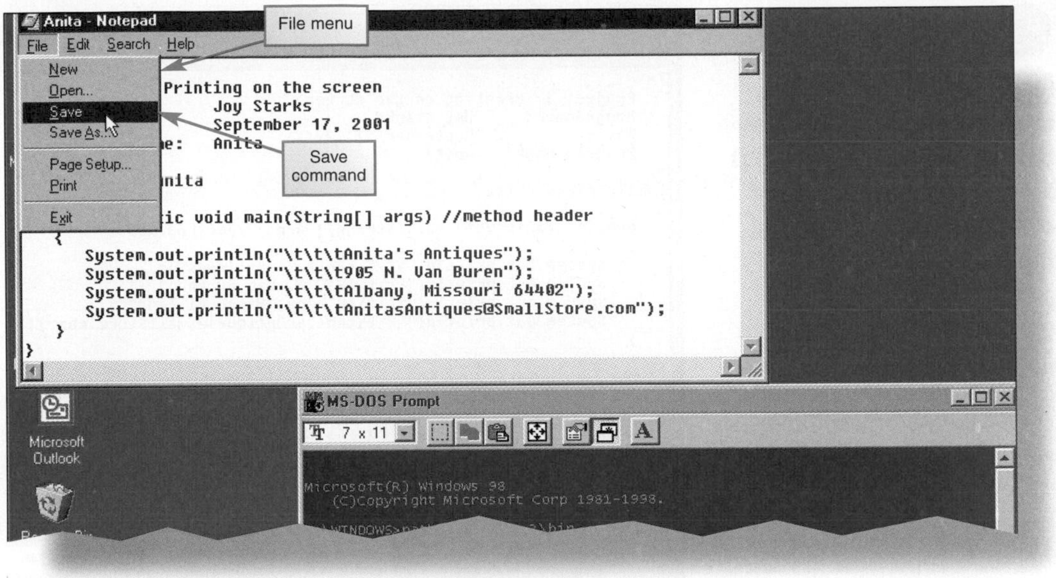

FIGURE 1-31

If you execute the program again, you will not see the newly formatted output. As you will see in the next series of steps, the program must be recompiled.

Recompiling and Running the Program

As you may remember, after compiling, Java created the file Anita.class that contains the bytecode or object code from your program. It is this object code that actually executes when you type Java and the file name. If you have not recompiled after editing, Java will execute the old bytecode and you will not see your updates. In order to run the most recent version of the program, you will compile Anita again and then run the new bytecode.

Follow these steps to recompile and run the program.

Steps **To Recompile and Run the Program**

1 **Click in the MS-DOS Prompt window or click the MS-DOS Prompt button on the taskbar to activate it. Type** `javac Anita.java` **and then press the ENTER key.**

The program compiles again (Figure 1-32).

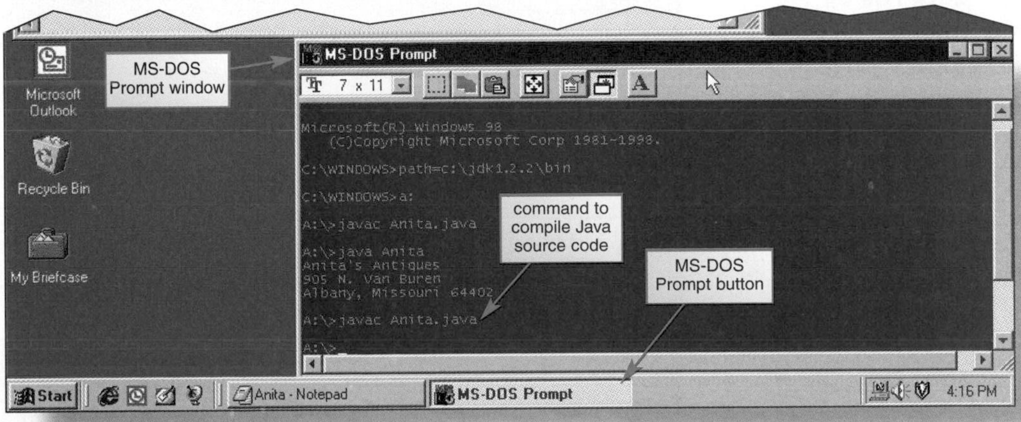

FIGURE 1-32

② **If the compiler displays errors, locate and fix them in the Notepad window, save the file again, and then repeat Step 1. Once the program compiles successfully, run the program by typing** java Anita **at the command prompt and then press the ENTER key.**

The program runs and the println methods send data to the monitor (Figure 1-33). The address lines display further to the right. The e-mail address also displays.

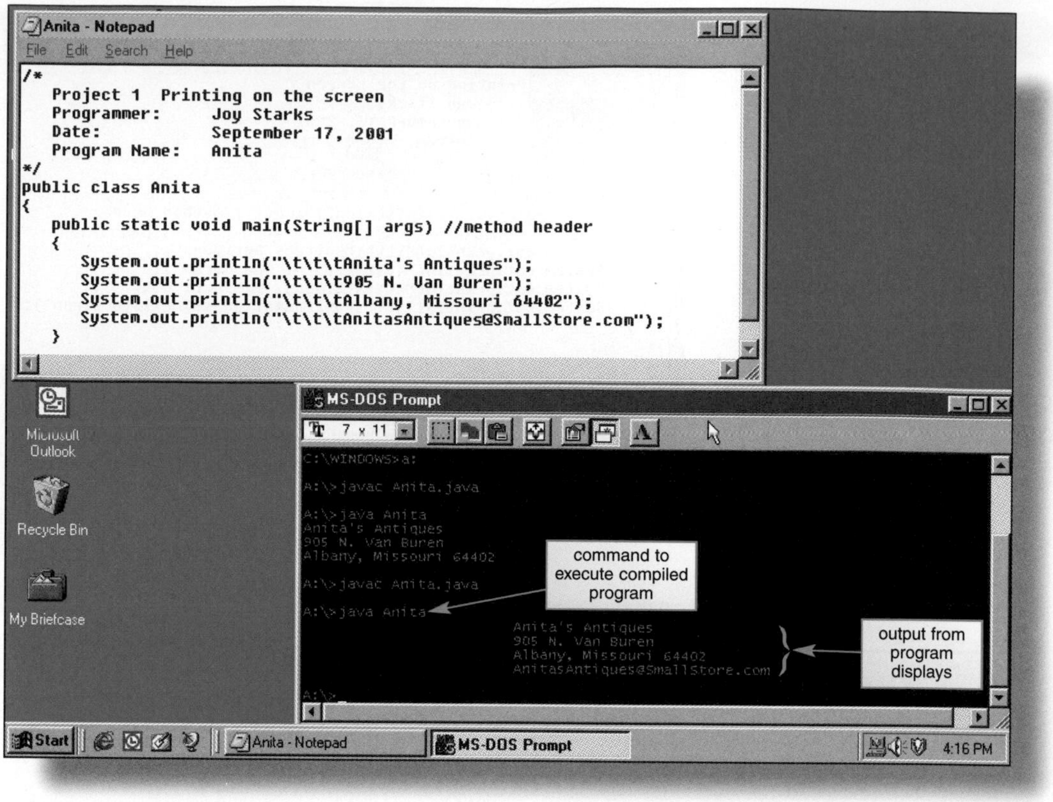

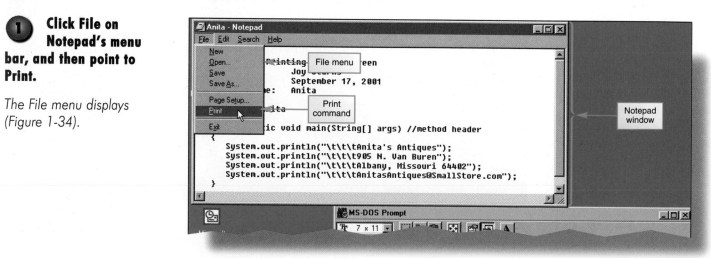

FIGURE 1-33

Printing the Source Code and Closing the Windows

In the following steps, you will print a copy of the source code using the Print command on Notepad's File menu. You also will use the title bar's Close button in the following steps to close both the Notepad and MS-DOS Prompt windows.

Steps To Print the Source Code and Close the Windows

① **Click File on Notepad's menu bar, and then point to Print.**

The File menu displays (Figure 1-34).

FIGURE 1-34

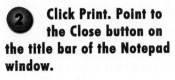

Click Print. Point to the Close button on the title bar of the Notepad window.

The source code for Anita.java prints on the system's default printer. The ScreenTip for the Close button displays (Figure 1-35).

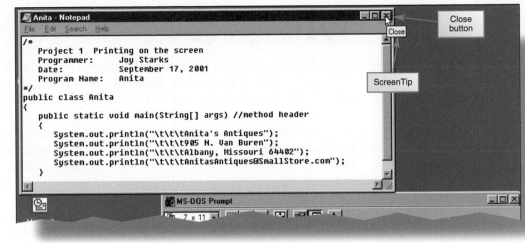

FIGURE 1-35

Click the Close button. Point to the Close button on the title bar of the MS-DOS Prompt window.

The Notepad window closes (Figure 1-36).

Click the Close button.

The MS-DOS Prompt window closes and the desktop again is completely visible.

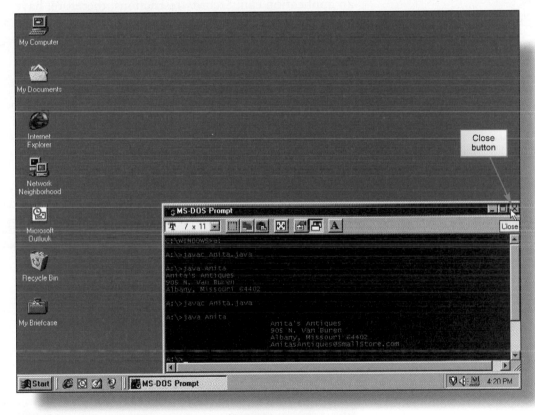

FIGURE 1-36

Notepad reminds you if you have not saved since changing any data in the Notepad window. Notepad does not save any resizing you may have done to the window. When you start Notepad again, you may have to move its window and resize it to customize your desktop.

The MS-DOS Prompt window does not save the path settings or drive changes you made when you exit to the desktop. However, the property changes you made on pages J 1.10 through J 1.13 for the font and window size will stay in effect when you open the window again.

Moving to the Web

One of the features that makes Java so useful is its ability to program applications that are machine-independent. Much of Java's portability lies in the use of small application programs that can run on the Web. These extremely popular mini-applications, which run as a part of a Web page, are called **applets**. An applet actually is any program called from within another language. Prior to the Web, the built-in writing and drawing programs that came with Windows sometimes were called applets. Java applets can perform interactive animations, immediate calculations, or other simple tasks without having to access the computer that is hosting the Web page.

There are major differences between Java applications and Java applets. One difference is the mode in which they are run; applications run in stand-alone or console mode, while applets run in a browser or viewer. Another difference is in their scope for data handling. An applet cannot be used to modify files stored on a user's system; an application can. Security restrictions, therefore, have less impact on applications. Another difference is that applications do not need a memory intensive browser or viewer in order to execute.

Opening Source Code Files

In the following steps, you will reopen the source code for the Anita program that was saved on your floppy disk. You then will edit and create an applet.

 ### To Start Notepad and Open a Java Source Code File

1 **Click the Start button on the taskbar and then point to Programs on the Start menu. Point to Accessories on the Programs submenu, and then click Notepad. When the Notepad window opens, drag its title bar to the upper-left corner of the desktop.**

The repositioned Notepad window displays (Figure 1-37).

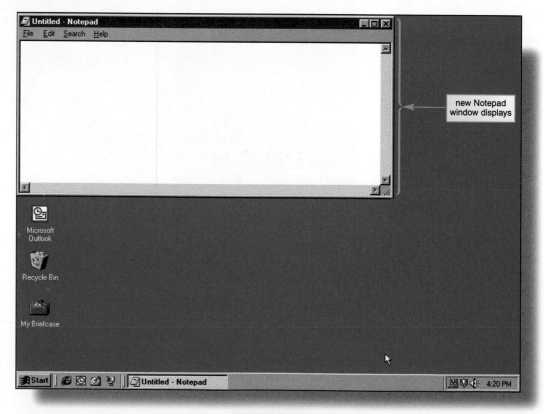

FIGURE 1-37

2 **Click File on the menu bar and then point to Open.**

The File menu displays (Figure 1-38).

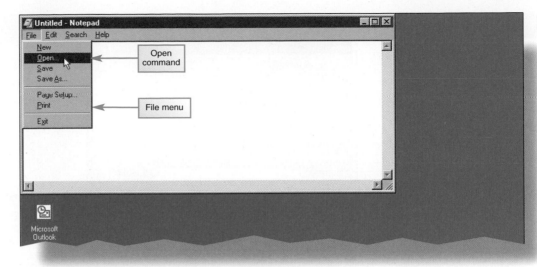

FIGURE 1-38

3 **Click Open. When the Open dialog box displays, point to the Files of type box arrow.**

The Open dialog box displays choices for the location, name, and type of files for Notepad to open (Figure 1-39).

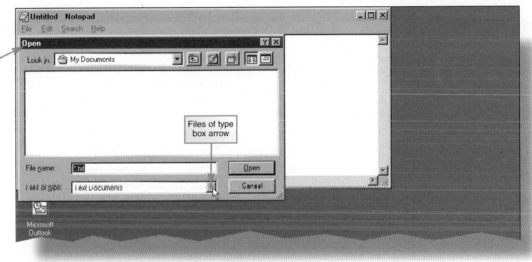

FIGURE 1-39

4 **Click the Files of type box arrow and then click All Files (*.*) in the list. Point to the Look in box arrow.**

Notepad will display files of all types (Figure 1-40).

FIGURE 1-40

5 Click the Look in box arrow and then click 3½ Floppy (A:) in the list. Point to the Java file named Anita.

Files from the floppy disk display (Figure 1-41). Both the Java source code and the compiled bytecode are named Anita. The source code usually displays with a Notepad. Your icons may differ depending on your installation of the JDK or JBuilder 3, and on the display detail.

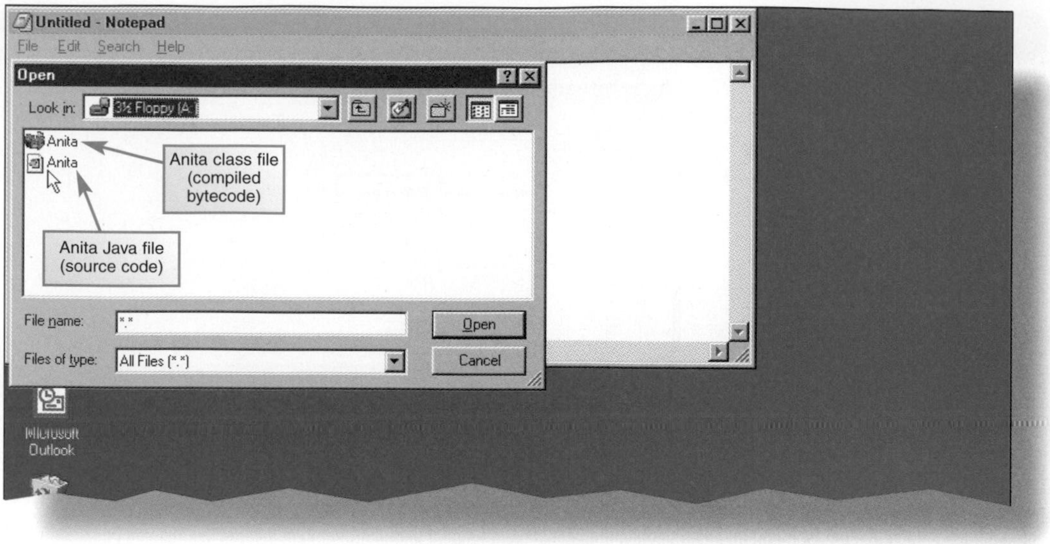

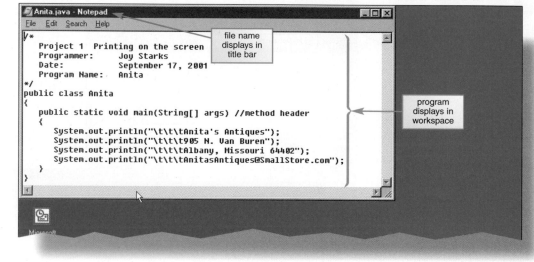

FIGURE 1-41

6 Double-click the source code file, Anita.

The Open dialog box closes and the Anita file displays in the Notepad workspace (Figure 1-42). The file name displays on the title bar.

FIGURE 1-42

Other Ways

1. Type complete path and name of file in File name box

When using the Open dialog box, if you do not choose All Files (*.*) in the Files of type list, Notepad will display only files with the extension .txt. Because Java programs have the extension .java, Notepad does not display Java source code files automatically.

Importing Packages

You will make modifications to the source code in order to direct the output to a Web window. The classes and methods needed to create such a window are not immediately available unless you tell the compiler, through the coding, to access the storage location. The JDK includes packages as part of the standard installation, packages that are used when creating an applet. **Packages** are collections of classes, sometimes called libraries, which contain portable Java bytecode files. Because there are hundreds of Java classes, the package is a convenient way to group them and maintain some order among this huge collection.

Some of the more significant packages and their descriptions are listed in Table 1-4. See Appendix A for information on downloading the JDK help files that contain a complete listing of which class resides in which package.

TABLE 1-4 JDK Provided Packages	
PACKAGE NAME	DESCRIPTION
java.applet	classes to facilitate using applets
java.awt	Abstract Window Toolkit; classes to facilitate graphics user interfaces
java.net	classes used for networking and client/server applications
java.io	classes to facilitate input and output
java.lang	classes to facilitate data types, threads, strings, and others
java.util	classes used for dates, vectors, and others

The java.lang package is the only package imported automatically without an explicit command; all other packages need an import command. The **import** command is placed at the beginning of java source code, most commonly right after the opening documentation. During compilation, the import command goes to the location where the JDK is stored and loads the appropriate class or classes. You may load all the classes within a package by typing an asterisk (*) or you may load individual classes by using their name.

Follow these steps to edit the Anita program you created earlier in this project and insert two import commands.

Steps To Insert the Import Command

1 **Make sure the Anita.java file is open in Notepad. Click at the end of line 6. Press the ENTER key.**

A new line displays in the source code (Figure 1-43).

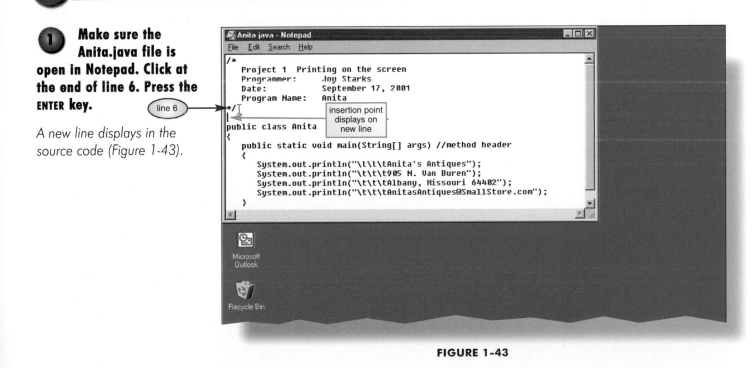

FIGURE 1-43

2 **Type** `import`
`java.applet.*;`
and then press the ENTER
key. Type `import`
`java.awt.*;` **on the new**
line.

The commands to import two
packages from the JDK display (Figure 1-44). All the
classes will be imported when
you include the asterisk.

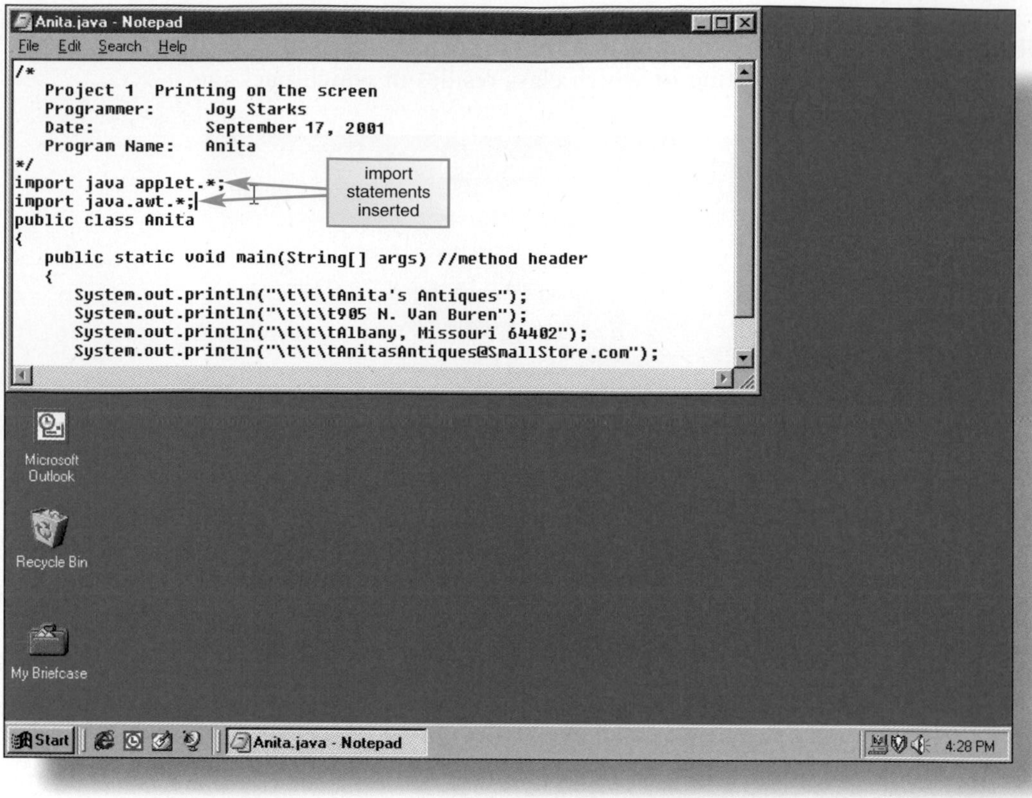

```
Anita.java - Notepad

File  Edit  Search  Help

/*
    Project 1  Printing on the screen
    Programmer:     Joy Starks
    Date:           September 17, 2001
    Program Name:   Anita
*/
import java applet.*;
import java.awt.*;
public class Anita
{
    public static void main(String[] args) //method header
    {
        System.out.println("\t\t\tAnita's Antiques");
        System.out.println("\t\t\t905 N. Van Buren");
        System.out.println("\t\t\tAlbany, Missouri 64402");
        System.out.println("\t\t\tAnitasAntiques@SmallStore.com");
```

import
statements
inserted

Microsoft
Outlook

Recycle Bin

My Briefcase

Start   Anita.java - Notepad   4:28 PM

FIGURE 1-44

Some programmers place the import statements before the block comments
instead of after them. Either way is acceptable, just as long as the import statements
are placed somewhere before the class header.

As you edit the remainder of the source code in order to adapt this program to
run on the Web, you will incorporate methods and classes that Java uses from these
two imported packages. Applets inherit certain attributes and manipulating classes
from the applet package. The **AWT** or **Abstract Window Toolkit** is a package included
with the JDK to provide you with access to color, draw methods, and other GUI
facilities commonly used in applets.

Editing the Applet

Because the purpose of this program now will be to run as an applet on the Web,
it is important to change the name of the class. You will change the program name in
the documentation, in the class header, and in the file name when you save. Additionally, you will **extend** the class, which means that this new Java class, created
specifically as an applet, must be a subclass of the general Applet class supplied with
the JDK applet package. The extends command is added to the class header along
with the name of the superclass. A superclass is a class that represents a broader,
higher category of the subclass object with a common structure and behavior. In this
case, Applet is the superclass you will use to create your specific applet subclass for
Anita's Antiques.

Perform the following steps to edit an applet.

Steps **To Edit an Applet**

1 **In the Notepad window, click after the word, Anita, in the documentation line. Without spacing, type** Applet **as shown in Figure 1-45.**

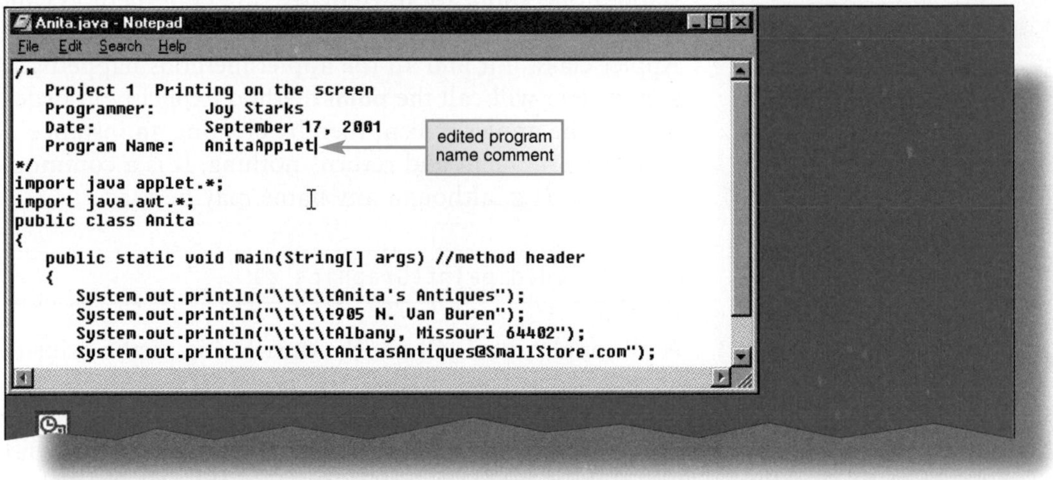

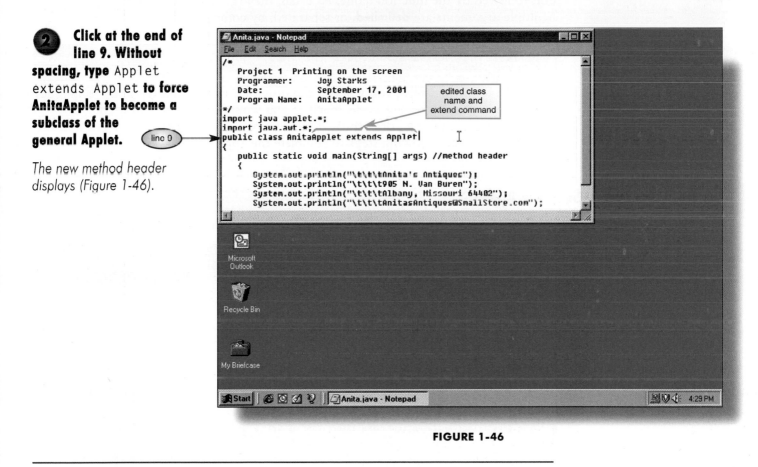

FIGURE 1-45

2 **Click at the end of line 9. Without spacing, type** Applet extends Applet **to force AnitaApplet to become a subclass of the general Applet.**

The new method header displays (Figure 1-46).

FIGURE 1-46

The relationship of the JDK to its packages, and the packages to their classes, is a perfect example of the superclass, class, and subclass hierarchy. You will learn more about creating subclasses and instances of existing classes in a later project.

The Paint Method and DrawString Method

The method header of an applet is not usually the main method, as it is in a stand-alone application. Actually, a default method called, **init**, initializes the applet and loads the initial setup of the applet. Because the previous steps extended the Applet class, init and all the applet methods happen automatically. However, in this applet, you will call the **paint** method explicitly in order to graphically draw some text on the applet screen, thereby creating an instance. The paint method takes a graphics argument and returns nothing. It is a common practice to identify the argument as g, although any name may be used.

```
public void paint(Graphics g)
```

Additionally, you will use the drawString method, instead of println. **DrawString**, which is a method of the AWT package, sends a message to a Graphics object. DrawString takes three arguments: a string to display, the horizontal (X) position at which to display the string, and the vertical (Y) coordinate at which to display the string. Notice that you use the variable name from the method header, followed by a dot, followed by the function name. As usual, the arguments are in parentheses. Multiple arguments are **delimited**, or separated, by commas.

```
g.drawString("Anita's Antiques", 15, 20)
```

In the following steps, you will edit the program. Use standard editing techniques to replace and enter the new code, much as you would for a word processing or spreadsheet program (i.e., drag through the text or use the DELETE and BACKSPACE keys). Perform the following steps to complete the applet and save it.

 ## To Complete and Save the Applet

1 **Edit the rest of the program as shown in Figure 1-47.**

The println methods have been replaced with the drawString method (Figure 1-47). The tab escape characters are replaced by coordinates following the string.

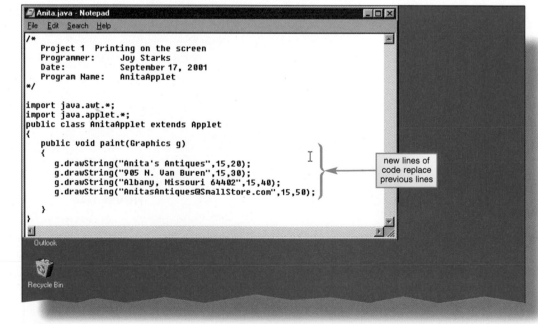

```
/*
    Project 1  Printing on the screen
    Programmer:     Joy Starks
    Date:           September 17, 2001
    Program Name:   AnitaApplet
*/

import java.awt.*;
import java.applet.*;
public class AnitaApplet extends Applet
{
    public void paint(Graphics g)
    {
        g.drawString("Anita's Antiques",15,20);
        g.drawString("905 N. Van Buren",15,30);
        g.drawString("Albany, Missouri 64402",15,40);
        g.drawString("AnitasAntiques@SmallStore.com",15,50);
    }
}
```

new lines of code replace previous lines

FIGURE 1-47

 **Click File on the menu bar and then point to Save As.**

The File menu displays (Figure 1-48).

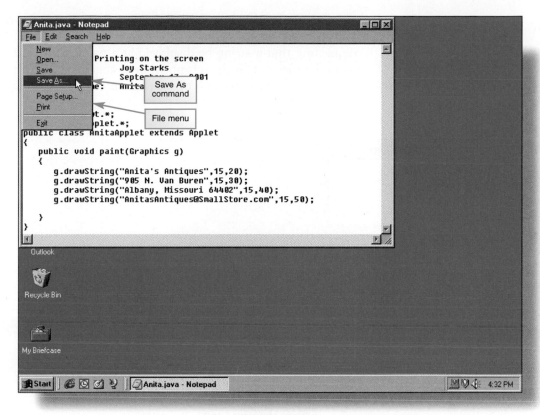

FIGURE 1-48

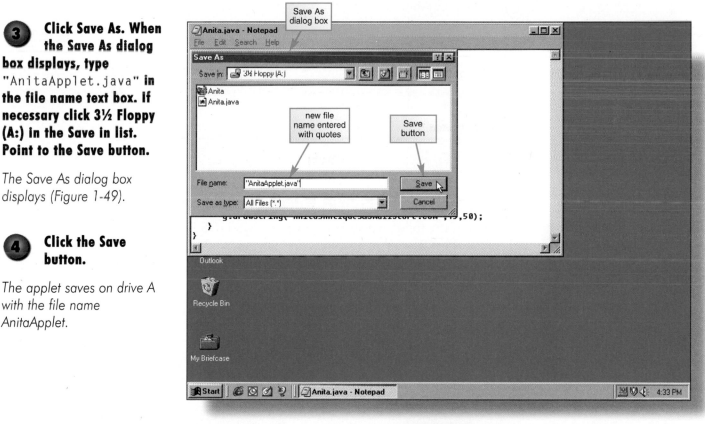

3 **Click Save As. When the Save As dialog box displays, type** `"AnitaApplet.java"` **in the file name text box. If necessary click 3½ Floppy (A:) in the Save in list. Point to the Save button.**

The Save As dialog box displays (Figure 1-49).

4 **Click the Save button.**

The applet saves on drive A with the file name AnitaApplet.

FIGURE 1-49

The Graphics argument is an object that models the drawing behavior of a portion of a screen, which means that it will respond to messages from a method requesting that a string be displayed at a particular location. The x-coordinate, as you might expect, is the left position of the string within the window, and the y-coordinate is the bottom or baseline of the string (Figure 1-50). Other methods used with the Graphics object draw shapes, add color, and return font information.

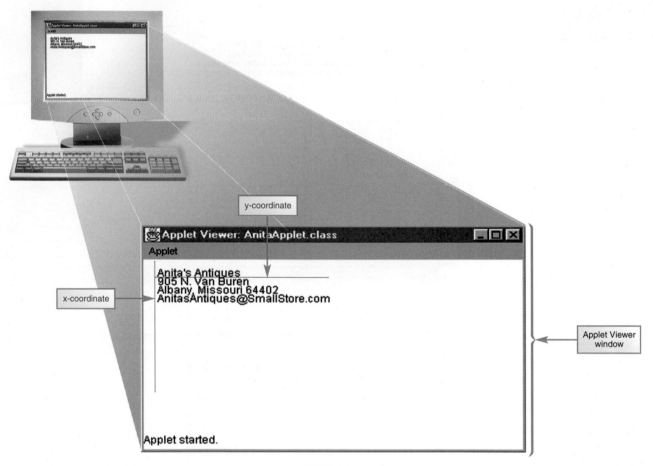

FIGURE 1-50

Opening the MS-DOS Prompt Window and Compiling the Applet

Perform the following steps to open the MS-DOS Prompt window and compile the applet. For detailed instructions on opening the MS-DOS Prompt window, see pages J 1.9 through J 1.13. For detailed instructions on compiling a program, see pages J 1.20 through J 1.21.

More About

Applet Color

Java's setBackground method allows you to change the background color of an applet window. For instance, the statement setBackground(Color.green); would change the background of the applet window to green.

TO OPEN THE MS-DOS PROMPT WINDOW AND COMPILE THE APPLET

 Click the Start button on the taskbar. Point to Programs. Click MS-DOS Prompt on the Programs submenu.

 When the MS-DOS Prompt window opens, if you downloaded Java from the Sun Web site, set the path by typing `path=c:\jdk1.2.2\bin` and then press the ENTER key. If you installed Java from the Inprise CD-ROM, set the path by typing `path=c:\jbuilder3\java\bin` at the command prompt. Press the ENTER key.

3 Specify drive A by typing `a:` and then press the ENTER key.

4 Type `javac AnitaApplet.java` and then press the ENTER key.

5 If an error message displays, correct the error in the Notepad window. Save the AnitaApplet.java file again, and repeat step 4.

The program compiles.

Again, possible errors include incorrect location for the Java compiler, typing mistakes, omitting special characters, case-sensitive errors, and file name errors. If you cannot determine your mistake based on what the Java compiler tells you about the error and the information about errors on pages J 1.22 through J 1.23, consult your instructor.

HTML Host Documents

Because an applet is initiated and executed from within another language or run as a part of a Web page, in order to view the applet in execution, you must create a **host,** or reference program to execute the applet. The applet for this project is called from a Web page. The HTML language is not really a language at all, because it cannot compute. It is a passive tool; in other words, it can present only the information that it carries. It cannot interact with the user to produce new information. That is why a Java applet is ideal for adding interactivity and programming to a Web page. You do not need to know the HTML language in order to program an applet; a few simple HTML commands are all that are necessary to create a host for a Java applet.

HTML Tags

HTML uses a concept called tags to reference Java applets. A **tag,** or markup, is a code specifying links to other documents, or code specifying how a Web page is to display. A tag has a beginning code word called a **start tag,** which is enclosed in angle brackets < >. The same code must be turned off after it is complete by using a slash before the code word called an **end tag,** again enclosed within angle brackets.

The tag at the beginning and end of the source code for a typical Web page is a perfect example. At the beginning, programmers insert a tag such as <HTML>. In order to end the code, programmers would need to insert </HTML>.

```
<HTML>
. . .
</HTML>
```

Tags

Other attributes that can be set with the applet tag include ALIGN, which sets how the applet is viewed: top, middle, or bottom, and VSPACE and HSPACE, which set the amount of space around the applet.

HTML

For more information on HTML code, visit the HTML Web page (www.scsite.com/html/more.htm).

In the following series of steps, you will create a simple HTML file to display the AnitaApplet you created earlier.

Steps **To Create the HTML Host Document**

1 **With the Notepad window still open, click File on the menu bar and then point to New. Be certain that any currently displayed files have been saved.**

The New command will clear the workspace (Figure 1-51).

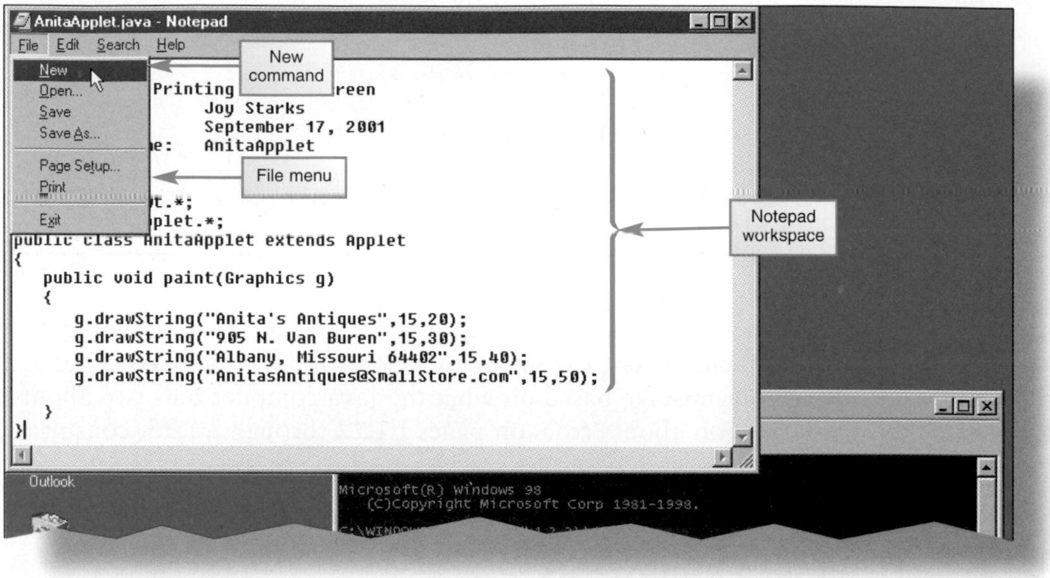

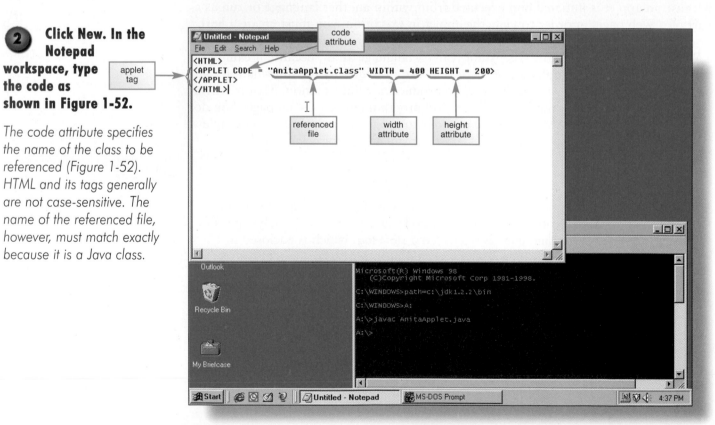

FIGURE 1-51

2 **Click New. In the Notepad workspace, type the code as shown in Figure 1-52.**

The code attribute specifies the name of the class to be referenced (Figure 1-52). HTML and its tags generally are not case-sensitive. The name of the referenced file, however, must match exactly because it is a Java class.

FIGURE 1-52

Click File on the menu bar and then click Save As. When the Save As dialog box displays, if necessary, click the Look in box arrow and click 3½ Floppy (A:) in the list. In the File name text box, type "AnitaApplet.html" **as the name of the file. Point to the Save button.**

The file will be saved on drive A with the name AnitaApplet.html (Figure 1-53). The quotation marks must be included to prevent Notepad from saving the file as a simple text file.

Click the Save button.

The file saves on drive A.

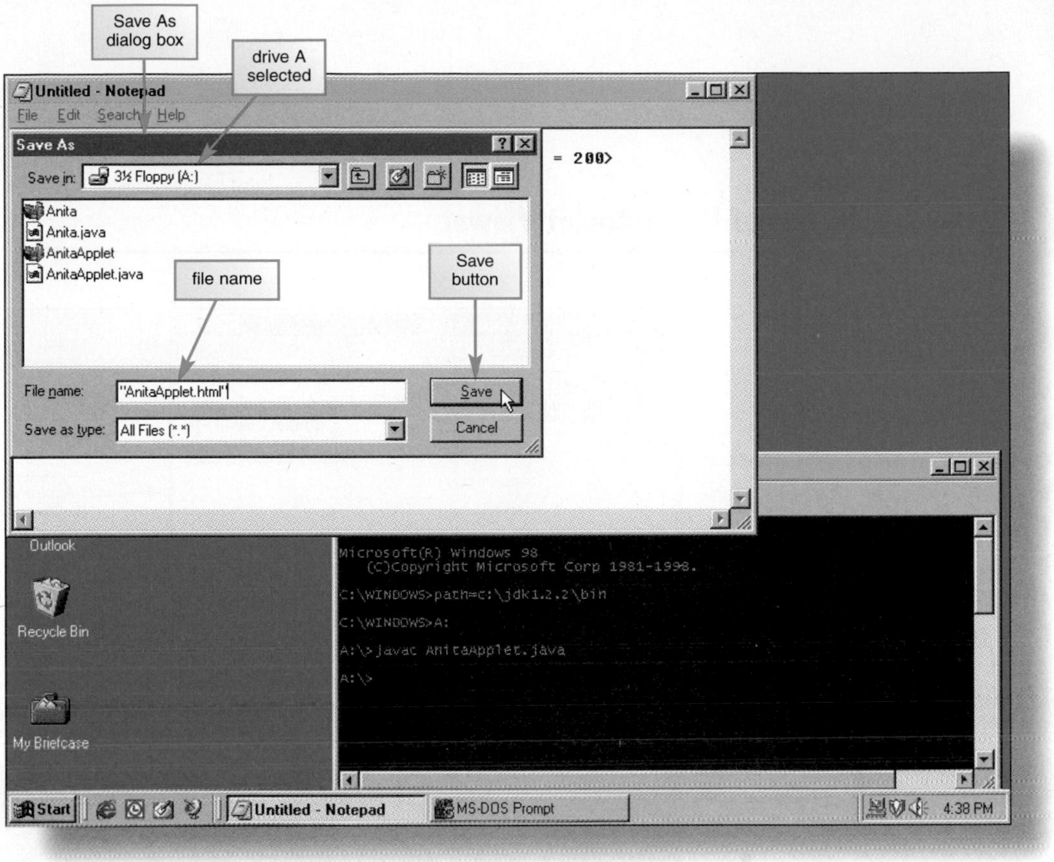

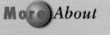

FIGURE 1-53

The applet tag, nested within the HTML beginning and ending tags, specifies three pieces of information that the Web page will need in order to access the Java applet: the name of the Java bytecode file, the width of the window, and the height of the window in which to run the applet (Figure 1-52).

The width and height attributes in the tag are measured in pixels. A **pixel,** or picture element, is the basic unit of programmable color on a computer display or in a computer image. You can think of it like a dot of light. Dots grouped together form characters and images. The physical size of a pixel depends on how you have set the resolution for your screen. For instance, if your screen resolution is 800 by 600 pixels, a width of 400 pixels means that the applet will display across approximately half the width of your screen.

Running an Applet Using Applet Viewer

The JDK provides an **appletviewer** command, which is a program to display Web page applets. At the command prompt, you type appletviewer, followed by the name of a host document, which is usually an HTML file. Applet Viewer displays each applet referenced by the host document in its own window.

Applet Viewer makes it possible to run a Java applet without using a browser. Applet Viewer ignores any HTML that is not immediately relevant to launching an applet. If the host document does not include a reference to an applet or similar object, Applet Viewer does nothing. If for some reason, you do not want to use Applet Viewer to execute the Java applet, you can display applets using a Web browser by entering the path and name of the host document in the browser's address text box.

More About

The Applet Tag

If your HTML file does not reference any applets using the OBJECT, EMBED, or APPLET tags, then Applet Viewer does nothing. For more information on the HTML tags that Applet Viewer supports, visit the Java Programming Web page (www.scsite.com/java/more.htm) and click Applet Viewer Tags.

The following step illustrates how to run an applet using Applet Viewer from the command prompt.

Steps To Run an Applet Using Applet Viewer

1 If the **A: prompt is not currently displayed in the MS-DOS window, type** a: **at the command prompt and press the ENTER key. In the MS-DOS Prompt window, type** appletviewer AnitaApplet.html **and then press the ENTER key.**

The applet displays on the screen (Figure 1-54). The name of the MS-DOS Prompt window changes to APPLET while the program is running.

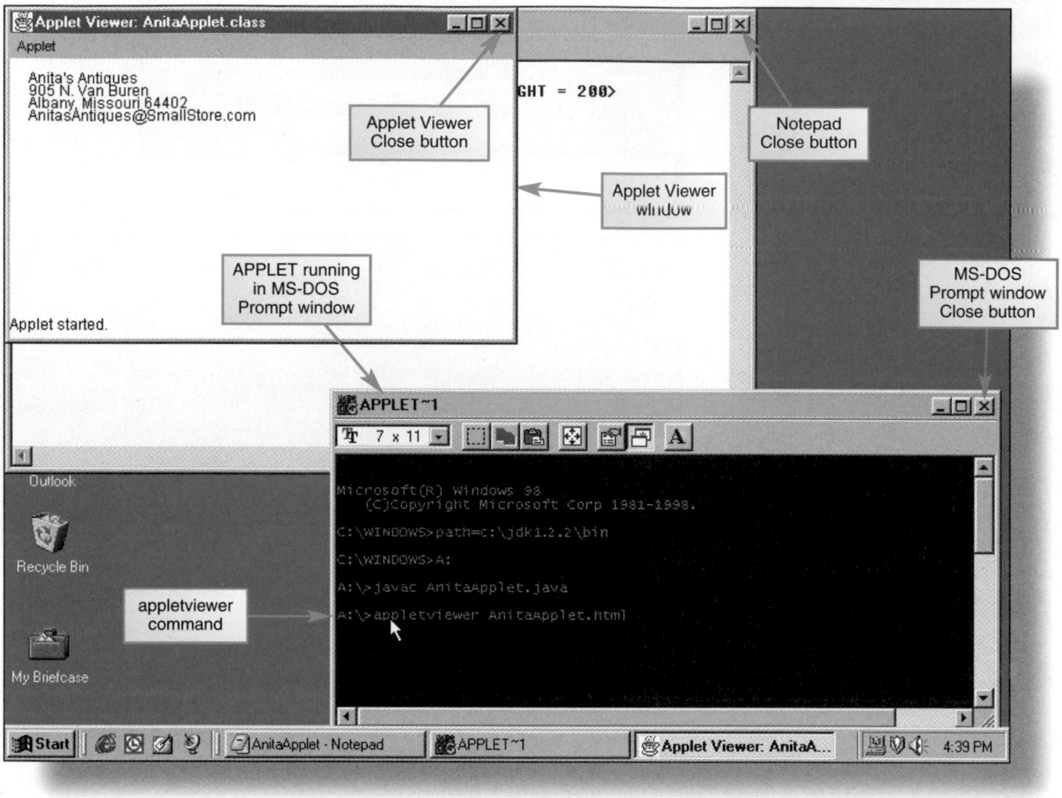

FIGURE 1-54

Applet Viewer does not contain any extra features like those in a browser. The advantage of using Applet Viewer is that you do not have to have access to a browser in order to view your applet. It also uses less memory than does a browser.

Closing the Open Applications

The project now is complete. Perform the following steps to close Applet Viewer, Notepad, and the MS-DOS Prompt windows.

TO CLOSE APPLET VIEWER, NOTEPAD, AND THE MS-DOS PROMPT WINDOWS

1 Click the Close button on the Applet Viewer title bar.

2 Click the Close button on the Notepad title bar.

3 Click the Close button on the MS-DOS Prompt title bar.

The applications close and the Windows desktop displays.

Summary

In this project, you learned the basic form of a Java program and an applet. You formatted the desktop to display both the Notepad window, used as an editor for Java source code, and the MS-DOS Prompt window, used to compile and run the Java programs in console, or stand-alone, mode. After inserting proper documentation, you learned the basic syntax of a class and method, along with naming conventions, arguments, and return values. You included sequential commands within the curly braces of the main method. After running and compiling the program, you edited the source code to include commands to create an applet that can run on the Web. Finally, you created a host program to display the applet and run it using Applet Viewer.

What You Should Know

Having completed this project, you now should be able to perform the following tasks:

▶ Close Applet Viewer, Notepad, and the MS-DOS Prompt Windows *(J 1.42)*

▶ Complete and Save the Applet *(J 1.36)*

▶ Create the HTML Host Document *(J 1.40)*

▶ Edit a Java Program and Save It with the Same File Name *(J 1.25)*

▶ Edit an Applet *(J 1.35)*

▶ Enter and Save Java Source Code *(J 1.17)*

▶ Insert the Import Command *(J 1.33)*

▶ Open and Format the Command Prompt Window *(J 1.9)*

▶ Open the MS-DOS Prompt Window and Compile the Applet *(J 1.39)*

▶ Print the Source Code and Close the Windows *(J 1.28)*

▶ Recompile and Run the Program *(J 1.27)*

▶ Run an Applet Using Applet Viewer *(J 1.42)*

▶ Run the Java Program *(J 1.24)*

▶ Set the Path and Compile the Program *(J 1.20)*

▶ Start Notepad *(J 1.8)*

▶ Start Notepad and Open a Java Source Code File *(J 1.30)*

Test Your Knowledge

1 True/False

Instructions: Circle **T** if the statement is true or **F** is the statement is false.

T F   1. Console mode refers to running Java programs from the command prompt.

T F   2. The Java Virtual Machine does not execute program comments.

T F   3. Two slashes (//) indicate a line comment.

T F   4. When a trigger sends a message to an object, an event occurs.

T F   5. Java code must begin with an access modifier.

T F   6. Java is not case-sensitive.

T F   7. The class name should be the same as the file name.

T F   8. Void means a method has no arguments.

T F   9. System.out usually is the default display.

T F 10. Java's println is a method.

2 Multiple Choice

Instructions: Circle the correct response.

1. IDE stands for _____ .
   a. Integration of Development Engineering
   b. Interactive Diagramming and Environments
   c. Interface Development Environment
   d. Integration of Diagnostic Encapsulation

2. Deciding on an exact sequence of steps to perform is done during the _____ phase of the Program Development Life Cycle.
   a. analysis
   b. design
   c. coding
   d. testing

3. The _____ is a way to interact with the operating system without using any specific application.
   a. command prompt
   b. Notepad
   c. Javac
   d. JBuilder 3

4. A(n) _____ is a piece of data or a data location, which is sent along with a method to help it perform its operation.
   a. identifier
   b. literal
   c. modifier
   d. argument

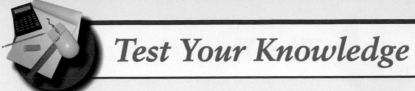

Test Your Knowledge

5. A(n) _____ is a programming language tool that translates source code into executable code.
   a. interpreter
   b. compiler
   c. IDE
   d. object code generator

6. Which of the following escape codes results in moving the insertion point 8 spaces to the right?
   a. \t
   b. \b
   c. \n
   d. \r

7. A misspelled method most likely would result in a _____ error.
   a. syntax
   b. message
   c. semantic
   d. logic

8. _____ are collections of classes, sometimes called libraries, which contain portable Java bytecode files.
   a. Methods
   b. Classes
   c. Packages
   d. Tables

9. The _____ command is placed at the beginning of java source code to load the appropriate class.
   a. system
   b. println
   c. main
   d. import

10. An extended class created specifically to be used as an applet must be a(n) _____ of the JDK Applet class.
   a. header
   b. superclass
   c. subclass
   d. application

Test Your Knowledge

3 Understanding the Desktop

Instructions: In Figure 1-55, arrows point to the parts of the two open windows on the desktop. Identify the various parts of those windows in the spaces provided.

FIGURE 1-55

Test Your Knowledge

4 Understanding Error Messages

Instructions: Figure 1-56(a) displays a Java program that prints a student's name and address on the screen. Figure 1-56(b) displays the compilation error messages. Rewrite the code to correct the errors.

```
Address.java - Notepad
File  Edit  Search  Help

/*
    Project 1  Printing on the screen
    Programmer:     Joy Starks
    Date:           September 9, 2001
    Program Name:   Address
//

public class Address
{
    public static void main(String[] args)
    {
        System.out.println("\t\t\tJason Frontera")
        System.out.println("\t\t\t1422 Stanley Blvd.");
        System.out.println("\t\t\tAurora, Colorado 80014");
    }

```

(a) Java Source Code

```
MS-DOS Prompt
 7 x 11

A:\>javac Address.java
Address.java:1: Comment not terminated at end of input.
/*
Address.java:12: Invalid type expression.
        System.out.println("\t\t\tJason Frontera")
                                                  ^
Address.java:13: Invalid declaration.
        System.out.println("\t\t\t1422 Stanley Blvd.");
                               ^
Address.java:15: '}' expected.
    }
    ^
4 errors

A:\>
```

(b) Java Compiler Error Messages

FIGURE 1-56

Apply Your Knowledge

1 Writing Java Code from a Flowchart

Instructions: Start Notepad. Open the file Apply1.java, from the Student Data Disk (see the inside back cover for instructions on how to obtain a copy of the Data Disk). Using the techniques you learned in the Introduction Project about reading flowcharts and the coding techniques you learned in this project, write the lines of code inside the main method to print the bibliographic entry as described in Figure 1-57.

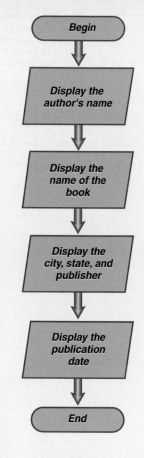

1. Open the file named Apply1.java on the Data Disk. With the Apply1.java program displayed in the Notepad window, locate the access modifier and class name Apply1. Change the class name to Biblio. Change the name to Biblio in the documentation lines as well.
2. Click inside the main method braces.
3. After studying the flowchart in Figure 1-57, enter the necessary lines of code to produce the output as shown in Figure 1-58.
4. Save the file on your floppy disk with the name "Biblio.java".
5. Open the MS-DOS Prompt window. If you downloaded JDK from the Sun Web site, set the path to the location of your Java bin by typing `path=c:\jdk1.2.2\bin` at the command prompt and press the ENTER key. If you installed the Java compiler from the JBuilder 3 CD-ROM that accompanies this text, type `path=c:\jbuilder3\java\bin` and press the ENTER key.
6. Change to drive A by typing `a:` and then press the ENTER key.
7. Compile your program by typing `javac Biblio.java` at the prompt. If the compilation is successful, proceed to step 8. Otherwise, return to step 3 and correct the errors.
8. Run the program by typing `java Biblio` at the prompt. If the program runs correctly, return to Notepad and print a copy for your instructor. Otherwise, return to step 3 and correct the errors.

FIGURE 1-57

```
MS-DOS Prompt

A:\>



Shelly, Gary B., Thomas J. Cashman, and Joy Starks.
       Java Programming: Introductory Concepts and Techniques.
       Cambridge, MA: Course Technology, 2001.




A:\>
```

FIGURE 1-58

In the Lab

1 Writing, Compiling, and Running a Java Program

Problem: In order to practice writing, compiling, and running Java, you decide to create a Java program that displays your name and address on the screen similar to the display in Figure 1-59.

FIGURE 1-58

Instructions:

1. To start Notepad, click the Start button. On the Start menu, click Programs and then click Accessories. On the Accessories menu, click Notepad.
2. Type the lines of code below, inserting your name and address in the appropriate places. (Remember: Java is case-sensitive.)
3. Save the program with the filename "Address.java" on your floppy disk.

```
/*
    Project 1, In the Lab 1, Printing my name and address on the screen
    Programmer:     Your Name
    Date:           September 9, 2001
    Program Name: Address
*/
public class Address
{
    public static void main(String[] args)
    {
        System.out.println("\t\t\tYour Name");
        System.out.println("\t\t\tYour Street Address");
        System.out.println("\t\t\tYour City, State, and Zip Code");
    }
}
```

4. To open the MS-DOS Prompt window, click the Start button. On the Start menu, click Programs and then click MS-DOS Prompt. Set your path and specify the floppy disk drive as explained on pages J 1.20 through J 1.21.
5. Compile the program by typing javac Address.java at the command prompt.
6. If necessary, fix any errors in the Notepad window and then save the program again. Once the program compiles correctly, run the program by typing java Address at the command prompt.
7. In the Notepad window, use the Print command on the File menu to print a copy of the coding for your instructor.
8. Close both the Notepad window and the MS-DOS Prompt window using the close button on each title bar.

In the Lab

2 Creating a Display Using Escape Code Sequences

Problem: Computer applications typically display a splash screen for users to view while waiting for the entire application to load. The computer science department at Middle Illinois College wants to display a splash screen with the school's initials, MIC, before each application. The display should use the characters themselves to make large versions of the letters M, I, and C (Figure 1-60).

Instructions:

1. Start Notepad.
2. Using a block comment beginning with /* type the text from the problem statement above. At the end of the text, type */ to finish the comment.
3. Enter the following code in the Notepad window, using the escape code sequence \t as indicated.
4. Add two or three more lines of code to complete the school's initials.

FIGURE 1-60

```java
public class MIC
{
    public static void main(String[] args)
    {
        System.out.println("\tMM          MM\tIIIIIIIIIIII\t CCCCCCCC");
        System.out.println("\tM M        M M\t        I      \tCC");
        System.out.println("\tM   M     M   M\t        I      \tCC");
        //Add new code here
    }
}
```

5. Save the program with the filename "MIC.java" on your floppy disk.
6. Open the MS-DOS Prompt window. If necessary, set your path. Compile your program by typing `javac MIC.java` at the command prompt.
7. If there are no compilation errors, execute the program by typing `java MIC` at the command prompt.
8. In the Notepad window, use the Print command on the File menu to print a copy of the coding for your instructor.
9. Close both the Notepad window and the MS-DOS Prompt window using the close button on each title bar.

In the Lab

3 Creating an Applet with a Background Color

Problem: In preparation for creating your own personal Web page, you would like to view some possible background colors that will be easy to read with black text. You decide to write a Java applet that displays black words on a colored background. You will use the setBackground method, which accepts a color argument in applets.

Instructions:

1. Start Notepad.
2. Type the following code, inserting your name as the programmer:

```
/*
        Project 1, In the Lab 3, Creating an Applet with a Background Color
        Programmer:   Your Name
        Date:         September 9, 2001
        Program Name: ColorApplet
*/
import java.awt.*;
import java.applet.*;
public class ColorApplet extends Applet
{
    public void paint(Graphics g)
    {
        setBackground(Color.yellow);
        g.drawString("Java is Cool!",15,20);
    }
}
```

3. Save the program with the filename "ColorApplet.java" on your floppy disk.
4. On the Notepad menu bar, click File and then click New. Type the following HTML code.

```
<HTML>
<APPLET CODE = "ColorApplet.class" WIDTH = 400 HEIGHT = 200>
</APPLET>
</HTML>
```

5. Save the HTML program with the filename "ColorApplet.html" on your floppy disk.
6. Open the MS-DOS Prompt window. If necessary, set your path. Compile your program by typing javac ColorApplet.java at the command prompt.
7. If there are no compilation errors, execute the applet by typing appletviewer ColorApplet.html at the command prompt.
8. Close the applet by clicking the Close button on the Applet Viewer title bar. Open the Java file named "ColorApplet.java" again. Change the word yellow to pink. Recompile and view the applet again. Try various colors.
9. Close Applet Viewer, Notepad, and the MS-DOS Prompt windows by clicking the Close button on each title bar.

Cases and Places

The difficulty of these case studies varies:
▶ are the least difficult; ▶▶ are more difficult; and ▶▶▶ are the most difficult.

1 ▶ Steve's Swimwear plans to move its line of swimwear to the Web next year. In preparation for Steve to begin e-commerce, write a Java program to display the name of the store on the screen. Use appropriate documentation lines. Compile the program and execute it. Once the program executes with no errors, edit the program to include Steve's e-mail address (SwimWithSteve@swimwear.com). Save, compile, and execute the program again. Convert the program to display as an applet. When it is complete, with no compilation errors, write the HTML code to run the applet.

2 ▶ Using the techniques from In the Lab 2 on page J 1.50, write a Java program to print your school's initials on the screen. Use the escape code characters and spacing to print the letters in the correct locations. Compile and execute your program. Print the source code.

3 ▶▶ Every applet you write is an instance of the Applet class. Use one of the following help sources to look for topics related to the Applet class: Sun's Java Web site http://java.sun.com/, Java API, Java Reference on the JBuilder 3 Help menu, other IDEs, or a Java reference book. Print out or write down what you found about the hierarchy of the Applet class. Create a hierarchy chart.

4 ▶▶ The Web contains many sites that boast of free Java applets that you may download. Search for Java applets using a search engine on the Web. When you find a page with some applets, use your browser's View Source command to look at the coding. Within that code, look for tags such as <APPLET CODE = >. Print two examples to submit to your instructor.

5 ▶▶▶ Companies sometimes use a splash screen on the Web to give the user something to look at while the longer, graphic intensive Web page downloads. Write a splash screen applet that displays the name of your company or school, the address, the Web address, and the toll-free phone number. Position the lines using the g.drawString method with the x and y coordinates. Position the applet window using WIDTH and HEIGHT attributes of the applet tag. Use both Applet Viewer and a browser to look at the splash screen. Compare the two results. Print both the source code for the applet and the HTML file.

6 ▶▶▶ In preparation for future Java programs, create a Java program named Center that displays a centered, opening screen with information about your program. Include the name of your program, your name, your instructor's name, the date, and any other necessary information. When maximized, the MS-DOS Prompt window displays approximately 25 lines that are 80 characters across. To center vertically, divide the number of lines of text by 25 (dropping any remainder) to determine how many blank lines (\n) to insert before each text line. To center horizontally, count your characters in the line of text, divide that by 2 (dropping any remainder), and then subtract that from 40 to determine how many spaces you should indent from the left margin. Remember that each tab character (\t) moves the text approximately 8 characters to the right. Use the SPACEBAR to insert fewer than 8 spaces. Compile and execute your program. Save your program for future use on a floppy disk.

Java Programming

Java Programming

Java Programming

PROJECT

2

Manipulating Data Using Methods

You will have mastered the material in this project when you can:

OBJECTIVES

- Enter sample data into a Java program
- Identify primitive data types
- Use proper naming conventions when creating identifiers
- Declare Java variables
- Use operators and parentheses correctly in formulas
- Use variables in output
- Round an answer using the Math.round method
- Find the exponential power of a number using the Math.pow method
- Wrap input streams from a keyboard buffer
- Create Java constructors
- Input data with the readLine method
- Convert strings to numbers using the parse method
- Add interactive components into an applet
- Implement the Java ActionListener
- Execute an interactive applet
- Identify Java source code files and Java class files on a storage device

A Circus Without Animals

Cirque du Soleil Stirs the Creative Spirit

A circus without elephants? Without a ringmaster's whistle, top hat, and tails? Yes, when the circus is Cirque du Soleil, a dazzling theatrical experience blending non-stop acrobatics, gymnastics, pantomime, dance, comedy, music, and lighting.

Cirque du Soleil, a French name that translates to Circus of the Sun, has humble beginnings as a festival of street performers in Quebec in 1984. Since that time, more than 23 million people in 120 cities have been mesmerized by a Cirque performance. Four of the shows are based permanently in the United States: *Alegría* in Biloxi, Mississippi; *Mystère* and O in Las Vegas; and *La Nouba* at the Walt Disney World Resort near Orlando, Florida. In addition, *Dralion*, *Quidam*, and *Saltimbanco* are traveling throughout North America, Europe, and Asia and are being performed in a giant tent containing an intimate, single ring.

Each show has an underlying theme based on such universal contrasts of reality and fantasy, good and evil, love and loneliness, and childhood and adulthood. Dancers, illusionists, and musicians are among the approximately 75 cast members who interpret these messages accompanied by synthesizers, electric guitars, reed instruments, percussion, and voice. More than 30 percent of the 450 full-time artists currently performing in the shows have an athletic background, particularly in gymnastics.

Each weekend, more than 50,000 people throughout the world witness Cirque's magic. Each day, more than 5,000 visit Cirque's Website, www.cirquedusoleil.com. This creative display of graphics and innovative effects features details of each production, RealVideo of *Mystère*, and virtual reality tours of the International Headquarters in Montreal. Lighting booths, costume shops, training rooms, and the lifts and platforms beneath the stage are displayed.

The Join Cirque section of the Web site describes diverse employment opportunities ranging from accountants to Web architects throughout the world. In addition, the site uses a flexible Java applet, Affiche.class (French for Displays), to show immediate needs for performers in specific shows. For example, if a dancer is needed for *Mystère*, the Web designers insert the words "DANCER WANTED — DANCER WANTED — DANCER WANTED" as the value in the text1 parameter code. When an interested viewer clicks the link below this text, the qualifications for the job and application procedures display.

The site also contains a handy online form to subscribe to the *Dralion* Internet Club, which gives members the opportunity to obtain advance tickets and to view audio and video clips of that show. Also available are a *Dralion* screensaver and wallpapers.

Likewise, you will create a practical Java applet in this project by developing a prototype program for a new car showroom kiosk. A shopper will enter values regarding the car price, loan terms, and down payment, and the program will process this data and then display a monthly payment.

Cirque returns nearly 1 percent of its box-office revenues to assist at-risk youth through the use of circus arts. This international philanthropic activity is an extension of Cirque's quest to awaken dreams and to kindle the imagination. Indeed, Cirque is much more than a circus.

Java Programming

Manipulating Data Using Methods

PROJECT 2

CASE PERSPECTIVE

Bert's car dealership, Bert's Banner Cars, wants to create an interactive kiosk in the new car show room. The kiosk, with a keyboard and screen, would run a question and answer program for customers to calculate sample monthly payments. Bert is hoping that this kiosk will ease the car buying process for customers.

Once customers have received the appropriate information from a salesperson at the dealership, Bert would like the program at the kiosk to prompt the customers for the price of the new car, their estimated down payment, their trade-in value, the current interest rate, and the number of payments to be made. After the user enters the information, Bert wants to display a message with the customer's projected monthly payment.

You decide to use the Java skills you have acquired to create a prototype program for Bert to consider. With some sample data that Bert provides, you can test your formula and then create an interactive stand-alone program for the kiosk. You also decide to create an applet to run from Bert's Web page.

Introduction

Manipulating data is integral to creating useful computer programs. Programmers must know how to retrieve and store different kinds of data efficiently. Data may come from a variety of sources, such as users, files, and other programs, as well. It is not unusual to imbed certain kinds of data, such as constant values that will not change, within the computer program and obtain other kinds of data, such as current rates or prices, from external files and users.

Java offers numerous ways to retrieve and manipulate data. Using lines of code that assign values to variables, Java can be used to store data temporarily for processing. Using classes and methods, Java can be used to set fields to specific values and create instances. When users provide data, Java can accept a stream of character input from a keyboard and then, using a method, can read the line and process it.

Project Two — Bert's Loan Kiosk

ANALYZING THE PROBLEM Bert wants a computer program that calculates a monthly payment on a car loan. Input values will include the customer's name, the price of the car, the amount of the down payment, the amount of the trade-in, the interest rate, and the number of payments. Output should include the customer's name and a message with the monthly payment amount (Figure 2-1a). Processing will involve using a standard formula that computes compound interest and then calculates a monthly payment.

The portability of Java across platforms makes it a good programming language to use for this type of application.

MS-DOS Prompt

```
A:\>java BertIO
What is your name?
Ben Boswick
What is the price of the car?
20000
What is the downpayment?
1000
What is the trade-in value?
1500
For how many months is the loan?
48
What is the decimal interest rate?
.075
The monthly payment for Ben Boswick is $423

A:\>
```

(a) Java Application

Applet Viewer: BertApplet.class

Applet

Please enter your name:

Ben Boswick

Enter the price of the car:

20000

Enter the down payment:

1000

Enter the trade in value:

1500

Enter the number of months:

48

Enter the yearly interest rate in decimal form:

.075

Calculate Monthly Payment

The monthly payment is $423

Applet started.

(b) Java Applet

FIGURE 2-1

DESIGNING THE PROGRAM The structure of the program will be sequential in nature. As you may remember from the Introduction Project, sequential processing means the computer is instructed to perform one action after another without skipping any steps or making any decisions that would affect the flow of the logic.

The program itself will be designed in three stages. The first stage will manipulate sample data that you will store in the code itself. By using sample data in the calculations, you will be able to test the formula and compare the results with known correct values. Second, you will modify the program to accept input from the keyboard. After storing the user's responses, the program will continue executing in a manner similar to the first stage. Finally, you will convert the application to an applet (Figure 2-1b). Each stage of the program should contain appropriate documentation and be saved for future use.

CODING THE PROGRAM You will create Java source code using the syntax and commands of the Java programming language. The following pages present a series of step-by-step instructions to write the code for each of the three stages as described in the preceding paragraph.

TESTING THE PROGRAM You will test the program by inserting sample data, compiling, and then executing it in console mode.

More About

Flowcharts

For more information on flow-charting sequential projects like this one, visit the Java Programming Web Page (www.scsite.com/java/more.htm) and then click Project 2 Flowchart.

FORMALIZING THE SOLUTION You will review the source code, use proper documentation, edit, recompile, and print a copy.

MAINTAINING THE PROGRAM You will modify the program to accept user input and then convert it to an applet.

Starting a New Java Program

In Project 1, you learned how to set up the desktop, opening both Notepad and the MS-DOS Prompt windows. Complete the following steps to set up the desktop.

TO SET UP THE DESKTOP

1. Click the Start button on the taskbar, point to Programs on the Start menu, and then point to Accessories on the Programs submenu. Click Notepad on the Accessories submenu.

2. In order to display both the Notepad window and the MS-DOS Prompt window on the desktop, drag the title bar of the Notepad window to the upper-left corner of the desktop. Drag the lower-right corner of the Notepad window so that it covers approximately one-third of the desktop.

3. With the Notepad window still open, click the Start button again. Point to Programs on the Start menu and then click MS-DOS Prompt (Windows 95 or 98) or Command Prompt (Windows NT).

4. If your system displays the MS-DOS Prompt window as a black, full screen, press and hold the ALT key while pressing the TAB key to minimize the window.

5. On the taskbar, right-click the MS-DOS Prompt button and then click Properties on the shortcut menu.

6. When the MS-DOS Prompt Properties dialog box displays, click the Font tab. In the Font size box, scroll, and then click the 7 x 11 or a similar font size.

7. Click the Screen tab. In the Usage area, click the Window option button to select it. In the Window area, make certain that the Display toolbar check box contains a check mark.

8. Click the OK button. If the MS-DOS Prompt window does not display, click the MS-DOS Prompt button so that the window displays. Drag it to the lower-right corner of the screen. If necessary, click in the MS-DOS Prompt window to activate it.

9. If you downloaded Java from the Sun Microsystems Web site, type `path=c:\jdk1.2.2\bin` at the prompt. If you installed the Java compiler from the JBuilder 3 CD-ROM that may accompany this text, type `path=c:\jbuilder3\java\bin` and then press the ENTER key.

10. With a floppy disk inserted in drive A, change to drive A by typing `a:` and then press the ENTER key.

The desktop displays the Notepad window in the upper-left portion of the screen and the MS-DOS Prompt window in the lower-right portion of the screen (Figure 2-2).

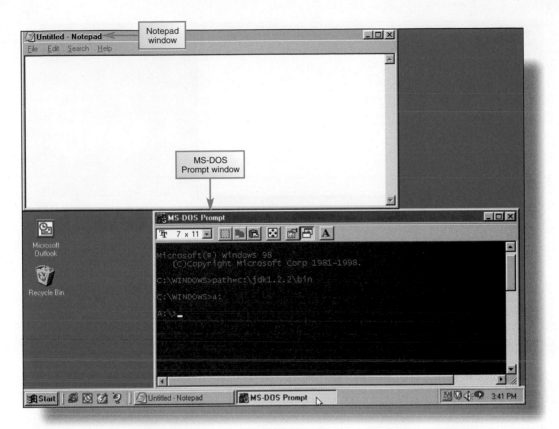

FIGURE 2-2

Entering Beginning Code

Similar to the program in Project 1, the program in this project for Bert's Banner Cars will include comments, an access modifier with the class name Bert, and a main method. Complete the following steps to enter beginning code.

Steps **To Enter Beginning Code**

1 **Click the Notepad window. Type the comments as shown in Figure 2-3, pressing the ENTER key after each line. Insert your own name as the programmer and the current date.**

The comments display (Figure 2-3). The beginning and ending block symbols delineate the indented comments.

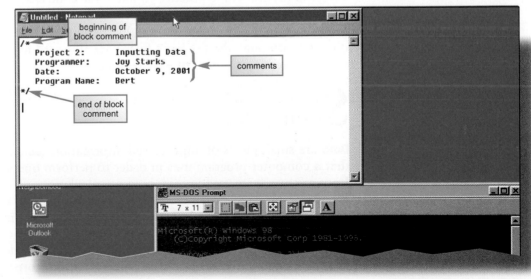

Other Ways

1. To start Notepad, right-click desktop, click New, click Text Document, double-click New Text Document icon on desktop

2. To open MS-DOS Prompt window, click Start button, click Run, type Command.com press ENTER key

FIGURE 2-3

2 **Type** public
class Bert **and
then press the ENTER key.
Type the opening brace
and then press the ENTER
key.**

*The access modifier and
class name display (Figure
2-4). The brace indicates
the beginning of the class
contents.*

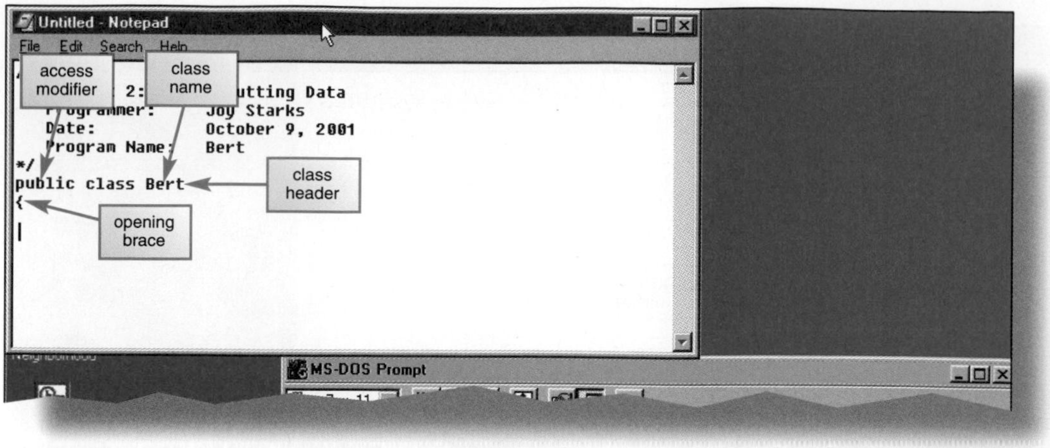

FIGURE 2-4

3 **In order to indent
the code, press the
SPACEBAR three times. Type**
public static void
main(String[] args)
**and then press the ENTER
key. Press the SPACEBAR
three times, type the
opening brace, and then
press the ENTER key.**

*The main method header that
begins most Java programs
displays (Figure 2-5).*

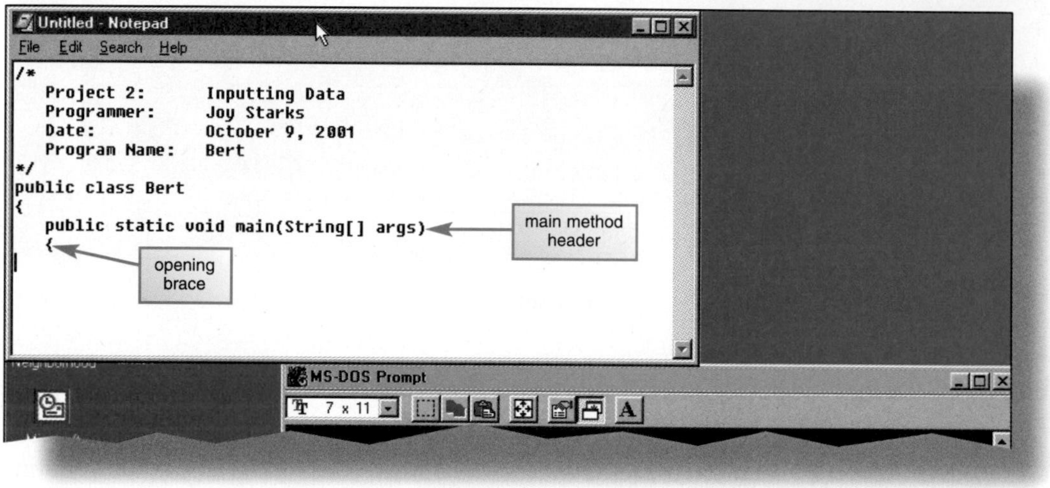

FIGURE 2-5

The indentation is not mandatory; Java ignores the space characters. However, it is good programming practice to make the code easy to read by using consistent indentation and to indent all code identically within a given set of braces. Two-space or three-space indentations are used by many programmers. You may use the TAB key to indent, although the TAB key's five space standard may make longer lines wrap around, defeating the goal of easy reading.

Storing Data

Data are small pieces of unprocessed information such as words, texts, or numbers that a computer program uses in order to perform operations and produce output. Data are raw facts used in reasoning or calculations. These data — datum is the singular form of the word — may come from the program itself, from users of the program, or from external files. For a computer program to make use of these pieces of data, they must be stored in the memory of the computer. Each storage location is **allocated**, or set up, before it is used with a declaration statement. The **declaration statement** identifies the type of data to store and assigns a logical name for the storage location.

Java Data Types

In Java, before you can store a piece of data, the storage location must be declared. **Declaring** means using a descriptive word or abbreviation to identify the type, or data type. A **data type** is a classification of a particular type of information that is a built-in feature of Java. It tells the computer how to interpret and store the data. It is easy for humans to distinguish between different types of data. You usually can tell at a glance whether a number is a percentage, a time, or an amount of money through special symbols, such as % or $, that indicate the data's type. Similarly, a computer uses special internal codes to keep track of the different types of data it processes.

Java is a **strongly typed language**, which means it enforces a set of rules about how you use the objects you create — especially when using data. For instance, you cannot declare a variable location as a single integer in Java and then try to insert a string of characters into that same location. First, there would not be enough room, because each data type has internal sizes associated with it. Second, the Java compiler would be confused and would possibly try to **cast**, or convert, the data from its original form to the declared data type with unpredictable results.

In this project, you will use some of Java's primitive data types. **Primitive data types** are data types that are structured by Java to hold simple kinds of data. Java's primitive data types help programmers by restricting the kind of data allowed in the declared variable location; Java displays an error message during compilation if you try to store some other type of value in that variable. The eight primitive data types are listed in Table 2-1. You will learn about other data types in a future project.

Integers

An integer is a positive or negative whole number. Java provides several types of integers, which are based on the number of bits in the integer's internal representation, such as byte, int, short, and long. You should choose the representation with the narrowest scope for your situation. When an integer literal, or actual value, is used in a Java program, it is considered an int value unless you type an L (designating long) after the value.

Table 2-1 Java Primitive Data Types	
TYPE	DESCRIPTION
boolean	stores data in only one of two states, as a logical value of true or false
byte	stores whole number values in 8-bit signed locations from −128 to +127
char	stores any one of the 65,436 single characters of the Unicode set, which includes characters and symbols from many languages
double	stores numbers with up to 14 or 15 decimal places as double-precision, floating-point values
float	stores numbers with up to 6 or 7 decimals as floating-point values
int	stores whole number values in 32-bit signed locations from -2^{31} to $+2^{31}-1$
long	stores whole number values in 64-bit signed locations from approximately $-9*10^{18}$ to $+9*10^{18}-1$
short	stores whole number values in 16-bit signed locations from −32,768 to +32,767

Data Types

Java's primitive data types are not considered objects. However, each primitive data type has a wrapper class, which encapsulates and helps perform certain data conversions like the parse method. For example, int is a primitive data type, but Integer is a wrapper class.

Variables and Identifiers

Along with the data type, each storage location is referenced by an identifier. An **identifier** is a word that the programmer chooses to label a storage address in memory. Every time the programmer needs to access that location, he or she uses the identifier name. Internally, storage locations have computer-assigned numeric addresses. Using an identifier is easier than remembering a nondescriptive number.

Identifiers also are used to represent classes, objects, and methods, but when referencing pieces of data, the identifier is naming the location for a variable or constant. A **variable** is a storage location for data that may change during the processing of the computer program. Examples might include calculated amounts, user-entered data, and accumulated totals. A **constant** is a value that does not change during the course of the program, such as a standard rate, a maximum or minimum value, or a constant scientific value such as *pi* or the boiling point of water.

Casting

In general, when a numeric expression contains values or operands of different data types, Java will promote the smaller type to a larger type. This is called implicit casting. An explicit cast is performed when the programmer forces a data type change by including the data type in parentheses before the value.

Identifiers should be meaningful to the purpose of the program. For instance, in a payroll program the name, x, is not as meaningful as the name, grosspay. Even though the programmer chooses the names of the identifiers, Java imposes a few rules to which programmers must adhere.

More About

Field Declarations

Some Java programmers refer to the declaration of a variable as a field declaration. Field declarations may include an access modifier that determines how the field can be accessed and its scope. For example, private double width; declares that the identifier width will not be available to other classes.

- The first character of an identifier must be a letter. Subsequent characters can be letters or numbers.
- Identifiers may not contain special characters such as percent signs or number signs. Identifiers may contain underscores (_) and the dollar sign ($), which are considered letters in Java.
- Identifiers may not contain spaces.
- Identifiers are case-sensitive.
- Identifiers may be spelled using any alphabet of any spoken language.
- Reserved words that are part of the Java language may not be used as identifiers (see Appendix B).

It is common practice among Java programmers to begin variable identifiers and object instances with a lowercase letter. Classes usually begin with a capital letter. Constants commonly are named in all uppercase letters. Java is case-sensitive, so you must be careful when typing code. Restrictions such as these may slow down the typing task, but it is easier to locate certain kinds of identifiers if a naming scheme is used.

Table 2-2 lists some legal and illegal examples of Java identifiers.

More About

Reference Variables

Java programmers use the term, reference variable, when the declaration is associated with an object. For instance, if you create an object called, Person, then the declaration would be Person student; which tells Java that student always must refer to a Person data type.

Table 2-2	Examples of Legal and Illegal Java Identifiers	
LEGAL	ILLEGAL	EXPLANATION
firstName first_Name	First Name	Java does not allow spaces; if spacing is desired for legibility, use an underscore (_) between words or capitalize the second word.
employee7	7employee	Identifiers must begin with a letter.
$amount	$amt.cents	The dollar sign ($) is allowed; however, special characters such as the period (.) are not allowed.
totalSales	Sales&Tax	Special characters (&) are not allowed.
invNo7123	7123	Identifiers may not begin with a number.
numberOfPeople	public	The reserved word, public, is not allowed.

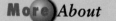

More About

Declaration Syntax

Every Java statement must end with a semicolon, but you can declare multiple identifiers of the same data type on the same line, as long as they are separated by commas. Identifiers, or variables, must be declared before they can be used, and the names are case-sensitive.

Declaring Variables

Declaring a variable means listing the data type and the identifier before it is used in the program.

```
int grandTotal;
```

This example code tells Java that an integer will be stored, and that you plan to reference it with the word grandTotal as an identifier. Declarations must take place before variables can be used; however, you may combine the declaration of a variable with its first value or assignment. In the following example, the interest rate is declared a float and assigned a value of nine percent in the same line.

```
float interestRate = .09;
```

As you declare your variables and add more lines of code, you will benefit by having a bigger window to display more workspace. Perform the following steps to maximize the Notepad window and then code the declaration statements of the program for Bert's Banner Cars.

 To Maximize the Notepad Window and Declare Variables

1 **If necessary, click the Notepad window to activate it. Point to the Maximize button on the Notepad title bar.**

The title bar displays buttons to minimize, maximize, and close the window (Figure 2-6).

2 **Click the Maximize button and then click below the lines of code in the Notepad window on line 11.**

The insertion point displays on line 11 (Figure 2-7).

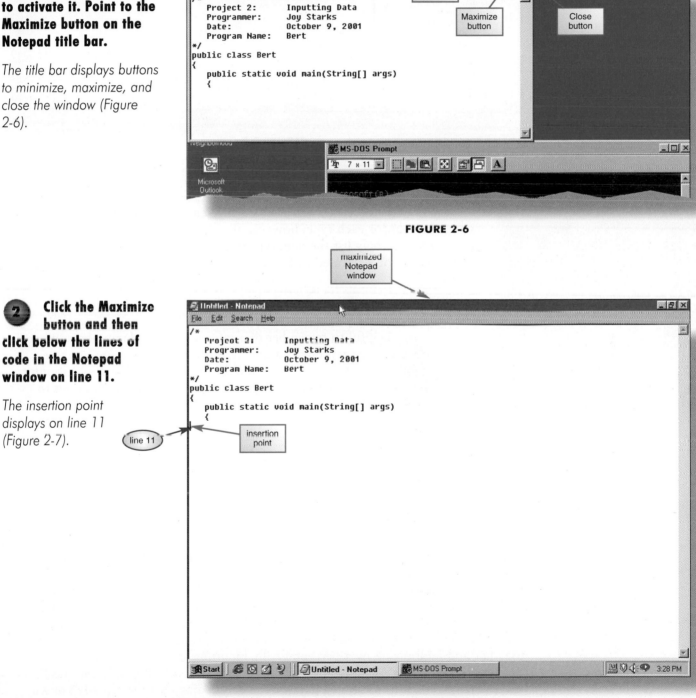

FIGURE 2-6

FIGURE 2-7

3 **Type the declaration section of code as shown in Table 2-3 using proper indentation.**

The declaration for the pieces of data display (Figure 2-8). No assignment of values is made.

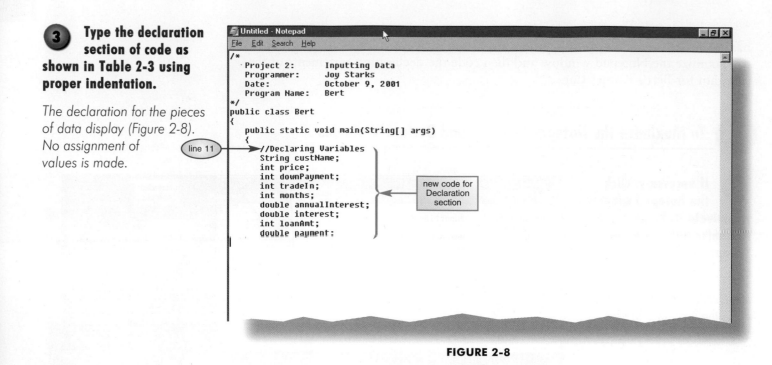

FIGURE 2-8

Table 2-3	
LINE	*CODE*
11	//Declaring Variables
12	String custName;
13	int price;
14	int downPayment;
15	int tradeIn;
16	int months;
17	double annualInterest;
18	double interest;
19	int loanAmt;
20	double payment;

If you want to declare variables of different types, you must use a separate statement for each type; however, if you have several variables of the same type, you may list the data type once, and then include each variable on the same line separated by commas.

```
double price, salary;
```

It may be helpful to remember that integers are whole numbers, whereas the double data type represents a double-precision, floating-point value. Table 2-1 on page J 2.9 describes a double as a number that is precise up to 14 decimal places. The word floating comes from scientists who refer to large numbers in scientific notation. For instance, 1,200,000 can be notated as 1.2 times 10 to the power of 6. The decimal point floated six places to the left.

Precision refers to the amount of storage allocated to hold the fractional part of a number. The higher that storage amount, the more precise the number.

Using Sample Data

Programmers use sample data to test their programs. **Sample data**, or test data, are pieces of information used in lieu of the real data in order to see if a program is functioning properly. For instance, if a programmer wants to test a formula to accumulate a total of all purchased items and then calculate sales tax, he or she might create a fictitious list of items to be purchased. The programmer then would use these amounts, instead of a real customer's bill, to practice adding the amounts together and multiplying by a percentage. By inputting sample data into the computer, the programmer manipulates data that would not affect a real customer. Additionally, results from sample data can be checked against the already known correct answers to assure that all formulas and calculations are correct.

Writing Code with Sample Data

You will use assignment statements to store sample data values in the computer's memory. An **assignment statement** is a line of code beginning with a location, followed by an equal sign (=) and the new value.

```
location = value
```

The value may be a number, a string, a formula, or reference to another piece of data. The location may be a variable identifier or an attribute of an object.

Perform the following step to assign sample data to the program.

More About

The Scope of Sample Data

An identifier's scope is simply that portion of the class where it may be used. Fields or instance variables in Java have class scope that extends throughout the entire body of the class definition in which they are declared. Class scope identifiers will not retain their value in other classes.

Steps **To Assign Sample Data**

1 **In the Notepad window, position the insertion point below the previous code in the workspace on line 21. Press the ENTER key to insert a blank line and then type the comment and code as displayed in Table 2-4 using proper indentation. After the last line of code is entered, press the ENTER key.**

The comments and assignment statements display (Figure 2-9). A blank line between sections of code makes it easier to read and understand.

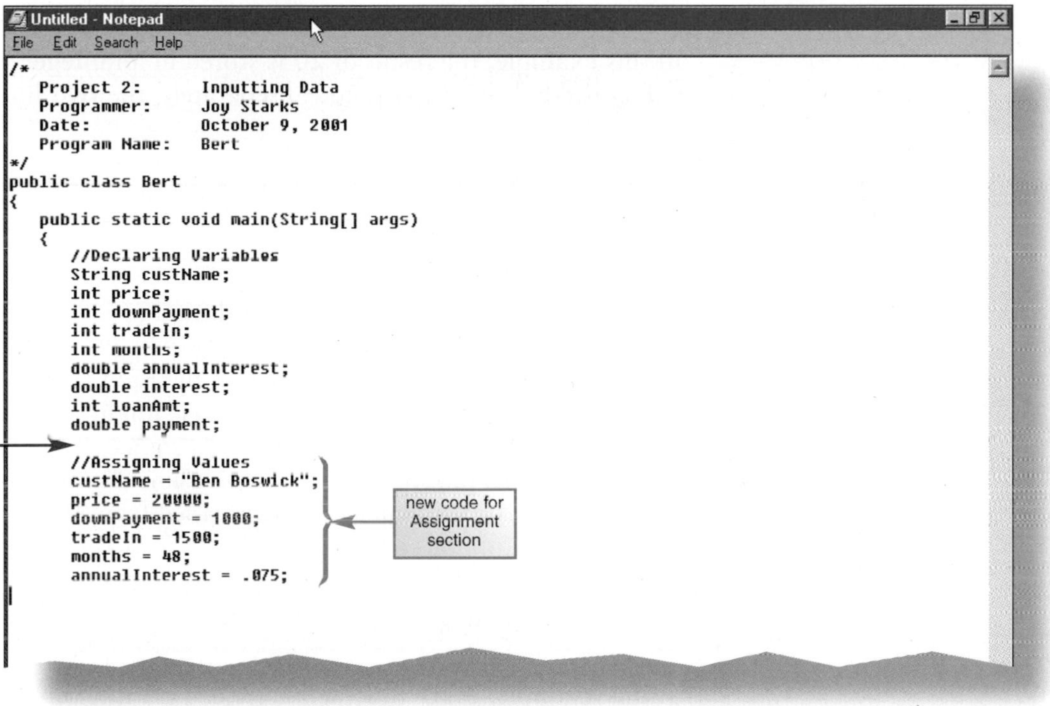

FIGURE 2-9

Table 2-4	
LINE	CODE
22	//Assigning Values
23	custName = "Ben Boswick";
24	price = 20000;
25	downPayment = 1000;
26	tradeIn = 1500;
27	months = 48;
28	annualInterest = .075;

Notice that assignment statements are code statements and end with a semicolon in Java. Later, when the program accepts data from a user, these assignment statements with sample data will be removed from the program.

Operators

Operators need not be preceded and followed by a space. Java basically ignores any white space between commands. Pressing the SPACEBAR key before and after operators simply makes the formulas easier to read.

Operators

Performing mathematical operations and using formulas in Java is similar to other programming languages. Values stored in the computer may need to be manipulated arithmetically, such as adding or subtracting values; or they may need to be evaluated logically, such as testing to see if the hours worked are greater than 40. Operator symbols in Java are similar to regular algebraic symbols. In the case of formulas, an assignment statement is used. The formula is placed on the right side of the equal sign and the location to store the result is on the left.

```
int answer = 15 + 5;
```

In this example, the result of 20 is stored in an integer variable named, answer. Alternately if the declaration is coded separately, the two lines of code would display as follows.

```
int answer;
answer = 15 + 5;
```

Both ways of assigning a formula's solution to a variable location are acceptable and produce the same result.

Because Java evaluates the code on the right side of the equal sign before assigning the value to the left side, a special case might arise where a value is manipulated and stored back in the same place. For instance, if you wanted to collect the number of hits on a web page, you might write a line of code to add one more to a storage location every time the page is downloaded from the Web server. The result is an accumulated total or counter.

```
counter = counter + 1;
```

In this example, every time Java executes the line of code, one more will be added to the counter. You will use accumulators and counters in a future project.

Arithmetic Operators

Arithmetic operators manipulate two or more numeric values. Table 2-5 lists the five arithmetic operators, their descriptions, examples, and example results. You may be familiar with most of the arithmetic operators. The unusual ones, with respect to Java, are integer and modular division. **Integer division** is performed when both the dividend and the divisor are integers. Java forces the result to be an integer because it is a primitive data type. **Modular division** is a way to store any truncated remainder value from integer division. The **modulus operator**, %, is sometimes called the remainder operator. It is entered between two integers and performs modular division. Modular division is common to many programming languages.

The Modulus Operator

The modulus operator can be used by itself without its corresponding integer division. Read as 10 mod 3, the result is 1. You do not have to know that 10/3 is 3. Many times, you want to know only if a remainder exists; therefore, modulus operations can stand alone.

Table 2-5 Arithmetic Operators in Java			
OPERATOR	DESCRIPTION	EXAMPLE	RESULT
+	Addition	20 + 3	23
–	Subtraction	20 – 3	17
*	Multiplication	20 * 3	60
/	Division with integers	20 / 3	6 (the remainder is dropped because the operands both are integers)
/	Division with floating point numbers	20.0 / 3.0	6.6666667 for float 6.666666666666667 for double
%	Modular division	20 % 3	2 (only the integer remainder is stored)

The first four arithmetic operators may manipulate any data type. However, if you divide integer values, the remainder will be dropped. Dividing float or double numbers will yield decimal results. If the operands in a division problem are of different data types, Java **promotes** the integers to floating point values before the expression is evaluated. Modular division can be performed only on integers, because an integer remainder results. You will learn about special operators that involve single value arithmetic in a later project.

Comparison Operators

Comparison operators involve two values, as do arithmetic operators; however, they compare the numbers. The result evaluates to be either true or false. Programmers use the term **boolean** to store a result that only has two states, such as true or false, yes or no, 1 or 0. As an example, the following statement would declare a boolean variable and store a true value if the variable, hours, is greater than 40.

```
boolean isOvertime = ( hours > 40 );
```

Comparison operations are enclosed in parentheses. The identifiers for boolean variables are recognized more easily if a form of the verb, to be, is used as part of the variable name, as in the example above.

Table 2-6 lists the six comparison operators, their descriptions, a true expression, and a false expression.

More About

Operators

Java actually has 12 different kinds of operators, including parentheses, incremental, unary, type casts, constructors, relational, equality, and Boolean, as well as the traditional operators.

Table 2-6 Comparison Operators in Java			
OPERATOR	DESCRIPTION	TRUE EXPRESSION	FALSE EXPRESSION
<	less than	(2 < 9)	(9 < 2)
>	greater than	(5 > 1)	(1 > 5)
<=	less than or equal to	(3 <= 4)	(5 <= 4)
>=	greater than or equal to	(8 >= 6)	(3 >= 7)
==	equal to	(9 == 9)	(5 == 9)
!=	not equal to	(4 != 2)	(2 != 2)

The first four comparison operators sometimes are referred to as **relational operators** because they compare the relation of two values; the last two commonly are called **equality operators.** The double equal sign (==) is used to differentiate "equal to" from the assignment statement's equal sign used in Java. Spaces are not included between comparison operator double symbols.

Precedence

With both arithmetic and comparison operators, operations enclosed within parentheses indicate precedence. An operation takes **precedence** if it is performed before another operation. After parentheses, multiplication and division are performed before addition and subtraction, in order from the left to the right. Relational operators take precedence over equality operators. When in doubt about the precedence, use parentheses to force the desired operation to take place first.

Formulas

A **formula** is a mathematical sentence that contains values — variables, constants, or numbers — and operators. Formulas may appear in assignment statements or as a part of a method, in which case the result becomes an argument or parameter. Three formulas will be used in this program.

- Divide the annual percentage rate by 12 for a monthly payment
- Calculate a loan amount by subtracting the down payment and trade-in values from the price of the car
- Calculate a monthly payment with compound interest

The formula for compound interest contains an exponent. Even though Java has no exponentiation operator, it easily is accomplished by using a prewritten method named, pow, which is from the Math class. The **Math class** is part of the java.lang package. It contains methods for a number of useful functions such as rounding, randomizing, and square roots. In this case, pow is a method for expressing exponentiation. The Math class methods have the following general form:

```
Math.method(arguments)
```

For example, if you want Java to calculate 17 to the power of 9, commonly written as 17^9, you would enter Math.pow(17,9).

Perform the following steps to enter the formulas.

More About

Precedence

Formulas that do not contain parentheses are hard to read. Java will perform multiplication, division, and modulus operations, left to right, before performing addition and subtraction. You later will learn about unary operators, which change that order. Unary operators are performed before all other operations and then they are performed right to left. To avoid confusion, use parentheses.

More About

Operator Overloading

Operator symbols are overloaded in Java, which means they can be used for more than one type-dependent operation. For example, the plus sign (+) may be used for addition and string concatenation, and the slash (/) is used for both integer and floating-point division.

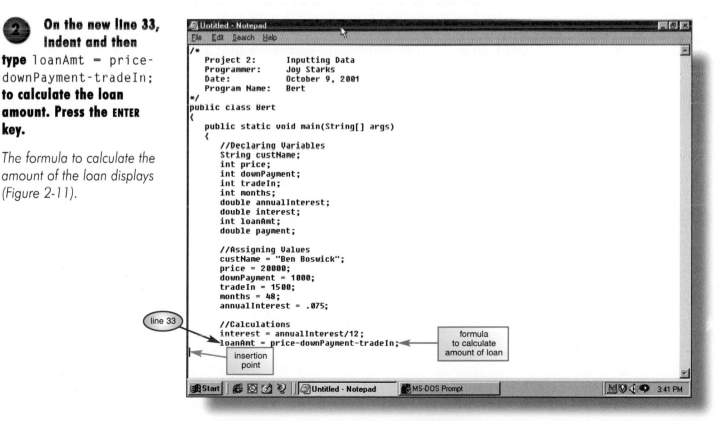

Steps: To Enter the Formulas

1 In the Notepad window, position the insertion point below the code previously entered. Press the ENTER key to insert a blank line and then press the SPACEBAR to indent as shown in Figure 2-10. Type the comment, `//Calculations` **and then press the ENTER key. Indent again, and then type** `interest = annualInterest/12;` **to calculate the interest rate. Press the ENTER key.**

The formula to divide the yearly interest rate by 12 displays (Figure 2-10).

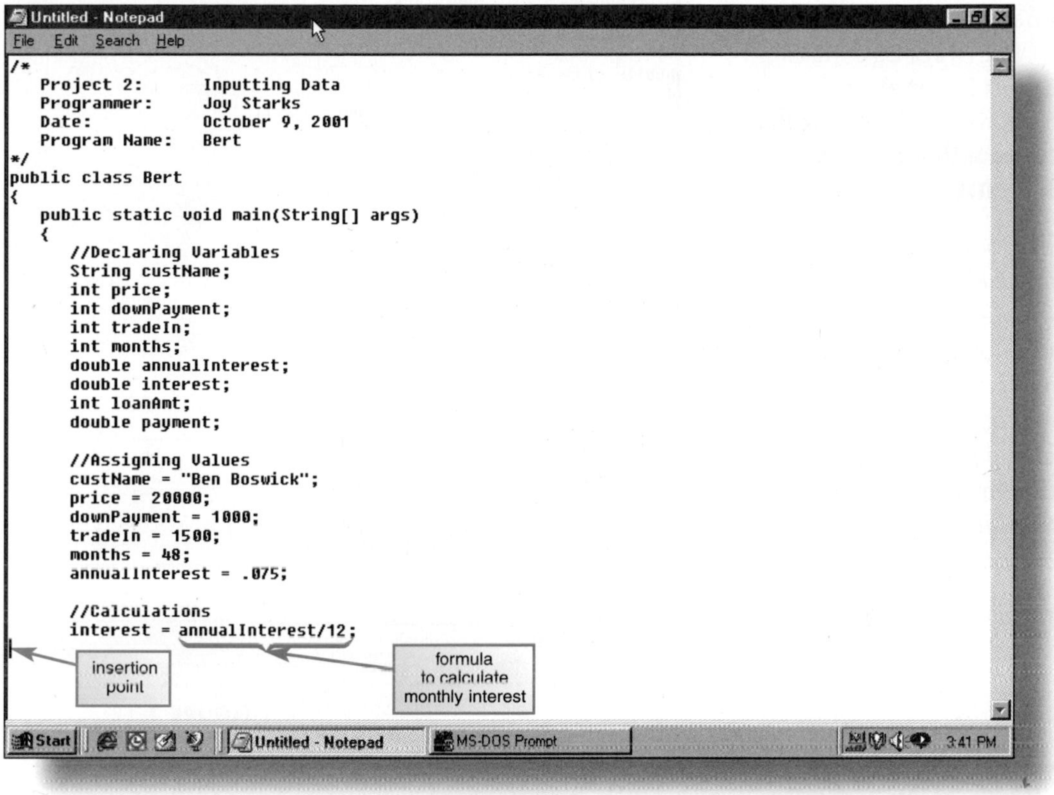

FIGURE 2-10

2 On the new line 33, indent and then **type** `loanAmt = price-downPayment-tradeIn;` **to calculate the loan amount. Press the ENTER key.**

The formula to calculate the amount of the loan displays (Figure 2-11).

FIGURE 2-11

3 On the new line 34, indent and then **type** payment = loanAmt/((1/interest) -(1/(interest*Math .pow(1+interest, months)))); **to calculate the monthly payment. Press the ENTER key.**

The formula to calculate the monthly payment displays (Figure 2-12). Notice this formula uses variables assigned in the previous formulas, as well as the method, pow. The formula is a standard one used by banks and other industries to compute compound interest.

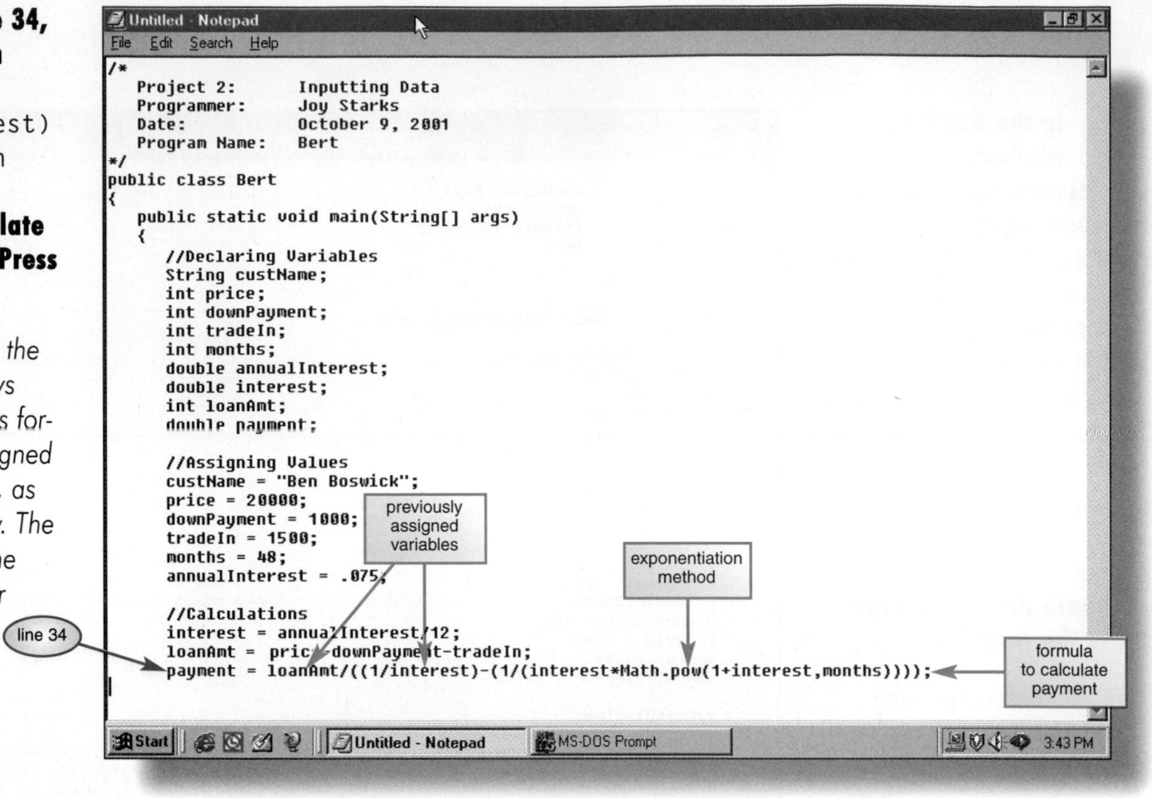

```
/*
    Project 2:      Inputting Data
    Programmer:     Joy Starks
    Date:           October 9, 2001
    Program Name:   Bert
*/
public class Bert
{
    public static void main(String[] args)
    {
        //Declaring Variables
        String custName;
        int price;
        int downPayment;
        int tradeIn;
        int months;
        double annualInterest;
        double interest;
        int loanAmt;
        double payment;

        //Assigning Values
        custName = "Ben Boswick";
        price = 20000;
        downPayment = 1000;
        tradeIn = 1500;
        months = 48;
        annualInterest = .075;

        //Calculations
        interest = annualInterest/12;
        loanAmt = price-downPayment-tradeIn;
        payment = loanAmt/((1/interest)-(1/(interest*Math.pow(1+interest,months))));
```

previously assigned variables

exponentiation method

line 34

formula to calculate payment

Untitled - Notepad

File Edit Search Help

Start | Untitled - Notepad | MS-DOS Prompt | 3:43 PM

FIGURE 2-12

In general, you invoke methods by typing the class name, followed by a period, followed by the method name. Recall that the values inside the parentheses are the arguments — the pieces of information the method needs to perform its task. The Math class is part of the java.lang package, which, as discussed in Project 1, is part of the JDK and needs no previous declaration or import.

Now that you have entered all the formulas, you are ready to code the output to the display.

Output

After all calculations are performed, the program should display appropriate responses on the screen. Output will include a message with the customer's name and the monthly payment for the car the customer wishes to purchase.

Using Variables in Output

The System.out.println, used in Project 1, commonly displays a string of characters, but it also can display values from variable locations. Remember that System.out refers to the default output device, usually the monitor. The only way for Java to display the values from variable locations to users is to send them to an output device. An identifier may be used instead of the literal string inside the println argument. In the following example, the value stored in amountBorrowed would display.

```
System.out.println(amountBorrowed);
```

If you want to combine strings of characters and variables on the same line, the code can take one of two forms. First, you can use the method, print, followed by println. The print method does not force a new line after displaying, so that any output following a print method will display on the same line. The following two lines of code display on one line on the screen.

```
System.out.print("The answer is ");
System.out.println(answer);
```

A second way to combine strings and variables on the same line is to use concatenation. Using a plus sign (+), Java allows a **concatenation**, or joining, of these types of data in a single output line of code.

```
System.out.println("The answer is " + answer);
```

In the example, the plus sign (+) concatenates the string with the variable to display both on the same line. Leaving a space after the word, is, keeps the message and the answer from running together in both examples.

Using Methods in Output

Additionally, programmers may invoke methods in their output. Adding the Math.round method to the above example, would round off any decimal places.

```
System.out.println(Math.round(answer));
```

Math is the name of the class; round is the method; answer is the argument.

Perform the steps on the next page to enter the code to produce output on the screen using variables, concatenation, and a method.

More *About*

Output

For more information on outputting to a file for printing on a printer, visit the Java Programming Web Page (www.scsite.com/java/more.htm) and click File Processing.

To Enter Output Code

1 **In the Notepad window, position the insertion point below the code previously entered. If necessary, press the ENTER key to begin a new line 36. Indent and then type** //Output **as a comment for this section. Press the ENTER key.**

The insertion point displays on a new line (Figure 2-13).

FIGURE 2-13

2 **Indent and then type** System.out. print("The monthly payment for " + custName + " is $"); **to enter the code for output on line 37. Press the ENTER key.**

The output line of code displays (Figure 2-14). The plus signs concatenate strings on either side of the variable. The print method will not create a new line during execution.

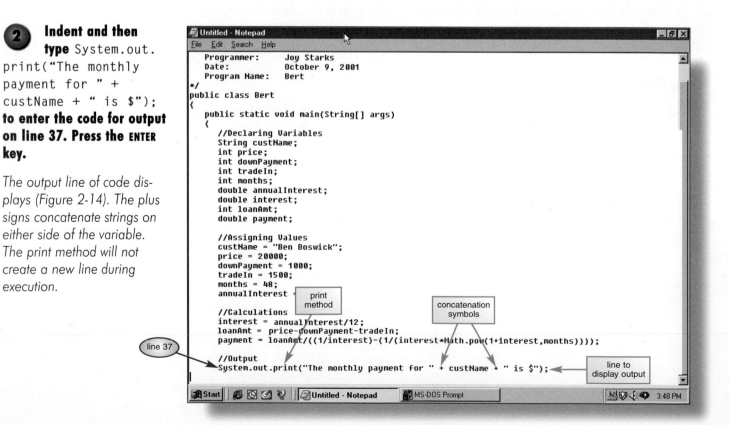

FIGURE 2-14

3 Indent and then type System.out. println(Math.round (payment)); **to code the monthly payment output on line 38. Press the ENTER key.**

The output line displays (Figure 2-15). The rounded monthly payment will display on the same line as the previous data.

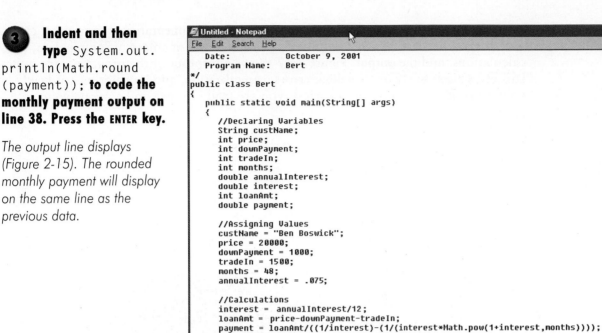

```
    Date:         October 9, 2001
    Program Name:   Bert
*/
public class Bert
{
    public static void main(String[] args)
    {
        //Declaring Variables
        String custName;
        int price;
        int downPayment;
        int tradeIn;
        int months;
        double annualInterest;
        double interest;
        int loanAmt;
        double payment;

        //Assigning Values
        custName = "Ben Boswick";
        price = 20000;
        downPayment = 1000;
        tradeIn = 1500;
        months = 48;
        annualInterest = .075;

        //Calculations
        interest = annualInterest/12;
        loanAmt = price-downPayment-tradeIn;
        payment = loanAmt/((1/interest)-(1/(interest*Math.pow(1+interest,months))));

        //Output
        System.out.print("The monthly payment for " + c            is $");
        System.out.println(Math.round(payment));
```

line 38 → (pointing to line 38)

output line with rounding method →

FIGURE 2-15

4 Indent and then type the closing brace for the main method. Press the ENTER key and then type the closing brace for the Bert class.

The two closing braces display on lines 39 and 40 (Figure 2-16).

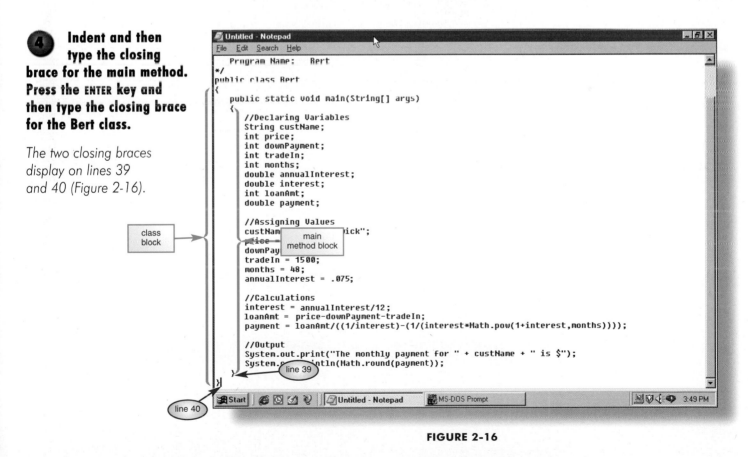

```
    Program Name:   Bert
*/
public class Bert
{
    public static void main(String[] args)
    {
        //Declaring Variables
        String custName;
        int price;
        int downPayment;
        int tradeIn;
        int months;
        double annualInterest;
        double interest;
        int loanAmt;
        double payment;

        //Assigning Values
        custName            ick";
        price               main
        downPay          method block
        tradeIn = 1500;
        months = 48;
        annualInterest = .075;

        //Calculations
        interest = annualInterest/12;
        loanAmt = price-downPayment-tradeIn;
        payment = loanAmt/((1/interest)-(1/(interest*Math.pow(1+interest,months))));

        //Output
        System.out.print("The monthly payment for " + custName + " is $");
        System.o         ntln(Math.round(payment));
    }
}
```

class block →

line 39 → (pointing to line 39)

line 40 → (pointing to line 40)

FIGURE 2-16

Your program now is complete. You coded the documentation, the opening class and method headers, the declaration of variables, the assignment of sample data, the calculations, and the output. Figure 2-17 shows a printout of the program code in its entirety. Check for syntax, spelling errors, capitalization, and indentations. When you are confident everything is correct, you are ready to save and compile your program.

```
                                                    Bert


/*
      Project 2:        Inputting Data
      Programmer:       Joy Starks
      Date:             October 9, 2001
      Program Name:     Bert
*/
public class Bert
{
   public static void main(String[] args)
    {
        //Declaring Variables
        String custName;
        int price;
        int downPayment;
        int tradeIn;
        int months;
        double annualInterest;
        double interest;
        int loanAmt;
        double payment;

        //Assigning Values
        custName = "Ben Boswick";
        price = 20000;
        downPayment = 1000;
        tradeIn = 1500;
        months = 48;
        annualInterest = .075;

        //Calculations
        interest = annualInterest/12;
        loanAmt = price-downPayment-tradeIn;
        payment = loanAmt/((1/interest)-(1/(interest*Math.pow(1+interest,months))));

        //Output
        System.out.print("The monthly payment for " + custName + " is $");
        System.out.println(Math.round(payment));
    }
}
```

FIGURE 2-17

Saving, Compiling, and Executing

You will save the program on a floppy disk, compile the source code with the javac compiler, and then execute the program by running the compiled bytecode.

Saving the Source Code

To save the source code, you must save the Notepad file with a .java extension. Complete the following steps to save the source code.

TO SAVE THE SOURCE CODE

① With a floppy disk in drive A, click File on Notepad's menu bar, and then click Save As.

② When the Save As dialog box displays, type "Bert.java" in the File name text box. You must type the quotation marks around the file name.

③ If necessary, click the Save in box arrow and then click 3½ Floppy (A:) in the list.

④ Click the Save button.

The file is saved on drive A.

Other Ways

1. Press ALT+F, press A

Compiling the Program

Remember that compiling must be done before executing. The compiler translates the source code into Java bytecode. To compile the program, you must issue the javac command at the command prompt, followed by the name of the file. Complete the following steps to compile the program.

TO COMPILE THE PROGRAM

① If you previously closed the MS-DOS Prompt window, or the MS-DOS Prompt button does not display on your taskbar, re-open it by following steps 3 through 10 on page J 2.6 in this project. Otherwise, click the MS-DOS Prompt button on the taskbar.

② In the MS-DOS Prompt window, type javac Bert.java at the A: prompt and then press the ENTER key.

The program compiles. If Java notifies you of compilation errors, fix them in the Notepad window, and then save and compile again.

Executing the Program

Now that the program has been compiled into bytecode, you are ready to execute, or run, the program and see the results of your coded calculations. Perform the steps on the next page to execute the program.

More *About*

Repeating Commands

The F3 function key can be used to repeat the most recent command in the MS-DOS Prompt window. For instance, say you compiled and got an error. After you fix the error and save in Notepad, pressing the F3 key will type the compile command again for you.

TO EXECUTE THE PROGRAM

① If necessary, click the MS-DOS Prompt window.

② Type `java Bert` and then press the ENTER key.

The output displays on the screen (Figure 2-18).

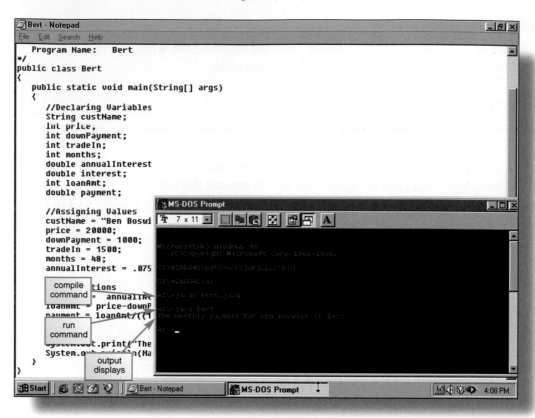

FIGURE 2-18

Notice the answer displays on one line. If your screen displays a different monthly payment than what is displayed in Figure 2-18, double check the formulas entered on pages J 2.11 and J 2.12. Fix any errors, save, and recompile. You may want to print a copy of the Bert source code to view as you modify the program for user input instead of sample data. You also may refer back to Figure 2-17 on page J 2.22.

User Input

Programmers who want to use timely data or data that changes on a regular basis usually do not type the data into their programs. For example, bank transaction data, such as deposits and checks, are recorded electronically. Programmers reference only the external data source in their program. Bank customers, not the programmer, can enter data such as PIN numbers using the ATM machine keyboard. In fact, it is more common to rely on data from external sources than it is to type the data into the program itself. External data allows for flexibility in programming and tailoring of the program to fit the company's or the user's needs.

Input from the Keyboard

Interactive is the term used with programs that allow the user to interact with the program by making choices, entering data, and viewing results. Interactive input and output in Java usually involves a user of the program entering data from a keyboard and viewing results on the screen.

Streams and Constructors

In Java, data flowing in or out of a program are called a **stream**. The System class, which you used in Project 1, actually has many different streams, which are defined as class variables, including the more popular ones: System.in, System.out, and System.err. Table 2-7 describes these three system classes.

Table 2-7	System Classes		
CLASS	FUNCTION	METHODS USED IN IN CONJUNCTION WITH CLASS	DEFAULT DEVICE
System.in	Accepts data from the keyboard buffer wrapped in the InputStreamReader	readLine( )	keyboard buffer
System.out	Sends output to the display or redirects to a designated file	print( ) println( ) flush( )	monitor
System.err	Sends output to the monitor, used for prompts and error messages	print( ) flush( )	monitor

Recall that System.out sent a stream to the standard output device, usually the monitor. System.out implemented the method, println, to transfer the stream of characters.

```
System.out.println("Anita's Antiques");
```

The result of System.out.println was a display of the literal string argument on the screen. In the above example, Anita's Antiques would appear on the display. System.in, however, is more complicated. The JDK contains no simple method for input like the println method for output.

System.in actually refers to a buffered input stream. As a user types, the keystrokes are sent to a buffer. A **buffer** is a data area shared by hardware devices or programs, where data are held until they are needed by the processor. Buffering ensures that if a user hits the BACKSPACE key to take out a character, the deleted characters are not sent when the program retrieves characters from the input buffer.

The JDK contains a special reader to read the input buffer called the InputStreamReader. The **InputStreamReader** (**ISR**) is a Java class or object that serves as an intermediary between the input buffer and the Java program. Java programmers use the word, **wrap**, to describe how the ISR envelops the stream from the input buffer. The Java code necessary to reference the buffer is an ISR class method, with System.in as the argument.

```
InputStreamReader(System.in)
```

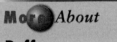

More About

Buffers

For more information on computer system buffers, visit the Java Programming Web Page (www.scsite.com/java/ more.htm) and click Buffers.

One more step must be completed before you can use the data from the ISR. It must be stored and named in an accessible way as described in the next section.

Instantiation and Constructors

Instantiation

Recall that an instance is a unique example of an object. With System.in, each time the buffer is read, it becomes an instance. Java Programmers use the verb, instantiate, when an instance is created.

As you may recall, storage locations must be declared and identified before they can be used. This is true for data from the ISR as well. Because the ISR data are special kinds of data from a buffer, its data type is not a primitive one. Complex data types must be created by the programmer or instantiated from a Java class. **Instantiation** is the process of creating an instance from a previously defined class. In the case of buffers, the previously defined class is called the BufferedReader. **BufferedReader** is a non-primitive class from a package of input and output utilities called java.io, which comes with the JDK.

The code necessary to instantiate is called a constructor, or constructor method. A **constructor** specifies the data type and assigns an identifier just like a declaration statement. The difference is that a constructor uses an assignment statement to declare the variable as an instance. A constructor takes the following form. The equal sign and the word, new, always are included.

```
Class identifier = new Class( );
```

In the case of instantiating for input, the BufferedReader is the class. Most programmers use a variable identifier such as myIn or dataIn to hold their input data. The resulting line of Java code may seem a bit cryptic; however, when broken down into its components, it is easier to understand.

```
BufferedReader dataIn = new BufferedReader(new InputStreamReader(System.in);
```

| class | identifier | instance constructor | | buffer | data from keyboard |

An identifier called dataIn is created from an instance of the BufferedReader class. It will contain the new data from System.in wrapped in the InputStreamReader each time the statement is executed. Figure 2-19 shows the flow of the data stream.

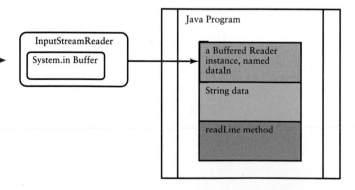

InputStreamReader
System.in Buffer

Java Program

a Buffered Reader instance, named dataIn

String data

readLine method

FIGURE 2-19

Modifying the Bert Program

As you modify this program to accept user input, it is appropriate to give this version of the program a new name, not only to distinguish it from the previous version, but also to better reflect the purpose. You will rename this program BertIO.java. Using a name such as BertIO, instead of BertVersion2, more closely represents the purpose of the program and is easier to remember.

Inserting an import statement before the class header will tell Java to expect references to classes from the java.io package, as it did in Project 1. Additionally, you will enter a constructor, creating a storage allocation for the instance of the buffered stream.

Perform the following steps to edit the code for interactive data input from the user.

More About

Class File Names

If you routinely edit, recompile, and execute the same file name, Java allows you to add an optional command to the java statement to re-compile if necessary. By typing java -cs and then the file name, the Java runtime system will recompile if a newer version of bytecode exists.

Steps **To Enter New Code**

---

1 If necessary, minimize the MS-DOS Prompt window so that the maximized Notepad window displays. Point to the end of the word, Bert, in line 5.

The mouse pointer displays as an I-beam over previously typed text at the end of the word Bert (Figure 2-20).

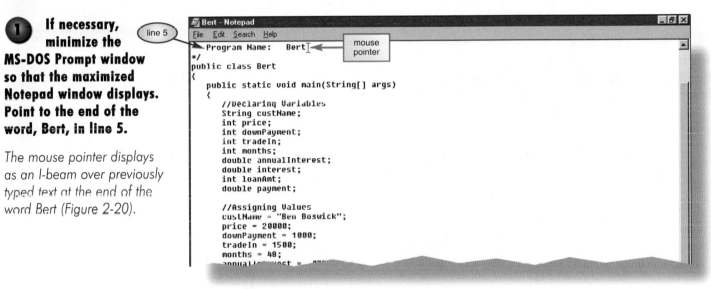

FIGURE 2-20

2 Click at the end of the word Bert. Without inserting a space, type IO to change the Program Name comment. Point to the end of the block comment.

The edited comment displays (Figure 2-21).

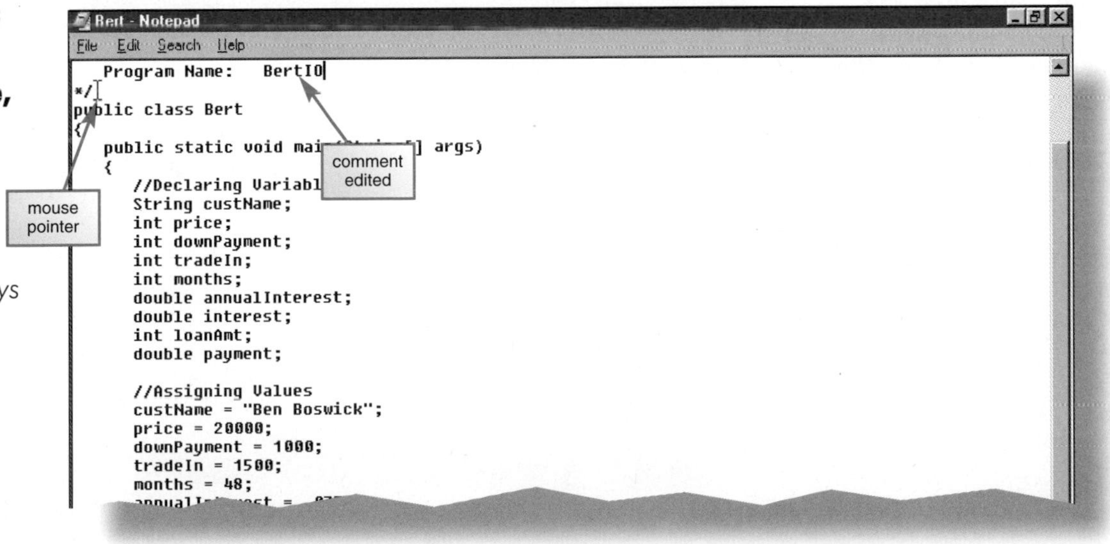

FIGURE 2-21

3 Click after the block comment. Press the ENTER key twice. Type `import java.io.*;` and then press the ENTER key. Point to the end of the word Bert in the class header.

The new line of code to import all of the classes in the java.io package displays (Figure 2-22). The semicolon ends the line.

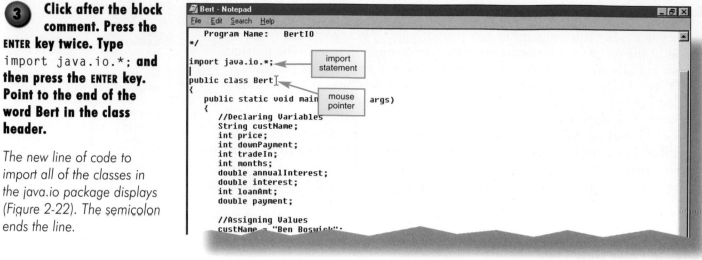

```
Program Name:    BertIO
*/

import java.io.*;          import
                           statement

public class Bert
{                          mouse
   public static void main      args)
   {                      pointer
      //Declaring Variables
      String custName;
      int price;
      int downPayment;
      int tradeIn;
      int months;
      double annualInterest;
      double interest;
      int loanAmt;
      double payment;

      //Assigning Values
      custName = "Ben Boswick";
```

FIGURE 2-22

4 Click after the word, Bert, in the class header. Type `IO` to change the class name to BertIO. Point to the opening brace of the main method.

The class name now is BertIO (Figure 2-23).

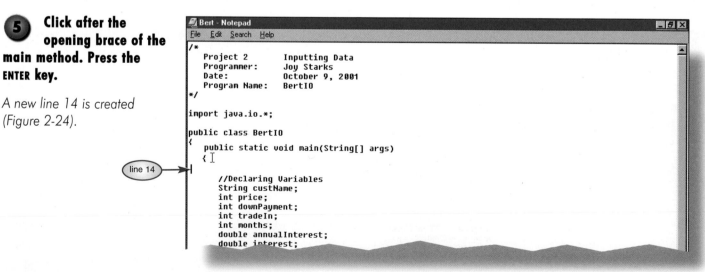

```
Program Name:      class
*/                 name edited

import java.io.*;

public class BertIO
{
   public static void main(String[] args)
   {
      //Declaring Variables
      String custName;          opening
      int price;                brace for main
      int downPayment;          method
      int tradeIn;
      int months;
      double annualInterest;
      double interest;
      int loanAmt;
      double payment;

      //Assigning Values
      custName = "Ben Boswick";
```

FIGURE 2-23

5 Click after the opening brace of the main method. Press the ENTER key.

A new line 14 is created (Figure 2-24).

```
/*
   Project 2        Inputting Data
   Programmer:      Joy Starks
   Date:            October 9, 2001
   Program Name:    BertIO
*/

import java.io.*;

public class BertIO
{
   public static void main(String[] args)
   {
                              line 14
      //Declaring Variables
      String custName;
      int price;
      int downPayment;
      int tradeIn;
      int months;
      double annualInterest;
      double interest;
```

FIGURE 2-24

6 **Indent and then type**
BufferedReader dataIn = new BufferedReader(new InputStreamReader (System.in)); **to enter the constructor code. Press the ENTER key.**

The new line of code for the constructor displays (Figure 2-25).

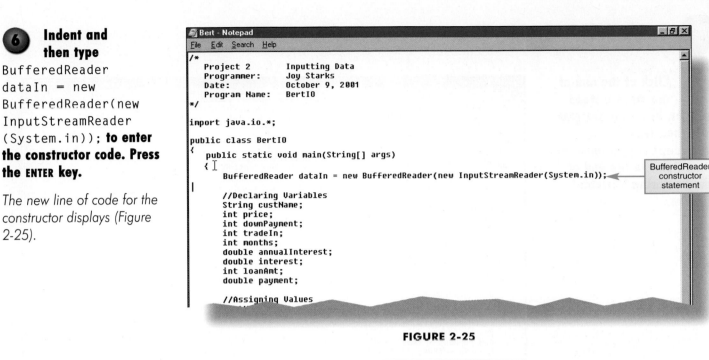

```
/*
    Project 2        Inputting Data
    Programmer:      Joy Starks
    Date:            October 9, 2001
    Program Name:    BertIO
*/

import java.io.*;

public class BertIO
{
    public static void main(String[] args)
    {
        BufferedReader dataIn = new BufferedReader(new InputStreamReader(System.in));

        //Declaring Variables
        String custName;
        int price;
        int downPayment;
        int tradeIn;
        int months;
        double annualInterest;
        double interest;
        int loanAmt;
        double payment;

        //Assigning Values
```

BufferedReader constructor statement

FIGURE 2-25

Many users and textbooks create their own classes for input and output to simplify the process of reading from the buffer. However, it is exactly this BufferedReader capability that makes Java easy to adapt to all kinds of input, such as strings, numbers, special characters, and foreign language symbols. It aids in Java's platform independence.

Data Handling

Users of this program will respond to prompts on the screen in order to enter the data. The sample data will be replaced by prompts that take the form of questions displayed with the System.out.println method. Then, using a method from the BufferedReader class called **readLine**, the data will be moved from the generic dataIn location to a location with an identifier that is more indicative of the data itself. For instance, a customer's name might be moved from dataIn to custName for use later in the program. Like all variables, these identifiers must be declared before being used.

Because the buffer stores input data one character at a time from the keyboard, a piece of data read from the buffer with the method, readLine, is a string of characters, and, therefore, must be declared as such. A string of characters is fine for data such as a person's name, but Java cannot perform mathematical operations on strings. Consequently, the data must be converted from string to numeric data types. Java has a **parse** method that you use to convert input strings to integers or doubles.

When you use the readLine method, you must warn Java that there is a possibility of errors. For instance, a user might not have authority to open a file that Java is trying to read, or the buffer on a particular system might be busy with other input. An easy way to keep the program from aborting prematurely due to these kinds of errors is to add the code: **throws IOException** to the end of the main method header. The program then acknowledges potential failures of this kind and will compile correctly.

Perform the steps on the next page to add exception handling to the main method header, to declare the input variables, and to parse the numbers.

More About

Parsing

Java allows several different parse methods to convert data types, including the wrappers for Long, Short, and Double - all of which convert values. The toString method is available for converting numbers to strings.

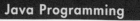

 Steps **To Edit Code for Data Handling**

1 **Click at the end of the main method header. Press the SPACEBAR and then type** throws IOException **to finish the line. Point to the end of the Declaring Variables section.**

The main method now acknowledges possible run-time errors (Figure 2-26).

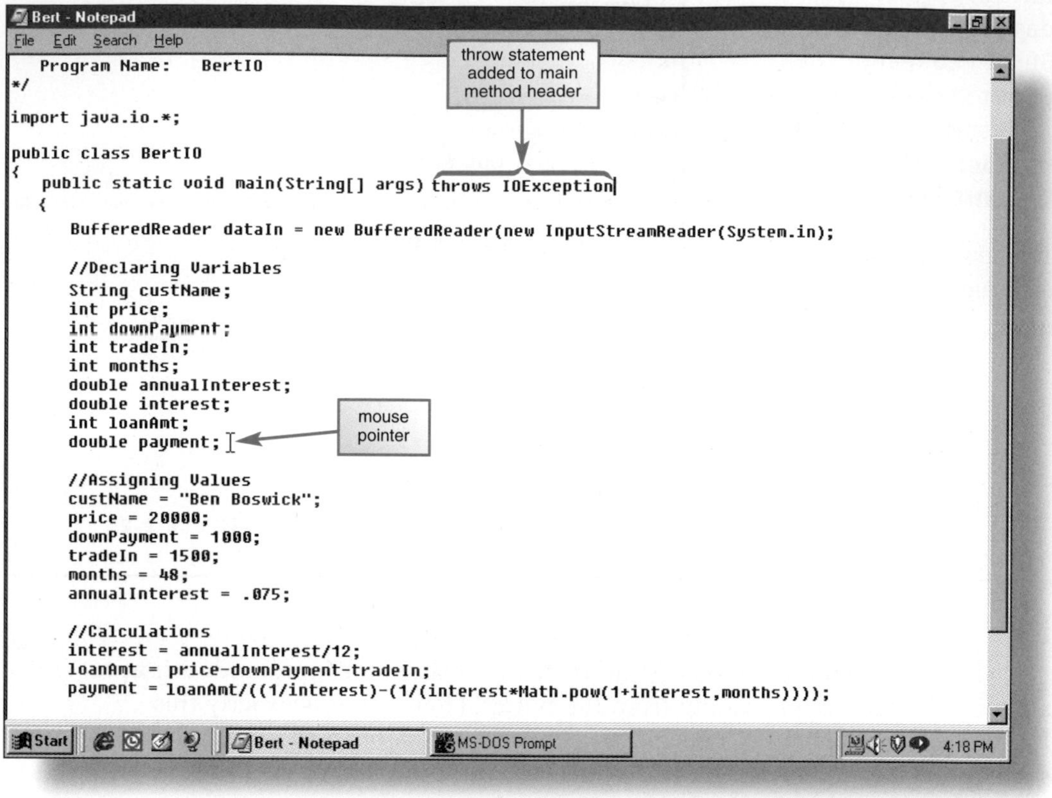

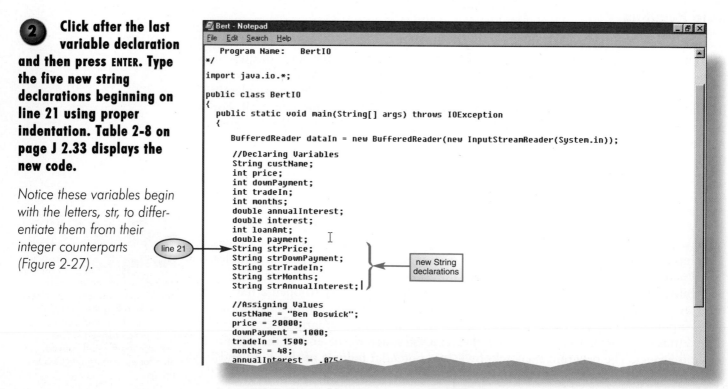

FIGURE 2-26

2 **Click after the last variable declaration and then press ENTER. Type the five new string declarations beginning on line 21 using proper indentation. Table 2-8 on page J 2.33 displays the new code.**

Notice these variables begin with the letters, str, to differentiate them from their integer counterparts (Figure 2-27).

FIGURE 2-27

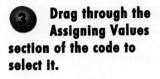 **Drag through the Assigning Values section of the code to select it.**

The comment line and assignments of sample data are selected (Figure 2-28).

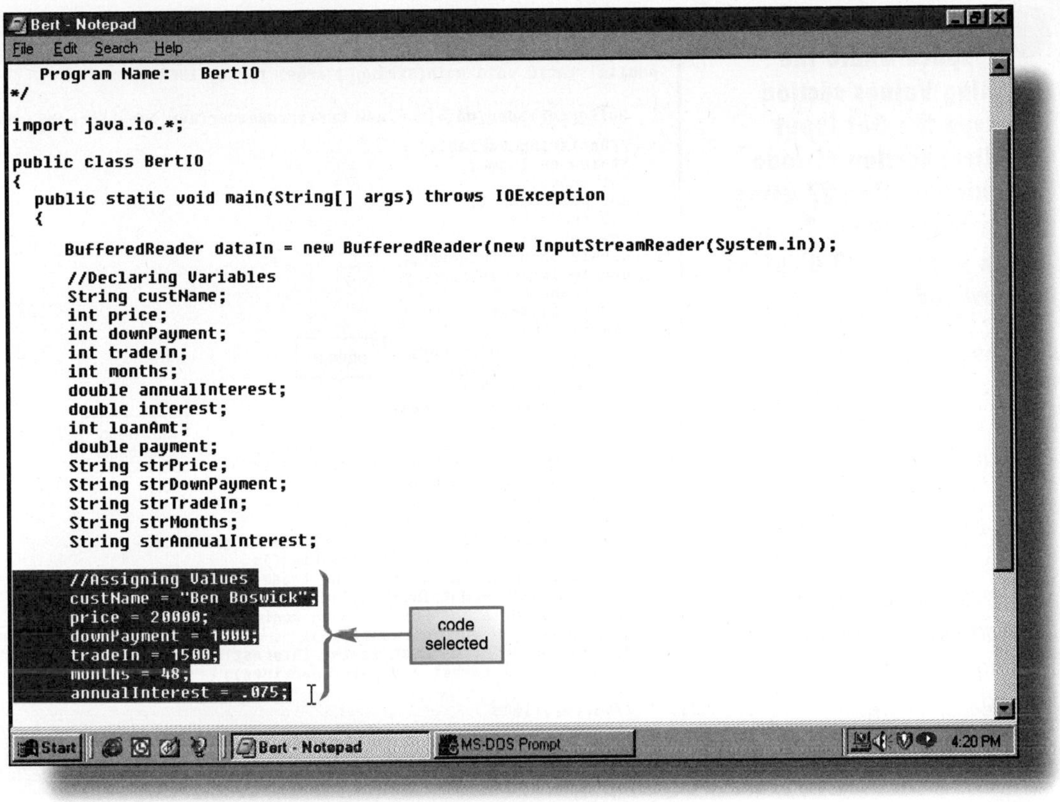

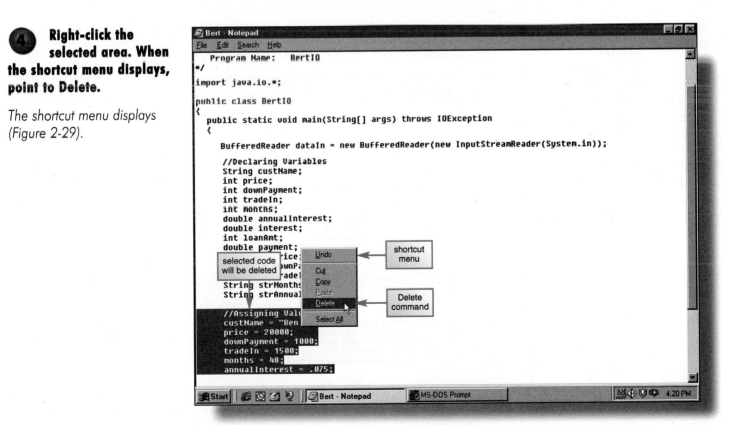

FIGURE 2-28

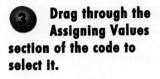 **Right-click the selected area. When the shortcut menu displays, point to Delete.**

The shortcut menu displays (Figure 2-29).

FIGURE 2-29

5 **Click Delete. In the space where the Assigning Values section was, type the Get Input from User section of code beginning on line 27 using proper indentation. Table 2-9 on page J 2.33 displays the new code.**

The System.out.println method displays the prompt as the argument for each question (Figure 2-30). The assignment statements below each prompt transfer data from the buffer to the appropriate variable location. Indentation and line spacing make the code easy to read.

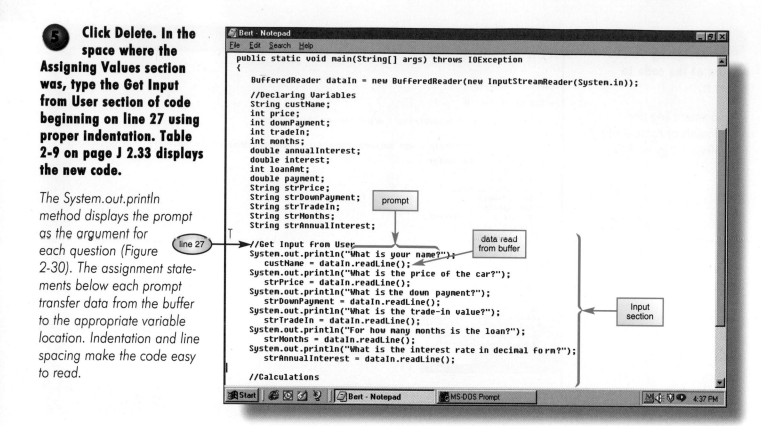

```
Bert - Notepad
File  Edit  Search  Help
public static void main(String[] args) throws IOException
{
    BufferedReader dataIn = new BufferedReader(new InputStreamReader(System.in));

    //Declaring Variables
    String custName;
    int price;
    int downPayment;
    int tradeIn;
    int months;
    double annualInterest;
    double interest;
    int loanAmt;
    double payment;
    String strPrice;
    String strDownPayment;          prompt
    String strTradeIn;
    String strMonths;
    String strAnnualInterest;
                                                          data read
    //Get Input from User                                 from buffer
    System.out.println("What is your name?");
        custName = dataIn.readLine();
    System.out.println("What is the price of the car?");
        strPrice = dataIn.readLine();
    System.out.println("What is the down payment?");      Input
        strDownPayment = dataIn.readLine();               section
    System.out.println("What is the trade-in value?");
        strTradeIn = dataIn.readLine();
    System.out.println("For how many months is the loan?");
        strMonths = dataIn.readLine();
    System.out.println("What is the interest rate in decimal form?");
        strAnnualInterest = dataIn.readLine();

    //Calculations
Start    Bert - Notepad    MS-DOS Prompt                        4:37 PM
```

line 27

FIGURE 2-30

6 **Press the ENTER key, then type the Conversions section of code beginning at line 41 using proper indentation. Table 2-10 on page J 2.33 displays the new code.**

The parse method displays in each assignment statement (Figure 2-31).

```
Bert - Notepad
File  Edit  Search  Help
    int downPayment;
    int tradeIn;
    int months;
    double annualInterest;
    double interest;
    int loanAmt;
    double payment;
    String strPrice;
    String strDownPayment;
    String strTradeIn;
    String strMonths;
    String strAnnualInterest;

    //Get Input from User
    System.out.println("What is your name?");
        custName = dataIn.readLine();
    System.out.println("What is the price of the car?");
        strPrice = dataIn.readLine();
    System.out.println("What is the down payment?");
        strDownPayment = dataIn.readLine();
    System.out.println("What is the trade-in value?");
        strTradeIn = dataIn.readLine();
    System.out.println("For how many months is the loan?");
        strMonths = dataI        ();
    System.out.println("          parse      e interest rate in decimal form?");
        strAnnualInterest        method      readLine();

    //Conversions
    price = Integer.parseInt(strPrice);
    downPayment = Integer.parseInt(strDownPayment);        Conversion
    tradeIn = Integer.parseInt(strTradeIn);               section
    months = Integer.parseInt(strMonths);
    annualInterest = Double.parseDouble(strAnnualInterest);

    //Calculations
Start    Bert - Notepad    MS-DOS Prompt                        4:25 PM
```

line 41

FIGURE 2-31

Table 2-8

LINE	CODE
21	String strPrice;
22	String strDownPayment;
23	String strTradeIn;
24	String strMonths;
25	String strAnnualInterest;

Table 2-9

LINE	CODE
27	//Get Input from User
28	System.out.println("What is your name?");
29	custName = dataIn.readLine();
30	System.out.println("What is the price of the car?");
31	strPrice = dataIn.readLine();
32	System.out.println("What is the downpayment?");
33	strDownPayment = dataIn.readLine();
34	System.out.println("What is the trade-in value?");
35	strTradeIn = dataIn.readLine();
36	System.out.println("For how many months is the loan?");
37	strMonths = dataIn.readLine();
38	System.out.println("What is the decimal interest rate?");
39	strAnnualInterest = dataIn.readLine();

Table 2-10

LINE	CODE
41	//Conversions
42	price = Integer.parseInt(strPrice);
43	downPayment = Integer.parseInt(strDownPayment);
44	tradeIn = Integer.parseInt(strTradeIn);
45	months = Integer.parseInt(strMonths);
46	annualInterest = Double.parseDouble(strAnnualInterest);

The interactive version of the program now is complete. You added the import statement, changed the name of the class, and declared the necessary string variables. You then entered code to prompt the user and to accept a string answer from the buffer. Finally, you included the parse method to convert the strings to numbers in order to use them in later calculations.

Figure 2-32 on the next page shows the printout of the program code in its entirety. Check for syntax, proper spelling, capitalization, and indentations. When you are confident everything is correct, you are ready to save and compile your program.

```
                              BertIO


     tradeIn = Integer.parseInt(strTradeIn);
     months = Integer.parseInt(strMonths);
     annualInterest = Double.parseDouble(strAnnualInterest);

     //Calculations
     interest = annualInterest/12;
     loanAmt = price-downPayment-tradeIn;
     payment = loanAmt/((1/interest)-(1/(interest*Math.pow(1+interest,months))));

     //Output
     System.out.print("The monthly payment for " + custName + " is $");
     System.out.println(Math.round(payment));
   }
}
```

Page 2

```
                              BertIO


     /*
         Project 2        Inputting Data
         Programmer:      Joy Starks
         Date:            October 9, 2001
         Program Name:    BertIO
     */

     import java.io.*;

     public class BertIO
     {
        public static void main(String[] args) throws IOException
        {

           BufferedReader dataIn = new BufferedReader(new InputStreamReader(System.in));

           //Declaring Variables
           String custName;
           int price;
           int downPayment;
           int tradeIn;
           int months;
           double annualInterest;
           double interest;
           int loanAmt;
           double payment;
           String strPrice;
           String strDownPayment;
           String strTradeIn;
           String strMonths;
           String strAnnualInterest;

           //Get Input from User
           System.out.println("What is your name?");
              custName = dataIn.readLine();
           System.out.println("What is the price of the car?");
              strPrice = dataIn.readLine();
           System.out.println("What is the down payment?");
              strDownPayment = dataIn.readLine();
           System.out.println("What is the trade-in value?");
              strTradeIn = dataIn.readLine();
           System.out.println("For how many months is the loan?");
              strMonths = dataIn.readLine();
           System.out.println("What is the interest rate in decimal form?");
              strAnnualInterest = dataIn.readLine();

           //Conversions
           price = Integer.parseInt(strPrice);
           downPayment = Integer.parseInt(strDownPayment);
```

Page 1

FIGURE 2-32

Executing an Interactive Program

Java program names must be the same as the class statement at the beginning of the code. Therefore, when you save the program, you must use the Save As command and indicate the new file name. You also will use the new file name when you compile the program.

Saving and Compiling

You will save this new version of the program that accepts input from the user with the file name BertIO.java. Perform the following steps to save the file on a floppy disk with a new name and then compile it. Perform the following steps to save and compile the source code.

TO SAVE AND COMPILE THE SOURCE CODE

1 With a floppy disk in drive A, click File on Notepad's menu bar, and then click Save As.

2 When the Save As dialog box displays, type "BertIO.java" in the File name text box.

3 If necessary, click the Save in box arrow and then click 3½ Floppy (A:) in the list.

4 Click the Save button.

5 Click the MS-DOS Prompt button on the taskbar. At the A: prompt, type javac BertIO.java and press the ENTER key to compile the program. If you have errors, correct them in the Notepad window and repeat the steps.

The command prompt again displays as the file on drive A is compiled successfully.

Again, if you want to print a copy of your program, the Notepad File menu contains the Print command, which sends a copy of your code to the default printer.

Other Ways

1. To save in Notepad, press ALT+F, press A

Running the Program

When you run an interactive Java program, the compiled bytecode runs in the MS-DOS Prompt window, pausing every time the readLine method is executed in order for the user to enter the data requested in the prompt. To test the program, programmers typically use the same sample data that they used in creating the original version of the code, this time entering it from a user's perspective as the program runs.

Perform the steps on the next page to run the interactive program, BertIO from the prompt line.

Steps: To Run the Program

1 At the A: prompt in the MS-DOS Prompt window, type java BertIO and then press the ENTER key.

The first prompt displays (Figure 2-33). The MS-DOS Prompt button on the taskbar changes to reflect the running Java program.

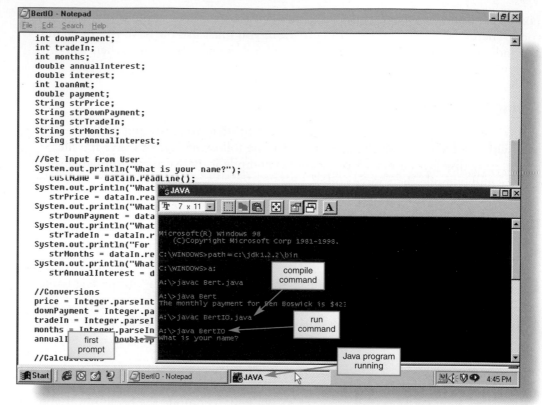

FIGURE 2-33

2 Type Ben Boswick and then press the ENTER key.

The customer name is entered and the next prompt displays (Figure 2-34).

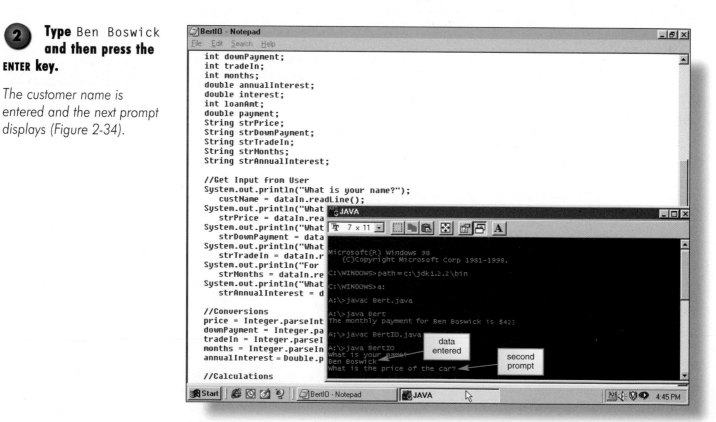

FIGURE 2-34

3 Type 20000 **in response to the prompt for the price of the car. Press the ENTER key.**

The price is entered and the next prompt displays (Figure 2-35). When entering numbers, do not type a comma.

FIGURE 2-35

4 **At the next four prompts, enter the corresponding sample data of** 1000 **for the down payment,** 1500 **for the trade-in,** 48 **for the number of months, and** .075 **for the interest rate, pressing the ENTER key after each entry.**

The final answer displays (Figure 2-36).

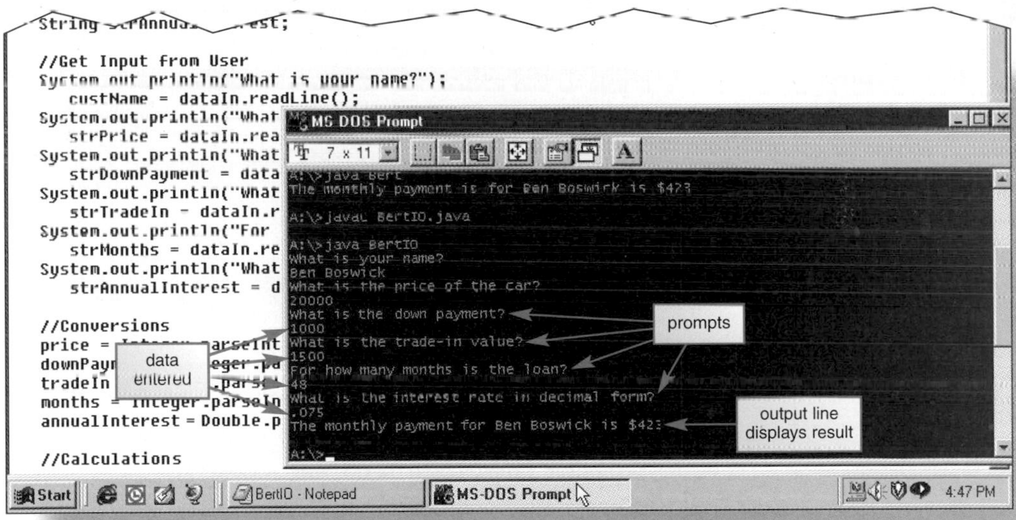

FIGURE 2-36

Interactive programs allow programmers the flexibility of running the program many times, using various sample data, without having to recompile. Obviously, many things could go wrong when users begin to enter data, such as entering incorrect information or unrealistic data. This project does not attempt to account for all of the possible errors that might occur; however, if the program is run with sensible data and the data are entered correctly, the correct answer will display.

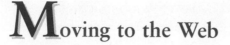
Moving to the Web

The final version of the program for Bert's Banner Cars is to create an applet. Recall that an applet is a program called from within another environment, usually a Web page. In order to convert the BertIO program from running at the command prompt into a program that will display as part of a Web page, you will need to create three kinds of applet objects. You will use labels, text fields, and buttons in the applet for Bert's Banner Cars.

Converting the Program to an Applet

In Project 1, you learned that an applet uses Java packages that are different from an application. Instead of the java.io package, an interactive applet must import the JDK-supplied java.awt package as well as the java.applet package. Applets must extend the program's class in the class header, in order to inherit attributes from the applet package.

This applet will be interactive, which requires implementing an interface handler provided with the JDK called **ActionListener**. ActionListener is contained in a special part of the java.awt package used for applet events. ActionListener listens for events such as mouse clicks during execution of the applet.

Perform the following steps to insert import statements into the BertIO program, extend the Applet, implement the ActionListener, and change the applet's name.

 To Enter Code

1 If necessary, minimize the MS-DOS Prompt window so that the maximized Notepad window displays. Point to the scroll box on the vertical scroll bar.

The Notepad window displays and is maximized (Figure 2-37).

```
BertIO - Notepad                                          Notepad
File  Edit  Search  Help                                  window

    int downPayment;
    int tradeIn;
    int months;
    double annualInterest;
    double interest;
    int loanAmt;
    double payment;
    String strPrice;
    String strDownPayment;
    String strTradeIn;
    String strMonths;
    String strAnnualInterest;

    //Get Input from User
    System.out.println("What is your name?");
        custName = dataIn.readLine();
    System.out.println("What is the price of the car?");
        strPrice = dataIn.readLine();
    System.out.println("What is the down payment?");      scroll
        strDownPayment = dataIn.readLine();               box
    System.out.println("What is the trade-in value?");
        strTradeIn = dataIn.readLine();
    System.out.println("For how many months is the loan?");
        strMonths = dataIn.readLine();
    System.out.println("What is the interest rate in decimal form?");
        strAnnualInterest = dataIn.readLine();

    //Conversions
    price = Integer.parseInt(strPrice);
    downPayment = Integer.parse        ment);
    tradeIn = Integer.parseInt(    BertIO –
    months = Integer.parseInt(    Notepad button
    annualInterest = Double.parseDouble(strAnnualInterest);

    //Calculations
```

Start | BertIO - Notepad | MS-DOS Prompt | 5:00 PM

FIGURE 2-37

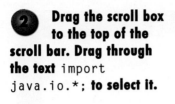

2 Drag the scroll box to the top of the scroll bar. Drag through the text import java.io.*; to select it.

The line of code displays selected (Figure 2-38).

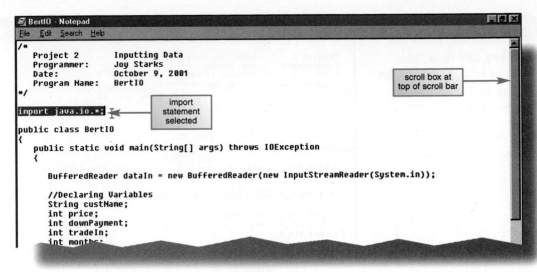

FIGURE 2-38

3 With the text still selected, press the DELETE key and then type the new import statements as shown in Figure 2-39.

The commands to import the Java packages display (Figure 2-39).

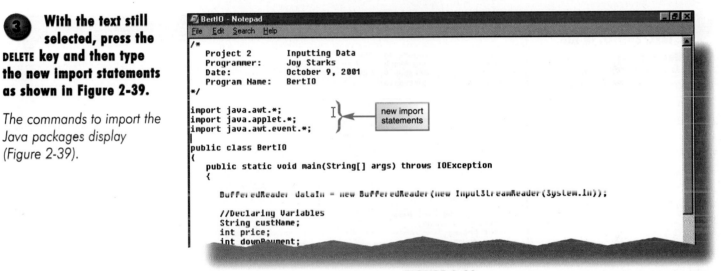

FIGURE 2-39

4 Select the text, BertIO, in the block comment.

The name of the class displays selected (Figure 2-40).

```
/*
    Project 2        Inputting Data
    Programmer:      Joy Starks
    Date:            October 9, 2001          comment
    Program Name:    BertIO                   text selected
*/

import java.awt.*;
import java.applet.*;
import java.awt.event.*;

public class BertIO
{
    public static void main(String[] args) throws IOException
    {

        BufferedReader dataIn = new BufferedReader(new InputStreamReader(System.in));

        //Declaring Variables
        String custName;
        int price;
        int downPayment;
```

FIGURE 2-40

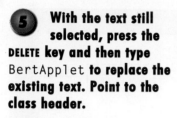

5 With the text still selected, press the DELETE key and then type BertApplet to replace the existing text. Point to the class header.

BertApplet replaces the old class name (Figure 2-41).

```
/*
    Project 2        Inputting Data
    Programmer:      Joy Starks
    Date:            October 9, 2001
    Program Name:    BertApplet|        new class
*/                                      name inserted

import java.awt.*;
import java.applet.*;
import java.awt.event.*;                class
                                        header
public class BertIO I

    public static void main(String[] args) throws IOException
    {

        BufferedReader dataIn = new BufferedReader(new InputStreamReader(System.in));

        //Declaring Variables
        String custName;
        int price;
        int downPayment;
```

FIGURE 2-41

6 Drag through the text, BertIO, in the class header.

The class name in the class header displays selected (Figure 2-42).

```
/*
    Project 2        Inputting Data
    Programmer:      Joy Starks
    Date:            October 9, 2001
    Program Name:    BertApplet
*/

import java.awt.*;
import java.applet.*;
import java.awt.event.*;
                                        class name
public class BertIO                     selected
{
    public static void main(String[] args) throws IOException
    {

        BufferedReader dataIn = new BufferedReader(new InputStreamReader(System.in));

        //Declaring Variables
        String custName;
        int price;
        int downPayment;
```

FIGURE 2-42

7 With the text still selected, press the DELETE key and then type BertApplet extends Applet implements ActionListener in the class header.

The class header displays the new class name, extension, and implementation (Figure 2-43).

```
/*
    Project 2        Inputting Data
    Programmer:      Joy Starks
    Date:            October 9, 2001
    Program Name:    BertAppl        extension
*/                                   statement

import java.awt.*;
import java.applet.*;
import java.awt.event.*;

public class BertApplet extends Applet implements ActionListener
{
    public static void main(String[] args) throws IOException
    {
                        new           implementation
        Buffere        class name     statement           treamReader(System.in));

        //Decla              les
        String custName;
        int price;
        int downPayment;
```

FIGURE 2-43

Import statements allow you to refer to a library class by its short name rather than spelling out the entire package and class name each time you want to use it. In the previous step, instead of referring to java.awt.event.ActionListener, the programmer simply uses the name of the event ActionListener in the code. The **asterisk** (*) is a wild card character that matches any public class name in the java.awt.event package.

In general, the purpose of importing classes is to avoid having to write common routines that already exist in Java.

Label Components

The java.awt package contains components that you can use in applets. A typical component called a **label**, is a class that displays text on the screen. Labels are assigned a string of characters, or a text value, by the programmer. A common usage is to create a constructor that assigns the string of characters to the component.

```
Label identifier = new identifier("message");
```

Recall that a constructor is a special kind of assignment statement that creates an instance of a class. The label instance is constructed during compilation. During execution, the label, displaying its message, is added to the applet window.

Text Field Components

A second kind of component that holds and displays text is a text field. A **text field** is a class that creates a box in which users enter text. Like the label, it displays inside the applet window. In the constructor, the programmer enters a width argument, which is the number of characters a user may input during execution. The difference between labels and text fields is a conceptual one. Only the programmer manipulates the text of a label, whereas a text field is created by the programmer for manipulation by the user. A common usage is to create a text field component that the user will fill in during execution.

```
TextField identifier = new TextField(width);
```

Button Components

A third type of component is a button. Most computer users are very familiar with command buttons. When you click a button you expect something to happen. Typically, buttons inherit their characteristics, such as color and shape, from the operating system, but programmers may determine the caption on the button, as well as the actions to be performed when it is clicked. In the constructor, the programmer enters a caption argument, which is the string of characters that displays on the face of the button during execution. The construct, or code, for a button is similar to a label constructor.

```
Button identifier = new Button("caption");
```

Programming Conventions

Component identifiers must follow the same Java naming rules as variable identifiers, but programmers differ in their specific naming conventions. A **naming convention** is the way you use words, case, prefixes, and underscores to name the identifiers in your program. The main reason for using a consistent set of naming conventions within a given program is to standardize the structure and coding style of an application, so that you and others may read and understand the code. For example, if you consistently use title case — capitalized first letters — for identifiers with more than one word, your program is easier to read and edit.

Some programmers name their applet components with a three-letter prefix similar to the ones used in the Visual Basic programming languages, such as lblTitle or txtName. Others use no component-specific letters, simply calling their components, label, title, or name. Such a convention makes it difficult in longer programs to remember and identify what kind of component is being used. In this text, the naming convention will identify the purpose beginning with a lowercase letter, followed by the component in title case. For example, a label might be named, titleLabel, and a text field, nameField. When naming buttons, the purpose will include a verb whenever possible, or a response caption such as OK. That purpose and/or response will be followed by the word Button. For example, a button might be named, calcButton or okButton. Whatever naming convention you decide to use in your own programs, your goals should be easy reading and consistency.

Recall that when you coded the prompt for the user, followed by the allocation of storage for the answer, you indented the allocation of storage to easily pair the two. You will do the same for the creation of labels and text fields that go together. This kind of indentation rule is part of a programmer's **coding convention**.

Unfortunately, there are no hard and fast rules about coding conventions, but as Java takes a firmer hold in application development, a system of standardized indentations and spacings will follow.

Perform the following steps to create label, text field, and button components in the applet.

Steps To Create Applet Components

1 **Select the text from the main method header through the Get Input from User section.**

The text is selected (Figure 2-44).

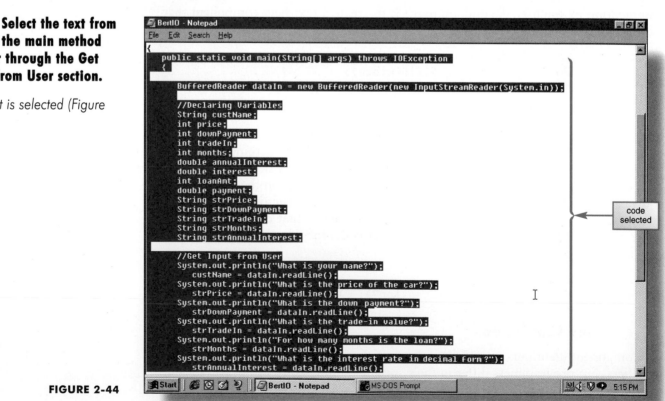

FIGURE 2-44

2 **Right-click the selected area and point to Delete on the shortcut menu.**

The shortcut menu displays (Figure 2-45).

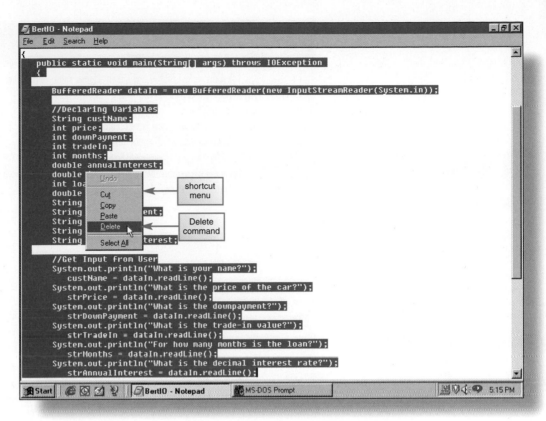

FIGURE 2-45

3 **Click Delete and then type the lines to display the labels, text boxes, and button as shown in Table 2-11 on the next page. Use proper indentation.**

The constructor lines display (Figure 2-46).

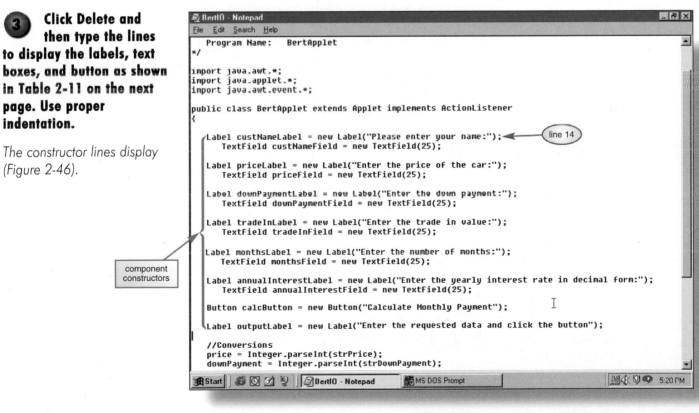

FIGURE 2-46

Table 2-11

LINE	CODE
14	Label custNameLabel = new Label("Please enter your name:");
15	TextField custNameField = new TextField(25);
16	
17	Label priceLabel = new Label("Enter the price of the car:");
18	TextField priceField = new TextField(25);
19	
20	Label downPaymentLabel = new Label("Enter the down payment:");
21	TextField downPaymentField = new TextField(25);
22	
23	Label tradeInLabel = new Label("Enter the trade in value:");
24	TextField tradeInField = new TextField(25);
25	
26	Label monthsLabel = new Label("Enter the number of months:");
27	TextField monthsField = new TextField(25);
28	
29	Label annualInterestLabel = new Label("Enter the yearly interest rate in decimal form:");
30	TextField annualInterestField = new TextField(25);
31	
32	Button calcButton = new Button("Calculate Monthly Payment");
33	
34	Label outputLabel = new Label("Enter the requested data and click the button");

More About

Applets

Applets do not include a main method because they do not start themselves. An applet is added to an already running program: the browser. The browser has predefined means for getting each applet to do what it wants. It does this by calling methods that it knows the applet may have, such as init, paint, or start.

You may save this program now by following the steps on page 2.23 or wait until you have finished entering the code and then save it.

Component objects have become more stable over time. With the advent of graphical user interfaces (GUI) in the 1980s, users have certain expectations of text boxes, and expect buttons to be "clickable." Java takes advantages of those expectations and provides the pre-built classes for typical GUI components. Programmers have these kinds of tools at their fingertips, with many ways to manipulate them.

Table 2-12

LINE	CODE
37	{
38	add(custNameLabel);
39	add(custNameField);
40	add(priceLabel);
41	add(priceField);
42	add(downPaymentLabel);
43	add(downPaymentField);
44	add(tradeInLabel);
45	add(tradeInField);
46	add(monthsLabel);
47	add(monthsField);
48	add(annualInterestLabel);
49	add(annualInterestField);
50	add(calcButton);
51	add(outputLabel);

The Init Method

The constructors for labels, text fields, and buttons are merely storage locations until the applet actually is displayed on the screen. Recall that in Project 1, you used the paint method to draw a string of text in the applet window. The init method is another applet method that is initialized when the applet actually begins to display on the screen or in the browser. The container method, add, is used to add the previously declared objects to the applet. A **container method** is a special method to manipulate a component that resides inside a larger structure such as a window, frame, or panel.

Perform the following steps to code the init method, which adds the components to the applet container.

Steps **To Code the Init Method**

1 **In the Notepad window, position the insertion point below the last label constructor. Press the ENTER key to insert a blank line. Indent three spaces and then type** `public void init()` **to code the init method header. Press the ENTER key again.**

The init header displays (Figure 2-47).

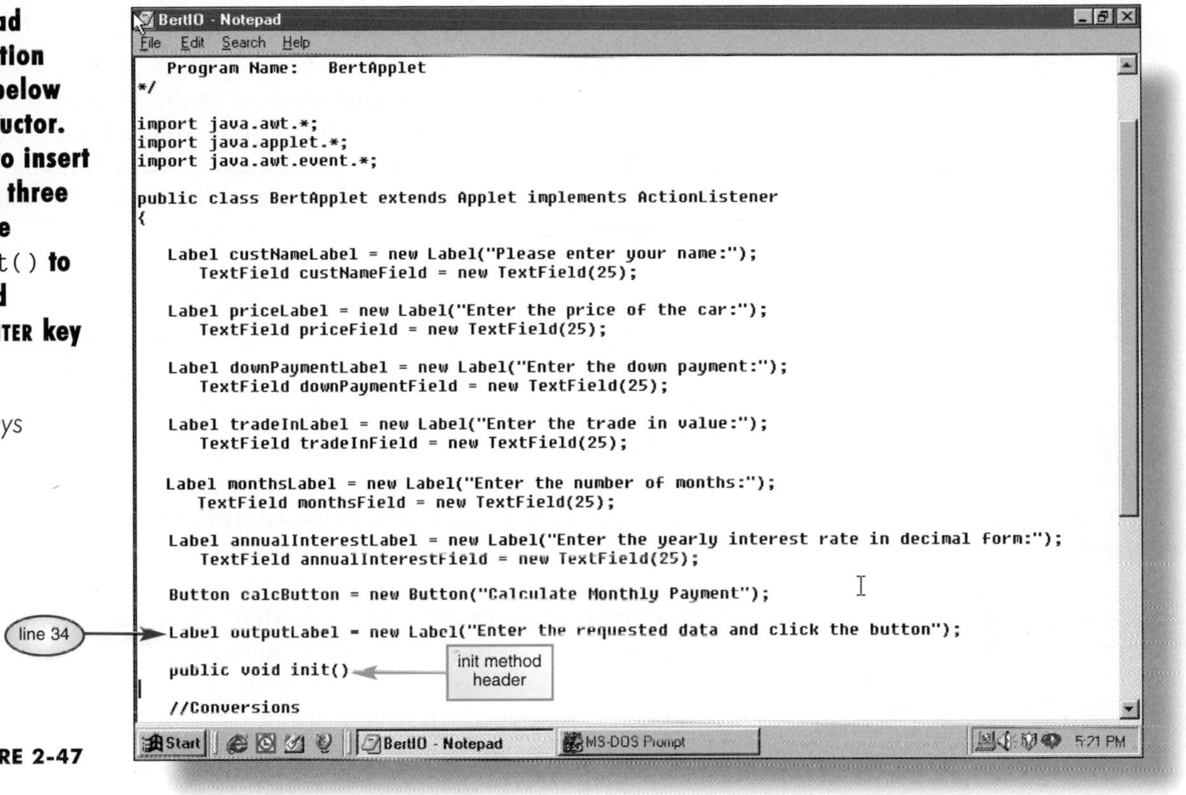

FIGURE 2-47

```
    Program Name:    BertApplet
*/

import java.awt.*;
import java.applet.*;
import java.awt.event.*;

public class BertApplet extends Applet implements ActionListener
{
    Label custNameLabel = new Label("Please enter your name:");
       TextField custNameField = new TextField(25);

    Label priceLabel = new Label("Enter the price of the car:");
       TextField priceField = new TextField(25);

    Label downPaymentLabel = new Label("Enter the down payment:");
       TextField downPaymentField = new TextField(25);

    Label tradeInLabel = new Label("Enter the trade in value:");
       TextField tradeInField = new TextField(25);

    Label monthsLabel = new Label("Enter the number of months:");
       TextField monthsField = new TextField(25);

    Label annualInterestLabel = new Label("Enter the yearly interest rate in decimal form:");
       TextField annualInterestField = new TextField(25);

    Button calcButton = new Button("Calculate Monthly Payment");

    Label outputLabel = new Label("Enter the requested data and click the button");

    public void init()          ← init method header

    //Conversions
```

line 34 → `Label outputLabel = new Label("Enter the requested data and click the button");`

init method header → `public void init()`

2 **Type the rest of the init method as shown in Table 2-12 using proper indentation. After the last line of code is entered, press the ENTER key.**

The code to add the labels, fields, and button displays (Figure 2-48).

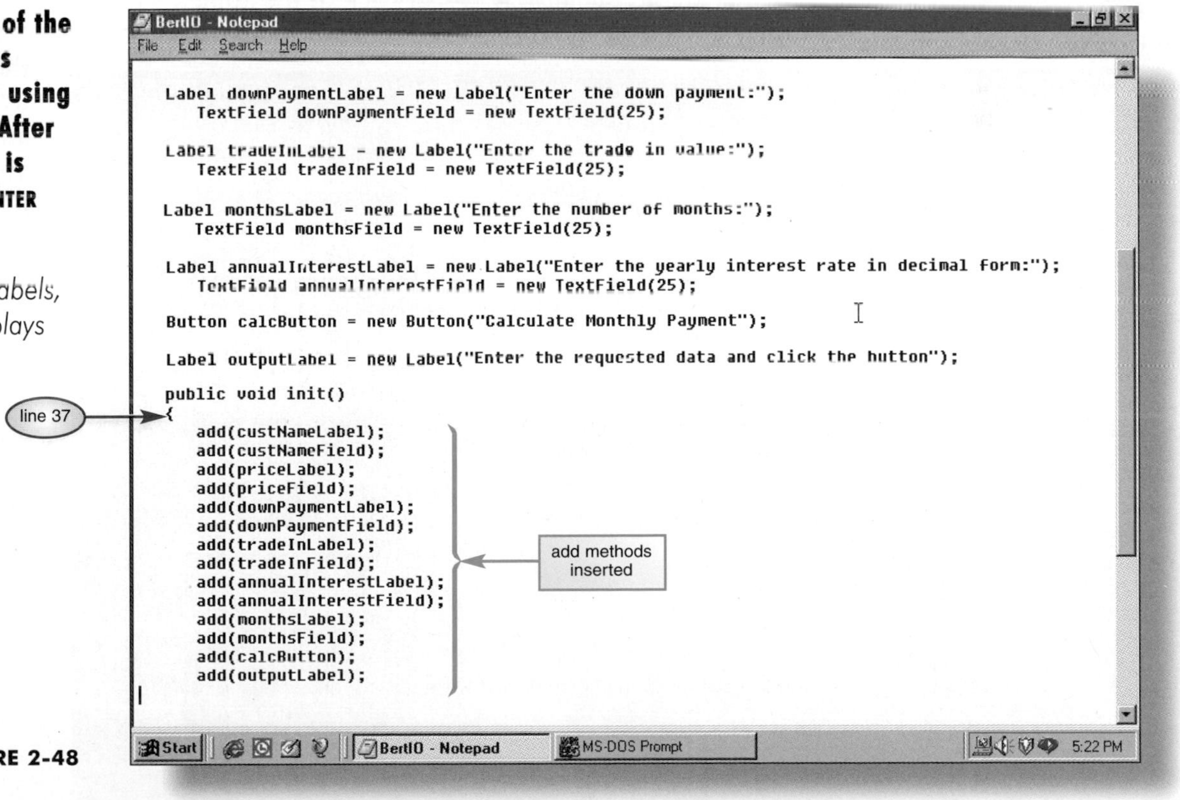

FIGURE 2-48

```
    Label downPaymentLabel = new Label("Enter the down payment:");
       TextField downPaymentField = new TextField(25);

    Label tradeInLabel = new Label("Enter the trade in value:");
       TextField tradeInField = new TextField(25);

    Label monthsLabel = new Label("Enter the number of months:");
       TextField monthsField = new TextField(25);

    Label annualInterestLabel = new Label("Enter the yearly interest rate in decimal form:");
       TextField annualInterestField = new TextField(25);

    Button calcButton = new Button("Calculate Monthly Payment");

    Label outputLabel = new Label("Enter the requested data and click the button");

    public void init()
    {
        add(custNameLabel);
        add(custNameField);
        add(priceLabel);
        add(priceField);
        add(downPaymentLabel);
        add(downPaymentField);
        add(tradeInLabel);
        add(tradeInField);
        add(annualInterestLabel);
        add(annualInterestField);
        add(monthsLabel);
        add(monthsField);
        add(calcButton);
        add(outputLabel);
```

line 37 → `{`

add methods inserted →

Notice that the code to construct the labels, fields, and button comes before the init method. This will speed processing during execution as the init method will already have the compiled data to add to the applet on the screen.

The final set of code will create the event behind the calculate button.

The ActionListener

Recall that the ActionListener, implemented at the beginning of the program, is a part of the java.awt.event package. The ActionListener detects keystrokes and mouse clicks. The programmer decides which component is going to be the external trigger for the user. The programmer then uses a method called addActionListener to make the component active.

```
calcButton.addActionListener(this);
```

In this example, the calcButton will be the hot component. The addActionListener method only needs one argument to perform its method. Recall that an argument is the information a function, procedure, or method needs in order to do its job. In the applet program, you will use a reserved word, this, as an argument. (See Appendix B for a complete list of reserved words in Java.) The reserved word, this, refers back to the container. In other words, you are asking the ActionListener to add an active button to this applet.

Although the reasons to use a keyword that refers back to the object itself are rather confusing, you can think of it as the ActionListener making the applet listen for the click, and the keyword, this, identifying the "clickable" component.

Once a click is received, a Java applet must perform a task; in this case, it must calculate the monthly payment just as it did in the previous two versions of the program. The **ActionPerformed** method is executed when the click occurs. Text field data items, entered by the user, are retrieved and converted to numbers. The formulas are calculated and the answer is sent back to the applet. The **getText** and **setText** methods are part of the java.awt package. Anytime you use a text box in Java, you can use these methods to easily transfer data back and forth from the applet user to the program, just as you did with the ISR when the program was a stand-alone application.

Finally, the ActionPerformed method (Table 2-13) will hold the code to perform the calculations.

More About

The Java AWT Package

See Appendix A for information on browsing the Java SDK documentation. Sun Microsystems provides a complete listing of the methods and classes for each of the packages.

Table 2-13

LINE	CODE
55	`public void actionPerformed(ActionEvent e)`
56	`{`
57	`    //Converting input to values`
58	`    int price = Integer.parseInt(priceField.getText());`
59	`    int downPayment = Integer.parseInt(downPaymentField.getText());`
60	`    int tradeIn = Integer.parseInt(tradeInField.getText());`
61	`    double annualInterest = Double.parseDouble(annualInterestField.getText());`
62	`    int months = Integer.parseInt(monthsField.getText());`
63	
64	`    //Variables used in formulas and output`
65	`    double interest;`
66	`    int loanAmt;`
67	`    double payment;`
68	
69	`    //Calculation`
70	`    interest = annualInterest/12;`
71	`    loanAmt = price-downPayment-tradeIn;`
72	`    payment = loanAmt/((1/interest)-(1/(interest*Math.pow(1+interest,months))));`
73	
74	`    //Output`
75	`    outputLabel.setText("The monthly payment is $" + Math.round(payment));`
76	`    }`
77	`}`

Perform the following steps to enter the code for the ActionListener and the
ActionPerformed method.

Steps To Code the ActionListener

1 In the Notepad
window, position
the insertion point directly
below the last add
command. Indent as shown
in Figure 2-49, type
`calcButton.`
`addActionListener`
`(this);` **and then press
the ENTER key. Indent three
spaces and then type a
closing brace to complete
the init method.**

*The last line of the init
method calls the
ActionListener
(Figure 2-49).*

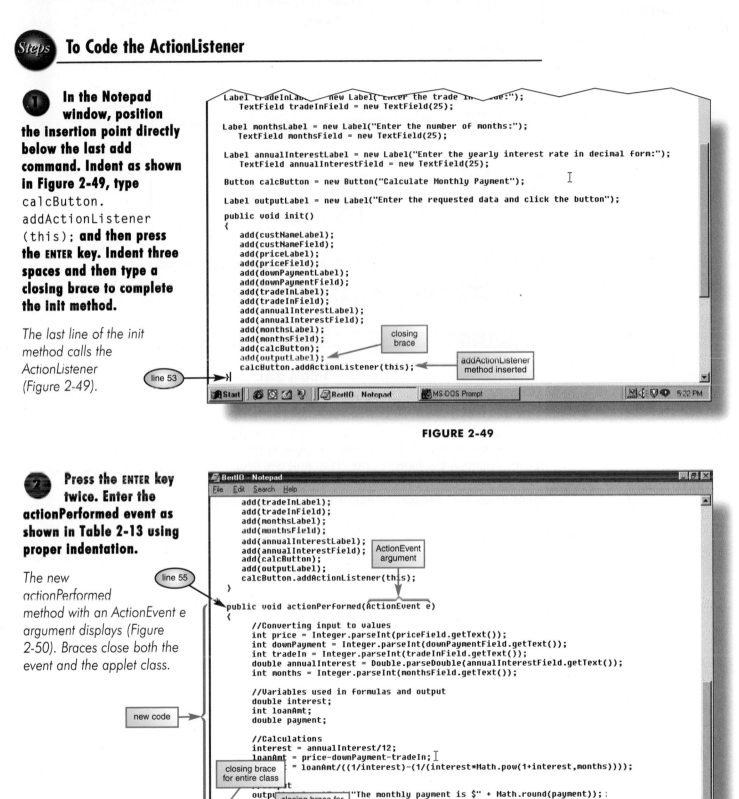

FIGURE 2-49

2 **Press the ENTER key
twice. Enter the
actionPerformed event as
shown in Table 2-13 using
proper indentation.**

*The new
actionPerformed
method with an ActionEvent e
argument displays (Figure
2-50). Braces close both the
event and the applet class.*

FIGURE 2-50

3 Drag through the remaining code left from the BertIO version of the program.

The code displays selected (Figure 2-51).

4 Right-click the selected text and then click Delete on the shortcut menu.

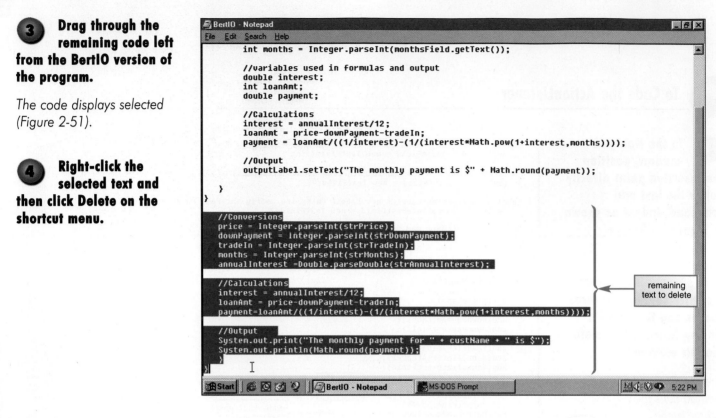

```
BertIO - Notepad
File  Edit  Search  Help
        int months = Integer.parseInt(monthsField.getText());

        //variables used in formulas and output
        double interest;
        int loanAmt;
        double payment;

        //Calculations
        interest = annualInterest/12;
        loanAmt = price-downPayment-tradeIn;
        payment = loanAmt/((1/interest)-(1/(interest*Math.pow(1+interest,months))));

        //Output
        outputLabel.setText("The monthly payment is $" + Math.round(payment));
    }
}

//Conversions
price = Integer.parseInt(strPrice);
downPayment = Integer.parseInt(strDownPayment);
tradeIn = Integer.parseInt(strTradeIn);
months = Integer.parseInt(strMonths);
annualInterest =Double.parseDouble(strAnnualInterest);

//Calculations
interest = annualInterest/12;
loanAmt = price-downPayment-tradeIn;
payment=loanAmt/((1/interest)-(1/(interest*Math.pow(1+interest,months))));

//Output
System.out.print("The monthly payment for " + custName + " is $");
System.out.println(Math.round(payment));
}
```

remaining text to delete

Start   BertIO - Notepad   MS-DOS Prompt   5:22 PM

FIGURE 2-51

The applet version of the program now is complete. You added the import statements, changed the name of the class, and constructed the applet components. You then entered code for the init() method. Finally, you included the actionPerformed event to convert the text to numbers, to calculate, and to display the answer.

Figure 2-52 shows the applet code in its entirety. Check your own code for syntax, proper spelling, capitalization, and indentations. When you are confident everything is correct, you are ready to save and compile your program.

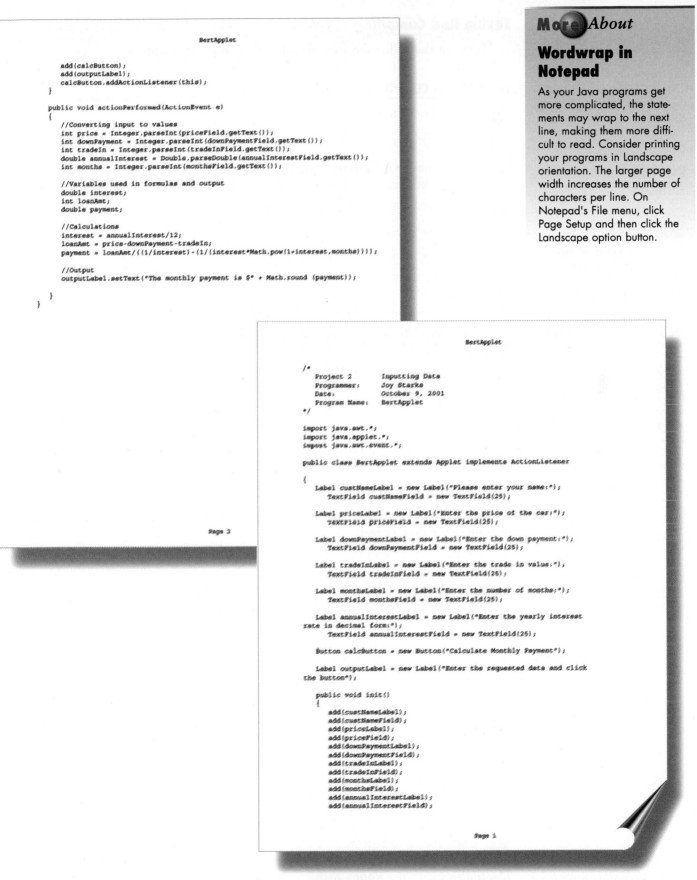

More About

Wordwrap in Notepad

As your Java programs get more complicated, the statements may wrap to the next line, making them more difficult to read. Consider printing your programs in Landscape orientation. The larger page width increases the number of characters per line. On Notepad's File menu, click Page Setup and then click the Landscape option button.

FIGURE 2-52

Saving And Compiling

Perform the following steps to save and compile the applet.

TO SAVE AND COMPILE THE APPLET

1 Click the Notepad window.

2 With a floppy disk in drive A, click File on the menu bar and then click Save As.

3 When the Save As dialog box displays, type "BertApplet.java" in the File name text box. You must type the quotation marks around the file name.

4 Click the Save in box arrow and then click 3½ Floppy (A:) in the list.

5 Click the Save button.

6 If the MS-DOS Prompt window is not on your desktop, open it, set your path, and change to drive A. Otherwise, click the MS-DOS Prompt button on the taskbar.

7 At the A: prompt in the MS-DOS Prompt window, type `javac BertApplet.java` and then press the ENTER key.

8 If you have errors, fix them in the Notepad window. Save the BertApplet.java file again, and repeat step 7.

The program compiles.

The HTML Host Document and Interactive Applets

You may remember that, in order to execute an applet in a browser or with Applet Viewer, you need a host document. This short, HTML file tells the browser, through the use of tags, the name of the applet and the size of the window. HTML hosts may contain other tags as well.

Creating the Host Document

You will use the <HTML> tag and the <APPLET> tag in the host document. Perform the following steps to create the HTML host document using Notepad.

TO CREATE THE HTML HOST DOCUMENT

1 If necessary, start Notepad. Be certain that you have saved any files that may display.

2 Click File on the menu bar and then click New.

3 In the Notepad workspace, type the code as shown in Figure 2-53.

4 Click File on the menu bar and then click Save As. When the Save As dialog box displays, if necessary, click the Look in box arrow and click 3½ Floppy (A:) in the list. In the File name text box, type "BertApplet.html" as the name of the file.

5 Click the Save button.

The file saves on the floppy disk.

More About

Editing in the MS-DOS Prompt Window

If you type doskey at the command prompt and then press the ENTER key, the operating system remembers your typed commands. You can add this command to your autoexec.bat file or type it each time you open a MS-DOS Prompt session. You then can use the arrow keys to display previously typed commands, which saves you time and eliminates the tedium of typing the commands again. The F3 key displays only the most recent command, whereas using doskey and the arrow keys keeps a record of all your previous command entries.

BertApplet - Notepad
File Edit Search Help
<HTML>
<APPLET CODE = "BertApplet.class" WIDTH = 320 HEIGHT = 400>
</APPLET>
</HTML>
HTML code

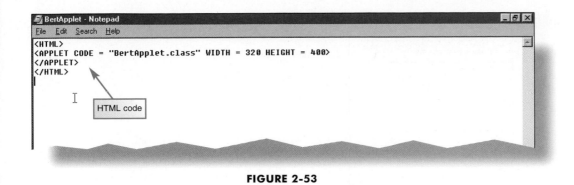

FIGURE 2-53

The applet tag nested within the HTML beginning and ending tags specifies three pieces of information that the Web page will need in order to access the Java applet: the name of the Java bytecode file, the width of the window, and the height of the window in which to run the applet.

Running an Interactive Applet Using Applet Viewer

Using the JDK Applet Viewer makes it possible to run a Java applet without using a Web browser. However, whether you use Applet Viewer or a browser, you can interact with the applet when prompted by entering data into text boxes and clicking buttons.

The following steps illustrate how to run an interactive applet using Applet Viewer from the command prompt.

Steps To Run an Interactive Applet Using Applet Viewer

1 Click the MS-DOS Prompt button on the taskbar. Type `appletviewer BertApplet.html` **and then press the ENTER key.**

The applet displays on the screen (Figure 2-54).

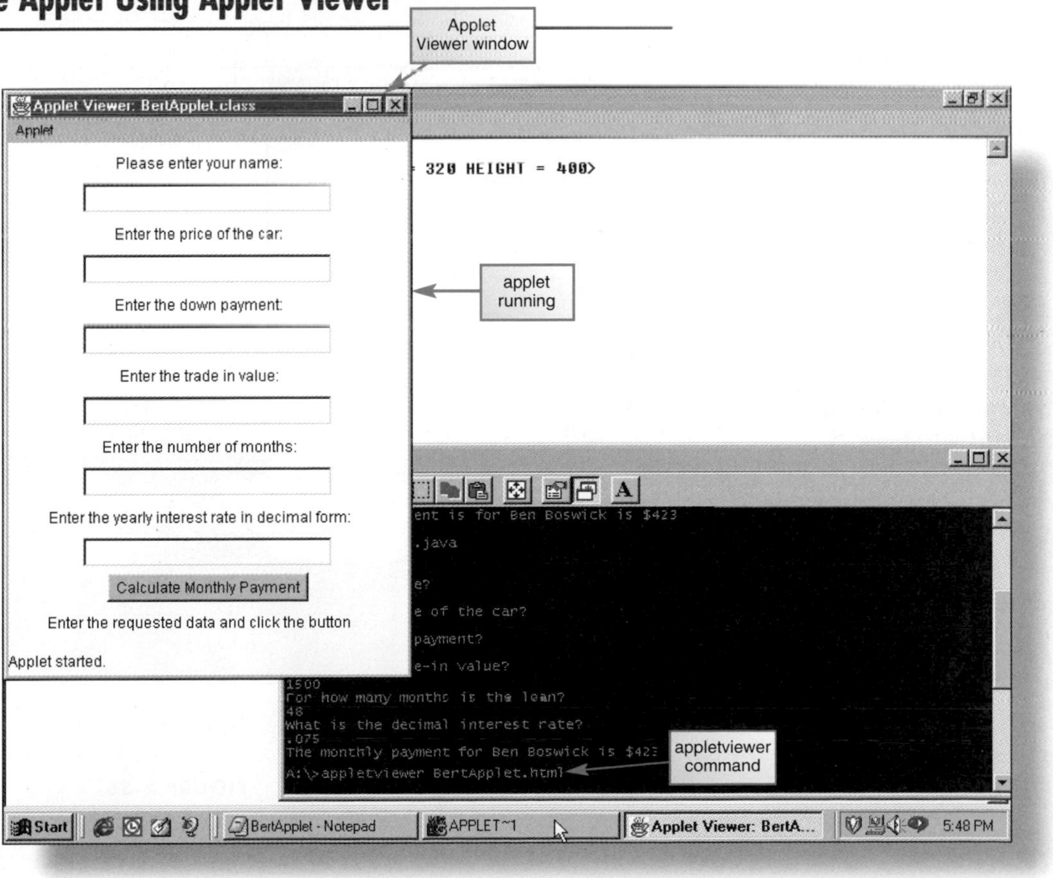

Applet Viewer window
Applet Viewer: BertApplet.class
Applet
Please enter your name:
Enter the price of the car:
Enter the down payment:
Enter the trade in value:
Enter the number of months:
Enter the yearly interest rate in decimal form:
Calculate Monthly Payment
Enter the requested data and click the button
Applet started.
320 HEIGHT = 400>
applet running
1500
For how many months is the loan?
48
What is the decimal interest rate?
.075
The monthly payment for Ben Boswick is $423
A:\>appletviewer BertApplet.html
appletviewer command
Start
BertApplet - Notepad
APPLET~1
Applet Viewer: BertA...
5:48 PM

FIGURE 2-54

2 **Click the first text box. Enter the sample information as shown in Figure 2-55. You may use the TAB key to move from field to field, or you may use your mouse to click inside each text box. When you are finished, point to the Calculate Monthly Payment button.**

Each text box displays the sample data (Figure 2-55).

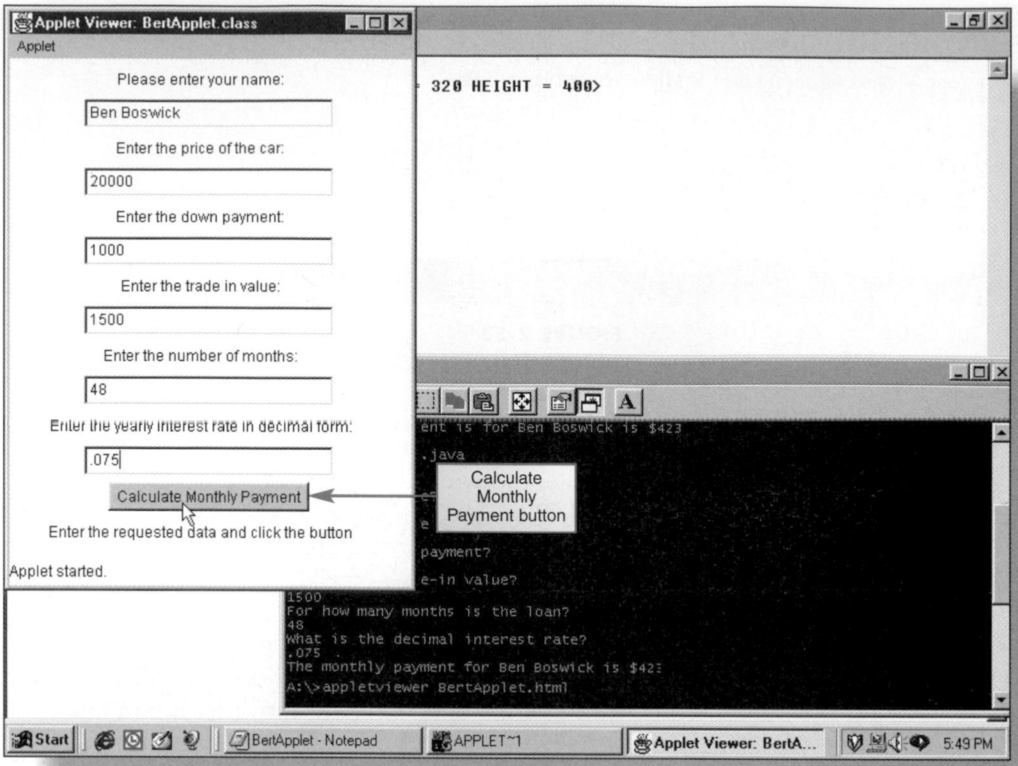

FIGURE 2-55

3 **Click the Calculate Monthly Payment button. Point to Applet Viewer's Close button.**

The monthly payment for the sample data displays (Figure 2-56).

4 **Click the Close button. Click the Close buttons on the Notepad and the MS-DOS Prompt windows.**

Applet Viewer, Notepad, and the MS-DOS window close and the Windows desktop displays.

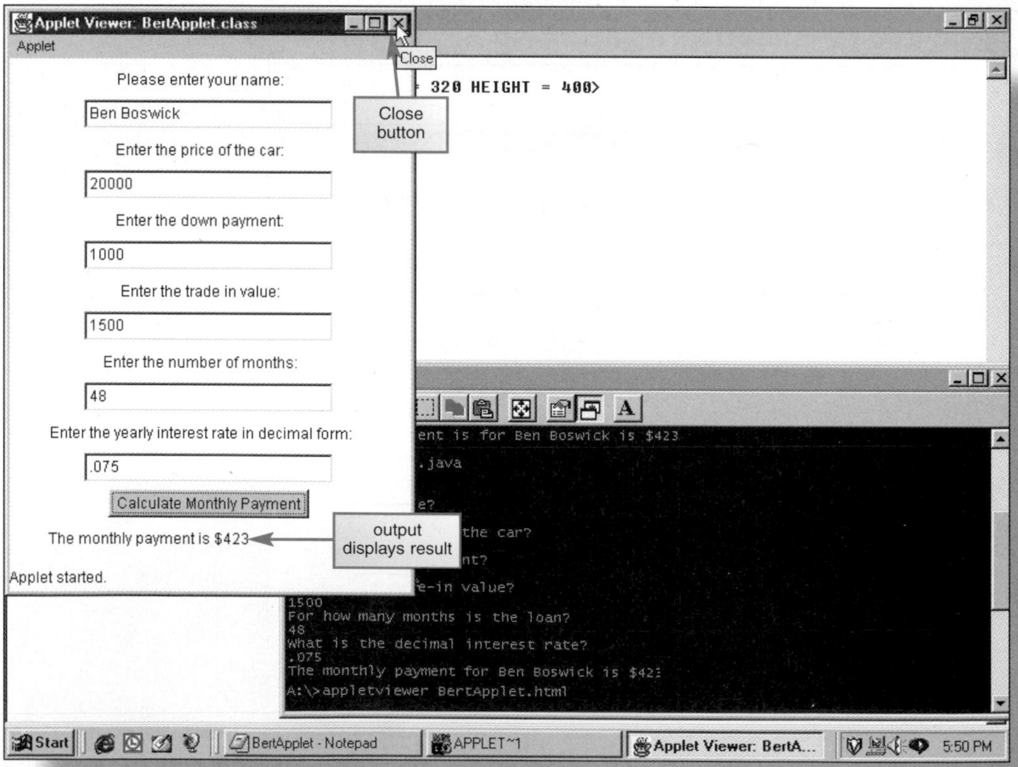

FIGURE 2-56

Each time you execute the applet with Applet Viewer, you can enter different data. In a later project, you will learn how to write a clear event that will clear the sample data for the next person, without having to close and execute the program again.

File Management

Performing the steps to code, save, compile, modify, and so on, creates several files on your storage device. File naming conventions and the operating system's capability of displaying icons associated with different file types can help you keep everything in logical order. In this project, you created a java file, which when compiled, created a class file on your floppy disk. You also modified that file twice, saving and compiling it both times. You created a HTML host file on your floppy disk, as well, for a total of seven files. Figure 2-57 displays a list of files on a floppy disk. Your icons may appear differently, based on your installation of the JDK and your default browser.

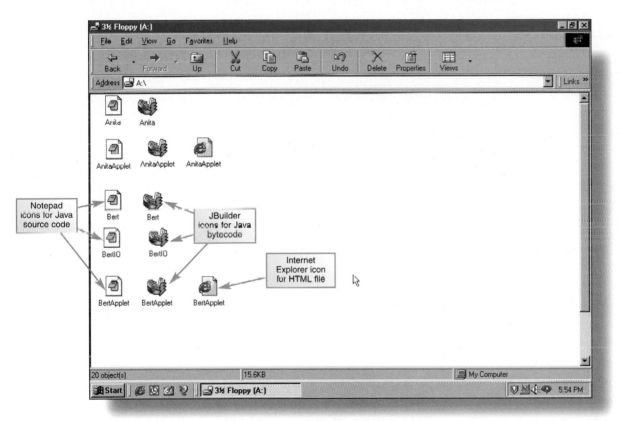

FIGURE 2-57

Project Summary

In this project, you learned how to write assignment statements in Java to store sample data with proper identifiers. You learned how to code formulas with mathematical operators. Two methods from the Math class, round and pow, were used to calculate a monthly payment. Output included variables, calculated amounts, and string data. You then modified the program to accept data from a user. The stand-alone version of the application read data from a buffer wrapped by the InputStreamReader (ISR). The readLine method made the program pause and wait for user input. You converted the application to an interactive applet. Using constructors for each of the components, you added labels, text fields, and a button. With the init method, you added the components to the applet. Finally, running the HTML host produced an applet that allowed user input and calculated when a button was clicked.

What You Should Know

Having completed this project, you should be able to perform the following tasks:

▶ Assign Sample Data *(J 2.13)*
▶ Code the ActionListener *(J 2.47)*
▶ Code the Init Method *(J 2.45)*
▶ Compile the Program *(J 2.23)*
▶ Create Applet Components *(J 2.42)*
▶ Create the HTML Host Document *(J 2.50)*
▶ Edit Code for Data Handling *(J 2.30)*
▶ Enter Beginning Code *(J 2.7)*
▶ Enter Code *(J 2.38)*
▶ Enter New Code *(J 2.27)*
▶ Enter Output Code *(J 2.20)*
▶ Enter the Formulas *(J 2.17)*
▶ Execute the Program *(J 2.24)*
▶ Maximize the Notepad Window and Declare Variables *(J 2.11)*
▶ Run an Interactive Applet Using Applet Viewer *(J 2.51)*
▶ Run the Program *(J 2.36)*
▶ Save and Compile the Applet *(J 2.50)*
▶ Save and Compile the Source Code *(J 2.35)*
▶ Save the Source Code *(J 2.23)*
▶ Set Up the Desktop *(J 2.6)*

Test Your Knowledge

1 True/False

Instructions: Circle **T** if the statement is true or **F** is the statement is false.

T F   1. The Java programming language is considered a strongly typed language.
T F   2. Java's use of primitive data types means Java is a primitive language.
T F   3. Math.pow is an operator to perform exponentiation.
T F   4. Declaring a variable involves listing the data type and the identifier.
T F   5. The following statement evaluates to true in Java: (7 == 7).
T F   6. Programmers use the term boolean to refer to a result that has only one state.
T F   7. Java's add method adds two numbers together.
T F   8. A buffer is a data area shared by hardware devices or programs, where data are held until they are needed.
T F   9. The parse method can convert integers to strings.
T F   10. Modular division truncates any remainder.

2 Multiple Choice

Instructions: Circle the correct response.

1. In Java, the process of joining two strings with a plus sign is called _____ .
   a. combination
   b. concatenation
   c. encapsulation
   d. compilation

2. Data flowing in or out of a program in Java are called _____ data.
   a. streaming
   b. sinuous
   c. buffering
   d. constructing

3. ISR stands for _____ .
   a. Internal Synchronous Reset
   b. Input Standard Return
   c. Intermediary System Reader
   d. Input Stream Reader

4. _____ is the process of creating an instance of an object with a constructor.
   a. Instantiation
   b. Buffering
   c. Wrapping
   d. Streaming

(continued)

Test Your Knowledge

Multiple Choice *(continued)*

5. If Java tries to open a non-existent file, _____ .
   a. the program needs to acknowledge the potential failure ahead of time
   b. the program throws an exception
   c. the program could abort prematurely
   d. all of the above

6. _____ listens for events in an applet.
   a. A component object
   b. The compiler
   c. ActionListener
   d. The Init method

7. All of the following are applet component objects *except* _____ .
   a. labels
   b. mice
   c. text fields
   d. buttons

8. ActionPerformed is an example of a(n) _____ .
   a. class
   b. instance
   c. object
   d. event

9. The main reason for using a consistent set of _____ is to standardize the structure and coding style of an application, so that you and others easily may read and understand the code.
   a. naming conventions
   b. instantiations
   c. methods
   d. programming applications

10. When evaluating the expression 4 + 8 / 2 * 3 – 2, which of the following is the correct answer?
    a. 16
    b. 22
    c. 6
    d. 14

Test Your Knowledge

3 Understanding the Code

Instructions: In Figure 2-58, arrows point to sections of Java code. Identify the code in the spaces provided using the appropriate word(s) from the following list.

comment	constructor	calculation	concatenation
declaration section	conversion	input from buffer	output section
	class name	package name	

```
/*
    Project 2:       Test Your Knowledge #3          1._____
    Programmer:      Joy Starks
    Date:            October 9, 2001
    Program Name:    FallingObjects
    Description:     Objects fall faster, the farther they fall. This program calculates
                     the average speed of a falling object.
*/
import java.io.*;                                    2._____

public class FallingObjects                          3._____
{
    public static void main(String[] args) throws IOException
    {
        BufferedReader dataIn = new BufferedReader(new InputStreamReader(System.in));   4._____

        double gravity = 32.174;
        double seconds;                              5._____
        String strSeconds;                           6._____
        double velocity;

        //Get Input from User
7._____ System.out.println("What is the number of seconds it takes the object to fall?");
            strSeconds = dataIn.readLine();


        seconds = Double.parseDouble(strSeconds);


        velocity  = 1.0/2.0 * gravity * Math.pow(seconds,2);    8._____

        System.out.print("Your objects travels at an average rate of ");   9._____
        System.out.print(Math.round(velocity) + " feet per second.");

    }
}
                                    10._____
```

FIGURE 2-58

Test Your Knowledge

4 Identifying Applet Components

Instructions: Figure 2-59 displays a Java applet. Identify the various parts of the applet in the spaces provided.

FIGURE 2-59

Apply Your Knowledge

1 Converting from Sample Data to User Input

Instructions: In order to start Notepad, click the Start button on the taskbar. Point to Programs and then point to Accessories on the Programs submenu. Click Notepad on the Accessories submenu. Open the file Apply2.java, from the Data Disk (see inside back cover for instructions on how to obtain a copy of the Data Disk). The program converts any number of coins into dollars and cents. Change the lines of code that assign sample data into lines of code that prompt the user and store the answers. The resulting prompts display with the calculated answer as shown in Figure 2-60.

Apply Your Knowledge

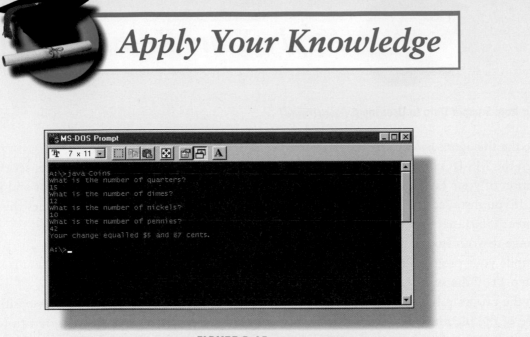

FIGURE 2-60

1. With the Apply2.java program displayed in the Notepad window, substitute your name and date in the block comment at the beginning.
2. In the class header, select the class name, Apply2. Type `Coins` as the new class name. Edit the name of the class in the documentation lines as well.
3. Save the file on your floppy disk with the name "Coins.java" as the file name.
4. Add four additional variable declarations for string inputs by typing:

```
String strQuarters;
String strDimes;
String strNickels;
String strPennies;
```

5. Delete the Assigning Values section of code. Replace it with the following:

```
System.out.println("What is the number of quarters?");
     strQuarters = dataIn.readLine();
System.out.println("What is the number of dimes?");
     strDimes = dataIn.readLine();
System.out.println("What is the number of nickels?");
     strNickels = dataIn.readLine();
System.out.println("What is the number of pennies?");
     strPennies = dataIn.readLine();
```

6. Delete the Calculations section of code. Replace the statements that multiply the number of coins by their face value, to lines of code that parse the values the user inputs by typing the following:

```
quarters = Integer.parseInt(strQuarters) * 25;
dimes = Integer.parseInt(strDimes) * 10;
nickels = Integer.parseInt(strNickels) * 5;
pennies = Integer.parseInt(strPennies) * 1;
```

(continued)

Apply Your Knowledge

Converting from Sample Data to User Input *(continued)*

7. Save the file again by clicking the Save command on the Notepad File menu.
8. Open the MS-DOS Prompt window. If you downloaded JDK from the Sun Web site, set the path to the location of your Java bin by typing `path=c:\jdk1.2.2\bin` at the command prompt and press the ENTER key. If you installed the Java compiler from the JBuilder3 CD-ROM that accompanies this text, type `path=c:\jbuilder3\java\bin` and press the ENTER key.
9. Change to your floppy disk drive by typing `a:` and then press the ENTER key.
10. Compile your program by typing `javac Coins.java` at the prompt. If the compilation is successful, proceed to step 11. Otherwise, correct the errors and return to step 7.
11. Run the program by typing `java Coins` at the prompt. Remember that Java is case-sensitive and that the name of the file must match the class name exactly. If the program runs correctly, return to Notepad and print a copy for your instructor. Otherwise, return to step 7 and correct the errors.

In the Lab

1 Income to Debt Ratio Calculator

Problem: Many financial institutions make decisions about extending credit and financing majors purchases based on a customer's income to debt ratio. This ratio is the percentage of a customer's income that is spent paying off other debts such as mortgages, automobile loans, credit cards, etc. Typically, all debts are added together and then that total is divided by the monthly income. Customers with a lower income to debt ratio are more likely to qualify for a loan.

As an intern at the Employee's Credit Union, you have been asked to create an interactive income to debt ratio calculation program that can run as a stand-alone application. Figure 2-61 displays the results from executing the program.

FIGURE 2-61

In the Lab

Instructions: Perform the following tasks.

1. To start Notepad, click the Start button. On the Start menu, point to Programs and then point to Accessories. On the Accessories submenu, click Notepad.

2. Begin your code by typing a block comment with the Lab Assignment number, your name, the current date, and the program name, DebtRatio.java.

3. Type the following lines that import the java.io package and begin blocks for the class header and main method header:

```
import java.io;
public class DebtRatio
{
    public static void main(String[] args) throws IOException
    {
```

4. Type the constructor for the buffered input:

```
BufferedReader dataIn = new BufferedReader(new InputStreamReader(System.in));
```

5. Declare the following variables to be Strings: strMonthlyIncome, strMortgage, strAutoLoan, and strOtherDebt.

6. Declare the following variables to be doubles: monthlyIncome, mortgage, autoLoan, otherDebt, and ratio.

7. Create an input section beginning with an appropriate line comment. Type the System.out.println methods to display the prompts as shown in Figure 2-61. In order to accept user input, type an indented readLine method for each string variable. The first two lines are as follows. Type them and the remaining prompts and readLine methods.

```
System.out.println("What is your monthly income?");
        strMonthlyIncome = dataIn.readLine();
```

8. Create a conversion section, beginning with an appropriate line comment, to parse each of the inputted values. For example, for the first input value, the code would be:

```
monthlyIncome = Double.parseDouble(strMonthlyIncome);
```

9. Create a calculation section, beginning with an appropriate line comment, to calculate the income to debt ratio by typing:

```
ratio = (mortgage + autoLoan + otherDebt) / monthlyIncome;
```

(continued)

In the Lab

Income to Debt Ratio Calculator (*continued*)

10. Create an output section, beginning with an appropriate line comment. Enter the code to display the answer by typing:

```
System.out.print("Your income to debt ratio is " + ratio);
```

11. Close both the main and class methods with closing braces.
12. Save the program with the file name "DebtRatio.java" on your floppy disk.
13. Open the MS-DOS Prompt window and set the path.
14. Compile your program by typing javac DebtRatio.java at the command prompt. Remember that Java is case-sensitive with respect to the name of the file.
15. If there are no compilation errors, execute the program by typing java DebtRatio at the command prompt. Enter the sample data from Figure 2-61 on the previous page. Run the program again with your own personal data.
16. In the Notepad window, use the Print command on the File menu to print a copy of the coding for your instructor.
17. Close Notepad and the MS-DOS Prompt windows by clicking the Close button on each title bar.

2 Interactive IO with Java

Problem: You would like a program to help you balance your checkbook. You decide to write a stand-alone Java application that accepts the beginning balance, the total of the checks you wrote, the total of your deposits, and the fees charged by the bank as inputs, and then display what the ending balance should be. Figure 2-62 displays the results from executing the application.

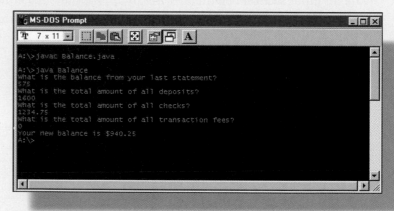

FIGURE 2-62

Instructions:

1. Open the Notepad window.
2. Begin your code by typing a block comment with the Lab Assignment number, your name, the current date, and the program name, Balance.java.
3. Type the import statement, class header, and main method header and their opening braces. Remember to use the phrase, throws IOException, as you will be using interactive statements.
4. Type a constructor for the Buffered Reader as described in this project on pages J 2.26 through J 2.29.

In the Lab

5. Declare both string and float variables for beginning balance, total deposits, total checks, and total fees. Declare a float variable for ending balance.

6. Using System.out.println methods, enter lines of code to prompt the user for each of the input variables as shown in Figure 2-62. Include a readLine method to accept each input and assign it to its corresponding declared string variable.

7. Enter code to convert each input variable to doubles or floats. For example, for the first input value, the code would be:

```
begBalance = Float.parseFloat(strBegBalance);
```

8. Write a formula that takes the beginning balance plus the total deposits, minus the checks and fees, and assigns the value to the ending balance.

9. Write an output section that displays an appropriate message and the ending balance on the screen.

10. Label each section with an appropriate line comment.

11. Save the program with the filename "Balance.java" on your floppy disk.

12. Open an MS-DOS Prompt window and set the path.

13. Compile your program by typing javac Balance.java at the command prompt. Remember that Java is case-sensitive with respect to the name of the file.

14. If there are no compilation errors, execute the program by typing java Balance at the command prompt. Enter the sample data from Figure 2-62. Run the program again with your own personal data.

15. In the Notepad window, use the Print command on the File menu to print a copy of the code for your instructor.

16. Close both the Notepad window and the MS-DOS Prompt windows by clicking the Close button on each title bar.

3 Creating an Applet

Problem: As webmaster for a chain of appliance stores, you have been asked to create an applet that will display as part of the store's e-commerce site. The applet will calculate the annual cost of running an appliance. Using text boxes, the applet will ask the user for the cost per kilowatt-hour in cents, and the number of kilowatt-hours the appliance uses in a year. Figure 2-63 displays the results from executing the applet.

Applet Viewer: KilowattApplet.class

Applet

Please enter the cost per kilowatt-hour in cents:

.0842

Please enter the number of kilowatt-hours this appliance is run:

653

Calculate Annual Appliance Cost

The cost of running this appliance is $55

Applet started.

FIGURE 2-63

(continued)

In the Lab

Instructions:

1. Open the Notepad window, and begin your code by typing a block comment with the Lab Assignment number, your name, the current date, and the program name, KilowattApplet.java.

2. Type lines of code to import the following packages:

```
import java.awt.*;
import java.applet.*:
import java.awt.event.*;
```

3. Type the following class header and opening brace:

```
public class KilowattApplet extends Applet implements ActionListener
{
```

4. Type the following Label constructor and a TextField constructor where costKwhr is the cost per kilowatt-hour:

```
Label costKwhrLabel = new Label("Please enter the cost per kilowatt-hour in cents:");
TextField costKwhrField = new TextField(25);
```

5. Type a similar Label and TextField constructor for the number of kilowatt-hours the appliance uses in a year.

6. Construct a button for the user to click by typing:

```
Button calcButton = new Button("Calculate Annual Appliance Cost");
```

7. Type a Label constructor to display the average.

8. Create an init method to add all of the above controls to the applet interface. The first few lines are as follows:

```
public void init()
{
    add(costKwhrLabel);
    add(costKwhrField);
```

9. Type the following command to add the ActionListener to the calcButton and close the init method with a brace:

```
    calcButton.addActionListener(this);
}
```

In the Lab

10. Create an actionPerformed event to convert the input and perform the calculations. The event header and first conversion are done for you. Enter the following lines and a line to accept the kilowatt-hours that the appliance uses in a year.

```
public void actionPerformed(ActionEvent e)
{
   //Converting input to values
   double costKwhr = Double.parseDouble(costKwhrField.getText());
```

11. Type a similar line to convert the annual kilowatt-hours.
12. Declare a float variable to hold the average, by typing the following:

```
//Variables used in formulas and output
double average;
```

13. Write a line of code to perform the calculation, which multiplies the cents by the kilowatt-hours in a year, and assigns it to the variable, average.
14. Round off the displayed result using the Math.round method and assign it to the output Label.
15. Close the init block with a closing brace and then close the applet with a closing brace.
16. Save the program with the file name "KilowattApplet.java" on your floppy disk.
17. Open the MS-DOS Prompt window. Set the path, if necessary. Compile the program by typing javac KilowattApplet.java at the command prompt. If there are compilation errors, fix them and recompile.
18. Print a copy of the coding for your instructor.
19. In the Notepad window, click New on the File menu and type the following code for the HTML file:

```
<HTML>
<APPLET CODE = "KilowattApplet.class" WIDTH = 400 HEIGHT = 200>
</APPLET>
</HTML>
```

20. Save the HTML code with the file name "KilowattApplet.html" on your floppy disk.
21. Execute the program from the MS-DOS Prompt window by typing appletviewer KilowattApplet.html at the command prompt. Enter the sample data from Figure 2-63 on page J 2.63. Run the program again with your own personal data.
22. Close both the Notepad window and the MS-DOS Prompt window by clicking the Close button on each title bar.

Cases and Places

The difficulty of these case studies varies:
▶ are the least difficult; ▶▶ are more difficult; and ▶▶▶ are the most difficult.

1 ▶ Bill's Burgers would like an applet that calculates the sales tax for their front counter help. The applet should let the worker enter the total amount of the customer's order and then calculate a 7 percent sales tax. When the worker clicks a calculate button, the applet should display the amount of the customer's order, the tax, and the total of the customer's order and tax added together.

2 ▶ Ohm's Law relates the resistance of an electrical device, such as a portable heater, to the electric current flowing through the device and the voltage applied to it. The law is: I = V/R. V is the voltage, measured in volts. R is the resistance, measured in ohms. The answer, I, is the electrical current, measured in amps. Write an applet with two label prompts and text fields. One label will ask the user to input the voltage; the other label will ask the user to input the resistance of a device. The applet then will display the current. Remember that because V and R will be entered as integers; your ActionListener event will have to parse the numbers into double values in order to perform the division.

3 ▶▶ Your younger brother is studying beginning geometry. He has to calculate the area of several different circles and would like to automate the process. Write a stand-alone application for him that calculates the area of a circle from the radius. The radius will be an integer read in from the keyboard. Create a method that will accept the integer and perform the calculation using the formula *pi* r^2; that is, the value of *pi* times the radius, squared. Use the PI method from the Math class for the value of *pi*.

4 ▶▶ Write a program that will display the number of dollars and cents based on user numeric input. For instance, if the user inputs 543, the program will print out 5 dollars and 43 cents. For this program you will use integer arithmetic and will need to avoid floating point arithmetic. Review the integer remainder modular operator % discussed in the project.

5 ▶▶▶ Because you are an outstanding student, a local civic organization has awarded you a generous sum of money to pursue your education in England. You also plan to do some sightseeing while you are in Europe. The award money is in U.S. dollars and you want to know how that will convert to British pounds, French francs, Italian lire, German Deutsche marks, and Spanish pesetas. Use the concepts and techniques presented in this project to create an application that will accept the U.S. dollar amount, convert the U.S. dollar amount, and display the English, French, Italian, German and Spanish equivalents. Use the Web, a newspaper, or a local financial institution to obtain the conversion rates.

6 ▶▶▶ Use the Sun Microsystems Java documentation Web site at http://java.sun.com/docs/searchabledocs.html to find documentation on Java packages. In particular, search the site for methods in the Math class. Make a list of 10 methods and describe their arguments and what they return.

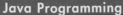

Java Programming

Java Programming

PROJECT 3

Decision, Repetition, and Components in Java

OBJECTIVES

You will have mastered the material in this project when you can:

- Design a program using components
- Test each component individually
- Differentiate between compile-time and run-time errors
- Define an exception
- Code a try and catch construct
- Use the throw statement to construct an exception
- Write a decision structure using the if statement
- Describe the use of AND, OR, and NOT
- Decide when to check data for reasonableness
- Create a user-defined method
- Send arguments and receive return values from a method
- Write a switch structure to test for multiple values in data
- Code a repetition structure using the while statement
- Describe the java.awt, java.applet, and java.awt.event packages
- Add a component with addItemListener in an applet
- Construct a check box group
- Differentiate between applications of a check box and a check box group
- Code an itemStateChanged event

A Virtual Green Thumb

Find Your Roots With Garden.com

Whether your rhododendrons are the envy of your neighborhood or your crabgrass is making you cranky, you can get back to your roots by digging in the virtual garden at Garden.com. This all-encompassing Web site runs the gamut from an online garden doctor with 24/7 office hours to a chat room filled with green thumb aficionados.

Plan to share the soil with many other nature-loving surfers. Gardening is the foremost recreational pastime for adults, says the Lawn and Garden Marketing and Distribution Association. Sixty-seven million Americans in two-thirds of American households call themselves gardeners, according to the National Gardening Association. They spend, on average, 10 hours per week planting, watering, fertilizing, and pulling weeds.

Garden.com offers more than 20,000 plants and products, Garden Escape Magazine, and weekend project plans. The Plant Finder feature selects plants based on user-specified conditions, such as sun exposure, soil pH and composition, moisture, color and foliage colors, and degree of maintenance. Another useful feature is the LandscapePlanner, a Java applet stored on the Garden.com server that lets users design their dream gardens. Gardeners begin either by creating their own custom palette from scratch or by choosing a professionally created template, such as a butterfly garden. The custom palette users start their plans by specifying the garden's dimensions on the design canvas, which has gridlines representing a one-foot scale. They then add plants and other accessories, such as furniture, statues, and arbors, by selecting the objects and dragging them to the desired locations on the grid.

The professional templates include a verbal description of the selected plants and the recommended soil and climate conditions, a photo or drawing showing how the finished garden might look at maturity, and links to relevant magazine articles providing additional insight. For example, the butterfly garden template has links to stories on monarch butterflies and on caterpillar cuisine.

Virtual gardeners then can view a list of the plants contained on their templates and make substitutions, additions, and deletions. Once they have finalized their plans, they add the plants to their virtual Wheelbarrow, which is Garden.com's version of a shopping cart. When ready to place an order, they view the Wheelbarrow, enter their name and mailing address, select the form of payment and choose the delivery method. Growers across the country then ship the plants directly to the user in as few as three days.

Placing an online order also is a factor of the Java applet you will create in the project for Candle Line, which sells designer candles and gifts. Your Java modules will accept customer input, test these values, and then calculate shipping charges. Based on the delivery times ranging from 1 to 7 days, you will use decision steps to compute the correct shipping fee and add it to a customer's order.

A delivery from Garden.com can make virtual gardeners' lives blossom as they really dig the results!

Java Programming

Decision, Repetition, and Components in Java

CASE PERSPECTIVE

CandleLine.com sells designer candles and personal gifts, catering to customers who want to send gifts for special occasions. CandleLine's e-commerce site is an interactive Web page. As customers choose the candles and gifts they wish to purchase, the items are added to an electronic shopping cart. Approximately 300 people per day are accessing CandleLine's Web site, but many have complained that the shipping charges are a hidden cost. In order to improve customer relations, the company would like to give its customers a choice in shipping methods and a way to calculate their shipping costs before finalizing their order.

You have been asked to create a sample Java program that calculates the shipping cost for customer purchases. Eventually the program will read the total price of purchases as data from the Web page, but for now you will enter the total price as an input value and then have the program calculate shipping charges.

After finalizing the solution, CandleLine wants you to convert the application to an applet that the webmaster eventually can link with the customer shopping cart, implemented from the Web page.

Introduction

The previous Java programming examples in this book have executed sequentially, from top to bottom without skipping any code or branching to another class, and without making any decisions. Realistically, programs need to interpret data and assess user input, which usually affects the direction the program should take. As discussed in the Introduction Project, a control structure is a standard progression of logical steps to control the sequence of statement execution. The logic controls the order in which the program instructions are executed.

A **sequence** of steps is performed one after another, whereas a **decision**, such as whether or not a user has entered data, is based on a condition. The evaluated condition causes the computer to execute one set of coding instructions as opposed to another. Multiple choices, sometimes presented in the form of menus, assist users in making correct decisions — decisions that then determine the coding path the program will take. Many times, programs must repeat a set of instructions for multiple instances of data or multiple users. A **loop** repeats a section of code while a condition is true or until a condition is met. The **case structure** executes one of several statement blocks depending on the value of an expression. In Java, programmers typically use the case structure when a menu is the best choice for user input.

In Project 2, you learned how to accept user input from the keyboard and manipulate it using Java's arithmetic operators and methods from the Math class. The program worked only if the user entered the data in an acceptable format. No validation of the data occurred. The data was not tested for reasonableness, data type errors, validity within a range, or for consistency errors. An important use of decision structures, in well-written programs, is to verify the correctness of the input data before using it in processing. Programs that terminate abruptly because of invalid input are poorly designed and extremely annoying to users. Allowing the user to try again to enter correct data involves transferring execution back to the beginning of that processing section. Therefore, programmers use a loop to repeat a section of code until valid, correct data has been entered. Java provides data validation techniques using both traditional and object-oriented design and control structures.

Breaking these tasks into small sections of code that can be reused for each data entry is known as **modularization.** In traditional languages, dividing a large problem into simpler sections, called **modules,** makes a program easier to understand and maintain. Most object-oriented languages like Java use the term **component,** which commonly means any of the object-oriented structures such as objects, classes, methods, and events. Eliminating duplicate code, improving understandability, and facilitating reusability are all reasons to write Java code using components.

More About

Object-Oriented Components

For more information on components and how they are used in object-oriented programming, visit the Java Programming Web page (www.scsite.com/java/more.htm) and then click Components.

Project Three — CandleLine Shipping Charges

ANALYZING THE PROBLEM A computer program is required that will accept the cost of a customer order; then, based on a shipping menu choice, the program will calculate a total charge. The values entered by the user must be valid numbers. Customers may choose the shipping options of priority, express, and standard delivery. Priority shipping is $14.95. Express delivery is $11.95. If the value of the order is more than $75.00, then standard shipping is free; otherwise, it is $5.95. Output will include the value of the order, the shipping charge, and the total of the two charges. Figure 3-1(a) displays the program as an application with sample user input. Figure 3-1(b) displays the program as an applet.

(a) Java Application

(b) Java Applet

FIGURE 3-1

DESIGNING THE PROGRAM Because this program will make decisions based on user input, appropriate prompts and messages need to be coded. The program should accept and test a numeric value from the user, display a menu and test for a valid choice, and then calculate and display results. Toward this end, the program will be designed in stages. Programmers commonly create a small portion of code and then thoroughly test it before moving on to the next section. The object-oriented nature of Java lends itself to this kind of design by component, creating reusable portions of code and breaking the programming task down into simpler, more manageable steps. Because this program involves making decisions based on user input, each decision can be designed and tested individually as it is added to the program.

Figure 3-2(a) through Figure 3-2(c) display a flowchart of the logic to input, store, and test the data. Notice that Figure 3-2(a) uses the predefined process symbols to reference Figures 3-2(b) and 3-2(c).

CODING THE PROGRAM You will create Java source code using the syntax and commands of the Java programming language. After creating a Java method to modularize the task of obtaining a shipping cost, you will use Java's ability to catch data type errors as they occur and create a module to display an appropriate error message. Entering a case structure will allow the use of a menu to direct user input. This project presents a series of step-by-step instructions to write the code, explaining its parts.

TESTING THE PROGRAM In this project, you will test the code in each component as you write it. You will compile and run the program at various stages with and without data. Evaluation of the program will take place by deliberately entering incorrect data to test for error checking. Finally, you will test the applet version of the program using Applet Viewer.

FORMALIZING THE SOLUTION You will review the source code, use proper documentation, edit, recompile, and execute the application.

MAINTAINING THE PROGRAM You will modify the program to run as an applet creating options for the three different shipping methods. The applet will calculate in a similar manner to the application.

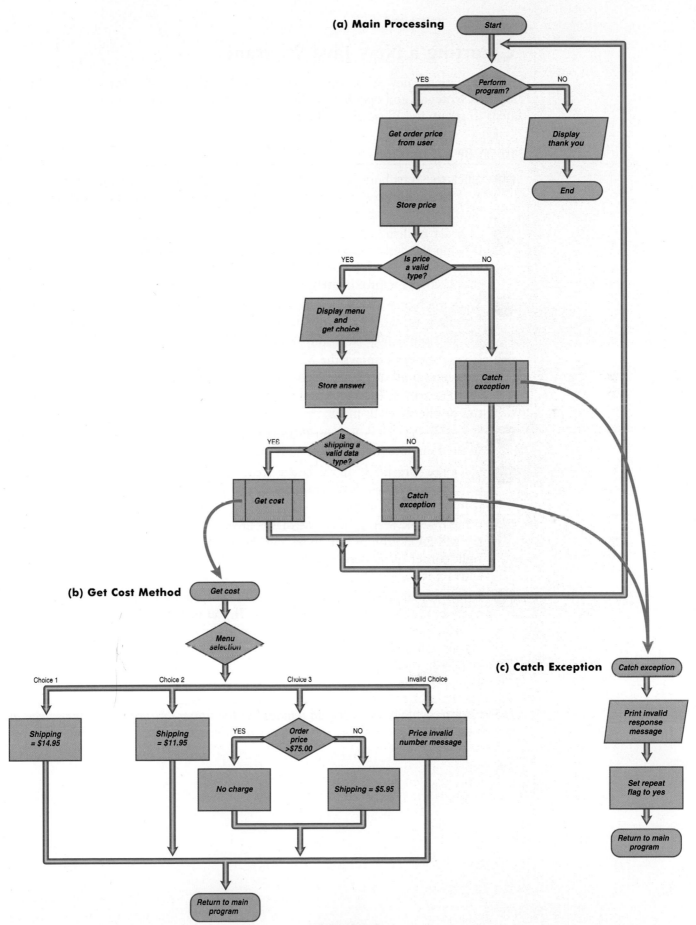

FIGURE 3-2

Starting a New Java Program

Before starting a new Java program, you should set up the Windows desktop by starting Notepad and opening the MS-DOS Prompt window. Perform the following steps to set up the Windows desktop.

TO SET UP THE DESKTOP

1. Click the Start button on the taskbar, point to Programs on the Start menu, and then point to Accessories on the Programs submenu. Click Notepad on the Accessories submenu.

2. In order to display both the Notepad window and the MS-DOS Prompt window on the desktop, drag the title bar of the Notepad window to the upper-left corner of the desktop. Drag the lower-right corner of the Notepad window so that it covers approximately one-third of the desktop.

3. With the Notepad window still open, click the Start button again. Point to Programs on the Start menu and then click MS-DOS Prompt (Windows 95 or 98) or Command Prompt (Windows NT).

4. If your system displays the MS-DOS Prompt window as a black, full screen, press and hold the ALT key while pressing the TAB key to minimize the window.

5. On the taskbar, right-click the MS-DOS Prompt button and then click Properties on the shortcut menu.

6. When the MS-DOS Prompt Properties dialog box displays, click the Font tab. In the Font size box, scroll to and then click the 7 x 11 or a similar font size.

7. Click the Screen tab. In the Usage area, click the Window option button to select it. In the Window area, make certain that the Display toolbar check box contains a check mark.

8. Click the OK button. If the MS-DOS Prompt window does not display, click the MS-DOS Prompt button so that the window displays. Drag it to the lower-right corner of the screen. If necessary, click in the MS-DOS Prompt window to activate it.

9. If you downloaded Java from the Sun Microsystems Web site, type path=c:\jdk1.2.2\bin at the prompt. If you installed the Java compiler from the JBuilder 3 CD-ROM that may accompany this text, type path=c:\jbuilder3\java\bin and then press the ENTER key.

10. With a floppy disk inserted in drive A, change to drive A by typing a: and then press the ENTER key.

The desktop displays the Notepad window in the upper-left portion of the screen and the MS-DOS Prompt window in the lower-right portion of the screen (Figure 3-3).

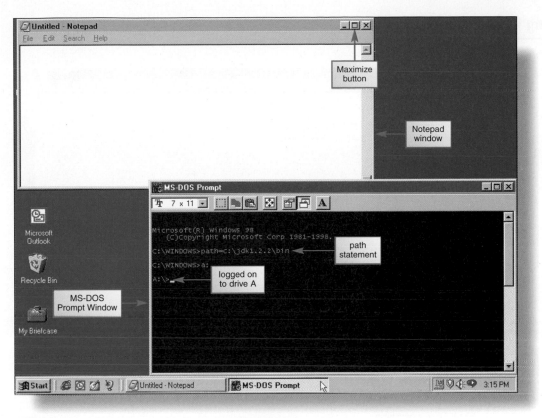

FIGURE 3-3

User Input

Several beginning statements and commands are common to all programs that require user input. These include import statements, comments, the class header, and the method header. Recall from Project 2 that programs requiring user input must import the java.io package. Normally, you should import the entire package by using the wildcard (*) if you plan to use more than one or two classes from that package. General comments and import statements usually precede the class header. In Project 2 you also learned that if there is a possibility that data might be entered incorrectly, you should warn the Java compiler by adding the statement, throws IOException, to the main method header. This statement acknowledges potential failures and allows the program to compile correctly.

Beginning Code

In the following steps you will create an application for the CandleLine company to calculate shipping charges. You will enter general comments about the program, import the java.io package, create the class named Candle, and enter the main method header. Even though this program has no code inside the braces, Java will compile and execute the program successfully. Programs designed as a kind of template in order to enter code at a later time are called **stubs**.

Steps **To Enter the Beginning Code**

1 Maximize the Notepad window by clicking the Maximize button on its title bar. Enter the block comment as shown in Figure 3-4, replacing the programmer name and date shown with your name and the current date.

The block comment for the program displays (Figure 3-4).

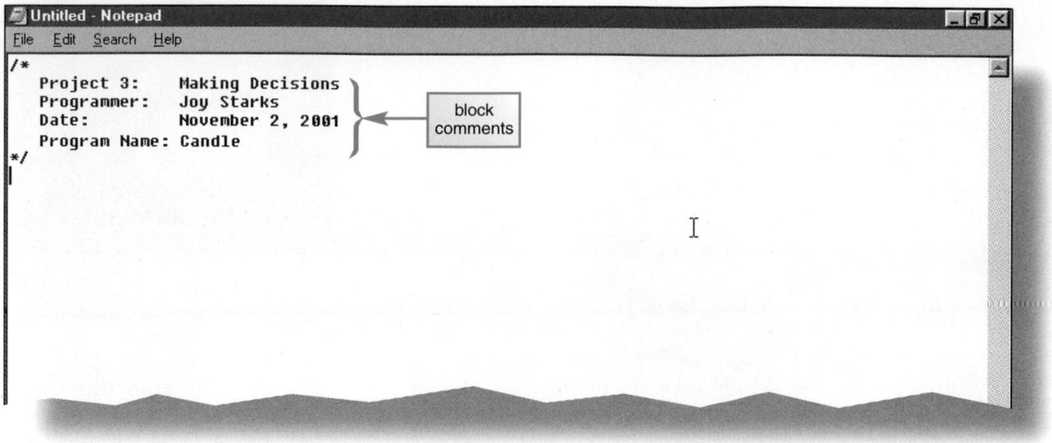

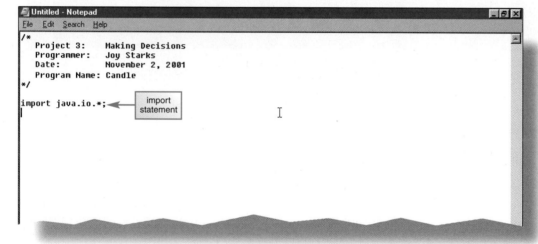

FIGURE 3-4

2 Enter the import statement as shown in Figure 3-5.

The java.io package will be imported to handle input and output methods (Figure 3-5).

FIGURE 3-5

3 Create the program stub by entering the class header and main method headers along with their opening and closing braces, as shown in Figure 3-6. Use proper indentation.

The name of the class will be Candle (Figure 3-6). The main method warns the compiler of a possible IOException.

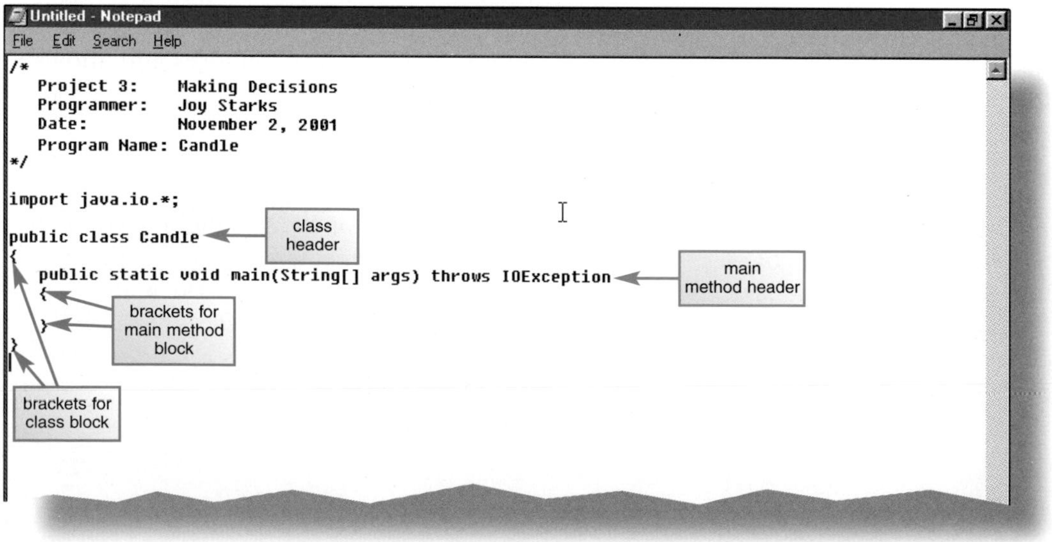

FIGURE 3-6

Remember that the name of the class must match exactly the name of the Java source code file that you save. You will save the source code with the name "Candle.java" on a floppy disk in the next series of steps.

Component Modularity

The object-oriented nature of Java lends itself to component modularity. **Modularity** means breaking a large program's source code down into smaller sections. Java source code needs only one public class header and one main method in order to compile. After that, it does not matter how many sections of code or components you add. **Components** might include classes, methods, blocks of code, or even calls to classes that are external of the program.

Designing component modularity from the beginning creates reusable portions of code, and breaks the programming task down into simpler, more manageable steps. Because this program involves making decisions based on user input, each decision can be designed and tested individually as it is added to the program, catching errors along the way.

Saving, Compiling, and Executing the Program Stub

Perform the following steps to save, compile, and execute the program stub.

TO SAVE, COMPILE, AND EXECUTE THE SOURCE CODE

1 With a floppy disk in drive A, click File on the Notepad menu bar, and then click Save As.

2 When the Save As dialog box displays, type "Candle.java" in the File name text box. You must type the quotation marks around the file name.

3 Click the Save in box arrow and then click 3½ Floppy (A:) in the list.

4 Click the Save button.

5 Click the MS-DOS Prompt button on the taskbar. If necessary, enter the path statement and log onto drive A. Type javac Candle.java and then press the ENTER key to compile the program.

6 If your program contains errors, fix them in the Notepad window and then recompile the program in the MS-DOS Prompt window.

7 When your program compiles successfully, execute it by typing java Candle at the command prompt and then press the ENTER key.

The program compiles but produces no visible output (Figure 3-7 on the next page). The program stub has no active statements or commands.

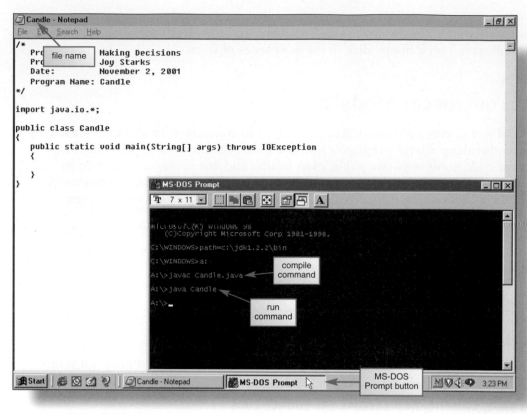

FIGURE 3-7

Exception Handling

Checking for an IOException during compilation is only the first step in handling potential errors. An IOException is an example of a **compile-time** exception — an event that occurs when you try to compile a program. An **exception** is a Java event that generates a new, logical object resulting from an unusual or erroneous situation. The **object** exception contains information about the exception, such as its location and type. **Run-time** exceptions and errors happen when the program is running and Java encounters a problem. When an exception occurs, the JVM run-time environment **throws** the object exception to the processor who looks for a **handler**, or a way to handle the problem. And, unless the programmer codes a way to **catch** the exception, the program will terminate prematurely and display an exception error message. For example, if Java expects an integer input, and the user types a decimal point, a number format exception displays and the program terminates. A **number format exception** indicates an operation was attempted using a number in an illegal format. The number format exception is only one of more than 100 different kinds of exceptions that Java throws. Appendix D lists some sample input and output exceptions.

Java also can throw an **error**, such as an out of memory error, which is a more serious problem representing an unrecoverable situation. Errors sometimes are called **unchecked exceptions** because programmers should not attempt to fix these kinds of system problems.

Exception handling is the general concept of planning for possible exceptions from the beginning by directing the program to deal with them gracefully, without aborting prematurely. Java provides several ways — both object-oriented and traditional — to write code that checks for exceptions.

Try and Catch

One object-oriented way to handle user input errors is to include the lines of code that might cause exceptions inside a **try and catch construct**. The **try statement** identifies a block of statements that potentially may throw an exception. If an exception occurs, the try block transfers execution to a handler. Table 3-1 shows the general form of the **try block**.

Table 3-1	The try Block
| **General form:** | ```
try
{
    . . . lines of code that might generate an exception;
    . . .throw new exception;
}
``` |
| **Comment:** | **Try** and **throw new** are reserved words. All statements within the try block braces are monitored for exceptions. Programmers may **explicitly**, or intentionally, cause an exception by typing the words, throw new, followed by the name of a standard Java exception object. A try block must be followed by a catch block. |
| **Examples:** | ```
try
{
    answer = 23 / 0; //Java throws exception automatically
    throw new DivideByZeroException(); //programmer explicitly throws exception
}
``` |

The try block notifies the JVM that you plan to deal with exceptions rather than just allowing them to happen. Any exception occurring as a result of code within the try block will not terminate the program.

The try block must be followed by a **catch block**. This is the destination of the thrown exception; in other words, execution will be transferred to the catch block when an exception occurs. The **catch statement** consists of the keyword catch, followed by a parameter declaration that identifies the type of exception being caught and an identifier name. The identifier name holds a Java-assigned error value that can access more information about the error through the use of messages. Inside the catch block, programmers include statements to either describe the error to the user or fix the error through programming. Table 3-2 shows the general form of the catch block.

Table 3-2	The catch Block
| **General form:** | ```
catch (exception identifier)
{
    . . . lines of code that handle the exception;
}
``` |
| **Comment:** | **Catch** is a reserved word. **Exception** is the name of a standard Java exception. **Identifier** is a variable name to hold a Java-assigned error value. Catch blocks optionally may be followed by a finally block to continue more processing. |
| **Examples:** | ```
catch(ArithmeticException errNum)
{
    System.out.println("An arithmetic error has occurred. " +
    errNum.getMessage());// message prints with Java-generated data
}
``` |

For example, if a user error causes a program to try to divide by zero, the program normally would abort with the following error message.

```
Exception in thread "main" java.lang.ArthmeticException: / by zero
```

However, if the code is put in a try block and the same error occurs, execution is thrown to the catch block. The programmer then can display a more descriptive message to the user, and perhaps let the user re-enter the information.

Java may generate the exception, as in the division by zero example above, or you may use the keywords, **throw new**, to explicitly or intentionally throw the exception yourself. For instance, Java would throw an ArithmeticException if you tried to calculate an average with no numbers. You might decide to throw the exception if the value were zero, as well. A decision structure could test for the zero value with a resulting throw to the same exception.

```
throw new ArithmeticException();
```

Alternately, you might want to create a new exception type. For example, when a user enters the wrong password you might enter the following line of code.

```
throw new WrongPasswordException();
```

The program then would call the class, WrongPasswordException. That new class must be defined by the programmer and be accessible to the class that contains the throw statement.

The throw statement causes execution to be transferred to the catch block. That way, control passes to the same error handling routine whether the exception is caught by the JVM, as in a data type error, or caught by a programmer testing for an invalid or unreasonable number.

As with the traditional control structures, the try and catch, object-oriented structure can be nested within any other structure. In addition, you can have more than one catch block in the same program or even within the same method, if you are trying to throw multiple exceptions. The try and catch blocks may be followed by an optional block, named with the reserved word, **finally**, which is placed after the catch block. The finally block can be used to perform an end of processing routine associated with the try and catch.

Table 3-3 displays the variable declaration and the try block for the Candle application. Table 3-4 displays the catch block. The catch block will execute only if a number format exception occurs when the program tries to parse the user input (lines 26 and 34).

Table 3-3

LINE	CODE
14	//Declaring Variables
15	BufferedReader dataIn = new BufferedReader(new InputStreamReader(System.in));
16	String strPrice;
17	String strDays;
18	double price
19	int days;
20	
21	try
22	{
23	//Get input from user
24	System.out.println("What is the total dollar amount of your order?");
25	strPrice = dataIn.readLine();
26	price = Double.parseDouble(strPrice);
27	
28	System.out.println("What is your shipping priority?");
29	System.out.println();
30	System.out.println("\t1) Priority (Overnight)");
31	System.out.println("\t2) Express (2 business days)");
32	System.out.println("\t3) Standard (3 to 7 business days)");
33	strDays = dataIn.readLine();
34	days = Integer.parseInt(strDays);
35	}
36	

Table 3-4

LINE	CODE
37	catch (NumberFormatException e)
38	{
39	System.out.println("\tYour response was not a valid number.");
40	System.out.println("\tPlease reenter your order using a numeric value.");
41	System.out.println();
42	}

In the following steps, you will enter the try and catch blocks. In the try block, you will instantiate the constructor method named BufferedReader (line 15) for the input stream from the keyboard buffer, just as you did in Project 2. You then will declare the variables for data input (lines 16 through 19). Finally, you will code lines to print prompts on the screen and accept user input (lines 24 through 34). In the catch block, you will display an appropriate message to the user if a number format exception occurs (lines 39 and 40). After all code has been entered, you will save the program. Perform the following steps to enter the try and catch blocks and then save the program.

To Enter the try and catch Blocks

1 Click the Notepad window between the two braces of the main block on line 14.

The insertion point displays on the blank line (Figure 3-8).

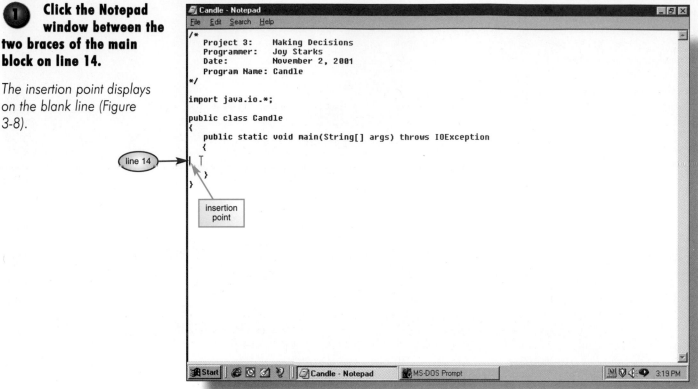

FIGURE 3-8

2 Using proper indentation, enter the code for the declaration section and the try block as shown in Table 3-3 on the previous page.

After the variable declarations, the try block contains the user interface statements for this program (Figure 3-9). As you type, the workspace will scroll.

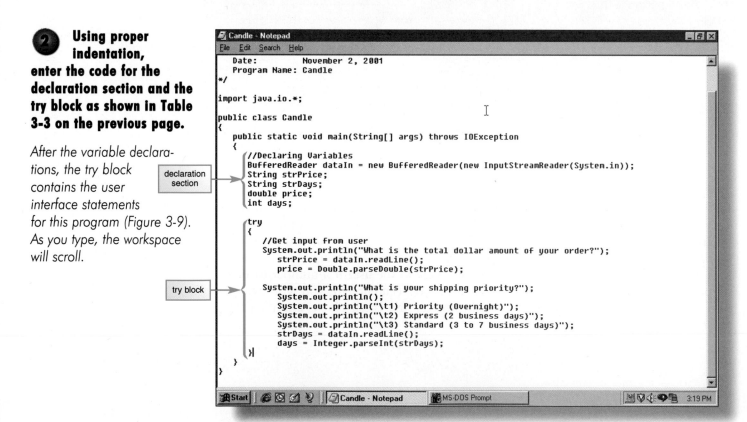

FIGURE 3-9

3 Press the ENTER key. Using proper indentation, enter the code for the catch block as shown in Table 3-4 on page J 3.15.

When an exception occurs, the println methods will print a user-friendly message (Figure 3-10).

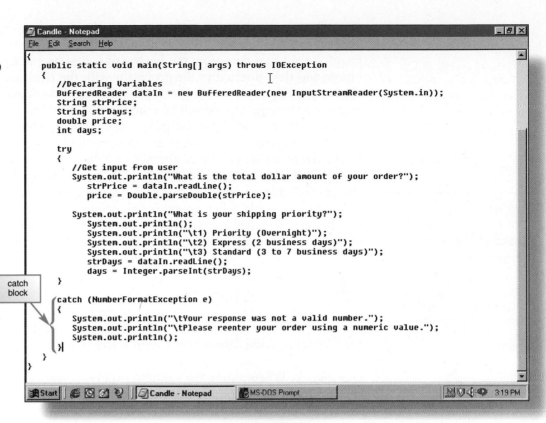

```
public static void main(String[] args) throws IOException
{
    //Declaring Variables
    BufferedReader dataIn = new BufferedReader(new InputStreamReader(System.in));
    String strPrice;
    String strDays;
    double price;
    int days;

    try
    {
        //Get input from user
        System.out.println("What is the total dollar amount of your order?");
            strPrice = dataIn.readLine();
            price = Double.parseDouble(strPrice);

        System.out.println("What is your shipping priority?");
            System.out.println();
            System.out.println("\t1) Priority (Overnight)");
            System.out.println("\t2) Express (2 business days)");
            System.out.println("\t3) Standard (3 to 7 business days)");
            strDays = dataIn.readLine();
            days = Integer.parseInt(strDays);
    }

    catch (NumberFormatException e)
    {
        System.out.println("\tYour response was not a valid number.");
        System.out.println("\tPlease reenter your order using a numeric value.");
        System.out.println();
    }
}
```

catch block

FIGURE 3-10

4 Click File on the Notepad menu bar and then point to Save.

The File menu displays (Figure 3-11). Because this program has been saved previously with the name Candle, clicking the Save command will save it with the same name, in the same location.

5 Click Save.

The program is saved on drive A with the same file name.

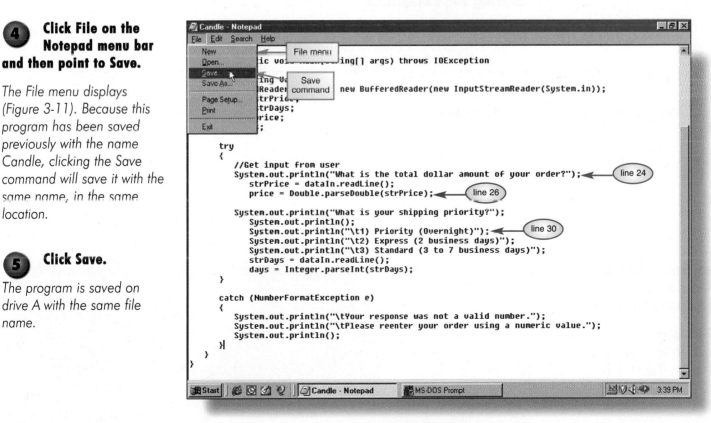

```
                            ic vo...........ing[] args) throws IOException
                            ing V..
    Reade...              new BufferedReader(new InputStreamReader(System.in));
    trPri..;
    trDays;
    rice;
    ;

    try
    {
        //Get input from user
        System.out.println("What is the total dollar amount of your order?");     line 24
            strPrice = dataIn.readLine();
            price = Double.parseDouble(strPrice);     line 26

        System.out.println("What is your shipping priority?");
            System.out.println();
            System.out.println("\t1) Priority (Overnight)");     line 30
            System.out.println("\t2) Express (2 business days)");
            System.out.println("\t3) Standard (3 to 7 business days)");
            strDays = dataIn.readLine();
            days = Integer.parseInt(strDays);
    }

    catch (NumberFormatException e)
    {
        System.out.println("\tYour response was not a valid number.");
        System.out.println("\tPlease reenter your order using a numeric value.");
        System.out.println();
    }
}
```

File menu

Save command

FIGURE 3-11

When the program is complete and ready for execution, the first prompt will instruct the user to enter a dollar amount (line 24 in Figure 3-11 on the previous page). Recall that data from the keyboard is sent as a stream of characters to the buffer and then directed to the processor with the readLine method. The string data then is parsed, or converted (line 26). Values with anticipated decimals, such as the price and shipping charge will be converted to doubles.

Lines 30 through 32 will display a small menu, which during execution will accept a numeric value. Because the choices all are whole numbers, the value will be converted to an integer. In an attempt to help the user to enter correct values, the user-friendly menu lists valid choices with explanations. Notice that the menu choices will display indented, for easier reading, due to the \t tab escape character.

In this example, when an exception occurs, a message will display on the screen and the program will terminate. Later in this project, you write code to further test user input and re-direct execution allowing the user to try again.

Running Java Programs

During execution, if you decide you want to stop entering data and terminate the program, you can press CTRL+C to stop the running program.

Testing Partial Programs

Testing partial programs before moving on to the next section is quite common. You can check for compilation errors with fewer lines of codes, see the results of just one condition or one set of inputs, or debug or look for exceptions within a narrower framework. When testing the running program, you can enter incorrect data to force specific types of exceptions without needing to account for a wide range of errors resulting from combinations of user mistakes.

Testing for Exceptions

Perform the following steps to compile and then execute the program. During execution, you will enter valid and invalid numbers to test for number format exceptions.

 To Test the Program for Exceptions

1 **Click the MS-DOS Prompt button on the taskbar. Type** javac Candle.java **at the command prompt and then press the ENTER key. If there are errors, fix them in the Notepad window and then recompile the program.**

The command prompt displays after a successful compilation (Figure 3-12).

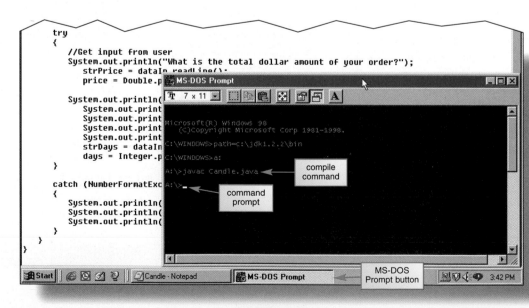

FIGURE 3-12

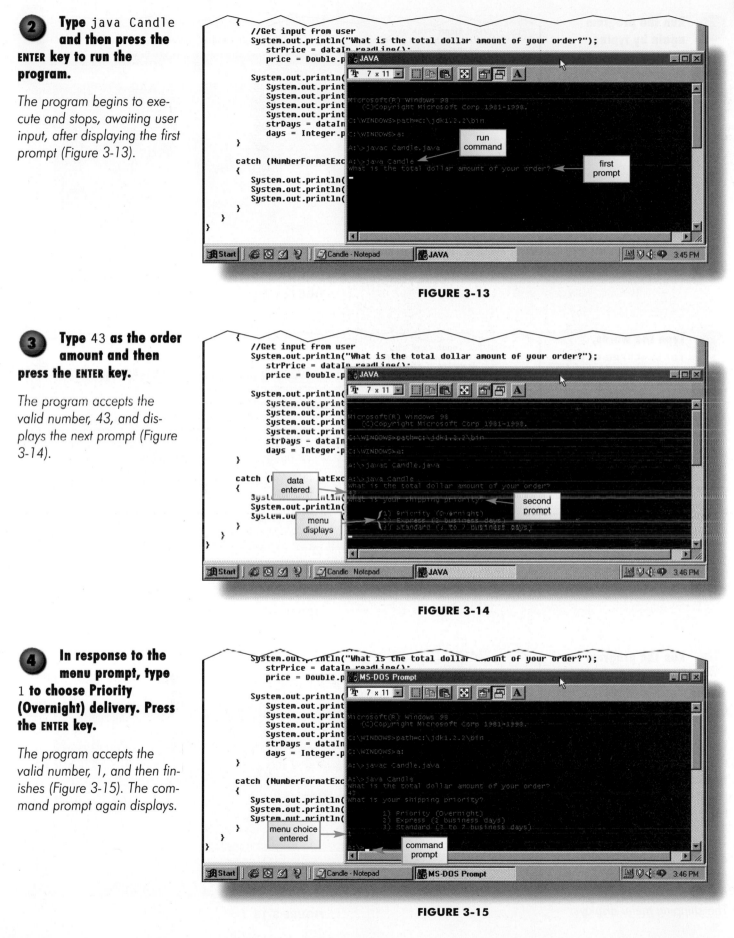

2 **Type** java Candle **and then press the ENTER key to run the program.**

The program begins to execute and stops, awaiting user input, after displaying the first prompt (Figure 3-13).

FIGURE 3-13

3 **Type** 43 **as the order amount and then press the ENTER key.**

The program accepts the valid number, 43, and displays the next prompt (Figure 3-14).

FIGURE 3-14

4 **In response to the menu prompt, type** 1 **to choose Priority (Overnight) delivery. Press the ENTER key.**

The program accepts the valid number, 1, and then finishes (Figure 3-15). The command prompt again displays.

FIGURE 3-15

5 **Run the program again by typing** `java Candle` **at the command prompt, and then press the ENTER key.**

The prompt for the dollar amount of the order again displays (Figure 3-16).

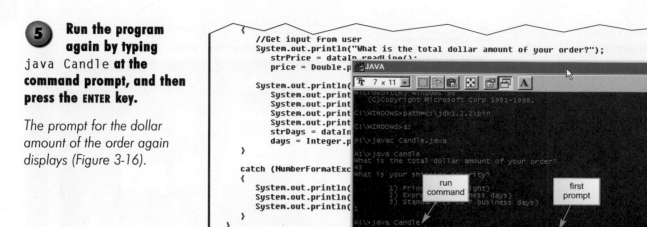

FIGURE 3-16

6 **Type the words,** `forty-three` **at the prompt and then press the ENTER key.**

Java redirects execution to the catch block and displays the error message (Figure 3-17). The words, forty-three, could not be converted to the double data type. The program terminates.

FIGURE 3-17

7 **Run the program again by typing** `java Candle` **at the command prompt, and then press the ENTER key. When the dollar amount prompt displays, type** `59.99` **to test a number with decimal points, and then press the ENTER key.**

The program accepts the decimal number because the input was converted to a double data type (Figure 3-18). The shipping menu displays.

FIGURE 3-18

8 **Type** 2.7 **in response to the shipping menu prompt and then press the ENTER key.**

Java again redirects execution to the catch block and displays the error message because the input for shipping accepts only an integer (Figure 3-19). The program terminates.

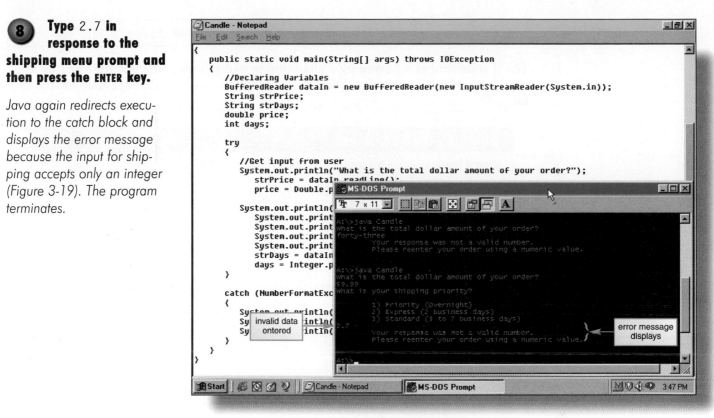

FIGURE 3-19

When execution transfers to the catch block, the program performs a validity check. A **validity** check looks for valid data such as correct data types. The exceptions for which you tested in the previous series of steps were both caused by entering values that did not match the type of data the program expects. You did not write the code to test for the condition yourself; you merely caught the JVM interpreter's throw of the number format exception. In the next series of steps, you will write Java statements to test for different kinds of errors.

The If Decision Structure

Merely because a user has input data that causes no exceptions in Java, it does not mean that it is acceptable data for the program's logic. Java, like other programming languages, has commands that allow the programmer to test or make decisions about data. The decision control structure, also known as the If...Then...Else structure, is used for testing a condition that executes one of two different sets of code. If the condition is true, one set of code is executed; if it is false, then another set of code is executed. These two paths do not have to match in the number of lines of code; for example, the false condition may result in no action being performed, while the true condition might have many lines of code that execute. The only restriction is that the two paths must come back together after the decision structure, in order to continue processing.

The **if** statement in Java can take one of three forms (Table 3-5 on the next page). The first form tests a condition and performs a single action. For example, in a payroll application, if a value named hours equals 40, you might wish to print a message indicating no overtime.

```
if (hours == 40) System.out.println("No overtime is paid");
```

The if statement is followed by a condition in parentheses, which is followed by the resulting code statement. **Conditions** are boolean expressions that evaluate to true or false.

Table 3-5 The if Construct	
General forms:	`if (condition) resulting statement;`

	`if (condition)`
	`{`
	`...statements to execute when true`
	`}`

	`if (condition)`
	`{`
	`...statements to execute when true`
	`}`
	`else`
	`{`
	`...statements to execute when false`
	`}`

Comment:	The words, **if** and **else**, are reserved words. The **condition** must evaluate to a boolean expression. If the condition is true, the statements following the if execute; otherwise, the statements following the word else are executed. Either way execution passes out of the construct to the next line of code following the block.

Examples:	`if (answer == correct)`
	`{`
	`    System.out.println("You got it right!");`
	`    numCorrect = numCorrect + 1;`
	`}`
	`else`
	`{`
	`    System.out.println("You did not answer it correctly");`
	`    System.out.println("The correct answer was " + correct);`
	`    numWrong = numWrong + 1;`
	`}`

The second form of the if construct (Table 3-5) allows for multiple statements to execute based on a condition. The resulting statements are enclosed in block braces. For example, if the hours are less than 40 you might want to calculate the grossPay on a rate times hours basis and then display the result.

```
if (hours < 40)
    {
        grossPay = rate * hours;
        System.out.println("The gross pay is "+ grossPay);
    }
```

However, when there are actions to perform when the condition is true, and other actions to perform when the condition is false, you must include the else statement as shown in the third form of the if construct (Table 3-5). As with the if statement, the else statement may be followed by one statement or multiple statements enclosed in braces. The keywords, if and else, are entered in lowercase. Statements within the blocks commonly are indented for easy reading. For example, if the hours are greater than 40, you might want to call an overtime method; otherwise, you might calculate the grossPay as before. Either way the structure comes back together to perform the next sequential step that displays the grossPay.

```
if (hours > 40)
    {
        grossPay = getOvertime(hours);
    }
else
    {
        grossPay = rate * hours;
    }
System.out.println("The gross pay is "+ grossPay);
```

In Project 2, you learned that different types of comparative operators are used in conditions. Comparative operators commonly are broken into three categories: equality, relational, and logical. All three are used to evaluate the relationship between two expressions or values. The values may be variables, constants, numbers, strings, or the result of a function or method.

Table 3-6 displays the equality, relational, and logical operators in Java.

More About

Spacing in Java Syntax

The Java programming language, like C and C++, is considered a freeform language, which means there are no special rules for positioning white spaces such as blanks, tabs, and new lines. The only limitation is that white space cannot be placed between the two characters of an operator, such as == or ++.

Table 3-6	Operator Results in Decision Structures			
OPERATOR	MEANING	EXAMPLE	RESULT	TYPE
==	equal to	2 == 2 1 == 6	true false	equality
!=	not equal to	7 != 4 4 != 4	true false	equality
<	less than	3 < 5 5 < 3	true false	relational
<=	less than or equal to	4 <= 6 7 <= 6	true false	relational
>	greater than	9 > 7 7 > 9	true false	relational
>=	greater than or equal to	8 >= 8 8 >= 10	true false	relational
&&	logical AND (both conditions must be true)	(7 > 3) && (0 < 1) (7 > 3) && (1 < 0)	true false	logical
||	logical OR (one of the conditions must be true)	(7 > 3) || (1 < 0) (3 > 7) || (1 < 0)	true false	logical
!	logical NOT (condition must evaluate to false in order to make the condition true)	! (5 == 4) ! (a == a)	true false	logical

Reasonableness Check with the if Statement

Input from the user may be checked for **reasonableness**. Any positive number might be a reasonable answer for the dollar amount, as you do not know how many items a customer may have purchased. Negative amounts and the number zero, however, would not be reasonable. If users input a negative number or zero, a message should display notifying them of their error. Because you have already coded a catch block for errors, you may create your own number format exception when the user inputs an unreasonable number. The throw statement, followed by the constructor keyword new, transfers execution to the catch block. Using the catch block for this exception, as well as for the previous exception, is an example of how Java promotes reusable objects.

Perform the following steps to enter code that performs a reasonableness check on the total dollar amount entered by the customer. After saving the program, you will run it and test a value of zero.

Steps To Code and Test the if Statement

1 **If necessary, click the Notepad window to activate it. Click on line 27 between the two sections requesting user input.**

The insertion point displays between the two sections that prompt the user for input (Figure 3-20). (line 27)

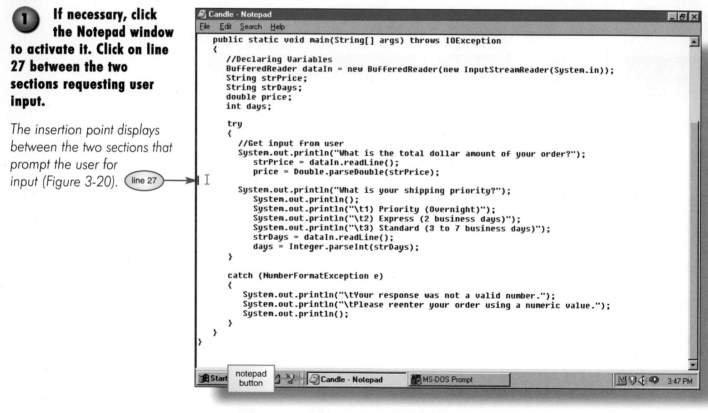

```java
public static void main(String[] args) throws IOException
{
    //Declaring Variables
    BufferedReader dataIn = new BufferedReader(new InputStreamReader(System.in));
    String strPrice;
    String strDays;
    double price;
    int days;

    try
    {
        //Get input from user
        System.out.println("What is the total dollar amount of your order?");
            strPrice = dataIn.readLine();
            price = Double.parseDouble(strPrice);

        System.out.println("What is your shipping priority?");
            System.out.println();
            System.out.println("\t1) Priority (Overnight)");
            System.out.println("\t2) Express (2 business days)");
            System.out.println("\t3) Standard (3 to 7 business days)");
            strDays = dataIn.readLine();
            days = Integer.parseInt(strDays);
    }

    catch (NumberFormatException e)
    {
        System.out.println("\tYour response was not a valid number.");
        System.out.println("\tPlease reenter your order using a numeric value.");
        System.out.println();
    }
}
```

FIGURE 3-20

2 Press the ENTER key to create a blank line. Indent and type the if statement and its block as shown in Figure 3-21. Press the ENTER key again to insert another blank line after the closing brace.

The if statement, braces, and two statements display (Figure 3-21).

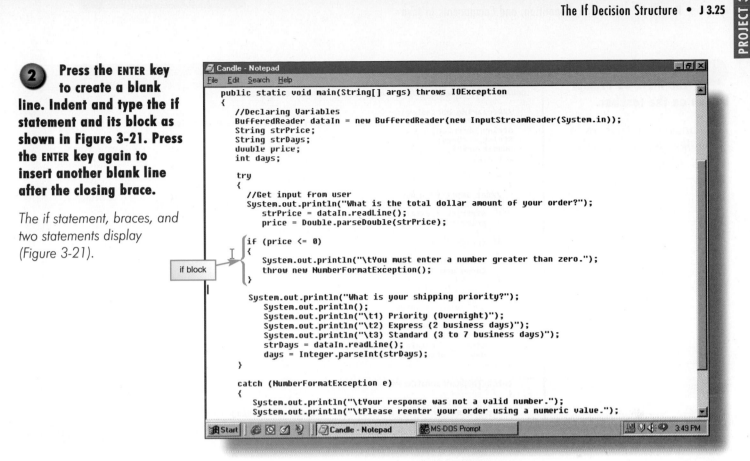

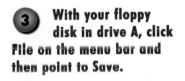

if block

FIGURE 3-21

3 With your floppy disk in drive A, click File on the menu bar and then point to Save.

The File menu displays (Figure 3-22). The program will save again in the same location, with the same file name.

FIGURE 3-22

4 **Click Save. Point to the MS-DOS Prompt button on the taskbar.**

The Candle.java file is saved on the floppy disk in drive A (Figure 3-23).

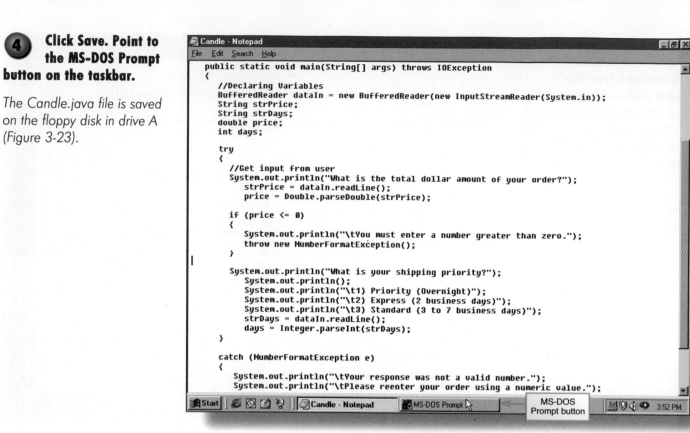

```
public static void main(String[] args) throws IOException
{
    //Declaring Variables
    BufferedReader dataIn = new BufferedReader(new InputStreamReader(System.in));
    String strPrice;
    String strDays;
    double price;
    int days;

    try
    {
        //Get input from user
        System.out.println("What is the total dollar amount of your order?");
        strPrice = dataIn.readLine();
        price = Double.parseDouble(strPrice);

        if (price <= 0)
        {
            System.out.println("\tYou must enter a number greater than zero.");
            throw new NumberFormatException();
        }

        System.out.println("What is your shipping priority?");
        System.out.println();
        System.out.println("\t1) Priority (Overnight)");
        System.out.println("\t2) Express (2 business days)");
        System.out.println("\t3) Standard (3 to 7 business days)");
        strDays = dataIn.readLine();
        days = Integer.parseInt(strDays);
    }

    catch (NumberFormatException e)
    {
        System.out.println("\tYour response was not a valid number.");
        System.out.println("\tPlease reenter your order using a numeric value.");
```

FIGURE 3-23

5 **Click the MS-DOS Prompt button. Type** `javac Candle.java` **and then press the ENTER key.**

The program compiles and the command prompt again displays (Figure 3-24). If you have errors, fix them in the Notepad window, save the file, and then recompile.

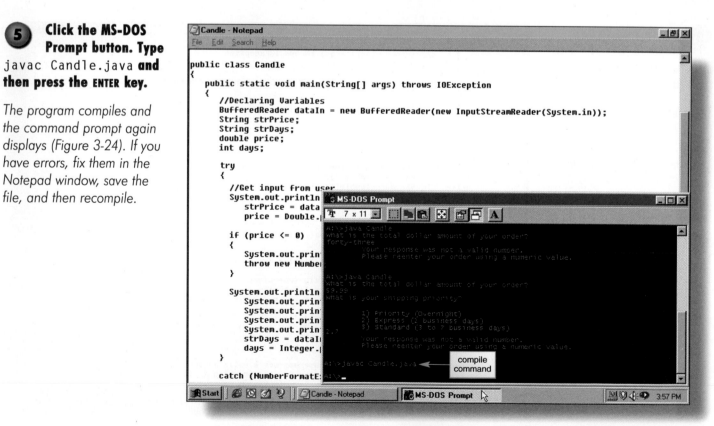

FIGURE 3-24

6 To test the program, type `java Candle` at the command prompt and then press the ENTER key.

The program begins to execute and the first prompt displays (Figure 3-25).

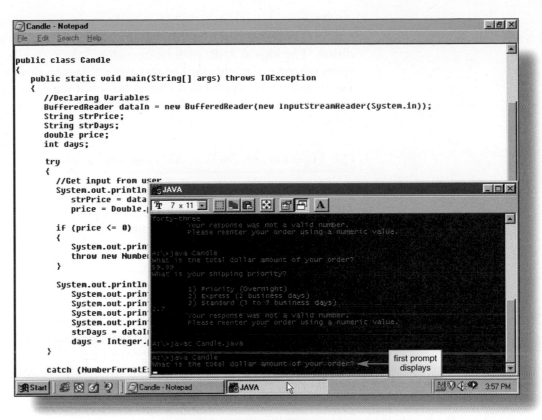

FIGURE 3-25

7 Type 0 and then press the ENTER key.

The program displays the error message (Figure 3-26).

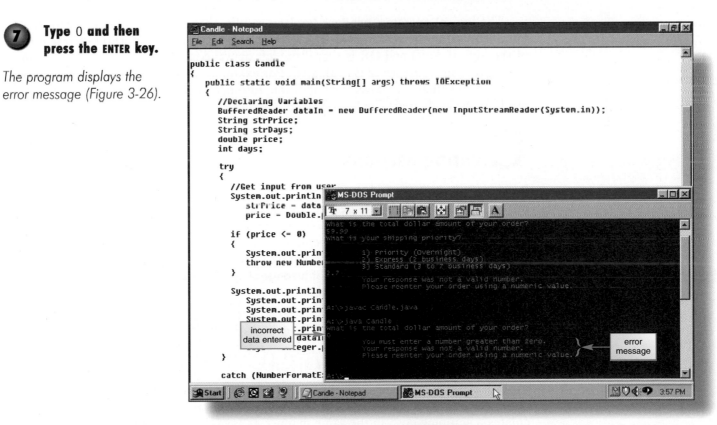

FIGURE 3-26

The previous steps included code that tested for only one condition at a time. While this is common, decision structures may check for more than one possible condition. The logical **AND**, with its operator, &&, typically would be used for situations where you might want to test more than one piece of data at the same time. For example, a program that checks for adult males to register for the selective service might compare the gender with a code for male, and the age with a numeric value. In this case, each condition is enclosed in its own set of parentheses.

```
if ((gender == "male") && (age >= 18))
```

The logical **OR**, with its operator, | |, typically would be used for testing the same piece of data in two different ways. For example, a program that tests an age for possible child or senior discount might compare the age against two different numeric values.

```
if ((age<18) | | (age > 65))
```

The logical **NOT**, with its operator, !, typically would be used for testing a boolean piece of data. For example, a programmer might assign a boolean true value to a variable named, done, in response to a user's input to quit the program. If done were not set, then processing would continue. The decision statement might display as follows.

```
if (!done)
```

The logical operators produce boolean results; that is, they evaluate to true or false. The values or operands used also must be boolean. An important characteristic of the logical AND and OR is that if the left operand is sufficient to decide the condition, the right side never is evaluated. For example if the left side of the AND operator, &&, evaluates to false, the condition automatically is false and the right side need not be evaluated. The left operand was sufficient to decide the condition.

Creating Methods

Breaking a large program's source code down into smaller sections applies to both the creation process and the design. So far, you have created the program by adding small pieces of code and testing the program after each new addition. Now you will write code to test user input for the menu selection. Java's NumberFormatException checked for an integer, which was a validity check. Checking to see if the menu choice is 1, 2, or 3 is an example of a **range check**. Instead of writing the code in the main method block, you will transfer execution to an external routine in an effort to keep portions of code in their own separate and reusable components. Java calls these external routines programmer-defined or user-defined methods.

Coding User-Defined Methods

A **method** is the code used to perform an operation or service. In this case, the method will be a service that tests for a correct menu response of 1, 2, or 3, and calculates a shipping cost. In the same manner as Java-defined methods, any method you create must follow certain syntax rules. Creating a method is a two-part process. You must write a call statement and write the code for the method itself.

When you reach the place in the program where the method is to perform its service, you must **call** it. The call is a line of code stating the name of the method along with any data the method needs to do its job enclosed in parentheses. The pieces of data, if any, are called **arguments**, or parameters. If you have no arguments, you still must include the parentheses with nothing inside. The call may be part of another method or statement as in the following example.

```
System.out.println(calculateAverage(payment));
```

The name of the method is calculateAverage. The argument in this example is payment.

Many of the methods you create calculate or assign a value. If you plan to use that value later in the program, you must assign it an identifier name. The following assignment statement, inserted in the main method, calls the user-defined method, getCost.

```
shipping = getCost(price, days);
```

The name of the method is getCost. Price and days are arguments. The answer is returned to a variable named, shipping. Shipping, price, and days must be declared before the call.

When a call statement is encountered, the Java compiler looks for a matching method, either from an imported package, embedded in the application, or from an external class. Table 3-7 displays a stub for the method. In this project, the method will be coded directly below the main method. The method must contain a header (line 56) and a block (lines 57 through 61).

The method header in line 56 contains an access modifier and a method modifier. You may remember that an access modifier specifies the circumstances in which the class can be accessed. The access modifier, public, indicates that the method can be accessed by all objects and can be extended, or used, as a basis for another class. A method modifier, such as static, enables you to set properties for the method, such as where it will be visible and how subclasses of the current class will interact with the method.

Table 3-7	
LINE	CODE
56	`public static double getCost(double price, int days)`
57	`{`
58	`    double shipping=0;`
59	
60	`    return shipping;`
61	`}`

If a method returns a value, the data type of the return value comes next. In this case, the method returns a double value. That value must be declared in the body of the method.

You then type the name of the method itself, getCost. The method accepts two values from the code statement that calls it, in this case, the values, price and days, in parentheses. Notice that those two values are included with their data types; this serves as their declaration. They need not be named the same as in the call statement.

The getCost method will execute the code inside its block using the declared values. It will send back the shipping charge to the main method that called it. Because it returns a value, the last line inside the block (line 60) must be is a return statement. The **return** statement indicates to the JVM that the method is finished and that execution may return to the main method. When a method is complete, execution always passes back to the next sequential line that follows the call.

Perform the following steps to declare the shipping variable, insert the code to call the getCost method, and then code a stub for the getCost method itself.

Steps To Enter Code for the getCost Method

1 **Click in the Notepad window to activate it. Click on line 21 to the right of the variable declaration for days.**

The insertion point displays (Figure 3-27).

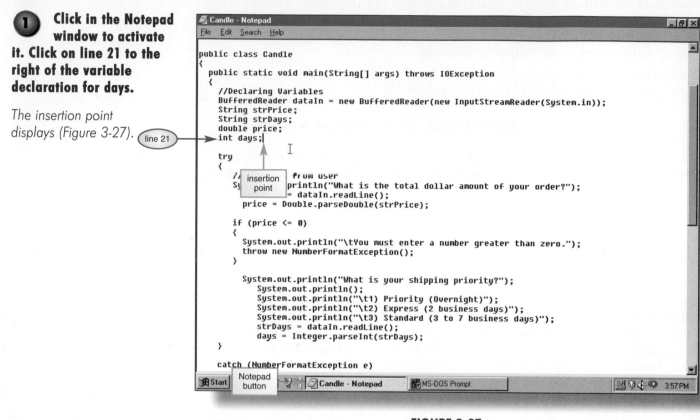

FIGURE 3-27

2 **Press the ENTER key. Indent and then type** double shipping; **to declare the new variable. Point to the end of the line 41, which parses strDays into days.**

The variable shipping is declared to be a double data type (Figure 3-28).

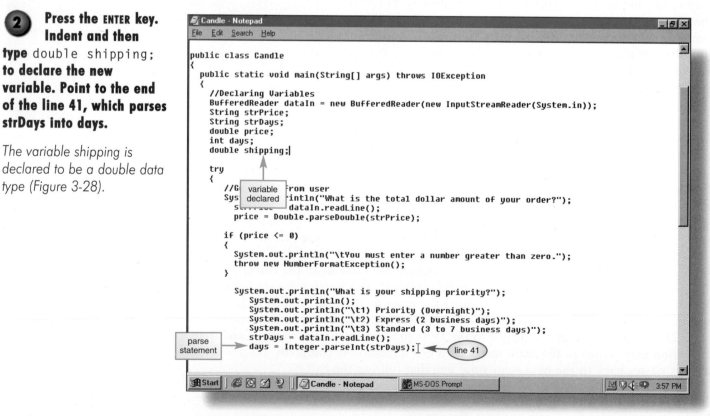

FIGURE 3-28

3 Click at the end of the line 41. Press the ENTER key twice and indent. Type //Call method to get a valid shipping charge **and then press the ENTER key.**

The comment displays (Figure 3-29).

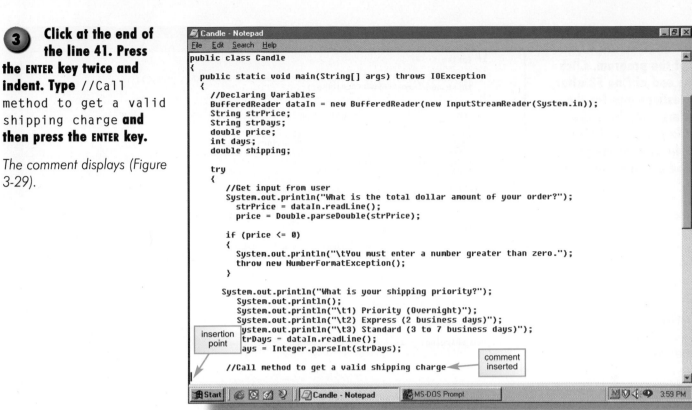

FIGURE 3-29

4 Indent and then **type** shipping = getCost(price, days); **to enter the code to call the method. Press the ENTER key twice. Point to the scroll box on the vertical scroll bar.**

The code to call the method displays (Figure 3-30). This call will send two values, price and days, to the method and return the value, shipping.

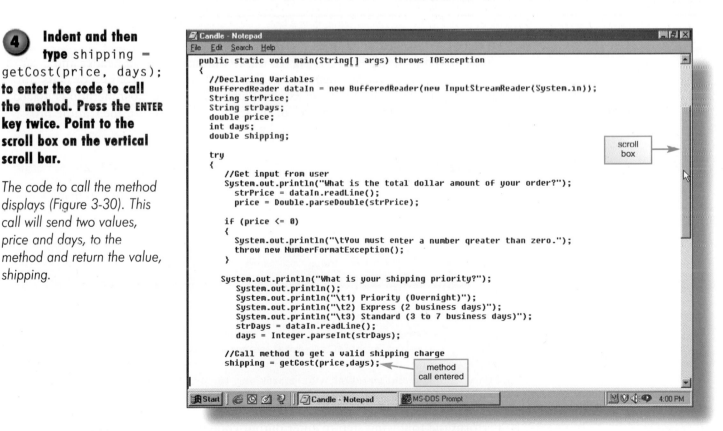

FIGURE 3-30

5 Drag the scroll box down to display the rest of the program. Click at the end of line 53 after the closing brace for the main method. Press the ENTER key twice and then type the stub of the getCost method as shown in Figure 3-31.

The method header is declared public and static (Figure 3-31). It accepts two arguments, a double and an int, and will return a double value. The shipping variable is declared set to zero and returned to the calling method in order for this stub to work.

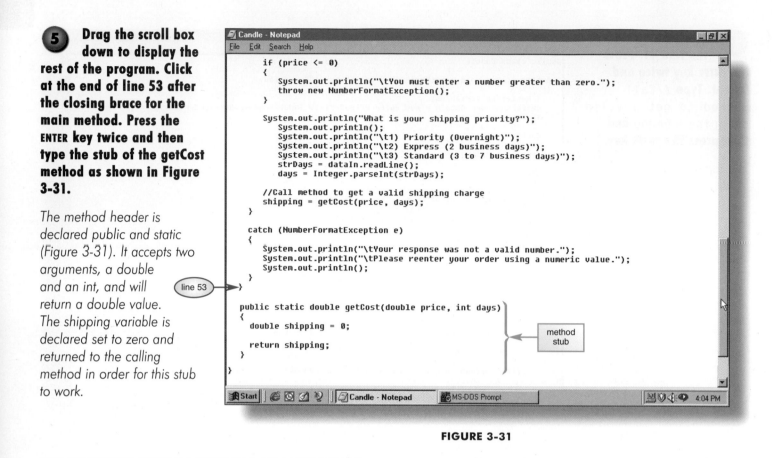

FIGURE 3-31

User-defined methods such as getCost must contain a method header and a set of braces. The only other requirement is that they reside inside a program or class. In this application, which does not use external methods, the getCost method is placed outside of main, but within the braces of the Candle class. So far, the Candle program has two internal methods, main and getCost.

Coding the Output

To display the shipping cost, you must code a few lines of output to display during execution (Table 3-8).

Table 3-8	
LINE	CODE
46	//Display Output
47	System.out.println();
48	System.out.println("The shipping charge is $" + (shipping));
49	System.out.println("The total charge will be $" + (price + shipping));
50	System.out.println();
51	System.out.println("\t\t\tThank you for ordering from CandleLine");

Perform the following step to enter output code in the main method.

TO ENTER OUTPUT CODE

1 Click at the end of line 44. Press the ENTER key twice, indent, and then type the output code as shown in Table 3-8.

The output code displays (Figure 3-32).

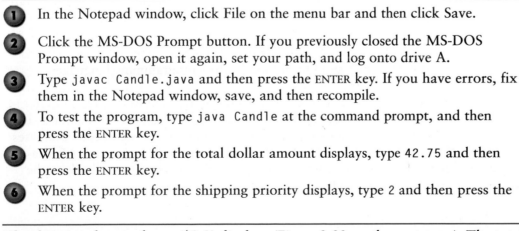

```
Candle - Notepad                                                    _ 8 X
File  Edit  Search  Help

        System.out.println("What is your shipping priority?");
            System.out.println();
            System.out.println("\t1) Priority ( vernight)");
            System.out.println("\t2) Express (2 business days)");
            System.out.println("\t3) Standard (3 to 7 business days)");
            strDays = dataIn.readLine();
            days = Integer.parseInt(strDays);

        //Call method to get a valid shipping charge
line 44 ──▶  shipping = getCost(price,days);  I

        //Display Output
        System.out.println();
output   System.out.println("The shipping charge is $" + (shipping));
code     System.out.println("The total charge will be $" + (price + shipping));
        System.out.println();
        System.out.println("\t\t\tThank you for ordering from CandleLine");|
    }

    catch (NumberFormatException e)
    {
        System.out.println("\tYour response was not a valid number.");
        System.out.println("\tPlease reenter your order using a numeric value.");
        System.out.println();
    }
}

public static double getCost(double price, int days)
{
    double shipping = 0;

    return shipping;
}
}

Start   🌐 📷 📝 ✏   📄 Candle - Notepad    📄 MS-DOS Prompt              🔊 🔅       4:13 PM
```

FIGURE 3-32

Testing the getCost Method

Perform the following steps to save, compile, and test the getCost method stub.

TO SAVE, COMPILE, AND TEST THE GETCOST METHOD STUB

1 In the Notepad window, click File on the menu bar and then click Save.

2 Click the MS-DOS Prompt button. If you previously closed the MS-DOS Prompt window, open it again, set your path, and log onto drive A.

3 Type `javac Candle.java` and then press the ENTER key. If you have errors, fix them in the Notepad window, save, and then recompile.

4 To test the program, type `java Candle` at the command prompt, and then press the ENTER key.

5 When the prompt for the total dollar amount displays, type `42.75` and then press the ENTER key.

6 When the prompt for the shipping priority displays, type `2` and then press the ENTER key.

The shipping charge of zero ($0.0) displays (Figure 3-33 on the next page). The total charge also displays.

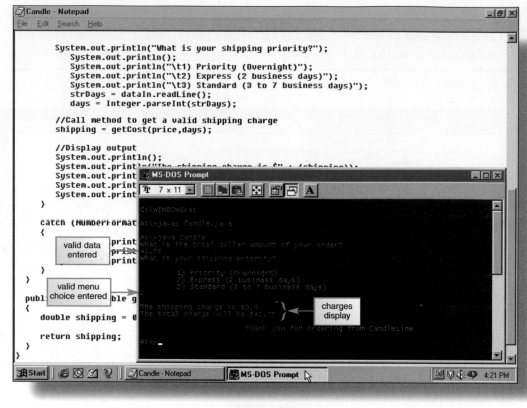

FIGURE 3-33

When you create a user-defined method, such as getCost, you may rename the argument identifiers in the method header parentheses. They need not have the same name as the arguments in the main method. The arguments are passed from the calling statement as values to the new identifiers. These values then are used only within the scope of the new method. **Scope** refers to the variable's visibility. In other words, if you use a new name, only the method itself will recognize that variable, thus preventing confusion or accidental overwriting of the original value. You will learn more about scope in a future project.

The Case Structure

Sending a value to a method where it will be tested is a convenient way to make the program easy to read and to test its components. In the case of a menu selection, there might be many possible, valid choices for the user to input. When there are more than two possibilities, the logical operators become cumbersome and hard to understand, even when AND and OR are used. Most programming languages, including Java, contain a variation of the decision structure called case. In the Introduction Project, you learned that **case** is a special selection control structure that allows for more than two choices when the condition is evaluated. For example, if a user can select from several choices on a menu, the logic of the menu code evaluates the choice. If a match is found, then the appropriate action is performed. Alternatively, if no match is found, the case control structure can provide feedback to the user or store the no match result for later use in the program.

The switch Statement

Java uses a **switch** statement to evaluate a multiple choice value. Then, depending on the value, control is transferred to a corresponding **case statement**. If the value following the case statement matches the switch value, then that case block is executed. Often, each case block contains a **break** statement at the end, which forces an exit of the structure because a match is found. After the break, no more statements within the structure are evaluated, thereby reducing processing time. Table 3-9 displays information about the switch statement.

Table 3-9	The switch Statement
General form:	```switch (variable)
{
case value1:
...statements to execute if value matches value1
break;
case value2:
...statements to execute if value matches value 2
break;
.
.
.
default:
...statements to execute if no match is found
}```
Comment:	**Switch, case, break,** and **default** are reserved words. The case value is any valid variable or constant. Switch compares the case value to the variable. If they match, the code following that case statement is executed.
Example:	```switch (flavor)
{
case 1:
System.out.println("chocolate");
break;
case 2:
System.out.println("vanilla");
break;
case 3:
System.out.println("strawberry");
break;
default:
System.out.println("Please choose one of our three flavors.");
}```

In the Candle program, the user will choose from three menu choices, so you will program cases for the choices, plus the possibility that the user enters an incorrect choice. Should a user enter 1, the program should assign shipping a value of $14.95. If the user enters a 2, the program should assign a shipping a value of $11.95. If a user enters a 3, then the program should evaluate the cost of the order. If the total cost of the order is more than $75.00, shipping will be assigned a value of zero; otherwise shipping will be $5.95.

If a user enters a number outside of the valid range, less than 1 or greater than 3, the program will again throw a number format exception. Java will throw its own NumberFormatException if the number is not an integer. When execution returns to the main method, the catch block then will be executed.

Table 3-10

LINE	CODE
65	switch(days)
66	{
67	case 1:
68	shipping = 14.95;
69	break;
70	case 2:
71	shipping = 11.95;
72	break;
73	case 3:
74	if (price > 75)
75	shipping = 0;
76	else
77	shipping = 5.95;
78	break;
79	default:
80	throw new NumberFormatException();
81	}

You will use the if structure nested inside the third case structure, as shown in Table 3-10. A control structure is **nested** when it is located completely within another structure. A nested structure must end before the outer structure may end. Java programs may have multiple layers of nesting.

Perform the following step to delete the initial assignment of shipping to zero and then add a switch case structure to the getCost method.

TO CODE THE SWITCH STRUCTURE

1 Click the Notepad window to activate it. Delete =0 from line 64. Below the shipping variable declaration, enter the Java code from Table 3-10.

The switch structure displays (Figure 3-34).

In the default case, the program will throw a number format exception. Because the getCost method was called from within the try block, execution will pass to the corresponding catch block, if a user enters a number other than 1, 2, or 3.

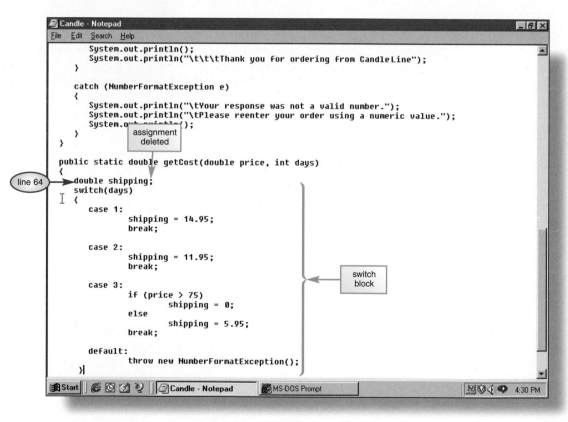

FIGURE 3-34

Testing the switch Structure

Perform the following steps to save, compile, and test the switch structure.

TO SAVE, COMPILE, AND TEST THE SWITCH STRUCTURE

1 In the Notepad window, click File on the menu bar and then click Save.

2 Click the MS-DOS Prompt button. If you previously closed the MS-DOS Prompt window, open it again, set the path, and log onto drive A.

3 Type `javac Candle.java` and then press the ENTER key. If you have errors, fix them in the Notepad window, save, and then recompile.

4 To test the program, type `java Candle` at the command prompt, and then press the ENTER key.

5 When the prompt for the total dollar amount displays, type 150 and then press the ENTER key.

6 When the prompt for the shipping priority displays, type 1 and then press the ENTER key.

The shipping charge displays (Figure 3-35).

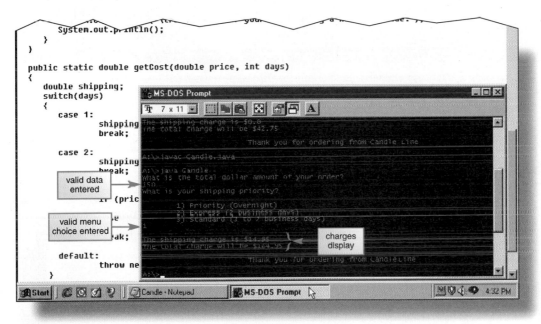

FIGURE 3-35

More About

Logos
Variables, such as done, that are tested to see if iteration should continue sometimes are called sentinel values, or flags. Programmers design a variable that is intentionally wrong and then reset it to a correct value when some phase of the processing has been finished. Testing against that flag allows the program to continue looping until the condition is met.

Run the program several more times and test each menu choice, as well as dollar values above, below, and exactly at 75.

Repetition Structure

So far in this project, when the user types in an invalid or unreasonable number, the program terminates. A message displays notifying the user of the error, but it does not allow the user to reenter the information and try again without rerunning the entire program. As you may recall from the Introduction Project, computer programs are capable of repeating a set of instructions a certain number of times, or indefinitely, based on a conditional factor. The logical structure that alters the flow of sequential execution by repeating a set of code is called **looping, repetition,** or an **iteration control structure.** In the case of the CandleLine company, the program should repeat the instructions while the user is attempting to enter the correct information.

The while Statement

Java uses the Do...While concept for looping when the exact number of repetitions is unknown. First you enter the keyword, **while**, and then a condition in parentheses. All code that should be repeated, based on the condition, is enclosed in braces. Table 3-11 shows the general form of the while statement.

Table 3-11	The while Statement

General form:	`while (condition)`
	`{`
	`...lines of code to repeat while above condition is true;`
	`}`

Comment:	The word, **while**, is a reserved keyword. Condition must be a boolean expression that evaluates to true or false. The condition must eventually evaluate to false in order to exit the loop.

Examples:	`while (!done)`
	`{`
	`    System.out.println("Are you done (yes or no)");`
	`    answer = dataIn.readLine();`
	`    if (answer == "yes") done;`
	`}`

Perform the following steps to add the code for the while loop.

Steps: To Loop Using the while Statement

1 **Click the Notepad window to activate it. Drag the scroll box to display the first part of the program. Click at the end of the declaration section on line 20.**

The first part of the program displays (Figure 3-36).

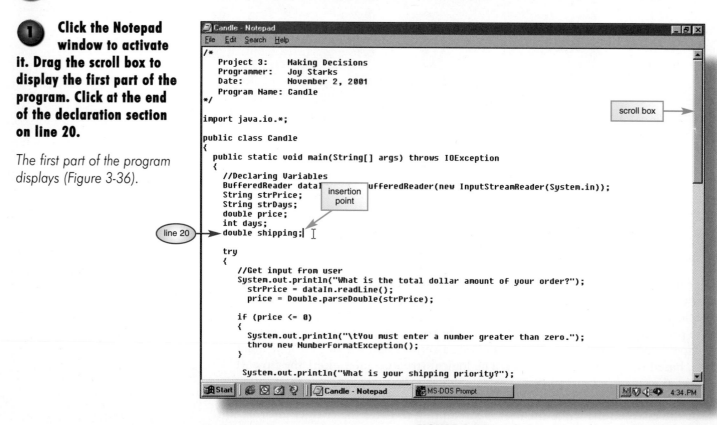

FIGURE 3-36

2 Press the ENTER key. Indent and then **type** boolean done = false; **to declare the beginning value for the while condition. Press the** ENTER **key twice.**

The declaration for the variable, done, displays (Figure 3-37). Boolean values equate to either true or false in Java.

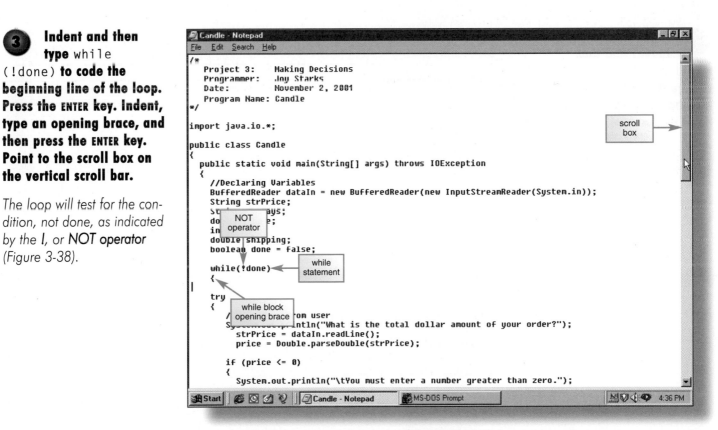

FIGURE 3-37

3 Indent and then **type** while (!done) **to code the beginning line of the loop. Press the** ENTER **key. Indent, type an opening brace, and then press the** ENTER **key. Point to the scroll box on the vertical scroll bar.**

The loop will test for the condition, not done, as indicated by the I, or NOT operator (Figure 3-38).

FIGURE 3-38

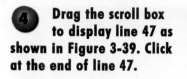

4 **Drag the scroll box to display line 47 as shown in Figure 3-39. Click at the end of line 47.**

The Display Output portion of the program displays (Figure 3-39). If the getCost method call does not throw an exception, then the user must have entered acceptable input.

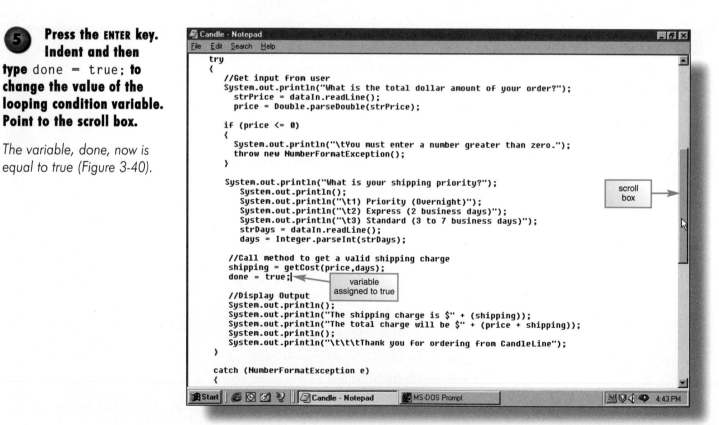

```
try
{
    //Get input from user
    System.out.println("What is the total dollar amount of your order?");
     strPrice = dataIn.readLine();
     price = Double.parseDouble(strPrice);

    if (price <= 0)
    {
       System.out.println("\tYou must enter a number greater than zero.");
       throw new NumberFormatException();
    }

    System.out.println("What is your shipping priority?");
       System.out.println();
       System.out.println("\t1) Priority (Overnight)");
       System.out.println("\t2) Express (2 business days)");
       System.out.println("\t3) Standard (3 to 7 business days)");
       strDays = dataIn.readLine();
       days = Integer.parseInt(strDays);

    //Call method to get a valid shipping charge
    shipping = getCost(price,days);

    //Display Output
    System.out.println();
    System.out.println("The shipping charge is $" + (shipping));
    System.out.println("The total charge will be $" + (price + shipping));
    System.out.println();
    System.out.println("\t\t\tThank you for ordering from CandleLine");
}

catch (NumberFormatException e)
{
```

scroll box

line 47

output code

FIGURE 3-39

5 **Press the ENTER key. Indent and then type done = true; to change the value of the looping condition variable. Point to the scroll box.**

The variable, done, now is equal to true (Figure 3-40).

```
try
{
    //Get input from user
    System.out.println("What is the total dollar amount of your order?");
     strPrice = dataIn.readLine();
     price = Double.parseDouble(strPrice);

    if (price <= 0)
    {
       System.out.println("\tYou must enter a number greater than zero.");
       throw new NumberFormatException();
    }

    System.out.println("What is your shipping priority?");
       System.out.println();
       System.out.println("\t1) Priority (Overnight)");
       System.out.println("\t2) Express (2 business days)");
       System.out.println("\t3) Standard (3 to 7 business days)");
       strDays = dataIn.readLine();
       days = Integer.parseInt(strDays);

    //Call method to get a valid shipping charge
    shipping = getCost(price,days);
    done = true;

    //Display Output
    System.out.println();
    System.out.println("The shipping charge is $" + (shipping));
    System.out.println("The total charge will be $" + (price + shipping));
    System.out.println();
    System.out.println("\t\t\tThank you for ordering from CandleLine");
}

catch (NumberFormatException e)
{
```

scroll box

variable assigned to true

FIGURE 3-40

6 Scroll down to the end of the catch block. Click after the closing brace on line 63. Press the ENTER key, indent, and then type a closing brace for the while loop.

The braces closing the catch block, the while block, and the main method display (Figure 3-41).

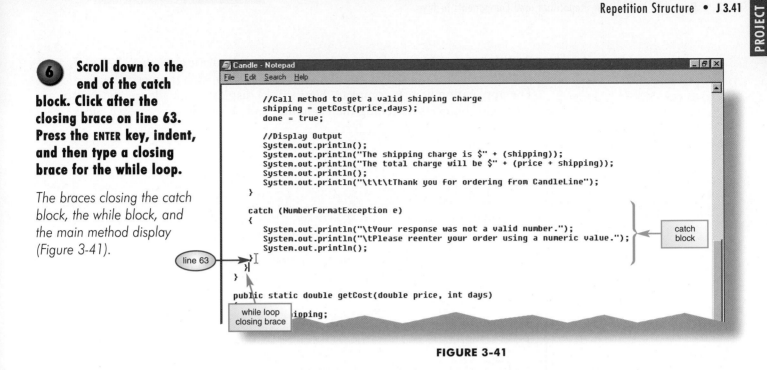

```
                //Call method to get a valid shipping charge
                shipping = getCost(price,days);
                done = true;

                //Display Output
                System.out.println();
                System.out.println("The shipping charge is $" + (shipping));
                System.out.println("The total charge will be $" + (price + shipping));
                System.out.println();
                System.out.println("\t\t\tThank you for ordering from CandleLine");
            }

            catch (NumberFormatException e)
            {
                System.out.println("\tYour response was not a valid number.");
                System.out.println("\tPlease reenter your order using a numeric value.");
                System.out.println();
            }
        }
    }

    public static double getCost(double price, int days)
    {
```

FIGURE 3-41

Testing the while Structure

Perform the following steps to save, compile, and then test the while structure.

TO SAVE, COMPILE, AND TEST THE WHILE STRUCTURE

1 In the Notepad window, click File on the menu bar and then click Save.

2 Click the MS-DOS Prompt button. If you previously closed the MS-DOS Prompt window, open it again, set your path, and log onto drive A.

3 Type javac Candle.java and then press the ENTER key. If you have errors, fix them in the Notepad window, save, and then recompile.

4 To test the program, type java Candle at the command prompt, and then press the ENTER key.

5 When the prompt for the total dollar amount displays, type -35 and then press the ENTER key.

6 When the program notifies you of an invalid number and displays the prompt to reenter the total dollar amount, type 35 and then press the ENTER key.

7 When the prompt for the shipping priority displays, type 3 and then press the ENTER key.

The shipping charge displays (Figure 3-42).

FIGURE 3-42

Run the program several more times and test each menu choice, 1, 2, and 3, as well as valid and invalid dollar amounts, such as zero or alphanumeric data.

The application now is complete. Figure 3-43 displays the code for the entire program with brackets matching the beginning and closing braces of each block.

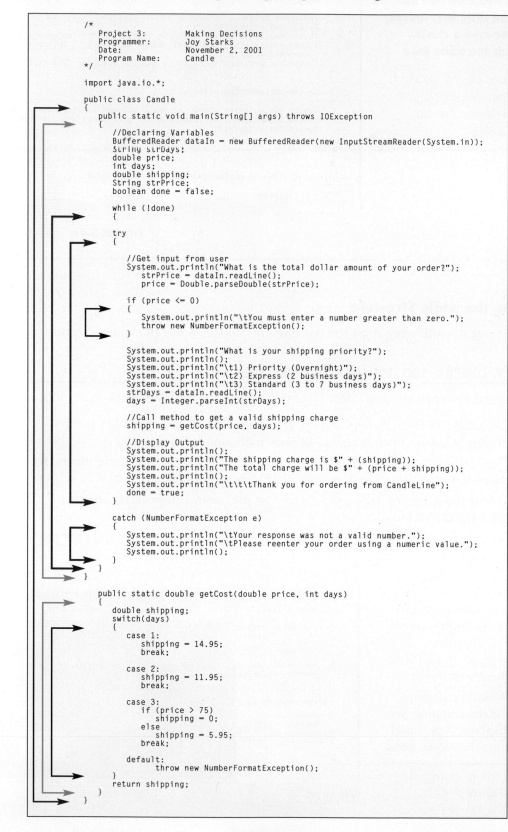

```java
/*
    Project 3:       Making Decisions
    Programmer:      Joy Starks
    Date:            November 2, 2001
    Program Name:    Candle
*/

import java.io.*;

public class Candle
{
    public static void main(String[] args) throws IOException
    {
        //Declaring Variables
        BufferedReader dataIn = new BufferedReader(new InputStreamReader(System.in));
        String strDays;
        double price;
        int days;
        double shipping;
        String strPrice;
        boolean done = false;

        while (!done)
        {
            try
            {

                //Get input from user
                System.out.println("What is the total dollar amount of your order?");
                strPrice = dataIn.readLine();
                price = Double.parseDouble(strPrice);

                if (price <= 0)
                {
                    System.out.println("\tYou must enter a number greater than zero.");
                    throw new NumberFormatException();
                }

                System.out.println("What is your shipping priority?");
                System.out.println();
                System.out.println("\t1) Priority (Overnight)");
                System.out.println("\t2) Express (2 business days)");
                System.out.println("\t3) Standard (3 to 7 business days)");
                strDays = dataIn.readLine();
                days = Integer.parseInt(strDays);

                //Call method to get a valid shipping charge
                shipping = getCost(price, days);

                //Display Output
                System.out.println();
                System.out.println("The shipping charge is $" + (shipping));
                System.out.println("The total charge will be $" + (price + shipping));
                System.out.println();
                System.out.println("\t\t\tThank you for ordering from CandleLine");
                done = true;
            }

            catch (NumberFormatException e)
            {
                System.out.println("\tYour response was not a valid number.");
                System.out.println("\tPlease reenter your order using a numeric value.");
                System.out.println();
            }
        }
    }

    public static double getCost(double price, int days)
    {
        double shipping;
        switch(days)
        {
            case 1:
                shipping = 14.95;
                break;

            case 2:
                shipping = 11.95;
                break;

            case 3:
                if (price > 75)
                    shipping = 0;
                else
                    shipping = 5.95;
                break;

            default:
                throw new NumberFormatException();
        }
        return shipping;
    }
}
```

FIGURE 3-43

Moving to the Web

As you create the applet version of the CandleLine company's application, you will use the same techniques to build component modularity into your applet. First, you will create the HTML host document to call the applet. Then you will create the applet stub and test it by compiling. As you add components to the applet and build decision structures into the applet's code, you will create new blocks, save them, and compile them. Finally, you will run the applet and try various sample data in order to test its error and exception handling capabilities.

Creating the Host Document

Recall from previous projects that each Java applet must be called from within another program or application. The host document usually is an HTML file with an applet tag. The code to create an HTML file to access the CandleApplet program is listed in Table 3-12.

Table 3-12	
LINE	CODE
1	<HTML>
2	<APPLET CODE = "CandleApplet.class" WIDTH = 350 HEIGHT = 300
3	</APPLET>
4	</HTML>

Perform the following steps to create the HTML file and save it on your floppy disk.

TO CREATE THE HOST DOCUMENT

1 Start a new session of Notepad. If Notepad already is on your desktop, click File on the Notepad menu bar and then click New.

2 Type the code from Table 3-12 in the Notepad workspace.

3 With a floppy disk in drive A, click File on the menu bar and then click Save. When the Save As dialog box displays, type "CandleApplet.html" in the File name text box. If necessary, click 3½ Floppy (A:) in the Save in list. Click the Save button.

The program saves on the floppy disk in drive A with the name, "CandleApplet.html" (Figure 3-44).

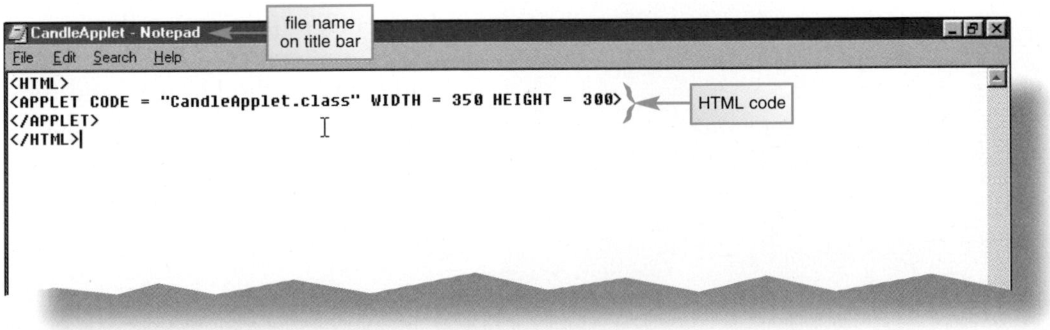

FIGURE 3-44

The HTML host document is complete. In the next section, you will create a stub for the applet itself.

Creating an Applet Stub

As you may recall from previous projects, applets typically use the Abstract Windows Toolkit provided with the JDK. Programmers commonly enter the statement to import the AWT.

```
import java.awt.*;
```

The **Abstract Windows Toolkit (AWT)** consists of resources that enable you to create rich, attractive, and useful interfaces in your applets. The **java.awt** package not only contains managerial classes for complete interface layouts, but it also has the container classes to add components such as buttons, text fields, and labels. The AWT's Graphics class is very powerful, allowing you to create shapes and display images. Applets additionally must import the **java.applet** package, which lays the foundation for all applets.

The other imported package used in many applets is the java.awt.event package. The **java.awt.event** package is not a subset of java.awt package; rather, it is a separate package enabling you to implement interfaces, such as the ActionListener and the ItemListener. You may recall that ActionListener listens for events related to command buttons, such as a mouse click or ENTER key during execution of the applet. **ItemListener** can be added to listen for when the user clicks components such as check boxes. Among ItemListener's methods are addItemListener and itemStateChanged, which enable you to enliven those components and test whether or not they are selected. The java.awt, java.applet, and java.awt.event packages may be imported in any order (lines 8, 9, and 10 in Table 3-13).

Recall that applets do not have a main method. Instead, applets use the init method to **initialize** the applet from the browser or Applet Viewer (line 14). When the applet is loaded, the browser calls the init method. This method is called only once no matter how many times you might return to the Web page.

Stubbing in the program will involve typing the general block comments, importing the three classes, and entering the applet header, init method header, and the itemStateChanged method header. Perform the following steps to stub in the applet with the code from Table 3-13.

More About

The ActionEvents

An ActionEvent is the type of event that occurs when a user clicks a component, such as a button. You tell applets to expect ActionEvents with the addActionListener method. Inside the body of the corresponding ActionPerformed method, you write any statements that you want to execute when the action takes place.

Table 3-13

LINE	CODE
1	/*
2	Project 3: Making Decision
3	Programmer: Joy Starks
4	Date: November 2, 2001
5	Program Name: CandleApplet
6	*/
7	
8	import java.awt.*;
9	import java.applet.*;
10	import java.awt.event.*;
11	
12	public class CandleApplet extends Applet implements ItemListener
13	{
14	public void init()
15	{
16	
17	}
18	
19	public void itemStateChanged(ItemEvent choice)
20	{
21	
22	}
23	}

TO CODE THE APPLET STUB

1 Start a new session of Notepad. If Notepad already is on your desktop, click File on the Notepad menu bar and then click New.

2 Enter the code from Table 3-13 using your name and the current date in the block comment.

The code for the program stub displays in the Notepad window (Figure 3-45).

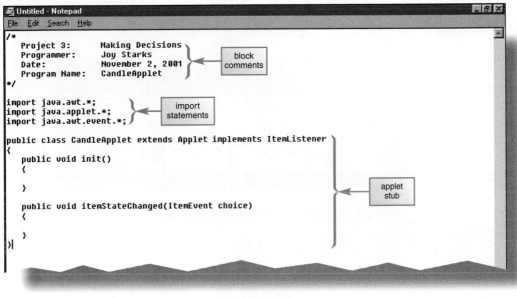

FIGURE 3-45

You can test the applet, even without any commands or data components. Perform the following steps to save, compile, and test the applet stub.

TO SAVE, COMPILE, AND TEST THE APPLET STUB

1 If necessary, click the Notepad window.

2 With a floppy disk in drive A, click File on the menu bar and then click Save As.

3 When the Save As dialog box displays, type "CandleApplet.java" in the File name text box. You must type the quotation marks around the file name.

4 Click the Save in box arrow and then click 3½ Floppy (A:) in the list.

5 Click the Save button.

6 Click the MS-DOS Prompt button on the taskbar. If you previously closed the MS-DOS Prompt window, open it again, set your path, and log onto drive A. Type javac CandleApplet.java and then press the ENTER key to compile the program.

7 If you have errors, fix them in the Notepad window, save, and then recompile the program in the MS-DOS Prompt window.

8 When your program compiles successfully, execute it by typing appletviewer CandleApplet.html at the command prompt and then press the ENTER key.

Applet Viewer displays the applet with no components (see Figure 3-46 on the next page). The program stub has no active statements or commands.

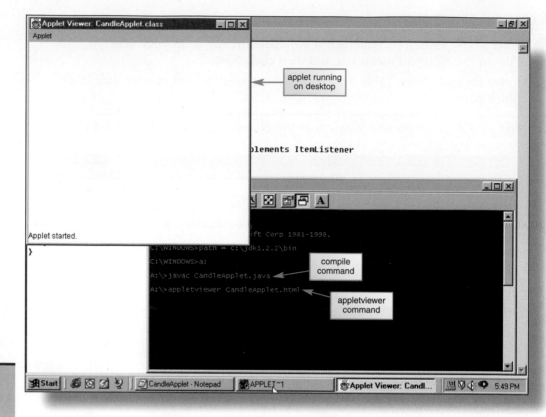

applet running
on desktop

lements ItemListener

compile
command

appletviewer
command

FIGURE 3-46

Making Decisions in Applets

As is true in applications, a Java applet does not always perform the same series of steps. Much of the time, the path that the applet takes depends upon the actions of the user. For example, if the user enters an invalid number, the applet should display an error message and then give the user a chance to enter another number. Alternatively, if the user makes a choice from a list of options, a Java applet should branch to a certain set of code statements based on that choice.

As with the application you created in this project, applet control structures may be either object-oriented in nature or programmed to make a decision. For instance, applets may use the object-oriented try and catch blocks described on pages J 3.13 through J 3.18. In a try block, the program may throw an exception or the programmer may throw the exception to the catch block based on a condition, such as the user entering a number that is out of range.

Through the use of check boxes, Java applets may allow the user to make choices that are evaluated by the applet. For instance, a user may select a check box by clicking it. Java then allows the applet, through the ItemListener, to listen for that click, and then perform a unique set of instructions associated with that component. Thus, a multiple-choice case structure can be implemented.

Java applets also support the traditional If...Then...Else structures, as well as the switch block.

Constructing Check Boxes

You have used constructors to create label, text field, and button components. In this project, you will create a constructor for a check box. Java has two different kinds of check boxes. The first is a traditional **check box** that displays as a small square with a caption. When selected, the check box displays a check mark (Figure 3-47). The check box has the toggled value of on or off depending on whether the check mark displays. The check box is an independent component that allows the user to select it, regardless of other choices in the interface.

The second kind of check box displays as a small circle or option button (Figure 3-47). This check box is one of a mutually exclusive group. Even though Java calls this a **grouped check box**, most people would think of it as an option button. When the user clicks one of the grouped check box components, the others automatically become deselected. Only one member of the grouped check boxes can be selected at any one time. Table 3-14 displays the code to construct the applet components.

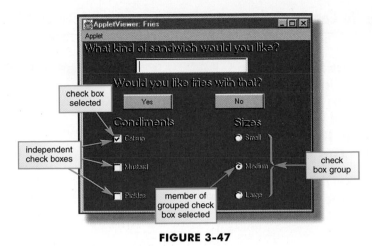

FIGURE 3-47

Table 3-14	
LINE	CODE
14	//Create components for applet
15	Label companyNameLabel = new Label ("CandleLine—Candles Online");
16	
17	Label priceLabel = new Label ("Please enter the total dollar amount of your order:");
18	TextField priceField = new TextField(35);
19	
20	Label shippingLabel = new Label ("Please choose your method of shipping:");
21	
22	CheckboxGroup shippingGroup = new CheckboxGroup();
23	Checkbox oneDayBox = new Checkbox("Priority (Overnight)",false,shippingGroup);
24	Checkbox twoDayBox = new Checkbox("Express (2 business days)",false,shippingGroup);
25	Checkbox moreDaysBox = new Checkbox("Standard (3 to 7 business days)",false,shippingGroup);
26	Checkbox hiddenBox = new Checkbox("",true,shippingGroup);
27	
28	Label outputLabel = new Label("We guarantee on time delivery, or your money back.");
29	

Two methods from the AWT are employed when using a grouping of check boxes to create options. An instance of the **CheckboxGroup** is constructed first (line 22), directing the Java compiler to create a mutually exclusive grouping. You then can construct individual instances of the check boxes with unique identifiers. The **Checkbox method**, which constructs each instance (lines 23 through 26), takes three arguments: the caption, the state, and the group name. The **caption** is the string you wish to display beside the check box. The **state** is true or false, depending on whether you want the member of the grouped check box filled in for true or not filled in for false. Because it is a mutually exclusive grouping, only one member of the group may have its state value set to true at any given time. The **group name** is the identifier previously used when the CheckboxGroup was constructed. The group name assigns membership.

Perform the steps on the next page to enter the code to construct the applet components.

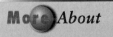

More About

Component States

The getStateChange method can be used to test a check box for its current state. The method will return either ItemEvent.SELECTED or ItemEvent.DESELECTED. For example, if a calculate button was to test a discount check box, you could write a line of code similar to this: if (discountBox.getStateChange() = ItemEvent.SELECTED) price = price - discount.

To Construct Components

1 **Close Applet Viewer by clicking the Close button on its title bar. Click the Notepad window at the end of line 13 and then press the ENTER key.**

The insertion point displays inside the CandleApplet block (Figure 3-48).

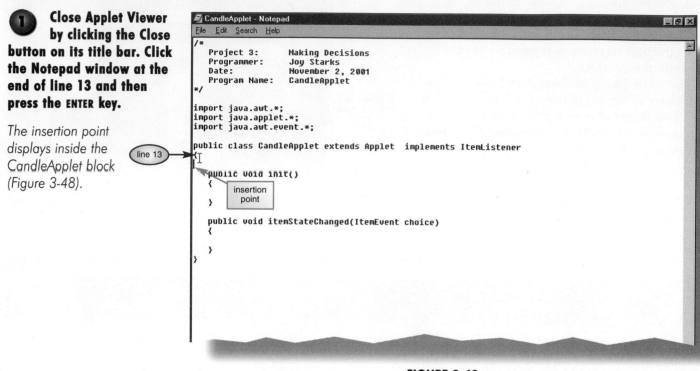

FIGURE 3-48

2 **Enter the code from Table 3-14 on the previous page to create the components for the applet.**

The code to construct the components displays (Figure 3-49). Notice the check box constructors are grouped with the name, shippingGroup.

3 **Click File on the Notepad menu bar and then click Save.**

The file is saved on the floppy disk in drive A.

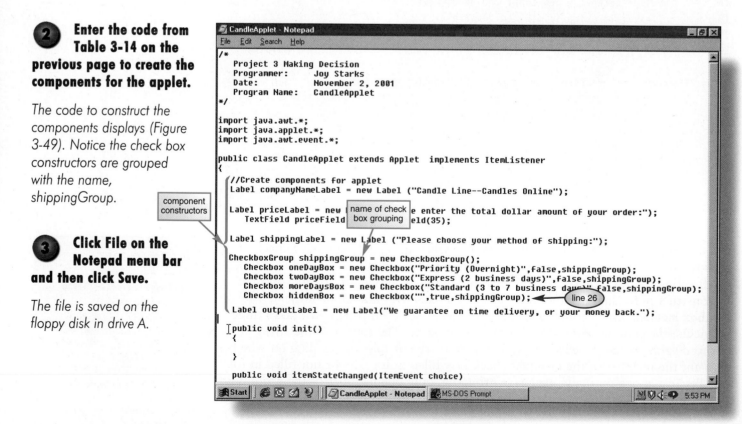

FIGURE 3-49

The hidden check box on line 26 is not added to the applet's viewing area, as you will see in the next series of steps. That way, if you want to clear all the other check boxes in the group, you can simply set the hidden check box to true, thus changing the others to false automatically.

Adding Components, Color, and Focus to the Applet

You may recall that the **add** method takes an argument of a declared component and adds it to the Applet Viewer window when the applet is initiated. The **addItemListener** event then causes the applet to listen for clicks initiated by the user. When the click occurs, a series of associated objects and methods change, including the getState method, the itemStateChanged method, and the ItemEvent object. Table 3-15 describes the general form of the addItemListener event.

Applets and Web pages rely on the use of graphics, animation, sound, and color to entice viewing and provide entertainment. While sophisticated graphics and animation may be best served with another design tool, Java can produce colors rather simply. Two methods help you change the color of your applet: the setBackground method and the setForeground method. Each method works the same way; each takes a color argument. The **setBackground** method changes the color behind the text. The **setForeground** method changes the text color. You may want to change the foreground color to draw attention to a certain component or use a lighter color to make the text display better on darker backgrounds. The following line sets the background of the entire applet to blue.

Table 3-15	The addItemListener Event
General form:	component.addItemListener(ItemListener object)
Comment:	The component must be declared with a constructor before triggering the event. The ItemListener object may be the self-referential, **this** object or a constructor of a new object.
Example:	optBlue.addItemListener(this);

```
setBackground(Color.blue);
```

If you want to set the color for a specific label or check box, you must precede the command with the name of the object.

```
myLabel.setForeground(Color.lightGray);
```

Color is an object that Java can reference. LightGray is an attribute. Table 3-16 lists valid attributes for the color object. The preset colors are medium gray for the background and black for the text.

Another method associated with applets that use text fields is the requestFocus method. The **requestFocus** method moves the insertion point to the control that calls it. In the case of text fields, the insertion point displays as a vertical flashing line in the text box.

Table 3-16	Valid Color Attributes	
VIVID COLORS		
black	green	red
blue	lightGray	white
cyan	magenta	yellow
darkGray	orange	
gray	pink	

More About

requestFocus

When a component has the focus, the insertion point will display or the button will have a dotted box around its caption. Java has no preset or default focus; you must set focus in the code. You may, however, move it from one component to the next as the user completes tasks.

```
myField.requestFocus();
```

Table 3-17

LINE	CODE
32	//Add components to window and set colors
33	setBackground(Color.cyan);
34	add(companyNameLabel);
35	add(priceLabel);
36	add(priceField);
37	priceField.requestFocus();
38	add(oneDayBox);
39	oneDayBox.addItemListener(this);
40	add(twoDayBox);
41	twoDayBox.addItemListener(this);
42	add(moreDaysBox);
43	moreDaysBox.addItemListener(this);
44	add(outputLabel);

Displaying the insertion point helps users focus on the appropriate spot to enter the next item of text and commonly is used when clearing an incorrect entry, to let the user try another entry.

Table 3-17 displays the code for the init method to set the background color, add the components to the applet, and set the focus to the text field. Perform the following steps to code the init method.

TO CODE THE INIT METHOD

1 Click the Notepad window inside the init method at line 32.

2 Enter the code from Table 3-17 to create the add methods, their corresponding ItemListener statements, color, and focus.

3 Click File on the Notepad menu bar and then click Save.

The add methods and addItemListener methods display (Figure 3-50). The file is saved on the floppy disk in drive A.

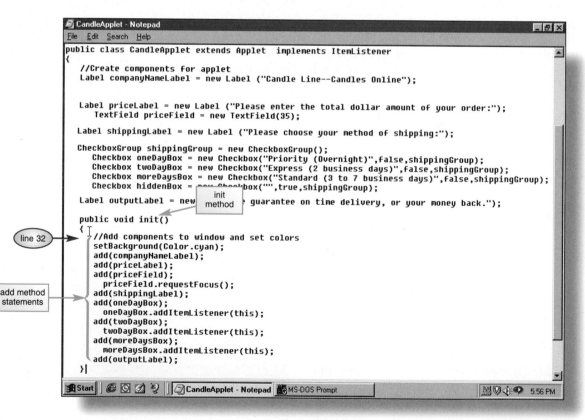

FIGURE 3-50

Now, during execution, the applet will display its labels, fields, and boxes, allowing the user to click one of the options created from the check box grouping. Perform the following steps to compile the applet and test the check box grouping.

Steps | **To Compile the Applet and Test the Check Box Grouping**

1 **Click the MS-DOS Prompt button on the taskbar. Type** `javac CandleApplet.java` **and then press the ENTER key to compile the program. If there are errors, fix them in the Notepad window, save, and then recompile. Type** `appletviewer CandleApplet.html` **at the command prompt and then press the ENTER key.**

The applet displays (Figure 3-51). Your colors may vary depending upon your system settings. Notice the insertion point in the text field. None of the options is selected, because the state value of the hidden one is set to true.

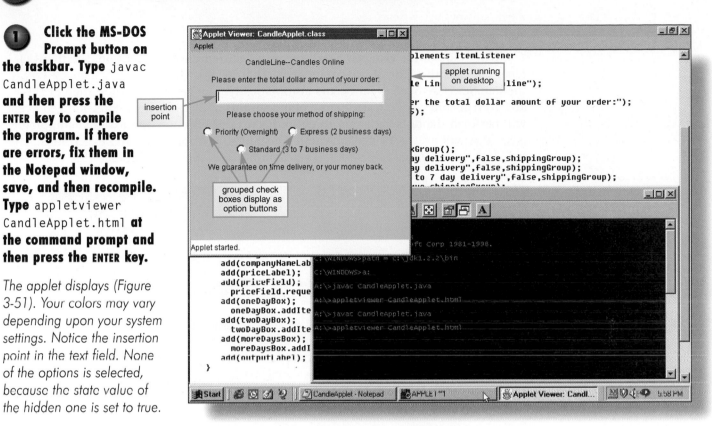

FIGURE 3-51

2 **Click Priority (Overnight), and then click Express (2 business days).**

When Express (2 business days) is selected, Priority (Overnight) automatically displays deselected (Figure 3-52).

3 **Close the applet by clicking the Close button on the Applet Viewer title bar.**

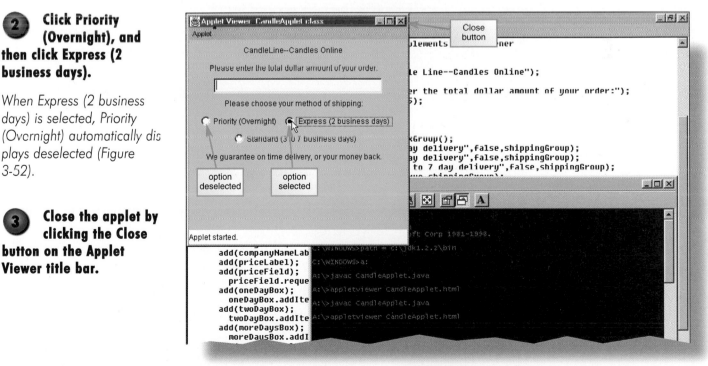

FIGURE 3-52

Using a hidden check box as part of the option group forces the user to make a decision, rather than letting a default selection dictate the course of the program.

Decisions in the Applet

When one of the grouped check boxes is selected during execution, the ItemListener changes the state of the component. That means when you click a check box, the itemStateChanged event occurs automatically. The getState method then evaluates to true and can be tested with coding. In this applet, the itemStateChanged event will perform the tests necessary to check for a valid selection and assign a shipping cost. You will use Java's try and catch constant to test for errors and exceptions. The try block is shown in Table 3-18. The catch block is shown in Table 3-19.

Table 3-18

LINE	CODE
48	`try`
49	`{`
50	`   double shipping;`
51	`   double price = Double.parseDouble(priceField.getText());`
52	
53	`   //Check to see if price is greater than zero`
54	`   if (price <= 0) throw new NumberFormatException();`
55	
56	`   //Check to see which option button is selected`
57	`   if (oneDayBox.getState())`
58	`      shipping = 14.95;`
59	`   else`
60	`      if (twoDayBox.getState())`
61	`         shipping = 11.95;`
62	`      else`
63	`         if (price > 75)`
64	`            shipping = 0;`
65	`         else`
66	`            shipping = 5.95;`
67	
68	`   //Display Output`
69	`   outputLabel.setForeground(Color.black);`
70	`   outputLabel.setText("Your total cost is $" + (price+shipping));`
71	`}`

Table 3-19

LINE	CODE
73	`catch (NumberFormatException e)`
74	`{`
75	`   outputLabel.setText("You must enter a dollar amount greater than zero");`
76	`   outputLabel.setForeground(Color.red);`
77	`   hiddenBox.setState(true);`
78	`   priceField.setText("");`
79	`   priceField.requestFocus();`
80	`}`

Perform the following steps to code the try and catch construct for the applet.

TO ENTER THE TRY AND CATCH BLOCKS IN THE APPLET

1 Click the Notepad window. Click the blank line inside the braces of the itemStateChanged block.

2 Enter the try block code from Table 3-18.

3 Enter the catch block code from Table 3-19.

4 Click File on the menu bar and then click Save.

The try and catch blocks display (Figure 3-53). The file is saved on the floppy disk in drive A.

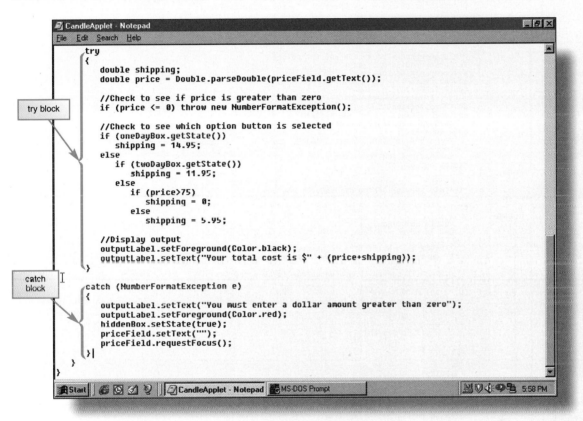

```
try
{
    double shipping;
    double price = Double.parseDouble(priceField.getText());

    //Check to see if price is greater than zero
    if (price <= 0) throw new NumberFormatException();

    //Check to see which option button is selected
    if (oneDayBox.getState())
        shipping = 14.95;
    else
        if (twoDayBox.getState())
            shipping = 11.95;
        else
            if (price>75)
                shipping = 0;
            else
                shipping = 5.95;

    //Display output
    outputLabel.setForeground(Color.black);
    outputLabel.setText("Your total cost is $" + (price+shipping));
}

catch (NumberFormatException e)
{
    outputLabel.setText("You must enter a dollar amount greater than zero");
    outputLabel.setForeground(Color.red);
    hiddenBox.setState(true);
    priceField.setText("");
    priceField.requestFocus();
}
```

try block

catch block

FIGURE 3-53

If the catch block is executed, a message will display in red, the visible options will be cleared, the text field will be cleared of any wrong input, and the focus will be reset to that text field.

Because the switch statement cannot test the boolean state of a check box, the nested if statements are used in the try block to determine which check box has been selected (Figure 3-53). You will learn other ways to check the state of components in a later project.

Executing the Applet

The applet is complete. Figure 3-54 on the next page displays the code for the entire program with brackets matching the beginning and closing braces of each block. Perform the following steps to compile and execute the applet.

```
/*
    Project 3:      Making Decision
    Programmer:     Joy Starks
    Date:           November 2, 2001
    Program Name:   CandleApplet
*/

import java.awt.*;
import java.applet.*;
import java.awt.event.*;

public class CandleApplet extends Applet implements ItemListener
{
    //Create components for applet
    Label companyNameLabel = new Label ("CandleLine--Candles Online");

    Label priceLabel = new Label ("Please enter the total dollar amount of your order:");
        TextField priceField = new TextField(35);

    Label shippingLabel = new Label ("Please choose your method of shipping:");

    CheckboxGroup shippingGroup = new CheckboxGroup();
        Checkbox oneDayBox = new Checkbox("Priority (Overnight)",false,shippingGroup);
        Checkbox twoDayBox = new Checkbox("Express (2 business days)",false,shippingGroup);
        Checkbox moreDaysBox = new Checkbox("Standard (3 to 7 business days)",false,shippingGroup);
        Checkbox hiddenBox = new Checkbox("",true,shippingGroup);

    Label outputLabel = new Label("We guarantee on time delivery, or your money back.");

    public void init()
    {
        //Add components to window and set colors
        setBackground(Color.cyan);
        add(companyNameLabel);
        add(priceLabel);
        add(priceField);
            priceField.requestFocus();
        add(shippingLabel);
        add(oneDayBox);
            oneDayBox.addItemListener(this);
        add(twoDayBox);
            twoDayBox.addItemListener(this);
        add(moreDaysBox);
            moreDaysBox.addItemListener(this);
        add(outputLabel);
    }

    public void itemStateChanged(ItemEvent choice)
    {
        try
        {
            double shipping;
            double price = Double.parseDouble(priceField.getText());

            //Check to see if price is greater than zero
            if (price <= 0) throw new NumberFormatException();

            //Check to see which option button is selected
            if (oneDayBox.getState())
                shipping = 14.95;
            else
            if (twoDayBox.getState())
                shipping = 11.95;
              else
                if (price>75)
                    shipping = 0;
                else
                    shipping = 5.95;

            //Display Output
            outputLabel.setForeground(Color.black);
            outputLabel.setText("Your total cost is $" + (price+shipping));
        }

        catch (NumberFormatException e)
        {
            outputLabel.setText("You must enter a dollar amount greater than zero");
            outputLabel.setForeground(Color.red);
            hiddenBox.setState(true);
            priceField.setText("");
            priceField.requestFocus();
        }
    }
}
```

FIGURE 3-54

Steps **To Compile and Execute the Applet**

1 **Click the MS-DOS Prompt button on the taskbar. Type** `javac CandleApplet.java` **to compile the program. If errors occur, fix them in the Notepad window, save, and then recompile. Type** `appletviewer CandleApplet.html` **and then press the ENTER key.**

Applet Viewer displays the CandleApplet (Figure 3-55). Notice the insertion point displays in the text field due to the requestFocus method statement.

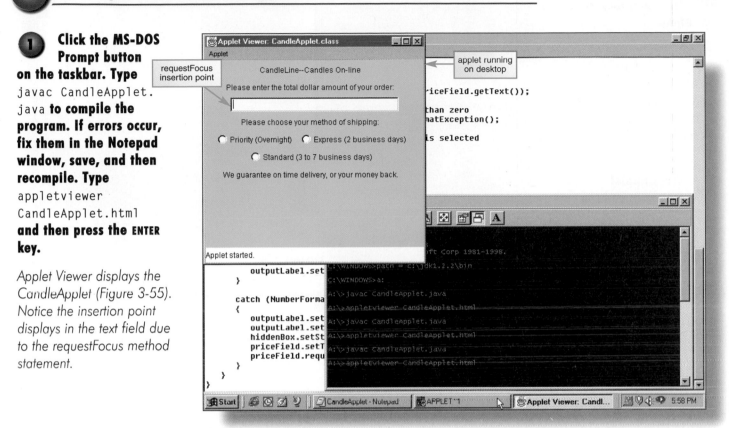

FIGURE 3-55

2 **Type** `forty-three` **in the text field. Click any of the options.**

The itemStateChanged event occurs (Figure 3-56). The alphabetic value created a number format exception, which then called the catch block. Notice the error message in red.

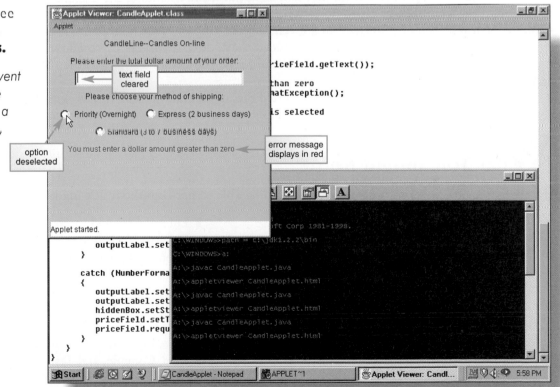

FIGURE 3-56

3 Type 43 **in the text field and then click any option.**

The valid number caused the try block to finish without calling catch, so a total charge displays (Figure 3-57). You may test other values and shipping options.

4 **Close Applet Viewer, Notepad, and the MS-DOS Prompt window by clicking the respective Close buttons on the title bars.**

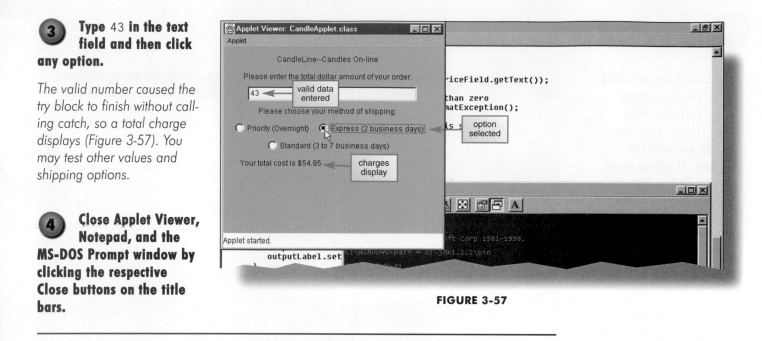

FIGURE 3-57

You also may run the applet using a browser. Simply type the complete path of the host document, a:\CandleApplet.html, in the Address or Location text box of the browser.

Project Summary

This project presented a series of steps and a discussion of a Java application to calculate shipping charges for an e-commerce site. You first coded the standalone application, including the try and catch blocks to handle possible exceptions. You used an if structure to test for valid prices. You created a user-defined method, called from main, to obtain a menu option within a given range. Using the switch structure, you calculated a shipping charge based on user input. Finally, you included the code in a while loop to allow users to try again, in case they enter inaccurate data. At each step of the process, you coded a stub and then tested small sections of code before moving on to the next component.

In the last part of the project, you converted the application into an applet with check boxes. You set the focus, changed the color, and instantiated a check box grouping for a mutually exclusive choice.

What You Should Know

Having completed this project, you now should be able to perform the following tasks:

▶ Code and Test the if Statement *(J 3.24)*
▶ Code the Applet Stub *(J 3.45)*
▶ Code the init Method *(J 3.50)*
▶ Code the switch Structure *(J 3.36)*
▶ Compile and Execute the Applet *(J 3.55)*
▶ Compile the Applet and Test the Check Box Grouping *(J 3.51)*
▶ Construct Components *(J 3.48)*
▶ Create the Host Document *(J 3.43)*
▶ Enter the Beginning Code *(J 3.10)*
▶ Enter Code for the getCost Method *(J 3.30)*
▶ Enter Output Code *(J 3.33)*

▶ Enter the try and catch Blocks *(J 3.16)*
▶ Enter the try and catch Blocks in the Applet *(J 3.53)*
▶ Loop Using the while Statement *(J 3.38)*
▶ Save, Compile, and Execute the Source Code *(J 3.11)*
▶ Save, Compile, and Test the Applet Stub *(J 3.45)*
▶ Save, Compile, and Test the getCost Method Stub *(J 3.33)*
▶ Save, Compile, and Test the switch Structure *(J 3.37)*
▶ Save, Compile, and Test the while Structure *(J 3.41)*
▶ Set up the Desktop *(J 3.8)*
▶ Test the Program for Exceptions *(J 3.18)*

Test Your Knowledge

1 True/False

Instructions: Circle T if the statement is true or F is the statement is false.

T F 1. Modularity means breaking a large program's source code down into smaller sections.

T F 2. A stub is a program that does not accept user input.

T F 3. Exceptions are non-primitive data types.

T F 4. The finally block can be used to perform an end of processing routine associated with the try and catch blocks.

T F 5. A method is the code used to perform an operation or service.

T F 6. A user-defined method must reside within a program or class.

T F 7. Scope is a data type.

T F 8. An end if command must close each If...Then...Else structure.

T F 9. Check boxes and grouped check boxes display identically in applets.

T F 10. A set of grouped check boxes creates a mutually exclusive group.

2 Multiple Choice

Instructions: Circle the correct response.

1. A control structure is referred to as _____ when it is located completely within another structure.

    a. hidden   b. never executed   c. local in scope   d. nested

2. Statements and commands common to the beginning of interactive programs include all of the following *except*_____.

    a. import statements   b. finally block   c. class and method headers   d. comments

3. Java uses a(n) _____ statement to evaluate a value for the case structure.

    a. scope   b. case   c. switch   d. if

4. An operation that attempts to use a float value in a location declared to be integer, is an example of a(n)

    _____.

    a. number format exception   c. IOException

    b. memory error   d. compile-time exception

5. A(n) _____ check might be used to look for data that fits the program's specifications for a correct data type.

    a. exception   b. reasonableness   c. range   d. validity

6. Conditions in Java are _____ expressions that evaluate to true or false.

    a. untested   b. boolean   c. variable   d. iterative

7. The control structure that allows for more than two choices when a condition is evaluated is called a(n)

    _____.

    a. case   b. if   c. try   d. while

8. Which of the following is not a conditional operator?

    a. &&   b. >   c. || d. *

(continued)

Test Your Knowledge

Multiple Choice *(continued)*

9. A hidden check box in a grouped set _____.
   a. can be used to clear others in the mutually exclusive set
   b. can receive the focus and be selected
   c. uses a constructor like other check boxes
   d. all of the above

10. When a check box is selected, the _____ method is called.
    a. itemStateChanged   b. click   c. add   d. listen

3 Understanding Applet Components

Instructions: In Figure 3-58, arrows point to components of a Java applet running on the desktop. Identify the various components of the applet in the spaces provided.

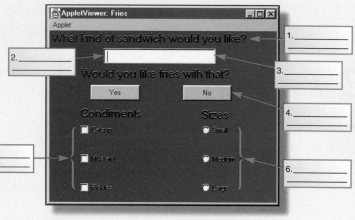

FIGURE 3-58

4 Understanding Conditions

Instructions: Study the following conditions and determine whether they evaluate to true or false. In those examples that display more than one condition, tell which condition confirms the true or false state.

1. $25 == 25$ _____
2. $(18 < 19)$ && $(12 > 14)$ _____
3. $(18 < 19)$ || $(12 > 14)$ _____
4. $31 <= 31$ _____
5. $!(5 == 5)$ _____
6. $(a == a)$ || $(b == b)$ || $(c == c)$ _____
7. $!((14 > 12)$ && $(27 => 26))$ _____
8. $(45 < 55)$ && $(55 > 45)$ _____
9. $(100 + 5) != (40 + 65)$ _____
10. $(a == a)$ || $!(a == a)$ _____

Apply Your Knowledge

1 Multiplication Quiz

Instructions: Start Notepad and maximize the window, if necessary. Open the file Apply3.java, from the Data Disk (see the inside back cover for instructions on how to obtain a copy of the Data Disk). This Multiplication Quiz asks students to enter the multiplication table they wish to practice and then prompts them for each answer, multiplying their table value by each integer from 0 to 12. Although the program tells students whether they are right or wrong, it does not provide error checking for invalid entries such as typing errors, decimals, or strings.

Using techniques learned in this project, write the try and catch blocks to display appropriate messages if students try to enter non-integer numbers. Also write a while loop to keep repeating the prompt if the students enter invalid values. Figure 3-59 displays the completed program during execution.

FIGURE 3-59

1. With the Apply3.java code displayed in the Notepad window, substitute your name and date in the block comment at the beginning. Type `Multiply` as the new class name. Edit the name of the class in the class header, as well.

2. Save the file on your floppy disk with the name, "Multiply.java" as the file name. Print a copy if you wish, to reference while completing this lab.

3. Open the MS DOS Prompt window. If you downloaded JDK from the Sun Web site, set the path to the location of your Java bin by typing `path=c:\jdk1.2.2\bin` at the command prompt and press the ENTER key. If you installed the Java compiler from the JBuilder3 CD-ROM that may accompany this text, type `path=c:\jbuilder3\java\bin` and then press the ENTER key.

4. Change to your floppy disk drive by typing `a:` and then press the ENTER key.

5. Compile your program by typing `javac Multiply.java` and then press the ENTER key.

6. Run the program by typing `java Multiply` and then press the ENTER key. As the program executes, enter an integer for the multiplication table value, such as 8. Respond to the prompts with whole numbers.

7. Now run the program again, but enter a non-integer value for the multiplication table value, such as 7.5. Java throws an exception, and you will receive a NumberFormatException message.

8. Click the Notepad window. In the main method, enclose the section of code labeled, //Calling the user-defined methods, in a try block. Remember to enter the try statement and an opening brace before the section and a closing brace after that section.

(continued)

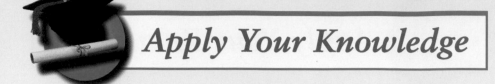

Apply Your Knowledge

Multiplication Quiz *(continued)*

9. Below the try block, enter a catch block for a NumberFormatException as follows:

```
catch(NumberFormatException e)
{
    System.out.println("I'm sorry, you may enter only whole numbers");
}
```

10. Save the file by clicking File on Notepad's menu bar and then click Save.

11. Click the MS-DOS Prompt button on the taskbar and then compile the program again with the javac command. If necessary, fix any errors in the Notepad window, save, and then recompile.

12. Run the program again, testing with both integer and non-integer values. Notice that an appropriate message now displays, but students still must run the program again to answer any additional questions.

13. Click the Notepad window and enclose both the try and catch blocks in a while loop by entering while(!done) and an opening brace before the section of code and a closing brace after that section.

14. Before the closing brace of the try block, enter a new line of code, done = true; to terminate the loop during execution. Save the file by clicking File on Notepad's menu bar and then click Save.

15. In the MS-DOS Prompt window, compile and run the program again, testing with both integer and non-integer values. Notice that students now are directed back to the beginning of the program after the message displays.

16. Click the Notepad window. In the takeQuiz method, find the statement, while (count <= 12). Click below the while block's opening brace. Enclose all the code within the while block in a try block. Include all the code statements in the try block, but not the opening or closing braces of the while block itself. The last inclusive line in the new try block will be: count = count + 1;

17. Below the try block, enter a catch block for a NumberFormatException as follows:

```
catch(NumberFormatException e)
{
    System.out.println("I'm sorry, your answer must be a whole number. Try again.");
}
```

18. Save the file by clicking File on Notepad's menu bar and then click Save.

19. In the MS-DOS Prompt window, compile and run the program again, testing with both integer and non-integer values. Students now are given a chance to answer the question again after the message displays.

20. Print a copy of your code for your instructor.

In the Lab

1 Using switch and try Blocks to Validate User Input

Problem: You would like to write a program to help beginning Java programmers understand data types. You have noticed that students have trouble differentiating among doubles, ints, strings, and other data types. You decide to create a menu-driven program to test their knowledge. Beginning with a try block, the program should allow users to choose a data type. Then, based on a switch structure, the user should be prompted to enter a value that would fit that specific data type. If the user enters correct data — data that parses correctly — the

program should display positive feedback. If the inputted data does not match the chosen data type, the parse statement will throw a NumberFormatException. In the catch block, the program should display an appropriate error message, and then allow the user to try again. A sample menu of choices displays in Figure 3-60.

```
JAVA
 Tᴛ  7 x 11  ▾   ▢ ▣ ▣   ▣ ▣  A
A:\>java Menu

        What's My Type?

    1) String
    2) Int
    3) Double
    4) Quit the program
```

FIGURE 3-60

Instructions:

1. Start Notepad.
2. Enter general documentation comments, including the name of this lab, your name, the date, and the file name, Menu.
3. Import the java.io.* package.
4. Type public class Menu and an opening brace to begin the class.
5. Type public static void main(String[] args) throws IOException and an opening brace to begin main.
6. Declare the following variables:

   BufferedReader dataIn = new BufferedReader(new InputStreamReader(System.in));
   String strChoice, strTryString, strTryInt, strTryDouble;
   int choice, tryInt;
   double tryDouble;
   boolean done = false;

7. Begin a while(!done) loop to repeat as long as the user does not enter the menu choice to quit.
8. Inside a try block, type System.out.println commands to print a menu with four choices, as shown in Figure 3-60.
9. Type strChoice = dataIn.readLine(); to allow user input. To parse the choice, type choice = Integer.parseInteger(strChoice); on the next line.
10. Create a switch structure to test for each of the four choices. Type the header, switch(choice) and then press the ENTER key. Type an opening brace.

(continued)

In the Lab

Using switch and try Blocks to Validate User Input *(continued)*

11. Create each case, using pages J 3.35 through J 3.37 as a guide for the switch, case and break statements.

   ▶ Case 1: Prompt the user for a string. Read the input as strTryString. Display a message that informs users they are correct, as *any* input can be saved as a string. Enter the break statement.

   ▶ Case 2: Create a try block that prompts the user for an int value. Read the input as strTryInt. Parse the value into tryInt. Display a message that informs users they are correct. Enter the break statement.

   ▶ Case 3: Create a try block that prompts the user for a double value. Read the input as strTryDouble. Parse the value into tryDouble. Display a message that informs users they are correct. Enter the break statement.

   ▶ Case 4: Set done equal to true. Display a closing message. Enter the break statement.

   ▶ Case default: Throw a new NumberFormatException

12. Close the switch block with a closing brace.

13. Create a catch block by typing, catch(NumberFormatException e) and then an opening brace.

14. Display an appropriate message directing the user to try again and then close the catch block with a closing brace.

15. Close the try block, the while block, and the main method with closing braces.

16. Save the file as "Menu.java" on your floppy disk.

17. Open the MS-DOS Prompt, set the path, and log onto drive A.

18. Compile the program. If necessary, fix any errors in the Notepad window, save, and then recompile.

19. Run the program. Enter various values for each menu choice. Check your answers.

20. Print a copy of the source code for your instructor.

21. As an extra credit assignment, add choices to the menu for longs, bytes, and boolean data types.

2 Writing User-Defined Methods

Problem: A small proprietary school that offers distance-learning courses would like an application that calculates total tuition and fees for their students. Users will input the number of hours and the program should calculate the total cost. Cost per credit hour for full time (greater than 15 hours) is $44.50 per credit hour; 15 hours or less costs $50.00 per credit hour.

Instructions:

1. Start Notepad.

2. Enter general documentation comments, including the name of this lab, your name, the date, and the file name, Tuition.

3. Import the java.io.* package.

4. Create a header for the public class, Tuition, followed by an opening brace.

5. Enter the standard main method header, which throws an IOException. Type the opening brace for the main header.

6. Declare an int identifier, hours. Declare double identifiers for fees, rates, and tuition.

In the Lab

7. Enter the following method calls and then close the main method with a closing brace.

```
displayWelcome();
hours = getHours();
rate = getRate(hours);
tuition = calcTuition(hours, rate);
fees = calcFees(tuition);
displayTotal(tuition+fees);
```

8. Code the corresponding methods:

   ▶ Type `public static void displayWelcome()` and then, within that block, code the statements to display a welcome message.

   ▶ Type `public static int getHours() throws IOException` and then, within that block, construct an instance of the BufferedReader. Declare strHours as a String and hours as an int, setting hours to an initial value of zero. Display a prompt that allows the user to enter a string value, strHours, for the total number of hours. Parse that value into the integer value, hours. This method also should include a try and catch block for non-integer input. This method will return the int, hours to main.

   ▶ Type `public static double getRate(int hours)` and then, within that block, include an if statement for hours greater than 15, which will calculate a rate per credit hour. This method will return the double, rate to main.

   ▶ Type `public static double calcTuition(int hours, double rate)` and then, within that block, code statements to accept two values, multiply them, and return a double value, tuition to main.

   ▶ Type `public static double calcFees(double tuition)` and then, within that block, code statements to accept the double value, tuition, multiply it by .08, and then return a double value, fees to main.

   ▶ Type `public static void displayTotal(double total)` and then, within that block use the System.out.println method to display the value passed by adding tuition and fees, along with a closing message.

9. Save the file as "Tuition.java" on your floppy disk.

10. Open the MS-DOS Prompt window, set the path, and log onto drive A.

11. Compile the program. If necessary, fix any errors in the Notepad window, save, and then recompile.

12. Run the program. Enter values both less than and greater than 15. Check your answers.

13. Print a copy of the source code for your instructor.

In the Lab

3 Creating an Applet with Check Boxes

Problem: Figure 3-58 on page J 3.58 displays an interface for an applet relating to fast food. Using the techniques you learned in Project 3, create the interface with all its components. Add enough functionality to make the selection of both grouped and individual check boxes work. The text field should receive the focus and allow data entry, but the itemStateChanged event may contain just a stub.

Instructions:

1. Start Notepad.
2. Enter general documentation comments, including the name of this lab, your name, the date, and the file name: FriesApplet.
3. Import the following packages: java.awt.*, java.applet.*, and java.awt.event.*. Remember to use the import statement and conclude each line with a semicolon.
4. Enter a public class header for Fries that extends Applet and implements ItemListener.
5. Create the components as shown in Figure 3-58 on page J 3.58, using a constructor for each: sandwichPromptLabel, sandwichInputField, friesPromptLabel, yesButton, noButton, condimentsLabel, sizesLabel, catsupBox, mustardBox, picklesBox, sizesGroup, smallBox, mediumBox, largeBox. Set the length of sandwichInputField to 25. The grouped check boxes represent the sizes, and the condiments are individual check boxes. Set all the condiment check boxes to false. Set the first of the grouped check boxes to true and the other sizes to false.
6. Create an init method by typing `public void init()` as the header and an opening brace.
7. Set the background color to red.
8. Enter add methods for each of the components created in Step 5. Use the requestFocus method to create an insertion point in the text field. Use an addItemListener(this) for each of the boxes and buttons. Type the closing brace for the init method.
9. Type `public void itemStateChanged(ItemEvent choice)` as the header for another method. Type an opening brace and closing brace to stub in the event.
10. Save the file as "FriesApplet.java" on your floppy disk.
11. Click New on Notepad's File menu and then enter the HTML code to display the applet. Be sure to include the beginning and ending HTML and APPLET tags. Use a width of 350 and a height of 300.
12. Save the file as "FriesApplet.html" on your floppy disk.
13. Open the MS-DOS Prompt window and set the path. Log onto drive A.
14. Compile your program by typing `javac FriesApplet.java` at the command prompt. Remember that Java is case-sensitive with respect to file names.
15. If no compilation errors occur, execute the applet by typing `appletviewer FriesApplet.html` at the command prompt. Click each of the buttons and boxes. Notice the check boxes toggle on and off, individually, while the grouped check boxes are mutually exclusive.
16. Print a copy of the source code for your instructor.
17. As an extra credit assignment, code the itemStateChanged event.

Cases and Places

1 ▶ You are serving an internship with the traffic court in the city where you live. The clerks in the traffic court office want a simple application that will allow them to enter the actual speed limit, the speed at which the offender was traveling, and the number of previous tickets that person has received. The application should have a menu system to allow users to exit the application, begin again, and calculate charges. The application should calculate and display how many miles over the speed limit the offender was traveling, the cost of the speeding ticket, and court costs. Use $10.00 as the amount to be charged for each mile per hour over the speed limit. The court cost should begin at $53.20 and increase by $20.00 for each subsequent offense up to the third offense (that will represent the maximum court cost).

2 ▶ Lions, Tigers, and Bears is a pet clinic with several locations. The office manager has asked you to create an applet that could run from a browser at all the offices. The applet should be designed with individual check boxes to select the various services such as office visits, vaccinations, hospitalization, heartworm prevention, boarding, dentistry, x-rays, laboratory work, and prescriptions. As each service is selected, the charge for the service should display . After all selections have been made, the charges should be added together to arrive at a total amount due and display when a command button is clicked. The office manager also would like to clear all the check boxes for the next customer.

3 ▶▶ You have been asked to develop an interactive applet that will run on a kiosk at the planetarium. The applet is to display the planet names with individual check boxes, and their gravities. Then, based on a grouped check box selection, the distance of the planet to the sun or distance of the planet to the earth should display beside the checked planet.

4 ▶▶ Reasonable Computers Corporation would like an applet to calculate the cost of adding peripherals to their basic PC system. Use at least six single check boxes for various types of peripheral devices including printers, monitors, modems, or other devices with which you are familiar. Assume a basic system price of $500 and then add appropriate prices based on user checks. Create a button to perform the calculation and display the final price.

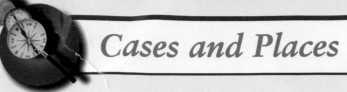

Cases and Places

5 ▶▶▶ Wright's Garage wants an interactive program that requires the mechanic to enter the tire pressure from four tires on any given car that comes into the garage. The program should first print out a menu for driving types: normal, hauling, and rugged. After the mechanic chooses a driving type, the program should ask for the four tire pressures with appropriate prompts. Finally, the program should tell the mechanic what adjustments to make. Assume the following:

▶ For normal driving, all four tires should be inflated between 33 and 43 pounds per square inch (psi).
▶ For hauling, the rear tires should be approximately 10% greater.
▶ For rugged terrain, the rear tires should be approximately 15% greater.

6 ▶▶▶ Your city library has hired you on a consulting basis to provide them with an application for overdue charges. The charges apply to overdue books, records, tapes, CDs, and videotapes. The books can be either hardbound or paperback. The librarians want an easy way to calculate the overdue charges, keeping in mind that a borrower could be returning multiple overdue items. Some method of looping to enter the next item is necessary. The total number of overdue items and the total amount due should display.

Java Programming

Java Programming

PROJECT

4

External Classes, Arrays, and Choices

You will have mastered the material in this project when you can:

- Create and implement a programmer-defined data type
- Describe forms of access between classes
- Construct a method to initialize instance variables
- Create an instance method
- Declare and construct an array
- Use correct array notation
- Reference array elements and subscript numbers
- Differentiate between an array of primitive data types and an object array
- Create a user-defined method
- Code a measured loop using the for statement
- Employ assignment and unary operators
- Use increment and decrement operators
- Discuss the general types of sorting algorithms
- Use a sort routine to sort array data
- Compare strings using the compareTo method
- Add a Choice component to an applet
- Retrieve data from fields using the getText and getSelectedItem methods
- Convert floats to Strings using the valueOf method
- Reset Choice components using the select method

Weather or Not

TWC Helps Ride Out the Storm

If you think you would find a Fujita-Pearson Scale in the produce department of your local supermarket and that nephelococcygia is a new rock band at your school, perhaps a visit to The Weather Channel (TWC) Web site (weather.com) would be of interest.

Millions of Internet users flock to this site, which they affectionately call TWC. It has become the 30th most popular site on the Internet with more than 130 million hits per month, and it constantly receives rave reviews for being one of the top five Internet news content sites.

Although more than 10,000 weather pages exist on the Web, TWC is one of the few offering free information 24/7. The site contains current conditions and five-day forecasts for more than 1,700 cities worldwide, maps, weather-related news, a customizable home page, flight information, and educational resources.

One of these tools is a weather glossary containing more than 800 definitions, including the Fujita-Pearson Scale, which classifies the intensity of wind damage and usually is used in the wake of tornadoes. A nephelococcygia is a person who finds familiar objects within the shape of a cloud.

Another impressive feature of the site is local and regional radar. Weather aficionados can select one of three infrared satellite pictures — local Doppler radar, regional Doppler radar, and regional satellite — to study the current cloud cover and precipitation intensity.

Of particular interest are the time-lapse loops showing the progression of storms and fronts during the past few hours. These loops are constructed using Java applets, which capture six consecutive radar images stored in approximately 15-minute increments and then display this sequence to create a moving picture.

In this Java project, you likewise will work with data of the same type that has been organized and stored when you build an application that automates performance summaries of students competing in National Forensics League tournaments. In

addition, you will convert this application into an applet so that users will be able to choose among several categories to enter debate tournament scores.

Landmark Communications, Inc. owns the Web site along with the cable television network with the same name, which is seen in more than 72 million U.S. homes and reaches more than 30 countries worldwide. TWC was launched in Atlanta in 1982, and it is one of the more profitable cable networks. It employs more than 80 full-time meteorologists, and some of its on-air weather personalities have become popular media figures.

Other The Weather Channel features are its interactive telephone service, wireless weather products accessible through PalmPilots™, telephones, pagers, and other personal digital assistants, The Weather Channel Radio Network, which provides local forecasts and severe weather warnings in more than 250 radio markets, and The Weather Channel Newspaper Services.

So the next time you are wondering if the weather is going to cooperate with your outdoor plans, log on to TWC. You might just find a ray of sunshine to brighten your day.

Java Programming

External Classes, Arrays, and Choices

PROJECT

4

Donna Reneau is president of the college chapter of the National Forensics League at Midland University. The chapter consistently has maintained a fine record in competition at intercollegiate forensics tournaments in the Midwest. Donna's chapter specializes in debate tournaments where students are given scores from 1 to 5, in categories such as content organization and delivery, with 1 being the best score. Each debater then is ranked among all competitors in the competition.

Because the debate team tours schools with a variety of computer platforms and Web access, Donna believes that a Java program might be the best way to automate performance summaries at these tournaments. Donna knows of your interest in Java and has asked you to build an application she can use to enter individual scores, average the categories, and calculate an overall team performance score. Once data is entered, the program then will display the averages and overall scores.

You also decide to try your hand at converting the application into an applet with a drop-down list for each of the categories.

Introduction

One of the most powerful features of Java and most modern programming languages is the ability to store more than single variables in memory. Storing a single value and then manipulating it is useful for some applications, but many times a program must deal with a large amount of data. Manipulating large numbers of variables with individual identifiers is cumbersome and tedious. Users need to summarize, search, and select data based on some criteria. Fortunately, data can be organized and processed systematically. Java uses **arrays**, or data lists, that employ a single, but inclusive, storage location to hold data of the same type with the same name. Arrays are useful for organizing and storing data. Arrays use one identifier to refer to a collection of elements. Like object variables, Java array variables are references to the array location in memory.

In previous projects, you have displayed small amounts of information on the screen, usually in some logical order based on user input or need. As you use arrays and manipulate larger amounts of data, it may become necessary to **sort**, or order, the data before displaying it. Obviously, data displayed in no specific order is hard to read and understand, as well as being difficult to search and select. Many software application programs, such as spreadsheets and databases, offer routines and GUI interfaces for sorting, available at the click of a button. In this project, you will look at the code behind a sorting algorithm and then use it to sort an array of names and associated data.

In this project, you also will learn about a new applet component called the Choice component. Similar to a drop-down list, the Choice component also stores data as elements with subscripts. It commonly is used to create a set of predetermined choices from which the user will select. When you convert the application to an applet, you will see the advantage of giving users a choice, which not only makes the program more user-friendly, but also prevents data entry errors.

Project Four — Donna's Debate Tournament Scores

ANALYZING THE PROBLEM A computer program is required that will allow the user to enter individual names and scores from a debate tournament and then average the categories of content, delivery, organization and rank for each individual. The program then should calculate an overall team performance score.

Figure 4-1a displays the program as an application with results from sample data. Figure 4-1b displays the program as an applet.

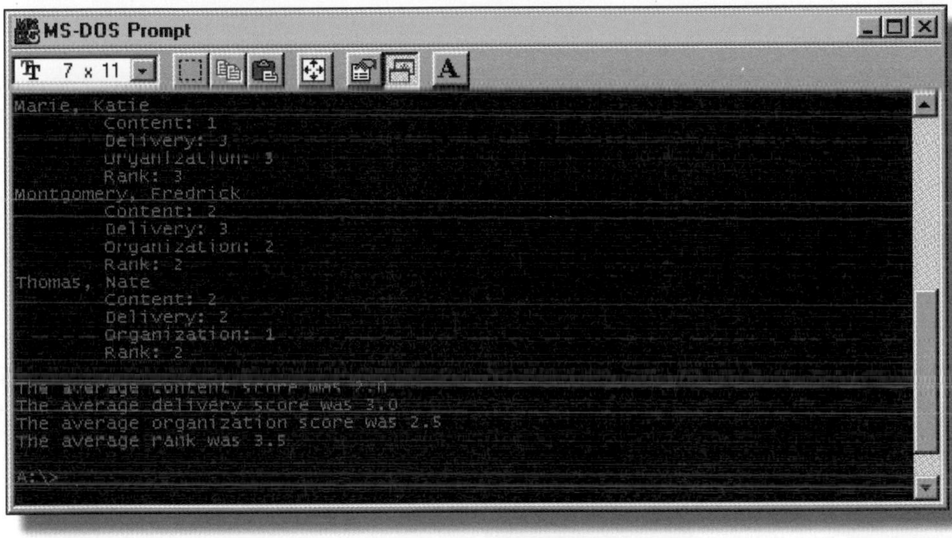

(a) Java Application

(b) Java Applet

FIGURE 4-1

DESIGNING THE PROGRAM The program will include creating a user-defined structure to hold information about each person on the debate team. Fields need to be created to hold the person's first name, last name, and the individual scores for content, delivery, organization, and rank. Once that data structure is in place, you will need to establish methods to access each piece of data. Figure 4-2 displays an object structure diagram for the Person structure.

Person
firstName lastName content delivery organization rank
instantiation methods getFirstName getLastName getContent getDelivery getOrganization getRank

FIGURE 4-2

Figure 4-3 displays a main processing module flowchart representing the major tasks of the application. The Person structure will be created in its own class. A second class, named Donna, will act as the driver class that provides the ability for data entry, sorting, and displaying results. A **driver class** is the term used to specify the main program that calls other classes.

The Donna program will use a repetition control structure to construct multiple Person instances. You may recall that a repetition control structure is a logical way to write code that instructs the computer to perform a set of actions over and over again. You will use the repetition structure to allow data entry of multiple records. Within that data entry loop, the steps will be sequential in nature, allowing the user to enter data that will be stored in an array. Once all the data is entered, the array will be sorted. A second loop then will display the data in alphabetical order by last name and calculate and display averages.

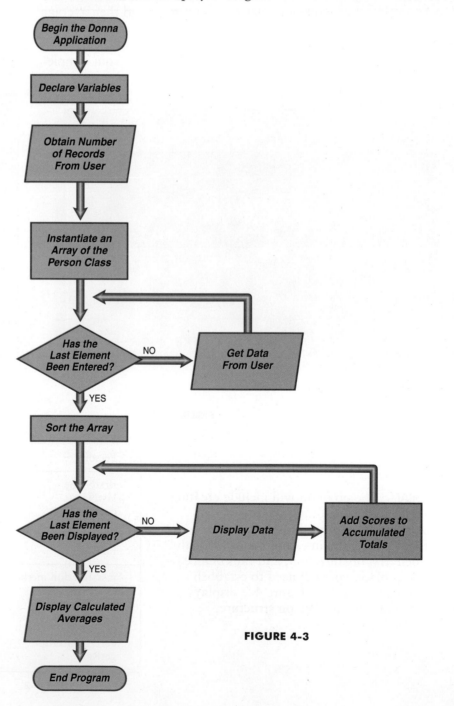

FIGURE 4-3

CODING THE PROGRAM You will create Java source code using the syntax and commands of the Java programming language. The application will use an external class to create an instance of each Person to store in an object array.

TESTING THE PROGRAM You will create, debug, and execute the program as a Java application. In this project, you will test the external class by calling it from the main class. You then will compile and run the program with sample data. Finally, you will test the applet version of the program using Applet Viewer.

FORMALIZING THE SOLUTION You will review the source code, use proper documentation, edit, recompile, and execute the application with sample data.

MAINTAINING THE PROGRAM You will modify the program to run as an applet using the Choice component for drop-down lists.

Starting A New Java Program

Before starting a new Java program, you should set up the Windows desktop by starting Notepad and opening the MS-DOS Prompt window. Figure 4-4 displays a typical desktop configuration. The desktop displays the Notepad window maximized and the MS-DOS Prompt window in the lower-right portion of the screen. The user has set the path and changed to drive A. If you are using JBuilder3, your path will differ.

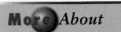

More About

Versions of the JDK

The release of J2SE version 1.3 promises to deliver substantial gains in performance and improved Web deployment for enterprise-grade, client-side applets, and applications written in the Java programming language. To download the latest version, visit the Java Programming Web Page (www.scsite.com/java/more.htm) and then click Downloading the JDK.

Notepad window maximized

MS-DOS Prompt window

path statement

changed to drive A

```
Microsoft(R) Windows 98
    (C)Copyright Microsoft Corp 1981-1998.

C:\WINDOWS>path = c:\jdk1.2.2\bin

C:\WINDOWS>a:

A:\>_
```

FIGURE 4-4

Creating the Person Class

The application in this project uses two classes. The Person class will contain the constructors and methods to create a single instance of a Person and their scores. The Donna class will contain the main method and calculations to allow the debate team president to enter scores and obtain averages. Separating these two processes into two different classes promotes reusability of the Person class for multiple applications. For example, Donna later may want to create an application to save all scores to an external data file. The new application also could call and use the Person class. Classes may call each other and use each other's public methods. A class or method that is not part of the running driver class is called an **external class**.

Entering Beginning Code for the Person Class

The Person class implements a **programmer-defined type**, which means that the programmer combines fields and data types to create a new data type. In the Person class, you first will assign a name to the class and then you will determine what data and methods will be part of the class.

The name of the class will be Person. The data will include pieces of information about each student participating in the debate tournament: firstName, lastName, content, delivery, organization, and rank. Table 4-1 displays the code for the comments, import statement, class header, and declarations. Notice in line 10 the class header contains only the access modifier, public; the keyword, class; and the identifier, Person.

Perform the following steps to enter the beginning code.

Table 4-1

LINE	CODE
1	`/*`
2	`    Project 4        Arrays`
3	`    Programmer:      Joy Starks`
4	`    Date:            December 12, 2001`
5	`    Program Name:    Person`
6	`*/`
7	
8	`import java.io.*;`
9	
10	`public class Person`
11	`{`
12	`    String firstName;`
13	`    String lastName;`
14	`    int content;`
15	`    int delivery;`
16	`    int organization;`
17	`    int rank;`
18	`}`

TO ENTER BEGINNING CODE

1 Start Notepad and maximize the Notepad window, if necessary.

2 Type the code as displayed in Table 4-1. Use your own name and the current date in lines 3 and 4.

3 With a floppy disk in drive A, click File on the Notepad menu bar and then click Save.

4 When the Save As dialog box displays, type "Person.java" in the File name text box. You must type the quotation marks around the file name.

5 Click the Save in box arrow and then click 3½ Floppy (A:) in the Save in list.

6 Click the Save button.

The Notepad window displays the name of the file on its title bar (Figure 4-5).

name of
file

```
/*
    Project 4        Arrays
    Programmer:      Joy Starks
    Date:            December 12, 2001          block
    Program Name:    Person                     comments
*/

import java.io.*;

public class Person          line 10
{
    String firstName;
    String lastName;
    int content;
    int delivery;
    int organization;
    int rank;
}
```

FIGURE 4-5

In line 10, the class, Person, was declared public. **Public classes** are accessible by all objects, which means that public classes can be **extended**, or used, as a basis for any other class. **Public access** is the most liberal form of access, which means that any other class may call it. If you develop a viable Person class, you can use it to extend additional, more specific classes, which keeps you from having to start over from scratch. Each new class can become an extension of the original Person class, inheriting its data and methods. Other modifiers, such as final or abstract, impose at least some limitation on extensibility. You will use the public access modifier for most of your classes.

Constructing an Instance

Declaring identifiers or variables in the class, actually does not create the Person object. A class is just an abstract description of what an object will be like if any objects ever are instantiated, or created. This kind of class definition is like a blueprint for the object. Just as you might understand all the characteristics of an item you intend to manufacture long before the first one rolls off the assembly line, you create a class before you create a working instance of that class.

Recall that an instance is a unique object or a specific occurrence of a class of objects. You can think of an instance as a proper noun. For example, the word, boy, is a noun; but the word, John, is a proper noun. John defines which boy you are talking about. In Java, listing the field declarations is similar to saying there is going to be a boy. Using a method, you then must state which boy (John). The resulting method, which creates a working instance by defining the components, becomes a constructor in Java. A **constructor method** initializes the instance variables.

Public Classes

Public is the most common class access modifier. A class declared without the public modifier has package visibility, meaning that it is visible only in its own package. Java provides these mechanisms for access control to prevent the users of a package or class from depending on unnecessary details of the implementation of that package or class.

Constructor Methods

Whether you call it a constructor method or a method constructor, it simply means that you are enabling the program to create and initialize objects. These special methods always have the same name as the class, and never have a return value. The arguments or parameters they accept may vary, however.

More About

Default Constructors

A constructor without any arguments or parameters is a default constructor. Java will create a default constructor if the programmer does not create any constructors for the class. If the programmer does create a constructor, even with one or more parameters, the compiler will not create a zero-argument (default) constructor.

A constructor method for a data type begins with an access modifier, followed by the identifier. Even though the constructor method seems to return no specified value, it does return an initialized object of the class type.

Table 4-2 lists the code to create a constructor method within the Person class. The method header in line 19 has the same name as the class, including six parameters. In this case, **parameters** are the values passed to the method from the point of the call. Many Java programmers use a single letter identifier in constructor method parameters.

Table 4-2	
LINE	**CODE**
19	`public Person(String f, String l, int c, int d, int o, int r)`
20	`{`
21	`    firstName = f;`
22	`    lastName = l;`
23	`    content = c;`
24	`    delivery = d;`
25	`    organization = o;`
26	`    rank = r;`
27	`}`

Lines 21 through 26 assign the parameter values to identifiers that are local to the constructor method. Local variables exist for use by the method and do not persist after the method code is exited.

Perform the following steps to enter the method constructor.

 **To Enter the Method Constructor**

1 **Click to position the insertion point at the end of line 17 and press the ENTER key twice.**

The new constructor method will be entered within the Person class, after the declarations (Figure 4-6). A blank line between these sections makes the program easier to read.

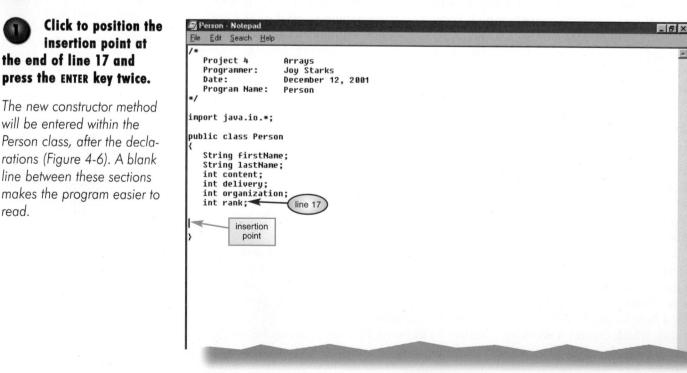

FIGURE 4-6

2 **Enter the code from Table 4-2 using proper indentation.**

The constructor method displays as entered (Figure 4-7).

3 **Click File on the Notepad menu bar and then click Save.**

The program saves in the same location with the same file name.

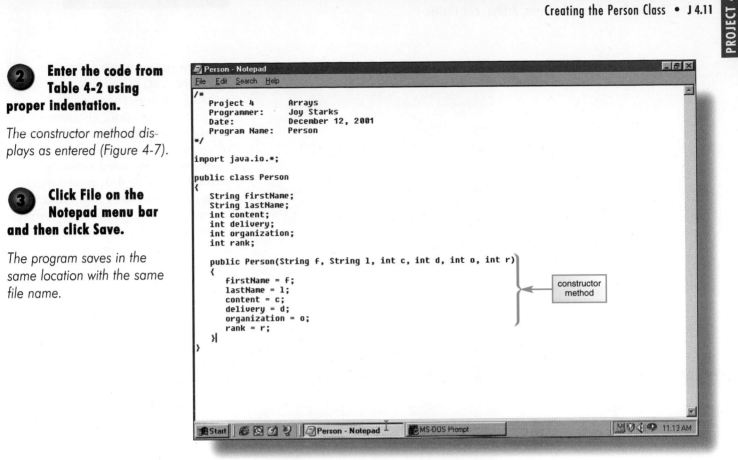

```
/*
    Project 4         Arrays
    Programmer:       Joy Starks
    Date:             December 12, 2001
    Program Name:     Person
*/

import java.io.*;

public class Person
{
    String firstName;
    String lastName;
    int content;
    int delivery;
    int organization;
    int rank;

    public Person(String f, String 1, int c, int d, int o, int r)
    {
        firstName = f;
        lastName = 1;
        content = c;
        delivery = d;
        organization = o;
        rank = r;
    }
}
```

constructor method

FIGURE 4-7

You can create multiple constructors of the same data type, if you anticipate multiple instances of the constructor with different arguments. For example, if you plan to use an instance of the Person class in a different application, one with only a first name and last name and no scores, you can include a second constructor with the same name using a different set of arguments.

```
public Person(String f, String 1)
```

Whether the calling application sends along just two arguments or the complete set, your programmer-defined data type will accept the call. This practice of defining more than one constructor method with the same name is called **method overloading**.

Using Instance Methods

Just as declaring the identifiers did not instantiate the Person class, creating an instance by itself does not provide a means to enter data into that instance — for that, you need a method. Recall that a method is the code used to perform an operation or service and can be thought of as an action verb. A programmer-defined class, such as the Person class, contains instance methods. Every time the Person class is instantiated, a new instance of the method is created as well. For example, an instance method you need for the Person object is a way to retrieve a specific score associated with a specific person.

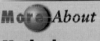

Method Overloading

Overloading means using one word to represent several different concepts. For instance, you use the word close to close a file, close your eyes, and close the door - all are closing actions, but each uses different tools with different results. Most people who understand the English language differentiate the meaning because of the accompanying noun. Method overloading is the same concept. You use the same method name with different parameters to perform a similar but slightly different function. The Java compiler understands the difference based on the number of arguments or parameters you send when you call the method.

Table 4-3

LINE	CODE
29	`public String getFirstName()`
30	`{`
31	`    return firstName;`
32	`}`
33	
34	`public String getLastName()`
35	`{`
36	`    return lastName;`
37	`}`
38	
39	`public int getContent()`
40	`{`
41	`    return content;`
42	`}`
43	
44	`public int getDelivery()`
45	`{`
46	`    return delivery;`
47	`}`
48	
49	`public int getOrganization()`
50	`{`
51	`    return organization;`
52	`}`
53	
54	`public int getRank()`
55	`{`
56	`    return rank;`
57	`}`

Java programmers typically use the word, get, in the title of these sorts of instance methods that retrieve information, also known as **accessor methods**. The word, set, is often used in a method that sets a value, which is called a **mutator method**. In Table 4-3, notice that each of the methods has public access, allowing its use in other programs, and each method returns the data to the calling program. For example, in line 29, public describes the method's access. String describes the return variable's data type, and getFirstName is the method identifier name.

Perform the following steps to enter the instance methods for the Person class.

Steps To Create Instance Methods

1 Click at the end of line 27 and press the ENTER key twice.

The new instance methods will be entered within the Person class, after the declarations (Figure 4-8). A blank line between these sections makes the program easier to read.

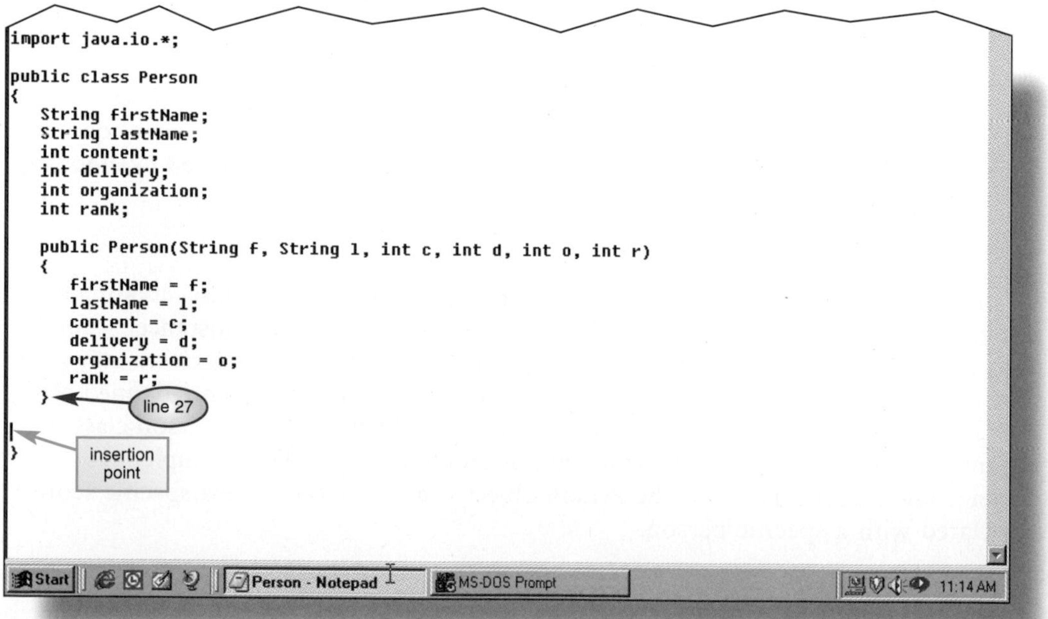

```
import java.io.*;

public class Person
{
    String firstName;
    String lastName;
    int content;
    int delivery;
    int organization;
    int rank;

    public Person(String f, String l, int c, int d, int o, int r)
    {
        firstName = f;
        lastName = l;
        content = c;
        delivery = d;
        organization = o;
        rank = r;
    }                    line 27

I                insertion
}                point
```

FIGURE 4-8

Start | Person - Notepad | MS-DOS Prompt | 11:14 AM

2 **Enter the code from Table 4-3 using proper indentation.**

The instance methods display as entered (Figure 4-9).

3 **Click File on the Notepad menu bar and then click Save.**

The program saves in the same location with the same file name.

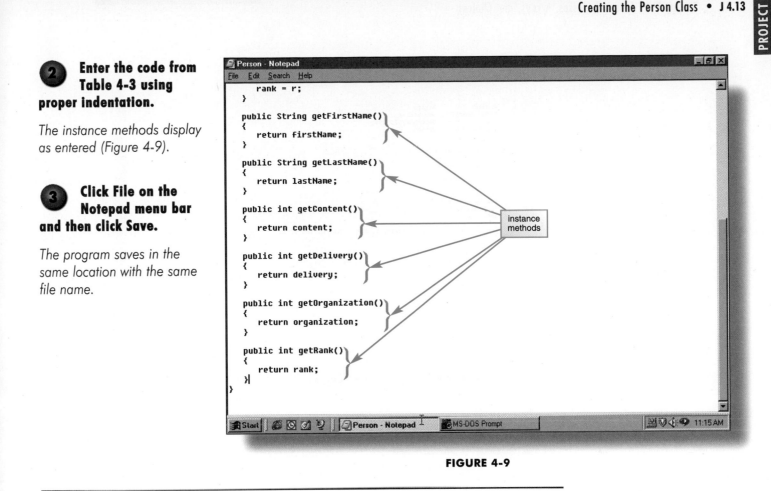

FIGURE 4-9

The Person class is complete. Figure 4-10 on the next page displays the code for the entire class.

Compiling the Source Code

You now are ready to compile the source code. You can print a copy of the code for later reference by clicking Print on the Notepad File menu. Perform the following steps to compile the Person class source code.

TO COMPILE THE PERSON CLASS SOURCE CODE

1 Open the MS-DOS Prompt window or click the MS-DOS Prompt button on the taskbar. If necessary, enter the path statement and log onto drive A. Type javac Person.java and then press the ENTER key to compile the source code.

2 If the Person class contains errors, fix them in the Notepad window, save, and then recompile the program in the MS-DOS Prompt window.

The program compiles (Figure 4-11 on the next page).

```
                                    Person

    /*
        Project 4        Arrays
        Programmer:      Joy Starks
        Date:            December 12, 2001
        Program Name:    Person
    */

    import java.io.*;

    public class Person
    {
        String firstName;
        String lastName;
        int content;
        int delivery;
        int organization;
        int rank;

        public Person(String f, String l, int c, int d, int o, int r)
        {
            firstName = f;
            lastName = l;
            content = c;
            delivery = d;
            organization = o;
            rank = r;
        }

        public String getFirstName()
        {
            return firstName;
        }

        public String getLastName()
        {
            return lastName;
        }

        public int getContent()
        {
            return content;
        }

        public int getDelivery()
        {
            return delivery;
        }

        public int getOrganization()
        {
            return organization;
        }

        public int getRank()
        {
            return rank;
        }
    }
```

Page 1

FIGURE 4-10

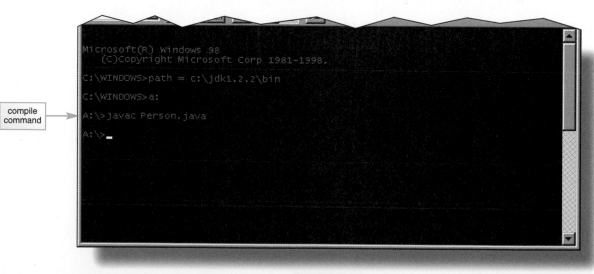

compile
command

```
Microsoft(R) Windows 98
    (C)Copyright Microsoft Corp 1981-1998.

C:\WINDOWS>path = c:\jdk1.2.2\bin

C:\WINDOWS>a:

A:\>javac Person.java

A:\>_
```

FIGURE 4-11

The Person class now can be used or called from any Java application that needs this kind of class. The next section in this project will create the driver application, Donna, to enter and analyze the debate team's scores using arrays.

Arrays

A single piece of data is stored with a unique name and a predetermined data type. When you manipulate that data, you reference its identifier name. A list of related values, stored in individual locations, requires a separate line of code to manipulate each value. Java and other programming languages use a data structure called an array to store lists and manipulate data more efficiently. An **array** stores multiple data items in a contiguous block of memory, divided into a number of slots. Think of an array as a stretched variable — a location that still has one identifier name, but is larger, or dimensional, in that it can hold more than one value. Each slot is referred to as a **member**, or **element**, of the array, and each slot may hold a different value. All of the values, however, must be of the same data type. The data type may be any valid data type including primitive, reference, or programmer-defined data types.

An **index number**, or **subscript**, is assigned to each member of the array, allowing the program and the programmer to access individual values when necessary. Index numbers are always integers. They begin with zero and progress sequentially by whole numbers to the end of the array. The practice of **zero-indexing** is common to many programming languages. It may help to think of the first array member as being zero members away from the beginning of the array.

Array Notation

Arrays must be declared, like all variables. You list the data type, followed by a set of square brackets, followed by the identifier name when declaring an array.

```
int[] ages;
```

An alternate declaration, similar to the C and C++ programming languages, places the brackets after the identifier.

```
int ages[];
```

Java uses brackets instead of parentheses for arrays, so as not to confuse them with methods.

In the above examples, an array named, ages, is declared that will hold int values; however, the actual array is not constructed by either of these declarations. You must construct the array and specify its length with a constructor statement.

```
ages = new ages[100];
```

Often an array is declared and constructed in a single statement.

```
int[] ages = new int[100];
```

This declaration tells the Java compiler that ages will be used as the name of an array containing ints, and to construct a new array containing 100 elements. Remember that Java uses zero-indexing, so the 100 constructed elements will be numbered 0 through 99.

An array is an object, and like any other object in Java, it is constructed out of main storage as the program is running and not at compile time. The array constructor uses different syntax than most object constructors because it must initialize the **length**, or total number of elements, in the array. The length of an array is established when the array is created at run-time. After creation, an array is a fixed-length structure. In other words, once an array has been constructed, the number of elements it contains does not change.

Once an array is declared and constructed, the stored value of each member of the array will be initialized to zero; however, reference data types such as Strings are not initialized to SPACEBAR blanks or an empty string. You must populate String arrays explicitly.

Later in the program, when referencing a single element, the programmer places the index number in brackets.

```
System.out.println(answer[5]);
```

In the above example, answer is the name of the array. The sixth element of the array will display during executing because array subscripts begin with zero.

You can use assignment statements to explicitly place values within arrays, just as you do with single variables.

```
temperature[3] = 78;
```

After it has been executed, the fourth member of the array, temperature, will hold the value 78.

Alternately, you can declare, construct, and assign values all at once, as in the following example.

```
boolean[] results = { true, false, true, true, false };
```

Java provides this shortcut syntax for creating and initializing an array. The length of this boolean array is determined by the number of values provided between the braces.

Array members can be used anywhere a variable can be used.

```
overtime = (hours[6] - 40) * rate[6] * 1.5;
```

In the example, overtime is calculated by taking the seventh member of the hours array, subtracting 40 and then multiplying it by the seventh member of the rate array and finally by 1.5 for time-and-a-half pay.

The index of an array is always an integer type, but it does not have to be a literal. It can be any expression that evaluates to an integer. For example, if the array has been declared properly, the following code is legal.

```
int index = 8;
myArray[index] = 71;
```

In the above example, the ninth element of myArray will be set to the value 71. Using an expression for an array subscript is a very powerful tool. Often a problem is solved by organizing the data into arrays, and then processing the data in a logical way using variables as indices.

Object Arrays

When an array contains values other than primitive data types, such as a reference data type or String, it is an **object array**. You can store an object array of programmer-defined data types or classes, such as the Person class created earlier in this project, in the same way that you can store an array of ints or booleans. Again, think of the array as a stretched variable location; in the case of an object array, however, it becomes almost three-dimensional because it refers to an entire set of data in each element. For example, the following code declares and constructs an array of type Person, a class you created earlier in this project.

```
Person[] debateGroup = new Person[size];
```

The name of the array is debateGroup. The length is set to the identifier, size. Assuming size has been declared previously and assigned a value, the code goes and looks for the class, Person, during execution and then opens an array storage location large enough to hold *size* number of people.

Creating an Application with Arrays

The application to enter data for Donna's debate team scores will use arrays, and call the Person class created earlier in this project. The first set of steps will be to enter the block comments, class and method headers, and declare the variables. The application will use variables to hold user input, parse the input, and accumulate totals. Additionally, you will code statements to prompt users for the total number of students they plan to enter as the program runs — that value will become the length used in declaring and constructing the array. Named debateGroup, the array will consist of six students and their scores from a recent debate tournament.

Perform the following steps to begin the program and save a copy of the beginning code.

More About

Data Structures

Using arrays is the first step in thinking about Java data structures. Organizing data using structures is an important step to make your programs run more efficiently. A Java array is a static structure meaning it does not change in size. Dynamic data structures grow or shrink as the data they hold changes. Vectors, lists, stacks, and trees are all dynamic structures. A vector is like a dynamic array that can grow in size. The cost of this flexibility is a decrease in performance compared to an array. Vectors are useful, however, in multithreaded applications where different parts of the program proceed in parallel, sharing the processor.

Steps **To Begin the Donna Application**

1. **Start Notepad. If Notepad already is running, click New on the Notepad File menu. Type the beginning comments of the Donna application as shown in Figure 4-12. Use your own name and the current date in the comments.**

The block comments display in a new Notepad window (Figure 4-12).

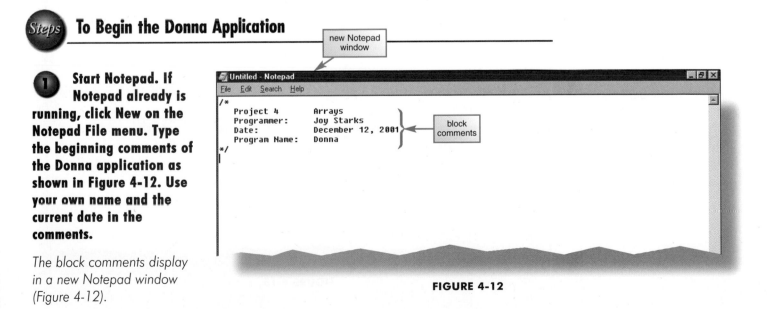

FIGURE 4-12

2 **Type the import statement, class header, and main method header of the Donna application as shown in Figure 4-13.**

The code and beginning braces of both the class header and the main method header display (Figure 4-13).

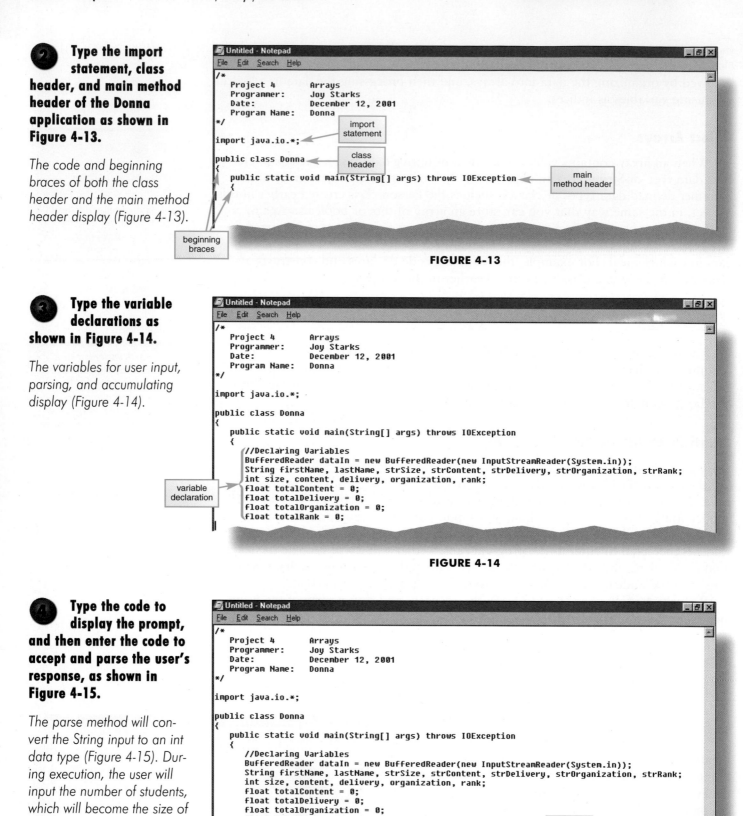

FIGURE 4-13

3 **Type the variable declarations as shown in Figure 4-14.**

The variables for user input, parsing, and accumulating display (Figure 4-14).

FIGURE 4-14

4 **Type the code to display the prompt, and then enter the code to accept and parse the user's response, as shown in Figure 4-15.**

The parse method will convert the String input to an int data type (Figure 4-15). During execution, the user will input the number of students, which will become the size of the array.

FIGURE 4-15

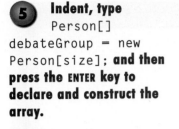

Indent, type
`Person[]`
`debateGroup = new`
`Person[size];` **and then
press the ENTER key to
declare and construct the
array.**

*The array, debateGroup,
is declared to be of type
Person, and of length, size
(Figure 4-16). During execution, the compiler will look at
the Person class and con-
struct an array of its objects,
with a length equal to the
size of the user input.*

```
/*
    Project 4        Arrays
    Programmer:      Joy Starks
    Date:            December 12, 2001
    Program Name:    Donna
*/

import java.io.*;

public class Donna
{
    public static void main(String[] args) throws IOException
    {
        //Declaring Variables
        BufferedReader dataIn = new BufferedReader(new InputStreamReader(System.in));
        String firstName, lastName, strSize, strContent, strDelivery, strOrganization, strRank;
        int size, content, delivery, organization, rank;
        float totalContent = 0;
        float totalDelivery = 0;
        float totalOrganization = 0;
        float totalRank = 0;

        System.out.print("How many students will you enter? ");
            strSize = dataIn.readLine();
            size = Integer.parseInt(strSize);

        Person[] debateGroup = new Person[size];
```

declare
and construct
the array

FIGURE 4-16

**Click File on the
Notepad menu bar
and then point to Save.**

*The File menu displays
(Figure 4-17).*

File menu

```
File  Edit  Search  Help
  New
  Open...
  Save
  Save As...

  Page Setup...
  Print

  Exit
```

Save
command

```
public class Donna
{
    public static void main(String[] args) throws IOException
    {
        //Declaring Variables
        BufferedReader dataIn = new BufferedReader(new InputStreamReader(System.in));
        String firstName, lastName, strSize, strContent, strDelivery, strOrganization, strRank;
        int size, content, delivery, organization, rank;
        float totalContent = 0;
        float totalDelivery = 0;
        float totalOrganization = 0;
        float totalRank = 0;

        System.out.print("How many students will you enter? ");
            strSize = dataIn.readLine();
            size = Integer.parseInt(strSize);

        Person[] debateGroup = new Person[size];
```

FIGURE 4-17

7   **Click Save. When the Save As dialog box displays, type "Donna.java" in the File name text box. If necessary, click the Save in box arrow and click 3½ Floppy (A:) in the Save in list. Point to the Save button.**

The code will save with the file name, "Donna.java" on the floppy disk in drive A (Figure 4-18).

8   **Click the Save button.**

The file saves on the floppy disk.

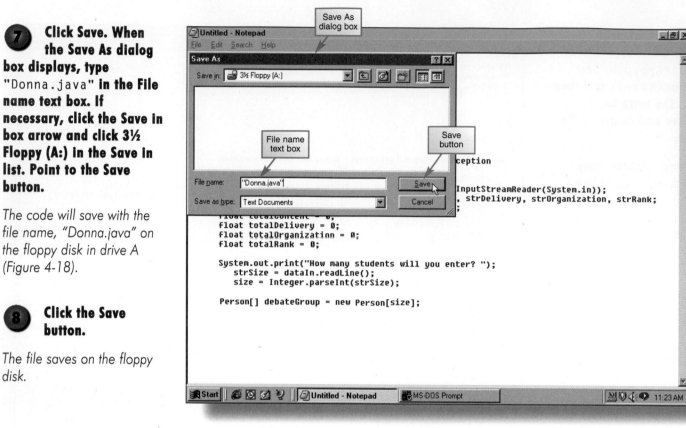

FIGURE 4-18

During execution, Donna will input the total number of students for whom she has scores. Notice that the variable for the size of the array is declared to be an int data type and the total accumulated scores are declared as floats. That way, when Java performs the math to divide the total by the size, an explicit cast will occur. When a formula contains two different data types, **casting** forces the answer to conform to the declaration of the broader data type — in this case, a float.

Measured Loops

Recall that when you wanted to repeat a set of instructions, you used a while loop. While loops work well when you need to perform a task some undetermined number of times. In previous programs, you may have initialized a boolean identifier, such as done, to false and then based on some condition or user input changed that value to true to exit the loop. Java provides a shorter, better mechanism, however, if you are sure how many times you want to loop. A loop that executes a specific number of times is called a **measured loop** or **counted loop**.

The for Loop

Java uses a **for statement** to list the parameters of a measured loop. The for statement needs to know the beginning value, when to stop, and by what increment to count. The three parameters are enclosed in parentheses and separated with semicolons. The for statement is followed by a block of statements, enclosed in braces, which execute the number of times as prescribed in the for statement.

Table 4-4 displays the for statement and examples.

Table 4-4	The for Loop

General form:	```for (start; stop; counter-control)```
	```{```
	```...lines of code to repeat;```
	```}```

Comment:	The word, **for**, is a reserved keyword. Start is typically a variable initialized to a beginning value and is executed only once per invocation of the loop. Stop is a condition that tests whether to continue the loop. As long as it evaluates to true, the loop continues. The counter-control, sometimes called the update, is typically an expression indicating how to increment or decrement the counter. Semicolons separate the three variables.

Examples:	```for (int j=1; j<=5; j++)```
	j is initialized to 1; the loop continues until j = 5; j is incremented at each pass of the loop; the loop will execute 4 times.
	```for (counter = 6; counter>=0; counter--)```
	counter is initialized to 6; the loop continues until counter is less than 0; counter is decremented at each pass of the loop; the loop will execute 7 times.
	```for (evenValues = 2; evenValues <= 100; evenValues+=2)```
	evenValues is initialized to 2; the loop continues until evenValues = 100; 2 is added to evenValues at each pass of the loop; the loop will execute 49 times.

Assignment and Unary Operators

Recall that to accumulate a running total, you declare a variable, give that variable a beginning value, and then add to it by including the identifier name on both sides of an assignment operator.

```
variable = variable + newValue;
```

In the above example, each time the line is executed, the old value is added to the new value and then reassigned to the original identifier name. Java's **assignment operators**, or **shortcut operators**, are a shortened form of that variable accumulation. For example, if you declare a variable with the identifier name, counter, and want to add five to it each time the line of code is executed, use the **add and assign operator** (+=).

```
counter += 5;
```

Each time the above code is executed, Java adds five to the previous value of counter and writes the new value back into the same storage location, effectively overwriting the earlier value.

An easy way to increment a counter is to use a special operator called a unary operator. A **unary operator** is an operator that needs only one value, or operand, to perform its function. With traditional operators, such as addition, you must supply at least two values to be added. With unary operators, you use a special symbol that performs a mathematical operation on a single value.

More **About**

Counting by Numbers other than 1

Sometimes you may want to set your counter to increment by numbers other than one. For example, if you want to display the multiplication table based on 5's, you might want to count from 0 to 100 by 5's. That way you can use your counter variable in the body of the loop without having to create a new variable to hold the multiplicand.

For example, if you want to increment the variable i, by one, you could write the following code using a traditional style.

```
i = i + 1;
```

Using an assignment operator, the code becomes a little shorter.

```
i+=1;
```

Using a unary operator, the code becomes even simpler.

```
i++;
```

An interesting feature of unary operators is that they behave differently depending upon which side of the variable they are located. If it is a **postfix operator**, coming after the variable, it is sometimes called a **postfix** the value is incremented after the line of code is executed. If it is a **prefix operator**, preceding the variable, the value is incremented before the line of code is executed. In a single incremental line of code, as above, it does not make any difference, but if the unary operator is included as part of a formula or in an assignment statement, the placement is crucial.

```
i = 5;
answer = ++i;
```

In the above example, answer will be equal to 6, because the variable, i, is incremented before the line of code is executed. Any later references to the value, i, will be evaluated at 6, as well.

If the unary operator comes after the variable, however, the answer changes.

```
i = 5;
answer = i++;
```

In this example, the answer will be equal to 5, because the variable, i, is incremented after the line of code is executed. Any later references to the value, i, will be evaluated as 6, because i was incremented after the assignment.

When you use the increment operator in a for loop, it is appropriate to place the operator after the operand, because you want the value to increment after the line is executed.

The **decrement operator** (– –) subtracts one from the operand. The timing of the decrement is dependent upon the placement of the operator as with the increment operator.

For example, a simple loop that is to be repeated 10 times may contain a for statement as follows.

```
for (int i = 1; i < 11; i++)
```

Many programmers use the identifier, i, for looping instead of spelling out the word increment; however, Java will accept any valid identifier. The first parameter declares and sets the i variable to 1. The second parameter tests i to make sure it is less than 11. The third parameter increments the variable by one, using the unary operator, ++.

Table 4-5 displays a series of Java code showing how the value of i might change using both prefix and postfix operators. The code is sequential.

Table 4-5	How a Value Changes Using the Increment and Decrement Operators		
LINE	CODE	DISPLAYED RESULT	REASON
1	i = 10;		
2	System.out.println(i);	10	i was assigned the value of 10 in line 1
3	i++;		
4	System.out.println(i);	11	i was incremented after line 3
5	System.out.println(i++);	11	i is not incremented until after line 5 is executed
6	System.out.println(i);	12	i was incremented after line 5
7	System.out.println(++i);	13	i is incremented before line 7 is executed
8	System.out.println(i);	13	i was not changed after line 7

Java's two unary operators and six arithmetic assignment operators are listed in Table 4-6. The sample results are independent — each based on a previous assignment of the value 10.

Table 4-6	Unary and Arithmetic Assignment Operators			
OPERATOR SYMBOL	OPERATOR NAME	TYPE OF OPERATOR	SAMPLE FORMULA WHERE ANSWER PREVIOUSLY IS SET TO 10	STORED RESULT OF ANSWER AFTER EXECUTION
++	increment	unary	answer++;	11
– –	decrement	unary	answer; – –;	9
=	assign	assignment	answer = 9;	9
+=	add and assign	assignment	answer += 10;	20
– =	subtract and assign	assignment	answer - = 3;	7
*=	multiply and assign	assignment	answer *= 4;	40
/=	divide and assign	assignment	answer /= 5;	2
%–	modulus and assign	assignment	answer %= 3;	1

Entering the for Loop

Table 4-7 on the next page displays the code for a loop of prompts and user inputs. Line 29 begins the for block. Notice the counter is named i and is declared an int data type. It is initialized to zero, then tested against size, a variable entered previously by the user. Finally, i, is incremented each time the loop is executed. In line 54, the value of i is used to identify at which debateGroup index number the program should save its newly constructed Person.

Line 54 also illustrates another reference to the Person class. Recall that earlier in the program you entered a line of code to declare and construct an object array called debateGroup.

```
Person[] debateGroup = new Person[size];
```

You now are assigning data to a member of that array with an instance method and six arguments.

```
debateGroup[i] = new Person(firstName, lastName, content, delivery, organization, rank);
```

Table 4-7

LINE	CODE
29	`for (int i=0; i<size; i++)`
30	`{`
31	`    //Get input from user`
32	`    System.out.print("What is the first name of student #" + (i+1) + ": ");`
33	`        firstName = dataIn.readLine();`
34	
35	`    System.out.print("What is the last name of student #" + (i+1) + ": ");`
36	`        lastName = dataIn.readLine();`
37	
38	`    System.out.print("\tWhat is the score for content? ");`
39	`        strContent = dataIn.readLine();`
40	`        content = Integer.parseInt(strContent);`
41	
42	`    System.out.print("\tWhat is the score for delivery? ");`
43	`        strDelivery = dataIn.readLine();`
44	`        delivery = Integer.parseInt(strDelivery);`
45	
46	`    System.out.print("\tWhat is the score for organization?  ");`
47	`        strOrganization = dataIn.readLine();`
48	`        organization = Integer.parseInt(strOrganization);`
49	
50	`    System.out.print("\tWhat is the rank? ");`
51	`        strRank = dataIn.readLine();`
52	`        rank = Integer.parseInt(strRank);`
53	
54	`    debateGroup[i] = new Person(firstName, lastName, content, delivery, organization, rank);`
55	`}`

Perform the following steps to enter the code from Table 4-7.

TO ENTER THE FOR LOOP

 If necessary, click at the end of the previous code on line 27. Press the ENTER key twice to create a blank line between the previous code and the new for loop.

2 Enter the code from Table 4-7.

3 Click File on the Notepad menu bar and then click Save.

The for loop code displays (Figure 4-19).

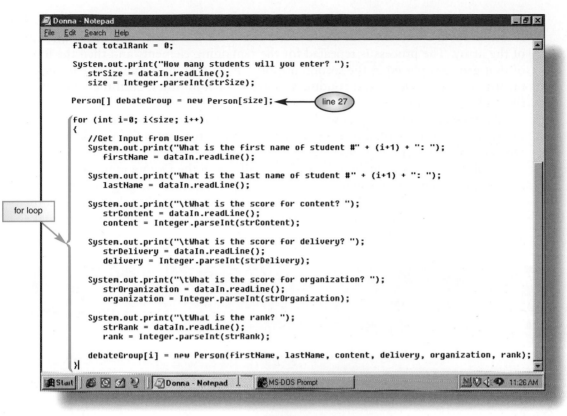

FIGURE 4-19

Notice the print method, instead of the println method, is used in the lines that prompt for data entry. The print method does not move the insertion point to the next line, allowing the user to be able to input on the same line as the question.

Now that the data has been entered, it is time to put it in some logical order.

Sorting an Array

Sorting is the process of arranging the array's elements in ascending or descending order. Anytime large amounts of data are maintained, the data usually needs to be arranged in a particular order for simplified searching or for logical retrieval. Banks sort transactions by check number or date. Telephone directories sort by last name and then by first name. Teachers sometimes sort exam grades from highest to lowest to look for patterns. No matter in what order Donna may input her debate students, it would be logical to have the information display and print in alphabetical order by last name.

Computer sorting algorithms have been used for many years; some have proven more efficient than others. A sorting algorithm needs to look at pairs of elements to see if they are in order. If not, that pair must be interchanged. The algorithm needs to traverse the array checking pairs until a complete pass yields no interchanges — a tedious task by hand, but one well suited for Java. A popular method of sorting is called the **bubble sort**, so named because when a pair of elements is examined, the interchanged value moves, or bubbles up, toward the top of the array.

More About

The Size of an Array

To get the size of an array, you write the array name followed by a dot and then the word length. Programmers new to the Java programming language are tempted to follow length with an empty set of parentheses. This does not work because length is not a method, it is a property provided by the Java platform for all arrays.

Another method of sorting is called the **selection sort**, in which the entire array is searched for the element with the lowest value. It then is positioned at the beginning of the array. The process is repeated for the remaining elements and then the lowest of that group is placed in the second position. Each search examines one fewer element than the previous, and continues to place them in order, until there are no remaining elements.

An **insertion sort**, which is well suited for small arrays, creates a new array and inserts the values in order. A **merge sort** takes two sorted arrays of the same data type and blends them in order.

Table 4-8 displays the bubble sort you will use in the Donna application. It uses a loop that progresses through the array in ascending order looking for elements that are out of order. If an interchange or swap is necessary, it makes the swap and then decrements a counter to look back through the array in descending order to make any secondary swaps that might now be necessary.

Table 4-8	
LINE	CODE
56	//Sort by last name
57	for (int i=1; i<size; i++)
58	{
59	int j = i;
60	String tempLastName = debateGroup[i].getLastName();
61	Person tempDebateGroup = debateGroup[i];
62	
63	while ((j>0) && (debateGroup[j-1].getLastName().compareTo(tempLastName)>0))
64	{
65	debateGroup[j] = debateGroup[j-1];
66	j--;
67	}
68	debateGroup[j] = tempDebateGroup;
69	}

Instances

In line 61, a new reference variable is created, not a new instance. Consequently, both tempDebateGroup and debateGroup[i] reference the same instance. To test this, try changing a value of an instance variable, say content, for the tempDebateGroup item (you will have to create a mutator method in the Person class to do this). Changing the variable will change its value when referenced by the tempDebateGroup reference or the DebateGroup[i] reference. Why? Because they both reference the same object. It is like two pointers pointing to the same data. Therefore, the assignment does not copy the data, just the reference.

The for statement in line 57 directs the application to perform a loop starting at 1 and going to the length of the array as input by the user. In line 59, the second identifier — to count backward checking to see if any secondary swaps are needed — is declared and initialized as j. Its value always is set to the current value of the for loop. The first time through the loop, both values will be 1.

Line 60 calls the getLastName method. Recall that getLastName is an instance method created in the Person class at the beginning of the project. Here the purpose of the getLastName method is to retrieve the last name of the debateGroup member. The first time through the loop, the counter i references the first element in the debateGroup array. Once retrieved, that name is stored in a temporary holding location called tempLastName. Storing the name in a temporary location prevents the data from being overwritten when the next name is retrieved.

Line 61 does not – by copying the entire first element into that instance, as you might think — literally construct a new instance of the Person class. It actually creates a new reference variable that points to, or references, the same instance of the Person class called, tempDebateGroup. The assignment, therefore, does not copy the data, only the reference. When a swap is necessary, the reference is transferred from its temporary location into its new position in the array as shown in line 68.

An interesting part of the sort routine is how Java compares the current name to the previous name. Line 63 uses a method called compareTo, which Java uses as a comparison operator. The **compareTo** method returns a value less than zero when the String object inside its parenthetical argument is less than the given string; a value of zero when the strings are equal; and a value greater than zero when the String object is greater than the given string. It is the comparison operator's return value that indicates whether the two names, and their corresponding fields, should be swapped. Line 63 compares the previous name to the current name, as stored in the temporary location.

```
debateGroup[j-1].getLastName().compareTo(tempLastName)
```

If that value is greater than zero, then a swap should be made. The first time through, the compareTo method will be looking at element 0 and comparing it to element 1 stored in the temporary location. Line 65 performs the swap and line 66 decrements the backward counter, j.

Line 63 also checks for the beginning of the array — ending the backward counting when necessary — by looking at the j counter.

Recall that a while loop tests a condition to see if the body of the loop should be performed. In this sort routine, the And operator, &&, separates the two parts of the condition. The body of the while loop, is only performed when both parts are true. The first part of the condition, j>0 checks to see if the counter is back at the beginning of the array. The second part, debateGroup[j-1].getLastName(). compareTo(tempLastName)>0, indicates a swap is necessary. At the end of the for loop, in line 68, the element data from the tempDebateGroup is transferred into the current location. It is important to remember that even though this sort routine compares last name to last name, reference to the entire data member with all its fields is swapped in line 68.

Perform the following steps to enter the search code.

TO ENTER THE SEARCH CODE

① If necessary, click at the end of the previous code. Press the ENTER key twice to create a blank line between the previous code and the new for loop.

② Enter the code from Table 4-8.

③ Click File on the Notepad menu bar and then click Save.

The search code displays (Figure 4-20).

More About

Comparing Strings

A String is a small array of characters. To compare one String to another, you must traverse the array and look at each pair of characters. The equal to operator, (= = or .equals) tests each member of the first String to the corresponding member of the second. If any deviation exists, the result of the comparison will be false. For more information about Strings, visit the Java Programming Web Page (www.scsite.com/java/ more.htm) and then click String Methods.

```
//Sort by last name
for (int i=1; i<size; i++)
{
    int j = i;
    String tempLastName = debateGroup[i].getLastName();
    Person tempDebateGroup = debateGroup[i];

    while ((j>0) && (debateGroup[j-1].getLastName().compareTo(tempLastName)>0))
    {
        debateGroup[j] = debateGroup[j-1];
        j--;
    }

    debateGroup[j] = tempDebateGroup;
}
```

search code

Start | Donna - Notepad | MS-DOS Prompt | 11:26 AM

FIGURE 4-20

Finishing the Donna Application

The final code to finish the Donna application is displayed in Table 4-9. First, a loop runs through the sorted array, printing the detail from each element of the array on the screen (lines 74 through 78). Individual scores then are added to an accumulated total using the add and assign operator (lines 81 through 84). Once the scores are totaled, dividing by the size of the array will produce the averages (lines 88 through 91).

Lines 88 through 91 contain formulas that divide a float by an int data type. The resulting cast will create a float answer during execution.

Table 4-9

LINE	CODE
70	
71	`//Display detail`
72	`for (int i=0; i<size; i++)`
73	`{`
74	`System.out.println(debateGroup[i].getLastName()+", "+debateGroup[i].getFirstName());`
75	`System.out.println("\tContent: "+debateGroup[i].getContent());`
76	`System.out.println("\tDelivery: "+debateGroup[i].getDelivery());`
77	`System.out.println("\tOrganization: "+debateGroup[i].getOrganization());`
78	`System.out.println("\tRank: "+debateGroup[i].getRank());`
79	
80	`//Calculate totals for each category`
81	`totalContent += debateGroup[i].getContent();`
82	`totalDelivery += debateGroup[i].getDelivery();`
83	`totalOrganization += debateGroup[i].getOrganization();`
84	`totalRank += debateGroup[i].getRank();`
85	`}`
86	
87	`System.out.println("");`
88	`System.out.println("The average content score was "+(totalContent/size));`
89	`System.out.println("The average delivery score was "+(totalDelivery/size));`
90	`System.out.println("The average organization score was "+(totalOrganization/size));`
91	`System.out.println("The average rank was "+(totalRank/size));`
92	`}`
93	`}`

Perform the following steps to enter the code to display the sorted array and accumulate grand totals to calculate averages.

Steps

To Enter the Display, Accumulation, and Averaging Code

1 **Click at the end of line 69 after the brace. Press the ENTER key twice.**

A blank line separates the previous sort routine and the final set of code (Figure 4-21).

```
strDelivery = dataIn.readLine();
delivery = Integer.parseInt(strDelivery);

System.out.print("\tWhat is the score for organization? ");
strOrganization = dataIn.readLine();
organization = Integer.parseInt(strOrganization);

System.out.print("\tWhat is the rank? ");
strRank = dataIn.readLine();
rank = Integer.parseInt(strRank);

debateGroup[i] = new Person(firstName, lastName, content, delivery, organization, rank);
}

//Sort by last name
for (int i=1; i<size; i++)
{
    int j = i;
    String tempLastName = debateGroup[i].getLastName();
    Person tempDebateGroup = debateGroup[i];

    while ((j>0) && (debateGroup[j-1].getLastName().compareTo(tempLastName)>0))
    {
        debateGroup[j] = debateGroup[j-1];
        j--;
    }

    debateGroup[j] = tempDebateGroup;
}    ← line 69
```
insertion point

FIGURE 4-21

2 **Type the code from Table 4-9 using proper indentation.**

The code to display the sorted array, accumulate totals, and display averages displays as entered (Figure 4-22). Final braces close both the main method and Donna class blocks.

3 **Click File on the menu bar and then click Save.**

The program saves.

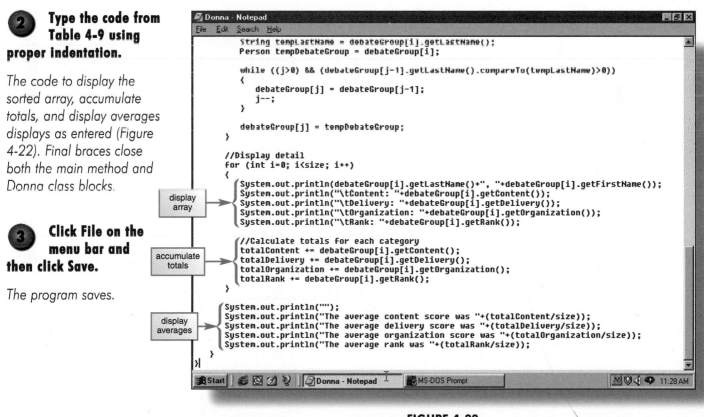

```
    String tempLastName = debateGroup[i].getLastName();
    Person tempDebateGroup = debateGroup[i];

    while ((j>0) && (debateGroup[j-1].getLastName().compareTo(tempLastName)>0))
    {
        debateGroup[j] = debateGroup[j-1];
        j--;
    }

    debateGroup[j] = tempDebateGroup;
}

//Display detail
for (int i=0; i<size; i++)
{
    System.out.println(debateGroup[i].getLastName()+", "+debateGroup[i].getFirstName());
    System.out.println("\tContent: "+debateGroup[i].getContent());
    System.out.println("\tDelivery: "+debateGroup[i].getDelivery());
    System.out.println("\tOrganization: "+debateGroup[i].getOrganization());
    System.out.println("\tRank: "+debateGroup[i].getRank());

    //Calculate totals for each category
    totalContent += debateGroup[i].getContent();
    totalDelivery += debateGroup[i].getDelivery();
    totalOrganization += debateGroup[i].getOrganization();
    totalRank += debateGroup[i].getRank();
}

    System.out.println("");
    System.out.println("The average content score was "+(totalContent/size));
    System.out.println("The average delivery score was "+(totalDelivery/size));
    System.out.println("The average organization score was "+(totalOrganization/size));
    System.out.println("The average rank was "+(totalRank/size));
}
```
display array

accumulate totals

display averages

FIGURE 4-22

Figure 4-23 displays the entire program for the Donna application.

Donna

```
//Sort by last name
for (int i=1; i<size; i++)
{
    int j = i;
    String tempLastName = debateGroup[i].getLastName();
    Person tempDebateGroup = debateGroup[i];

    while ((j>0) && (debateGroup[j-1].getLastName().compareTo(tempLastName)>0))
    {
        debateGroup[j] = debateGroup[j-1];
        j--;
    }
    debateGroup[j] = tempDebateGroup;
}

//Display detail
for (int i=0; i<size; i++)
{
    System.out.println(debateGroup[i].getLastName()+", "+debateGroup[i].getFirstName());
    System.out.println("\tContent: "+debateGroup[i].getContent());
    System.out.println("\tDelivery: "+debateGroup[i].getDelivery());
    System.out.println("\tOrganization: "+debateGroup[i].getOrganization());
    System.out.println("\tRank: "+debateGroup[i].getRank());

    //Calculate totals for each category
    totalContent += debateGroup[i].getContent();
    totalDelivery += debateGroup[i].getDelivery();
    totalOrganization += debateGroup[i].getOrganization();
    totalRank += debateGroup[i].getRank();
}

System.out.println("");
System.out.println("The average content score was "+(totalContent/size));
System.out.println("The average delivery score was "+(totalDelivery/size));
System.out.println("The average organization score was "+(totalOrganization/size));
System.out.println("The average rank was "+(totalRank/size));
}
}
```

Page 2

Donna

```
/*
    Project 4        Arrays
    Programmer:      Joy Starks
    Date:            December 12, 2001
    Program Name:    Donna
*/

import java.io.*;

public class Donna
{
    public static void main(String[] args) throws IOException
    {
        //Declaring Variables
        BufferedReader dataIn = new BufferedReader(new InputStreamReader(System.in));
        String firstName, lastName, strSize, strContent, strDelivery, strOrganization, strRank;
        int size, content, delivery, organization, rank;
        float totalContent = 0;
        float totalDelivery = 0;
        float totalOrganization = 0;
        float totalRank = 0;

        System.out.print("How many students will you enter? ");
            strSize = dataIn.readLine();
          size = Integer.parseInt(strSize);

        Person[] debateGroup = new Person[size];

        for (int i=0; i<size; i++)
        {
            //Get Input from User
            System.out.print("What is the first name of student #" + (i+1) + ": ");
                firstName = dataIn.readLine();

            System.out.print("What is the last name of student # :" + (i+1) + ": ");
                lastName = dataIn.readLine();

            System.out.print("\tWhat is the score for content? ");
                strContent = dataIn.readLine();
                content = Integer.parseInt(strContent);

            System.out.print("\tWhat is the score for delivery? ");
                strDelivery = dataIn.readLine();
                delivery = Integer.parseInt(strDelivery);

            System.out.print("\tWhat is the score for organization? ");
                strOrganization = dataIn.readLine();
                organization = Integer.parseInt(strOrganization);

            System.out.print("\tWhat is the rank? ");
                strRank = dataIn.readLine();
                rank = Integer.parseInt(strRank);

            debateGroup[i] = new Person(firstName, lastName, content, delivery, organization, rank);
        }
```

FIGURE 4-23

Page 1

Compiling and Running the Application

Perform the following steps to compile the program. You then will enter sample data from Table 4-10 as you run the program. The application will sort the data and display it with averages for the debate team.

Table 4-10	Sample Data for Donna Application				
FIRST NAME	LAST NAME	CONTENT	DELIVERY	ORGANIZATION	RANK
Katie	Marie	1	3	3	3
Michael	Louks	3	5	4	7
Nate	Thomas	2	2	1	2
Fredrick	Montgomery	2	3	2	2
Marsha	Elana	3	4	3	6
Jon	Arthur	1	1	2	1

 ## To Compile and Run the Application

1 **Click the MS-DOS Prompt button on the taskbar. If you previously closed the MS-DOS Prompt window, open it again, set your path, and log onto drive A. At the command prompt, type** `Javac Donna.java` **and then press the ENTER key.**

The program compiles (Figure 4-24). If you have errors, fix them in the Notepad window, save, and then recompile.

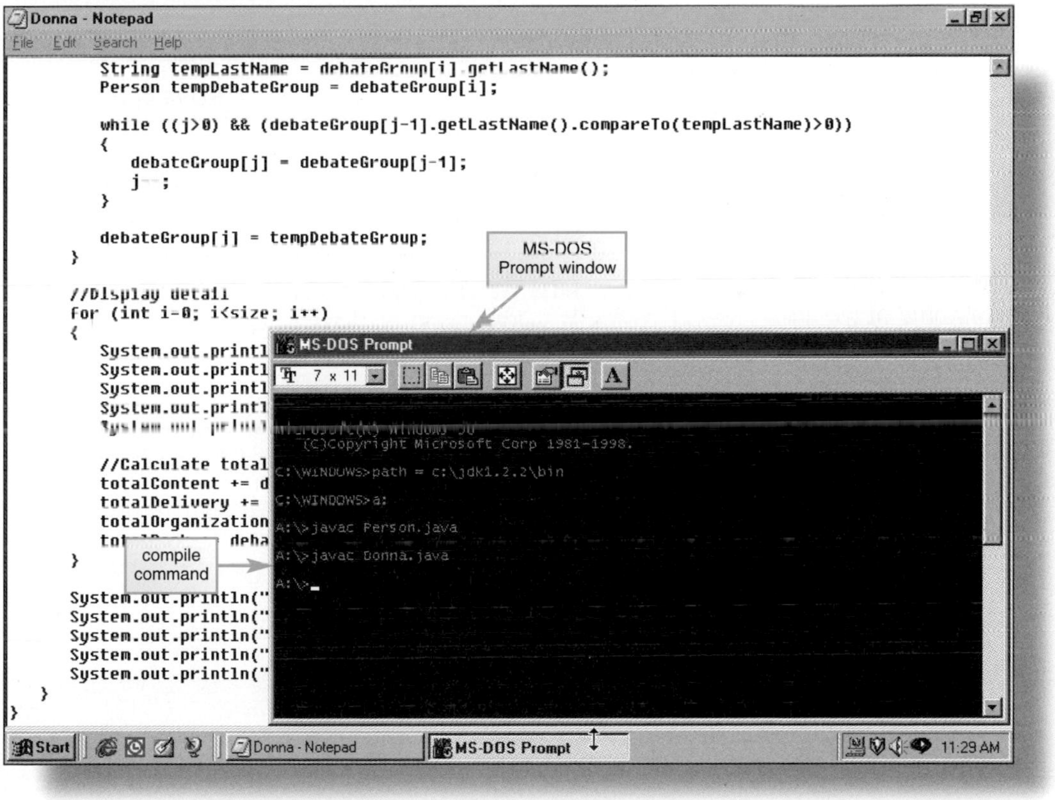

FIGURE 4-24

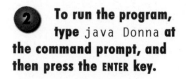
2 **To run the program, type** java Donna **at the command prompt, and then press the** ENTER **key.**

The first prompt displays (Figure 4-25). Notice that while the program is running, both the title bar and the taskbar display JAVA instead of MS-DOS Prompt.

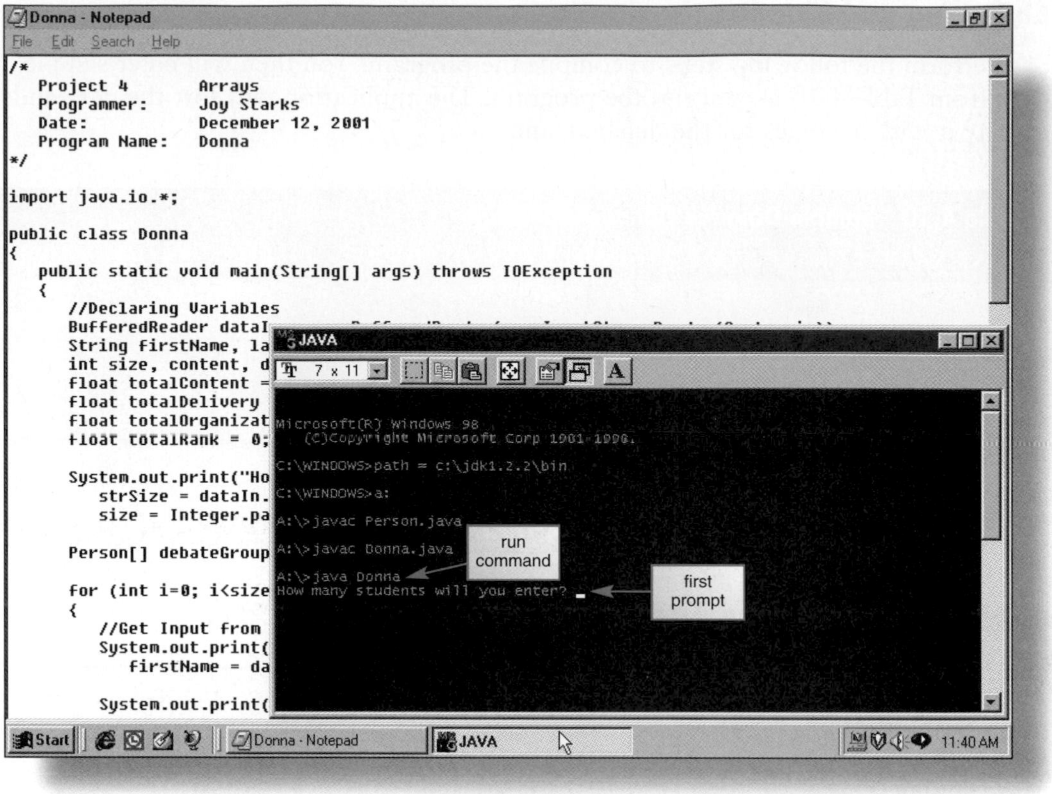

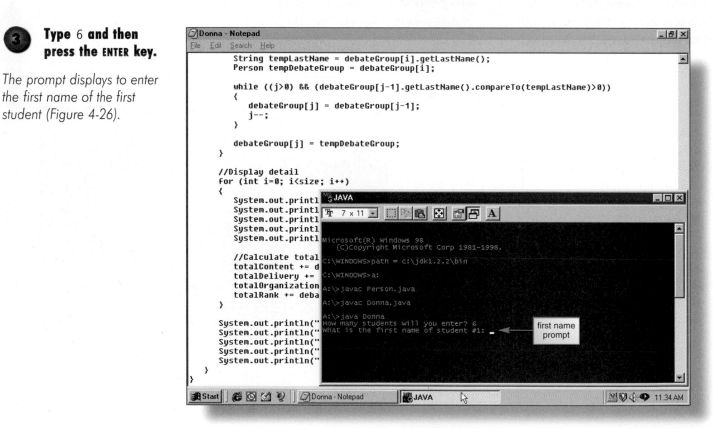

FIGURE 4-25

3 **Type** 6 **and then press the** ENTER **key.**

The prompt displays to enter the first name of the first student (Figure 4-26).

FIGURE 4-26

4 **Enter the data from Table 4-10 on page J 4.31 as the prompts display, pressing the ENTER key after each piece of data is entered.**

After all the data is entered, Java sorts the array and displays the answers (Figure 4-27).

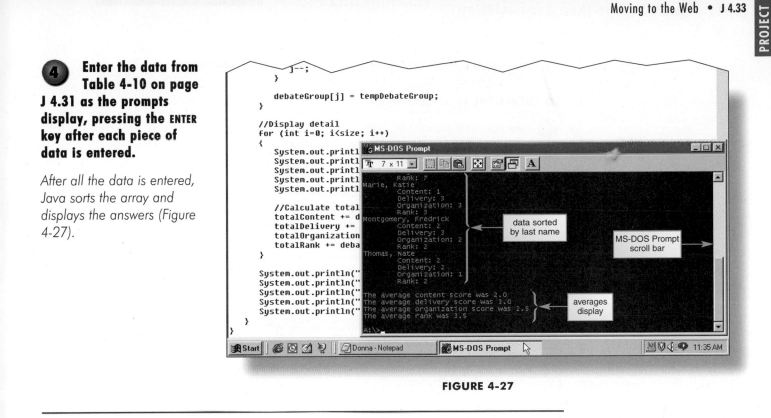

FIGURE 4-27

The formula, which divided a float by an int, produced a float answer for the averages. To see the sorted results from all the data, you can use the MS-DOS Prompt scroll bar on the right side of the window.

Moving to the Web

Creating an applet version of the Donna application involves the use of an applet component called Choice. A **Choice** displays as a drop-down list box with an arrow. The possible scores of 1 through 5 will display for each category. The team member's name and rank will be inserted in text fields, as those entries may vary widely. As you create the applet, you will use the same techniques as in previous projects to create the HTML host document to call the applet. Then you will create the applet itself.

Creating the Host Document

Recall from previous projects that each Java applet must be called from within another program or application. The host document usually is an HTML file with an applet tag. The code to create an HTML file to access the DonnaApplet program is listed in Table 4-11.

Table 4-11

LINE	CODE
1	`<HTML>`
2	`<APPLET CODE = "DonnaApplet.class" WIDTH = 205 HEIGHT = 500>`
3	`</APPLET>`
4	`</HTML>`

More About

Viewing the Host Document with a Browser

If you are having trouble displaying applets in Internet Explorer (IE) 5.5 or higher, it may be that your browser is set to read applets only from the hard drive. Sometimes the problem is due to a security violation that happens only when IE is trying to fetch a class from a floppy drive. Try creating a folder on your desktop and copy into it the compiled bytecode and the host HTML document from your floppy disk. Your applet may run correctly from the desktop.

Perform the following steps to create the host document.

TO CREATE THE HOST DOCUMENT

 1 Start a new session of Notepad. If Notepad already is on your desktop, click File on the Notepad menu bar and then click New.

2 In the Notepad workspace, type the code from Table 4-11.

3 With a floppy disk in drive A, click File on the menu bar and then click Save. When the Save As dialog box displays, type "DonnaApplet.html" in the File name text box. If necessary, click 3½ Floppy (A:) in the Save in list. Click the Save button.

The program saves on the floppy disk in drive A with the name, "DonnaApplet.html" (Figure 4-28).

```
DonnaApplet - Notepad
File  Edit  Search  Help
<HTML>
<APPLET CODE = "DonnaApplet.class" WIDTH = 205 HEIGHT = 500>     ← HTML code
</APPLET>
</HTML>
```

FIGURE 4-28

Table 4-12	
LINE	CODE
1	`/*`
2	`    Project 4        Arrays`
3	`    Programmer:    Joy Starks`
4	`    Date:          December 12, 2001`
5	`    Program Name:  DonnaApplet`
6	`*/`
7	
8	`import java.awt.*;`
9	`import java.applet.*;`
10	`import java.awt.event.*;`
11	
12	`public class DonnaApplet extends Applet implements ActionListener`
13	`{`
14	`    //Declaring Variables`
15	`    String firstName, lastName;`
16	`    int size, content, delivery, organization, rank;`
17	`    int i = 1;`
18	`    float totalContent = 0;`
19	`    float totalDelivery = 0;`
20	`    float totalOrganization = 0;`
21	`    float totalRank = 0;`
22	`    Person[] debateGroup = new Person[50];`
23	

The HTML host document is complete. In the next section, you will create the applet.

Writing Code to Begin the Applet

The DonnaApplet will begin like other applets, with comments, import statements, and a class that extends the Applet and implements ActionListener. You will declare variables to hold the seven fields of information about each student, as well as variables to hold the averages.

The DonnaApplet will differ from the application; you will not recreate the sort routine. The DonnaApplet will allow data entry and calculate the averages. Ask your instructor for ways to expand this applet and include a sort button.

Table 4-12 lists the beginning code.

Perform the following step to write the beginning code for the applet.

TO WRITE CODE TO BEGIN THE APPLET

1 If necessary, click File on the Notepad menu bar and then click New. If you plan to cut and paste code from the Donna application, open a second copy of Notepad and open the Donna file. Enter the code or edit it, from Table 4-12 using your name and the current date in the block comments.

The code is entered in the Notepad window (Figure 4-29).

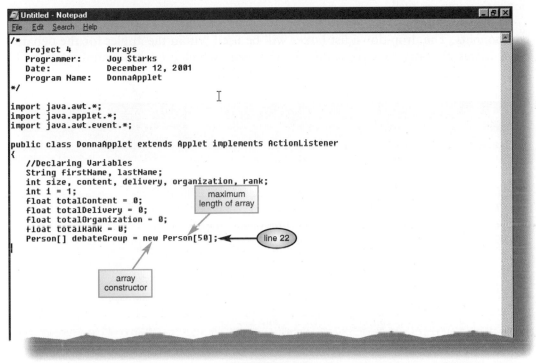

FIGURE 4-29

In lines 8 through 10, the usual import statements display. The variables are declared in lines 15 through 22. Most of the declared variables are the same in both the Donna application program and the DonnaApplet. Of special interest is the array constructor in line 22. It is initialized to be a length of 50, based on the maximum number of people on the debate team.

Creating Choices

Choice is a Java applet component just like buttons, labels, and fields; however, the Choice component displays as a drop-down list box with a box arrow. Computer users expect drop-down lists to display when they click the arrow. The click is the event that Java associates with a Choice event and performs automatically. The Choice event of clicking the arrow to display the list, and then choosing from that list is polymorphic — it happens without any additional components or coding. When you add the Choice component, the functionality comes with it. As you will see later in this project, Choice components have some unique features with regard to their creation and population, but they must be constructed with a name and then added to the applet in a manner similar to other components.

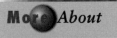
Components

For more information on applet components including Choice and List, visit the Java Programming Web Page (www.scsite.com/java/more.htm) and then click Components.

Using an = new constructor, the Choice component must be given a name.

```
Choice myChoice = new Choice();
```

Choice is the type of component; myChoice is the name of this specific instance of the Choice component. As with the CheckBox group component you learned about in an earlier project, the Choice component's argument list is null — nothing is listed inside the parentheses during construction. Construction takes place in the applet class, before the init method. The component type, Choice, must be capitalized. It is common practice to use the word, Choice, as the last part of the new component's name, as well.

Table 4-13 displays the code to construct the labels, text fields, and three Choice components. The drop-down list boxes will be used within the applet for the debate team scores of content, delivery, and organization, which are whole numbers from 1 to 5. The other input data will use regular text fields.

Table 4-13

LINE	CODE
24	//Create components for applet
25	Label headerLabel = new Label("Please enter forensic score data");
26	
27	Label firstNameLabel = new Label("First Name:");
28	TextField firstNameField = new TextField(15);
29	
30	Label lastNameLabel = new Label("Last Name:");
31	TextField lastNameField = new TextField(15);
32	
33	Label contentLabel = new Label("Content Score:");
34	Choice contentChoice = new Choice();
35	
36	Label deliveryLabel = new Label("Delivery Score:");
37	Choice deliveryChoice = new Choice();
38	
39	Label organizationLabel = new Label("Organization Score:");
40	Choice organizationChoice = new Choice();
41	
42	Label rankLabel = new Label("Rank:");
43	TextField rankField = new TextField(4);
44	
45	Button submitButton = new Button("Submit Scores");
46	Button displayButton = new Button("Display Averages");
47	
48	Label avgContentLabel = new Label("Average Content");
49	Label displayAvgContentLabel = new Label("");
50	Label avgDeliveryLabel = new Label("Average Delivery");
51	Label displayAvgDeliveryLabel = new Label("");
52	Label avgOrganizationLabel = new Label("Average Organization");
53	Label displayAvgOrganizationLabel = new Label("");
54	Label avgRankLabel = new Label("Average Rank");
55	Label displayAvgRankLabel = new Label("");

Perform the following steps to construct the components.

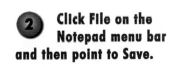 **To Construct the Components**

1 **Below the previous code, type the code to construct the applet components from Table 4-13.**

The code is entered in the Notepad window (Figure 4-30).

```
float totalRank = 0;
Person[] debateGroup = new Person[50];

//Create components for applet
Label headerLabel = new Label("Please enter forensic score data");

Label firstNameLabel = new Label("First Name:");
    TextField firstNameField = new TextField(15);

Label lastNameLabel = new Label("Last Name:");
    TextField lastNameField = new TextField(15);

Label contentLabel = new Label("Content Score:");
    Choice contentChoice = new Choice();

Label deliveryLabel = new Label("Delivery Score:");
    Choice deliveryChoice = new Choice();

Label organizationLabel = new Label("Organization Score:");
    Choice organizationChoice = new Choice();

Label rankLabel = new Label("Rank:");
    TextField rankField = new TextField(4);

Button submitButton = new Button("Submit Scores");
Button displayButton = new Button("Display Averages");

Label avgContentLabel = new Label("Average Content");
    Label displayAvgContentLabel = new Label("");
Label avgDeliveryLabel = new Label("Average Delivery");
    Label displayAvgDeliveryLabel = new Label("");
Label avgOrganizationLabel = new Label("Average Organization");
    Label displayAvgOrganizationLabel = new Label("");
Label avgRankLabel = new Label("Average Rank");
    Label displayAvgRankLabel = new Label("");
```

Choice constructor

Button constructor

FIGURE 4-30

File menu

2 **Click File on the Notepad menu bar and then point to Save.**

The Save As dialog box displays (Figure 4-31).

Save command

```
        Rank = 0;
        bateGrou    erson[50];

mponents    et
rLabel = new Label("Please enter forensic score data");

NameLabel = new Label("First Name:");
d firstNameField = new TextField(15);

Label lastNameLabel = new Label("Last Name:");
    TextField lastNameField = new TextField(15);

Label contentLabel = new Label("Content Score:");
    Choice contentChoice = new Choice();

Label deliveryLabel = new Label("Delivery Score:");
    Choice deliveryChoice = new Choice();

Label organizationLabel = new Label("Organization Score:");
    Choice organizationChoice = new Choice();

Label rankLabel = new Label("Rank:");
    TextField rankField = new TextField(4);

Button submitButton = new Button("Submit Scores");
Button displayButton = new Button("Display Averages");

Label avgContentLabel = new Label("Average Content");
    Label displayAvgContentLabel = new L
```

File menu items: New, Open..., Save, Save As..., Page Setup..., Print, Exit

FIGURE 4-31

3 **Click Save. Type**

"DonnaApplet.java" **in the File name text box. You must type the quotation marks around the file name. If necessary, click the Save in box arrow and then click 3½ Floppy (A:) in the Save in list. Point to the Save button.**

The new file name displays (Figure 4-32). The file will save on drive A.

4 **Click the Save button.**

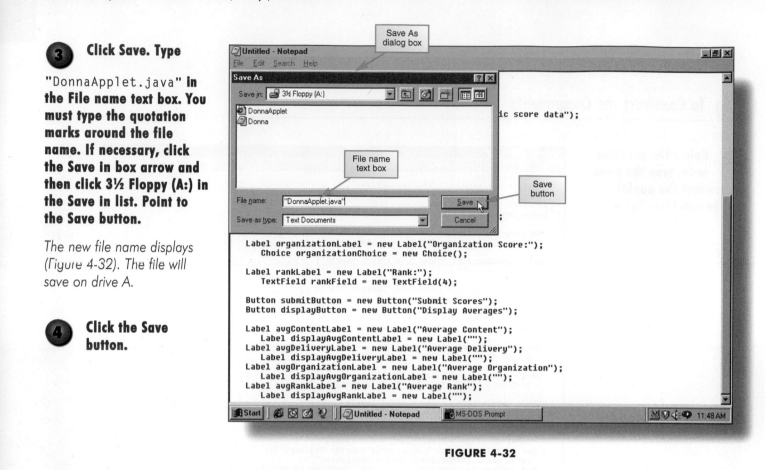

FIGURE 4-32

Lines 34, 37, and 40 construct the Choice components. Indenting the components underneath their associated labels makes the code easier to read.

The addItem Method

Inside the applet's init block, the Choice component is added to the applet in the same way other components have been added.

```
add(myChoice);
```

The add method's argument, inside the parentheses, is the identifier name of the component, myChoice, as constructed previously. It is added in order from top to bottom or left to right. You will learn more about specific placement of components on the screen in a later project.

After the component is added, you must **populate**, or insert data into, the drop-down list. The **addItem** method is used to specify the data.

```
myChoice.addItem("green");
```

In the above example, myChoice is the name of the component, and addItem is the method. Notice that a period separates the object and its method, as is usual in object-oriented languages. The word, green, is a String that becomes the first member of the list. Choice components must be populated with Strings only. If you later need to use the data in a numeric fashion, you must parse or convert it.

The population of a drop-down list is similar to adding data to an array. As the data is entered, it is given an index number that begins with zero and increases by one each time new data is entered. You may use as many addItem methods as you like, populated explicitly as in the above example, or populated from user input with variables. Each subsequent addItem method is placed in order in the given object's list. Programmers often place the addItems together in the code, directly after the addition of the object itself.

Table 4-14 displays the init method and the add methods. Notice that line 70 adds a label identifying the Choice component in line 71. Lines 72 through 76 then populate the Choice component with addItem methods. The indentation is optional, but adds to the applet code's legibility. The order of the population is crucial. You must list the addItem methods in the order you want them to display in the list.

Table 4-14

LINE	CODE	LINE	CODE
57	`public void init()`	86	`add(organizationLabel);`
58	`{`	87	`add(organizationChoice);`
59	`//Add components to window and set colors`	88	`organizationChoice.addItem("1");`
60	`setBackground(Color.green);`	89	`organizationChoice.addItem("2");`
61	`add(headerLabel);`	90	`organizationChoice.addItem("3");`
62		91	`organizationChoice.addItem("4");`
63	`add(firstNameLabel);`	92	`organizationChoice.addItem("5");`
64	`add(firstNameField);`	93	
65	`firstNameField.requestFocus();`	94	`add(rankLabel);`
66		95	`add(rankField);`
67	`add(lastNameLabel);`	96	
68	`add(lastNameField);`	97	`add(submitButton);`
69		98	`submitButton.addActionListener(this);`
70	`add(contentLabel);`	99	
71	`add(contentChoice);`	100	`add(displayButton);`
72	`contentChoice.addItem("1");`	101	`displayButton.addActionListener(this);`
73	`contentChoice.addItem("2");`	102	
74	`contentChoice.addItem("3");`	103	`add(avgContentLabel);`
75	`contentChoice.addItem("4");`	104	`add(displayAvgContentLabel);`
76	`contentChoice.addItem("5");`	105	`add(avgDeliveryLabel);`
77		106	`add(displayAvgDeliveryLabel);`
78	`add(deliveryLabel);`	107	`add(avgOrganizationLabel);`
79	`add(deliveryChoice);`	108	`add(displayAvgOrganizationLabel);`
80	`deliveryChoice.addItem("1");`	109	`add(avgRankLabel);`
81	`deliveryChoice.addItem("2");`	110	`add(displayAvgRankLabel);`
82	`deliveryChoice.addItem("3");`	111	`}`
83	`deliveryChoice.addItem("4");`		
84	`deliveryChoice.addItem("5");`		
85			

Perform the following steps to enter the init block with its add methods into the DonnaApplet program.

To Enter the add Methods

1 **If necessary, click at the end of the code on line 55. Press the ENTER key twice, to create a blank line between the label constructors and the init method.**

The insertion point displays on line 57 (Figure 4-33).

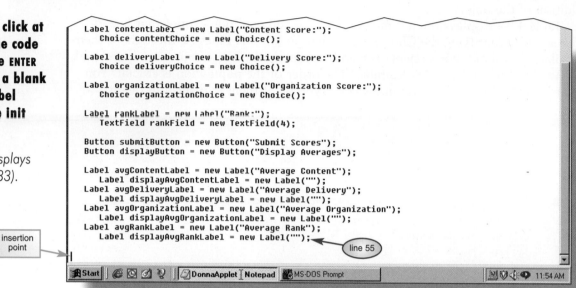

```
Label contentLabel = new Label("Content Score:");
    Choice contentChoice = new Choice();

Label deliveryLabel = new Label("Delivery Score:");
    Choice deliveryChoice = new Choice();

Label organizationLabel = new Label("Organization Score:");
    Choice organizationChoice = new Choice();

Label rankLabel = new Label("Rank:");
    TextField rankField = new TextField(4);

Button submitButton = new Button("Submit Scores");
Button displayButton = new Button("Display Averages");

Label avgContentLabel = new Label("Average Content");
    Label displayAvgContentLabel = new Label("");
Label avgDeliveryLabel = new Label("Average Delivery");
    Label displayAvgDeliveryLabel = new Label("");
Label avgOrganizationLabel = new Label("Average Organization");
    Label displayAvgOrganizationLabel = new Label("");
Label avgRankLabel = new Label("Average Rank");
    Label displayAvgRankLabel = new Label("");
```

insertion point

line 55

FIGURE 4-33

2 **From Table 4-14 on the previous page, type the code using appropriate indentations.**

The init method block displays as entered (Figure 4-34). Some code will scroll out of view.

3 **Click File on the Notepad menu bar and then click Save.**

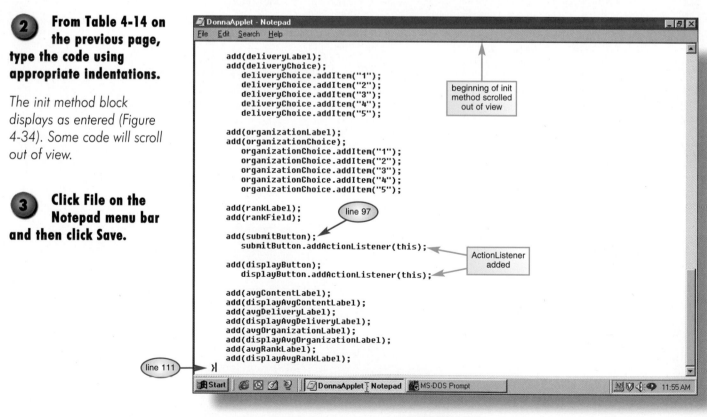

DonnaApplet - Notepad
File   Edit   Search   Help

```
    add(deliveryLabel);
    add(deliveryChoice);
        deliveryChoice.addItem("1");
        deliveryChoice.addItem("2");
        deliveryChoice.addItem("3");
        deliveryChoice.addItem("4");
        deliveryChoice.addItem("5");

    add(organizationLabel);
    add(organizationChoice);
        organizationChoice.addItem("1");
        organizationChoice.addItem("2");
        organizationChoice.addItem("3");
        organizationChoice.addItem("4");
        organizationChoice.addItem("5");

    add(rankLabel);
    add(rankField);

    add(submitButton);
        submitButton.addActionListener(this);

    add(displayButton);
        displayButton.addActionListener(this);

    add(avgContentLabel);
    add(displayAvgContentLabel);
    add(avgDeliveryLabel);
    add(displayAvgDeliveryLabel);
    add(avgOrganizationLabel);
    add(displayAvgOrganizationLabel);
    add(avgRankLabel);
    add(displayAvgRankLabel);
```

beginning of init method scrolled out of view

line 97

ActionListener added

line 111

FIGURE 4-34

In line 65 (Table 4-13 on page J 4.31), the requestFocus method will force the insertion point to display in the first text field. Lines 97 through 101 add two buttons to the applet, one to submit the scores to the array and the second to display averages. Each button is given the ability to be clicked by the addActionListener event that you learned about in a previous project.

The actionPerformed Event

Because the applet contains two buttons, the actionPerformed event must be able to distinguish which one the user has clicked. The actionPerformed event begins whenever an ActionListener button is clicked. With code, you must direct the actionPerformed event to perform a different set of instructions based on the individual buttons. To test the button's command, if statements will be used. Table 4-15 lists the actionPerformed event code.

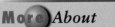

More About

The repaint Method

Java's repaint method (line 150) refreshes the applet screen after a data change. For more information on applet methods, visit the Java Programming Web Page (www.scsite.com/java/more.htm) and then click Applet Methods.

Table 4-15

LINE	CODE
113	`public void actionPerformed(ActionEvent e)`
114	`{`
115	`    String arg = e.getActionCommand();`
116	`    if (arg == "Submit Scores")`
117	`    {`
118	`        //Assigning data`
119	`        firstName = firstNameField.getText();`
120	`        lastName = lastNameField.getText();`
121	`        content = Integer.parseInt(contentChoice.getSelectedItem());`
122	`        delivery = Integer.parseInt(deliveryChoice.getSelectedItem());`
123	`        organization = Integer.parseInt(organizationChoice.getSelectedItem());`
124	`        rank = Integer.parseInt(rankField.getText());`
125	
126	`        size = i++;`
127	`        debateGroup[i] = new Person(firstName, lastName, content, delivery, organization, rank);`
128	
129	`        //Accumulate totals for each category`
130	`        totalContent += debateGroup[i].getContent();`
131	`        totalDelivery += debateGroup[i].getDelivery();`
132	`        totalOrganization += debateGroup[i].getOrganization();`
133	`        totalRank += debateGroup[i].getRank();`
134	
135	`        firstNameField.setText("");`
136	`        lastNameField.setText("");`
137	`        contentChoice.select(0);`
138	`        deliveryChoice.select(0);`
139	`        organizationChoice.select(0);`
140	`        rankField.setText("");`
141	`        firstNameField.requestFocus();`
142	`    }`
143	
144	`    if (arg == "Display Averages")`
145	`    {`
146	`        displayAvgContentLabel.setText(String.valueOf(totalContent/size));`
147	`        displayAvgDeliveryLabel.setText(String.valueOf(totalDelivery/size));`
148	`        displayAvgOrganizationLabel.setText(String.valueOf(totalOrganization/size));`
149	`        displayAvgRankLabel.setText(String.valueOf(totalRank/size));`
150	`        repaint();`
151	`    }`
152	`}`
153	`}`

Sorting Data in an Applet

If your instructor wishes you to add a sort button to the applet, you must enlarge the applet display in the host document and add a text field to display the results. In the applet itself, you would create or construct the button and the new field at the beginning of the class, add them to the applet in the init method, and then code an if statement to test the button's caption. A sort routine would need to be coded if the condition were true.

Line 115 uses a **getActionCommand** to assign the clicked button's caption to an identifier variable, arg. Then, arg is compared against the caption "Submit Scores" in line 116 and again against "Display Averages" in line 144. If the condition is true, the code inside the corresponding block will be performed.

If the user clicks Submit Scores the fields are assigned to variables. The **getText** method retrieves information from the text fields (lines 119, 120, and 124). The **getSelectedItem** method retrieves data from the Choice component (lines 121 through 123), which then is parsed into integers and stored.

In order to store the information in an array, the variable i is incremented in line 126. The value is assigned to the location, size, which will be used later in the calculation of averages. Line 127 assigns the data to the array element, just as in the application created earlier in this project.

Java's assignment operators are used to accumulate the totals. After the data is stored, the text fields and choices boxes are set back to their original values (lines 135 through 141).

If the stored command, arg, is equal to Display Averages, then the user must have clicked the Display Averages button. At this point, the display labels which previously were blank are assigned the String values corresponding to the calculated answers. The **valueOf** method converts the float answers to Strings for display purposes.

Perform the following steps to enter the actionPerformed event block.

Steps: To Enter the actionPerformed Event

1 **If necessary, click at the end of all previous code on line 111. Press the ENTER key twice to create a blank line between the init method and the actionPerformed event.**

The insertion point displays on line 113 (Figure 4-35).

```
        add(deliveryChoice);
            deliveryChoice.addItem("1");
            deliveryChoice.addItem("2");
            deliveryChoice.addItem("3");
            deliveryChoice.addItem("4");
            deliveryChoice.addItem("5");

        add(organizationLabel);
        add(organizationChoice);
            organizationChoice.addItem("1");
            organizationChoice.addItem("2");
            organizationChoice.addItem("3");
            organizationChoice.addItem("4");
            organizationChoice.addItem("5");

        add(rankLabel);
        add(rankField);

        add(submitButton);
            submitButton.addActionListener(this);

        add(displayButton);
            displayButton.addActionListener(this);

        add(avgContentLabel);
        add(displayAvgContentLabel);
        add(avgDeliveryLabel);
        add(displayAvgDeliveryLabel);
        add(avgOrganizationLabel);
        add(displayAvgOrganizationLabel);
        add(avgRankLabel);
        add(displayAvgRankLabel);
    }
```

line 111

insertion point

FIGURE 4-35

2 From Table 4-15 on page J 4.41, type the code using appropriate indentations.

The actionPerformed event block displays as entered (Figure 4-36). The three closing braces close the if construct, the actionPerformed event, and the DonnaApplet class.

3 Click File on the Notepad menu bar and then click Save.

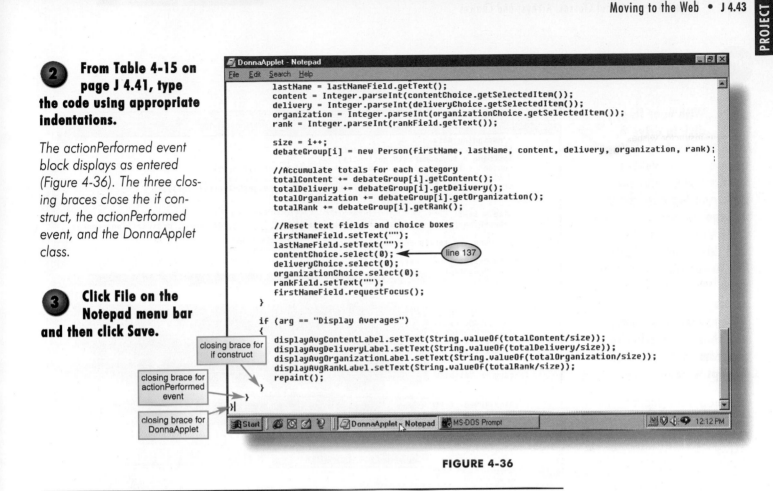

```
lastName = lastNameField.getText();
content = Integer.parseInt(contentChoice.getSelectedItem());
delivery = Integer.parseInt(deliveryChoice.getSelectedItem());
organization = Integer.parseInt(organizationChoice.getSelectedItem());
rank = Integer.parseInt(rankField.getText());

size = i++;
debateGroup[i] = new Person(firstName, lastName, content, delivery, organization, rank);

//Accumulate totals for each category
totalContent += debateGroup[i].getContent();
totalDelivery += debateGroup[i].getDelivery();
totalOrganization += debateGroup[i].getOrganization();
totalRank += debateGroup[i].getRank();

//Reset text fields and choice boxes
firstNameField.setText("");
lastNameField.setText("");
contentChoice.select(0);          <- line 137
deliveryChoice.select(0);
organizationChoice.select(0);
rankField.setText("");
firstNameField.requestFocus();
}

if (arg == "Display Averages")
{
    displayAvgContentLabel.setText(String.valueOf(totalContent/size));
    displayAvgDeliveryLabel.setText(String.valueOf(totalDelivery/size));
    displayAvgOrganizationLabel.setText(String.valueOf(totalOrganization/size));
    displayAvgRankLabel.setText(String.valueOf(totalRank/size));
    repaint();
}
```

closing brace for if construct

closing brace for actionPerformed event

closing brace for DonnaApplet

FIGURE 4-36

The **select** method is used to reset the Choice components (lines 137 through 139). Its argument is the subscript of the item in the list you wish to display. The text fields are cleared, and focus is returned to the First Name text box.

Now that the applet is done, you are ready to compile and test the running applet.

Compiling the DonnaApplet

Perform the steps on the next page to compile and run the DonnaApplet. You may use any sample data you would like, or you may enter the same data you used in the Donna application, from Table 4-10 on page J 4.31.

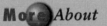

More About

Displaying Applets

Do your applets appear differently? Why do applet components move around when I resize the applet window? If you have asked yourself these questions, you are ready to progress to Project 5. Up to now, you have used the default applet layout manager that places components left to right as they fit within the window. Your screens may differ because your monitor resolution is different. To control placement exactly, you will use one of Java's five layout managers, which automatically resizes your components and places them where you want them, as the user resizes the applet window.

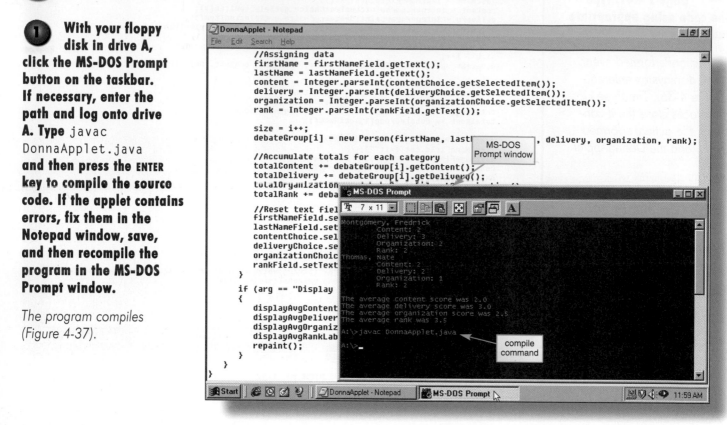

Steps **To Compile and Run the DonnaApplet**

1 **With your floppy disk in drive A, click the MS-DOS Prompt button on the taskbar. If necessary, enter the path and log onto drive A. Type** javac DonnaApplet.java **and then press the ENTER key to compile the source code. If the applet contains errors, fix them in the Notepad window, save, and then recompile the program in the MS-DOS Prompt window.**

The program compiles (Figure 4-37).

FIGURE 4-37

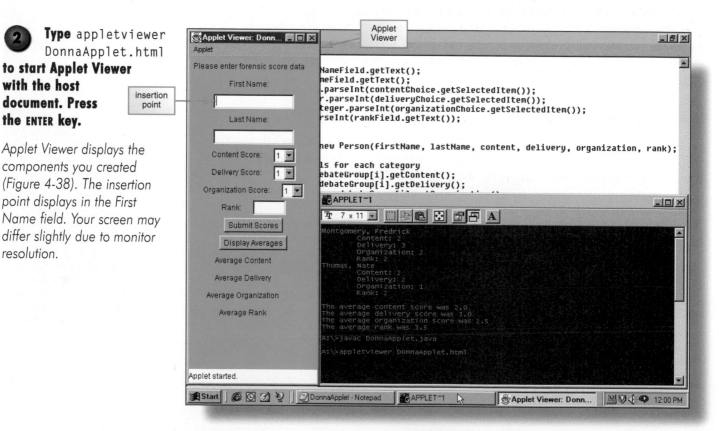

2 **Type** appletviewer DonnaApplet.html **to start Applet Viewer with the host document. Press the ENTER key.**

Applet Viewer displays the components you created (Figure 4-38). The insertion point displays in the First Name field. Your screen may differ slightly due to monitor resolution.

FIGURE 4-38

Type Katie **or another sample data name in the First Name text field. Press the TAB key.**

The name displays and the insertion point moves to the Last Name text field (Figure 4-39).

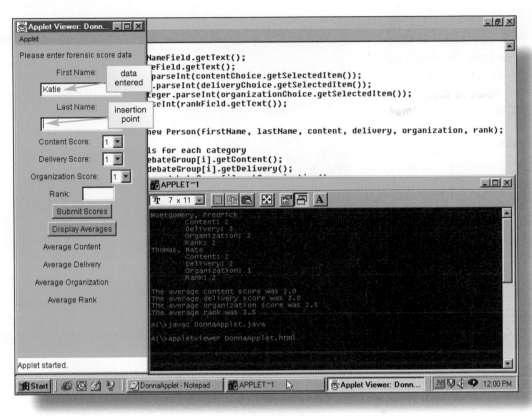

FIGURE 4-39

Type Marie **or another sample data name in the Last Name text field. Point to the first drop-down box arrow for the Content Score.**

The Last Name displays (Figure 4-40).

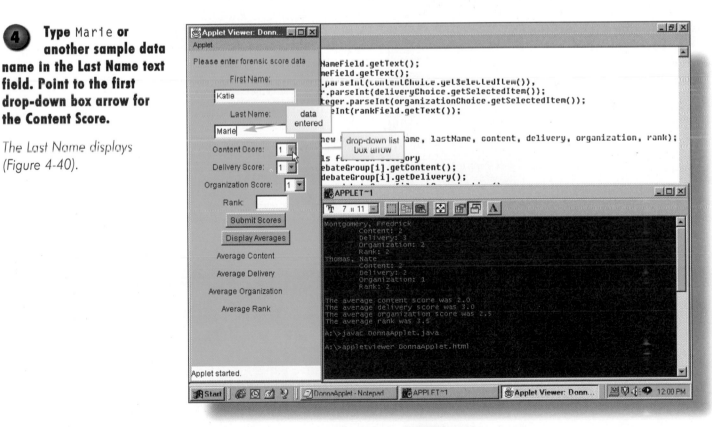

FIGURE 4-40

5 Click each box arrow and select sample scores from the displayed lists. If you are using the same data from Table 4-10 on page J 4.31, the data will display as shown in Figure 4-41.

The scores 1, 3, and 3 display respectively in the Content Score, Delivery Score, and Organization Score Choice components (Figure 4-41).

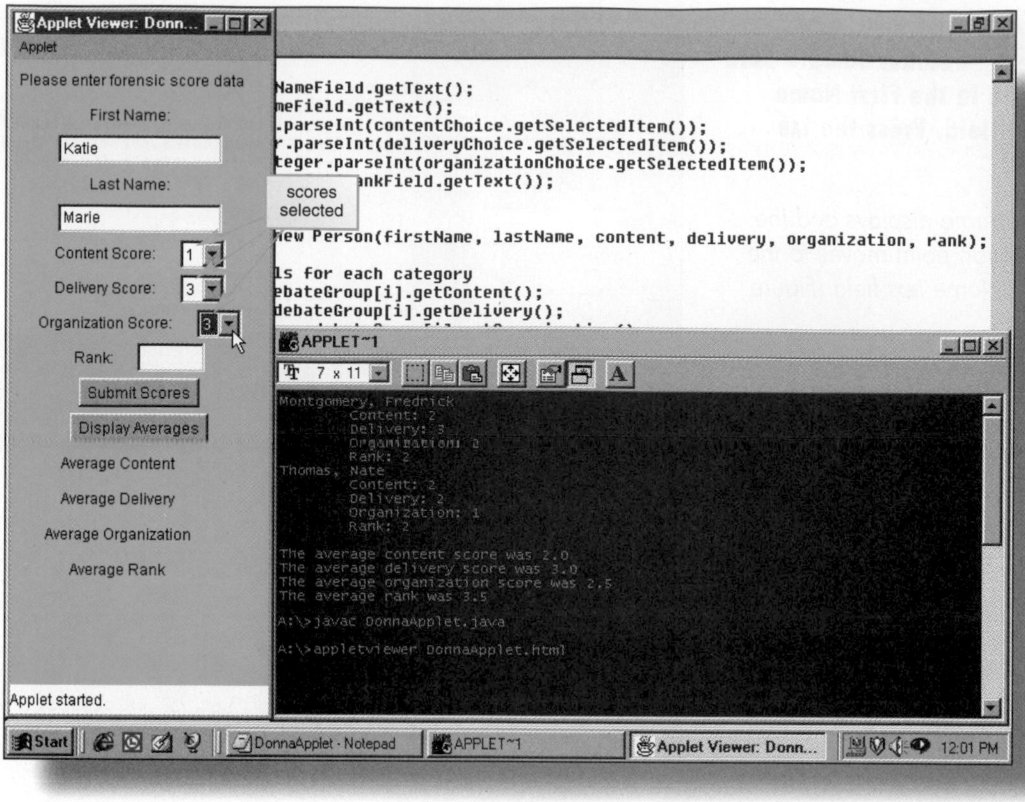

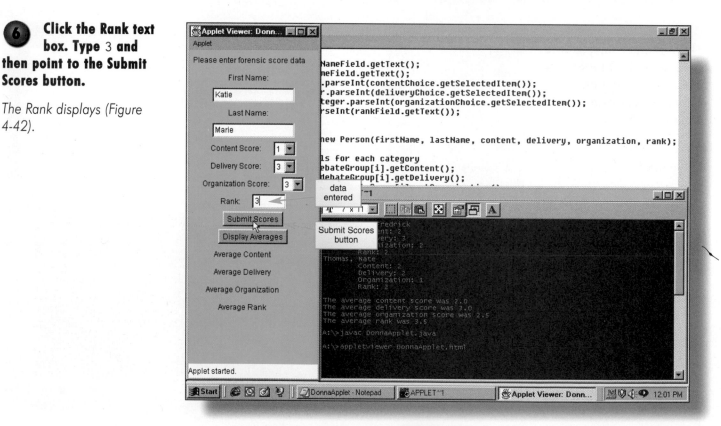

FIGURE 4-41

6 Click the Rank text box. Type 3 and then point to the Submit Scores button.

The Rank displays (Figure 4-42).

FIGURE 4-42

7 **Click the Submit Scores button.**

The data is sent to the array and the components are reset back to their original values (Figure 4-43).

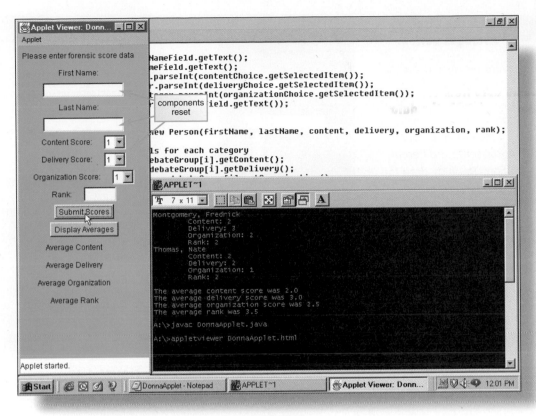

FIGURE 4-43

8 **Repeat Steps 3 through 7 for each student. After you have submitted all the scores, point to the Display Averages button.**

The last submission clears the text fields as you prepare to display the averages (Figure 4-44).

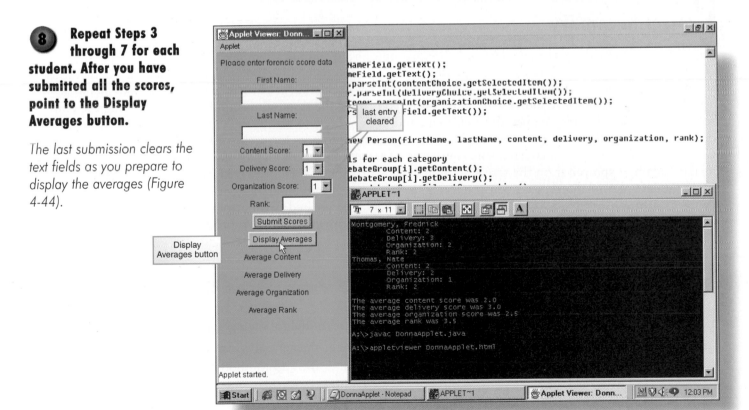

FIGURE 4-44

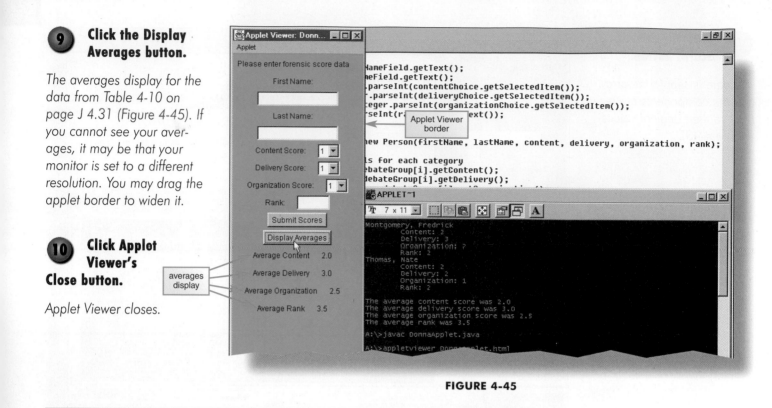

⑨ **Click the Display Averages button.**

The averages display for the data from Table 4-10 on page J 4.31 (Figure 4-45). If you cannot see your averages, it may be that your monitor is set to a different resolution. You may drag the applet border to widen it.

⑩ **Click Applet Viewer's Close button.**

Applet Viewer closes.

FIGURE 4-45

Project Summary

This project presented a series of steps and a discussion of a Java application to enter student scores from a recent debate tournament. First, you coded an external method named Person, which instantiated the methods to create a user-defined structure with the six data fields for each student's scores. The method also included instance methods to retrieve individual fields. Then, you coded the stand-alone application, including the construction of an object array named debateGroup, and lines of code to accept the data from the user. You used a for loop with the unary increment operator, ++, to repeat the prompts for each student's data. Once the data was stored in the array, you coded a sort routine to alphabetize the data by last name. A final loop ran through the data again, displayed it on the screen in alphabetical order, and then displayed calculated averages.

In the last part of the project, you converted the application into an applet with Choice components that displayed as drop-down lists, as well as text fields and labels. You created two buttons, one to submit the scores to an array and the other to display averages. Using an actionPerformed event, you tested which button the user chose.

What You Should Know

Having completed this project, you now should be able to perform the following tasks:

▸ Begin the Donna Application (J 4.17)
▸ Compile and Run the Application (J 4.31)
▸ Compile and Run the DonnaApplet (J 4.44)
▸ Compile the Person Class Source Code (J 4.13)
▸ Construct the Components (J 4.27)
▸ Create Instance Methods (J 4.12)
▸ Create the Host Document (J 4.34)
▸ Enter Beginning Code (J 4.8)

▸ Enter the actionPerformed Event (J 4.42)
▸ Enter the add Methods (J 4.40)
▸ Enter the Display, Accumulation, and Averaging Code (J 4.29)
▸ Enter the for Loop (J 4.24)
▸ Enter the Method Constructor (J 4.10)
▸ Enter the Search Code (J 4.27)
▸ Write Code to Begin the Applet (J 4.35)

Test Your Knowledge

1 True/False

Instructions: Circle T if the statement is true or F if the statement is false.

T F   1. A class or method that is not part of the running application class is called an external class.

T F   2. If you omit the access modifier in a class header, Java considers the class public.

T F   3. Defining more than one method with the same name is called reinstantiating.

T F   4. A subscript is a number referencing an array element.

T F   5. The length of the array is declared when it is constructed.

T F   6. The unary operator, ++, works the same way whether it is placed before or after an operand.

T F   7. The for statement parameters are separated by semicolons.

T F   8. The Choice component presents a list of option button choices.

T F   9. The addItem method adds a new data element to a standard array.

T F   10. Because it is impossible to tell which button a user has clicked, a separate actionPerformed event must be created for each one.

2 Multiple Choice

Instructions: Circle the correct response.

1. Which of the following declares an integer array named scores?
   a. int scores;
   b. int[] scores;
   c. new int scores[];
   d. int scores = int[];

2. What are the legal subscripts for the array evenNumbers, given the declaration int[] evenNumbers = {2, 4, 6, 8 }?
   a. 0, 1, 2, 3
   b. 1, 2, 3, 4
   c. 2, 4, 6, 8
   d. all even numbers

3. For which of the following applications is an array NOT suitable?
   a. storing the scores on 12 midterm exams of a class
   b. storing the name, social security number, age, and income of one individual
   c. storing the temperature readings taken every hour throughout a day
   d. storing a list of animals at the local zoo

4. Which of the following initializes an instance variable?
   a. a constructor method
   b. an overload
   c. an initializer
   d. a for statement

(continued)

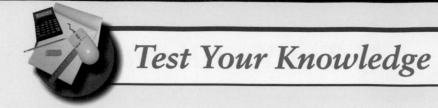

Test Your Knowledge

Multiple Choice *(continued)*

5. A(n) _____ stores data in a contiguous block of memory, divided into a number of slots.
   a. overload
   b. array
   c. element
   d. constructor

6. Sorting String data in _____ order results in an alphabetical listing from A to Z.
   a. descending
   b. forward
   c. ascending
   d. any

7. Which one of the following sort routines creates a new, sorted array by merging two previously sorted arrays?
   a. bubble sort
   b. selection sort
   c. insertion sort
   d. merge sort

8. Which of the following is NOT an assignment operator?
   a. +=
   b. =\
   c. *=
   d. /=

9. Which of the following methods correctly adds a new item to a Choice component?
   a. addItem()
   b. add()
   c. insertItem()
   d. addChoice()

10. In a formula with mixed data types, Java's conversion of the answer to the broader type is called _____.
   a. data typing
   b. floating
   c. classifying
   d. casting

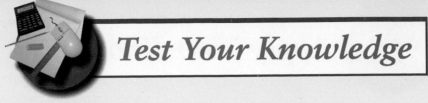

Test Your Knowledge

3 Coding a Choice Component

Instructions: Figure 4-46 displays a drop-down list. In the spaces provided, write the Java code to declare and construct the component, add the component to the applet, and then populate the drop-down list. The name of the component is zoomChoice.

_____

_____

_____

_____

_____

_____

_____

_____

_____

_____

_____

```
90%          ▼
500%
200%
150%
100%
75%
50%
25%
10%
Page Width
Text Width
Whole Page
Two Pages
```

FIGURE 4-46

4 Understanding Arrays and Operators

Instructions: In the spaces provided, list the displayed value after the line of code is executed. The first one has been completed for you. In the example, the first line of code declares and constructs an array of ints. Because no values have been assigned, the next line results in the display of a zero, which is the value stored at the zero element of the array. Assume the coding progresses sequentially, as you fill in the remaining spaces.

```
int[] myArray = new int[10];
    System.out.println(myArray[0]);              0
myArray[1] = 28;
    System.out.println(myArray[1]);              _____
myArray[2] = myArray[1];
    System.out.println(myArray[2]);              _____
myArray[3] = ++myArray[2];
    System.out.println(myArray[3]);              _____
myArray[4] = myArray[1]—;
    System.out.println(myArray[4]);              _____
myArray[5] += 7;
    System.out.println(myArray[5]);              _____
myArray[6] = myArray[1] /= myArray[5];
    System.out.println(myArray[1]);              _____
for (int i = 0; i<myArray.length; i++)
{
    myArray[i] = i;
}
    System.out.println(myArray[9]);              _____
```

Apply Your Knowledge

1 Using an Applet to Search an Array

Instructions: This exercise will use the file Apply4.java from the Data Disk (see the inside back cover for instructions on how to obtain a copy of the Data Disk). It will also create an HTML host file.

Many e-commerce Web sites and intranets require a login and password in order to access data from the site. You recently have taken a work-study job in the Computer Administration Department and have been asked to finish a login applet started by a previous student. The applet will ask the user for an ID and password. Once the user presses the Login button, the applet will search through an array of IDs and passwords for verification. The applet then will display an appropriate message. The file includes a method called setEchoCharacter, which displays asterisks as the user types the password and a setLayout method to align the components.

Using techniques learned in this project, write the code to create two arrays, one for the IDs and one for the corresponding passwords, assigning some sample IDs and passwords to elements of the arrays. You will write a loop to progress through the array, searching for a valid ID and password. You will use a sequential or linear search that looks at each member of the array and sets a flag to true if the ID and password match an array element. Finally, after compiling, you will use appletviewer and the HTML host document to run the applet.

Figure 4-47 displays the completed applet.

FIGURE 4-47

Part A: *Creating the Host Document*

1. Start a new session of Notepad.
2. Type the HTML tag and then, on the next line, begin the APPLET tag.
3. Use a CODE statement to access the PasswordApplet.class. Use a WIDTH statement of 300 and a HEIGHT statement of 300.
4. Close the APPLET and HTML tags.
5. Save the file as "PasswordApplet.html" on your floppy disk.

Apply Your Knowledge

Part B: *Creating the Applet*

1. Open the Apply4.java file in the Notepad window. Substitute your name and date in the block comment at the beginning. Type `PasswordApplet` as the new class name. Edit the name of the class in the class header as well.

2. Save the file on your floppy disk with "PasswordApplet.java" as the file name. Print a copy if you wish, to reference while completing this lab.

3. Insert three import statements after the block comments to import the java.awt.*, java.applet.*, and java.awt.event.* packages.

4. Insert the following array declaration and assignment statements at the end of the Declaring variables section. Fill in your own choice of passwords and IDs. Separate each element of the array with a comma, and enclose each password and ID in quotations.

   String idArray[] = {"id", ...};
   String passwordArray[] = {"password", ...};

5. In the actionPerformed event, below the line `//Sequential search`, construct a for loop that uses i as its counter. The loop should begin at 0, continue while the counter is less than idArray.length, and increment by 1 using the unary operator.

6. Inside the loop, enter the following code that uses the compareTo method to look for a match in both the id and password.

`if ((idArray[i].compareTo(id)==0) && (passwordArray[i].compareTo(password)==0)) success=true;`

7. After the loop, write an if and else structure to test the success of the user entry. If it is true, use the setText method to change the headerLabel to read "Login Successful" and then repaint. If it is false, display a message in the headerLabel to read "Unsuccessful, Try Again", and then clear both text fields and reset the focus. The repaint() method already is called at the end of the event.

8. Save the applet again.

9. Open the MS DOS Prompt window. If you downloaded JDK from the Sun Web site, set the path to the location of your Java bin by typing `path=c:\jdk1.2.2\bin` at the command prompt and then press the ENTER key. If you installed the Java compiler from the JBuilder3 CD-ROM that may accompany this text, type `path=c:\jbuilder3\java\bin` and then press the ENTER key.

10. Change to your floppy disk drive by typing `a:` and then press the ENTER key.

11. Compile your program by typing `javac PasswordApplet.java` and then press the ENTER key. If you have errors, fix them in the Notepad window, save, and then recompile.

12. Print a copy for your instructor.

Part C: *Running the Applet*

1. Click the MS-DOS Prompt button on the taskbar. Type `appletviewer PasswordApplet.html` at the MS-DOS prompt.

2. Enter an invalid ID and password. Click the Login button.

3. After the applet displays the error message and clears the fields, type a valid ID and password from the list you entered in Step 4 in Section B, above. Click the Login button.

4. Try various combinations of valid IDs and passwords.

In the Lab

1 Writing External Methods

As an intern at Jamco Incorporated, you have been asked to write a Java class named PayRec that, when called, creates a programmer-defined payroll record. As Jamco hires new employees, it will use the PayRec class, along with an accessor method, to input data about each employee. The fields should include last name, first name, position, rate, and hours. You also should include corresponding get methods to allow for future searching and sorting.

Instructions: Using the techniques you learned in creating the Person class from the Project, create a PayRec class by performing the following steps:

1. Start Notepad.
2. Include a block comment with your name, date, and the class name, PayRec.
3. Import the java.io.* package.
4. Write the public class header. Declare variables as shown in Table 4-16.

Table 4-16 Variables for the PayRec Application	
DATA TYPE	VARIABLE NAME
String	firstName
String	lastName
String	position
float	rate
float	hours

5. Begin a method constructor called PayRec that accepts the five arguments, f, l, p, r, and h, which correspond to the variables in Table 4-16.
6. Within the method constructor, assign each of the single letter identifiers to its corresponding variable name as you did in the project.
7. Create a second method constructor, also called PayRec, which overloads the class but accepts only l, f, and p corresponding to the last name, first name, and position.
8. Create instance methods that begin with the word get, for each of the variables from Table 4-16. Return the variable in each method.
9. Save the program with the file name, "PayRec.java" on your floppy disk.
10. Compile the program at the MS-DOS Prompt. If you have errors, fix them in the Notepad window, save, and then recompile.
11. Print a copy of the source code for your instructor.

In the Lab

2 Creating an Applet with Drop-Down Lists

David's Campground would like an applet to help their customers fill out a reservation on the Web. His paper reservation system includes fields for the customers' personal information, the date they plan to arrive, and the number of nights they will stay. His paper reservation form also lists the type of hookups the customer wants. David writes down the type of camping vehicles, such as pop-up, trailer, tent, etc.

In the Web form, David would like these fields and lists easily available. Additionally, he would like a Submit button and a Clear button. You do not have to add functionality to the Submit button. This is a prototype.

Part A: Creating the Host Document

1. Start a new session of Notepad.
2. Type the HTML tag and then, on the next line, begin the APPLET tag.
3. Use a CODE statement to access the DavidApplet.class. Use a WIDTH statement of 550 and a HEIGHT statement of 400.
4. Close the APPLET and HTML tags.
5. Save the file as "DavidApplet.html" on your floppy disk.

Part B: Creating the Applet Source Code

1. Start a new session of Notepad.
2. Type a block comment including your name, the current date, the file name "DavidApplet.java", and a brief description of the purpose of the program.
3. Import the java.awt.*, java.applet.*, and java.awt.event.* packages.
4. Include a header for the DavidApplet class, which extends Applet and implements the ActionListener.
5. Declare the following string variables: firstName, lastName, address, city, state, zip, arrivalDate. Declare the following int: numberNights.
6. Create components for the applet, including the labels, text fields, buttons and drop-down lists as shown in Figure 4-48.
7. Create an init method. Set a background color of your choice. Add the labels you created in step 6 in order from left to right and then top to bottom. Set the focus to the first text field. Use addItem methods to populate the drop-down lists as follows: Camping Vehicles: tent, pop-up, travel trailer, fifth-wheel, motor home Hook-ups: water only, water and electricity, full hook-ups, no hook-ups

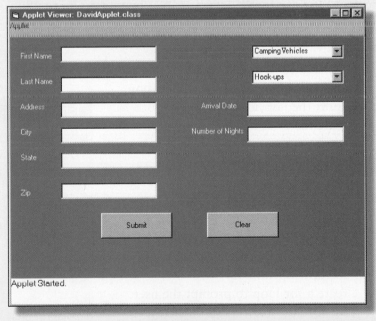

FIGURE 4-48

(continued)

In the Lab

Creating an Applet with Drop-Down Lists *(continued)*

8. Use the addActionListener method to make the buttons clickable.
9. Create an actionPerformed method that tests for which button was clicked with the code displayed in Table 4-17.
10. Add functionality to the Clear button using setText and select.
11. Type the closing brace to close the DavidApplet class.
12. Save the applet as "DavidApplet.java" on your floppy disk. Compile and execute the applet.
13. Your component placement may not match the figure exactly. You may experiment with field widths and the Width and Height of the applet itself in the HTML file. As an extra credit assignment, browse the Web for information on exact placement using Java's Layout Manager methods and incorporate that into your applet.

Table 4-17

CODE

```
public void actionPerformed(ActionEvent e)
{
    String arg = e.getActionCommand();
    if (arg == "Submit")
    {


    }
    if (arg == "Clear")
    {


    }
}
```

3 Sorting Arrays

ZoosRUs is a non-profit organization that assists zoos in keeping up with the endangered species list and helps with animal registries all over the United States. They would like a Java program to alphabetize all the animal species housed at zoos throughout the country. Many of the zoos have different computer platforms, so they would like a Java application that can run on any of the systems. ZoosRUs has given you list of 16 endangered species to use as sample data. Create a Java program to allow the user to enter the list, sort it, and then display it in columns on the screen.

Instructions:

1. Open Notepad and enter block comments to describe the purpose of the program, your name, the current date, and the name of the application.
2. Import the java.io package.
3. Create the class header and main header with their opening braces. Remember that the main header must throw an IOException due to user input.
4. Enter the constructor for the BufferedReader.
5. Declare an array of 16 animals named animalArray. Declare a String variable named, tempAnimal.
6. Create a for loop to prompt the user and store the answers in the array elements.

Table 4-18

CODE

```
//Sort the animals
for (int i = 1; i<animalArray.length; i++);
{
    int j = i;
    tempAnimal = animalArray[i];
    while ((j>0) && (animalArray[j-1].compareTo(tempAnimal)>0))
    {
        animalArray[j] = animalArray[j-1];
        j--;
    }
    animalArray[j] = tempAnimal;
}
```

In the Lab

7. Enter the sequential sort routine from Table 4-18.

8. Write a closing loop that increments by fours, using the add and assign operator. Use the \t escape character to print the list four across.
   Hint: System.out.println(animalArray[i]+"\t"+animalArray[i+1]+"\t"+animalArray[i+2]+...);

9. Save the application on your floppy disk. Open an MS-DOS Prompt window and set the path.

10. Compile the application and run it using the sample data from Table 4-19. When the sorted output displays, press the PRINTSCREEN button.

Table 4-19			
ENDANGERED SPECIES IN THE UNITED STATES			
shrew	bat	wolf	jaguar
ocelot	cougar	puma	sea lion
grizzly	whale	lemming	petrel
condor	tortoise	elimia	vole

11. Paste the print screen caption to Microsoft Word or Paint, or see your instructor for a suitable program on your system. Print the screen capture.

12. Print a copy of your source code from Notepad.

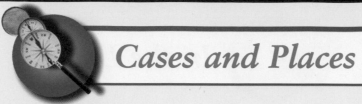

Cases and Places

The difficulty of these case studies varies:
▶ are the least difficult; ▶▶ are more difficult; and ▶▶▶ are the most difficult.

1 ▶ Write a Java program that allows you to enter your grades in this course into an array of floats. At the beginning of the program, the application should prompt you for the total number of grades you intend to enter. After entering the grades, the application should call a method to average the grades. Display the grades and the resulting average.

2 ▶ Encore Movies wants an applet that allows the user to choose a movie and then a number of tickets from drop-down lists. A check box should display for users to click so they can receive a discount for matinee movies. Consult a local movie theater for sample prices and attractions. The user should be able to click a calculate price button to display the total cost, and a clear button to clear each drop-down list and the check box.

3 ▶▶ Write a Java program to call an external method that creates a programmer-defined data type called CD. The CD data type will store information about the title of music CDs, the artist's name, and the style of music. The program should allow the user to enter an array of 15 CDs. Finally, the program should sort the CDs by artist and then display the results. Run the program and enter all or part of your own CD collection. Use the PRINTSCREEN key to generate results for your instructor.

4 ▶▶ Donna Reneau, advisor to the debate team, would like the ability to sort her team's information by various categories other than last name. Make the appropriate changes to the project program to allow Donna to choose by which category she would like to sort: content, delivery, organization, or rank. Once Donna chooses a category, use a switch structure to evaluate Donna's choice and call the appropriate get method.

5 ▶▶▶ Using a Web search engine, enter the keywords, Java applets, to surf the Web looking for examples of Java applets that use drop-down lists. If the source code is not given, use your browser's View menu to look at the source code for the applet. Print the source code and write comments for each line of code describing what the code does, how the drop-down lists are populated, and how the user's choices are evaluated.

6 ▶▶▶ An airfreight company has hired you to improve its maintenance tracking. After a certain combination of miles and hours, airplanes are required to be serviced or maintained. The airfreight company would like a program that allows the user to enter the plane's data and then display which maintenance schedule should be performed. After the program asks for the number of planes to enter, users will enter the tail number, hours flown, miles flown, excess hours, and excess miles into arrays. Use a loop to go back through the array, checking the hours flown. If the hours are greater than 75 or the miles flown greater than 500, then the program should display the tail number on the plane and the words, Maintenance Schedule A. If the hours are greater than 150 or the miles greater than 1000, the program should display the tail number and the words, Maintenance Schedule B. Planes with more than 200 hours or 1500 miles should display the tail number and the words, Maintenance Schedule C.

Java Programming

PROJECT

5

Using Java's Abstract Windows Toolkit

OBJECTIVES

You will have mastered the material in this project when you can:

- Define and describe the use of containers in GUI-based applications
- Differentiate among windows, frames, and panels
- Distinguish among the five layout managers
- Use BorderLayout and GridLayout to place objects in containers
- Convert values using the valueOf method
- Register a WindowListener event
- Create an actionPerformed event to use with a button array
- Set boolean flag variables to determine the current status of an event
- Perform a sequential search of a component array
- Write code to implement the setText and setEditable methods
- Program multiple case solutions
- Set frame attributes using setBounds, setTitle, and setAttributes
- Convert a GUI-based application to an applet

Making It Count

Voters View Presidential Election Tallies

The photo-finish 2000 U.S. Presidential election caused millions of Americans and worldwide spectators to turn to the Web for the latest vote tallies. The Internet became a vast source of information, particularly concerning the Florida vote totals for Texas Governor George W. Bush, Vice President Al Gore, Green Party candidate Ralph Nader, and Reform Party candidate Pat Buchanan.

As the nation anxiously waited for results, the Florida Division of Elections Web site was strained, with only a 22.8 percent response rate. The one-in-five visitors who were able to log in successfully were greeted by a Java applet scrolling one of seven messages: Contact Your Supervisor of Elections, Apply to Register to Vote Today!, Y2K Dates to Remember, 2000 Presidential Preference Primary, Calendar: See What's Coming Up, Federal Qualified Candidate List, and Florida Mock Election 2000.

On the other coast, California voters also encountered a Java

PRESIDENT	▶ Exit polls	Popular vote	% of vote	States won	Electoral votes won*
Candidate					
Al Gore (DEM)		49,244,746	48	19	255
Bush (REP)		49,026,305	48	29	246
(GRN)		2,702,640	3	0	0
(RFM)		441,003	0	0	0

s reporting. *270 electoral votes needed

▶ Exit polls	Current	Projected	Change
	54	50	-3
	46	49	3
	0	0	0
r polls close	--	1	--

▶ Exit polls	Current	Projected*	Change
	223	222	-1
	210	211	1
	2	2	0

Tampa –
St. Petersburg
10, 11

Miami
1-19, 21, 22

application when they loaded their state's VOTE2000 Web page in their browsers. The CALVOTER II Java-based system published the results from the state's 58 counties in real time. Residents also could use the Java Custom Video Player to select particular contests and display scrolling vote results for these races.

Like the user-friendly calculator program you create in Java Project 5 for e-commerce Web sites, the California calculator tabulates ballot results for state residents. It also provides secure transmission of voting results, validates the numbers, stores the data in the Secretary of State's database, and posts the results to the Web site within minutes of the polls' closing. These totals are updated every five minutes.

CALVOTER II's roots began in 1998 when the California Secretary of State's office implemented a statewide voter registration database under the CALVOTER I program. The project was expanded during the next two years to replace the state's aging election-management mainframe computer system, which required programmers to spend 4,000 hours coding new changes between each election.

Fourteen team members completed the new personal computer-based system in time for the

Presidential Primary election in March 2000. The programming team used Java technology to interface with each county's election system, which was no easy feat. Some counties, such as Los Angeles, are technologically sophisticated; one county in the northern part of the state, however, saw the CALVOTER II system as its first county-level personal computer.

The system is composed of three separate Java applications. The first, the Candidate Filing Application, electronically allows candidates to file applications and fee payments. Second, the Elections Reporting Application lets each county enter its vote totals and transmit this data to the Secretary of State's office. That office then automatically shares the data with the media, including the Associated Press, United Press International, newspapers, and broadcasters. The third component, the Systems Administration Application, manages system accounts and sorts the votes by jurisdiction.

Despite the candidates' pre-election promises regarding education, Medicare, and taxes, United States citizens knew the Web and the Java-based applications helped make Election Night and the subsequent weeks of waiting a little less taxing.

Java Programming

Using Java's Abstract Windows Toolkit

PROJECT 5

Introduction

Web site design and hosting is big business. More and more companies want to go online for e-commerce and exposure, and Internet service providers have eagerly risen, if not jumped, to the challenge. Web site designers want to offer their customers a large portfolio of possibilities from which they can choose, as well as offer customers the ability to custom design sites. Java programs and applets make sense in that kind of environment, not only for their cross-platform capabilities, but in their ability to load quickly and attach to Web pages as applets.

In this project, you will design a calculator program that can run as a stand-alone application and then modify it to run as an applet from a Web page. Even though most Windows operating system software comes with a calculator accessory, not every location that offers an interactive service wants to open up their entire system to the public, as is the case with kiosks and computers in libraries, museums, and pay-for-use systems. Additionally, many Web pages want to offer their visitors accessible services, rather than relying on the user to find his or her own tools, such as a calculator, timer, or multimedia viewer.

In previous projects, you have used Java's Abstract Windows Toolkit (AWT) only in applets. In this project, you will use AWT components in a stand-alone application, as well as in an applet. The calculator program you will design uses buttons and a text field to display calculations, all positioned inside a GUI-based window with its usual attributes.

Project Five — Calculator Program

ANALYZING THE PROBLEM A Web site design company wants a calculator program written in Java to use in both a stand-alone environment and as an applet. In order to make the calculator as user-friendly as possible, it should display in a standard window with Minimize, Maximize, and Close buttons. In addition, the user should be able to resize the window by dragging its border. The calculator should have the ten numeral buttons (numbered 0-9), four operator buttons, a decimal point, and an equal button. Figure 5-1(a) displays the Calculator window. As the buttons are clicked, the digits should display at the top of the window in a small area similar to an LCD screen on a hand-held calculator. When the user clicks the equal button, the answer should display.

DESIGNING THE INTERFACE Utilizing Java's Abstract Windows Toolkit to take advantage of some of the GUI-based objects, you will design a user-friendly window. The Frame should be the size and shape of a simple hand-held calculator with appropriately sized buttons. Within the Calculator display, 16 buttons are placed in a 4 x 4 grid, and a text field is positioned across the top for the display. Each button should have a label with its digit or symbol. In order to simplify the declaration, construction, adding, and labeling of the buttons, you will create an array of Button components. To practice inserting and editing components, the applet, displayed in Figure 5-1(b), also includes a clear button labeled CLR.

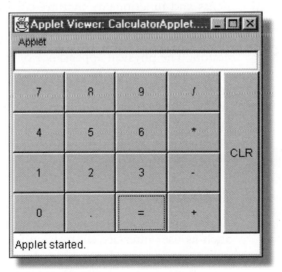

(a) Java Application   (b) Java Applet

FIGURE 5-1

The title bar of both the application and applet should display an appropriate caption. In order to make the application and applet similar, you will use components and objects that work in both applets and applications.

CODING THE PROGRAM   You will create Java source code using the syntax and commands of the Java programming language. This project presents a series of step-by-step instructions to write the code for both the application and applet. You will use Notepad to enter and save the Java source code. Then, you will compile and execute the program from the MS-DOS Prompt window. To run the applet, you will use Applet Viewer.

TESTING THE PROGRAM   By running the program and entering sample calculations using the digit and operator buttons, you will be able to check each button's performance. Additionally, you will test the Minimize, Maximize, and Close buttons, as well as the ability to drag the border for resizing.

FORMALIZING THE SOLUTION   You will review the source code, use proper documentation and programming practices, edit, recompile, and print a copy of the program.

MAINTAINING THE PROGRAM   You will modify the program to include a clear button, labeled CLR, to clear previous calculator entries, and make other appropriate changes to convert the application into an applet.

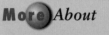

The AWT

For more information on the components of the AWT, visit the Java Programming Web page (www.scsite.com/java/more.htm) and then click AWT.

Abstract Windows Toolkit

Recall that the Abstract Windows Toolkit is the basic set of Java classes used to build graphical user interfaces for Java applets and applications. Using the AWT, programmers have access to tools for creating common graphical objects such as windows, dialog boxes, buttons, areas in which to manipulate text, and much more. The AWT also specifies an event-handling model that enables a Java program to respond to the keystrokes and mouse-clicks entered by a user.

The AWT is abstract, or conceptual, in that it provides only the essential components and functionality that are common to all major windowing systems. For example, the Microsoft Windows environment, the Apple Macintosh environment, and the various Unix environments all supply a button that is clicked to execute an action. The physical appearance of the button, precise behavior, and the application program interface (API), however, differ significantly between all three environments. Java abstracts the essential behavior of a button and provides an API that is presented to the developer in the AWT. When an instance of the Java Button class is compiled, the actual button presented to the user is obtained from the native, or user's, environment. The same is true for many of the other AWT components, including the window itself.

Containers

A **container** is a special category of Java objects that contains other components, such as user interface controls and components. For example, a window is a familiar container to users. It can hold icons, buttons, frames, and even other windows. Java containers defined in the AWT include: Windows, Panels, Frames, Canvases, Dialogs, ScrollPanes, and other containers.

The Calculator program will use a Frame container. Similar to a window, a **Frame** is used in stand-alone application with similar characteristics and attributes. Frames contain their own title bars, borders, icons, and Minimize, Maximize, and Close buttons.

Figure 5-2 displays the hierarchy of components. Notice that Frames inherit attributes and methods from the Window class. Frames may have pull-down menus and may use a number of different cursor shapes. Frames are a powerful feature of the AWT, because you may use Frames to build stand-alone graphical applications or to create separate windows for your applets, as is the case when running an applet outside the main window of a Web browser.

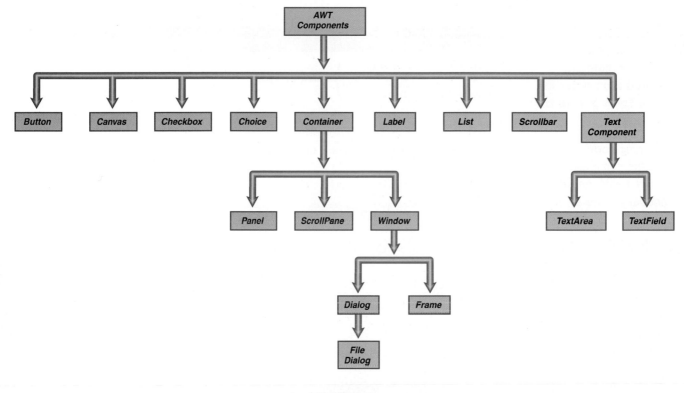

FIGURE 5-2

Programs that use a Frame need to explicitly say so in their class headers by using the word, extend. Recall that a program may **extend**, or build upon, a super-class that Java provides, or it may extend a programmer-defined class. Table 5-1 displays the beginning code to start the Calculator application. Notice that in line 11 the Calculator class extends Frame. The Frame class is the application equivalent of the Applet class — it is a logical and visual object in which components are placed.

By extending from the Frame class, the Calculator class will be a subclass or working copy of a Frame. The Calculator class will behave in a similar manner and will inherit all of the fields and methods declared or inherited in the Frame class. Programs that use a window, or GUI-based interface, typically extend the Frame class and are called **frame-based applications**.

Table 5-1	
LINE	CODE
1	`/*`
2	`    Project 5:    Using Frames`
3	`    Programmer:   Joy Starks`
4	`    Date:         January 9, 2002`
5	`    Program Name: Calculator`
6	`*/`
7	
8	`import java.awt.*;`
9	`import java.awt.event.*;`
10	
11	`public class Calculator extends Frame implements ActionListener`
12	`{`

The Calculator class also will implement the ActionListener because it will receive input, in the form of clicks, from a user. Perform the following steps to enter the beginning code.

Steps: To Enter Beginning Code

1 **Start Notepad on your system. Maximize the Notepad window and then enter the code from Table 5-1 on the previous page.**

The beginning code displays, including the comments, import statements, and the class header (Figure 5-3).

2 **Click File on the menu bar and then click Save. When the Save As dialog box displays, click 3½ Floppy (A:) in the Save in list. In the File name text box, type** "Calculator.java" **as the name of the file, being certain to include the quotation marks. Click the Save button in the Save As dialog box.**

The file is saved on drive A with "Calculator.java" as the file name.

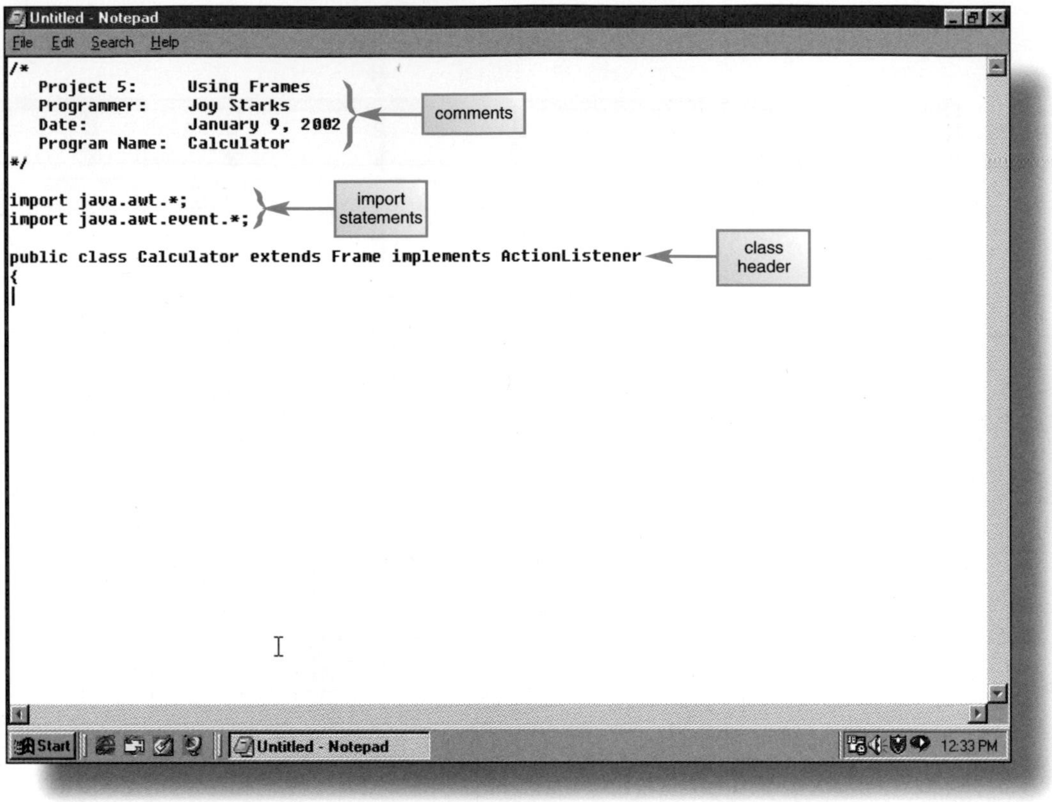

```
Untitled - Notepad
File  Edit  Search  Help
/*
    Project 5:      Using Frames
    Programmer:     Joy Starks              comments
    Date:           January 9, 2002
    Program Name:   Calculator
*/

import java.awt.*;                          import
import java.awt.event.*;                    statements

public class Calculator extends Frame implements ActionListener    class
{                                                                   header

```

FIGURE 5-3

Remember that Notepad will save your file as a text file with the extension, .txt unless you force it to be a Java source file by including the file name within quotation marks.

Panels

Several components with which you already may be familiar can be added to a Frame. Buttons, Fields, Choices, and Checkboxes are constructed, declared, and assigned in a similar manner in both applications and applets. In this project, you will declare a new component called a Panel. A **Panel** is a container used to organize other components and inherits from the Container class. A Panel is similar to a Frame in that it may contain other components, but it does not have a title bar or any automatic features. You must program any buttons contained within a Panel.

The Panel constructor that you will enter later takes no arguments because it needs no data for the title bar. Usually Java programmers create Panels inside the application Frame in order to help organize sections of the Frame or to group buttons and options.

Additionally, you will add a TextField to display clicked numbers and the answers to any calculations. The buttons of the Calculator keypad each will be Java Button components, declared in an array. Later you will initialize the array to be of length 16 — one for each number on the keypad, the four operators, an equal sign, and a decimal point. When you add the CLR button for the applet, the length will be 17.

Other int, boolean, and double variables will be used to make the Calculator work properly. Table 5-2 displays a variable dictionary, which lists the identifiers, the type of variable or data they will hold, and their purpose in the program.

More About

Double Values

A double value is used to store the result of user calculations in the Calculator program. A double allows you to calculate a 64-bit double precision floating-point number, which should be big enough for most calculations.

Table 5-2	Variable Dictionary for the Calculator Program	
IDENTIFIER	TYPE OF VARIABLE	COMPONENT OR PURPOSE
keysArray	array of type, Button	buttons on the Calculator keypad
keyPad	Panel	container to hold keypad buttons
lcdField	TextField	text field to display the calculation results
Result	double data type	stores calculation result
First	boolean data type	stores whether or not a first operand has been entered
foundKey	boolean data type	signals a button has been clicked
clearText	boolean data type	stores whether or not the lcdField display is clear
prevOperator	int data type	stores the location of the chosen operator button
calcFrame	instance of type, Calculator	specific occurrence of the Calculator frame with unique attributes
i	int data type	an increment in for loops

Table 5-3 displays the code for variable declarations. Most of the variables are declared, at the beginning of the program. Others will be declared within methods later in the program.

Table 5-3	
LINE	CODE
13	`private Button keysArray[];`
14	`private Panel keyPad;`
15	`private TextField lcdField;`
16	`private double result;`
17	`private boolean first;`
18	`private boolean foundKey;`
19	`static boolean clearText;`
20	`private int prevOperator;`
21	

More About

Doubles on the Web

The double.parseDouble method, which converts a value into a double, cannot be used for applets enabled with Java 1. Neither IE 5, nor Netscape 4 will recognize the method in an applet. For those applications, a float value works better. Sun Microsystems added the parseDouble method in the SDK2 release.

Perform the following steps to enter the code to declare variables.

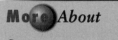 **To Enter Code to Declare Variables**

1 **With the Calculator program still displaying in the Notepad window, enter the code from Table 5-3 on the previous page.**

The declared variables display (Figure 5-4).

line 13

2 **Click File on the menu bar and then click Save.**

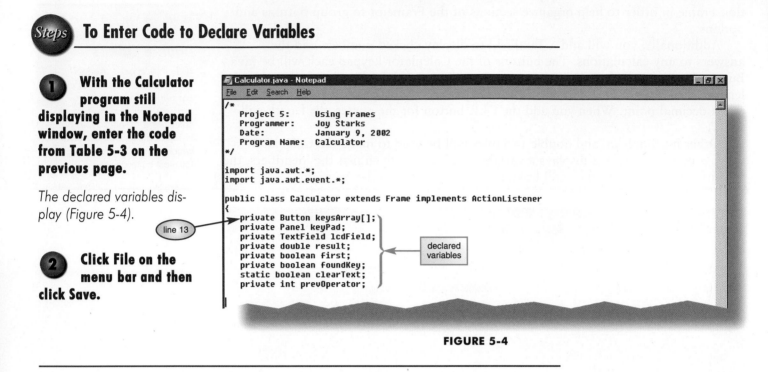

FIGURE 5-4

Notice that most of the identifiers are declared private. Recall that the access modifier, private, forces those components and instance variables to have class scope. **Class scope** means that these components and instance variables are not accessible outside the class. Other classes, or clients, create instances of the Calculator, then can use the class without knowing the internal details of how it is implemented or the variables it uses. By making the variables **local**, or limited to the class, you also save memory and make the program easier to follow.

The variable, clearText, is declared **static**, which means it remains the same whenever Java creates an instance of the Calculator class. Static variables sometimes are called **class variables**, because their scope extends beyond the local instance to all instances of the class.

Layout Managers

In previous projects, Java or Applet Viewer automatically has determined the placement of components by the size of the window listed in the HTML host document. Alternatively, you might have positioned components using coordinates, in order to determine placement. When you position components by absolute coordinates, it can cause problems when someone using a monitor with 640 x 380 resolution tries to run a program designed to fit on a 1280 x 1024 screen.

To assist in component placement inside containers, Java provides **layout managers** that help the programmer organize the containers, rather than allowing Java to place them left to right within the space provided. By using layout managers, you can program the AWT to place your components relative to other components. The five layout managers are FlowLayout, BorderLayout, GridLayout, CardLayout, and GridBagLayout.

More About

Scope

Variables declared at the beginning of the class to be private are visible to the entire class, but may be instantiated. Static variables are more like constants. Even when Java creates an instance of the class, static variables will remain the same. Variables declared inside a method are only visible to that method. Declaring your variables in as narrow a scope as possible saves computer memory.

Table 5-4 displays a quick reference table of the five layout manager configurations and features.

Table 5-4 Layout Managers		
LAYOUT MANAGER	COMPONENT PLACEMENT	COMPONENT HANDLING
FlowLayout	places components left to right	three alignment possibilities: LEFT, RIGHT, and CENTER
BorderLayout	places components at compass points; north, south, east, and west	placement in five possible areas in the container; specify horizontal and vertical gaps
GridLayout	places components left to right in a predetermined grid	specify number of rows and number of columns
CardLayout	places components in a stack	use methods such as first, last, previous, and next to display stack components
GridBagLayout	places components in grids; components may vary in size	specify grid and location of components

FlowLayout

FlowLayout is the default, or preset, layout manager for Panels and Applets. If you do not program a layout manager, Java assumes the FlowLayout, which treats a container as a set of rows. As components are added to the container, FlowLayout places them in rows, from left to right. The height of the item placed in the row determines the height of that entire row. The number of rows is determined by the size of the container. If the component cannot fit on the current row, FlowLayout moves it to the next row. Components are centered left to right, by default, if they do not fill the row.

If you decide to change back to FlowLayout from a different layout manager, the layout manager must be constructed with the **setLayout** method.

```
setLayout(new FlowLayout());
```

If you want to change FlowLayout's alignment, you must specify one of three different **alignment constants** as an argument or parameter to FlowLayout: **LEFT**, **RIGHT**, or **CENTER**.

```
setLayout(new FlowLayout(FlowLayout.RIGHT));
```

All constants, such as LEFT, RIGHT, or CENTER, are entered in capital letters in Java.

Once FlowLayout has been specified, components can be added to the container with the usual add method. The component name is the argument.

```
add(custNameLabel);
```

Figure 5-5 on the next page displays a sample applet that uses FlowLayout to place five buttons in the container at the default CENTER location.

More About

FlowLayout

If you resize a window that uses a FlowLayout Panel or Applet, the components in the window will automatically adjust to fill the rows. The number of rows changes as the window is resized, but the components remain in the same order. By default, the number of pixels between components is five. You may change the horizontal and vertical gaps between components by adding two more parameters to the FlowLayout method, such as FlowLayout (FlowLayout.LEFT, 10, 20).

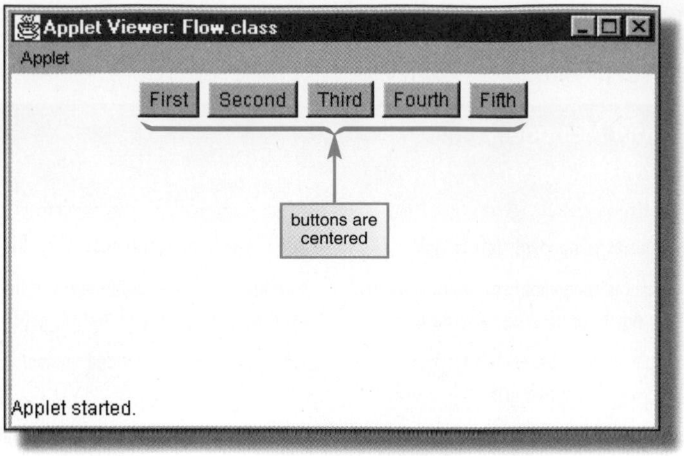

FIGURE 5-5

BorderLayout

BorderLayout is the next most popular layout manager in Java after FlowLayout. **BorderLayout** places components into five areas within the container: North, South, East, West, and Center. With BorderLayout, you also can specify the number of pixels between components.

```
setLayout(new BorderLayout(10,8));
```

This line of code instructs the layout manager to use the BorderLayout with ten pixels horizontally and eight pixels vertically between components.

Components are added to the container by specifying their geographical placement using the add method.

```
add(myButton, BorderLayout.SOUTH);
```

An alternate form adds and constructs a button with a caption in one line of code.

```
add("South", new Button("Okay"));
```

Up to five components may be added in any order, but only one component can be added to each area. The components placed in the North and South areas extend horizontally to the edge of the container and are as tall as the tallest component. The components in the East and West areas expand vertically between the North and South areas and are as wide as the widest component. The Center component expands to take up all the remaining space. If a North, South, East, or West component is not present, the adjacent components fill the space. If a Center component is not present, the area is left blank.

Figure 5-6 displays a sample applet that uses BorderLayout to place five buttons, one in each area.

FIGURE 5-6

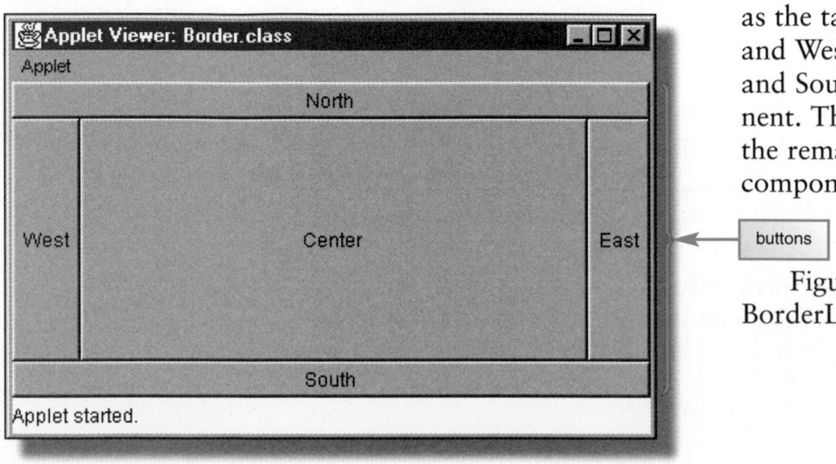

GridLayout

GridLayout divides the container into a grid so components can be placed in rows and columns, left to right within the grid.

```
setLayout(new GridLayout(3,3));
```

The line of code instructs the layout manager to use the GridLayout with three rows and three columns.

Figure 5-7 displays a sample applet with nine buttons placed in a 3 x 3 grid, using the GridLayout manager.

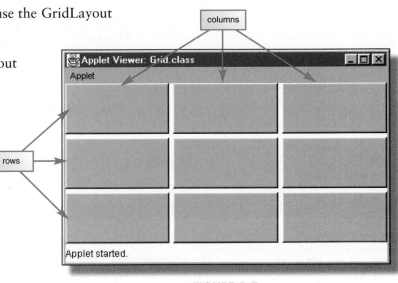

FIGURE 5-7

CardLayout

A more flexible, but slightly more complicated, layout manager is CardLayout. **CardLayout** is used primarily to house other containers. It places them in a stack similar to a deck of cards. Each container in the stack then can use its own layout manager. The container at the top of the deck is visible when the program is executed.

Often, an instance of CardLayout is constructed for use later in the program.

```
myCards = new CardLayout();
```

Containers are created and then used to construct the instance.

```
deck = new Panel();
deck.setLayout(myCards());
```

The add method then can be used to add the internal containers to the deck.

```
deck.add(myPanel);
deck.add(myDialog);
```

Only one card is visible at any one time. CardLayout uses four methods — first, previous, next, and last — to display the cards, with the name of the container as an argument.

```
myCards.previous(deck);
```

Figure 5-8 on the next page displays an applet that is typical of how Java programmers combine some of the different layout managers to achieve certain visual effects. The applet combines both the GridLayout and the CardLayout. On the left is a set of buttons positioned using the GridLayout manager. On the right are panels placed on top of one another, positioned using the CardLayout manager. The buttons then are programmed to bring a specific panel to the front. The first panel's background color has been set to green to better display its location.

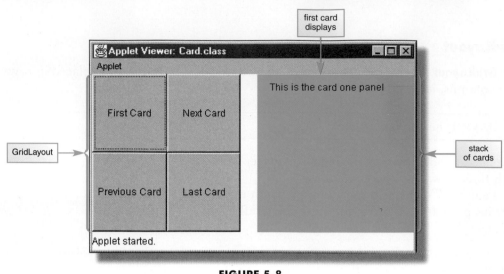

FIGURE 5-8

first card displays

GridLayout

stack of cards

More About

GridLayout

You can declare and construct the layout in a single line, such as setLayout(new GridLayout(2, 4, 10, 10)); using four parameters. In that case, the four parameters are: rows, columns, horizontal gap, and vertical gap.

GridBagLayout

Perhaps the most flexible of all the Java layout managers is the GridBagLayout. **GridBagLayout** is created in a manner similar to GridLayout, but each component can vary in size. The GridBagLayout aligns components horizontally and vertically without requiring that the components be the same size. Each GridBagLayout manager uses a rectangular grid of cells, with each component occupying one or more cells. Components may be added in any order. Figure 5-9 displays a sample applet whose components were placed using GridBagLayout.

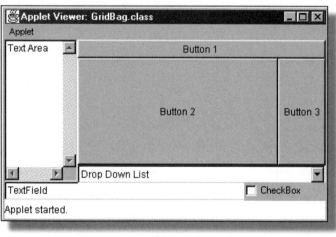

FIGURE 5-9

Programmers sometimes use other more tedious and more difficult layout options. You might want to place each of your containers and components manually. Using a layout manager, however, offers other benefits, such as adjusting your components automatically, if the user resizes your Frame.

The Calculator Frame itself will use BorderLayout; the Panel, created inside the Frame to hold the keypad, will use GridLayout. Combining and subsetting containers permits maximum flexibility, as well as control.

Creating the Calculator Frame and Layout

In the next series of steps, you enter the code to create an internal class or method for the Calculator. This Calculator class will construct its own Frame and embed the following components: a TextField, a Panel, and an array of buttons. It will initialize variables, establish a layout manager for itself, and set the display so the user cannot edit it. Later in this project, the main method will construct an instance of this Calculator class with a unique name and some specific attributes.

Table 5-5 displays the code to begin the Calculator Frame. Notice that in line 24, a TextField is created with space for 20 characters. In line 35, the TextField's user-input ability then is constrained. The **setEditable method**, which takes a boolean argument, is set to false – the field will be read only. Users cannot type into a TextField if the setEditable method is set to false. This especially is effective when you want the display to be distinctive, such as black letters on a white background, or when a label component does not seem appropriate or is not needed. In the Calculator program, the TextField will look more like an LCD display, but users will not be able to type into it.

Perform the following steps to create the Calculator Frame.

Table 5-5	
LINE	CODE
22	`public Calculator()`
23	`{`
24	`    lcdField = new TextField(20);`
25	`    keyPad = new Panel();`
26	`    keysArray = new Button[16];`
27	`    result = 0.0;`
28	`    prevOperator = 0;`
29	`    first = true;`
30	`    clearText = true;`
31	
32	`    //Set frame layout manager`
33	`    setLayout(new BorderLayout());`
34	
35	`    lcdField.setEditable(false);`
36	

Steps   To Create the Calculator Frame

1 With the **Calculator.java** program still displayed in the Notepad window, enter the code from Table 5-5.

The code displays to construct components and set the BorderLayout for the Frame (Figure 5-10).

2 Click File on the menu bar and then click Save.

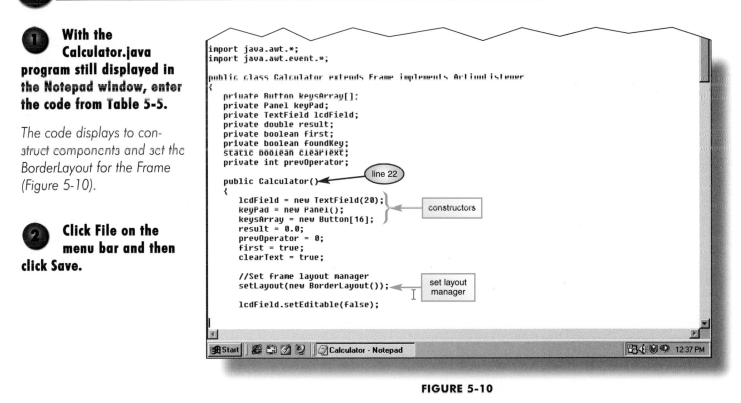

FIGURE 5-10

Now that the layout is set, it is time to create the subsetted keypad Panel.

Creating the Keypad

The Calculator program creates a numeric keypad complete with the digits 0 through 9, the decimal point, equal sign, and four arithmetic operators (addition, subtraction, multiplication, and division). Figure 5-11 displays the application running in stand-alone mode. Notice that the Frame contains a Panel and a TextField. The buttons are placed inside the Panel using a 4 x 4 GridLayout.

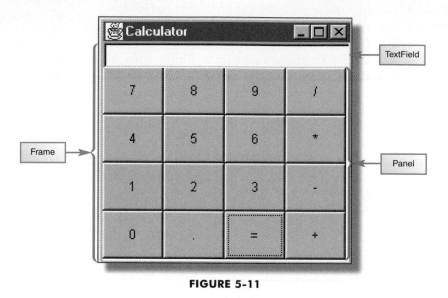

FIGURE 5-11

It makes sense to use an array for the buttons. Recall that an array is a list that employs a single, but inclusive, storage location to hold data of the same type with the same identifier name. In the case of the Button array named keysArray, using an array allows construction and labeling of the digit buttons using a for loop, with two lines of code instead of ten: one line of code for the for statement and another for the assignment. Symbol buttons are assigned one at a time. Additionally, a loop can be used to add buttons to the keypad grid. Adding the actionListener to each of the buttons also can be accomplished with two lines of code.

Constructing Buttons and Setting the Layout

Table 5-6 displays the code to construct and label the keypad buttons. It also displays the method to establish the GridLayout.

Lines 38 and 39 show a for loop that uses an integer, i, to increment through the ten digits and assign numeric labels. Buttons receive their labels as arguments to the Button method. Java's valueOf method converts the numeric value of i to a String. Therefore, in line 39, the argument in the Button constructor becomes the label of the button itself. Because line 39 is the only code in the for loop, block braces are unnecessary. Indenting line 39 makes the code easier to read and understand.

Table 5-6

LINE	CODE
37	//Create buttons
38	for (int i = 0; i <= 9; i++)
39	keysArray[i] = new Button(String.valueOf(i));
40	keysArray[10] = new Button("/");
41	keysArray[11] = new Button("*");
42	keysArray[12] = new Button("-");
43	keysArray[13] = new Button("+");
44	keysArray[14] = new Button("=");
45	keysArray[15] = new Button(".");
46	
47	//Set panel layout manager
48	keyPad.setLayout(new GridLayout(4,4));
49	

Lines 40 through 45 explicitly assign the labels for the other buttons. Line 48 sets the keypad Panel to the GridLayout manager with 4 rows and 4 columns.
Perform the following steps to construct the buttons and set the layout manager.

Steps To Construct the Buttons and Set the Layout Manager

1 With the Calculator.java program still displayed in the Notepad window, enter the code from Table 5-6.

The code displays to construct the buttons and set the panel's layout (Figure 5-12).

2 Click File on the menu bar and then click Save.

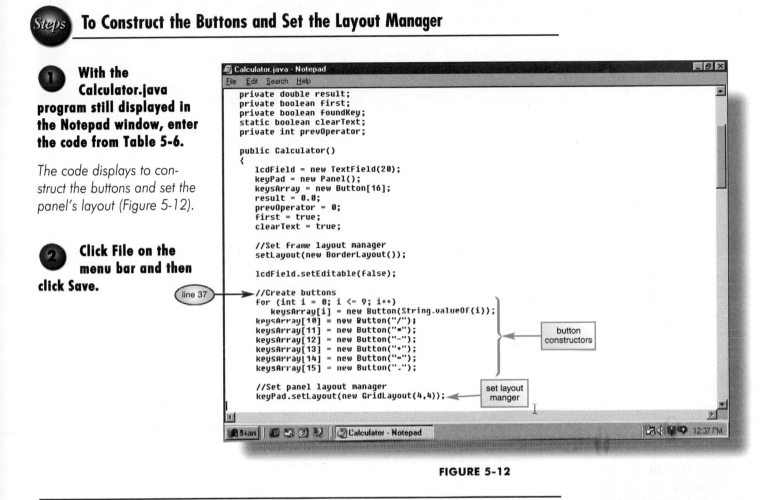

```
Calculator.java - Notepad
File   Edit   Search   Help

    private double result;
    private boolean first;
    private boolean foundKey;
    static boolean clearText;
    private int prevOperator;

    public Calculator()
    {
        lcdField = new TextField(20);
        keyPad = new Panel();
        keysArray = new Button[16];
        result = 0.0;
        prevOperator = 0;
        first = true;
        clearText = true;

        //Set frame layout manager
        setLayout(new BorderLayout());

        lcdField.setEditable(false);

        //Create buttons
        for (int i = 0; i <= 9; i++)
            keysArray[i] = new Button(String.valueOf(i));
        keysArray[10] = new Button("/");
        keysArray[11] = new Button("*");
        keysArray[12] = new Button("-");
        keysArray[13] = new Button("+");
        keysArray[14] = new Button("=");
        keysArray[15] = new Button(".");

        //Set panel layout manager
        keyPad.setLayout(new GridLayout(4,4));
```

line 37 →

button constructors →

set layout manger →

Start | Calculator - Notepad | 12:37 PM

FIGURE 5-12

Now that labeled buttons have been created, you are ready to add them to the Panel.

Adding Buttons to a Panel

Because the keypad panel is using a GridLayout, Java adds buttons beginning at the upper-left corner. Table 5-7 on the next page displays the code to add the 16 buttons to the panel using the 4 x 4 grid. Comments within the code will help you to understand how each loop and/or add method takes its turn. Examine the code before entering it.

More About

TextAreas

TextAreas are different from TextFields. TextAreas have their own special features. Because TextAreas normally are used for editing text, they contain methods for inserting, appending, and replacing text. You may use mouse and keyboard events in a TextArea, but the more common practice is to include a command button that users click when they are finished editing. The Comments area in a File Properties dialog box is an example of a TextArea of which you may be familiar.

Table 5-7

LINE	CODE
50	`//Add buttons to keyPad panel`
51	`for (int i = 7; i <= 10; i++)   //adds buttons 7, 8, 9, and divide to Panel`
52	`    keyPad.add(keysArray[i]);`
53	
54	`for (int i = 4; i <= 6; i++)   //adds buttons 4, 5, and 6 to Panel`
55	`    keyPad.add(keysArray[i]);`
56	
57	`keyPad.add(keysArray[11]);       //adds multiply button to Panel`
58	
59	`for (int i = 1; i <= 3; i++)   //adds buttons 1, 2, and 3 to Panel`
60	`    keyPad.add(keysArray[i]);`
61	
62	`keyPad.add(keysArray[12]);       //adds subtract button to Panel`
63	
64	`keyPad.add(keysArray[0]);        //adds 0 key to Panel`
65	
66	`for (int i = 15; i >= 13; i--)`
67	`    keyPad.add(keysArray[i]);    //adds decimal point, equal, and addition keys to Panel`
68	

Perform the following steps to add buttons to the Panel.

 To Add Buttons to the Panel

1 **With the Calculator.java program still displayed in the Notepad window, enter the code from Table 5-7.**

In the Notepad window, the code displays to add 16 buttons to the Panel (Figure 5-13).

2 **Click File on the menu bar and then click Save.**

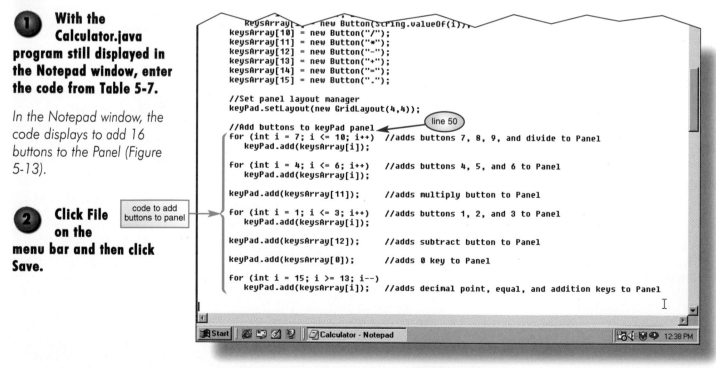

FIGURE 5-13

The Panel now is complete with 16 buttons. It is a **composite** component, or a container with added components, so the act of adding the Panel to the Frame will add all the buttons at once in the next series of steps.

Adding Components to the Frame

Line 69 in Table 5-8 adds the lcdField to the Frame itself. Recall that the Frame's layout manager is BorderLayout (the Panel used a GridLayout). Therefore, in order to add something to the Frame, you must specify the border area. The lcdField will be added in the North area. Line 70 adds the Panel, with all of its buttons, in the Center area.

Table 5-8

LINE	CODE
69	`add(lcdField, BorderLayout.NORTH);  //adds text field to top of Frame`
70	`add(keyPad, BorderLayout.CENTER);   //adds Panel to center of Frame`
71	
72	`for(int i = 0; i < keysArray.length; i++)`
73	`    keysArray[i].addActionListener(this);`
74	

In lines 72 and 73, the array of Buttons is run through a loop again in order to add the actionListener to each button. You learned that the self-referential, this, is an object that refers back to its own control, in this case, the keysArray. The for loop, begun in line 72, has only one statement, so braces are unnecessary.

Perform the following steps to code the keypad by adding the Panel and lcdField inside the Calculator Frame. You also will activate the ActionListener for the array of buttons.

More About

The Order of Adding the Buttons to the Panel

In the Calculator keypad, the buttons were added left to right, top to bottom. After all of the number keys were added, including 0, three more places existed in the bottom row of buttons. The decrement operator used in line 66, caused the layout manager to add the period, equal, and plus buttons in that order: button 15, button 14, and button 13. To add them using the increment operator, the definitions and assignments would need to be reversed.

Steps: To Code the Keypad

1 With the Calculator.java program still displayed in the Notepad window, enter the code from Table 5-8.

The add methods display (Figure 5-14).

2 Click File on the menu bar and then click Save.

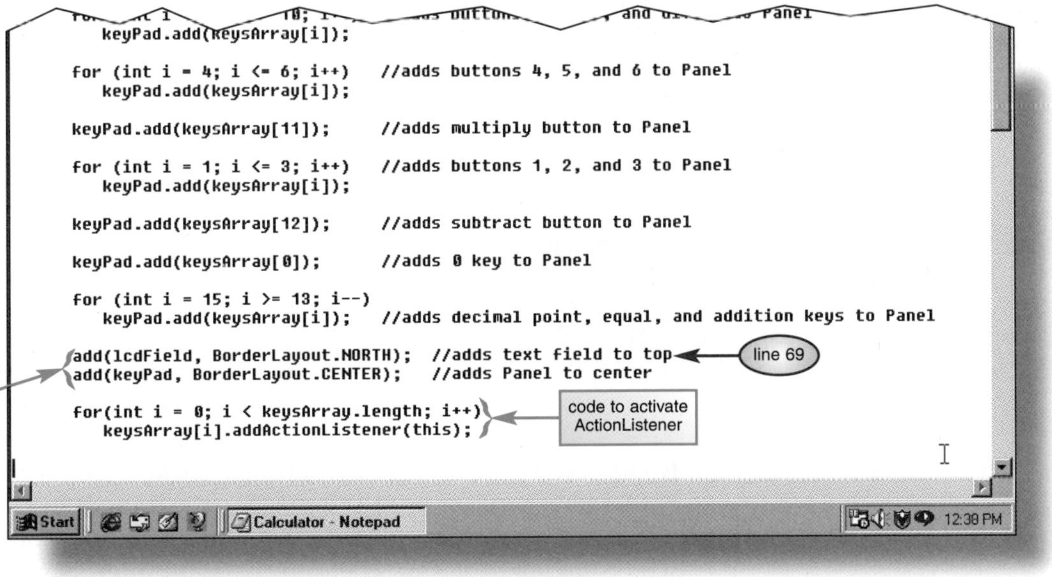

```
for (int i = 10; i ...  ... buttons ... and ... ... Panel
    keyPad.add(keysArray[i]);

for (int i = 4; i <= 6; i++)    //adds buttons 4, 5, and 6 to Panel
    keyPad.add(keysArray[i]);

keyPad.add(keysArray[11]);      //adds multiply button to Panel

for (int i = 1; i <= 3; i++)    //adds buttons 1, 2, and 3 to Panel
    keyPad.add(keysArray[i]);

keyPad.add(keysArray[12]);      //adds subtract button to Panel

keyPad.add(keysArray[0]);       //adds 0 key to Panel

for (int i = 15; i >= 13; i--)
    keyPad.add(keysArray[i]);   //adds decimal point, equal, and addition keys to Panel

add(lcdField, BorderLayout.NORTH);   //adds text field to top
add(keyPad, BorderLayout.CENTER);    //adds Panel to center

for(int i = 0; i < keysArray.length; i++)
    keysArray[i].addActionListener(this);
```

code to add components to Frame

line 69

code to activate ActionListener

Start | Calculator - Notepad | 12:38 PM

FIGURE 5-14

Later in the program, you will call the actionPerformed method to determine what will happen when each button is clicked.

Window Methods

You do not have to write all the code for the event loop that controls a GUI-based program because the JVM handles some of the functionality. Recall that the JVM, or Java Virtual Machine, is the run-time interpreter portion of the JDK or SDK. It handles building the system-specific frame, title bar, and window control buttons in the title bar. You do have to use event handlers, however, to respond to events such as the user closing the Frame, which is the top-level container in the application. Table 5-9 displays the code to add a WindowListener for the frame. Java's **addWindowListener event** in line 75, registers the listener with the frame. When you **register** a listener with a frame, you connect two objects so that events from one object, the frame, are sent to the other object, the listener. It tells the frame object to listen for such events and respond accordingly.

The argument inside the parentheses for the addWindowListener is unusual. It extends through line 83 where you see the closing parenthesis and the semicolon. In between, a new occurrence of the WindowAdapter class occurs. **Adapter classes** implement an abstract class, providing prewritten methods for all of the methods in the abstract class. In this particular case, WindowAdapter is a class of seven window event-handling methods. Table 5-10 displays the seven methods and how they are generated.

Each method in the WindowAdapter class is an event listener for a Window or a Frame event. In Java, programmers have the choice of implementing the WindowListener and then writing all the methods themselves, or using WindowAdapter and providing only the methods they wish to change or override. It is appropriate to use the WindowAdapter in this case because the program needs to handle only one of the events.

In lines 78 through 81, the program overrides the windowClosing event, telling the program what to do when the user clicks the Close button in the Frame. Normally, the windowClosing event simply closes the window or frame, making it invisible. It does not necessarily stop the program. In this case, it is overridden so that the program terminates and the window closes.

Internally, Java sends this method a Window-Event object when the Close button is clicked. The method disposes of the current Frame object and then calls System.exit in line 80 to exit the application.

You are familiar with the System.out method to direct the operating system to send a stream of characters to the default output device, usually the monitor. When encountered, the **System.exit** method causes the operating system to terminate the program. System.exit has one argument, which is sent to the operating system in

Table 5-9

LINE	CODE
75	addWindowListener(
76	new WindowAdapter()
77	{
78	public void windowClosing(WindowEvent e)
79	{
80	System.exit(0);
81	}
82	}
83	);
84	}
85	

Table 5-10   Window Event-Handling Methods

WINDOW EVENT-HANDLING METHOD	HOW THE EVENT IS GENERATED
WindowActivated	user starts the application or applet
windowClosed	operating system has closed the window
windowClosing	user clicks the Close button
windowDeactivated	user clicked in the application to give it the focus
windowDeiconified	user clicks the minimized icon
windowIconified	user clicks the Minimize button
windowOpened	operating system has opened the window

which the program is running. Traditionally, System.exit returns a zero (0) to the operating system when a program ends normally and a one (1) when a program ends due to an error. The exit method is used with applications only. If necessary, the exit method's argument is used by the JVM when the application terminates.

Programmers indent these kinds of chained-together methods in different ways. The intention is to facilitate the matching of beginning and ending parentheses and braces.

Perform the following steps to enter the code to close the window.

Steps **To Code the windowClosing Event**

1 **With the Calculator.java program still displayed in the Notepad window, enter the code from Table 5-9.**

The WindowListener method displays (Figure 5-15).

2 **Click File on the menu bar and then click Save.**

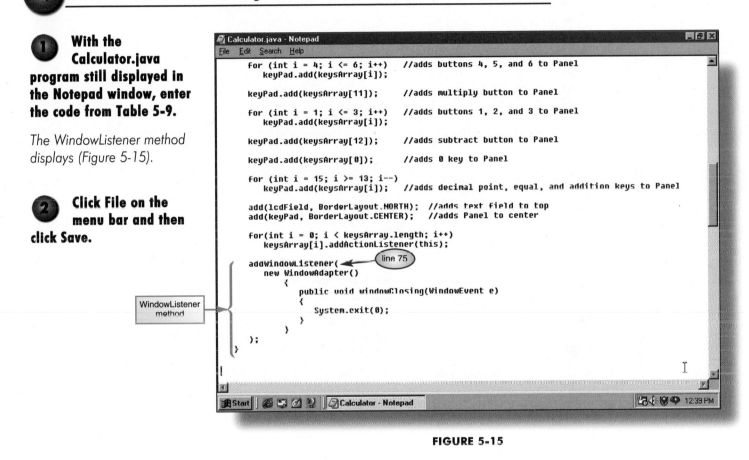

FIGURE 5-15

Although a WindowListener is an interface, an object actually is created — a WindowAdapter — which implements the interface.

The actionPerformed Method

In order to make the Calculator keypad functional, you must code an actionPerformed method. Recall that the actionPerformed method is required by the ActionListener coded previously (line 73 in Table 5-8 on page J 5-19). When the user clicks one of the buttons on the keypad, ActionListener activates the actionPerformed event where the *action* takes place. Also, recall that the method takes one argument, usually identified by e, which represents the object passed to it from the ActionListener.

The following paragraphs discuss each portion of the code individually.

Searching the Buttons

The first stage of the actionPerformed event is to determine which button was clicked. Table 5-11 displays the code to search the array and add functionality to the numeric buttons and the decimal point with the actionPerformed event.

Table 5-11

LINE	CODE
86	`public void actionPerformed(ActionEvent e)`
87	`    {`
88	`        foundKey = false;`
89	
90	`        //Search for the key pressed`
91	`        for (int i = 0; i < keysArray.length && !foundKey; i++)`
92	`            if(e.getSource() == keysArray[i])        //key match found`
93	`            {`
94	`                foundKey = true;`
95	`                switch(i)`
96	`                {`
97	`                    case 0: case 1: case 2: case 3: case 4:    //number buttons`
98	`                    case 5: case 6: case 7: case 8: case 9:    //0 - 9`
99	`                    case 15:                                   //decimal point button`
100	`                        if(clearText)`
101	`                        {`
102	`                            lcdField.setText("");`
103	`                            clearText = false;`
104	`                        }`
105	`                        lcdField.setText(lcdField.getText() + keysArray[i].getLabel());`
106	`                        break;`
107	

In line 88, a flag variable named, foundKey, is set to false.

```
foundKey = false;
```

In error, the user might click the display field, the title bar, or a border of the Frame. Setting a boolean **flag** variable such as this to false will allow testing later to prevent the rest of the actions from being performed unless a button is clicked directly. If a button click is detected, foundKey flag will be toggled to true.

Next, the event performs a sequential search, checking each button. In line 91, the code first looks for which key was pressed by **traversing**, or going through, the array one item at a time.

```
for (int i = 0; i < keysArray.length && !foundKey; i++)
```

Notice that the end of the for loop search occurs when the increment goes beyond the length of the array, and foundKey is false. Either way, the loop will terminate. It is better to use the **length** method than to enter the actual numeric length of 16, because if you wish to add more buttons to the calculator, the search will execute accurately without having to change the number in that line of code.

Notice that the for loop has no braces even though there are multiple lines of code. A brace is not necessary here, although it can be added, because the multiple lines constitute one large control structure, if, which begins in line 92.

```
if(e.getSource() == keysArray[i])        //key match found
```

If the **source** of the click, stored in the object e, matches one of the buttons in the keysArray, then code inside the if block begins. Line 94 toggles the foundKey variable to true when a match is found. The location of the match, at the i position in the array, becomes the variable used in the subsequent switch structure.

The switch Structure

The **multiple case** possibilities of the switch structure deserve special consideration. You learned that in a switch structure, Java tests a variable against multiple possibilities. Each case ends with a break statement; however, you can combine cases if one action can serve for multiple cases. In the Calculator program, the first possibility is that the user may click one of the buttons or the decimal point. Lines 97 through 99 combine cases. The line comments differentiate the cases for ease in reading, although any order is acceptable.

```
case 0: case 1: case 2: case 3: case 4:     //number buttons
case 5: case 6: case 7: case 8: case 9:     //0 - 9
case 15:                                    //decimal point button
```

Java allows multiple cases to perform the same action, as long as they are not separated by break statements.

The action displays in lines 100 through 106. An if statement tests clearText. Recall that the variable clearText was initialized to true at the beginning of the program. Therefore, the first button click will execute the code inside the if statement automatically.

The code clears the lcdField by setting lcdField's text to a null String (line 102). The **setText** method can be used with any component that contains a caption. Its argument is a String assigned to that component during execution. In this case, the lcdField will be assign a blank caption – essentially clearing the field. Line 103 sets the clearText flag to false. Then, as the actionPerformed event is called with each click, no matter whether it is the first click or subsequent clicks, the lcdField is set to display the labels from the buttons (line 105). The result of the **getLabel method** is concatenated with previous text from the lcdField.

For example, assume that the user begins the program and enters the number 27. When the user clicks the 2 button, the actionPerformed event picks up the click, and then clears the lcdField. The label from keysArray[2] then is displayed. When the user then clicks a 7, the label from keysArray[7] is concatenated (+) with the previous text in the field, and 27 displays. The integers 0 through 9 and the decimal points are entered this way.

Perform the following steps to code the first part of the actionPerformed event.

Steps **To Code the First Part of the actionPerformed Event**

1 **With the Calculator.java program still displayed in the Notepad window, enter the code from Table 5-11 on page J 5.22.**

The actionPerformed event code is shown in the Notepad window (Figure 5-16). When executed, the array will be searched, actionPerformed event *and the switch structure will look for numeric buttons and the decimal point. When found, the labels from the buttons will display in lcdField.*

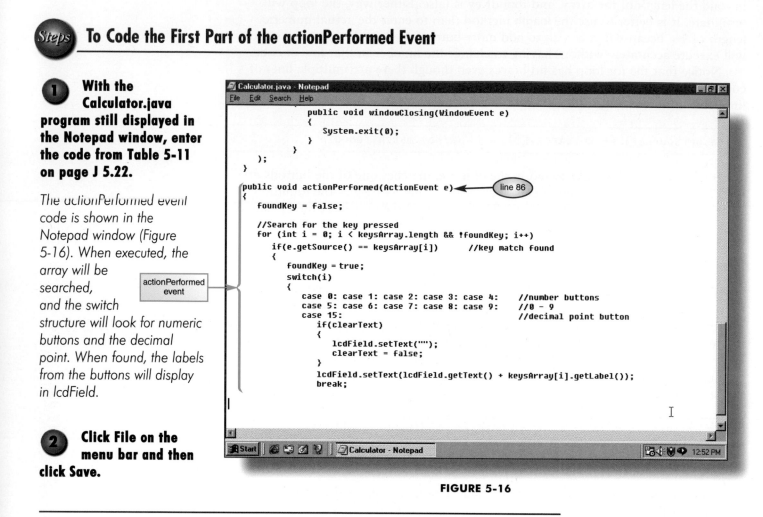

```
Calculator.java - Notepad
File  Edit  Search  Help
                        public void windowClosing(WindowEvent e)
                        {
                            System.exit(0);
                        }
                    }
                );
        }

    public void actionPerformed(ActionEvent e)          line 86
    {
        foundKey = false;

        //Search for the key pressed
        for (int i = 0; i < keysArray.length && !foundKey; i++)
            if(e.getSource() == keysArray[i])         //key match found
            {
                foundKey = true;
                switch(i)
                {
                    case 0: case 1: case 2: case 3: case 4:    //number buttons
                    case 5: case 6: case 7: case 8: case 9:    //0 - 9
                    case 15:                                    //decimal point button
                        if(clearText)
                        {
                            lcdField.setText("");
                            clearText = false;
                        }
                        lcdField.setText(lcdField.getText() + keysArray[i].getLabel());
                        break;
```
Start | Calculator - Notepad | 12:52 PM

FIGURE 5-16

2 **Click File on the menu bar and then click Save.**

Clicking the Operators

Table 5-12 displays the code for the multiple case of the operator buttons.

LINE	CODE
Table 5-12	
108	case 10: //divide button
109	case 11: //multiply button
110	case 12: //minus button
111	case 13: //plus button
112	case 14: //equal button
113	clearText = true;
114	if (first) //first operand
115	{
116	if(lcdField.getText().length()==0)
117	result = 0.0;
118	else
119	result = Double.valueOf(lcdField.getText()).doubleValue();
120	first = false;
121	prevOperator = i; //save previous operator
122	}

Lines 108 through 112 are the case statements that correspond to the operator buttons in the keysArray. These cases could have been included all on one line, but to better identify them, they are listed individually. Either way, execution of the code passes to the first non-case statement, which is seen in line 113.

Line 113 sets the clearText field to true. Recall that the identifier clearText was set to false in line 103 after the first operand was entered. Now that an operator is entered, setting clearText back to true will cause the display to clear again before the next number is entered.

Lines 114 through 122 are an if block executed only when the first operand is clicked. If there is nothing in the display, clicking an operator will store 0.0 in result (line 117). Ordinarily, a number will have been entered, and its value will be stored in result (line 119). The first flag will be set to false (line 120) and the location index of the operator will be stored for later use (line 121).

Perform the following steps to code what happens when the first operator is clicked.

Steps   To Code the First Operator

1 With the Calculator.java program still displayed in the Notepad window, enter the code from Table 5-12.

The code for the first operator click displays in the Notepad window (Figure 5-17).

2 Click File on the menu bar and then click Save.

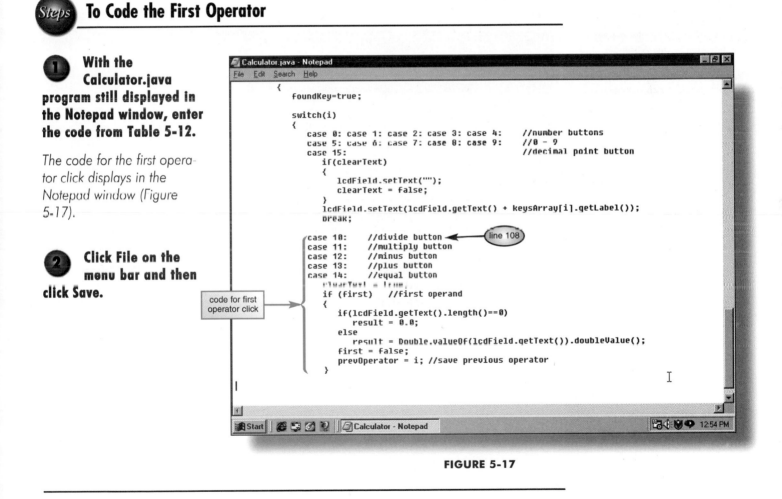

FIGURE 5-17

Period (.) delimiters link together two methods in line 116. The name of the field is followed by the getText method and then by the length method. Once Java determines the text of the lcdField using the getText method, it then can count the characters to return the length.

Subsequent Operator Clicks

Table 5-13 displays the else portion of code that is executed when a second or subsequent operator button is clicked and a calculation performed. Again, notice that a switch structure is used to determine which one of the operators was clicked, but this time the variable is prevOperator. The program tests that variable in line 125 to determine which calculation to perform. The four possible cases — lines 127, 130, 133, and 136 — each use an assignment operator to accumulate the result. The valueOf method converts text from the lcdField to doubles in order to perform the operation.

Table 5-13

LINE	CODE
123	`else  //second operand already entered, so calculate total`
124	`{`
125	`    switch(prevOperator)`
126	`    {`
127	`        case 10:    //divide button`
128	`            result /= Double.valueOf(lcdField.getText()).doubleValue();`
129	`            break;`
130	`        case 11:    //multiply button`
131	`            result *= Double.valueOf(lcdField.getText()).doubleValue();`
132	`            break;`
133	`        case 12:    //minus button`
134	`            result -= Double.valueOf(lcdField.getText()).doubleValue();`
135	`            break;`
136	`        case 13:    //plus button`
137	`            result += Double.valueOf(lcdField.getText()).doubleValue();`
138	`            break;`
139	`    }`
140	`    lcdField.setText(Double.toString(result));`

Finally, in line 140, the result is converted back to a String with the **toString** method and then assigned to the text of lcdField.

Perform the following steps to code for subsequent operator button clicks.

To Enter Code for Subsequent Operator Button Clicks

1 With the Calculator.java program still displayed in the Notepad window, enter the code from Table 5-13.

The code for subsequent operator button clicks displays in the Notepad window (Figure 5-18).

2 Click File on the menu bar and then click Save.

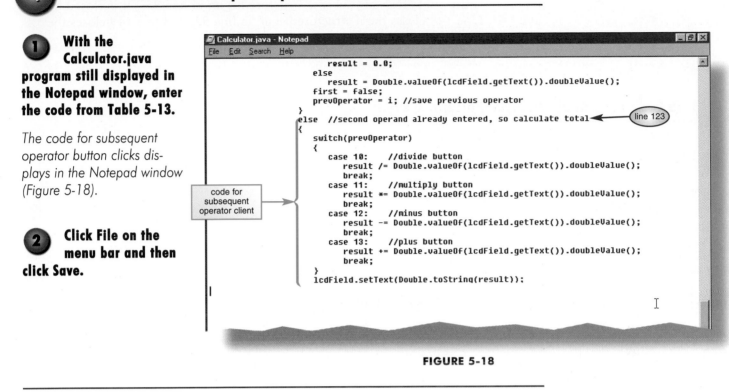

FIGURE 5-18

Notice that no case for the equal button is contained within this switch structure. When the user clicks the equal button, the prevOperator would be assigned a value of 14 – the index number of the equal button. Because a value of 14 does not match any of the cases, execution will pass directly to line 140, which will display the accumulated result in lcdField.

Coding the End of the actionPerformed Event

Table 5-14 displays the final portion of code for the actionPerformed event. If the user clicks the equal button, the first flag is set to true (line 142) in preparation for the next calculation, otherwise the prevOperator location is saved (line 144).

Table 5-14

LINE	CODE
141	`                    if(i==14)  //equal button`
142	`                        first = true;`
143	`                    else`
144	`                        prevOperator = i; //save previous operator`
145	`                }`
146	`                break;`
147	`            }`
148	`        }`
149	`    }`
150	

Line 145 closes the if-then-else structure for the first operand begun in line 113. Line 146 is the final break for the case structure begun in line 95 – it is closed in line 147. Line 148 closes the if structure begun in line 92, and line 149 closes the actionPerformed event entirely.

Perform the following steps to finish the actionPerformed event.

Steps **To Code the End of the actionPerformed Event**

1 With the Calculator.java program still displayed in the Notepad window, enter the code from Table 5-14.

The code to conclude the actionPerformed event displays in the Notepad window (Figure 5-19).

code to finish actionPerformed event

2 Click File on the menu bar and then click Save.

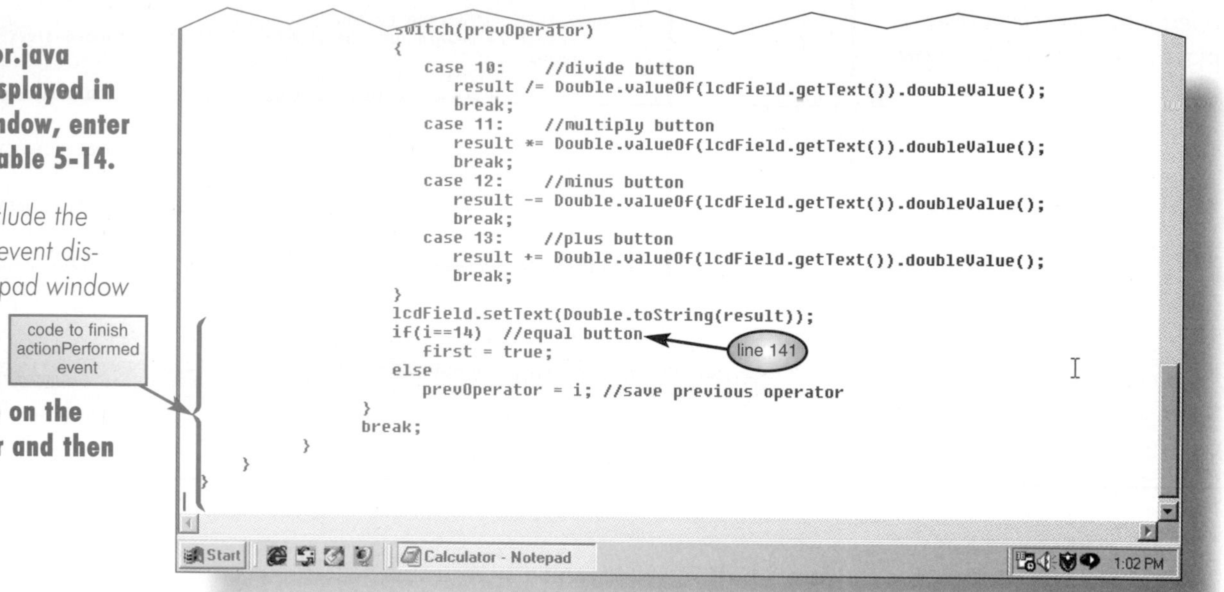

```
switch(prevOperator)
{
    case 10:    //divide button
        result /= Double.valueOf(lcdField.getText()).doubleValue();
        break;
    case 11:    //multiply button
        result *= Double.valueOf(lcdField.getText()).doubleValue();
        break;
    case 12:    //minus button
        result -= Double.valueOf(lcdField.getText()).doubleValue();
        break;
    case 13:    //plus button
        result += Double.valueOf(lcdField.getText()).doubleValue();
        break;
}
lcdField.setText(Double.toString(result));
if(i==14)   //equal button              line 141
    first = true;
else
    prevOperator = i; //save previous operator
}
break;
```

Start | Calculator - Notepad | 1:02 PM

FIGURE 5-19

One of the most common errors made by beginning Java programmers is the mismatching of opening and closing braces in control structures and class blocks. Some programmers insert a short line comment for each ending brace specifying what structure is closing. Your instructor may advise you to add other line comments.

Coding Main

Recall that all Java applications must contain a main method in order to compile and run. The main method for the Calculator application constructs an instance of the Calculator class and then sets three attributes. Table 5-15 displays the coding.

Table 5-15	
LINE	**CODE**
151	`    public static void main(String args[])`
152	`    {`
153	`        //Create a new instance of the Calculator object`
154	`        Calculator calcFrame = new Calculator();`
155	
156	`        //Set frame attributes`
157	`        calcFrame.setBounds(100,100,200,200);`
158	`        calcFrame.setTitle("Calculator");`
159	`        calcFrame.setVisible(true);`
160	`    }`
161	`}`

Frame Attributes

The **setBounds** method in line 157 takes four arguments. They are the pixel measurements to place the left, top, width, and height of the Frame with respect to the screen. In other words, calcFrame will display 100 pixels from the top and 100 pixels from the left of the user's screen; calcFrame will be 200 pixels wide and 200 pixels tall.

The **setTitle** method in line 158 takes a String argument, literal or variable. The argument displays as the title bar caption of the running application.

The **setVisible** method in line 159 takes a boolean argument. Positioning this method within the main method affects whether or not the Frame displays at the beginning of the application. The setVisible method is especially useful when several Frames are being used. With coding, you can decide exactly when or what event will make any given Frame visible.

Perform the following steps to code the main method.

Steps To Code the main Method

1 With the Calculator.java program still displayed in the Notepad window, enter the code from Table 5-15.

The main method displays (Figure 5-20).

2 Click File on the menu bar and then click Save.

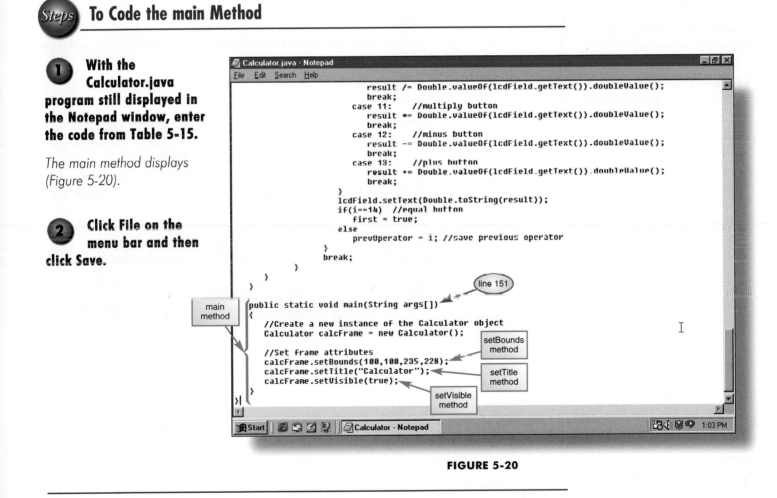

FIGURE 5-20

The application program now is complete. In the next steps, you will compile and execute the Calculator application testing the Frame's attributes and the functionality of the buttons. You may wish to print a copy of the source code to follow as you test the application.

Testing the Application

You have learned that testing the application involves trying out all possible clicks and entering sample data both correctly and incorrectly. In the next series of steps, you will compile and execute the Calculator program. You can enter other data and try different kinds of calculations in order to test the application fully. The following steps will test the border and perform one calculation.

To Test the Application

1 **Click the Start button on the taskbar, point to Programs, and then click MS-DOS Prompt on the Programs submenu. When the MS-DOS Prompt window opens, set the path for your system and change to drive A if necessary. Type** `javac Calculator.java` **and press the ENTER key. If you have errors, fix them in the Notepad window, save the file, and then compile again in the MS-DOS Prompt window.**

The program compiles (Figure 5-21).

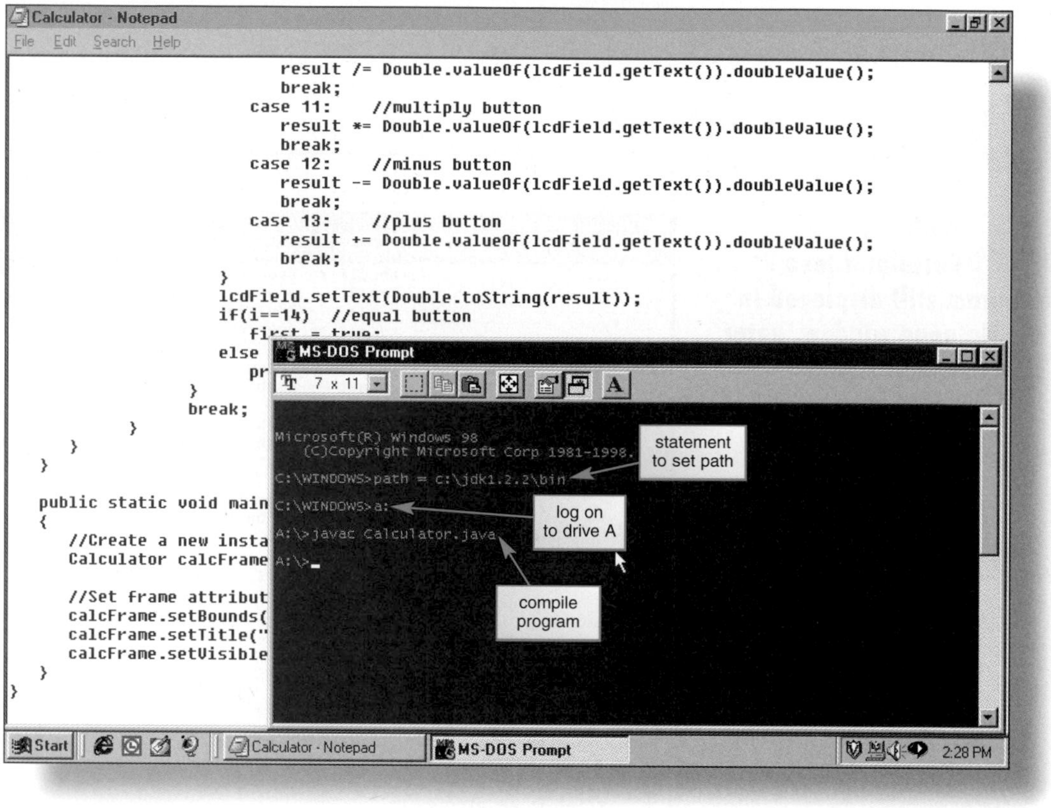

FIGURE 5-21

2 **Type** java Calculator **and then press the ENTER key. When the Calculator window displays, point to its border.**

The Calculator window displays with its title bar and components (Figure 5-22). Your display size may differ. Notice the mouse pointer becomes a double-headed arrow over the window border.

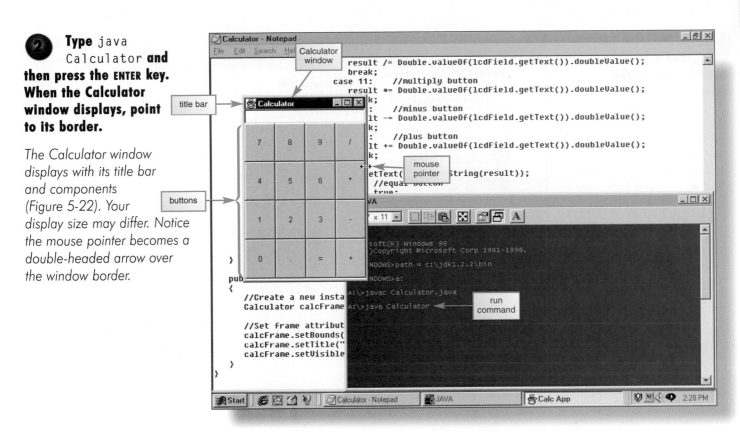

FIGURE 5-22

3 **Drag the border to increase the size of the window.**

Along with resizing the window, the buttons within the window resize (Figure 5-23). This component resizing functionality is part of the Frame component.

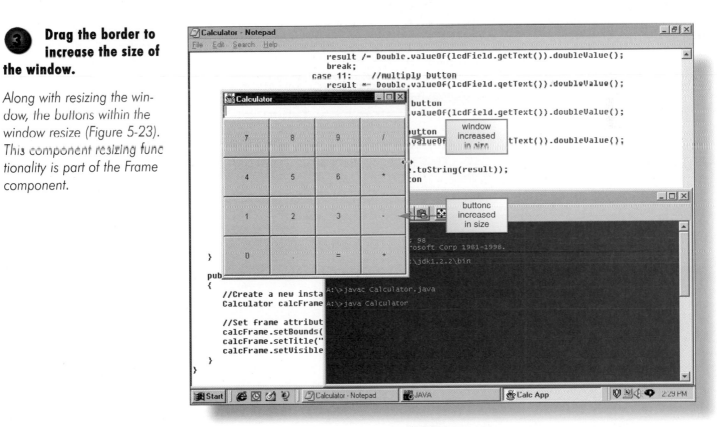

FIGURE 5-23

4 **Click 2 and then click 7 on the keypad. Point to the division button.**

The digits display in the lcdField at the top of the window (Figure 5-24). The actionPerformed event is executed each time a button is clicked.

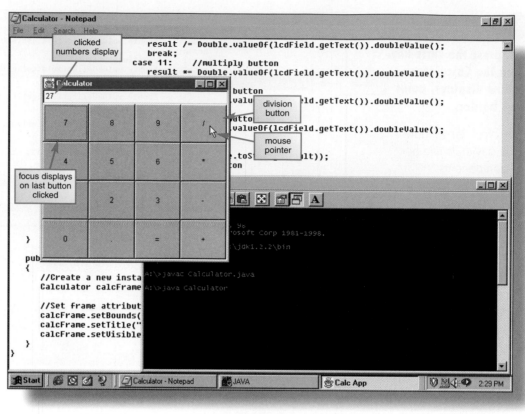

FIGURE 5-24

5 **Click the division button, and then click 3 on the keypad. Point to the equal button.**

The number 27 is cleared from the display and is replaced with the number 3 (Figure 5-25).

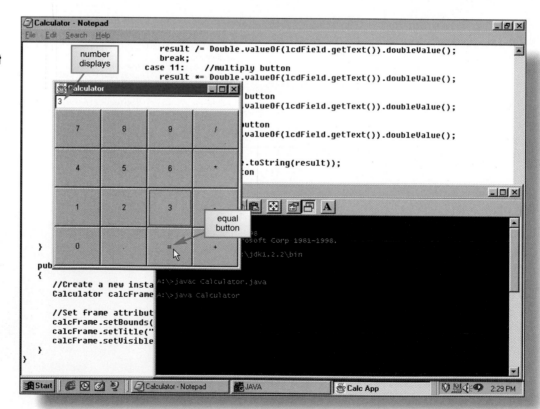

FIGURE 5-25

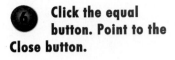

Click the equal button. Point to the Close button.

The answer, 9.0, displays (Figure 5-26). After the equal button is clicked, the calculator is ready for the next calculation, even though the display is not cleared. Notice also that when you point to the Close button, a ScreenTip displays automatically.

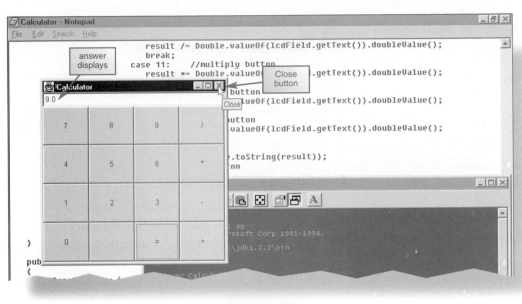

FIGURE 5-26

Click the Close button.

The program terminates and the MS-DOS Prompt window becomes active (Figure 5-27).

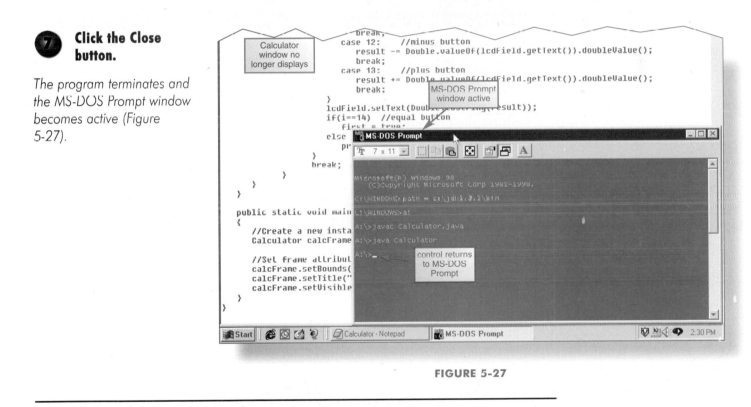

FIGURE 5-27

When a program contains an internal class with the same name as the hosting file, Java compiles them separately. If you examine the directory on your floppy disk, you will see the usual Java bytecode named Calculator and also one named Calculator$1. Calculator$1 is the compiled frame object that you constructed in the Calculator program.

Even though each calculation is new after the equal button is clicked, a clear display functionality would be helpful. As you convert this application to an applet, you will add a CLR button to clear a previous answer or erase numbers entered in error.

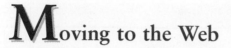

Moving to the Web

During execution, a frame-based application looks more like an applet than it does an application. Its window, title bar, and components are GUI-based, similar to an applet. Therefore, the conversion process to make the Calculator an applet is easy. Rather than starting an entirely new program, you will edit the existing code. First, you will make a host document and then you will edit the applet.

Creating a Host Document

The HTML file that will host the applet will be very similar to previous host documents. The code is listed in Table 5-16.

Table 5-16	
LINE	CODE
1	`<HTML>`
2	`<APPLET CODE = "CalculatorApplet.class" WIDTH = 400 HEIGHT = 200>`
3	`</APPLET>`
4	`</HTML>`

The Calculator application program used a setBounds method to specify the size of the frame. Because applets extend Applet rather than frame, you still need to specify a window size in the HTML code.

Perform the following steps to create an HTML host document for the Calculator applet.

TO CREATE A HOST DOCUMENT

1 In Notepad, click File on the menu bar and then click New, or start a new session of Notepad.

2 Enter the code from Table 5-16.

3 Save the file as "CalculatorApplet.html" on your floppy disk. Remember to include the quotation marks when you save the file.

Converting the Application to an Applet

In the following steps, you will make the necessary changes to make the program run as an applet, as well as add a new CLR button to the calculator. First, you will open the Calculator application, extend Applet, and change the internal Calculator class to init, removing the application's main. Then, you will enlarge the array to include another button, add it to the keypad Panel, and write the code to make it functional.

Implementing the Applet Package

The first step in converting to an applet involves making changes to the application to ensure it inherits from the Applet package. These edits include changing the name of the program, importing the Applet class, and extending Applet instead of Frame. You also will save the file with a new name.

Perform the following steps to convert the application to an applet.

More About

Attaching Your Applet to a Web Page

If you want to attach the Calculator Applet to an existing Web page, include the Applet Code tag and its attributes in your HTML file. Applets can be accessed from a hyperlink, as well. For more information, visit the Java Programming Web page (www.scsite.com/java/more.htm) and then click Attaching Applets to Web Pages.

Steps: To Edit the Application for the Applet Package

1 If necessary, open the Calculator source code file from your floppy disk or click the Notepad button on the taskbar if Calculator is still open. Scroll to the beginning of the code.

The Calculator application code displays (Figure 5-28). Your taskbar buttons may differ depending on the order in which you opened the windows.

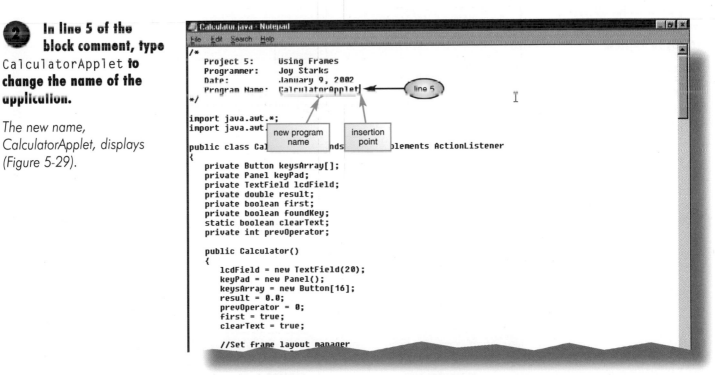

FIGURE 5-28

2 In line 5 of the block comment, type `CalculatorApplet` to change the name of the application.

The new name, CalculatorApplet, displays (Figure 5-29).

FIGURE 5-29

3 **Click the end of line 9. Press the ENTER key and then type** import java.applet.*; **to import the applet package.**

The new line displays (Figure 5-30).

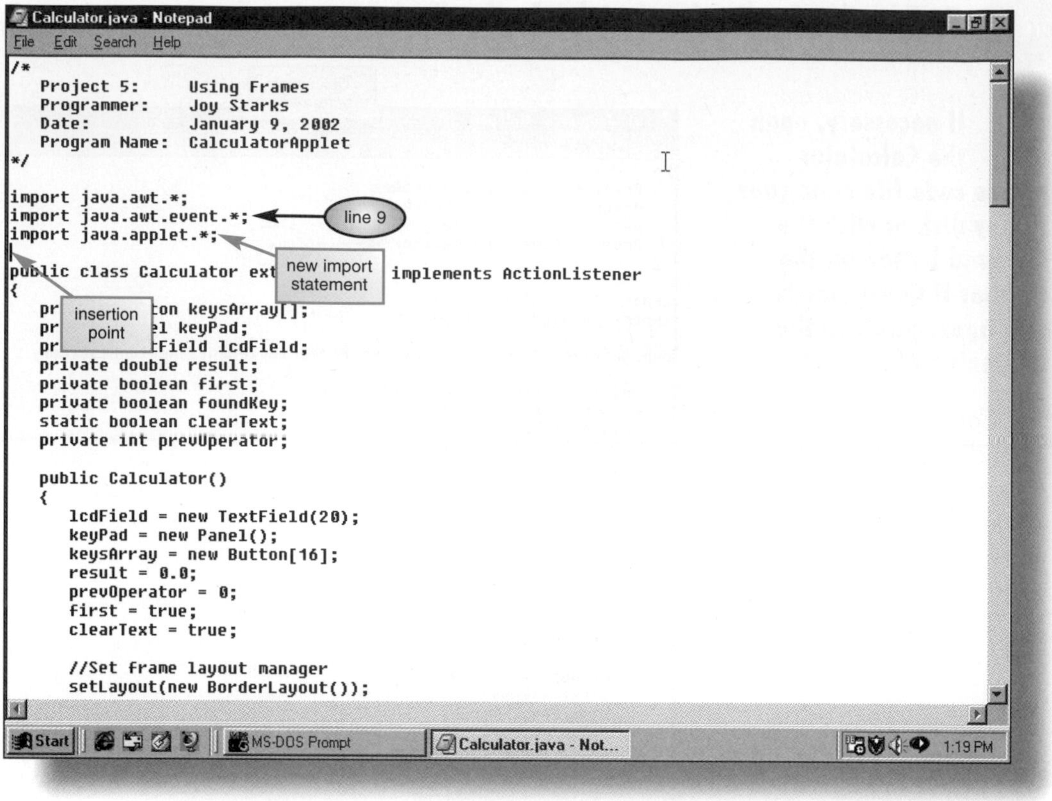

FIGURE 5-30

4 **In line 12, change the name of the class to CalculatorApplet, and change the word Frame, to Applet.**

Applications extend Frame; applets extend the Applet class (Figure 5-31).

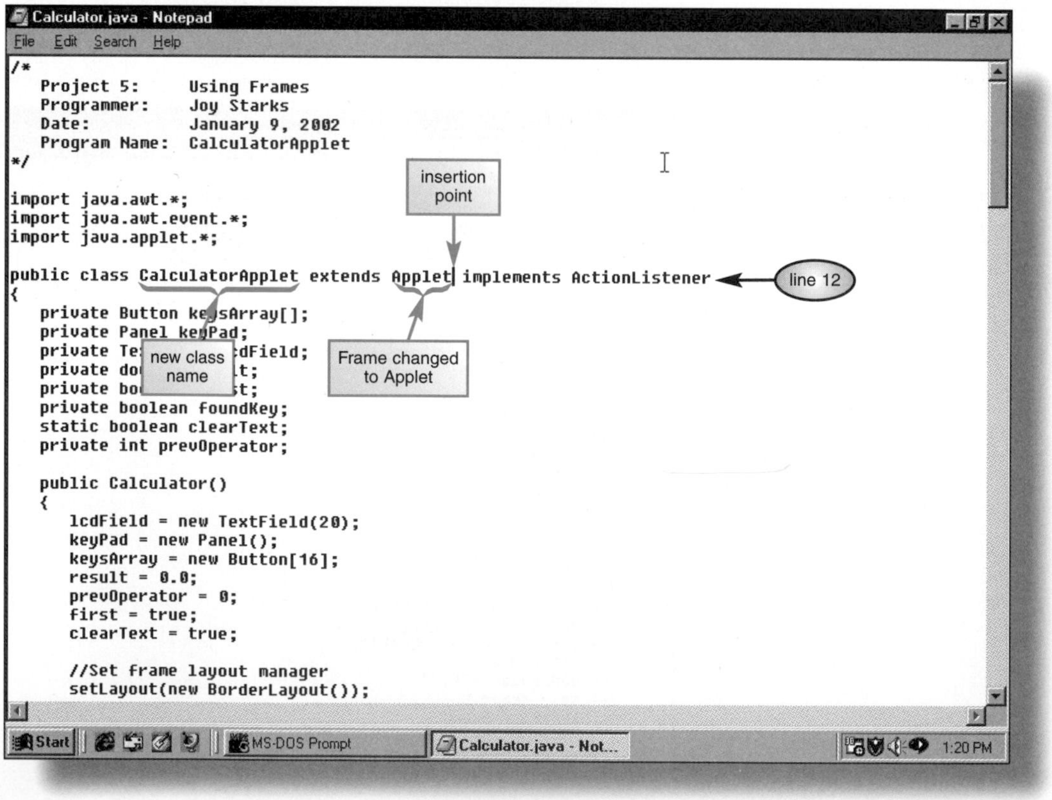

FIGURE 5-31

5 Click File on the menu bar and then click Save As. When the Save As dialog box displays, click 3½ Floppy (A:) in the Save in list and then type "CalculatorApplet.java" in the File name text box. Point to the Save button.

The new name of the program will be CalculatorApplet (Figure 5-32). The files on your floppy disk may differ.

6 Click the Save button.

The file saves on drive A with the new file name.

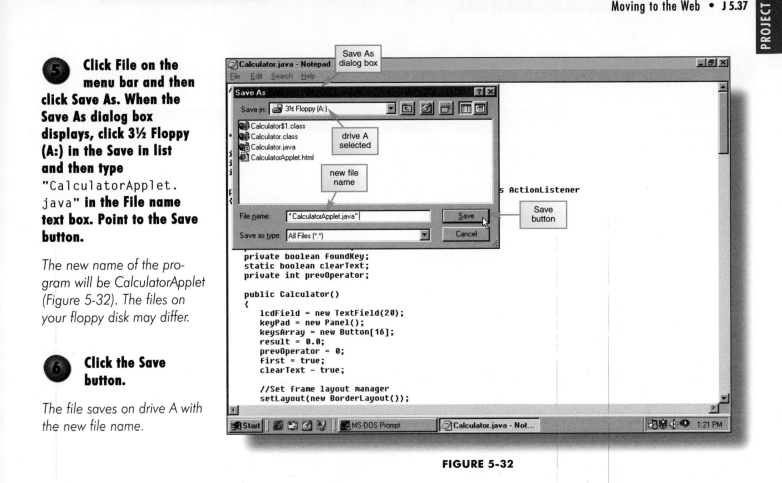

FIGURE 5-32

Changing the Calculator Class

Recall that all applets must have an init method. You will replace the Calculator constructor method with the init method.

In order to add a CLR button, you will need to change the length of the Button array to 17, construct a new button with a label, and then add it to the right side of the Frame, as shown in the steps on the next page.

More About

Java Text Editing Freeware

For more information on obtaining freeware to assist you in editing Java source code, visit the Java Programming Web page (www.scsite.com/java/more.htm) and then click Java Text Editing Freeware.

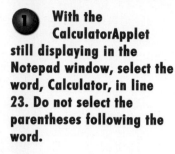

To Add a CLR Button

1 **With the CalculatorApplet still displaying in the Notepad window, select the word, Calculator, in line 23. Do not select the parentheses following the word.**

Calculator is highlighted in the Notepad window (Figure 5-33).

```
/*
    Project 5:      Using Frames
    Programmer:     Joy Starks
    Date:           January 9, 2002
    Program Name:   CalculatorApplet
*/

import java.awt.*;
import java.awt.event.*;
import java.applet.*;

public class CalculatorApplet extends Applet implements ActionListener
{
    private Button keysArray[];
    private Panel keyPad;
    private TextField lcdF
    private double result;
    private boolean first;
    private boolean foundK
    static boolean clearText;
    private int prevOperator;

    public Calculator()
    {
        lcdField = new TextField(20);
        keyPad = new Panel();
        keysArray = new Button[16];
        result = 0.0;
        prevOperator = 0;
        first = true;
        clearText = true;

        //Set frame layout manager
        setLayout(new BorderLayout());
```

name of constructor method selected

line 23

FIGURE 5-33

2 **Type the words** `void init` **to replace Calculator. Select the number 16 in line 27.**

Applets must have an init method (Figure 5-34). Recall that 16 is the original length of the button array in the application.

```
/*
    Project 5:      Using Frames
    Programmer:     Joy Starks
    Date:           January 9, 2002
    Program Name:   CalculatorApplet
*/

import java.awt.*;
import java.awt.event.*;
import java.applet.*;

public class CalculatorApplet extends Applet implements ActionListener
{
    private Button keysArray[];
    private Panel keyPad;
    private TextField lcd
    private double result
    private boolean first
    private boolean foundKey;
    static boolean clearText;
    private int prevOperator;

    public void init()
    {
        lcdField = new TextField(20);
        keyPad = new Panel();
        keysArray = new Button[16];
        result = 0.0;
        prevOperator = 0;
        first = true;
        clearText = true;

        //Set frame layout manager
        setLayout(new BorderLayout());
```

init method replaces Calculator constructor method

length of array selected

line 27

FIGURE 5-34

3 **Type** 17 **to replace the text.**

The length of the Button array now will be 17 (Figure 5-35).

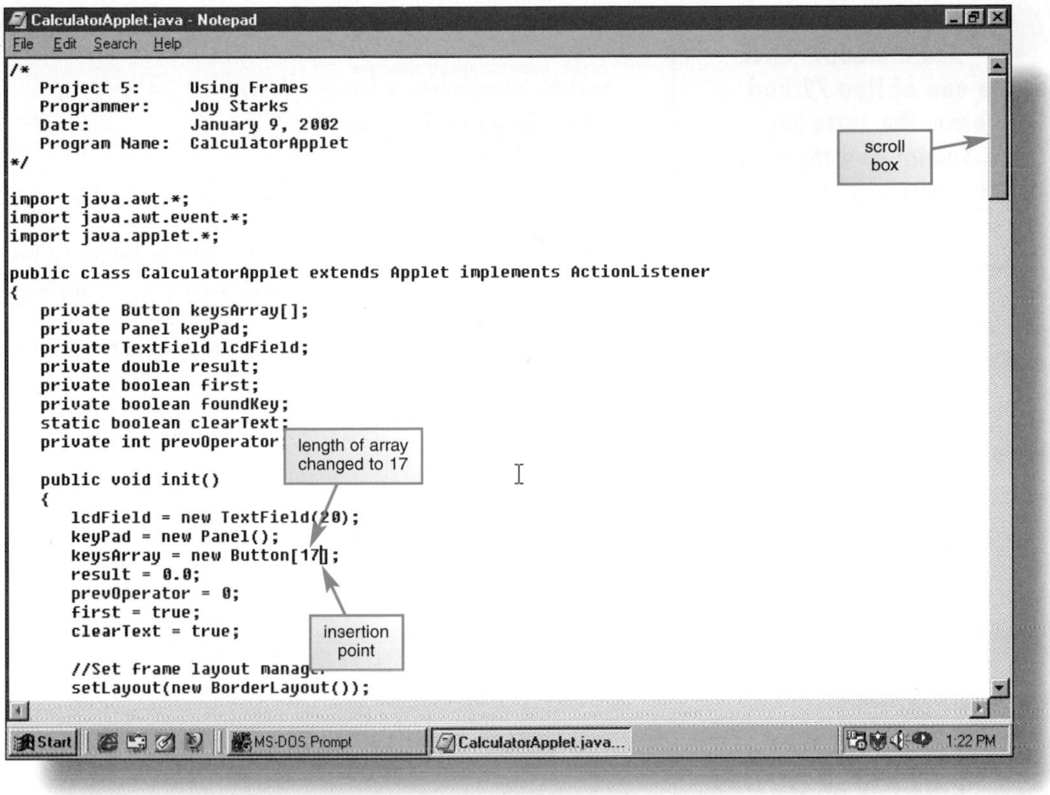

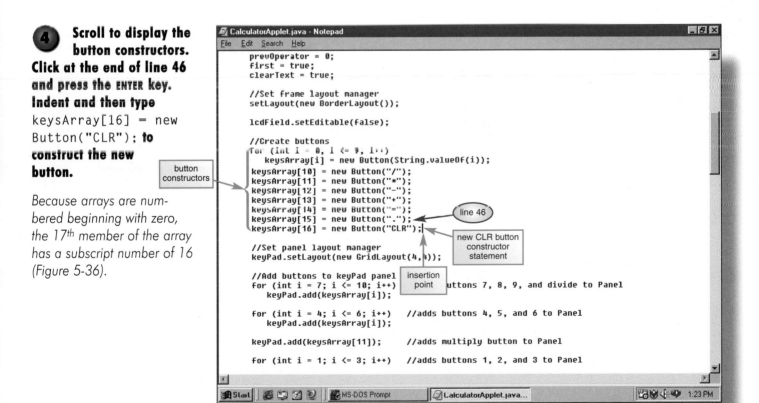

FIGURE 5-35

4 **Scroll to display the button constructors. Click at the end of line 46 and press the ENTER key. Indent and then type** keysArray[16] = new Button("CLR"); **to construct the new button.**

Because arrays are numbered beginning with zero, the 17th member of the array has a subscript number of 16 (Figure 5-36).

FIGURE 5-36

Step 5 Scroll to display the add methods. Click at the end of line 72 and then press the ENTER key twice. Indent and then type `add(keysArray[16], BorderLayout.EAST); //adds Clear key to right side of applet` to enter the add method and the comment.

The CLR button will be added in the East area, or right side, of the Frame (Figure 5-37). The comment after the semicolon (;) is not necessary, but it adds readability to the code and helps the programmer keep track of buttons.

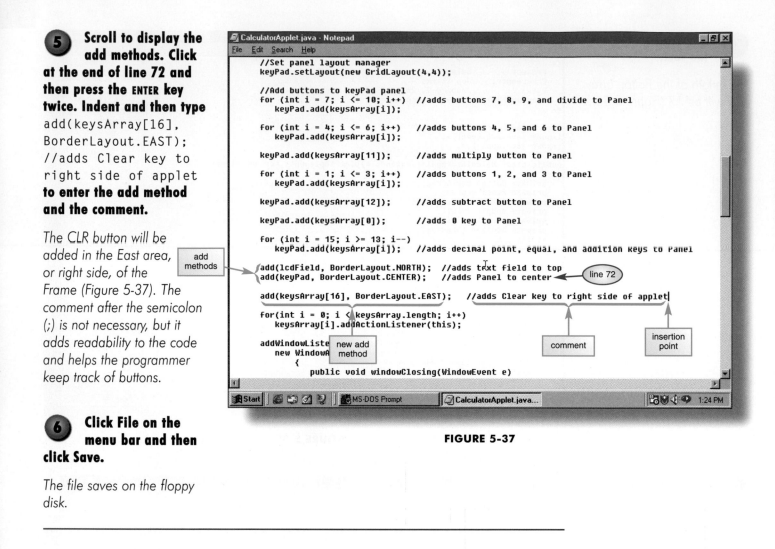

FIGURE 5-37

Step 6 Click File on the menu bar and then click Save.

The file saves on the floppy disk.

Editing the Applet for Functionality

Now that the Applet package has been imported, and the new button created and added to the Frame, you must add additional functionality to the applet.

First, you will delete the addWindowListener event. Then, you will add functionality to the CLR button. After a calculation is performed, the variables first and clearText both will be false. The CLR button will set both the variables to true in anticipation of beginning a new calculation. The CLR button also will set the text field lcdField to a null string and will set the variables, result, and prevOperator to zero.

Finally, you will remove the main method. Applet windows are governed by the browser and HTML host document and do not have a main method.

Perform the following steps to add functionality to the new button.

Steps **To Edit the Applet for Functionality**

1 **In the Notepad window, with CalculatorApplet.java still displaying, select the entire addWindowListener event.**

The entire event, with its closing parenthesis and semi-colon, displays selected (Figure 5-38). The Applet package provides its own closing mechanism, so the WindowListener no longer is needed.

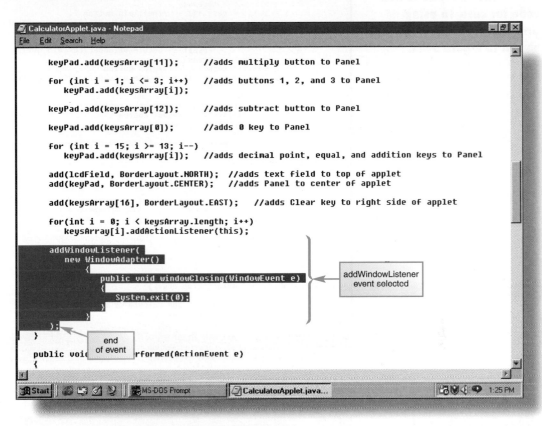

```
keyPad.add(keysArray[11]);      //adds multiply button to Panel

for (int i = 1; i <= 3; i++)    //adds buttons 1, 2, and 3 to Panel
    keyPad.add(keysArray[i]);

keyPad.add(keysArray[12]);      //adds subtract button to Panel

keyPad.add(keysArray[0]);       //adds 0 key to Panel

for (int i = 15; i >= 13; i--)
    keyPad.add(keysArray[i]);   //adds decimal point, equal, and addition keys to Panel

add(lcdField, BorderLayout.NORTH);  //adds text field to top of applet
add(keyPad, BorderLayout.CENTER);   //adds Panel to center of applet

add(keysArray[16], BorderLayout.EAST);   //adds Clear key to right side of applet

for(int i = 0; i < keysArray.length; i++)
    keysArray[i].addActionListener(this);

addWindowListener(
    new WindowAdapter()
        {
            public void windowClosing(WindowEvent e)
            {
                System.exit(0);
            }
        }
);
}
public void                 rformed(ActionEvent e)
{
```

addWindowListener event selected

end of event

FIGURE 5-38

2 **Press the DELETE key. Scroll to display the end of the actionPerformed event. Click at the end of line 142, after the last break; statement.**

The mouse pointer displays (Figure 5-39).

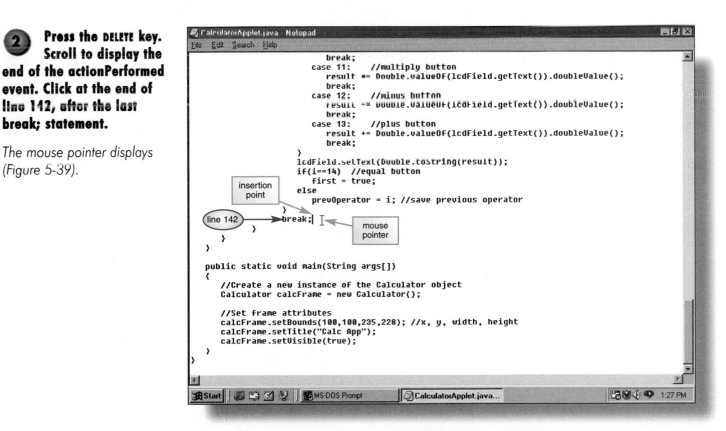

```
                break;
    case 11:    //multiply button
        result *= Double.valueOf(lcdField.getText()).doubleValue();
        break;
    case 12:    //minus button
        result -= Double.valueOf(lcdField.getText()).doubleValue();
        break;
    case 13:    //plus button
        result += Double.valueOf(lcdField.getText()).doubleValue();
        break;
    }
    lcdField.setText(Double.toString(result));
    if(i==14)  //equal button
        first = true;
    else
        prevOperator = i; //save previous operator
    }
    break;
    }
}

public static void main(String args[])
{
    //Create a new instance of the Calculator object
    Calculator calcFrame = new Calculator();

    //Set Frame attributes
    calcFrame.setBounds(100,100,235,228); //x, y, width, height
    calcFrame.setTitle("Calc App");
    calcFrame.setVisible(true);
}
}
```

insertion point

line 142

mouse pointer

FIGURE 5-39

3 **Press the ENTER key twice. Type the new code for case 16 using proper indentation as shown in Figure 5-40.**

The code to execute when the user clicks the CLR button displays (Figure 5-40).

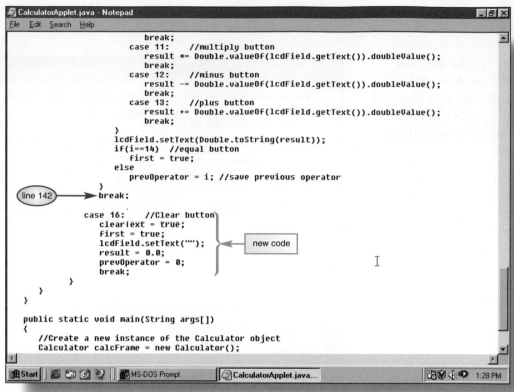

```
                                break;
                case 11:    //multiply button
                    result *= Double.valueOf(lcdField.getText()).doubleValue();
                    break;
                case 12:    //minus button
                    result -= Double.valueOf(lcdField.getText()).doubleValue();
                    break;
                case 13:    //plus button
                    result += Double.valueOf(lcdField.getText()).doubleValue();
                    break;
            }
            lcdField.setText(Double.toString(result));
            if(i==14)  //equal button
                first = true;
            else
                prevOperator = i; //save previous operator
        }
        break;

        case 16:    //Clear button
            clearText = true;
            first = true;
            lcdField.setText("");
            result = 0.0;
            prevOperator = 0;
            break;
        }
    }
}

public static void main(String args[])
{
    //Create a new instance of the Calculator object
    Calculator calcFrame = new Calculator();
```

line 142 → break;

new code →

FIGURE 5-40

4 **Select the entire main method.**

The main method displays selected (Figure 5-41). Be careful not to include the closing brace for the entire CalculatorApplet class.

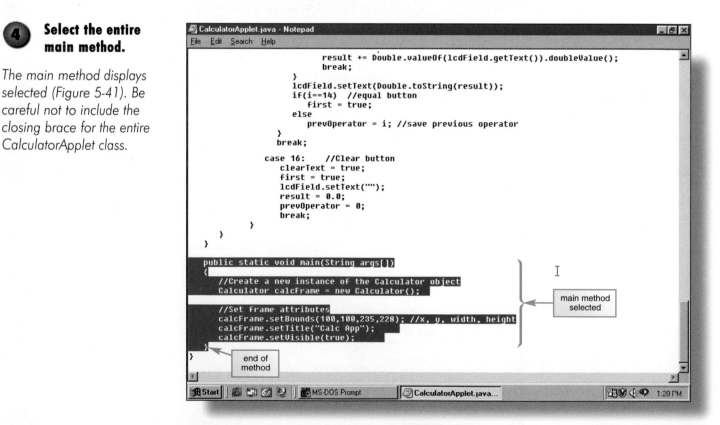

```
                    result += Double.valueOf(lcdField.getText()).doubleValue();
                    break;
            }
            lcdField.setText(Double.toString(result));
            if(i==14)  //equal button
                first = true;
            else
                prevOperator = i; //save previous operator
        }
        break;

        case 16:    //Clear button
            clearText = true;
            first = true;
            lcdField.setText("");
            result = 0.0;
            prevOperator = 0;
            break;
        }
    }
}

public static void main(String args[])
{
    //Create a new instance of the Calculator object
    Calculator calcFrame = new Calculator();

    //Set frame attributes
    calcFrame.setBounds(100,100,235,228); //x, y, width, height
    calcFrame.setTitle("Calc App");
    calcFrame.setVisible(true);
}
}
```

main method selected →

end of method →

FIGURE 5-41

⑤ Press the DELETE key.

The entire main method is deleted (Figure 5-42). Applets do not have a main method; the HTML host document governs placement attributes.

⑥ Click File on the menu bar and then click Save.

The file saves on the floppy disk.

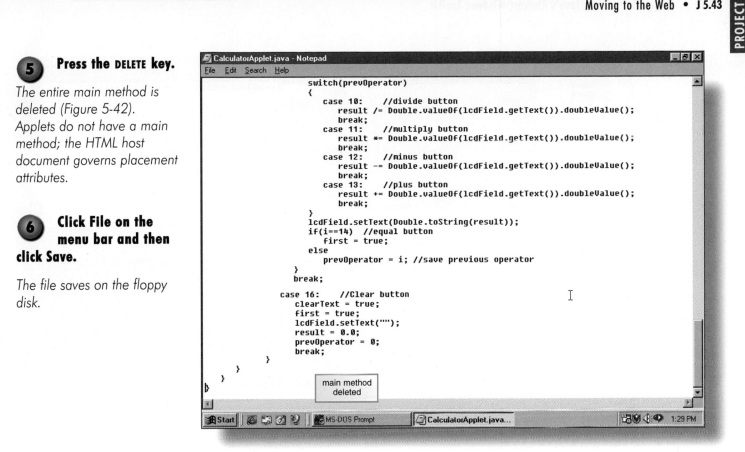

```
                        switch(prevOperator)
                        {
                           case 10:    //divide button
                              result /= Double.valueOf(lcdField.getText()).doubleValue();
                              break;
                           case 11:    //multiply button
                              result *= Double.valueOf(lcdField.getText()).doubleValue();
                              break;
                           case 12:    //minus button
                              result -= Double.valueOf(lcdField.getText()).doubleValue();
                              break;
                           case 13:    //plus button
                              result += Double.valueOf(lcdField.getText()).doubleValue();
                              break;
                        }
                        lcdField.setText(Double.toString(result));
                        if(i==14)  //equal button
                           first = true;
                        else
                           prevOperator = i; //save previous operator
                     }
                     break;

                  case 16:    //Clear button
                     clearText = true;
                     first = true;
                     lcdField.setText("");
                     result = 0.0;
                     prevOperator = 0;
                     break;

               }
            }
         }
```

main method deleted

FIGURE 5-42

Testing the CLR Button

Now that you have edited and saved the applet with the new CLR button, you should run it and test the button. Perform the following steps to run the applet using the Applet Viewer and then test the CLR button.

TO TEST THE CLR BUTTON

① Open the MS-DOS Prompt window, if necessary. Set the path and log onto drive A.

② Compile the applet by typing `javac CalculatorApplet.java` and then press the ENTER key.

③ If you have errors, fix them in the Notepad window, and then save the "CalculatorApplet.java" file again. Repeat Step 2.

④ Once the program has compiled, run the program using Applet Viewer. Type `appletviewer CalculatorApplet.html` and then press the ENTER key.

⑤ When the Calculator applet displays, test the CLR button by performing your choice of calculations, and then click the CLR button.

The CLR button causes the display field to clear any previous calculations or entries (Figure 5-43 on the next page). The size of your Applet Viewer window might differ.

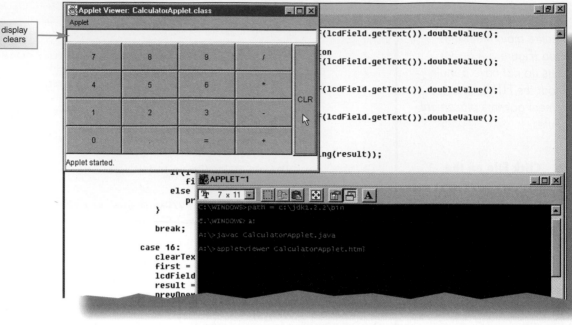

display clears

FIGURE 5-43

Project Summary

In this project, you learned about using Java's Abstract Windows Toolkit with layout managers in both applications and applets. First, you learned about the different kinds of containers and components that Java uses in conjunction with the five layout managers. With BorderLayout and GridLayout, Java places objects in containers, including containers within other containers. As you created the Calculator application, you added an array of buttons to a Panel and coded their functionality.

You learned that registering a WindowListener event and overriding the windowClosing allows you to customize exactly what will happen when the user clicks the Close button in a frame-based application. In order to set a window's other attributes, Java uses the setBounds, setTitle, and setVisible methods, among others.

Finally, the project showed you how to make small changes to a Java application that employs a GUI, to convert it to an applet. Because applets do not have a main method, you changed the Calculator constructor method to an init method. You added an extra CLR button to the Calculator, compiled, and executed it using Applet Viewer.

What You Should Know

Having completed this project, you now should be able to perform the following tasks:

- Add Buttons to the Panel (J 5.18)
- Add a CLR Button (J 5.38)
- Code the End of the actionPerformed Event (J 5.28)
- Code the First Operator (J 5.25)
- Code the First Part of the actionPerformed Event (J 5.24)
- Code the Keypad (J 5.19)
- Code the main Method (J 5.29)
- Code the windowClosing Event (J 5.21)
- Construct the Buttons and Set the Layout Manager (J 5.17)

- Create a Host Document (J 5.34)
- Create the Calculator Frame (J 5.15)
- Edit the Applet for Functionality (J 5.41)
- Edit the Application for the Applet Package (J 5.35)
- Enter Beginning Code (J 5.8)
- Enter Code for Subsequent Operator Button Clicks (J 5.27)
- Enter Code to Declare Variables (J 5.10)
- Test the Application (J 5.30)
- Test the CLR Button (J 5.43)

Test Your Knowledge

1 True/False

Instructions: Circle T if the statement is true or F if the statement is false.

T F 1. A container is a special category of Java objects that contains other components, such as user interface controls and components.

T F 2. Frames inherit their attributes and methods from the Applet class.

T F 3. Java automatically applies ScreenTips to the Minimize, Maximize, and Close buttons of a Frame.

T F 4. Subsetting of containers is not allowed in Java.

T F 5. The windowClosing event must be overridden in order for a Frame's Close button to terminate the application.

T F 6. The layout manager that uses a north, south, east, and west configuration is called MapLayout.

T F 7. The setBounds method is used to set the location of an applet.

T F 8. A component array can be constructed with one line of code.

T F 9. A flag usually is a boolean data type.

T F 10. Java uses a method named, Multiple, to assign a single action to multiple clicks.

2 Multiple Choice

Instructions: Circle the correct response.

1. AWT stands for _____.
   a. All Windows Toolkit
   b. Abstract Windows Toolkit
   c. Abstract Windowing Toolbar
   d. Adding Windows Technology

2. _____ is not a Java layout manager.
   a. GrabBagLayout
   b. BorderLayout
   c. CardLayout
   d. FlowLayout

3. _____ is the default layout manager.
   a. FlowLayout
   b. GridLayout
   c. BorderLayout
   d. NoLayout

4. _____ is not a Java component.
   a. TextField
   b. Panel
   c. Button
   d. Icon

(continued)

Test Your Knowledge

Multiple Choice (continued)

5. The delimiter between an object and its method is a(n) _____.
   a. dot
   b. parenthesis
   c. underscore
   d. comma

6. The method that governs the action taken when a user clicks the Close button is called the _____ method.
   a. Close
   b. windowMethod
   c. closeWindow
   d. windowClosing

7. Which of the following is a layout manager constant?
   a. center
   b. Center
   c. CENTER
   d. c.Center

8. If a variable remains the same when Java creates an instance of the class, it should be declared _____.
   a. global
   b. public
   c. static
   d. private

9. In the line of code, setLayout(new BorderLayout(10,8)); the arguments represent _____.
   a. pixels
   b. rows and columns
   c. twips
   d. array indices

10. The setEditable method takes a(n) _____ argument.
    a. String
    b. boolean
    c. int
    d. read/write

Test Your Knowledge

3 Understanding Components

Instructions: Using Figure 5-44, answer the following questions.

1. Does the figure display an applet or an application?
2. What is the name of the program?
3. Which layout manager is being used?
4. What is the probable container used to place the Buttons?
5. What internal or subsetted layout managers were used, if any?
6. Which of the components is a Choice component?
7. What method was used to place the word, TextField, in its component?
8. How would you increase the size of the space between Buttons?
9. What determines the size of this interface?
10. In what order were the components added to the interface?

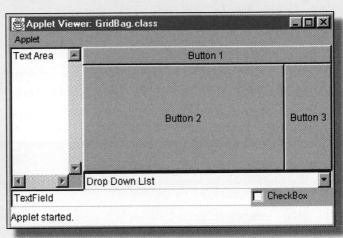

FIGURE 5-44

4 Understanding Java Code

Instructions: Find and fix the error in each line of code. Each line contains only one error. Assume variables have been declared correctly.

1. public class myFrame extends ActionListener
2. myArray[1] = Button("=");
3. myPad.setGridLayout(4,4);
4. add(myField, BorderLayout.TOP);
5. myButton.addActionListener;
6. Case 1:
7. myArray[i] = new Button(valueOf(i));
8. addSystem.exit(0);
9. myField.setEditable("");
10. myFrame.setCaption("Project 5");

Apply Your Knowledge

1 Using Java's BorderLayout in an Applet

Instructions: Start Notepad. Open the file Apply5.java, from the Data Disk (see inside back cover for instructions on how to obtain a copy of the Data Disk).

1. Change the name of the program to TestApplet, both in the class header and in the block comments. Insert your name and the current date in the comments.
2. Save the file as "TestApplet.java" on your floppy disk. Print a copy of the source code.
3. In Notepad, click File on the menu bar and then click New. Enter the code from Table 5-17. Save it with the name "TestApplet.html" on your floppy disk.

Table 5-17	
LINE	CODE
1	`<HTML>`
2	`<APPLET CODE = "TestApplet.class" WIDTH = 400 HEIGHT = 200>`
3	`</APPLET>`
4	`</HTML>`

4. Open the MS-DOS Prompt window and set the path. Change the drive location to your floppy disk.
5. Compile the program by typing `javac TestApplet.java` and then press the ENTER key.
6. Run the program by typing `appletviewer TestApplet.html`. The program displays running as shown in Figure 5-45.
7. Open the TestApplet.java source code file again in the Notepad window. Make the following changes to the program:
   a. In the init method, set the background color to red.
   b. Enter two arguments for the BorderLayout, which indicate the spacing between components. Use 20 pixels horizontally and 5 pixels vertically.
8. Save the source code in Notepad with the same name. Compile the program and fix any errors, if necessary. Run the applet from the MS-DOS Prompt window using Applet Viewer. Print a copy of the source code.
9. Make the following changes to the program:
   a. Implement the ActionListener in the class header.
   b. Change the names of the buttons to red, yellow, cyan, magenta, and white.
   c. Below the init method, but still within the class block, enter an actionPerformed event with the header, `public void actionPerformed(ActionEvent e)` and an opening brace.
   d. Declare and assign a variable arg, by typing, `String arg = e.getActionCommand();` within the block.

FIGURE 5-45

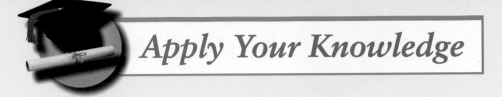

Apply Your Knowledge

e. Test the click of each button by writing an if statement similar to the following: if (arg == "red"), followed by a line of code to change the background color of the applet.

10. Save the source code. Compile, correct any errors, and then run the applet. Print a copy of the source code.

11. Finally, as an extra credit assignment, make the following changes to the program:
    a. Delete the button in the center area.
    b. Construct a Choice component.
    c. Use the addItem method to populate the Choice component with the colors from step 9b.
    d. Add an ActionListener to the Choice component and then add the Choice component to the center area of the BorderLayout.
    e. Write a switch structure to test for each item in the choice component and add functionality to change the background color.

12. Save the source code. Compile, correct any errors, and then run the applet. Print a copy of the source code.

In the Lab

1 Creating a Telephone Keypad

Problem: Many computer systems are connected to modems, telephones, and fax systems. As part of the programming team at WebPhone, you have been asked to design the user interface — a telephone keypad that displays on the screen. Figure 5-46 displays a sample of how the window should look.

Instructions: Using the techniques you have learned so far, including the steps you performed in this project, write a Java application that displays a telephone keypad. Add functionality so that when a button is clicked the number or symbol displays in the TextField. Perform the following steps to create the Telephone program.

1. Start Notepad. Create a block comment with your name, date, program name, and purpose.
2. Import Java's awt and awt.event packages.
3. Create a class named Telephone that extends Frame and implements the ActionListener.

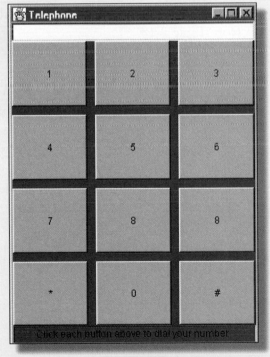

FIGURE 5-46

(continued)

In the Lab

Creating a Telephone Keypad *(continued)*

4. Declare public variables as follows:
   - an array of buttons
   - keypad
   - TextField
   - Label
   - variable named foundKey

5. Create an internal method, also called Telephone. Include the following:
   a. Write a constructor for the TextField with a length of 20.
   b. Write a constructor to create the keypad Panel.
   c. Write a constructor to set the array with a length of 12.
   d. Set the label to match the text in the lower part of Figure 5-46 on the previous page.
   e. Set the TextField to be uneditable.
   f. Type `setBackground(Color.magenta);` to change the color of the Frame's background.
   g. Type `setLayout(new BorderLayout());` to declare the layout manager for the Frame.
   h. Type `keyPad.setLayout(new GridLayout(4,3,10,10));` to declare the layout manager for the Panel.
   i. Add the buttons to the keyPad in order from upper-left to lower-right.
   j. Add the TextField to the North area of the Frame.
   k. Add the Panel to the Center area of the Frame.
   l. Add the Label to the South area of the Frame.

6. Register a WindowListener by typing the code from Table 5-18.

7. Create an actionPerformed event to include the following:
   a. Write a loop to traverse the array. Test the member of the array at the index number to see if it matches the argument passed to the actionPerformed event. Your code will look similar to `if(e.getSource() == keysArray[i])`. Your variable names may differ.
   b. When a match is found, transfer the label from the button to TextField, concatenating any previous entries. Your code will look similar to `lcdField.setText(lcdField.getText() + keysArray[i].getLabel( ));` however, your variable names may differ.

8. Create a main method with the following code:
   a. Construct an instance of the Telephone.
   b. Set the bounds of the Frame to 50, 100, 200, and 300.
   c. Set the title of the Frame to Telephone.
   d. Set the visibility of the Frame to true.

Table 5-18

CODE

```
addWindowListener(
    new WindowAdapter()
        {
            public void windowClosing(WindowEvent e)
            {
                System.exit(0);
            }
        }
    );
} //end of Telephone method
```

In the Lab

9. Enter the closing brace for the class. Print a copy to double-check the matching of braces and parentheses before compiling.
10. Save the file as "Telephone.java" on your floppy disk.
11. Compile the source code. Fix any errors and recompile, if necessary.
12. Run the application several times, trying each number and symbol.
13. Print a copy of the source code for your instructor.
14. If directed by your instructor, as an extra credit assignment, add a CLR button.

2 Using a Component Array and Measured Loop

Problem: You are tutoring programming students and want an application to demonstrate arrays and looping structures. You decide to create a panel containing an array of 16 TextFields that change color to correspond with the start, stop, and step values entered by the user. You want to start with a looping structure that allows the student to specify how many times the loop statements will be executed.

Instructions: Perform the following tasks to create the Checkerboard Array application as shown in Figure 5-47(a). When the user enters the start, stop, and step fields and then clicks the Go button, the results display as shown in Figure 5-46(b).

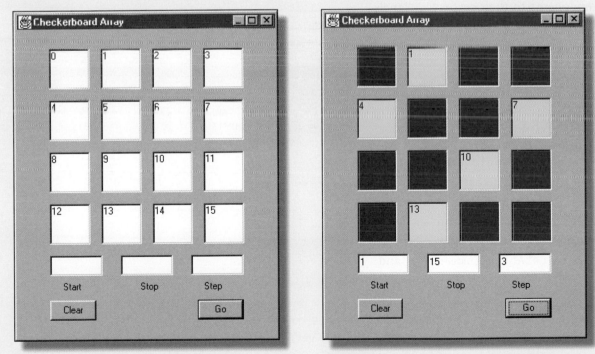

(a) Checkerboard application at startup   (b) Results after clicking the Go button

FIGURE 5-47

(continued)

In the Lab

Using a Component Array and Measured Loop *(continued)*

1. Open Notepad. Create a block comment with your name, date, program name, and purpose.
2. Import Java's awt and awt.event packages.
3. Create a class named Checkerboard that extends Frame and implements the ActionListener. Declare variables for the following components included in the frame:
   ▶ an array of 16 TextFields
   ▶ a Panel to hold the array
   ▶ three individual TextFields
   ▶ three int variables to receive the start, stop, and step data
   ▶ two buttons, Clear and Go
   ▶ a Panel to hold the three fields and two buttons
4. Create a class named Checkerboard.
   a. Construct each of the components declared above and set the start, stop, and step variables to zero.
   b. Set the frame layout manager to BorderLayout.
   c. Write a loop to traverse the array and set each of the 16 TextFields in that array so they cannot be edited. Within the same loop set each TextField's text to match the loop increment. (*Hint*: Use the setEditable and setText methods.)
   d. Set the upper Panel to GridLayout, 4 x 4. Set the lower Panel to GridLayout, 2 x 3.
   e. Add the components to their respective Panels.
   f. Use the addActionListener method to enliven the two buttons.
   g. Place the panels in the Frame using the appropriate area.
5. Enter the method displayed in Table 5-19, to close the Frame.
6. To make the Go button work, code an actionPerformed event.
   a. Type the header, `public void actionPerformed(ActionEvent e)` using the identifier, e, as an argument.
   b. Use the getActionCommand to store the label from the button in the identifier, arg. Type `String arg = e.getActionCommand();` and press the ENTER key.
   c. Then within the body of the event, check to see if the button clicked is the Go button. Type `if (arg == "Go")` and then type an opening brace.
   d. Convert the data from the input fields to ints, using the getText method along with the parseInt method. Store the result in the variables declared for that purpose in step 3 above.
   e. Write a loop that goes through the array setting every background color to a darker color, such as magenta.
   f. Write a loop based on the user input values. Each time the loop is executed, change the background color to a lighter color, such as yellow.

Table 5-19

CODE

```
addWindowListener(
    new WindowAdapter()
        {
            public void windowClosing(WindowEvent e)
            {
                System.exit(0);
            }
        }
    );
}
```

In the Lab

g. To make the Clear button work, write an if statement that compares arg to Clear. If true, a loop should be performed that sets all the background colors back to white, and clears the input fields by setting their texts to a null string.

h. Enter the closing brace for the actionPerformed event.

7. Write a main method that creates an instance of the Checkerboard Frame.

a. Set the bounds of the Frame to 50, 100, 300, and 400.

b. Set the title bar caption to Checkerboard Array.

c. Use the setVisible method to display the application Frame during execution.

8. Save the file as "Checkerboard.java" on your floppy disk.

9. Compile the source code. Fix any errors and recompile, if necessary.

10. Run the application several times, trying different numbers for the start, stop, and step. Remember the array has a length of 16, so the highest allowable stop value is 15.

11. Print a copy of the source code for your instructor.

3 Adding a Graphic to an Applet

Problem: Figure 5-48 displays an applet with a graphic. The buttons in the Panel at the bottom of the applet direct the movement of the graphic. The Java cup graphic is on the Data Disk that is provided with this text. If you wish, you may substitute your own graphic. Be sure to place the graphic in the same directory as your program.

Instructions: In this applet, you will use the getDocumentBase method to import a graphic. You will use the repaint method along with drawImage. The four arguments needed by drawImage are the name of the image, the top pixel, the left pixel, and the self-referential, this. Perform the following steps to create the host document and source code file.

1. In the Notepad window, enter the code from Table 5-20 to create a host document for the applet you plan to create.

FIGURE 5-48

Table 5-20	
LINE	CODE
1	`<HTML>`
2	`<APPLET CODE="MoveIt.class" WIDTH=325 HEIGHT=250>`
3	`</APPLET>`
4	`</HTML>`

(continued)

In the Lab

Adding a Graphic to an Applet *(continued)*

2. Save the file as "MoveIt.html" on your floppy disk.
3. Open a new Notepad file.
4. Enter the usual block comments.
5. Import java.awt.*; java.awt.event.*; and java.applet.*;.
6. Create a public class header with the name, MoveIt, which extends Applet and implements the ActionListener.
7. Declare the following variables:

```
private Image cup;
private Panel keyPad;
public int top = 10;
public int left = 10;
```

8. Begin an init method with the following code:

```
public void init()
{
    cup = getImage( getDocumentBase(), "cup.gif" );
    Canvas myCanvas = new Canvas();
```

9. Construct the keypad Panel and the five buttons labeled: Up, Left, Right, Down, and Center.
10. Set the background color to blue.
11. Set the layout manger of the Frame to be BorderLayout, then set the keypad layout manager to be BorderLayout.
12. Add the buttons to the keypad Panel in the appropriate areas.
13. Add myCanvas to the North and keypad to the South of the Frame.
14. Enter five addActionListener methods with the self-referential, this, for each of the buttons.
15. Enter the code to move the image using the paint method:

```
public void paint( Graphics g )
{
    g.drawImage( cup, left, top, this );
}
```

16. Create an actionPerformed event. (*Hint*: Remember to use the getActionCommand method and assign it to a variable, as you did in the project.)
17. Within the actionPerformed event, write an if statement to test each of the buttons as follows:
    a. If the user clicks the Up button, subtract 10 from the top variable.
    b. If the user clicks the Down button, add 10 to the top variable.
    c. If the user clicks the Left button, subtract 10 from the left variable.
    d. If the user clicks the Right button, add 10 to the left variable.
    e. If the user clicks the Center button, set the top and left variables to 50.
18. Enter the code to refresh the screen: repaint();
19. Save the file as "MoveIt.java" on your floppy disk. Compile the source code. Fix any errors and recompile, if necessary.
20. Run the application several times, trying all the buttons.
21. Print a copy of the source code for your instructor.

Cases and Places

The difficulty of these case studies varies:
▶ are the least difficult; ▶▶ are more difficult; and ▶▶▶ are the most difficult.

1 ▶ The WebPhone company now would like an applet that produces a telephone keypad. Create an applet that displays a text area across the top, similar to the LCD panel of most cellular phones. Include buttons for the ten digits, a star key (*), and a pound key (#) as shown in Figure 5-46 on page J 5.49. When clicked, the appropriate digit or symbol should display in the text area. No additional functionality is required until WebPhone approves your prototype.

2 ▶ Figures 5-5 through 5-9 on pages J 5.12 through J 5.14 display the five different layout managers available with Java's setLayout method. Choose one of the five, other than BorderLayout, and create the applet. No functionality is required.

3 ▶ Fred's Foods has a self-scan check out lane that accepts cash payment similar to a vending machine. Customers can scan their own UPC labels and the prices display on a monitor. Fruit, vegetables, and other produce without a UPC label must be placed on the scale. Fred wants to post a printed table with produce codes. Write an applet that accepts a produce number and weight, and then displays the calculated price. Using the Layout Manager, design a frame that allows the user to enter the produce codes and weight on a keypad. The frame should include a text area for display and three buttons: one for produce code, one for weight, and one to calculate price. Create and store ten different produce codes in an array with local market prices. Once both pieces of data are entered, your program should search for a match in the produce code and multiply it times the weight.

4 ▶▶ Create a frame-based application that displays an array of 16 buttons on a Panel. Assign the panel to the North area of your frame. Each button should display the name of a course in your department. Include a TextField in the South area of the Frame. When the user clicks a button, the course should display in the TextField.

5 ▶▶ Project 5 uses a method called setBounds to set certain attributes of a Frame. It is one of the methods inherited from Component. Use the online Java documentation at `http://java.sun.com/products/jdk/1.2/docs/api/index.html` to look up the setBounds method. You will find two setBounds with different arguments. Write a paragraph describing each and explain the difference. Draw a picture of the object hierarchy of the setBounds method.

6 ▶▶▶ Use a user reference manual or the online Java documentation at `http://java.sun.com/products/jdk/1.2/docs/api/index.html` to create a tree or hierarchy chart of the java.applet. Applet class similar to Figure 5-2 on page J 5.9. Include both superclasses and subclasses. Explain how the AWT intermingles with the applet class to use panels in both applications and applets.

Java Programming

PROJECT

6

Using External Data

You will have mastered the material in this project when you can:

O B J E C T I V E S

- Differentiate between volatile and non-volatile data
- Extend the Frame and Dialog classes to create windows
- Construct composite objects in an application using subsetted layout managers
- Define bit, byte, field, record, file, and database
- Explain the difference between sequential and random access files
- Create a sequential file using Java's FileOutputStream and write methods
- Code the requestFocus method to position the insertion point
- Differentiate between modal and non-modal windows and dialog boxes
- Create a derived class
- Use the super keyword to override a class to accept arguments
- Create a rectangle component in a frame
- Create and call an external class
- Place components using the getBounds and setLocation methods
- Resize all components in a frame using the pack method
- Explain the meaning of client/server architecture
- Identify the parts of a two-tier, three-tier, and multi-tier system
- Define client, server, and servlet

Mission Possible

Explore Mars without Leaving Earth

The Red Planet – Mars – has fascinated mankind for thousands of years. First identified as a red star that grew ominously brighter every few years, it became a symbol of fear and destruction. Ancient Babylonians called it the Star of Death, the Greeks named it after their god of war, Ares, and the Romans renamed it Mars after their god of war.

Thousands of years later, the fascination has spread to Hollywood. Astronauts Val Kilmer and Carrie-Anne Moss are stranded on Mars in 2050 in the science-fiction thriller, *Red Planet*. Tim Robbins and Gary Sinise participate in a NASA rescue mission in *Mission to Mars*. And James Cameron's mini-series and IMAX 3-D film *Mars* profile missions to the Red Planet.

You, too, can tap into the Mars fascination, thanks to NASA and Java. When NASA's *Mars Pathfinder* spacecraft landed on Mars on July 4, 1997, it carried a rover named *Sojourner* that became the first vehicle to explore the planet.

Scientists at the Jet Propulsion Laboratory (JPL) at the California Institute of Technology used a Java applet, Web Interface for Telescience

(WITS), and commanded the rover remotely for 83 days to investigate the landing site and study rocks.

The rover had a 2 MHz CPU, 768 KB of memory, and a large temporary data storage area. It communicated with the *Pathfinder* regularly, and then the *Pathfinder* relayed more than 300 MB of data back to earth.

NASA launched another spacecraft on January 3, 1999, to the Red Planet in its *Mars Polar Lander* mission. JPL scientists had planned to use WITS to control remotely robotic arm and camera operations mounted on the *Lander*. The *Lander*, however, was lost on December 3 of that year.

Using a public version of WITS, which contains the same code the scientists used for the missions, you can experience simulations of this command software. Once you download the Web Interface from the WITS *Mars Polar Lander* Headquarters site (mars.graham.com/mplwits/), you can generate command sequences to move a

simulated *Mars Polar Lander* robotic arm and robotic arm camera and view the Martian rock-strewn landscape in panoramic, overhead, and simulated 3-D views. You also can simulate sending scripted commands to the *Sojourner* rover by plotting targets for the rover to visit, computing distances, specifying hazards to avoid, and assigning tasks to be executed at the destinations. A third action you can perform is to control the rover interactively in 3-D view.

The Java applet you create in Project 6 of this book retrieves non-volatile data stored in a database regarding people who buy city vehicle stickers. Likewise, the WITS database contains non-volatile data retrieved from the *Pathfinder* and *Mars Polar Lander* missions. By using the interfaces in both of these applications, you will witness fascinating missions to the Department of Motor Vehicles and the Red Planet.

Java Programming

Using External Data

PROJECT

6

CASE PERSPECTIVE

The city of Flora, New Mexico wants to automate its collection of data about the people who buy city stickers. City stickers, which are displayed in vehicle windshields, are a way to keep track of vehicles and generate tax revenue. Currently, residents ordering or renewing a city sticker are required to appear in person at a downtown office. If the city could maintain a computer database so that residents could order stickers from remote locations, it would save time and money. City officials would like to provide a standardized program to different locations around the city, such as public libraries, Department of Motor Vehicles (DMV) branches, and other city Departments for the convenience of residents. These locations would submit updated data files on a regular basis.

You have been asked to develop an application that would operate the same on any computer platform. Once residents submit a request, the DMV will send an invoice along with the sticker.

You decide to investigate Java's Abstract Windows Toolkit to create a GUI-based application that creates a data file.

Introduction

Many businesses are converting their computer applications from those written in a traditional language to applications written in object-oriented languages. Java's reusable objects, portability, and efficiency make it ideal to run on multiple machines, a wide variety of operating systems, and across networks. Companies want the look and feel of window-based GUIs, even for their transaction-oriented programs, such as updating accounts or payroll processes — programs that traditionally have run from a command prompt. Java programs can create user interfaces that are efficient and typically small in size; a complied program may be smaller than 5 KB.

One of the most powerful features of any programming language is its capability of creating sophisticated database applications with minimal programming. A **database** is simply a collection of related facts organized in a systematic manner. Databases do not have to be electronic. A telephone book is an example of a database that contains the names, addresses, and telephone numbers of individuals and businesses in a community. Many database management products, such as Microsoft Access, are available for personal computers and are used to store, maintain, and retrieve data quickly and efficiently.

The programs you have written so far, however, deal with only volatile data. **Volatile data**, or electricity-dependent data, is stored in the computer's memory while the electricity is supplied to the computer and while the program is running. After the computer is powered off, the data is gone. In this project, you will learn how to store data in an external file on a secondary storage device. That **non-volatile** data then can be retrieved later or copied into a database management system (DBMS). Java can be used to build applications that display, edit, and update information from databases created by many different database software programs such as Access, dBase, Oracle, and Paradox. This project provides an introductory exposure to external data files by building an application that accepts vehicle registration data in order to obtain a city sticker.

Project Six — Flora City Stickers

ANALYZING THE PROBLEM The city of Flora requires all vehicles to display a city sticker verifying that the vehicle is registered and that taxes have been paid. City officials want to have a computer program to order or renew city stickers for residents. The application program should accept the vehicle identification number (VIN); make, model, and year of the vehicle; and the name and address of the owner. When the user clicks a command button, successful completion of all fields should send the information, along with a code for a new sticker or renewal, to a data file. If a field is blank, a message box should display. The program should generate a message on the screen saying the customer will receive his or her sticker and the bill through the mail.

Figure 6-1(a) displays the data entry screen. Figure 6-1(b) displays the window with a Data Entry Error dialog box.

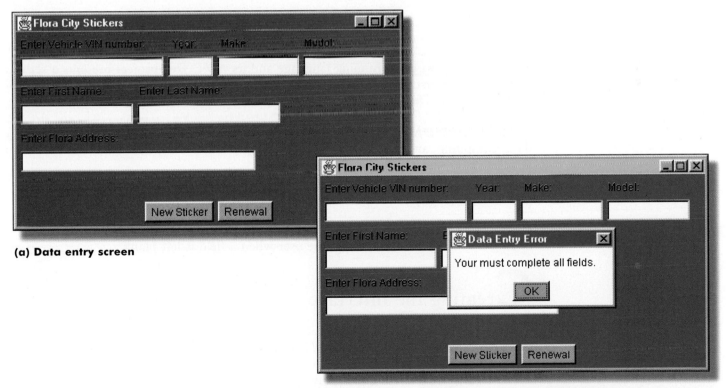

(a) Data entry screen

(b) Data entry error dialog box

FIGURE 6-1

DESIGNING THE PROGRAM   You will design the program in three stages. First, you will create the window. Second, you will add the components to the interface with appropriate fields and buttons. Finally, you will add functionality to the components so that users can enter data and store it in an external data file. Figure 6-2 displays a **storyboard**, which is a tool programmers use to layout the components of the interface. Notice that each row of components is a Panel. Using Java's BorderLayout manager, the Row Panels containing Labels and TextFields are placed within a Data Fields Panel in the North area; the Panel containing the buttons is placed in the South area.

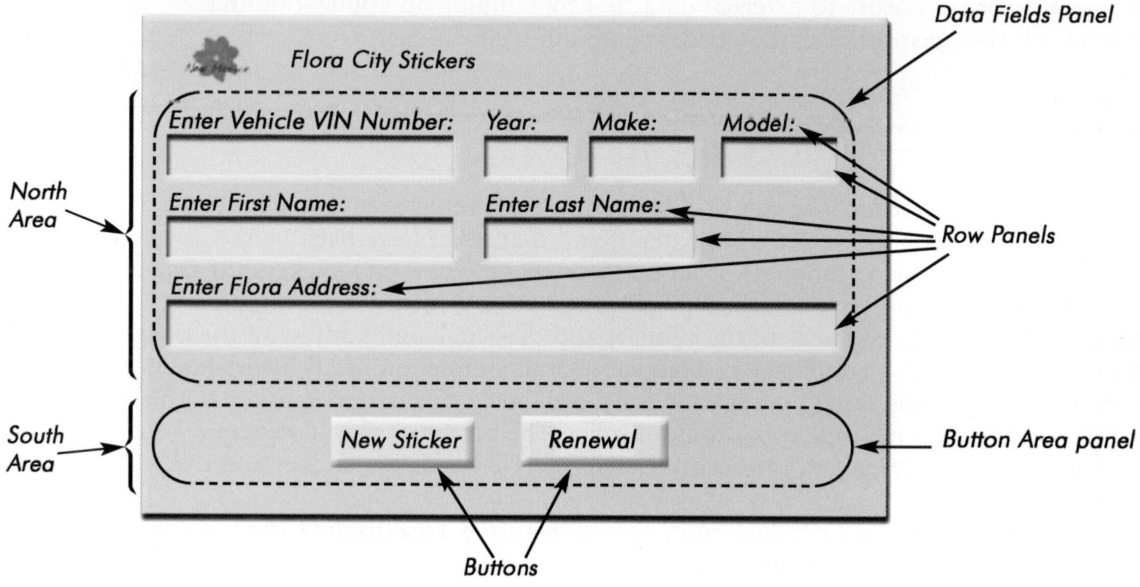

FIGURE 6-2

CODING THE PROGRAM   You will create Java source code using the syntax and commands of the Java programming language and its AWT. This project presents a series of step-by-step instructions to write the code for each of the three stages as described in the preceding Designing the Program section.

TESTING THE PROGRAM   You will test each stage of the program by inserting sample data, compiling, and then executing the program in console mode.

FORMALIZING THE SOLUTION   Once each button works properly, you will review the source code, use proper documentation, edit, recompile, and print a copy.

MAINTAINING THE PROGRAM   You will add further functionality to the program by adding a message box that warns the user when a field is left blank.

Creating the Interface

The first step in creating a GUI-based application, such as the one for the city of Flora, involves creating the window. You will create a class named Flora that will construct an instance of a window and set properties in its main method. Because user interaction will be required, the Flora class will use an ActionListener.

Creating a Window

Table 6-1 displays the beginning code to start the Flora application. Notice that in line 12 the Flora class extends Frame. Recall that a Java program may **extend**, or build upon, a superclass that Java provides or classes that you create. The **Frame** class is the application equivalent of the applet class which you have used before. By extending from Frame, Flora will be a subclass, or working copy, of the Frame class. It will behave identically to the original class and will have all of the fields and methods declared in, or inherited, from the Frame class. Programs that use a window or GUI-based interface typically extend Frame and therefore are called **frame-based applications**. The Flora class also implements ActionListener. Recall that ActionListener enables the application to listen for mouse clicks from the user.

Table 6-2 displays the main method to create a Frame. In keeping with Java's object-oriented philosophy, creating a Frame is accomplished best by the extension of an existing component rather than the construction of a component from scratch. You learned that Frames typically construct an instance of a window in the main method. Most programmers name the instance and the entire class with the same name; in this case, the shared name is Flora. Recall that the setTitle, setSize, and setVisible methods are all methods to set attributes of the Frame.

To run a test of the Frame itself, you must construct the instance of Flora and add a WindowListener. Table 6-3 displays the constructor class, Flora. In line 25, the background color is set to magenta. Lines 27 through 36 display the addWindowListener method. Recall that this method adds functionality to the Close button in Java applications. Line 37 is the closing brace for the Flora constructor.

Table 6-1

LINE	CODE
1	`/*`
2	`   Project 6:      AWT and Data Files`
3	`   Programmer:    Joy Starks`
4	`   Date:          January 9, 2002`
5	`   Program Name:  Flora`
6	`*/`
7	
8	`import java.io.*;`
9	`import java.awt.*;`
10	`import java.awt.event.*;`
11	
12	`public class Flora extends Frame implements ActionListener`
13	`{`

Table 6-2

LINE	CODE
14	`    public static void main(String[] args)`
15	`    {`
16	`        Flora window = new Flora();`
17	`        window.setTitle("Flora City Stickers");`
18	`        window.setSize(450, 250);`
19	`        window.setVisible(true);`
20	`    }`
21	

Table 6-3

LINE	CODE
22	`    public Flora()`
23	`    {`
24	`        //Set background and layout managers`
25	`        setBackground(Color.magenta);`
26	
27	`        //Construct window listener`
28	`        addWindowListener(`
29	`          new WindowAdapter()`
30	`          {`
31	`              public void windowClosing(WindowEvent e)`
32	`              {`
33	`                  System.exit(0);`
34	`              }`
35	`          }`
36	`        );`
37	`    }`
38	

Table 6-4

LINE	CODE
39	`public void actionPerformed(ActionEvent e)`
40	`{`
41	
42	`}`
43	`}`

Finally, because the class, Flora, implements the ActionListener, you must stub in an actionPerformed event. Recall that **stubbing in** means creating just enough code to compile and run your program, but not enough code to make the program fully functional. The code so far will display the window and make its Close button functional. Table 6-4 displays the header in line 39 and an empty block. Line 43 is the ending brace for the Flora class.

Perform the following steps to create the Flora window.

 To Create the Flora Window

① **Start Notepad and maximize its window. Enter the beginning code from Table 6-1 on the previous page.**

The comments, import statements, and class header display (Figure 6-3).

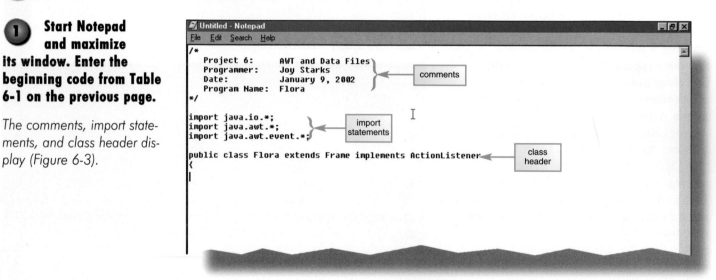

FIGURE 6-3

② **Starting on line 14 and using proper indentation, enter the code from Table 6-2 on the previous page to create a window.**

The code to create a window and set its attributes displays (Figure 6-4).

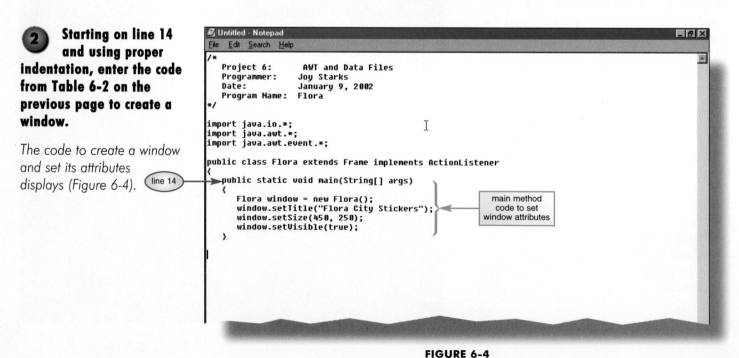

FIGURE 6-4

3 Starting on line 22 and using proper indentation, enter the code from Table 6-3 on page J 6.7 to construct an instance of the Flora window.

The window constructor code to create an instance displays (Figure 6-5).

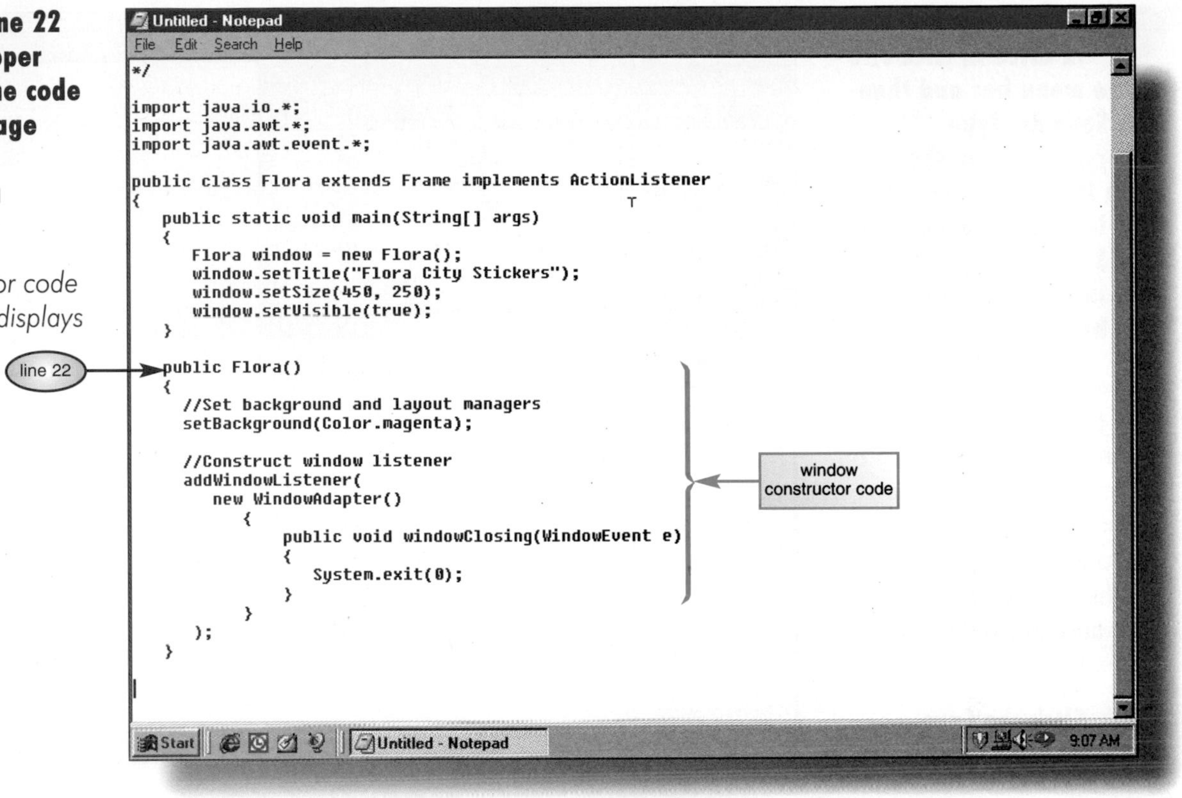

line 22

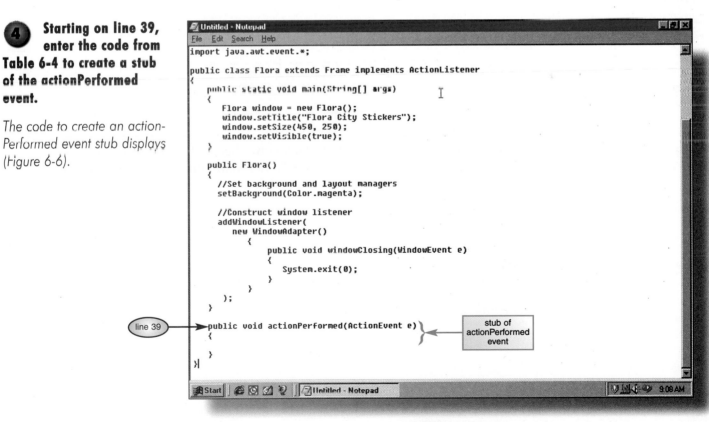

FIGURE 6-5

4 Starting on line 39, enter the code from Table 6-4 to create a stub of the actionPerformed event.

The code to create an action-Performed event stub displays (Figure 6-6).

line 39

FIGURE 6-6

5 **With a floppy disk in drive A, click File on the menu bar and then click Save As. Type "Flora.java" in the File name text box. Click the Save in box arrow and then click 3½ Floppy (A:) in the Save in list. Point to the Save button.**

The Save As dialog box displays (Figure 6-7). The file will be saved as Flora.java on the floppy disk. Recall that quotation marks are necessary to force Notepad to save with the .java extension. Your list of files may differ.

6 **Click the Save button.**

The file is saved on the floppy disk in drive A.

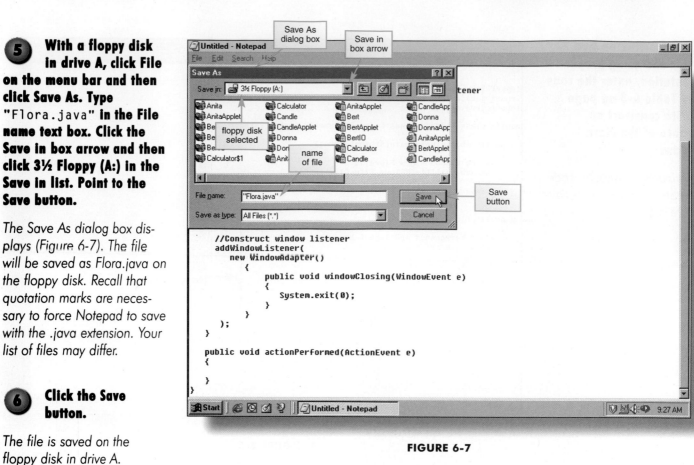

FIGURE 6-7

To test the functionality of the window created by the Flora class, you must compile and then execute the application, as shown in the following steps.

TO TEST THE FLORA WINDOW

1 Open the MS-DOS Prompt window by clicking the Start button, pointing to Programs, and then clicking MS-DOS Prompt on the Programs submenu. Set the path and then change to drive A if necessary.

2 Type javac Flora.java and press the ENTER key. If the program will not compile because of programming errors, fix them in the Notepad window, save the file, and then compile again in the MS-DOS Prompt window.

3 Type java Flora and then press the ENTER key.

The Flora City Stickers window displays (Figure 6-8). You may close the window by clicking its Close button.

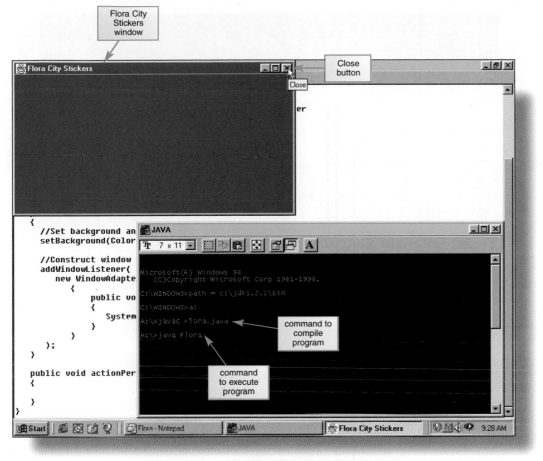

FIGURE 6-8

Testing your program's interface for the ability to open and close a window is one way to build an application in stages and test individual objects, such as the Close button, before complicating the application with more components.

Adding Components to the Interface

Adding components to the Flora interface involves constructing the components themselves, implementing layout managers for placement, and then using the add methods to insert the components into the Frame. The Java components in the Flora interface include the Frame, which you have already created; Labels to hold words, instructions, or prompts; TextFields to allow for user data-entry; Buttons to add functionality to the interface; and Panels to assist with component placement. Panels and Frames are **composite objects**, which are special Java objects that house other components, such as user interface controls and other containers.

Constructing the Components

Table 6-5 on the next page displays the constructors for the Flora interface. Eight panel containers are created in lines 15 through 22. Recall from the storyboard in Figure 6-2 on page J 6.6, that each row of Labels and TextFields will be a panel; a larger panel, named dataFields, will contain all of the rows; and another panel, named buttonArea, will hold the buttons. The table also displays the constructors to create the Button, Label, and TextField components.

More**About**

Main

Some programmers place main at the end of their application, others at the beginning. Java does not care; however, main is executed first when you run the program.

More**About**

Composite Objects

For more information about using composite objects in Java interfaces, visit the Java Programming Web Page (www.scsite.com/java/more.htm) and then click Composite Objects.

Table 6-5

LINE	CODE
14	//Construct components
15	Panel dataFields = new Panel();
16	Panel firstRow = new Panel();
17	Panel secondRow = new Panel();
18	Panel thirdRow = new Panel();
19	Panel fourthRow = new Panel();
20	Panel fifthRow = new Panel();
21	Panel sixthRow = new Panel();
22	Panel buttonArea = new Panel();
23	
24	Button newSticker = new Button("New Sticker");
25	Button renewal = new Button("Renewal");
26	
27	Label vinLabel = new Label("Enter Vehicle VIN number: ");
28	TextField vin = new TextField(20);
29	Label yearLabel = new Label("Year: ");
30	TextField year = new TextField(4);
31	Label makeLabel = new Label("Make: ");
32	TextField make = new TextField(10);
33	Label modelLabel = new Label("Model:");
34	TextField model = new TextField(10);
35	Label firstNameLabel = new Label("Enter First Name: ");
36	TextField firstName = new TextField(15);
37	Label lastNameLabel = new Label("Enter Last Name:");
38	TextField lastName = new TextField(20);
39	Label addressLabel = new Label("Enter Flora Address:");
40	TextField address = new TextField (35);

Perform the following steps to enter the constructor code. Make certain you use proper indentation as shown in the table and figure.

Steps **To Construct the Components**

1 **Click the Flora-Notepad button on the taskbar. With the Flora.java source code still displayed, scroll to display the beginning of the code and then click at the end of line 13.**

The insertion point displays to the right of the beginning brace of the class block (Figure 6-9).

```
Flora - Notepad

File  Edit  Search  Help

/*
    Project 6:      AWT and Data Files
    Programmer:     Joy Starks
    Date:           January 9, 2002
    Program Name:   Flora
*/

import java.io.*;
import java.awt.*;
import java.awt.event.*;

public class Flora extends Frame implements ActionListener
{
    public static void main(String[] args)
    {
        Flora window = new Flora();
        window.setTitle("Flora City Stickers");
        window.setSize(450, 250);
        window.setVisible(true);
    }

    public Flora()
```

line 13

insertion point

FIGURE 6-9

2 **Press the ENTER key and then enter the code from Table 6-5.**

The constructors display (Figure 6-10).

3 **Save the program by clicking File on the menu bar and then click Save.**

The program saves on the floppy disk.

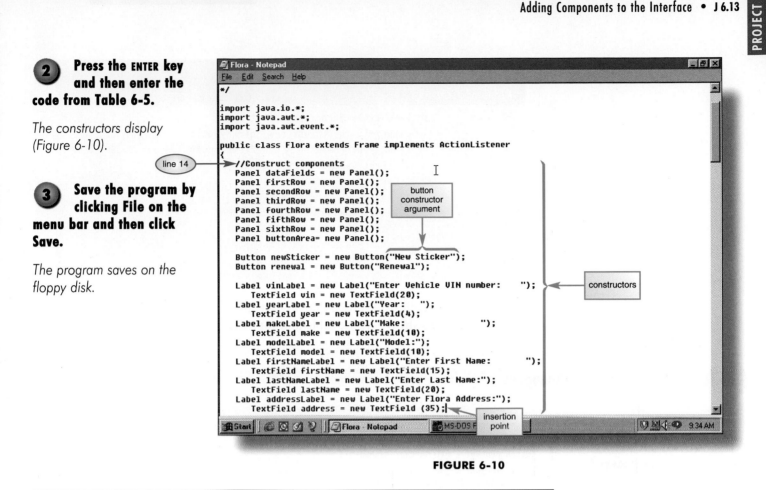

```
/*

import java.io.*;
import java.awt.*;
import java.awt.event.*;

public class Flora extends Frame implements ActionListener
{
    //Construct components
    Panel dataFields = new Panel();
    Panel firstRow = new Panel();
    Panel secondRow = new Panel();
    Panel thirdRow = new Panel();
    Panel fourthRow = new Panel();
    Panel fifthRow = new Panel();
    Panel sixthRow = new Panel();
    Panel buttonArea= new Panel();

    Button newSticker = new Button("New Sticker");
    Button renewal = new Button("Renewal");

    Label vinLabel = new Label("Enter Vehicle VIN number:    ");
        TextField vin = new TextField(20);
    Label yearLabel = new Label("Year:      ");
        TextField year = new TextField(4);
    Label makeLabel = new Label("Make:              ");
        TextField make = new TextField(10);
    Label modelLabel = new Label("Model:");
        TextField model = new TextField(10);
    Label firstNameLabel = new Label("Enter First Name:        ");
        TextField firstName = new TextField(15);
    Label lastNameLabel = new Label("Enter Last Name:");
        TextField lastName = new TextField(20);
    Label addressLabel = new Label("Enter Flora Address:");
        TextField address = new TextField (35);
```

line 14

button constructor argument

constructors

insertion point

FIGURE 6-10

Recall that Button constructors, such as lines 24 and 25, may contain an argument for the caption of the button itself. Later, that argument will be passed to the actionPerformed event to evaluate which button was clicked.

Setting the Layout Managers

Once the components have been constructed, you must plan for their placement. Layout managers help the programmer organize the containers, rather than allowing Java to place them automatically, left to right, within the space provided. The dataFields and buttonArea Panels will be placed using the BorderLayout manager. The other panels will use the FlowLayout manager. Java programmers typically combine and subset layout managers to produce attractive interfaces with exact placement of components.

Table 6-6 on the next page displays the setLayout methods for the Flora interface. Line 54 sets BorderLayout as the layout manager for the entire Frame. In line 55, the panel to hold all the rows, named dataFields, uses the GridLayout manager and is set to contain six rows and one column. Notice in line 56, an instance of the FlowLayout manager is created with left justification and with pixel settings for the horizontal and vertical placement of the components. The instance, named rowSetup, then is used in lines 57 through 62 as the layout manager for each row.

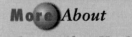

More About

The setSize Method

The setSize method can be used on any component to set its height and width. The method, public void setSize(int width, int height), allows you to enter the height and width in pixels.

Table 6-6

LINE	CODE
54	`setLayout(new BorderLayout());`
55	`dataFields.setLayout(new GridLayout(6,1));`
56	`FlowLayout rowSetup = new FlowLayout(FlowLayout.LEFT,5,2);`
57	`firstRow.setLayout(rowSetup);`
58	`secondRow.setLayout(rowSetup);`
59	`thirdRow.setLayout(rowSetup);`
60	`fourthRow.setLayout(rowSetup);`
61	`fifthRow.setLayout(rowSetup);`
62	`sixthRow.setLayout(rowSetup);`
63	`buttonArea.setLayout(new FlowLayout());`

Perform the following steps to set the layout managers, making certain to use proper indentation as shown in the table and figures.

 To Set the Layout Managers

1 **With the Flora.java source code still displayed in the Notepad window, scroll to display the beginning of the Flora constructor method and then click at the end of line 53.**

The insertion point displays at the end of the setBackground method (Figure 6-11).

```
Flora - Notepad
File  Edit  Search  Help

    Button renewal = new Button("Renewal");

    Label vinLabel = new Label("Enter Vehicle VIN number:      ");
        TextField vin = new TextField(20);
    Label yearLabel = new Label("Year:     ");
        TextField year = new TextField(4);
    Label makeLabel = new Label("Make:                ");
        TextField make = new TextField(10);
    Label modelLabel = new Label("Model:");
        TextField model = new TextField(10);
    Label firstNameLabel = new Label("Enter First Name:        ");
        TextField firstName = new TextField(15);
    Label lastNameLabel = new Label("Enter Last Name:");
        TextField lastName = new TextField(20);
    Label addressLabel = new Label("Enter Flora Address:");
        TextField address = new TextField (35);

    public static void main(String[] args)
    {
        Flora window = new Flora();
        window.setTitle("Flora City Stickers");
        window.setSize(450, 250);
        window.setVisible(true);
    }

    public Flora()
    {
        //Set background and layout managers
        setBackground(Color.magenta);

        //Construct window listener
        addWindowListener(
            new WindowAdapter()
            {
                public void win    g(WindowEvent e)
```

line 53

insertion point

Start   Flora - Notepad   MS-DOS Prompt   9:39 AM

FIGURE 6-11

2 **Press the ENTER key and then enter the code from Table 6-6.**

The setLayout methods display (Figure 6-12).

3 **Click File on the menu bar and then click Save to save the file again.**

The program saves on the floppy disk.

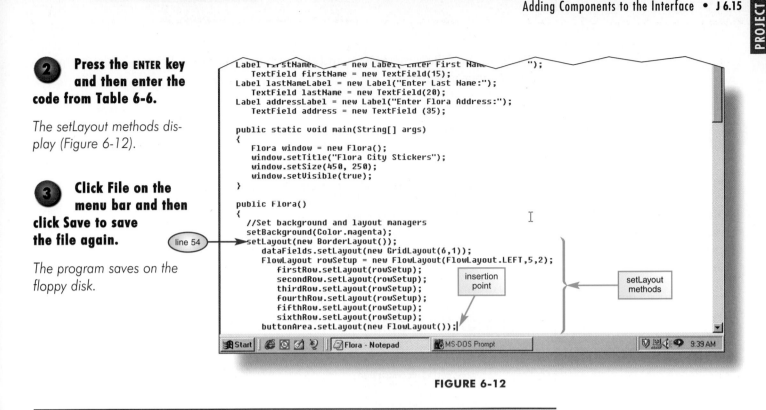

```
Label firstName      = new Label("Enter First Name     ");
     TextField firstName = new TextField(15);
Label lastNameLabel = new Label("Enter Last Name:");
     TextField lastName = new TextField(20);
Label addressLabel = new Label("Enter Flora Address:");
     TextField address = new TextField (35);

public static void main(String[] args)
{
    Flora window = new Flora();
    window.setTitle("Flora City Stickers");
    window.setSize(450, 250);
    window.setVisible(true);
}

public Flora()
{
    //Set background and layout managers
    setBackground(Color.magenta);
    setLayout(new BorderLayout());
        dataFields.setLayout(new GridLayout(6,1));
        FlowLayout rowSetup = new FlowLayout(FlowLayout.LEFT,5,2);
            firstRow.setLayout(rowSetup);
            secondRow.setLayout(rowSetup);
            thirdRow.setLayout(rowSetup);
            fourthRow.setLayout(rowSetup);
            fifthRow.setLayout(rowSetup);
            sixthRow.setLayout(rowSetup);
        buttonArea.setLayout(new FlowLayout());
```

line 54

insertion point

setLayout methods

Start | Flora - Notepad | MS-DOS Prompt | 9:39 AM

FIGURE 6-12

Adding Components to the Frame

The last step in creating the Frame is to add the previously constructed components to the interface. Table 6-7 displays the add methods and explanatory comments. The components are added in order from left to right and top to bottom.

Table 6-7

LINE	CODE	LINE	CODE
65	//Add fields to rows	84	sixthRow.add(address);
66	firstRow.add(vinLabel);	85	
67	firstRow.add(yearLabel);	86	//Add rows to panel
68	firstRow.add(makeLabel);	87	dataFields.add(firstRow);
69	firstRow.add(modelLabel);	88	dataFields.add(secondRow);
70		89	dataFields.add(thirdRow);
71	secondRow.add(vin);	90	dataFields.add(fourthRow);
72	secondRow.add(year);	91	dataFields.add(fifthRow);
73	secondRow.add(make);	92	dataFields.add(sixthRow);
74	secondRow.add(model);	93	
75		94	//Add buttons to panel
76	thirdRow.add(firstNameLabel);	95	buttonArea.add(newSticker);
77	thirdRow.add(lastNameLabel);	96	buttonArea.add(renewal);
78		97	
79	fourthRow.add(firstName);	98	//Add panels to frame
80	fourthRow.add(lastName);	99	add(dataFields, BorderLayout.NORTH);
81		100	add(buttonArea, BorderLayout.SOUTH);
82	fifthRow.add(addressLabel);		
83			

Perform the following steps to add the components to the Frame. Make certain you use proper indentation.

Steps **To Add the Components to the Frame**

1 **With the Flora.java source code still displayed in the Notepad window, if necessary, click after the last setLayout method in line 63.**

The insertion point displays at the end of line 63 (Figure 6-13).

```java
Label addressLabel = new Label("Enter Flora Address:");
    TextField address = new TextField (35);

public static void main(String[] args)
{
    Flora window = new Flora();
    window.setTitle("Flora City Stickers");
    window.setSize(450, 250);
    window.setVisible(true);
}

public Flora()
{
    //Set background and layout managers
    setBackground(Color.magenta);
    setLayout(new BorderLayout());
        dataFields.setLayout(new GridLayout(6,1));
        FlowLayout rowSetup = new FlowLayout(FlowLayout.LEFT,5,2);
            firstRow.setLayout(rowSetup);
            secondRow.setLayout(rowSetup);
            thirdRow.setLayout(rowSetup);
            fourthRow.setLayout(rowSetup);
            fifthRow.setLayout(rowSetup);
            sixthRow.setLayout(rowSetup);
        buttonArea.setLayout(new FlowLayout());
```

line 63 →

insertion point

Start | Flora - Notepad | MS-DOS Prompt | 9:39 AM

FIGURE 6-13

2 **Press the ENTER key and then enter the code from Table 6-7 on the previous page.**

The add methods display (Figure 6-14).

3 **Click File on the menu bar and then click Save to save the file again.**

The program saves on the floppy disk.

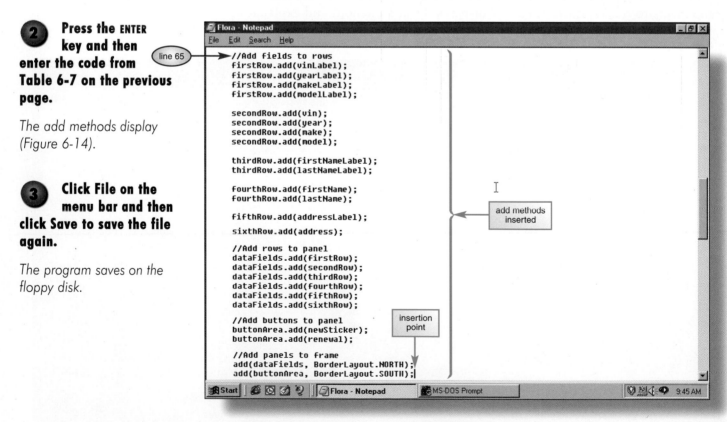

```java
//Add fields to rows
firstRow.add(vinLabel);
firstRow.add(yearLabel);
firstRow.add(makeLabel);
firstRow.add(modelLabel);

secondRow.add(vin);
secondRow.add(year);
secondRow.add(make);
secondRow.add(model);

thirdRow.add(firstNameLabel);
thirdRow.add(lastNameLabel);

fourthRow.add(firstName);
fourthRow.add(lastName);

fifthRow.add(addressLabel);

sixthRow.add(address);

//Add rows to panel
dataFields.add(firstRow);
dataFields.add(secondRow);
dataFields.add(thirdRow);
dataFields.add(fourthRow);
dataFields.add(fifthRow);
dataFields.add(sixthRow);

//Add buttons to panel
buttonArea.add(newSticker);
buttonArea.add(renewal);

//Add panels to frame
add(dataFields, BorderLayout.NORTH);
add(buttonArea, BorderLayout.SOUTH);
```

line 65 →

add methods inserted

insertion point

Start | Flora - Notepad | MS-DOS Prompt | 9:45 AM

FIGURE 6-14

To test the Flora window layout managers, you must compile and then execute the application, as shown in the following steps.

TO TEST THE FLORA WINDOW COMPONENTS

 Click the MS-DOS Prompt button on the taskbar or open an MS-DOS Prompt window from the Programs menu. If necessary, set the path and change to drive A.

② Type javac Flora.java and then press the ENTER key. If the program will not compile because of programming errors, fix them in the Notepad window, save the file, and then compile again in the MS-DOS Prompt window.

③ Type java Flora and then press the ENTER key.

The Flora City Stickers window displays with its components (Figure 6-15). Your display may differ. You may close the window by clicking its Close button.

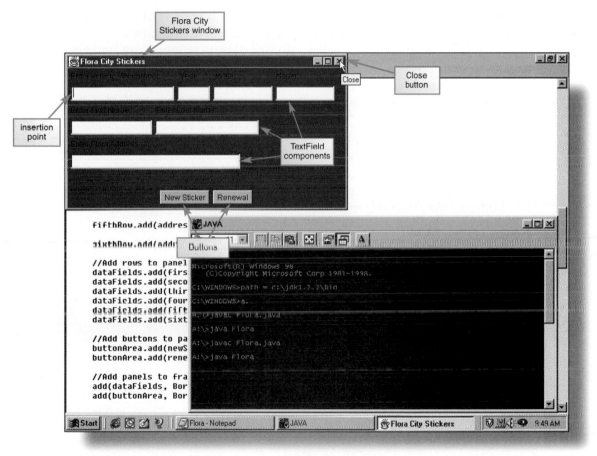

FIGURE 6-15

Recall that Java's BorderLayout manager stretches components to fill empty areas. The dataFields component fills the North, East, West, and Center areas (Figure 6-15).

External Data

Often programs need to bring in data from an external source or send out data to an external destination. Storing data in variable locations is temporary — data easily can be overwritten and lost when the computer is turned off. Therefore, any permanent storage of data must take place on a secondary storage device. Data typically are stored in **files**, which are stored collections of data fields and records.

The data can be anywhere, for example, in a file, on a disk, in memory, somewhere on the network, or in another program. In addition, data can be of any type: objects, characters, numbers, images, or sounds. To bring in data, a Java program must open a stream to an information source (for example, a file, memory, a socket) and then read the information serially. Similarly, a Java program can send information to an external destination by opening a stream to that destination and writing the information out serially.

Data Hierarchy

Data are organized in a hierarchy in which each higher level is made up of one or more elements from the lower level preceding it. The levels in the hierarchy of data include bit, byte, field, record, and file (Figure 6-16).

▶ **Bit** Inside the computer, all data appear as combinations of zeros and ones because electronic devices can assume one of two stable states: off and on. This **binary digit**, or **bit**, is the smallest piece of data a computer can understand. Usually a bit is combined with other bits to represent data.

▶ **Byte** The combination of bits with some kind of coding scheme is called a **byte**. A byte can represent a character such as a letter (A), a number (7), or a symbol (&).

▶ **Field** A logical grouping of bytes to form a piece of meaningful data (such as a last name or an ID number) is called a **field**.

▶ **Record** A **record** is a group of related fields. For example, an employee record would contain all the fields about an employee, such as name, date of birth, address, social security number, etc.

▶ **File** A **file** is a collection of related records stored under a single name. A school's student file, for example, would consist of thousands of individual student records. Each student record would contain the same fields as the other records.

More About

Organization of Data

The organization of data in the record usually is determined by the programming language that defines the record's organization and/ or by the application that processes it. Typically, records can be of fixed-length or variable length with the length information contained within the record.

HIERARCHY OF DATA		
DATA ELEMENT	*CAN CONTAIN*	*EXAMPLE*
Bit	Binary digit 0 or 1	Bits can represent any two-state condition, such as on or off, but usually are combined into bytes to represent data.
Byte	One character or other unit of information consisting of eight bits	01000001 (letter A)
Field	Individual elements of data such as a person's first name	Amy
Record	Related groups of fields such as a person's name and address data	Amy Lee, 123 Hill Street, Seattle, WA. 99999 206-555-1234
File	Many related records	Amy Lee, 123 Hill Street . . . Tom Sanchez, 1401 Reeder Ct. . . . Irving Brown, 1813 Ryan Ave. . . .

FIGURE 6-16

The java.io package contains a collection of file and stream classes that support algorithms for reading and writing. Java is not concerned about the concept of a record; it is the programmer's responsibility to organize and structure the data to meet the requirements of the application.

Sequential versus Random Access Files

Java views each file as a sequential stream of bytes. **Sequential** means to place items in a specific sequence, or in order, one after another. Java reads and writes sequential files as streams of bytes from beginning to end. Sequential files are used when data elements are manipulated in the order they are stored. For example, a Java programmer might create a sequential file to receive input data from a user, or to back up a set of transactions in a batch. The advantages of using sequential files include an increase in the speed at which the program reads and writes data, as well as contiguous storage of that data. Storing data sequentially, however, is somewhat tedious. You can think of a sequential file as being like a cassette tape. It plays from one end to the other. To add a new song in the middle would involve playing the tape and recording it on another tape, stopping at some point to add the song to the new tape, and then continuing to record the rest of the tape.

If constant updating – inserting, deleting, and changing – is involved, or if direct access is needed, Java provides another file mechanism that does not involve playing the entire file. **Random access** files store data in non-contiguous locations; their records can be retrieved in any order. Because they can locate a particular record directly, without reading all of the preceding records, random access files also are called **direct access** files.

The java.io package, imported at the beginning of the Flora application, provides classes that deal with input and output for both sequential and random access files.

The **InputStream** and **OutputStream** classes are abstract classes in the java.io package. The most common subclasses, **FileInputStream** and **FileOutputStream**, are used to read and write data, respectively, to a given file. For example, instead of sending data to System.out, you can send that data to a FileOutputStream. Implementing the FileOutputStream involves declaring an identifier to be of OutputStream type.

```
OutputStream output;
```

Then, a constructor creates an instance of the File object and names it.

```
File outFile = new File("myData.dat");
```

Finally, the data is sent to the file.

```
output = new FileOutputStream(outFile);
```

The **DataOutputStream** and **DataInputStream** classes are wrapper classes, which can be chained or connected to the corresponding File stream classes to implement the reading or writing of formatted data. Recall that you wrapped the InputStreamReader to accept the keyboard buffer.

```
BufferedReader dataIn = new BufferedReader(new InputStreamReader(System.in));
```

More About

Files

There are two types of files in Java: binary files and text files. Both kinds store data as a sequence of bits. The main difference is in how Java reads and writes the file. A binary file is processed as a sequence of bits, whereas a text file is processed as a sequence of characters. Java's input and output streams typically are used for binary files; the reader and writer streams are used for text files.

In the same way, you can wrap the FileInputStream inside the DataInputStream for formatted data.

```
input = new DataInputStream(new FileInputStream("Sticker.dat"));
```

Table 6-8 displays Data Stream class methods that transfer data to and from external files. Notice that there is no writeString method. Instead, Java Strings are read or written using a UTF method. **UTF** stands for **Unicode Text Format**, which is an encoding scheme that assigns a number to each symbol. The UTF methods provide a way to read and write formatted data without worrying about the specific data type, although the underlying mechanism still is reading one byte at a time.

More About

Opening Files

Placing the constructor to open a file inside a try block, allows you to catch an exception if there is an error opening the file. Possible input/output errors might include the disk not being available or the file not existing on the specified drive. Catching the IOException, allows for a graceful exit of the program if file problems occur.

Table 6-8 Read and Write Methods from the Data Stream Class			
TYPE OF DATA	INPUT METHOD	OUTPUT METHOD	EXAMPLE
boolean data	readBoolean	writeBoolean	true or false, stored as a 1 or 0
single character data	readChar	writeChar	a
integer	readInt	writeInt	7
double	readDouble	writeDouble	3.12E+10
float	readFloat	writeFloat	5.21
long	readLong	writeLong	9 * 1018
Strings	readUTF	writeUTF	Cashman's

The RandomAccessFile class also contains methods to read, write, close, and seek. The **seek** method allows programmers to select a beginning position within a file before they read or write data. The syntax is as follows:

```
myFile.seek(147);
```

The line of code, when executed, would select or point to the 148th byte in the file. This is because numbering starts with zero, just as it did with array index numbers. A subsequent read or write method then would begin at that location. Obviously, as Java considers data in bytes, the programmer needs to know how many bytes are in the given records. You may both read and write random access files, unlike sequential files that must be either input or output, but not both.

The Flora application will create a sequential file on your floppy disk, which then could be used to update the city database. Each time the user clicks one of the two buttons, formatted output stored as UTFs will be sent to the file. As with the BufferedReader, when Java attempts input or output, you must provide a way to catch possible errors. You will use the try and catch structure in the next series of steps.

More About

Random Access Files

When you construct an instance of a random access file, you must include a second argument. After the name of the file, an "r" indicates the file is read only; an argument of "rw" indicates the file will be used for both reading and writing. For example the code, RandomAccessFile inFile = new RandomAccessFile ("A:\\payroll.dat","r"); constructs an instance named inFile that opens a payroll data file from the floppy disk as a read only file.

Adding the ActionListener and Opening the Data File

Table 6-9 displays the code to add the ActionListener to the two buttons (lines 103 and 104); and to open a data file on the floppy disk (lines 107 through 114). Because the possibility of error always is present when Java is working with external data, Java requires any errors to be caught. Recall that a try structure (lines 107 through 110) encompasses code that may cause errors. A corresponding catch structure (lines 111 through 114) contains code to execute if or when the error occurs. In this case, if the file, Sticker.dat, cannot be opened in line 109, the application will close with the System.exit command in line 113.

Table 6-9

LINE	CODE
102	`//Add functionality to buttons`
103	`  newSticker.addActionListener(this);`
104	`  renewal.addActionListener(this);`
105	
106	`  //Open the file`
107	`  try`
108	`  {`
109	`    output = new DataOutputStream(new FileOutputStream("Sticker.dat"));`
110	`  }`
111	`  catch(IOException ex)`
112	`  {`
113	`    System.exit(1);`
114	`  }`
115	

Perform the following steps to add the ActionListener to the buttons and write the code to open the data file. Make certain you use proper indentation.

Steps To Add the ActionListener and Open the Data File

1 If necessary, click after the add methods at the end of the previous code on line 100. Press the ENTER key twice and then type the code from Table 6-9.

The new code displays (Figure 6-17).

2 Save the program by clicking File on the menu bar, then click Save.

The program saves on the floppy disk.

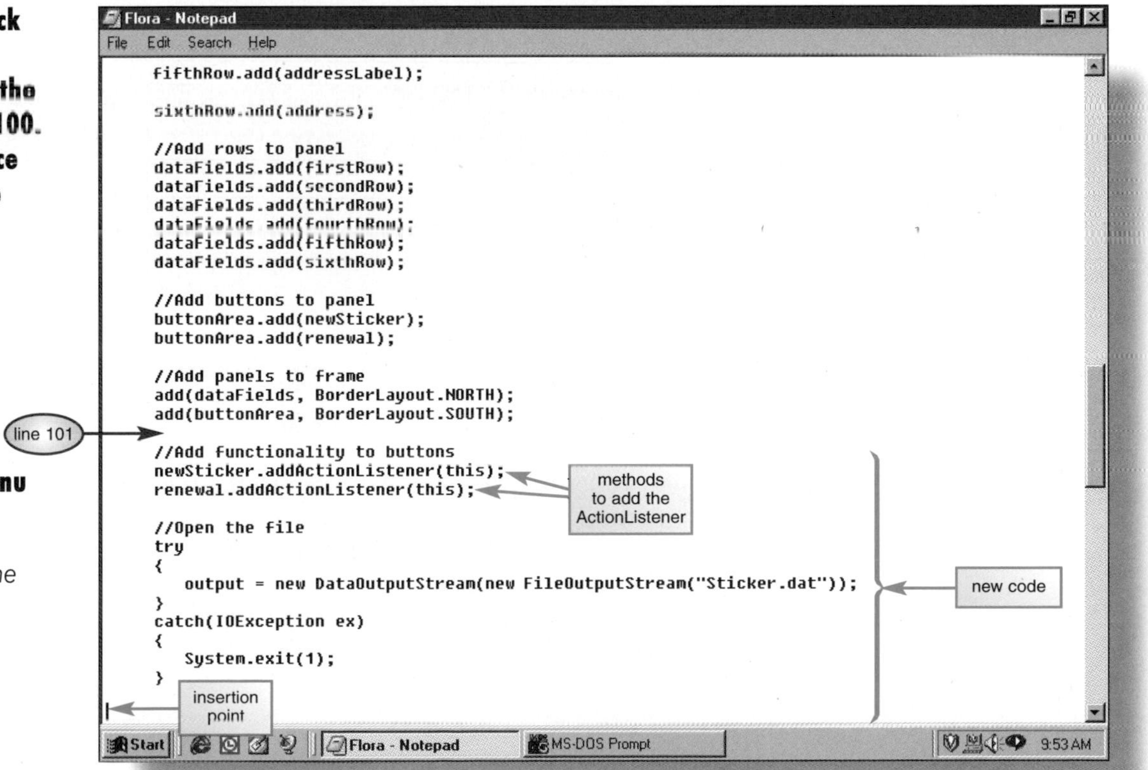

```
fifthRow.add(addressLabel);

sixthRow.add(address);

//Add rows to panel
dataFields.add(firstRow);
dataFields.add(secondRow);
dataFields.add(thirdRow);
dataFields.add(fourthRow);
dataFields.add(fifthRow);
dataFields.add(sixthRow);

//Add buttons to panel
buttonArea.add(newSticker);
buttonArea.add(renewal);

//Add panels to frame
add(dataFields, BorderLayout.NORTH);
add(buttonArea, BorderLayout.SOUTH);

//Add functionality to buttons
newSticker.addActionListener(this);
renewal.addActionListener(this);

//Open the file
try
{
    output = new DataOutputStream(new FileOutputStream("Sticker.dat"));
}
catch(IOException ex)
{
    System.exit(1);
}
```

line 101

methods to add the ActionListener

new code

insertion point

FIGURE 6-17

The System.exit argument is usually one (1) if the application terminates for an error and zero (0) if the program proceeds to its natural conclusion (i.e., the user clicks the Close button). If the window is closed successfully, then the open data file also will close.

Writing Data to the File

In order for the city officials of Flora to know whether a resident is ordering a new sticker or just renewing, a code field will be assigned to each record. When a user clicks the New Sticker button, an N code will be assigned. When a user clicks the Renewal button, a code will be assigned with a value of R. That code, along with the data from the TextFields, will be written to the disk. Again, because input and output is prone to errors, Java requires that you try to catch those errors. Table 6-10 displays the code to test the buttons and write to the disk.

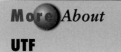

More About

UTF

For more information about the Unicode Text Format (UTF), visit the Java Programming Web Page (www.scsite.com/java/more.htm) and then click UTF.

Table 6-10	
LINE	CODE
142	`String arg = e.getActionCommand();`
143	`String code;`
144	`if (arg == "New Sticker")`
145	`    code = "N";`
146	`else`
147	`    code = "R";`
148	`try`
149	`{`
150	`    output.writeUTF(code);`
151	`    output.writeUTF(vin.getText());`
152	`    output.writeUTF(year.getText());`
153	`    output.writeUTF(make.getText());`
154	`    output.writeUTF(model.getText());`
155	`    output.writeUTF(firstName.getText());`
156	`    output.writeUTF(lastName.getText());`
157	`    output.writeUTF(address.getText());`
158	`}`
159	`catch(IOException c)`
160	`{`
161	`    System.exit(1);`
162	`}`
163	`clearFields();`

In line 163, after the data is written to the file, the program will call a user-defined method named clearFields, which you will code later in the project. The clearFields method will erase the data from each TextField on the screen and move the insertion point to the first field.

Perform the following steps to test which button was clicked and then code the write statements. Use proper indentation.

Steps ### To Code the Write Statements

1 **With the Flora.java source code still displayed in the Notepad window, scroll to display the beginning of the program and then click at the end of line 13.**

The insertion point displays at the beginning of the class block (Figure 6-18).

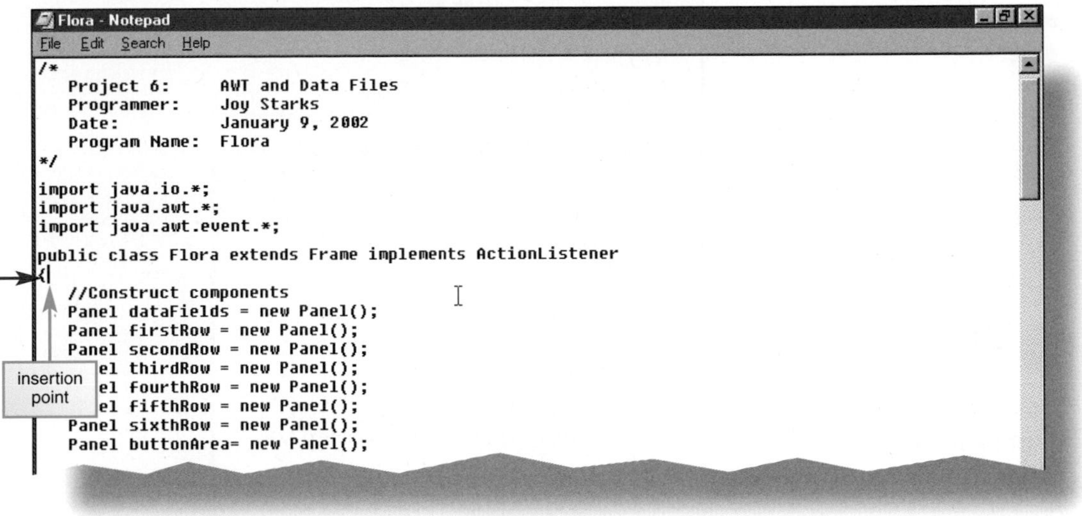

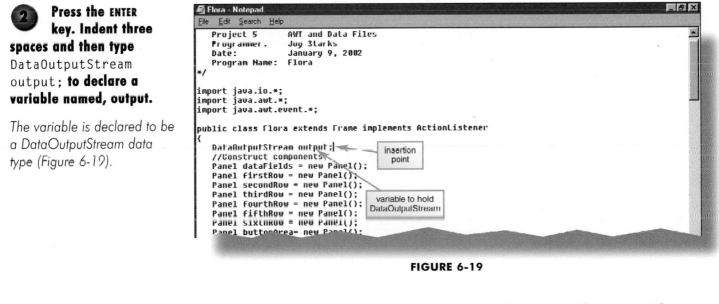

FIGURE 6-18

2 **Press the ENTER key. Indent three spaces and then type** DataOutputStream output; **to declare a variable named, output.**

The variable is declared to be a DataOutputStream data type (Figure 6-19).

FIGURE 6-19

3 **Scroll to the actionPerformed event and click at the end of line 141.**

The insertion point displays at the beginning of the actionPerformed block (Figure 6-20).

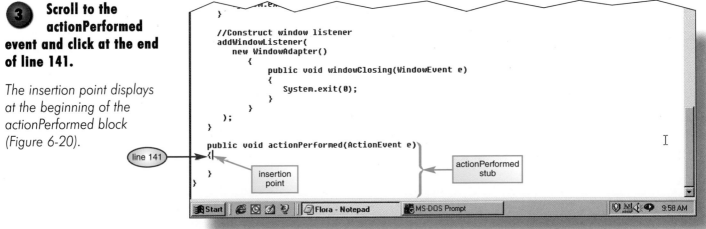

FIGURE 6-20

4 Press the ENTER key. Using proper indentation, type the code from Table 6-10 on page J 6.22.

The new code displays (Figure 6-21). The actionPerformed event sends data to the disk when a button is clicked.

5 Click File on the menu bar and then click Save to save the program again.

The program saves on the floppy disk.

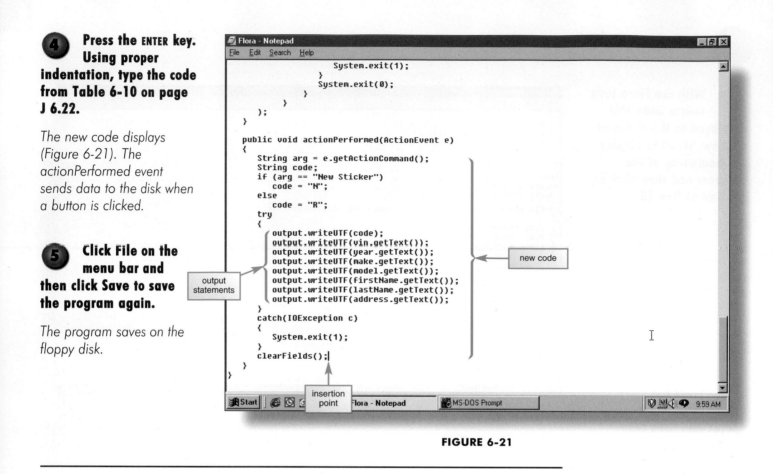

FIGURE 6-21

Recall that the try and catch structure must be used whenever you plan to use input or output operations. The clearFields method, called in line 163 will be created and coded in the next series of steps.

Table 6-11

LINE	CODE
166	`public void clearFields()`
167	`{`
168	`    //Clear fields and reset the focus`
169	`    vin.setText("");`
170	`    year.setText("");`
171	`    make.setText("");`
172	`    model.setText("");`
173	`    firstName.setText("");`
174	`    lastName.setText("");`
175	`    address.setText("");`
176	`    vin.requestFocus();`
177	`}`

Adding a Method to Clear the Fields and Return the Focus

The clearFields method is a user-defined method that clears the TextFields in the window and returns the focus to the first field. It is called after the user clicks either the New Sticker or the Renewal button. Table 6-11 displays the code for the clearFields method. Lines 169 through 175 set each field's text to a **null**, or empty, string (" "). Line 176 then moves the insertion point to the vin field with the **requestFocus** method.

Perform the following steps to code the clearFields method.

Steps To Code the clearFields Method

1 With the Flora.java source code still displayed in the Notepad window, scroll to display the end of the program. Click immediately to the left of the final closing brace in line 165.

The insertion point displays before the closing brace of the Flora class (Figure 6-22).

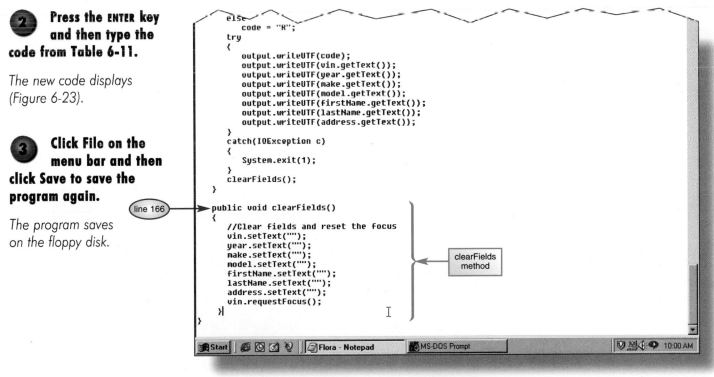

```
                        System.exit(1);
                }
                    System.exit(0);
                }
        }
    );
}

    public void actionPerformed(ActionEvent e)
    {
        String arg = e.getActionCommand();
        String code;
        if (arg == "New Sticker")
            code = "N";
        else
            code = "R";
        try
        {
            output.writeUTF(code);
            output.writeUTF(vin.getText());
            output.writeUTF(year.getText());
            output.writeUTF(make.getText());
            output.writeUTF(model.getText());
            output.writeUTF(firstName.getText());
            output.writeUTF(lastName.getText());
            output.writeUTF(address.getText());
        }
        catch(IOException c)
        {
            System.exit(1);
        }
        clearFields();
    }
}
```

insertion point

line 165

FIGURE 6-22

2 Press the ENTER key and then type the code from Table 6-11.

The new code displays (Figure 6-23).

3 Click File on the menu bar and then click Save to save the program again.

The program saves on the floppy disk.

```
        else
            code = "R";
        try
        {
            output.writeUTF(code);
            output.writeUTF(vin.getText());
            output.writeUTF(year.getText());
            output.writeUTF(make.getText());
            output.writeUTF(model.getText());
            output.writeUTF(firstName.getText());
            output.writeUTF(lastName.getText());
            output.writeUTF(address.getText());
        }
        catch(IOException c)
        {
            System.exit(1);
        }
        clearFields();
    }

    public void clearFields()
    {
        //Clear fields and reset the focus
        vin.setText("");
        year.setText("");
        make.setText("");
        model.setText("");
        firstName.setText("");
        lastName.setText("");
        address.setText("");
        vin.requestFocus();
    }
}
```

line 166

clearFields method

FIGURE 6-23

In this example, the clearFields method is coded at the end of the Flora class, although the placement of this method could be anywhere in the program.

Testing the Buttons

To test the buttons, you must compile and then execute the application. You will enter three records as displayed in Table 6-12.

Table 6-12 Sample Data for the Flora Application			
FIELD	RECORD 1	RECORD 2	RECORD 3
VIN	1Z37F54504016	2X98G12345678	3Y76H13579246
Year	1993	1998	2000
Make	CHE	FORD	CHR
Model	Corvette	Aerostar	LeBaron
First Name	Fred	Auggie	Patrick
Last Name	Starks	Schulke	See
Flora Address	8006 Howard Ave.	1718 Neely Dr.	5258 Minnesota St.
New Sticker or Renewal	New Sticker	Renewal	New Sticker

Perform the following steps to compile and execute the program, testing both the New Sticker and Renewal buttons.

Steps **To Test the Buttons**

① Click the MS-DOS Prompt button on the taskbar or open an MS-DOS Prompt window from the Programs submenu. If necessary, set the path and drive. Type `javac Flora.java` **and then press the ENTER key. If the program will not compile because of programming errors, fix them in the Notepad window, save the file, and then compile again in the MS-DOS Prompt window.**

The program compiles (Figure 6-24).

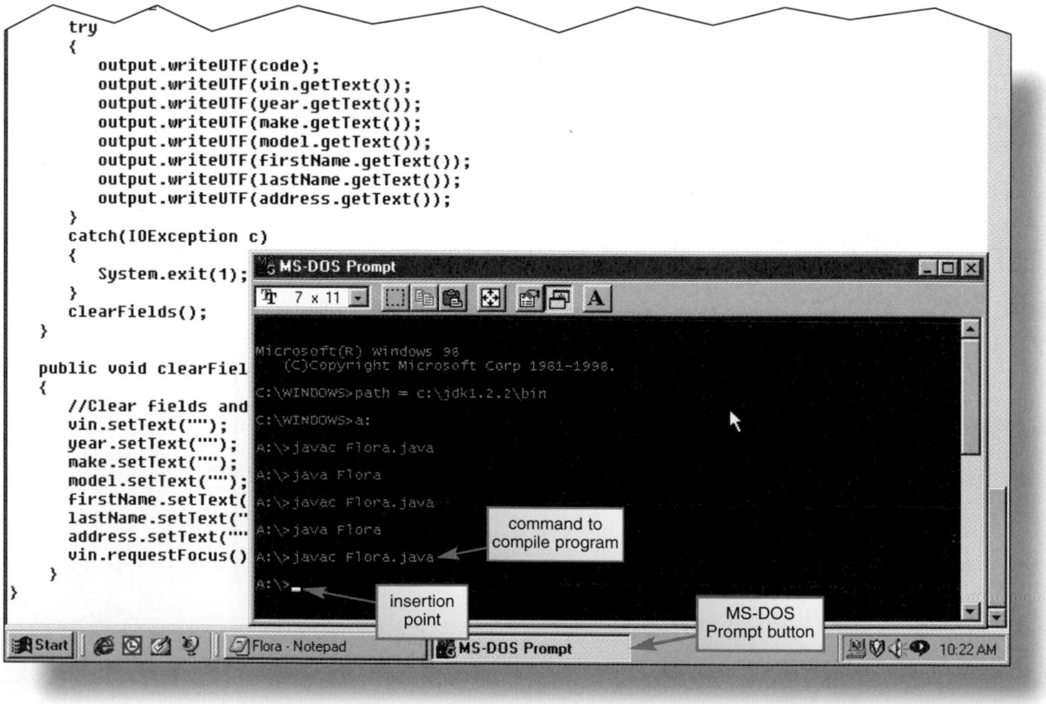

FIGURE 6-24

2 **Type** java Flora **and then press the ENTER key.**

The Flora City Stickers window displays (Figure 6-25). The insertion point displays in the first TextField.

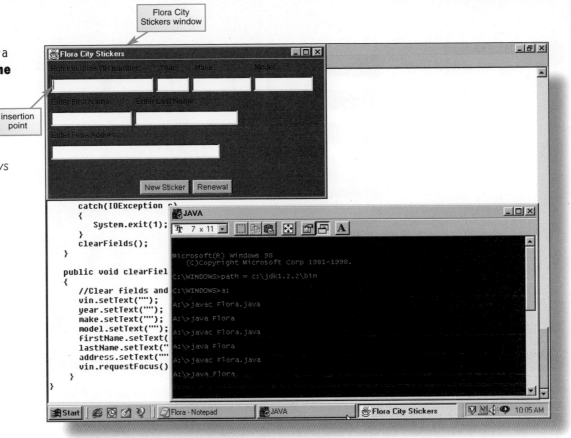

FIGURE 6-25

3 **Enter the first data record from Table 6-12, pressing the TAB key to move to each new field. With your floppy disk in drive A, point to the New Sticker button.**

Fields in the first record display (Figure 6-26). Your display may differ.

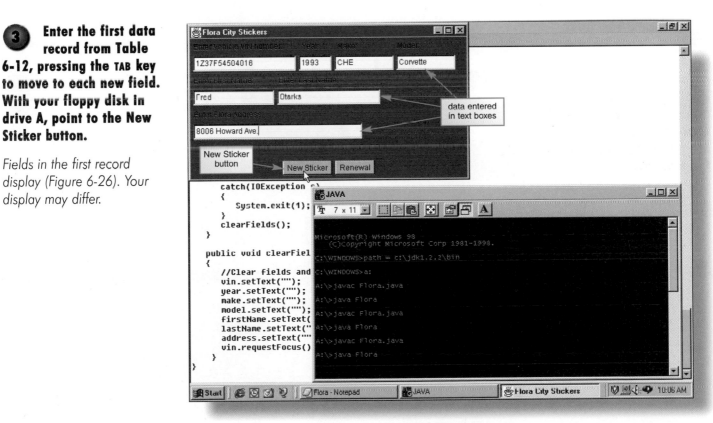

FIGURE 6-26

Click the New Sticker button.

The record writes to the disk drive, the fields clear, and the insertion point returns to the first TextField (Figure 6-27).

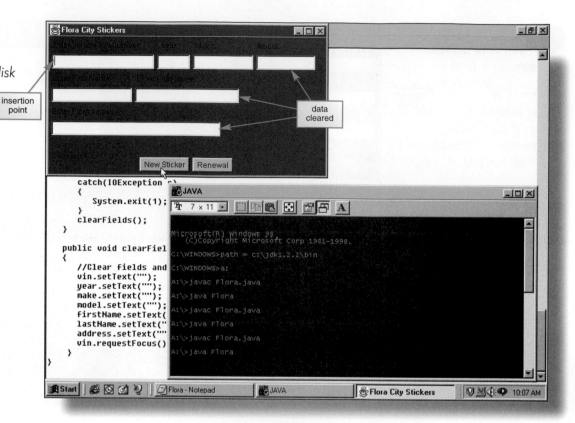

FIGURE 6-27

Repeat step 3 for the second and third records, clicking the appropriate button (either New Sticker or Renewal) after each record is completed. When you are finished, point to the Close button.

The fields clear and the ScreenTip displays (Figure 6-28). The records have been written to the disk.

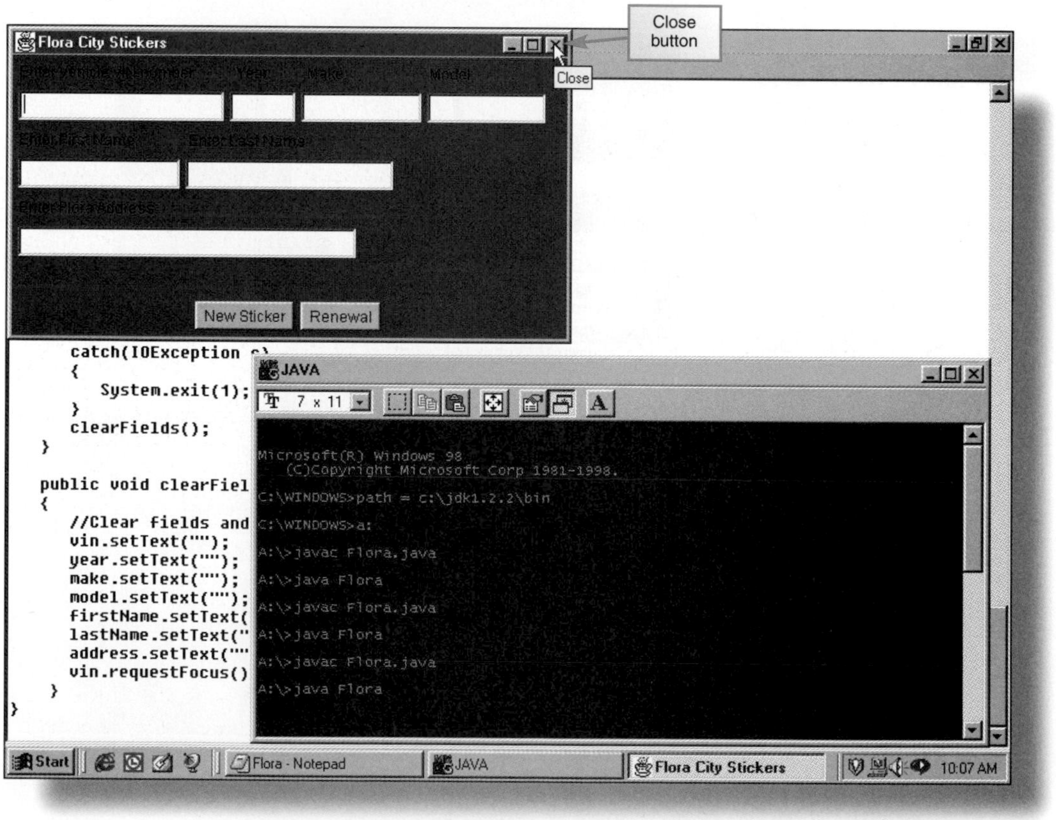

FIGURE 6-28

6 **Click the Close button and then click anywhere in the MS-DOS Prompt window.**

The Flora City Stickers window closes, as does the data file on the floppy disk (Figure 6-29). Control returns to the MS-DOS Prompt window.

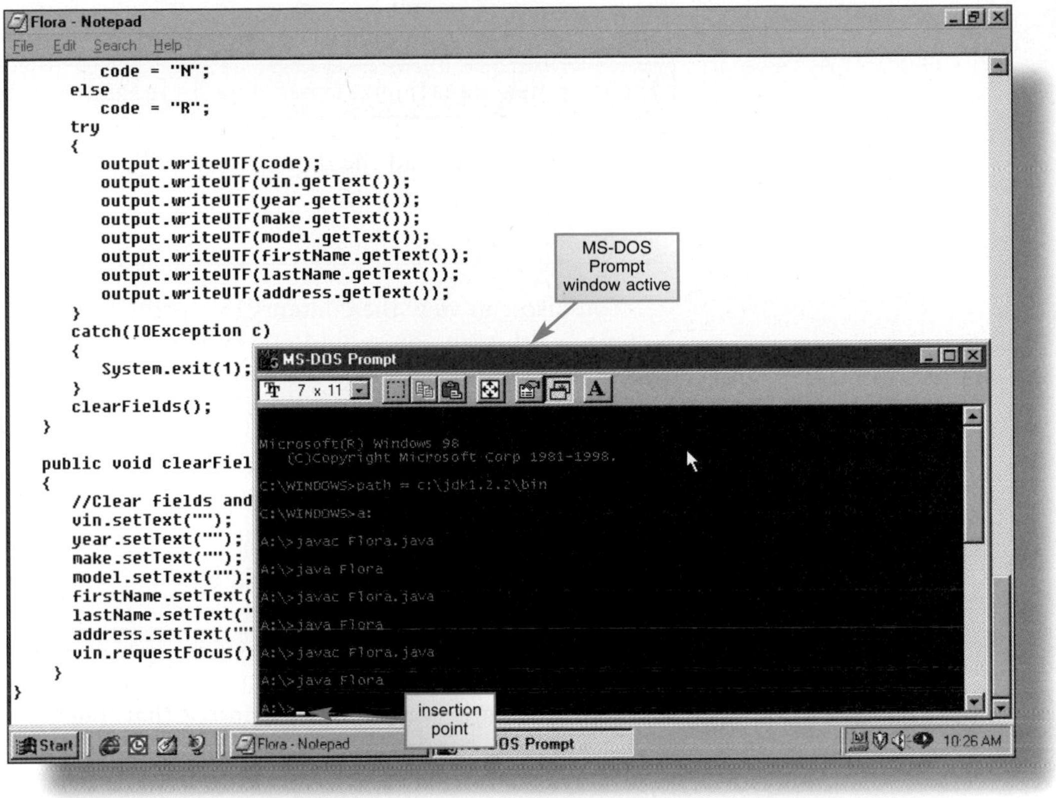

FIGURE 6-29

7 **With the MS-DOS Prompt window active, type** `dir/w` **and then press the ENTER key.**

A directory listing of drive A displays (Figure 6-30). Your directory may display differently. Notice that Sticker.dat now is saved on your floppy disk.

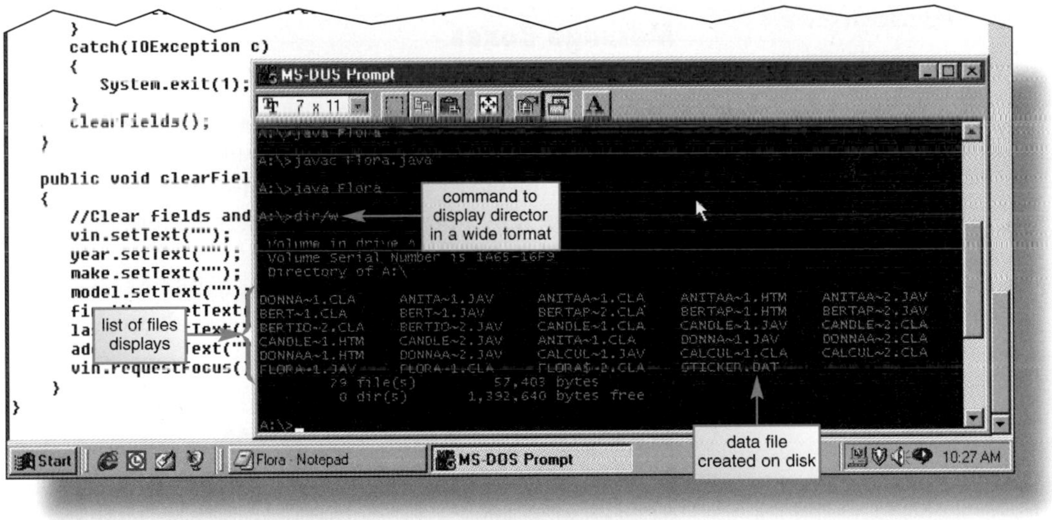

FIGURE 6-30

You may view the contents of the Sticker.dat file by reading it into a program that creates an instance of the DataInputStream and then uses the readUTF methods, in the same way as Flora used the DataOutputStream and writeUTF methods. For example, if you wanted to create a program to read the sticker data, you would declare a variable with the data type, InputStream.

```
InputStream input;
```

Then, wrap it in the FileInputStream buffer.

```
input = new DataInputStream(new FileInputStream("Sticker.dat"));
```

Finally, you would read the data from the file.

```
name.setText(readUTF());
```

You also can view the contents by opening the file in a text editor such as Notepad, although you should not save it because text editors will corrupt the binary nature of the file. Field separators might display as commas or special characters in a text editor window.

Error Checking

Users make mistakes. Data-entry is a tedious, boring, and mundane process; it is not difficult to see how a data entry operator might omit a field of data or make an error. Although Java inherently provides more error checking capabilities than most other programming languages when it compiles, it probably is impossible while programming to anticipate every other error that might occur. Providing error-checking routines to plan for possible problems that Java does not catch is an essential part of good programming. Most errors can be fixed if caught before data is written to the disk. A **prompt**, or message, to the user with some information about the problem and/or the solution is a common way to address errors.

Message Boxes

Creating a message box is one way of notifying a user of important information or actions that must be taken. A **message box** is a dialog box with a title bar, a message, and usually an OK button. When an error occurs, the program should generate or call the message box. After the user has read the message, he or she responds by clicking the OK button. As with most windows in Java, a message box is an instance of a frame.

You will create an **external class** called MessageBox, then instantiate and call it from the Flora program when an error occurs or when you want to present a message.

Creating the MessageBox Class

The MessageBox class displays in Table 6-13. Notice in line 10 that the MessageBox class extends **Dialog**, which is a Java class used to create smaller windows, such as dialog boxes, message boxes, information boxes, and alert messages. Dialog classes have several methods in common with the Frame class, including setTitle, getTitle, and isResizable. Dialog boxes can be declared **modal**, which blocks input to other windows while shown, or they can be declared **non-modal**, which allows the user to click outside the dialog box and continue working in the application. The default value is modal; therefore, if you do not specify in its constructor, the dialog box will force the user to respond to its message before continuing. The class header in line 10 also implements the ActionListener, because the message box has a button that will be clicked.

More About

The MessageBox Class Hierarchy

For more information about the hierarchy of the MessageBox Class, including a diagram of the class hierarchy, visit the Java Programming Web page (www.scsite.com/java/more.htm) and then click Class Hierarchies.

Table 6-13

LINE	CODE
1	`/*`
2	`    Project 6:      AWT and Data Files`
3	`    Programmer:     Joy Starks`
4	`    Date:           January 9, 2002`
5	`    Program Name:   MessageBox`
6	`*/`
7	
8	`import java.awt.*;`
9	`import java.awt.event.*;`
10	`class MessageBox extends Dialog implements ActionListener`
11	`{`
12	`    private String result;`
13	`    private Button OKButton;`
14	
15	`    public MessageBox(Frame frame, String title, String messageString)`
16	`    {`
17	`        //Call Dialog's constructor`
18	`        super(frame, title, true);`
19	
20	`        //Determine the size of the message box`
21	`        Rectangle bounds = frame.getBounds();`
22	`        setBackground(Color.white);`
23	`        setLocation(bounds.x+bounds.width/3, bounds.y+bounds.height/3);`
24	
25	`        //Create a Panel to hold the message`
26	`        Panel messagePane = new Panel();`
27	`        Label message = new Label(messageString);`
28	`        messagePane.add(message);`
29	`        add(messagePane, BorderLayout.CENTER);`
30	
31	`        //Create a Panel to hold the button`
32	`        Panel buttonPane = new Panel();`
33	`        OKButton = new Button("  OK  ");`
34	`        buttonPane.add(OKButton);`
35	`        add(buttonPane, BorderLayout.SOUTH);`
36	
37	`        //Add the ActionListener to the button`
38	`        OKButton.addActionListener(this);`
39	
40	`        //Reorganize internal components to fit window`
41	`        pack();`
42	`    }`
43	
44	`    public void actionPerformed(ActionEvent e)`
45	`    {`
46	`        setVisible(false);`
47	`    }`
48	`}`

A constructor method header displays in line 15. The method accepts three arguments: a frame and two strings. When the calling program instantiates this message box, it will send the name of the frame, the caption that should appear in the message box title bar, and the message itself.

Because MessageBox extends Dialog, inheriting all Dialog attributes, Java actually writes the constructor for you internally at compile time, creating a **derived** class. When Java constructs a derived class such as this, however, it receives no arguments. With MessageBox, you will want to receive arguments, such as the message and title, from the calling class. If you wish to receive arguments, you must override Java's construction. You could write the entire constructor yourself with the arguments, or you can use a shortcut that Java provides. The **super** keyword in line 18 is a way to refer back to that superclass of Dialog, without having to write it out again. Programmers use the super keyword to take the place of a class name and to invoke an overridden base class method in a derived class. In this example, the three arguments of super are the frame, the title of the Dialog box, and the frame's modal state, which is either true or false. Super overrides Java's constructor to read the frame, title, and modality that were passed to the constructor method.

Line 21 is a new component called Rectangle. The constructor names it with the identifier, bounds. A **Rectangle** component is any rectangular-shaped area within the frame. In this case, it is assigned the boundaries of the frame with the **getBounds** method. Line 23 then sets the location of the message box to begin one-third of the way across the frame. The **setLocation** method accepts an x and y grid coordinate to place the top left corner of the message box.

Recall constructor statements, such as lines 26 and 27, create new components, while add methods, such as lines 28 and 29, actually add the components to their respective containers. The same process occurs in lines 32 through 35. The OKButton is constructed and then added to the buttonPane. Line 38 makes the button clickable by adding the ActionListener.

Finally, the **pack** method in line 41 adjusts all the internal components to fit the designated size of the message box. This rendering of the message box is performed by the layout manager, which determines how much space each of the components needs, and then adjusts the component positions.

When the message box's OKButton is clicked, Java transfers execution of the program to the actionPerformed event. In line 46, the message box becomes invisible after the click.

Perform the following steps to create the MessageBox.java file, and compile it into the MessageBox.class file.

More About

Packing

A Window (which is also a Component and thus can use the setSize method) can be packed, which causes it to be sized to fit the size and layouts of its components (otherwise, some items may not be visible, or completely visible). If packing, you allow the Window to resize accordingly. If using setSize, you must know the height and width you need to accommodate the components of the Window.

TO CREATE THE MESSAGEBOX CLASS

1 Open Notepad and maximize it. If Notepad already is open, click File on the menu bar and then click New to open a new Notepad window.

2 Enter the code from Table 6-13 on the previous page, using proper indentation.

3 Save the file as "MessageBox.java" on your floppy disk.

4 Open an MS-DOS Prompt window and set the path, if necessary. On drive A, compile the program by typing `javac MessageBox.java` at the command prompt.

5 If errors occur during compilation, fix them in the Notepad window and then save the file again. Recompile MessageBox.java.

The program compiles (Figure 6-31).

The final step in implementing the message box is to create an instance of the MessageBox and call it with appropriate data.

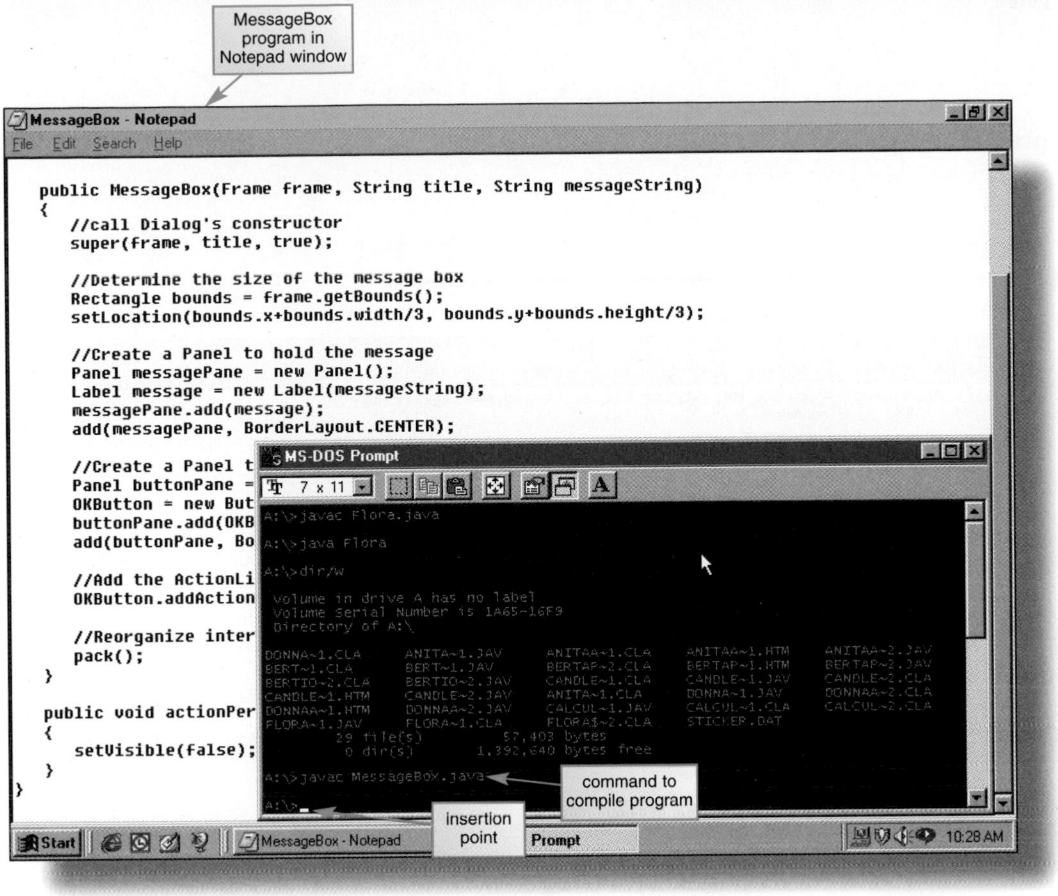

FIGURE 6-31

Calling the MessageBox Class

You will call a message box in two places in the Flora program. A warning message box should display if the user omits data in any of the TextFields. A confirmation message box should display if the data is written to the disk successfully.

Table 6-14 displays the if statement to test for an empty TextField. The getText method looks at each field and compares it to a null string using the compareTo method. If the return value is one, the field contains data. If it is less than one, no data are in the field. The or (| |) operators cause the if statement to test each of the fields.

Table 6-14

LINE	CODE
150	if (
151	(vin.getText().compareTo("")<1) ||
152	(year.getText().compareTo("")<1) ||
153	(make.getText().compareTo("")<1) ||
154	(model.getText().compareTo("")<1) ||
155	(firstName.getText().compareTo("")<1) ||
156	(lastName.getText().compareTo("")<1) ||
157	(address.getText().compareTo("")<1)
158	)
159	{
160	errorBox = new MessageBox(this, "Data Entry Error", "You must complete all fields.");
161	errorBox.setVisible(true);
162	}
163	else
164	{

Perform the following steps to edit the Flora program so that it will call appropriate message boxes.

Steps) To Call the Message Boxes

1 **Click File on Notepad's menu bar and then click Open. When the Open dialog box displays, click the Look in box arrow and then click 3½ Floppy (A:) in the Look in list. Type** Flora.java **in the File name text box. Point to the Open button.**

The Flora.java program will open from drive A (Figure 6-32). Alternately, you may choose All Files in the Files of Type box and then click the file in the displayed list.

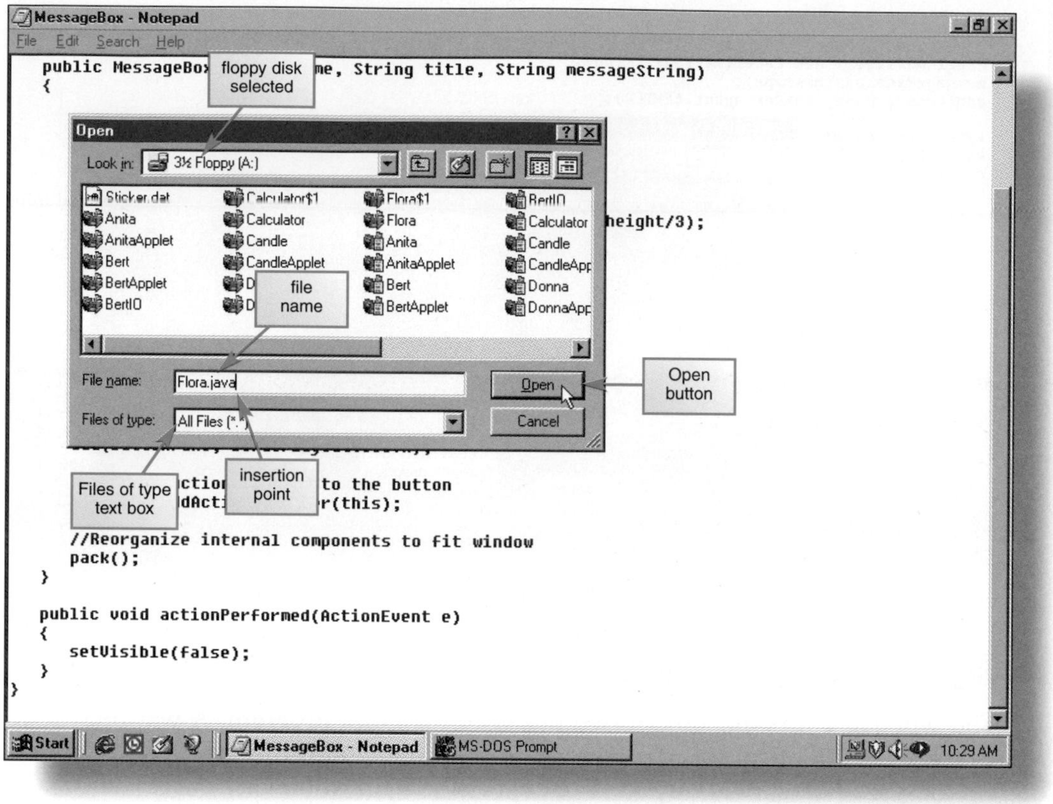

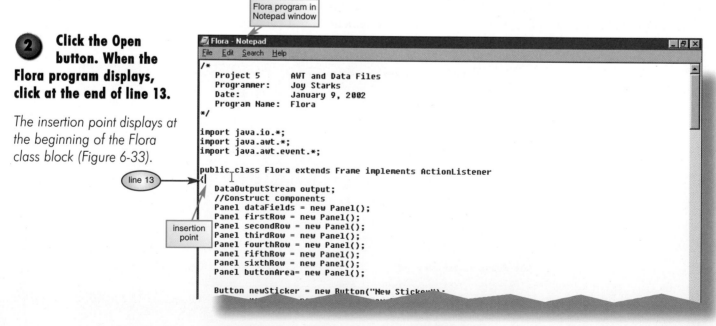

FIGURE 6-32

2 **Click the Open button. When the Flora program displays, click at the end of line 13.**

The insertion point displays at the beginning of the Flora class block (Figure 6-33).

FIGURE 6-33

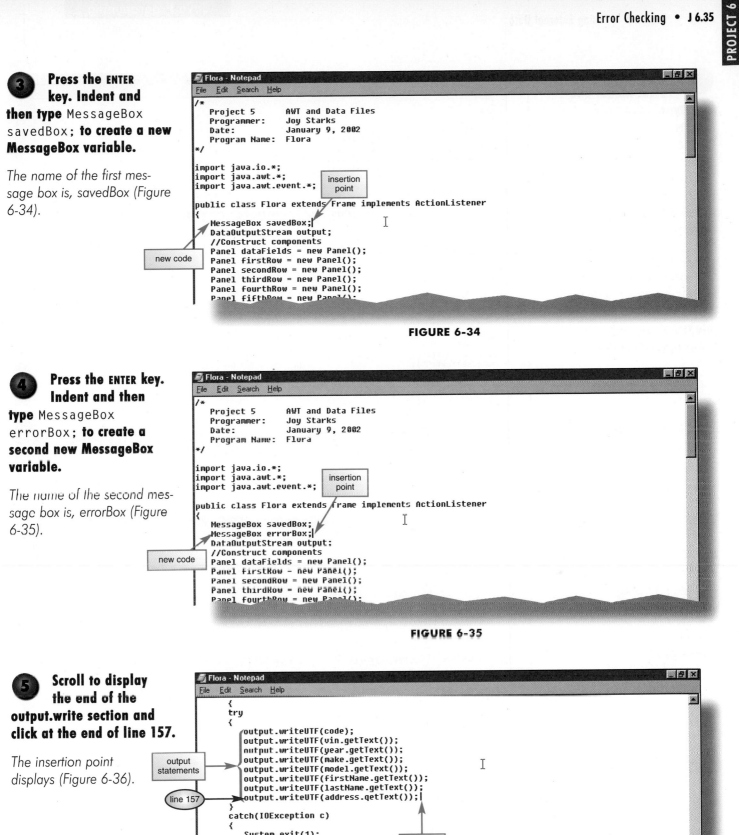

3 Press the ENTER key. Indent and then type MessageBox savedBox; **to create a new MessageBox variable.**

The name of the first message box is, savedBox (Figure 6-34).

```
/*
   Project 5        AWT and Data Files
   Programmer:      Joy Starks
   Date:            January 9, 2002
   Program Name:    Flora
*/

import java.io.*;
import java.awt.*;
import java.awt.event.*;          insertion point

public class Flora extends Frame implements ActionListener
{
    MessageBox savedBox;
    DataOutputStream output;
    //Construct components
    Panel dataFields = new Panel();
    Panel firstRow = new Panel();
    Panel secondRow = new Panel();
    Panel thirdRow = new Panel();
    Panel fourthRow = new Panel();
    Panel fifthRow = new Panel();
```

new code

FIGURE 6-34

4 Press the ENTER key. Indent and then type MessageBox errorBox; **to create a second new MessageBox variable.**

The name of the second message box is, errorBox (Figure 6-35).

```
/*
   Project 5        AWT and Data Files
   Programmer:      Joy Starks
   Date:            January 9, 2002
   Program Name:    Flora
*/

import java.io.*;
import java.awt.*;
import java.awt.event.*;          insertion point

public class Flora extends Frame implements ActionListener
{
    MessageBox savedBox;
    MessageBox errorBox;
    DataOutputStream output;
    //Construct components
    Panel dataFields = new Panel();
    Panel firstRow = new Panel();
    Panel secondRow = new Panel();
    Panel thirdRow = new Panel();
    Panel fourthRow = new Panel();
```

new code

FIGURE 6-35

5 Scroll to display the end of the output.write section and click at the end of line 157.

The insertion point displays (Figure 6-36).

```
    {
    try
    {
        output.writeUTF(code);
        output.writeUTF(vin.getText());
        output.writeUTF(year.getText());
        output.writeUTF(make.getText());
        output.writeUTF(model.getText());
        output.writeUTF(firstName.getText());
        output.writeUTF(lastName.getText());
        output.writeUTF(address.getText());
    }
    catch(IOException c)
    {
        System.exit(1);
    }
    clearFields();
    }
}

public void clearFields()
{
    //Clear fields and reset the focus
    vin.setText("");
```

output statements

line 157

insertion point

FIGURE 6-36

6 **Press the ENTER key twice. Indent and then type** savedBox = new MessageBox(this, "Data Submitted", "The vehicle information has been saved."); **to call the MessageBox class.**

The new code displays (Figure 6-37). Your line might wrap at a different place in the line. The self-referential, this, refers back to this constructed instance.

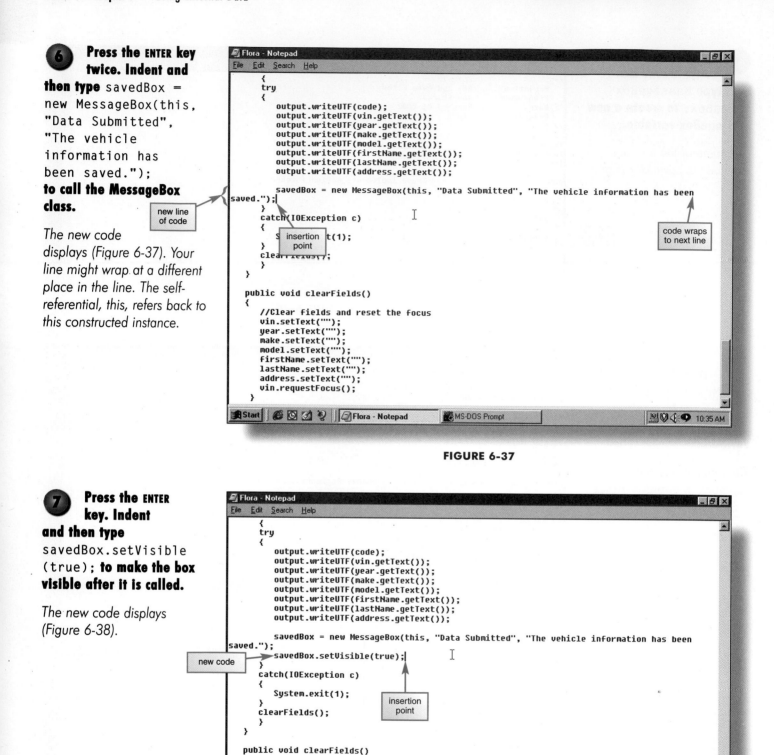

FIGURE 6-37

7 **Press the ENTER key. Indent and then type** savedBox.setVisible (true); **to make the box visible after it is called.**

The new code displays (Figure 6-38).

FIGURE 6-38

8 Scroll up and then click at the end of line 149, after the statements to set the code variable. Press ENTER and then type the code from Table 6-14 on page J 6.33.

The if command checks for blanks in any of the fields (Figure 6-39).

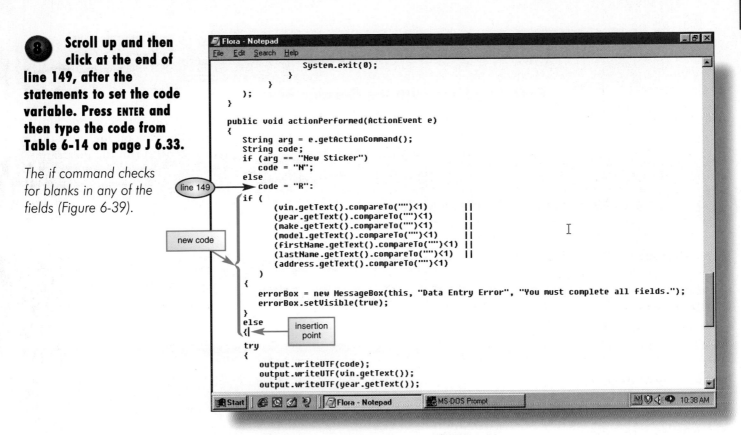

FIGURE 6-39

9 Scroll to the end of the actionPerformed event and click at the end of the clearFields() method in line 183. Press the ENTER key and then type a closing brace for the else block.

Two braces are needed here: one for the else block and one for the actionPerformed event (Figure 6-40).

10 Click File on the menu bar and then click Save to save the file again.

The program saves on the floppy disk.

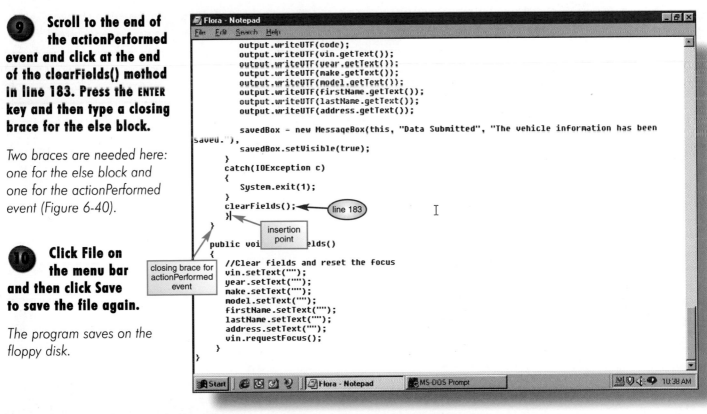

FIGURE 6-40

The program now is complete. You may print a copy by clicking File on the Notepad menu bar and then click Print.

Executing Flora with the Message Boxes

To test the MessageBox class and the calling statements, you must compile Flora again, and then run it. The compiled MessageBox class needs to be on the same disk and in the same directory as Flora. Perform the following steps to run the program.

To Execute Flora and Test The Message Boxes

1 **Click the MS-DOS Prompt button on the taskbar or open an MS-DOS Prompt window. If necessary, set the path and change to drive A. Type** javac Flora.java **and then press the ENTER key. If the program will not compile because of programming errors, fix them in the Notepad window, save the file, and then compile again in the MS-DOS Prompt window.**

The program compiles (Figure 6-41).

```
        output.writeUTF(lastName.getText());
        output.writeUTF(address.getText());

        savedBox = new MessageBox(this, "Data Submitted", "The vehicle information has been
saved.");
        savedBox.setVisible(true);
    }
    catch(IOException c)
    {
        System.exit(1);
    }
    clearFields();
    }
}

public void clearFiel
{
    //Clear fields and
    vin.setText("");
    year.setText("");
    make.setText("");
    model.setText("");
    firstName.setText(
    lastName.setText("
    address.setText(""
    vin.requestFocus()
    }
}
}
```

```
A:\>javac Flora.java
A:\>java Flora
A:\>dir/w
 Volume in drive A has no label
 Directory of A:\

[PROJEC~1]      FLORA~1.CLA     TEMP.DAT        201-6TXT.DOC    FLORA~1.JAV
MENUWI~1.JAV    MESSAG~1.JAV    FLORA$~2.CLA    MENUWI~1.CLA    MENUWI~2.CLA
MENUWI~3.CLA    MESSAG~1.CLA    STICKER.DAT     UNNAME~1.DEP    FLORAB~2.JAV
FLORAW~2.JAV    FLORA~1.JA      FLORA3~3.JAV    MESSAG~1.TXT
       18 file(s)        167,373 bytes
        1 dir(s)      1,089,024 bytes free
A:\>javac MessageBox.java
A:\>javac Flora.java
A:\>
```

command to compile the program

FIGURE 6-41

2 **Type** java Flora **and press the ENTER key. When the Flora City Stickers window displays, enter some sample data or use the data from Table 6-12 on page J 6.26. Enter all fields and then point to the New Sticker button.**

The Flora City Stickers window displays (Figure 6-42).

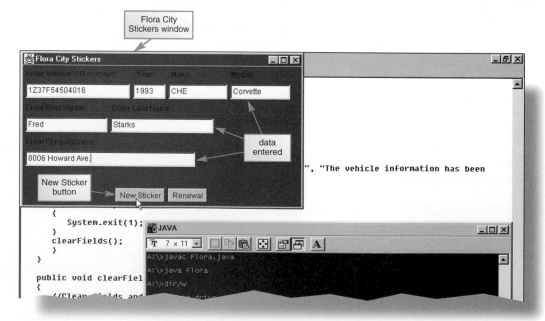

Flora City Stickers window

data entered

New Sticker button

FIGURE 6-42

Click the New Sticker button. When the Data Submitted dialog box displays, point to its OK button.

The message box displays (Figure 6-43).

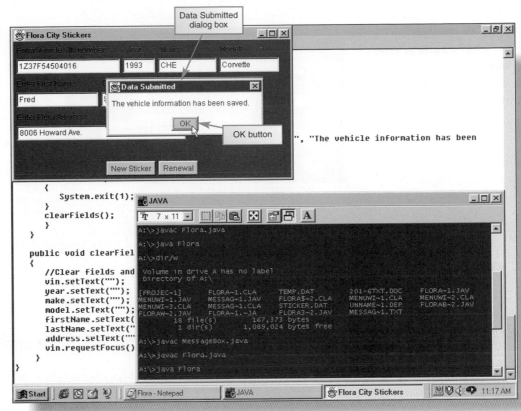

FIGURE 6-43

Click the OK button. When the fields clear, enter another record, but leave one of the fields empty. Point to the New Sticker button.

The data for all the fields, except the Year, display (Figure 6-44).

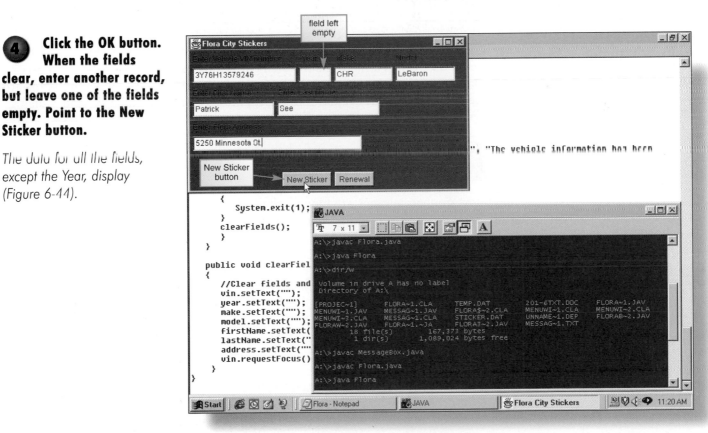

FIGURE 6-44

5 **Click the New Sticker button. When the Data Entry Error dialog box displays, point to the OK button.**

Because the Year field was left blank, the program called the messageBox with the error message (Figure 6-45).

6 **Click the OK button and then click the Close button.**

The program terminates.

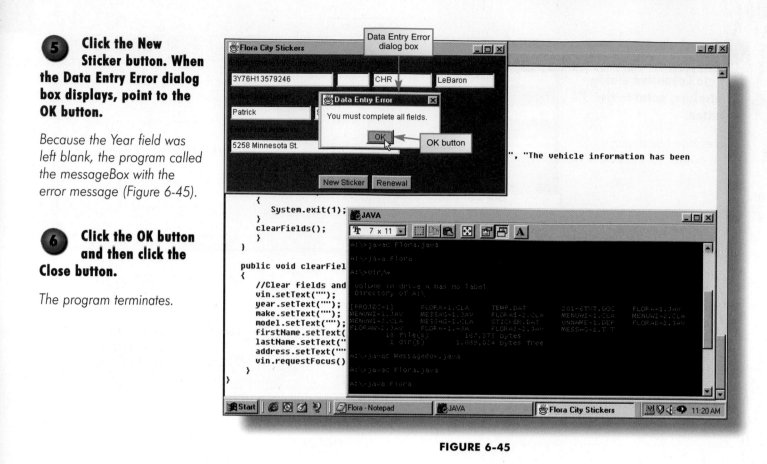

FIGURE 6-45

When a user omits a field, the if statement evaluates to true, so the Data Entry Error dialog box displays (line 161 in Table 6-14 on page J 6.33). When all fields are complete, the if statement evaluates to false, data is written to the disk, and a dialog box displays indicating successful data entry.

Moving to the Web

Many government agencies are moving their services to the Web. As individuals and companies continue to expand their e-commerce, city, state, and federal agencies are eager to jump on the Web bandwagon. Most financial-based institutions such as banks, credit card companies, and stock brokerage firms offer services 24 hours a day over the Web. The anytime, anywhere capability of the Internet allows information and services to be more available to more people with greater convenience and lower cost to customers. Not only do government agencies see the Web as a way to save time and money while serving the citizens around the clock, they also do not want to be outdated or left behind. Analysts predict that by the year 2004, the number of U.S. households with Internet access will rise to 90 million, doubling from the year 2000.

It is easy to think of the Web exclusively as new technology. It is far more useful to think of it as a new way to deliver services. Web services combine traditional functions, such as publishing, business transactions, information gathering, data search and retrieval, and others, into a single form of presentation. Web services also have some unique characteristics that require special policy, management, and technical attention. The most obvious of these is the speed of technological change and the rapidly expanding variety of tools and technologies. A less obvious, but perhaps more important, characteristic is the completely public nature of the interaction between an agency and a Web user. In theory, anyone, anywhere, at anytime can have access to an agency on the Web. Customer service on a Web site can be linked to other sites without permission or knowledge. Material can be copied, distributed, and used in ways you have neither planned nor expected. This characteristic gives the Web its excitement and vitality, but it means a new way of thinking for most government organizations.

Because it would not represent the way programmers and database administrators use Java, you will not convert the data file application in this project to an applet. Due to security issues relating to applet constraints and database integrity, most Web interfaces use a layer of security between the applet and the database. As you read the next section, you will learn about the layers of security and the client/server concepts typically employed by computer installations and database administrators.

Client/Server Concepts

In the past, the Internet interface for businesses has been written in C++, Visual Basic, or PowerBuilder. The database behind the interface typically has been Microsoft Access or Oracle. The **client**, which is a person or a computer system, sees the interface; and the **server**, which is a computer that houses a network or database, handles data manipulation and connectivity issues. **Client/server architecture** is a general description of a networked system where a client program initiates contact with a separate server program for a specific purpose. The client requests a service provided by the server. This separation of the interface and the database is called a **two-tier system**. The two-tier system, also called a first generation system, contains application logic typically tied to the client, with heavy network utilization required to mediate the client/server interaction.

A second generation of client/server implementations takes this a step further and adds a middle tier to achieve a three-tier architecture, or system. In a **three-tier system**, the application is split into three parts: the Web browser, the application server, and the database server. A program to handle both input and output separates the GUI and database, providing the logic to both of the other parts of the system, which leads to faster network communications, greater reliability, and improved overall performance.

With the advent of Java and the Internet, many businesses have taken a **multi-tier approach**, in which data moving from a client to a server goes through several stages. The middle tier is expanded to provide connections to various types of services, integrating and coupling them to the client, and also to each other. Partitioning the application logic among various hosts also can create a multi-tier approach. This encapsulation of distributed functionality provides significant advantages such as reusability and, therefore, reliability.

In a multi-tier approach, Java applets with their own objects and methods create the interface. A Java applet has a very distinct set of capabilities and restrictions within the language framework, especially from a security standpoint. Java applets can neither read nor write files on a local system, unless special permissions are assigned and accepted. Applets cannot create, rename, or copy files or directories on a local system. They also cannot make outside network connections except to the host machine from which they originated.

Most businesses, therefore, will create a client interface, with HTML or a scripting tool, to allow users to enter data. The database itself is separated from the interface by a Web server, usually complete with a firewall to protect the database from the Internet. The program on the Web server that runs the connectivity is in charge.

Sun Microsystems Inc., provides an Application Program Interface (API) called the **Java Database Connectivity (JDBC)** that has its own set of objects and methods to interact with underlying databases. Java programs can open a connection to a database and then create a transaction object, such as an insert, delete, or update. The transaction statements are passed to the underlying database management system (DBMS) by the program.

Another solution is to use a Java servlet. **Servlets** are modules that run inside request/response-oriented servers, such as Java-enabled Web servers, and extend them. For example, a servlet might be responsible for taking data in an HTML order-entry form and then applying the logic necessary to update a company's order database. Servlets replace cumbersome and non-robust scripting tools such as JavaScript or CGI. A servlet API, used to write servlets, knows nothing about how the servlet is loaded. This allows servlets to be used with many different Web servers.

Servlets are effective substitutes for other kinds of scripting tools because they provide a way to generate dynamic documents that are both easier to write and faster to run. Because they are written in Java, they also address the problem of doing server-side programming with platform-specific APIs. Servlets also offer substantial performance advantages for developers and webmasters, because — unlike code from other scripting tools — servlets do not create, or fork off, additional processes each time a request is made from a browser. Servlets are developed with the Java Servlet API, a standard Java extension. Many popular Web servers already support servlets.

Project Summary

In Project 6, you built an application that allowed the user to enter records into a data file. First, you constructed an interface window with Labels, TextFields, Buttons, and Panels. You used multiple layout managers to place components in the window and then wrapped the data from the FileOutputStream inside the DataOutputStream to construct a new file. Then, using the writeUTF method, you transferred data from the interface to the sequential file. To incorporate additional functionality and user-friendly features, you created and called a MessageBox class to inform users when data was submitted successfully, as well as to warn them when a field was left empty.

Finally, you learned about client/server architectures, the core of information technology from databases to the Web. You also learned that two-tier, three-tier, and multi-tier systems allow for protection of databases and world access.

What You Should Know

Having completed this project, you now should be able to perform the following tasks:

Add the ActionListener and Open the Data File (J 6.21)
Add the Components to the Frame (J 6.16)
Call the Message Boxes (J 6.34)
Code the clearFields Method (J 6.25)
Code the Write Statements (J 6.23)
Construct the Components (J 6.12)
Create the Flora Window (J 6.8)

Create the MessageBox Class (J 6.32)
Execute Flora and Test the Message Boxes (J 6.38)
Set the Layout Managers (J 6.14)
Test the Buttons (J 6.26)
Test the Flora Window (J 6.10)
Test the Flora Window Components (J 6.17)

Test Your Knowledge

1 True/False

Instructions: Circle T if the statement is true or F if the statement is false.

T F   1. Panels and Frames are composite objects.

T F   2. Non-volatile data is stored in the computer's memory while the electricity is supplied to the computer and while the program is running.

T F   3. FileInputStream and FileOutputStream are used to read data from the keyboard and write data to the printer.

T F   4. Dialog boxes that block input to other windows are called non-modal.

T F   5. The Rectangle component displays a rectangle in the Frame.

T F   6. A client is a person or system that sees the interface, whereas a server is the computer than houses the network or a database.

T F   7. The writeUTF method is used to write numeric data to a storage device.

T F   8. Java provides more error checking capabilities at compile time than most programming languages.

T F   9. The DataOutputStream and DataInputStream classes are wrapper classes.

T F 10. Sequential access files use the seek method to look for data.

2 Multiple Choice

Instructions: Circle the correct response.

1. Programs that use a window or GUI-based interface typically extend Frame, and are called _____.
   a. frame implementations
   b. applets
   c. ActionListener events
   d. frame-based applications

2. The binary state representing the smallest piece of data a computer can understand is called a(n) _____.
   a. bit
   b. byte
   c. field
   d. record

3. A message box usually contains all of the following except a(n) _____.
   a. title bar
   b. menu
   c. message
   d. OK button

4. The _____ method adjusts all the internal components to fit the designated size of the message box.
   a. repaint
   b. pack
   c. setSize
   d. render

(continued)

Test Your Knowledge

Multiple Choice *(continued)*

5. The DataOutputStream is a member of the _____ package.
   a. java.awt
   b. java.awt.event
   c. java.io
   d. java.applet

6. Files that must be read from beginning to end when looking for a piece of data are called _____ access files.
   a. sequential
   b. random
   c. stream
   d. ordered

7. A _____ is a collection of related records.
   a. record
   b. field
   c. file
   d. database

8. The keyword used to invoke a superclass constructor is called _____.
   a. method
   b. construct
   c. Dialog
   d. super

9. In a _____ system, the application uses a Web browser, an application server, and a database server which leads to faster network communications, greater reliability, and improved overall performance.
   a. two-tier
   b. three-tier
   c. multi-tier
   d. firewall

10. JDBC stands for _____.
    a. Java Data Building Computer
    b. Java Direct Business Connection
    c. Java's DataBase Creation program
    d. Java Database Connectivity

3 Debugging Java Code

Instructions: Figure 6-46 displays a dialog box method with ten errors. Find the lines of code that contain errors and write the corrected version in the spaces provided.

1. _____

2. _____

3. _____

4. _____

Test Your Knowledge

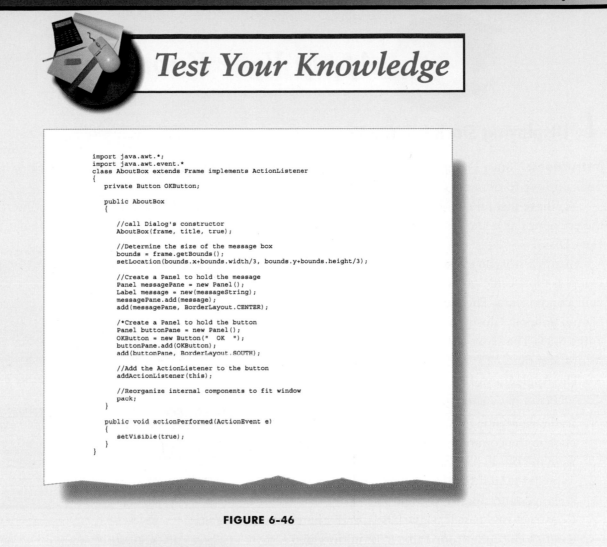

```
import java.awt.*;
import java.awt.event.*;
class AboutBox extends Frame implements ActionListener
{
    private Button OKButton;

    public AboutBox
    {

        //call Dialog's constructor
        AboutBox(frame, title, true);

        //Determine the size of the message box
        bounds = frame.getBounds();
        setLocation(bounds.x+bounds.width/3, bounds.y+bounds.height/3);

        //Create a Panel to hold the message
        Panel messagePane = new Panel();
        Label message = new(messageString);
        messagePane.add(message);
        add(messagePane, BorderLayout.CENTER);

        /*Create a Panel to hold the button
        Panel buttonPane = new Panel();
        OKButton = new Button("  OK  ");
        buttonPane.add(OKButton);
        add(buttonPane, BorderLayout.SOUTH);

        //Add the ActionListener to the button
        addActionListener(this);

        //Reorganize internal components to fit window
        pack;
    }

    public void actionPerformed(ActionEvent e)
    {
        setVisible(true);
    }
}
```

FIGURE 6-46

5. _____

6. _____

7. _____

8. _____

9. _____

10. _____

4 Understanding Layout Managers

Instructions: Figure 6-47 displays a Java program that creates a window interface used by Ye Olde Ice Cream Shoppe in order to fill ice cream orders. Draw two different storyboards to explain how the layout managers might have been subsetted in order to achieve the components' placement.

FIGURE 6-47

Apply Your Knowledge

1 Displaying Stock Information

Instructions: Start Notepad. Open the file, Apply6.java, from the Data Disk (see inside back cover for instructions on how to obtain a copy of the Data Disk).

You have just taken a job as an intern at a stock brokerage. Your first job is to create an interface to read in the previous day's "hottest" stocks that are stored sequentially in a binary file named, Apply6.dat (also on the Data Disk).

Create a storyboard similar to the application interface displayed in Figure 6-48. Decide on your colors, layout manager(s), and the names of your components. The data file contains the following fields: Stock Name, Volume, Closing Price, and Percentage Change as displayed in Table 6-15. The Next button should progress through the data, one record at a time.

The Apply6.java file contains comments to assist you in entering Java statements in the correct places within the program.

FIGURE 6-48

1. In the Apply6.java file, change the name of the class in the comments and class header to Stock. Save the file as "Stock.java" on your floppy disk.
2. Type `DataInputStream input;` to declare an input stream connection to the data file.
3. Construct two panels, eight labels, and a button by entering the code from Table 6-16 in the class block.
4. In the instance method, Stock, set the background color to blue and the foreground color to white so the interface will have white letters on a blue background. Set the next button's foreground color to black by typing `next.setForeground(Color.black);` so that the button will have black letters.
5. Type `setLayout(new BorderLayout());` to set the Frame's layout.
6. Type `dataFields.setLayout(new GridLayout(4,2));` to set the data panel layout.
7. Type `buttonArea.setLayout(new FlowLayout());` to set the button area's layout.
8. Add the components and the ActionListener to the interface by entering the methods from Table 6-17.

Table 6-15 Stock Data			
STOCK NAME	VOLUME	CLOSING PRICE	PERCENTAGE CHANGE
Cisco	89,147,500	59.31	+2
Intel	65,323,400	44.44	+.56
WrldCom	60,709,500	29	+2.94
DellCptr	40,835,400	33.44	+1
JDSUni	30,433,200	97.38	-.38
GlblCrss	26,358,300	31.88	+2
Microsft	25,092,700	61.31	+.69
ExodusC	24,999,200	49.13	-4.13
EricTel	23,418,800	15.94	-.13
ApldMat	22,579,400	63.88	...

Table 6-16

CODE

```
Panel dataFields = new Panel();
Panel buttonArea= new Panel();
Label stockLabel = new Label("Stock Name:");
Label stock= new Label("                    ");
Label volumeLabel = new Label("Volume:");
Label volume = new Label("                ");
Label priceLabel = new Label("Closing Price:");
Label price = new Label("              ");
Label changeLabel = new Label("Change:");
Label change = new Label("              ");
Button next = new Button("Next->");
```

Apply Your Knowledge

9. In the try block of the actionPerformed event, enter the code from Table 6-18 to read the String data into the appropriate labels.

10. When the end of the file is reached, a message should display and the fields should be cleared. Enter the code from Table 6-19 in the catch block of the actionPerformed event.

11. Save the file. Open an MS-DOS Prompt window, set the path, and then compile the program. If errors occur, correct them in the Notepad window, save the file, and then compile the program again.

12. Run the program. Click the Next button to look at all ten stocks. When you are done, click the Close button in the application's title bar.

13. Print a copy of the source code for your instructor.

Table 6-17

CODE

```
dataFields.add(stockLabel);
dataFields.add(stock);
dataFields.add(volumeLabel);
dataFields.add(volume);
dataFields.add(priceLabel);
dataFields.add(price);
dataFields.add(changeLabel);
dataFields.add(change);
buttonArea.add(next);
add(dataFields, BorderLayout.NORTH);
add(buttonArea, BorderLayout.SOUTH);
next.addActionListener(this);
```

Table 6-18

CODE

```
stock.setText(input.readUTF());
volume.setText(input.readUTF());
price.setText(input.readUTF());
change.setText(input.readUTF());
```

Table 6-19

CODE

```
stock.setText("End of File");
volume.setText("");
price.setText("");
change.setText("");
```

In the Lab

1 Entering Course Substitutions

Problem: The registrar at your college would like an interface to enter course information for transfer students. The created data file should be sequential in nature, with the student's name, ID number, the course number from the previous college, and the accepted course number at your college. The registrar then will give the data file to the transcript officer who will update the student's permanent files. Figure 6-49 displays the interface.

Instructions: Using the concepts you learned in Project 6, perform the following steps.

1. Start Notepad. Enter the program comments, then import the java.io.*, java.awt.*, and java.awt.event.* packages.
2. Create a class header named, Transfer, which extends Frame and implements ActionListener.
3. Save the file as "Transfer.java" on your floppy disk.
4. Type `DataOutputStream output;` to declare an output stream connection to the data file.
5. Construct two panels, four labels, four TextFields, and two buttons. Give them user-friendly names.
6. Create a main method that instantiates a Transfer window, and then sets its title, size, and visibility.
7. Create an instance method named, Transfer, that sets the frame to a BorderLayout, sets the first panel to a 4 x 2 GridLayout, and set the second panel to a FlowLayout.
8. Additionally, within the Transfer method, add the labels and TextFields to the first panel and the buttons to the second panel. Add the panels to North and South of the BorderLayout. Add the ActionListener to each button.
9. Type the code, `output = new DataOuputStream(new FileOutputStream("Transfer.dat"));` inside a try block.
10. Type the code, `System.exit(1);` inside the catch(IOException ex) block.
11. Lines 27 through 36 in Table 6-3 on page J 6.7 display the addWindowListener method. Enter those lines to construct the window listener at the end of the Transfer instance method.
12. Create an actionPerformed event. Within the block, type `String arg = e.getActionCommand();` to assign the button's argument, which is passed to the actionPerformed event when the user clicks a button.
13. Type `if (arg == "Submit" )` and then press the ENTER key. Type an opening brace to begin the if block.
14. Create a try block that contains output.writeUTF statements to send each of the four TextFields to the data file. For example, if your TextField is called student, the code `output.writeUTF(student.getText());` would send that data to the data file. After the four statements, close the try block.
15. Create a catch(IOException ex) block that calls the System.exit.
16. Call a method named clearFields and then close the if block.
17. Create an else block by typing the code from Table 6-20.
18. Close the actionPerformed event.
19. Create a clearFields method similar to the one in Table 6-11 on page J 6.24.

FIGURE 6-49

Transfer Course Substitutions

Name:

Student ID:

Transfer Course Number:

Local Course Number:

Submit   Exit

In the Lab

Table 6-20

CODE

```
else  //code to execute if the user clicks Exit
{
   try
   {
      output.close();
   }
   catch(IOException c)
   {
      System.exit(1);
   }
   System.exit(0);
}
```

20. Save the file, set the path, and then compile the program in an MS-DOS Prompt window. If errors occur, fix them in the Notepad window, save the file, and then compile the program again.
21. Run the program and enter sample data for five students with fictitious ID numbers and transfer courses.
22. Print the source code for your instructor.

2 Calling a Message Box

Problem: You would like to create an about box that would display your name, the date, and the name of your program to attach to one of your Java applications. The about box should display when the user clicks an About button.

Instructions: Perform the following steps to create the About class.

1. If you did not perform the steps in Project 6 to create the MessageBox class, enter and compile the method from Table 6-13 on page J 6.31. If you did create it, make sure you create this lab on the same disk and in the same directory as the compiled class.
2. Using Notepad, create a class named, About, that imports java.io.*, java.awt.*, and java.awt.event.*. The About class extends Frame and implements ActionListener. Use comments to describe the program.
3. Declare a variable, aboutBox, of the type MessageBox.
4. Construct a button named, aboutButton.
5. Create a main method that instantiates a window named, About. Set the window's title to, Testing the About Button. Set the size of the window to 250 x 150 pixels, and set its visibility to true.
6. Create an instance method of About. Set the background to red and the layout to FlowLayout. Add the aboutButton and then add the ActionListener to the button.
7. Using the code from Project 6, add the window listener event to activate the application's Close button.

(continued)

In the Lab

Calling a Message Box *(continued)*

8. Create an actionPerformed event. Within the event type `aboutBox = new MessageBox(this, "About the Program", "Your Name, Date, and Purpose");` and fill in the information about you. Type `aboutBox.setVisible(true);` to make the message box visible.

9. Save the program on your floppy disk using "About.java" as the file name. In the MS-DOS Prompt window, set the path and then compile the program. If there are errors, fix them in the Notepad window, and then compile again. Run the program and test your buttons. As an extra credit project, set the color of the background of the application window to be a different color than the message box window.

10. Print a copy of the About application code, as well as the code for the MessageBox class.

3 Adding a Menu to a Program

Problem: Your Java professor has asked you to try adding a menu to an application program. You decide to open the source code to a file you have created previously and create a menu that would display an About box and exit the program.

Instructions: Make a backup copy of the program you plan to change. To implement the About box, you also need to have created the MessageBox method in Project 6. Consult your instructor for the best way to complete this lab.

1. Start Notepad. Open an application that you have successfully created and compiled in the past, which extends Frame and implements the ActionListener. The Calculator and Flora programs are good examples.

2. In the declaration section at the beginning of your class, type `MessageBox aboutBox;` to declare a variable of the type, MessageBox.

3. In the instance method that creates your window frame, type the code from Table 6-21 to create an instance from Java's **MenuBar class**, declare two items on the menu from the **Menu class**, and declare two submenu items from Java's **MenuItem** class. Comments have been added to each line to help you understand the purpose.

Table 6-21

CODE

```
MenuBar mnuBar = new MenuBar();  //creates an instance of the menu bar
Menu mnuFile, mnuAbout; //declares two menu items in the menu bar
MenuItem mnuFileExit, mnuAboutProgrammer; //declares two submenu items
setMenuBar(mnuBar); //method to set the Menu bar
    mnuFile = new Menu("File", true); //Construct first menu item
        mnuBar.add(mnuFile); //Add menu item to menu bar
        mnuFileExit = new MenuItem("Exit"); //Construct submenu item
        mnuFile.add(mnuFileExit);  //Add submenu item to menu
    mnuAbout  = new Menu("About", true);//Construct second menu item
        mnuBar.add(mnuAbout); //Add menu item to menu bar
        mnuAboutProgrammer = new MenuItem("About the Programmer");//Create submenu item
        mnuAbout.add(mnuAboutProgrammer); //Add submenu item to menu
```

In the Lab

4. Next, add the ActionListener to the menu options by entering the code from Table 6-22. The **setActionCommand** method will allow you to test the click argument in the actionPerformed event.

5. At the beginning of your actionPerformed event, after the first code statement in the block that usually declares a String args to receive the action of the click, enter the code from Table 6-23. Enter your name where appropriate.

6. At the end of the actionPerformed event, insert a closing brace for the else block.

7. Save the program and compile it. Run the program and test your menu options.

8. Print a copy of your source code, or attach the Java class to an e-mail and send it to your instructor.

Table 6-22

CODE

```
mnuFile.addActionListener(this);
mnuAbout.addActionListener(this);
mnuFileExit.addActionListener(this);
mnuAboutProgrammer.addActionListener(this);
mnuFileExit.setActionCommand("Exit");
mnuAboutProgrammer.setActionCommand("About");
```

Table 6-23

CODE

```
if(arg == "Exit")
{
    System.exit(0);
}
if(arg == "About")
{
    aboutBox = new MessageBox(this, "About the Programmer", "Your Name");
    aboutBox.setVisible(true);
}
else
{
```

Cases and Places

The difficulty of these case studies varies:
▶ are the least difficult; ▶▶ are more difficult; and ▶▶▶ are the most difficult.

1 ▶ Your friend is majoring in meteorology. As a class project, she has been recording manually the daily rainfall amounts from the last 30 days. She now would like to generate an electronic data file to store the information. Create a Java application with a for loop that runs from 1 to 30. Components should include an input TextField, a submit button, and appropriate prompts. Store the data file with the name Rainfall.dat on your floppy disk.

2 ▶ Bowery Heating and Cooling wants an interface that will allow its dispatcher to enter service calls for the day and store them in a data file on a floppy disk. Fields should include time of call, customer name, address, phone, and description of the problem. Store the generated data file with the name, Dispatch.dat on your floppy disk. Enter seven sample customers and then open the data file with Notepad. Print its contents.

3 ▶ Add an About message box to any applet that you have created in the past, perhaps from a previous project. Include your name, the creation date, and your title (or Student Extraordinaire) in the message. Add a button or menu event to display the About message box.

4 ▶▶ Add a message box to any frame-based application that you have created in this project or the previous project. The message box should display the words, Are you sure you want to quit?, in its message. The box should display when the user clicks the Close button on the title bar. Change the caption of the internal button to say, Yes. Place the MessageBox call statement before the System.exit command. Consider adding a second button to the MessageBox class with the caption, No. Add functionality to both buttons. Save, compile, and execute your program. Print a copy of the source code.

5 ▶▶ Create an interface that will let you enter a description of your Java lab assignments and the grades you receive, storing them in a file on your floppy disk. Create a submit button to submit each grade, and a done button to close the file. When you click the done button, the submit button should disappear and a retrieve button should take its place. Add functionality to each button. Print a copy of the source code.

6 ▶▶▶ Assume that employee W-2 information has been stored in a sequential access file. Obtain a copy of a sample W-2 form from your local post office and then create an applet on the screen that looks like the form. Name each field appropriately and write the code to retrieve the information and fill in the form. Print a copy of the source code.

Java Programming

PROJECT 7

Using the JBuilder IDE

OBJECTIVES

You will have mastered the material in this project when you can:

- List the advantages and disadvantages of using an IDE
- Start the JBuilder software and set paths
- Define JBuilder's use of the term project and the .jpr extension
- Set Project Properties for a new project
- Identify parts of the JBuilder screen
- Identify the purpose of each pane in the AppBrowser
- Add source code to a project
- Use JBuilder's editing tools
- Differentiate between the Make, Rebuild, and Run commands
- List reasons to create a JAR file
- Create an applet project using JBuilder
- Use JBuilder's Help System

Gaze the Night Sky
Space Enthusiasts Track Satellites from Home

D id you ever gaze into the night sky and see a small white light moving overhead? Could it have been a falling star? The International Space Station? A UFO? More than 8,000 artificial objects are orbiting Earth right now, including 2,500 operative and inoperative satellites, items that have escaped from manned spacecraft, hatch covers, and rocket bodies.

Each of the operative satellites serves a specific purpose. Twenty-four of the satellites are part of the Global Positioning System (GPS) launched by the U.S. Department of Defense for identifying earth locations. Drivers hikers, boaters, and pilots use this GPS to specify their exact positions on the planet. National Oceanic and Atmospheric Administration (NOAA)

satellites follow weather patterns. Others are used for communication, such as transmitting cellular telephone conversations and sending television and radio signals. Search satellites help save lives by watching for distress beacons from airplanes, boats, and ground personnel. NASA researchers use some satellites to increase their knowledge of Earth and space.

To discover which satellites will be passing over your house and the locations of the Hubble Space Telescope, the International Space Station, and the Space Shuttle during missions, NASA has developed several spacecraft trackers that use Java. In Java Project 7, you will use an Integrated Development Environment (IDE) that provides editing, wizard, and project management tools for Java programmers. Likewise, software developers in the Mission Operations Laboratory at the Marshall Space Flight Center in Huntsville, Alabama, have used Java to develop the sophisticated J-Pass program that allows space enthusiasts to track more than 500 satellites.

J-Track 3D is the latest J-Pass version; as the name implies, it plots the position of these satellites in three dimensions over a world map. Users can zoom in and out on the satellites and rotate them to see different perspectives. They also can print custom maps of the specific times the satellites will be above their hometowns.

J-Track works by using orbit propagation, in which it takes the satellite's current location and direction, called a vector, and then calculates where the object should be in the future if no direction changes occur. The *Space Shuttle* has its own propulsion capability, so it changes its vectors often. The Java applet requires access to NASA's network to download the satellite and weather information.

The satellite tracking system is part of NASA's Liftoff to Space Exploration program. Its Web site, liftoff.msfc.nasa.gov, contains many useful science tools, including descriptions of spacecraft, stories of astronauts, details of the universe, including space, the solar system, stars, and galaxies, and fundamentals of science and engineering. The site uses another Java applet, DigitalClock, to synchronize the display with the exact countdown time until the next *Space Shuttle* launch.

The International Space Station brings 16 nations together in space with the goal of improving life on Earth. By using Java applets to view this satellite and hundreds of others in the sky and on your monitor, you too can participate in this new era of space exploration.

Java Programming

Using the JBuilder IDE

PROJECT

7

CASE PERSPECTIVE

Ellison Web, Incorporated (EWI) recently purchased the JBuilder Integrated Development Environment (IDE) software to assist their programmers with writing Java programs. Up until now, the programmers had written Java code using Notepad, and then compiled and executed it from the MS-DOS Prompt window in console mode.

EWI has included the Calculator program you created for them in various client packages. They now have hired you as an intern to create more Java programs. EWI chose JBuilder because it uses pure Java code and offers some editing, wizard, and project management tools not available with the JDK.

You decide to set up a JBuilder project and then bring in the code from the Calculator program so you can see how JBuilder works. You want to compare the creating, saving, compiling, and executing of Java programs to that of Notepad and the console mode.

Introduction

An **Integrated Development Environment** (**IDE**) is a tool used to increase productivity while programming in a computer language. Many languages are supported by IDEs that provide a visual development tool to assist with coding, syntax, compilation, and execution.

Selecting an Integrated Development Environment for Java is not an easy task. Many IDEs are on the market. While Java is the language of choice for many applications, the available tools for use with Java still are maturing and developing. Some of the major IDEs on the market now include VisualAge for Java, J++, Visual Café, and JBuilder/JDeveloper.

IDE software has some advantages over the JDK. Most IDEs present a graphical user interface, which is more user-friendly than Notepad. IDEs usually contain buttons, menus, navigation controls, and graphics; they typically provide more debugging assistance than what is available in the JDK compiler. Additionally, IDEs are distributed on CD-ROM, which avoids the extremely long download time associated with the JDK. The biggest disadvantage of an IDE is its cost; the Java download on the Sun Web site, on the other hand, is free. Table 7-1 displays some advantages and disadvantages of using IDEs.

No single Java IDE is able to meet all the needs of Java programmers at all of the stages of their skill development. When programmers are learning Java for the first time — or any language for that matter — they need to be able to concentrate on the language itself, and most IDEs actually hide some aspect of the language as part of their effort to make program development easier. When programmers gain more experience, they appreciate having some of the details looked after by an IDE, making them more productive than when they use a command-line oriented compiler. When a developer takes on a large collaborative project, or one that has very specialized class requirements, a more specialized IDE is appropriate, especially if it is from the vendor whose other hardware and software already is in use.

Some IDEs also add their own packages or code statements to make their programs unique or more user-friendly. Some software applications, such as Microsoft's J++, have changed the Java language within their IDE. For example, Visual J++ builds screens from widgets (on-screen controls, like buttons and check boxes) drawn from a library of pre-built Java objects called the **Windows Foundation Classes** (**WFC**). WFC is a Microsoft product that makes direct use of the underlying facilities of the Windows operating system. It therefore cannot be used for cross-platform Java development — the kind of development promoted by Sun. Sun Microsystems' attempt to keep Java a pure language, with cross-platform capabilities, has led Sun to sue companies who attempt to change Java technologies and pass them on to their own customers.

Borland's JBuilder 3, University Edition, which comes packaged with this book, supports pure Java with no extra packages or classes. The JDK is included as part of JBuilder's installation (see Appendix A). JBuilder uses visual tools, menus, toolbars, and Help screens to assist programmers in writing Java code. The interface's **AppBrowser** runs in a window similar to a Web browser. It provides support for the latest Java standards, including Java 2, JavaBeans, Java 2 JFC/Swing, Graphics 2D, Serialization, Collections, Java Archive file formats (JARs), and Java Native Interface (JNI), among others. JBuilder 3 includes a visual component palette, fully integrated Application Browser, project manager, visual designers, and numerous wizards.

Table 7-1	Advantages and Disadvantages of Using an IDE
ADVANTAGES	**DISADVANTAGES**
No download time	Large size of installed software
Help files	Some are very expensive
Large installed base of developers	Most IDEs are a version behind Sun
Many IDEs have online support	It takes more time to learn the interface
Options to use Sun Java 2 JDK	Some IDEs are slower than the JDK
Visual debugger	Installation is sometimes tedious
Can produce native PC executables	Online support is not as extensive as support from Sun
Capable of the full range of Java entities	

Project Seven — Using the JBuilder IDE

JBuilder is an application software. **Application software**, as opposed to system software, increases productivity and provides output to the user. JBuilder is a Windows-based application and, when installed, becomes a program on the Programs submenu.

After opening the application, you will set the paths and then use JBuilder's Project Wizard to set a new project's properties. You will add the code from the Calculator program to your new project. If you did not complete the Calculator program in Project 5, see your instructor for a copy, or use another Java source code file you have created.

Starting JBuilder and Setting the Paths

Just as you set the path and logged onto the floppy drive in the MS-DOS Prompt window in console mode, so must you set the path for the Source and Output of JBuilder's Java files.

More About

Installing JBuilder 3

If you want to install JBuilder 3 over an existing version of JBuilder, be sure to uninstall the previous version of JBuilder. On the Start button menu, point to Settings, and then click Control Panel. Double-click Add/Remove Programs and then click JBuilder 3. Manually delete the jbuilder2\bin and the jbuilder2\lib directories that may remain after uninstalling to avoid any conflicts with this version of JBuilder.

Perform the following steps to start JBuilder and set the paths.

 Steps | ## To Start JBuilder and Set the Paths

1 **Click the Start button on the taskbar. Point to Programs, point to Borland JBuilder 3 University, and then point to JBuilder 3.**

The Borland JBuilder 3 University submenu displays (Figure 7-1). Your menus may differ.

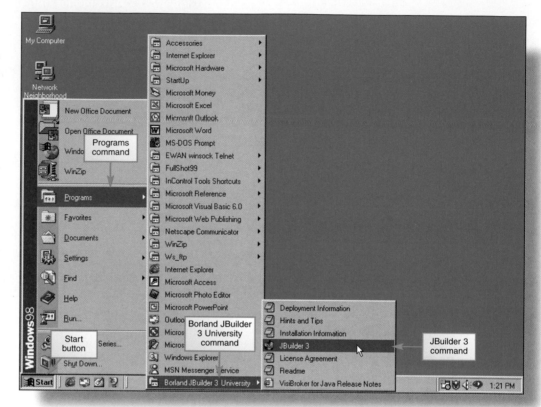

FIGURE 7-1

2 **Click JBuilder 3. When you first start JBuilder, the Welcome Project (welcome.jpr) opens, with its HTML file displayed in Web format. If the Welcome Project does not display, click Welcome Project (Sample) on the Help menu.**

The Welcome to JBuilder! window displays (Figure 7-2). Scroll down and read the presented information.

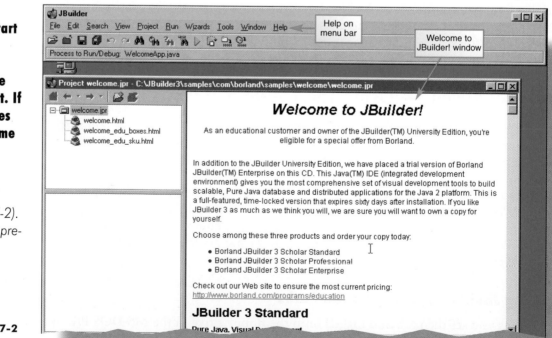

FIGURE 7-2

3 **Click Project on the menu bar and then point to Default Properties.**

The Project menu displays (Figure 7-3).

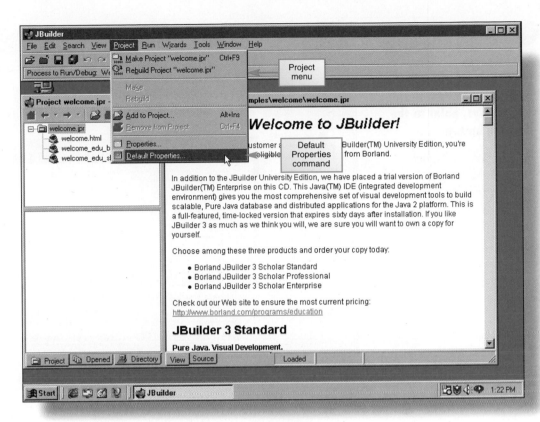

FIGURE 7-3

4 **Click Default Properties. When the Default Project Properties dialog box displays, point to the button to the right of the Source text box.**

The Default Project Properties dialog box displays (Figure 7-4). The button displays an ellipsis.

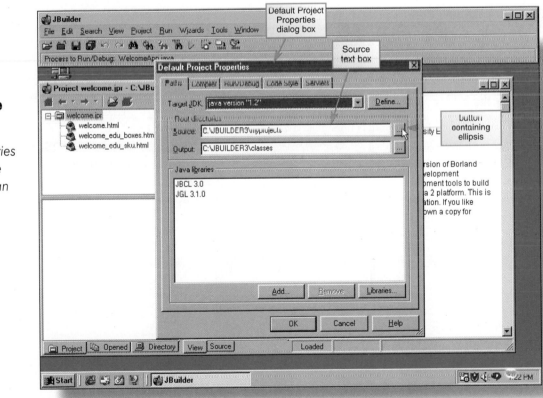

FIGURE 7-4

5 Click the button located to the right of the Source text box. When the Edit Default Project Source Path dialog box displays, point to the Add Path button.

The Edit Default Project Source Path dialog box displays the path JBuilder will take to look for your Java source code files (Figure 7-5).

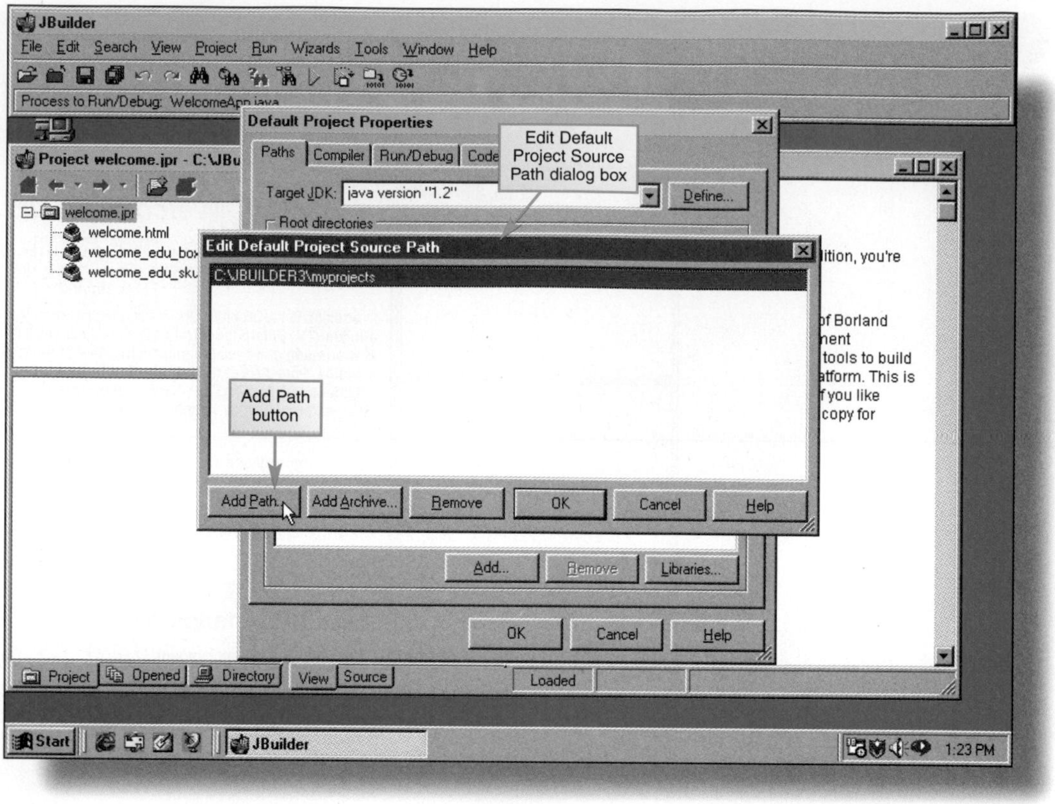

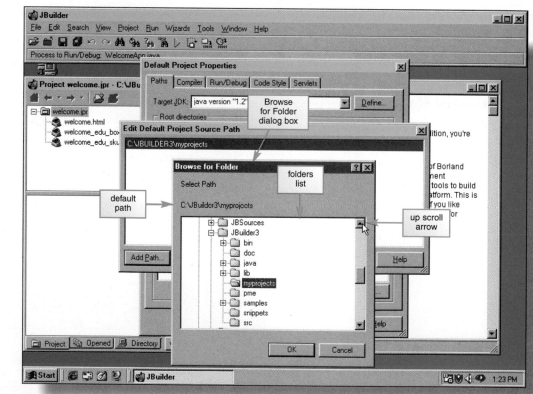

FIGURE 7-5

6 Click the Add Path button. When the Browse for Folder dialog box displays, point to the up scroll arrow in the list displaying the folder names.

The Browse for Folder dialog box displays (Figure 7-6). The default path is c:\JBuilder3\myprojects. Depending on your installation, your path may differ.

FIGURE 7-6

7 If necessary, click the up scroll arrow and then click 3½ Floppy (A:) in the list. Point to the OK button.

You will use your floppy disk to store your Java source code and classes (Figure 7-7).

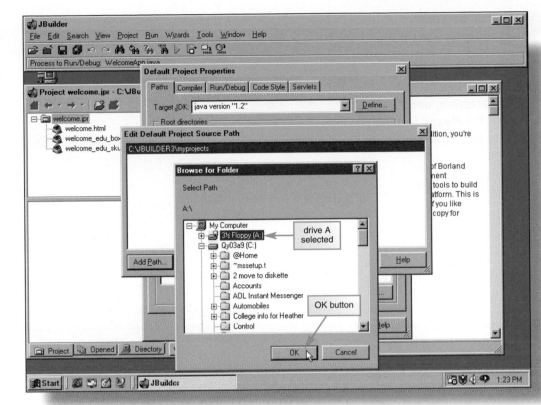

FIGURE 7-7

8 Click the OK button. When the Edit Default Prompt Source Path dialog box again is visible, click its OK button. When the Default Project Properties dialog box again is visible, point to the button containing the ellipses to the right of the Output text box.

You now will edit the path to contain the .class files created by JBuilder (Figure 7-8).

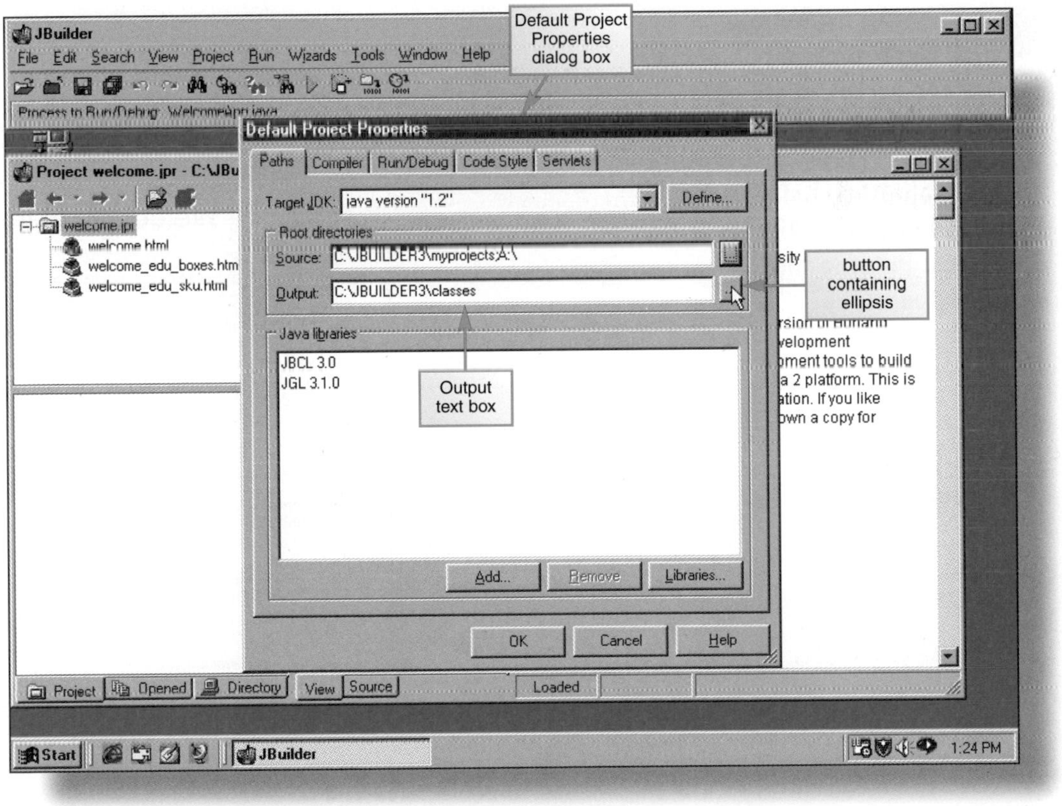

FIGURE 7-8

9 Click the button located to the right of the Output text box. When the Browse for Folder dialog box displays, scroll if necessary, and then click 3½ Floppy (A:) in the folder list. Point to the OK button.

The floppy drive is selected (Figure 7-9).

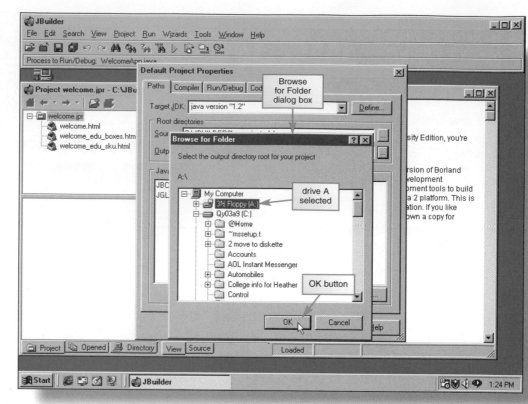

FIGURE 7-9

10 Click the OK button. If the Browse for Folders dialog box again displays, click its OK button. When the Default Project Properties dialog box again displays, click its OK button. Point to the Close button in the Welcome to JBuilder! Window.

11 Click the Close button.

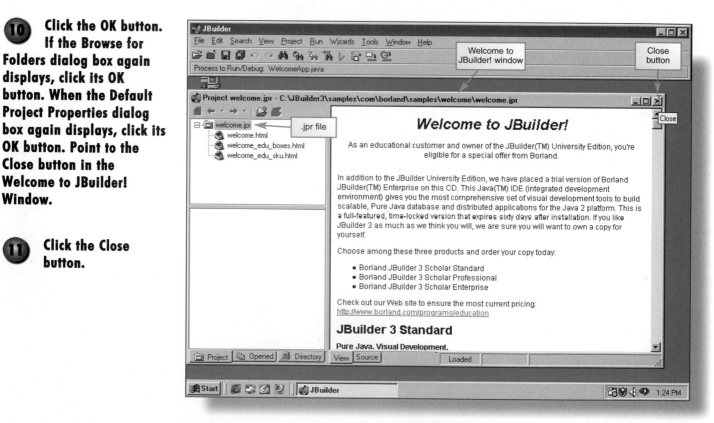

FIGURE 7-10

JBuilder provides several interactive tutorials to help you learn how to navigate and use the software. On JBuilder's Help menu, you can click Help Topics to view the JBuilder documentation.

Setting Up a New Project

JBuilder provides a Project Wizard to assist you in setting up a new project. A **project** is a container of files. Generally, a project is used to hold the files that make up a JBuilder application or applet. These files can be in any directory. Details about each JBuilder project are stored in a file with the extension **.jpr**. The .jpr file contains a list of all the files in the project, plus the project properties. JBuilder uses this information when you load, save, or build a project. You do not edit a .jpr file directly; it is modified whenever you use the JBuilder development environment to add files, remove files, or set project properties. The .jpr file displays in the upper-left corner of the AppBrowser window (Figure 7-10). Listed below it are all the files in the project.

While you can include any type of file in a JBuilder project, Table 7-2 displays the types of files that JBuilder automatically recognizes.

Table 7-2 Project Files and Descriptions

FILE EXTENSION	FILE DESCRIPTION
.jpr	JBuilder project file
.java	Java source file
.class	Compiled class file, one for each class in a .java source file
.gif	Graphics file
.jpg	Graphics file
.bmp	Graphics file
.au	Sound file
.wav	Sound file
.html	HTML document
.txt	Text file
.dat	Data file
.bat	Batch file

Setting Project Properties

Project properties are fields of information about your Java program, including the name of the file, the title of the project, the author, the company, and a description. Perform the following steps to set some initial project properties and create the project file in a folder on your floppy disk.

 Steps **To Set Project Properties for a New Project**

① Click File on the menu bar and then point to New Project.

The File menu displays (Figure 7-11).

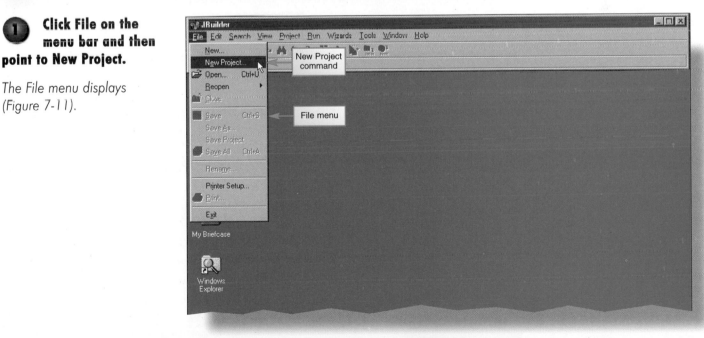

FIGURE 7-11

Click New Project. When the Project Wizard: Step 1 of 1 dialog box displays, double-click the File text box.

The File text box displays selected (Figure 7-12).

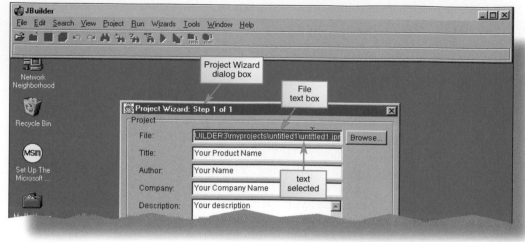

FIGURE 7-12

3 **Type** `A:\Project7\App\Calculator.jpr` **in the File text box.**

The new project file (.jpr) will be created in a folder named, App, within a folder named Project7 (Figure 7-13).

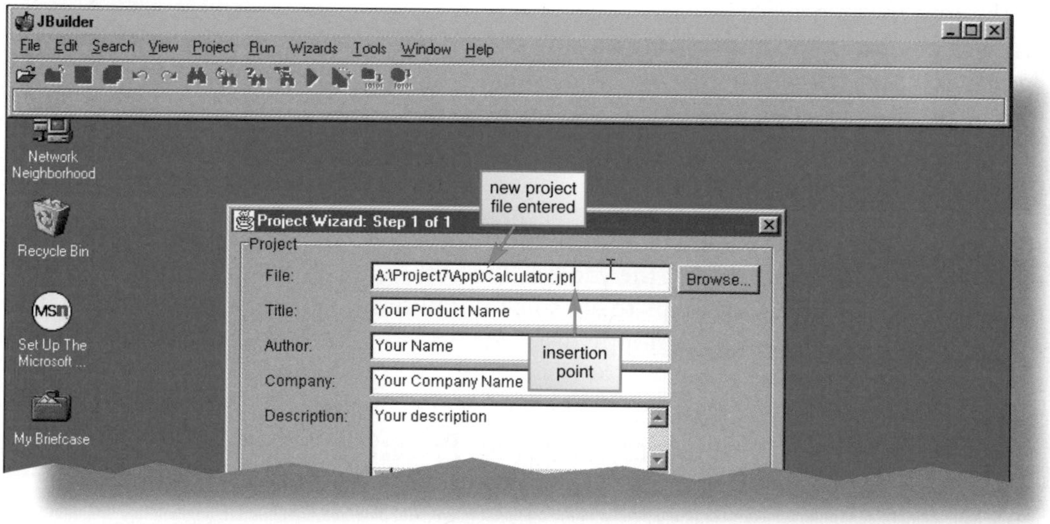

FIGURE 7-13

4 **Select each of the remaining text boxes in the Project Wizard: Step 1 of 1 dialog box one at a time. Enter the information as displayed in Figure 7-14, using your name in the Author text box. When you have completed all fields, point to the Finish button.**

The new project property fields display (Figure 7-14).

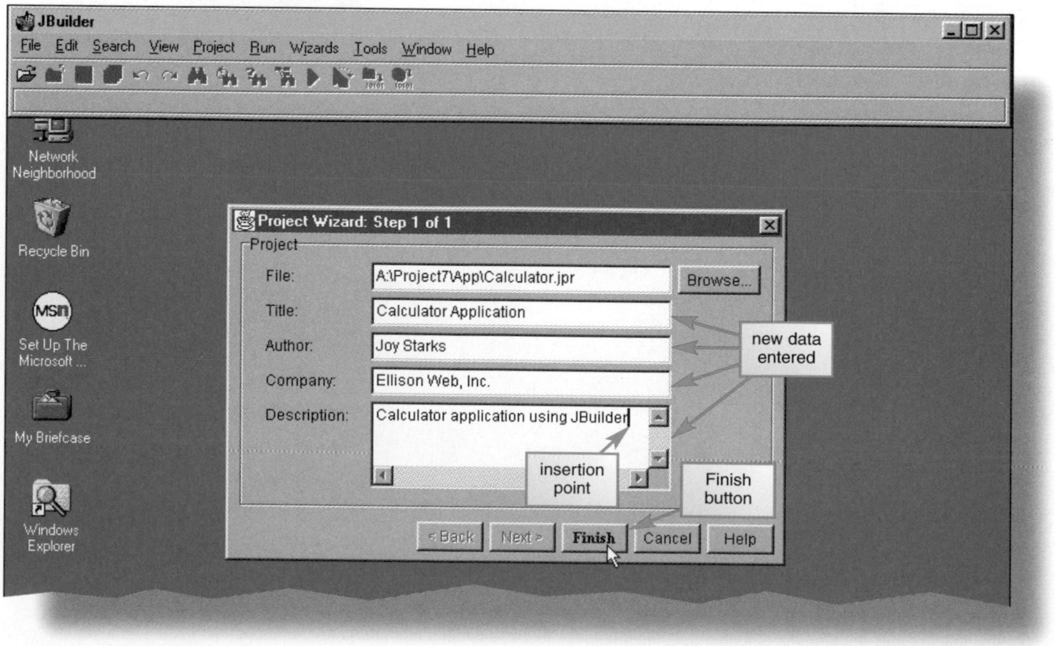

FIGURE 7-14

5 Click the Finish button.

The Calculator.jpr project file displays in the Navigation Pane (Figure 7-15). Project Notes display in the Content Pane.

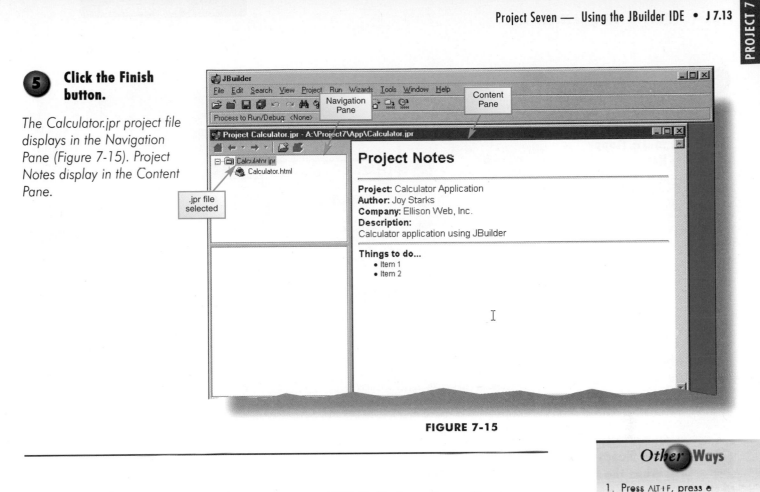

FIGURE 7-15

JBuilder creates the Project Notes page as an HTML file in every application, which is why you see one file already in the project's Navigation Pane (Figure 7-15).

Adding Source Code to an Existing Project

Perform the following steps to add source code to the project.

Steps To Add Source Code

1 Click Project on the menu bar and then point to Add to Project.

The Project menu displays (Figure 7-16). You will add the Calculator source code to the existing project.

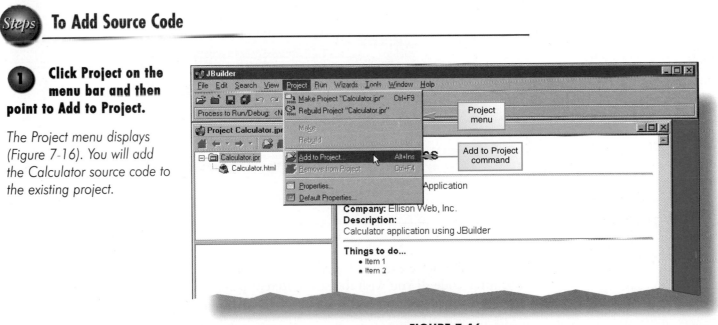

FIGURE 7-16

2 Click Add to Project. When the Open dialog box displays, click the Look in box arrow and then point to 3½ Floppy (A:) in the list.

Your list of locations and folders may differ (Figure 7-17).

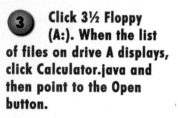

FIGURE 7-17

3 Click 3½ Floppy (A:). When the list of files on drive A displays, click Calculator.java and then point to the Open button.

The list of folders and files on the floppy disk in drive A displays (Figure 7-18). Your list may differ.

4 Click the Open button.

The Calculator source code displays as shown in Figure 7-19.

FIGURE 7-18

Other Ways

1. Click Add to Project button in Navigation Pane toolbar
2. Press ALT+INSERT

If you did not create the Calculator program, see your instructor for a copy of the source code. If you wish to use a different program, you still can perform the steps in this project, but your screens will differ.

The JBuilder Interface

Figure 7-19 displays the JBuilder interface for the Calculator program you just opened. At the top of the interface are a **menu bar**, **toolbar**, and **status bar**. These toolbars can be turned on and off from the View menu. Below the toolbars is the **AppBrowser window**, which includes the Navigation Pane (upper-left corner), the Structure Pane (lower-left corner), and the Content Pane (right side of the AppBrowser). If you want to use more than one program at a time, you may open multiple AppBrowsers.

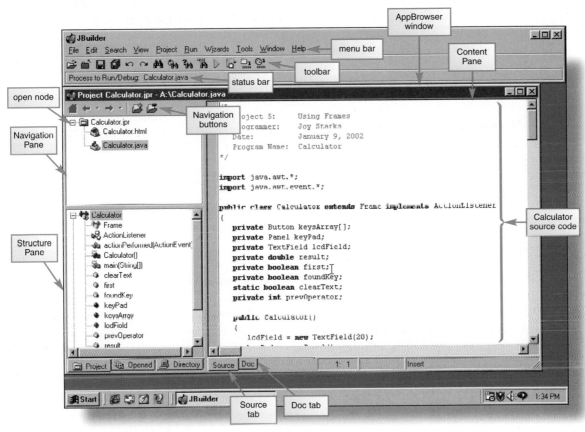

FIGURE 7-19

The Navigation Pane

The **Navigation Pane** is used to select the file you wish to view. In Figure 7-19, the name of the file, Calculator.java, is selected. The Navigation Pane shows different types of information, depending on the AppBrowser mode. You perform most project management tasks in the Navigation Pane, such as switching between the applet code and the associated HTML file, handling file dependencies, and setting build options. The directory tree displayed in the pane visually represents the application being built and provides easy access to all dependent files.

Navigation buttons display at the top of the Navigation Pane, with options to move back and forth, as well as to add and remove projects. The project file displays an **open node** with a minus symbol in the Navigation Pane hierarchy. When the .jpr file is selected, the Project Notes display. When a .java file is selected, the source code displays in the Content Pane.

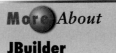

The Content Pane

The **Content Pane** displays the detailed content of the file selected in the Navigation Pane. In Figure 7-19 on the previous page, the Content Pane displays Java source code for the Calculator program. The type of data differs, however, depending on which tab you have selected at the bottom of the Content Pane.

With the **Source tab** selected in a .java file, JBuilder presents an editing window with tools such as searching, color-coding of commands, ScreenTips, AutoComplete tips, and the capability of jumping to a specific line number. When you select the **Doc tab**, you see the corresponding reference documentation for the selected class or file, if documentation exists.

If you select an .html file in the Navigation Pane, the Content Pane displays two tabs: View and Source. A **Source tab** selects an editor that lets you see and edit the file as raw HTML source code. A **View tab** lets you see the rendered HTML file, as you would see it in a Web browser.

If you select a .gif, .jpg, or .bmp image file in the Navigation Pane, an image viewer identified by an added View tab displays.

The Structure Pane

The **Structure Pane**, located in the lower-left of the AppBrowser, performs some interesting navigation and assistance functions. A structural analysis of the selected file is displayed as a hierarchical tree — a table of contents for the file. You can use the Structure Pane as a quick navigation tool to the various structural elements in the file.

Using the AppBrowser Editing Tools

Many times, when you have a compile error in Java, the javac compiler displays the location of the error with a line number in the MS-DOS Prompt window. Notepad does not support line numbers, which sometimes makes it difficult to find the error. On the Search menu, JBuilder has a **Go to Line Number** command; it also has the capability of printing line numbers in source code printouts.

Jumping to a specific occurrence of a command or class is a useful tool, especially when you are trying to match braces or double-check the class header. **Clicking** the component in the Structure Pane highlights the component code in the Content Pane. **Double-clicking** a component will open the Java package associated with that component so that you can view its hierarchy and associated methods.

JBuilder's AutoComplete tool, called **Code Insight**, uses context-sensitive pop-up windows within the editor, with lists of available classes, commands, and arguments. As you type a new command, a small box displays with appropriate choices for code completion, parameter lists, and tool tip expression evaluation. Code Insight will try to highlight illegal class references and statements that are not available within imported packages.

JBuilder also offers **color-coding** of keywords, comments, and data. Keywords are displayed in dark blue, comments in green, and data in light blue.

Perform the following steps to edit the Calculator program using the AppBrowser editing tools.

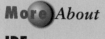

More About

IDEs

More IDEs are coming on the market very soon. In addition, the existing ones are changing and upgrading. For more information on the features of various IDEs, visit the Java Programming Web Page (www.scsite.com/java/more.htm) and then click IDEs.

More About

Code Insight

For performance reasons, if you have a machine slower than 166mhz, you may want to turn off all of the Code Insight Options. Click Tools on the menu bar, and then click Environment Options. Remove all the Code Insight check-boxes on the Code Insight tab. You still can use Code Insight, but it will be on demand by pressing the hotkeys CTRL+SPACEBAR, CTRL+SHIFT+SPACEBAR, or CTRL+ALT+SPACEBAR.

To Use JBuilder's Editing Tools

1 **To go directly to a specific line number, click Search on the menu bar, and then point to Go to Line Number.**

The Search menu displays (Figure 7-20). The Search menu offers search and replace features similar to a word processing program.

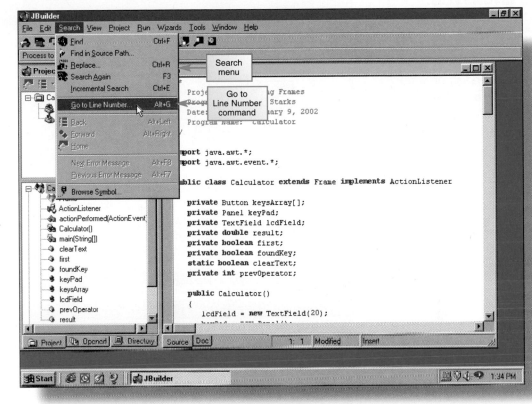

FIGURE 7-20

2 **Click Go to Line Number. When the Go To Line Number dialog box displays, type 73 in the Enter new line number box, and then point to the OK button.**

The Enter new line number dialog box displays (Figure 7-21). When clicked, the box arrow displays recently used line numbers.

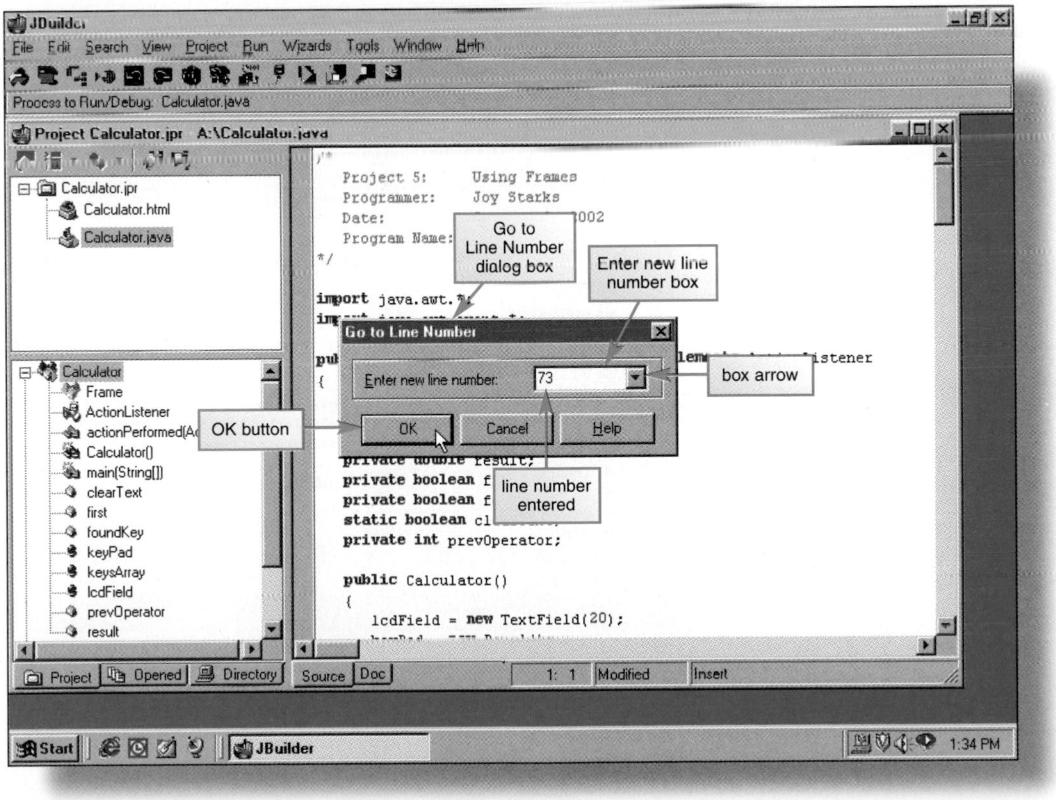

FIGURE 7-21

3 **Click the OK button. Point to Frame in the Structure Pane.**

JBuilder moves the insertion point to line 73 (Figure 7-22). Your specific line at 73 may differ depending on what Java program you are using. Notice that keywords are in dark blue.

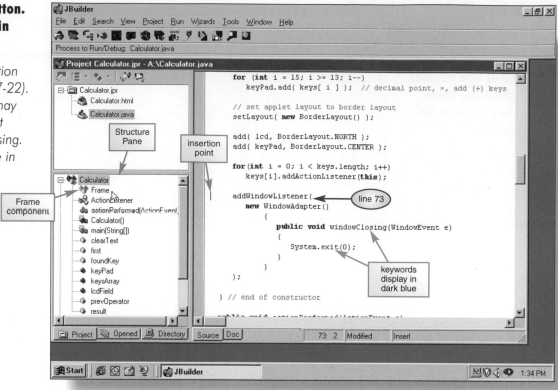

FIGURE 7-22

4 **Click Frame in the Structure Pane to see how the Structure Pane works.**

Notice that the Content Pane has highlighted the line of code in which Frame was used (Figure 7-23). The comments at the beginning of the program display in green.

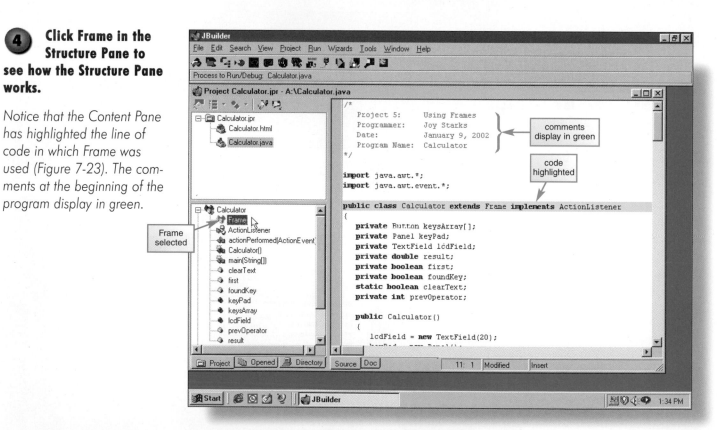

FIGURE 7-23

5 **Double-click Frame.**

The Frame package information displays in the Content Pane (Figure 7-24). Scroll down and read about Frame's properties and methods.

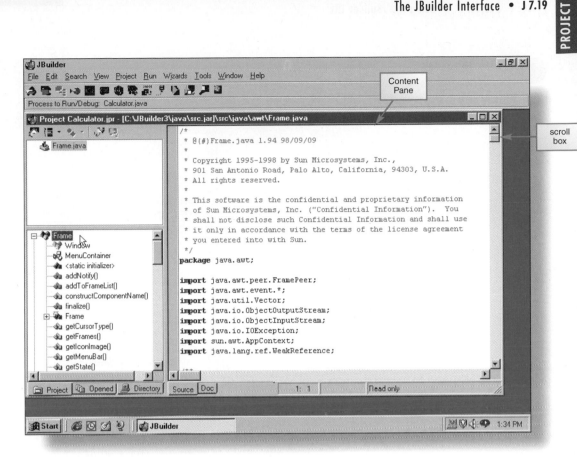

FIGURE 7-24

6 **To demonstrate Navigation buttons, point to the Back button in the Navigation Pane.**

The ScreenTip displays (Figure 7-25).

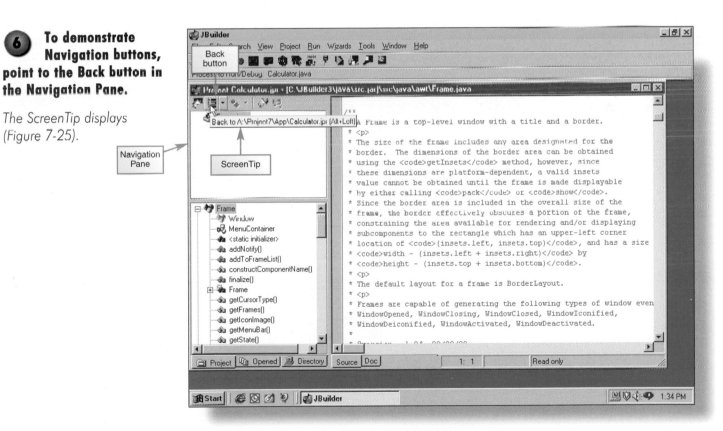

FIGURE 7-25

7 Click the Back button, and then click below the two import statements in line 10.

The Calculator source code again displays (Figure 7-26). Notice that data display in light blue.

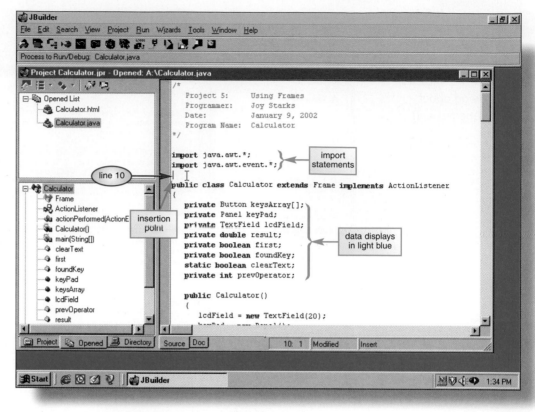

FIGURE 7-26

8 To demonstrate Code Insight, type `import java` on line 10. When the AutoComplete box displays, point to applet.

The AutoComplete box displays (Figure 7-27).

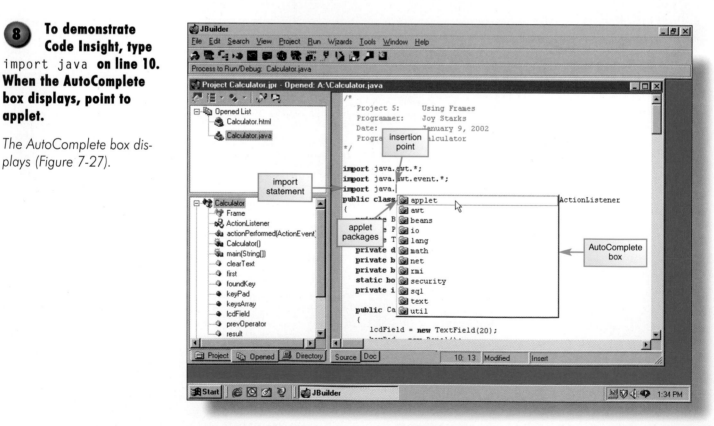

FIGURE 7-27

9 **Double-click applet.**

JBuilder completes the import package name (Figure 7-28).

10 **Select the import statement and press the DELETE key to remove it from the code.**

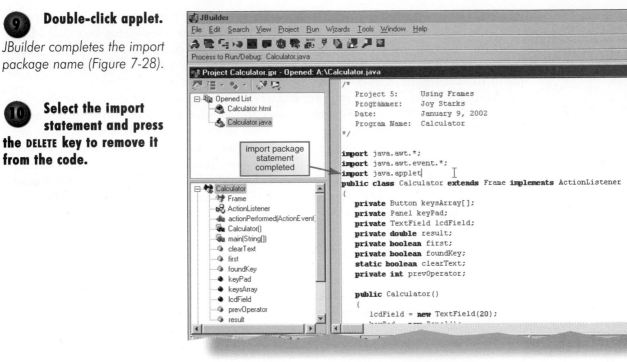

FIGURE 7-28

Other Ways

1. To go to a line number, press ALT+G

2. To display class information, right-click class name in Navigation Pane, on shortcut menu click Class Hierarchy

3. To go back in Navigation Pane, press ALT+LEFT ARROW

4. To go forward in Navigation Pane, press ALT+RIGHT ARROW

On the Tools menu, the Environment Options command displays a dialog box with additional editing tools. You can set tab usage, colors, fonts, and turn on cutting and pasting options.

Compiling a Program Using JBuilder

JBuilder uses the **Make** command to compile any Java source code files within the selected node that have outdated or nonexistent class files. An **outdated** class file is one that was not generated by the current version of the source code and, therefore, has an earlier internal date/time stamp than its associated source file. The Make command also compiles any imported files. The selected node can be a project, package, or .java file. Making a package or project compiles all the Java files within the package or project, including those within nested packages. The Make command is on JBuilder's Project menu, but you also can press CTRL+F9, click the Make button on the JBuilder toolbar, or click Make on the shortcut menu to access the Make command.

JBuilder's **Rebuild** command compiles all .java files within the selected node, regardless of whether or not their .class files are outdated. The Rebuild command also compiles the imported files, regardless of whether their .class files are outdated. Rebuild can be used to recompile Java source code, but it is not as fast as the Make command. The selected node can be a project, package, or .java file. Rebuilding a package or project includes all the .java files within the package or project, including those within nested packages and any other imported files. To Rebuild a node, select the node in the Navigation Pane, and then click Rebuild on the Project menu. Alternately, you may click the Rebuild button on the toolbar, or click Rebuild on the shortcut menu.

The **Run** command runs your application without debugging it, by using parameters specified in the Run/Debug sheet of the Project Properties dialog box. JBuilder opens a command prompt window and loads the javac compiler to run the program. As with the Make and Rebuild commands, you may use a button, menu, or shortcut menu to execute the Run command.

Saving a file is the most important part of creating an application or applet. Clicking **Save** on JBuilder's File menu saves the selected file to the same location with the same name. The **Save As** command is used so that you can change the name or location of the file. The necessary changes are made automatically inside the file to correspond with the new file name. In either case, JBuilder stores a date/time stamp that indicates the time of the last edit, not the time of the last save. The **Save Project** command saves the current project and all files in that project, such as the HTML file associated with an applet.

Making, Running, and Saving the Program

Even though you may have a current version of the Calculator class file on your floppy disk, you will use the Make command to practice compiling in JBuilder. You then will execute the program with the Run command. Both Make and Run are available as buttons on the JBuilder toolbar. You also will save the program again.

Perform the following steps to make, run, and save the program.

More About

Running Programs in JBuilder

If your project does not contain a .java file, JBuilder will set an .html file as the default. After adding a .java file that contains a main function, if you select that file in the Navigation Pane, JBuilder will run that file. Then, if you set that file as the default run file via the shortcut menu or on the Run tab of the Project Properties dialog, the setting will be saved with the project.

 Steps ## To Make, Run, and Save the Program

1 **With the Calculator.java file selected in the Navigation Pane, point to the Make button on the JBuilder toolbar.**

The ScreenTip displays the name of the selected file (Figure 7-29).

FIGURE 7-29

2 **Click the Make "Calculator.java" button.**

The program compiles (Figure 7-30). A message displays on the status bar. Any errors in the program will display in a window below the Content Pane.

FIGURE 7-30

3 **With the Calculator.java file still selected in the Navigation Pane, point to the Run button on the JBuilder toolbar.**

The ScreenTip displays the word, Run (F9); F9 means that as an alternative, you can press the F9 function key to run the program (Figure 7-31).

FIGURE 7-31

4 **Click the Run button.**

The program executes and the Calculator window displays (Figure 7-32). The size of your Calculator window may vary. Notice that JBuilder also opens an MS-DOS Prompt window and displays all buttons on the taskbar.

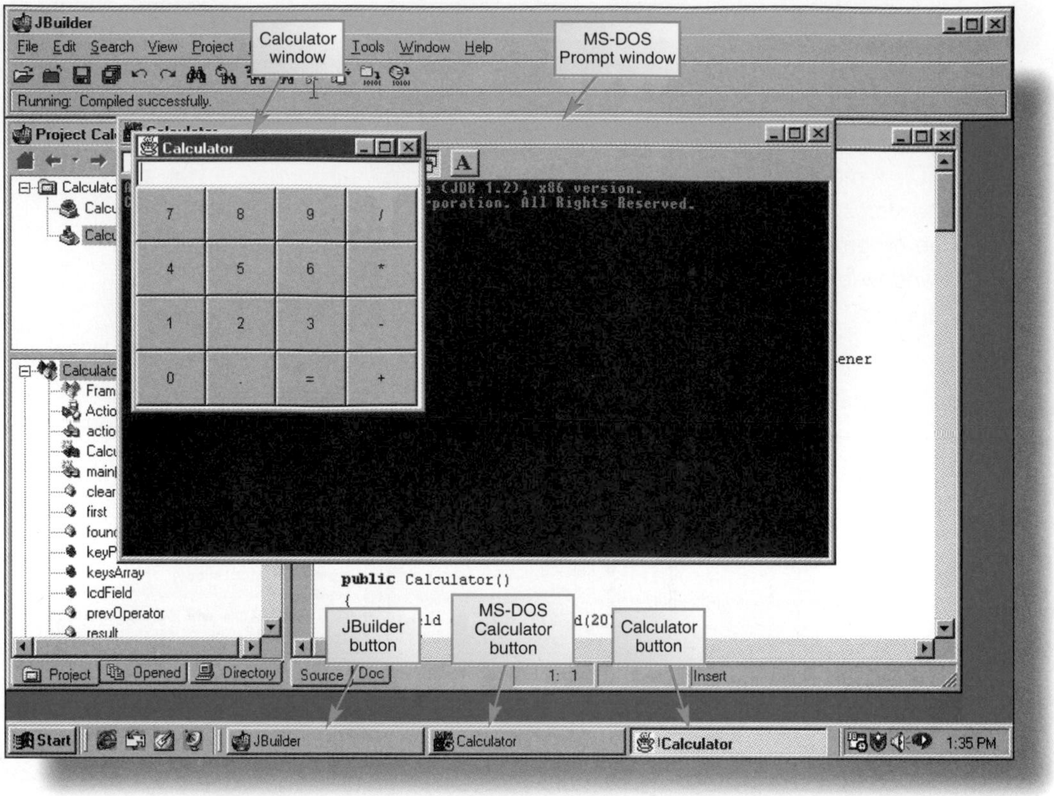

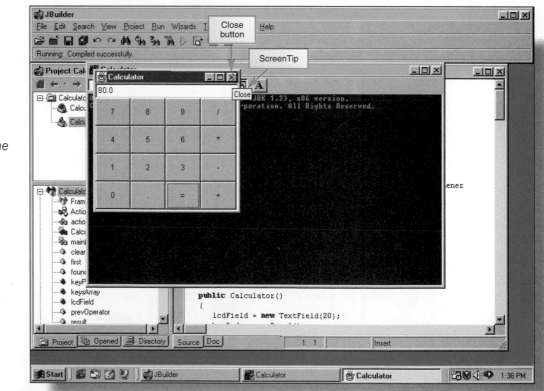

FIGURE 7-32

5 **Perform some test calculations using the buttons in the Calculator window. When you are finished, point to the Close button in the Calculator window.**

The ScreenTip displays for the Close button (Figure 7-33).

FIGURE 7-33

6 Click the Close button. Point to the Close button in the AppBrowser window.

JBuilder closes both the Calculator and MS-DOS Prompt windows and returns to the AppBrowser window (Figure 7-34).

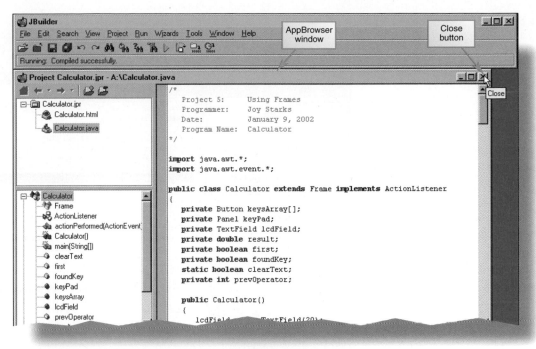

FIGURE 7-34

**7** Click the AppBrowser window's Close button. When the Save Modified Files dialog box displays, point to the OK button.

The list of modified files displays (Figure 7-35). Your list may differ if you made any changes to the source code.

8 Click the OK button.

The AppBrowser window closes. JBuilder still is open, however, and its toolbars still display.

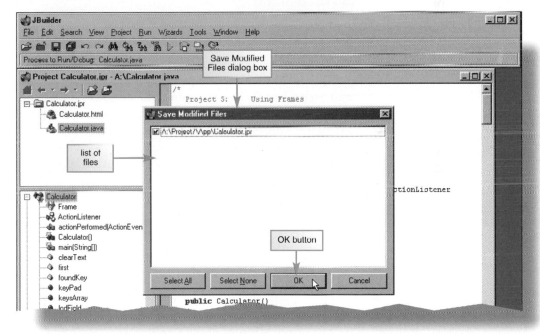

FIGURE 7-35

Saving a file does not necessarily cause the file to be recompiled. To force a recompile so the date/time stamp will show the last edit action, use the Rebuild command.

When you try to compile a program with errors, JBuilder opens a message window below the Content Pane (Figure 7-36 on the next page). The line numbers with errors are listed. In the Content Pane, JBuilder positions the insertion point at the beginning of the first line containing an error.

Other Ways

1. To compile, right-click source code file in Navigation Pane, click Make
2. To execute, right-click source code file in Navigation Pane, click Run
3. To execute, press F9
4. To save, press CTRL+S or click Save All on the File menu

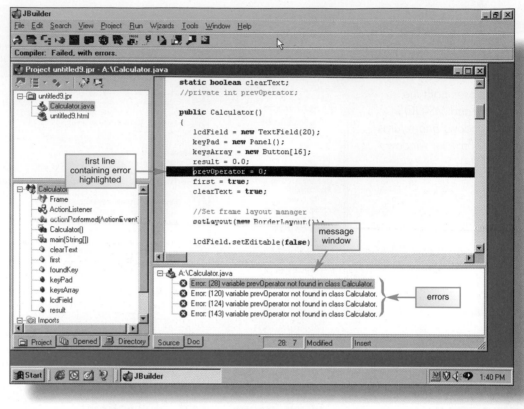

FIGURE 7-36

The Run menu contains other debugging options, including Debug, Trace Into, and Step Over. When you run your program under the control of the **Debugger**, it behaves as it normally would – your program creates windows, accepts user input, calculates values, and displays output; however, you can watch the behavior of your application in the windows it creates. By viewing the values of variables, the methods currently executing, and the program output, you can ensure that the area of code you are examining is performing as it should.

Using Applets in JBuilder

Creating source code for an applet in JBuilder is similar to creating an application. You can start from scratch, or add source code that you already have created. JBuilder supports both the source code and the associated HTML file as part of the package. If you already have created the HTML file, you can add it to the project. If you have not, JBuilder will help you create the file.

When you run an applet from within the IDE, the applet is displayed in the Applet Viewer, just as it does in console mode. The following steps add the Calculator Applet to the JBuilder interface.

More About

JBuilder Icons

JBuilder associates icons with each type of Java file, sometimes making it difficult to distinguish among .java, .jpr, and .class files. In the Windows operating system, the display of file types and extensions may be turned off. To display the file types for each icon, in a My Computer window, or Explorer window, click the Views button and then click Details. To display the dot (.) extensions on file names, click the View menu, click Folder Options, click the View tab, and then click to clear the Hide file extensions for known file types checkbox.

Steps **To Create an Applet Project in JBuilder**

1 Click File on the menu bar, and then click New Project. When the Project Wizard: Step 1 of 1 dialog box displays, enter the information shown in Figure 7-37, using your name in the Author text box. After completing all fields, point to the Finish button.

The project properties for the applet display (Figure 7-37).

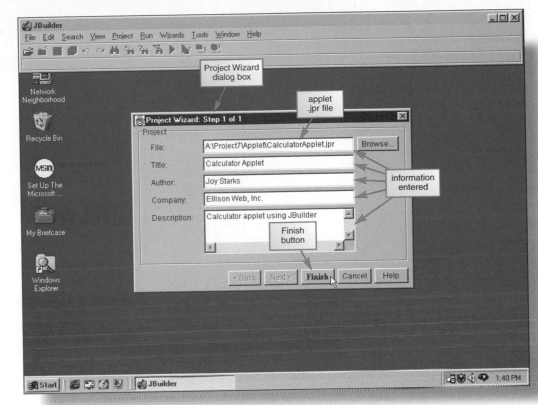

FIGURE 7-37

2 Click the Finish button. When the AppBrowser window opens, click Project on the menu bar and then point to Add to Project.

You will add the applet source code to this new project (Figure 7-38).

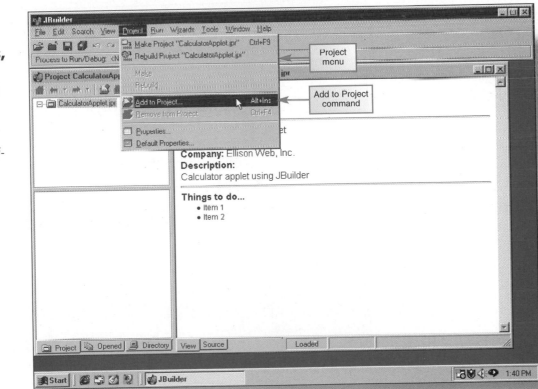

FIGURE 7-38

3 Click Add to Project. When the Open dialog box displays, click 3½ Floppy (A:) in the Look in list, and then click CalculatorApplet.html when the list of files on drive A displays.

CalculatorApplet.html is selected (Figure 7-39). Your list may vary.

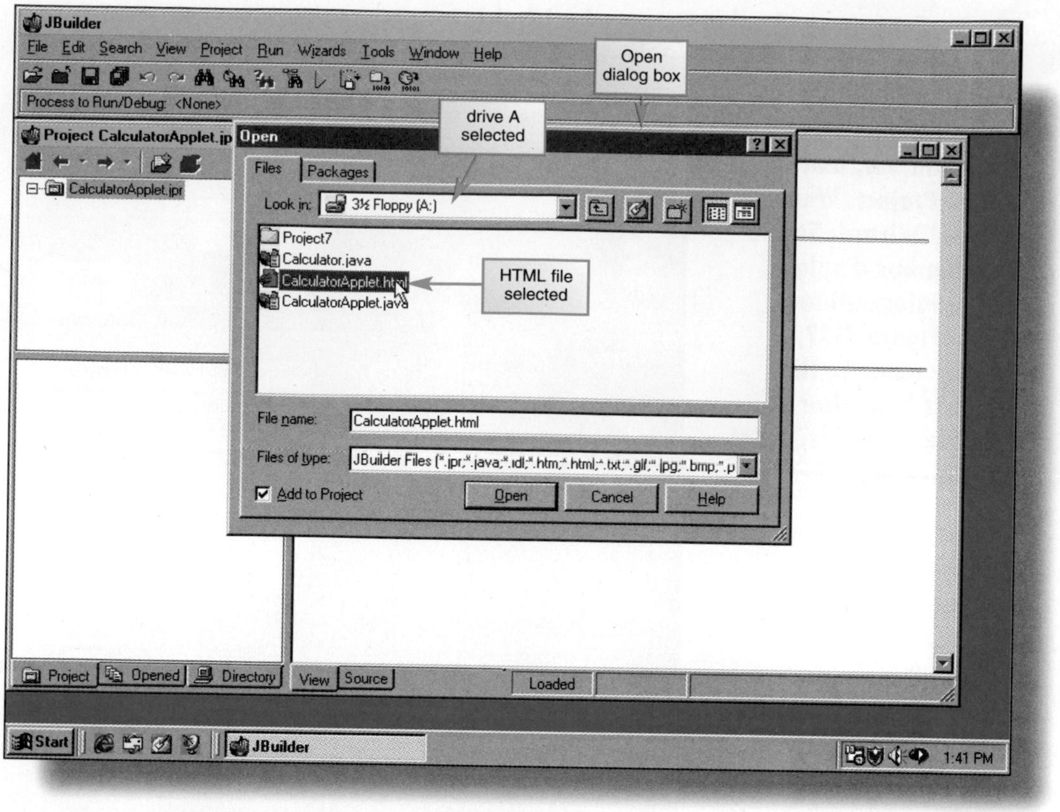

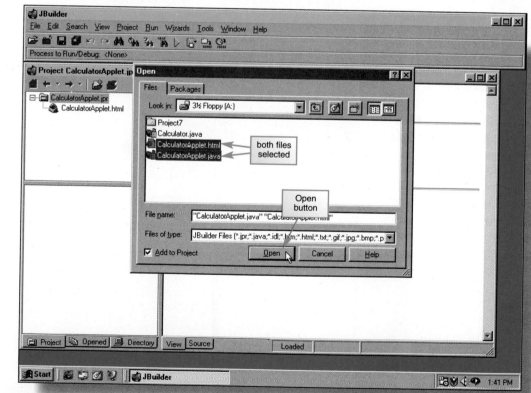

FIGURE 7-39

4 Press and hold the CTRL key while you click CalculatorApplet.java in the list. Point to the Open button.

Both files now display selected (Figure 7-40).

FIGURE 7-40

5 Click the Open button. When the AppBrowser window opens, click CalculatorApplet.html in the Navigation Pane and then point to the Source tab at the bottom of the Content Pane.

Notice that both files display in the Navigation Pane (Figure 7-41).

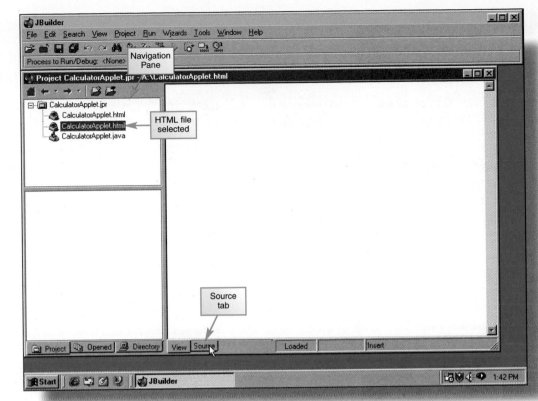

FIGURE 7-41

6 Click the Source tab to display the HTML code. Point to the Make button on the toolbar.

As the ScreenTip suggests, you also may press CTRL+F9 (Figure 7-42). Your HTML code may differ.

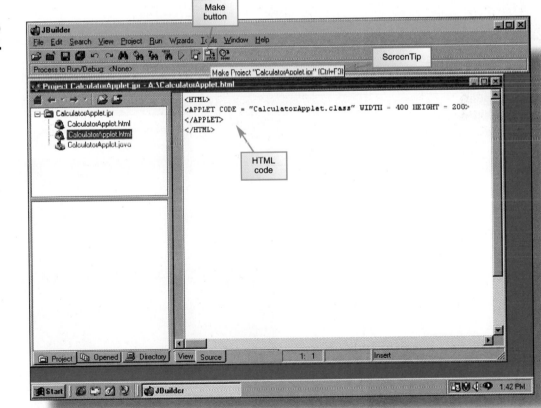

FIGURE 7-42

7 **Click the Make button. Point to the Run button on the toolbar.**

The project compiles (Figure 7-43). Recall that compiling the project also compiles the source code, even if it is not selected in the Navigation Pane. If errors occur, fix them in the Content Pane, and then recompile.

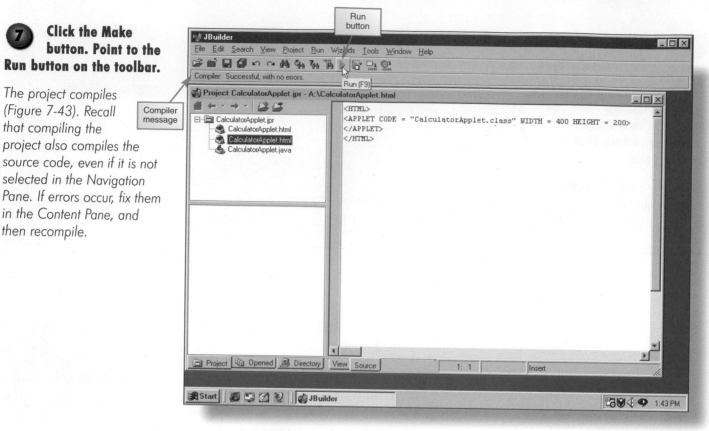

FIGURE 7-43

8 **Click the Run button. When the Applet Viewer window opens, click any buttons to perform test calculations. When you are finished, point to the CLR button.**

Recall that the CLR button clears the display at the top of the window (Figure 7-44).

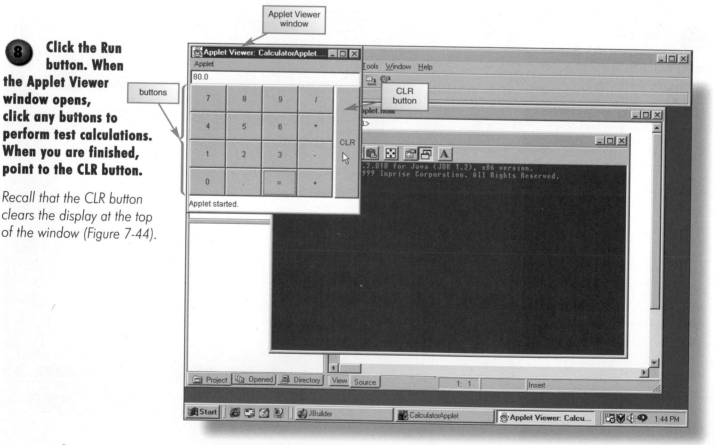

FIGURE 7-44

Click the CLR button. Point to the Close button in the Applet Viewer window.

The Calculator output display clears (Figure 7-45).

 Click the Applet Viewer Close button.

The Applet Viewer window closes and the AppBrowser window again is visible.

FIGURE 7-45

Other Ways

1. To add project, click Add to Project button in Navigation Pane toolbar
2. To add project, press ALT+INSERT
3. To compile, press CTRL+F9
4. To execute, press F9

JBuilder also contains an Applet Wizard, which you can access by clicking New on the File menu, and then clicking Applet. The **Applet Wizard** creates an .html file containing an APPLET tag referencing your applet class. Within the files, the wizard creates comments, parameters, links, and HTML code. It also creates a class that extends both Applet and JApplet for advanced Java Swing components. **Swing** refers to the new library of GUI controls that slowly is replacing the previous AWT controls. Java Swing, which is a separate Web download from the JDK, boasts a larger set of built-in controls, including trees, image buttons, tabbed panes, sliders, toolbars, color choosers, tables, and text areas. Most browsers do not yet support Swing controls without special plug-ins.

Another JBuilder wizard is the Deployment wizard. The **Deployment wizard** collects all the files and packages needed to distribute your application or applet to other users. The wizard creates compressed Java Archive (.jar) files. The Deployment wizard uses the files in your project as the basis for creating a **deployment set**.

Using JBuilder Help

At anytime while you are working in JBuilder, you can answer your JBuilder questions by using **Help**. Used properly, this form of online assistance can increase your productivity and reduce your frustration by minimizing the time you spend learning how to use JBuilder. Table 7-3 on the next page summarizes the six categories of JBuilder Help available to you.

The following sections show examples of some of the types of Help described in Table 7-3.

Using the Contents Tab to Obtain Help

The Contents tab provides access to the Contents sheet. The **Contents sheet** in the JBuilder Help window offers assistance when you know the general category of the topic in question, but not the specifics. Use the Contents sheet in the same manner you would use a table of contents at the front of a textbook. The steps on the next page show how to use the Contents sheet to obtain information on getting assistance from the JBuilder Help window.

More About

Deployment from the University Edition

Inprise grants you the right to use the software packaged with this book solely for educational or training purposes. No rights are granted for deploying or distributing applications created with this software. For more information, see your JBuilder 3 licensing agreement.

Table 7-3   JBuilder Help

HELP CATEGORY	DESCRIPTION	HOW TO ACTIVATE
Contents Sheet	Groups Help topics by general categories. Similar to a table of contents in a book.	Click Help on the JBuilder menu bar and then click the Contents tab.
Index Sheet	Accesses Help topics by subject. Similar to an index in a book.	Click Help on the JBuilder menu bar and then click the Index tab.
Find Sheet	Searches the index for all phrases that include the term in question.	Click Help on the JBuilder menu bar and then click the Find tab.
Question Mark button	Used to identify unfamiliar items on the screen.	In a dialog box, click the Question Mark button and then click an item in a dialog box; or right-click the object and choose Help on the shortcut menu.
F1 function key	Used to obtain context-sensitive Help on the current problem.	Press the F1 function key.
Class-specific Help	Used to reference documentation for a specific class.	Double-click a class name in the structure pane and then click the Doc tab; or click a class name in the structure pane and press the ENTER key; or right-click a class name in the source pane and choose Browse Symbol At Cursor. Click the Doc tab.

More About

Accessing the API from Help

On the Help menu, click Java Reference. The Help system will display the Java Platform 1.2 API Specification, complete with a list of Java packages hyperlinked to their specifications. This API document contains a menu, an index, links, and hierarchy trees. JBuilder's Java Reference especially is useful if you are not connected to the Web and cannot access the Sun Microsystems API site.

TO OBTAIN HELP USING THE CONTENTS SHEET

1 Click Help Topics on the JBuilder Help menu.

2 When the JBuilder Help window opens, double-click its title bar to maximize it.

3 If necessary, click the Contents tab. Double-click the Quick Start book icon.

4 Click the plus sign node beside Using JBuilder's Online Help.

5 Click the subtopic, The main parts of the Help Viewer.

JBuilder displays Help information on the topic, The main parts of the Help Viewer (Figure 7-46).

Once the information on the subtopic displays, you can scroll through and read it, or click the Print button on the JBuilder Help toolbar to obtain a hard copy. If you decide to click another subtopic on the left, or a link on the right, you can return to the Help page shown in Figure 7-46 by clicking the Back button.

Each topic in the Contents sheet is preceded by a book icon or a plus or minus sign node. A **book icon** indicates subtopics are available. A **plus sign node** indicates more subtopics are available. A **minus sign node** indicates all subtopics are displayed.

Using the Index Tab to Obtain Help

The Index tab provides access to the Index sheet. Use the **Index sheet** when you know a keyword or the first few letters of the keyword for which you want help. Use the Index sheet in the same manner you would use an index at the back of a textbook. As an example, the following steps show how to use the Index sheet to obtain postfix operators.

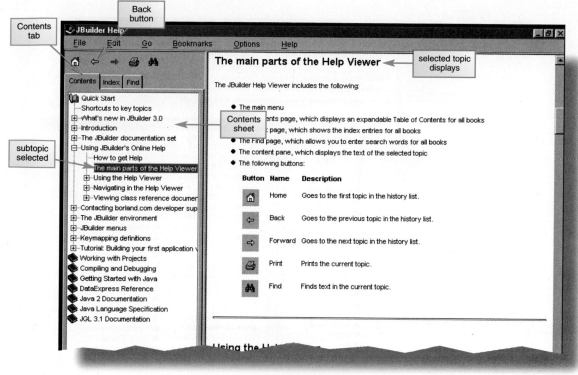

FIGURE 7-46

TO OBTAIN HELP USING THE INDEX SHEET

1 If necessary, click Help Topics on the JBuilder Help menu.

2 When the JBuilder Help window opens, if necessary, double-click its title bar to maximize the window.

3 Click the Index tab. Type code insight in the text box at the top of the sheet.

4 When the Index entry for Code Insight displays, double-click it.

5 When the topics display at the bottom of the sheet, double-click Getting coding assistance.

JBuilder displays Help information on the topic, Getting coding assistance (Figure 7-47 on the next page).

If the topic, Getting coding assistance, does not include the information you want, click another topic in the box or type a new word in the text box. As you begin typing a new keyword, JBuilder jumps to that point on the list.

Using the Find Tab to Obtain Help

The Find tab provides access to the Find sheet. The **Find sheet** in the JBuilder Help window is used to locate a Help topic on a particular word. The Find sheet searches the Help files for all phrases that include the word for which you are searching. The steps on the next page show how to use the Index sheet to obtain help about the Deployment wizard.

Opening JBuilder Files from Windows

In accordance with Windows conventions, JBuilder automatically updates your registry to add a file association for .java, .jpr, .class, and .idl files. This means JBuilder launches automatically when you double-click one of these file icons. If you wish to change these file associations, for example, you might want the ability to open Java files in Notepad, click the View menu in any folder window, and then click Options. On the File types Tab, select the file type and then click the Edit button. You then may update the open action for that file type. As a result, right-clicking the file icon will allow you to open a JBuilder file with another application.

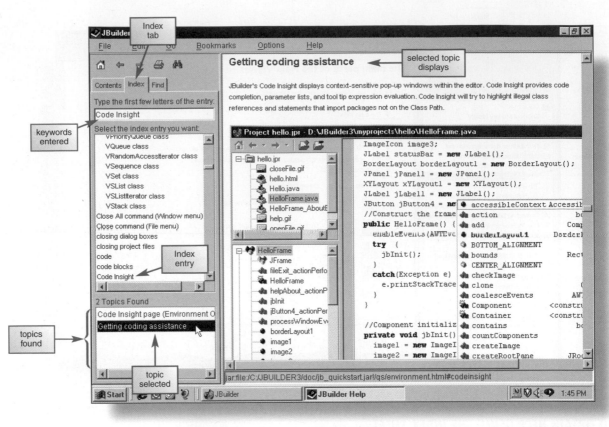

FIGURE 7-47

TO OBTAIN HELP USING THE FIND SHEET

① If necessary, click Help Topics on the menu bar.

② When the JBuilder Help window opens, if necessary, double-click its title bar to maximize it.

③ Click the Find tab. Type `deployment` in the text box at the top of the sheet.

④ When the Find entry for Deployment displays, double-click it.

⑤ When the topics display at the bottom of the sheet, double-click the topic, F1 Help: Deployment wizard.

JBuilder displays Help on the topic, F1 Deployment wizard (Figure 7-48).

An alternative to typing a keyword in the text box is to scroll through the list below the text box. When you locate the keyword, double-click it to display Help on the related topic. The Topics Found box displays other topics that relate to the new keyword.

The JBuilder Help Window Menu

The JBuilder Help window has its own menu bar. The **File menu** contains options to open, reload, print, and exit. The **Edit menu** contains options to copy, paste, and find. The **Go menu** contains options to navigate forward and backward through Help pages, and an option to return to the Home page. The **Bookmarks menu** has options to add and edit your own bookmarks in the JBuilder Help files. The **Options menu** contains options to display hyperlinks and URLs. Finally, the **Help menu** displays one option on how to use Help.

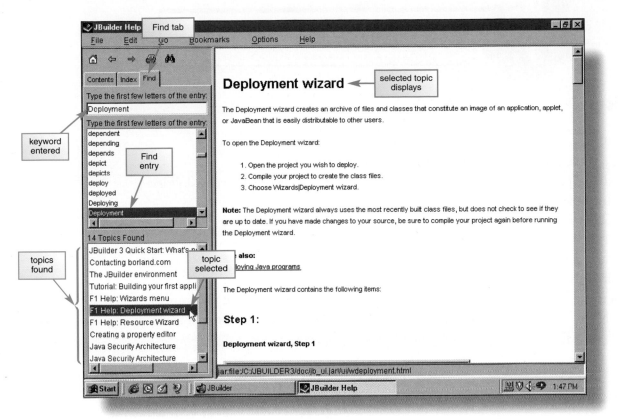

FIGURE 7-48

Project Summary

This project presented a discussion of the JBuilder Integrated Development Environment. You learned about the features, advantages, and disadvantages of using an IDE rather than the JDK. First, you learned how to start JBuilder and set the paths and properties. Then, you added the Calculator program to the project and saw how JBuilder sets up its interface with panes, menus, and toolbars. You practiced some editing techniques including jumping to line numbers, identifying code through colors, and looking at class hierarchies. Using the Make and Run commands, you compiled, executed, and then saved the application. Finally, you created a project and added an applet and its associated HTML file to the project. You saw how JBuilder displays applets with Applet Viewer and you looked at an example of the debugging window.

What You Should Know

Having completed this project, you now should be able to perform the following tasks:

- Add Source Code *(J 7.13)*
- Create an Applet Project in JBuilder *(J 7.27)*
- Make, Run, and Save the Program *(J 7.22)*
- Obtain Help Using the Contents Sheet *(J 7.32)*
- Obtain Help Using the Find Sheet *(J 7.34)*

- Obtain Help Using the Index Sheet *(J 7.33)*
- Set Project Properties for a New Project *(J 7.11)*
- Start JBuilder and Set the Paths *(J 7.6)*
- Use JBuilder's Editing Tools *(J 7.17)*

Test Your Knowledge

1 True/False

Instructions: Circle T if the statement is true or F if the statement is false.

T F   1. The only disadvantage of Sun's JDK is the cost.

T F   2. No single Java IDE is able to meet all of a programmer's needs at every skill level.

T F   3. JBuilder uses pure Java code.

T F   4. JBuilder assigns project properties from the comments in your code.

T F   5. The Project Notes page is an HTML file.

T F   6. The Navigation Pane contains all the source code.

T F   7. JBuilder uses the AppBrowser window to view Web pages.

T F   8. Java contains some editing tools that are similar to word processing programs.

T F   9. The Make command is preferred over the Rebuild command because it is faster.

T F   10. JBuilder displays any errors in a window below the source code.

2 Multiple Choice

Instructions: Circle the correct response.

1. JBuilder is a(n) _____.
   a. application software package
   b. IDE
   c. windows-based program
   d. all of the above

2. Which of the following is not an advantage of an IDE?
   a. cost
   b. wizards
   c. visual debugger
   d. toolbars

3. The file extension for a JBuilder Project is _____.
   a. .jdk
   b. .jbp
   c. .jpr
   d. .class

4. JBuilder's interface can recognize and display all of the following except _____.
   a. .doc
   b. .java
   c. .gif
   d. .html

5. The JBuilder IDE contains _____.
   a. a menu bar
   b. a toolbar
   c. a status bar
   d. all of the above

Test Your Knowledge

6. Which of the following is not a pane in the AppBrowser window?
   a. Structure Pane
   b. Content Pane
   c. Source Pane
   d. Navigation Pane

7. When you want to position the insertion point at a certain line, you should use the _____.
   a. Go to Line Number command
   b. Jump command
   c. Cursor command
   d. JBuilder Debugger

8. The Make command is equivalent to the _____ command in console mode.
   a. java
   b. path
   c. javac
   d. dir

9. JBuilder contains all of the following tools except _____.
   a. Trace Into command
   b. Applet Wizard
   c. Applet Viewer
   d. Spell Checker

10. The Content Pane displays comments in the color _____.
    a. light blue
    b. dark blue
    c. green
    d. black

3 Understanding the JBuilder Screen

Instructions: In Figure 7-49 on the next page, arrows point to components of the JBuilder screen running on the desktop. Identify the various components in the spaces provided.

1. _____
2. _____
3. _____
4. _____
5. _____
6. _____
7. _____
8. _____
9. _____
10. _____

(continued)

Test Your Knowledge

Understanding the JBuilder Screen *(continued)*

FIGURE 7-49

4 Understanding JBuilder Terminology

Instructions: Figure 7-50 displays a crossword puzzle. Fill in the puzzle using the clues listed below.

Across

3. type of software that increases productivity and provides output to the user
6. class file not generated by the current source code
10. in the Structure pane, the method to open the Java package associated with a component and to view its hierarchy and associated methods
12. Code _____ is JBuilder's AutoComplete tool
13. extension for JBuilder's project
14. JBuilder's container of files
15. JBuilder's compile command

Test Your Knowledge

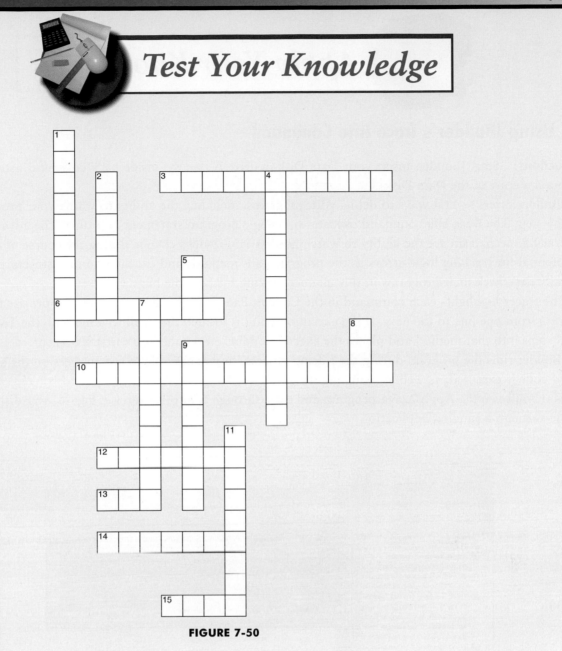

FIGURE 7-50

Down

1. upper-left pane to select files to view
2. pane that displays source code
4. displaying keywords and data in different colors to assist users in coding
5. acronym for software such as JBuilder
7. JBuilder's user interface for a Java program
8. JBuilder's execution command
9. a tool to watch the behavior of your application
11. a structural analysis of the selected file is displayed as a hierarchical tree in this pane

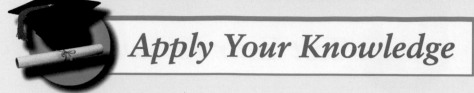

Apply Your Knowledge

1 Using JBuilder's Trace Into Command

Instructions: Start JBuilder. Insert your Data Disk in drive A (see the inside back cover for instructions on how to obtain a copy of the Data Disk).

JBuilder offers several ways to debug your programs, including the ability to watch your program executing step-by-step. The **Trace Into** command executes one single program statement at a time. The advantages of using this tracing mechanism are the ability to watch how variable values change during the course of execution and its potential for tracking logic errors as the program calls methods and executes control structures. Programmers typically **deskcheck** their programs in this manner looking for possible bugs.

The tracer highlights each command in the Content Pane, as it is executed. The user presses the F7 key to progress from one line to the next. If the execution point is located on a call to a method, the Trace Into command steps into that method and places the execution point on the method's first statement.

JBuilder runs the program during the tracing process, so you are able to see answers on the screen as each line of code is executed, as well as watching the variables change.

You will open the Apply7.java program and trace through it in this exercise. Figure 7-51 displays JBuilder tracing through a running application.

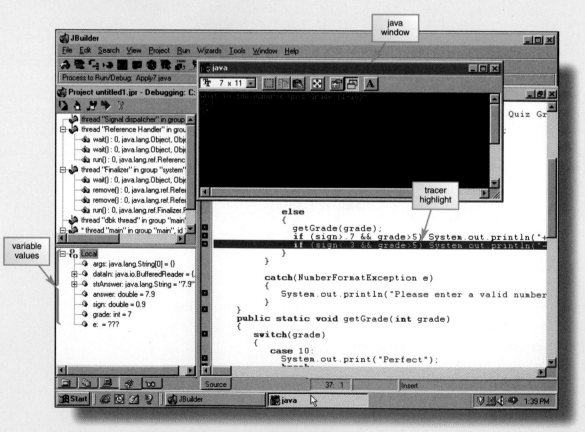

FIGURE 7-51

Apply Your Knowledge

1. With JBuilder running on your desktop and your Data Disk in drive A, click Default Properties on the Project menu to set the paths as you did in Project 7.
2. Click New Project on the File menu to set the Project properties for a new program using the Project Wizard.
3. When the Project Wizard: Step 1 of 1 dialog box displays, type A:\Project7\App\Apply7.jpr as the project name.
4. Select each of the remaining text boxes in the dialog box, one at a time. Enter Apply Your Knowledge as the title. Enter your name in the Author text box. Click the Finish button.
5. To add the Apply7.java source code, click Project on the menu bar and then click to Add to Project.
6. When the Open dialog box displays, click the Look in box arrow and then click 3½ Floppy (A:) in the list. Double-click the file named, Apply7.java.
7. Ready the printer on your system. Click the File menu and then click Print. When the Print Selection dialog box displays, click the Line numbers check box, and then click the OK button. Look at the printout noting the control structures. The program, which runs in console mode, asks the user for a numeric quiz grade and then prints out the corresponding letter grade.
8. Click at the beginning of the program, if necessary. On the Run menu, click Trace Into.
9. JBuilder will pause at each active line of code. Press the F7 key to move from one line to the next. When F7 no longer moves the highlighted tracer, it is either waiting for data from the user or it is complete. If it is waiting for input, the running application's java button will display on the taskbar. If necessary, click the java button on the task bar to display the application running in console mode. The java window asks you to enter a numeric quiz grade. Type 7.9 and then press the ENTER key. Click the JBuilder window again to continue tracing.
10. Each time you press the F7 key, follow the execution of the program as it moves from one command to the next. It will jump from the main method to the getGrade method and traverse the switch structure. When the tracer finishes, the insertion point again will display at the beginning of the Content Pane and the java window will close.
11. Run the Trace Into command again, entering a different number between one and ten. This time, as JBuilder traces through the program, watch the lower left pane of the AppBrowser. The values of each variable will display as the program progresses. When you click the java window to input the grade, drag the window out of the way, if necessary.
12. Run the tracer again and enter an alphabetic character. Click the java window frequently to see what output displays.

In the Lab

1 Making a JAR

Problem: Your employer would like you to create an archive of files and classes that constitute an image of an application that is easily distributable to other users, known as a JAR file.

Instructions: Use JBuilder's Deployment Wizard to make a JAR version of the Calculator or Flora program (or program of your choice). The Wizard will create a deployment set.

1. Start JBuilder on your system.
2. Choose Deployment wizard on the Wizards menu.
3. When the Deployment wizard displays, make sure all files in the project are selected. Click each plus sign node to see a list of classes that are referenced directly or indirectly by that file. By default, all files and packages in a project are selected to be deployed.
4. For Archive type, choose Compressed JAR. Do not change the entry in the Manifest File text box; JBuilder automatically will generate this file for you.
5. Enter a name, such as CalcJar, for your JAR in the Output file text box.
6. Click the Finish button. The Deployment wizard stores your settings in a .properties file in the same directory as your project file. The file extension will be .deployment.properties. For example, if your project is named CalcJar.jpr, the deployment settings will be stored in the file CalcJar.deployment.properties.
7. All classes and files associated with your program now are stored in a single file. E-mail that file as an attachment to your instructor.
8. Open an MS-DOS Prompt window, set the path, and change to the drive and folder that contains your JAR file.
9. Type jar tf CalcJar.jar (or the name of your JAR) to display the files inside the file. The t option indicates that you want to view the table of contents of the JAR file. The f option indicates that the JAR file to be viewed is specified on the command line. Without the f option, the Jar tool would expect a standard input device, such as a floppy disk.

2 Using Help

Problem: Your Java instructor wants you to research variable scope. You decide to use JBuilder's Help files as source to learn why placement of the variable declaration is so important to the variable's visibility within the program and outside the program.

Instructions: Perform the following steps to start JBuilder and obtain information about scope.

1. Start JBuilder on your system.
2. Click Help on the JBuilder menu bar, and then click Help Topics.
3. When the JBuilder Help window opens, click the Contents tab.
4. Double-click the book node, Getting Started with Java.
5. Click the plus node, Java Language Basics.
6. Click the plus node, Java's Data Types.
7. Click Scope rules. Figure 7-52 displays the Content sheet with the nodes open.
8. Read about global and local variables in the Content pane. Scroll to finish reading the Help information on Scope Rules.

In the Lab

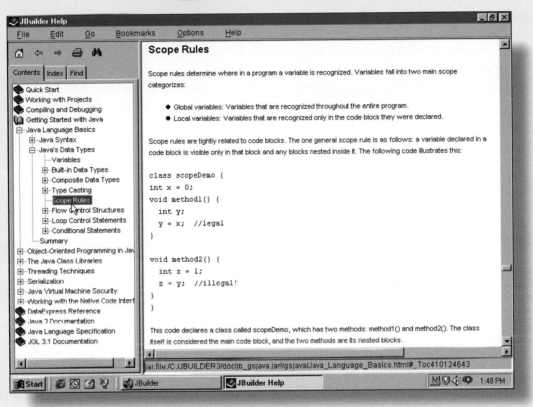

FIGURE 7-52

9. Click the Index tab.
10. Type scope in the text box at the top of the Index sheet.
11. Use the down scroll arrow at the bottom of the Index sheet to look at other topics related to scope. Click the topic, scope of local variable declarations. (The light blue background of the Index pane indicates the information is taken from *The Java Language Specification*, an online book provided with JBuilder 3.)
12. Read the information about scope listed as 14.3.2. (As an extra credit assignment, try copying some of the coding examples, pasting them into JBuilder, and then compiling them.)

3 Exploring JBuilder Features

Problem: As a teaching assistant for a continuing education Java course, you have been asked to develop a lab exercise for the students. The exercise should cover a feature of JBuilder not previously covered in this Project. Some sample topics might include: managing files in JBuilder, global vs. local variables, the New dialog box, or Java beans. The lead instructor has given you the following instructions:

1. The lab should state the purpose, problem, or learning objectives.
2. The lab should present a complete view of the intended concept.
3. Cite reading references, either from the Web or from JBuilder's Help system.

(continued)

In the Lab

Exploring JBuilder Features *(continued)*

4. Include a step-by-step list of instructions for menu clicks, dialog box responses, and the opening or closing of windows, files, and panes.

5. Include at least two of the following categories of assessment: questions to answer about the tasks performed, printouts of source code, printouts of screen, files on disk.

6. The lab should take students one hour or less to complete.

7. Your final product should include a disk with any files the students may need, a printout of the lab and any instruction sheet(s), sample answers, a copy of any printouts generated by the students who complete the lab, and any other materials you feel the lead instructor or student should have.

Cases and Places

The difficulty of these case studies varies:
▶ are the least difficult; ▶▶ are more difficult; and ▶▶▶ are the most difficult.

1 ▶ Obtain a copy of a Java program that has been created and compiled in console mode. Use JBuilder to load, compile, and execute it. Note the differences and similarities. Write several paragraphs describing your experiences.

2 ▶ Use JBuilder's Applet Wizard to create an applet that displays your name, the course number, and the date in an applet window. Use JBuilder's Print command to print the applet source code with line numbers.

3 ▶▶ Use JBuilder's Help menu to go through the Quick-start Tutorial on Nested Panel Layouts. Save the application you create through the tutorial on a floppy disk. Print the source code.

4 ▶▶▶ Obtain a review copy of another IDE besides JBuilder, or contact your system administrator for other IDE packages your school may own. Start the IDE and try to import a Java program you already have created. Note the differences between that IDE and JBuilder. Write a paper describing whether or not you think JBuilder is better. Give specific reasons and examples from both IDEs.

5 ▶▶▶ Search the Web for articles about IDEs. Find three different articles discussing some of the advantages and disadvantages. Go to the JBuilder Web site and compare their features with another IDE, such as Visual Café or J++. Write a paper or e-mail the Web sites and a short description to your instructor.

APPENDIX A
Installing Java

Installing Java

Sun Microsystems calls its recent release of Java the **Java 2 Standard Development Kit** (**SDK**). The SDK includes the compiler and run-time system you will need to execute the Java projects in this textbook. You can obtain the Java 2 SDK and its documentation in one of several different ways. For more information, visit the Java Programming Web page (www.scsite.com/java/more.htm) and then click Installing Java.

Downloading Java 2 SDK from the Sun Microsystems Web Site

If you download the free SDK from the Sun Microsystems Web site, you will get the most recent version of the Java SDK. A major drawback of downloading the SDK from the Sun Web site is the time it takes to download the necessary files. The speed is dependant upon the speed of your computer system, the speed of your modem, the connection rate, and the operation of the site itself. It may take anywhere from 20 minutes to an hour or more.

The Java 2 SDK download will save a 20-megabyte file on your hard drive. You then must run or execute that file to decompress the downloaded files and install the components on your system. The files, when installed on your system, will use approximately 44 megabytes of storage. Make sure you have a total of 64 megabytes of storage space before you begin the download process: 44 megabytes for the installed file and 20 megabytes for the download file. After the installation, you may delete the original download file because you no longer will need it.

Perform the following steps to download the SDK from the Sun Microsystems Web site.

TO DOWNLOAD THE SDK

1 With your system connected to the Web, start your browser. Type `www.scsite.com/java/more.htm` in the Address or Go To textbox. Press the ENTER key. When the page displays, click the Installing Java link.

2 When the Sun Microsystems Java Web page displays, scroll to the section titled Production Releases. Click the link, Java™ 2 SDK v 1.2.2-001 Windows 95/98/NT Production Release, or the link to the most recent version of Java on the page.

3 When the Download Web page displays, scroll to the section titled, Download Java 2 SDK v 1.2.2-001 for Windows 95 / 98 / NT 4.0 (Intel Platform). Be sure that the One large bundle option button is selected and then click the continue button.

4 When the License & Export page displays, read the terms of agreement, and then click the Agree button. When the Download Java Development Kit Web page displays, click the FTP download button.

5 If a File Download dialog box displays, make sure the Save this program to disk option button is selected. At this point, some browsers automatically may begin downloading the file with the default name and the default location. If your browser begins the download, skip to Step 8.

6 If your browser displayed a File Download dialog box, click its OK button. When the Save As dialog box displays, if necessary, choose Desktop in the Save in list. Click the Save button.

7 When the download is complete, the message, Download Complete, will display in the File Download dialog box. Click the Close button.

8 Close the browser. Double-click the file, jdk1_2_2-001-win, on the desktop or in the folder to which you downloaded.

After a few seconds, the Welcome dialog box of the Java Development Kit Setup wizard will display. Click the Next button.

 At each of the setup screens, after reading the screen, click the Next or Yes button to proceed. Click the Yes or OK button to accept the default folder locations for the installation when prompted. When the installation is complete, click the Finish button.

Once you have extracted the files for the Java 2 SDK, you may delete the executable file that you downloaded. Simply right-click the file and then click Delete on the shortcut menu.

An alternative to downloading is to purchase the Java 2 SDK on a CD-ROM from Sun Microsystems. Purchasing the product avoids the long download time and serves as a backup if you need to reinstall.

Using the Java 2 SDK Documentation

Sun Microsystems also provides free documentation on the Java 2 SDK platform. Available in a wide variety of formats, including HTML and PDF files, the documentation on the Sun Microsystems Web site is updated regularly. You may browse, search, or download the documentation. For more information, visit the Java Programming Web Page (www.scsite.com/java/more.htm) and then click Documentation.

The Java 2 SDK documentation files contain a wide variety of information about Java topics including the release notes, language specifications, basic features, and the **application program interface (API)**. The Java API is the accumulation of all the specific classes and methods prescribed by Java.

Perform the following steps to browse the Java 2 SDK Documentation on the Sun Microsystems Web site.

TO BROWSE THE JAVA 2 SDK DOCUMENTATION

 With your system connected to the Web, start your browser. Type `www.scsite.com/java/more.htm` in the Address or Go To text box. Press the ENTER key. When the page displays, click Documentation.

 When the Sun Microsystems Web page displays, click the Browse the Java 2 SDK Documentation link.

③ When the documentation page displays, read the various available documentation topics and then scroll to the section titled, Java Foundation Classes (JFC).

④ Click a topic, such as Swing Components. One at a time, click at least three different links on the page and print a copy of each page you choose for your instructor.

The Java documentation files include links to tutorials, articles about implementation, and sample programs and applets that you may run on the Web or download.

Installing Inprise's JBuilder 3 Software

Another way to obtain the SDK and its documentation is to obtain an Integrated Development Environment (IDE) that includes the SDK. An **IDE** is a third party software tool developed to assist with the writing of Java programs. Usually, it is **GUI-based**, which means that the IDE contains buttons, menus, and Help files to support the software. A growing number of IDEs, such as JBuilder 3, have come on the market in the past few years. These IDEs provide programmers with a set of development tools, which may include color-coded editors, wizards, and pre-written Java classes. A copy of JBuilder 3 may be included on a CD-ROM with this textbook.

JBuilder 3 requires approximately 188 megabytes of storage space on your hard disk. An advantage of this software is the quick installation of the SDK compared with downloading files from the Sun Microsystems Web site. You also can use the JBuilder IDE to create Java programs and applets.

Perform the following steps to install Inprise's JBuilder 3 software that may be included with this textbook. Installing this software also will install the SDK, the compiler, and run-time environment to run applications and applets from the command prompt.

To Install Inprise's JBuilder 3 Software

1 Insert the Inprise JBuilder 3 CD-ROM in your CD-ROM drive. When the Install Launcher screen displays, point to JBuilder 3 University. If the installation procedure does not begin automatically, perform the steps listed in the Other Ways at the end of these steps.

The Install Launcher displays (Figure A-1). The installation procedure begins.

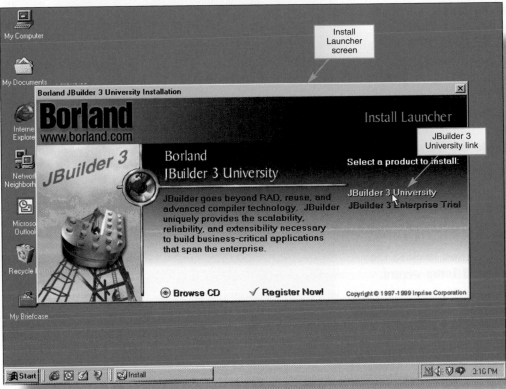

FIGURE A-1

2 Click JBuilder 3 University. When the Welcome dialog box of the JBuilder 3 Setup wizard displays, point to the Next button.

The Welcome screen is the first of several screens that display as part of the setup (Figure A-2).

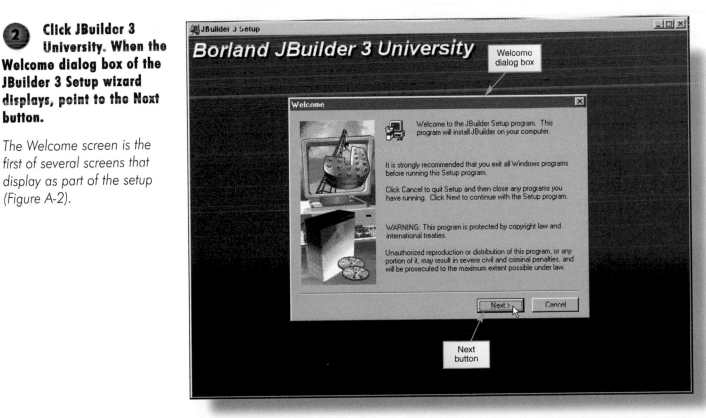

FIGURE A-2

3 Click the Next button. At each of the setup screens, after reading the screen, click the Next or Yes button to proceed. Accept the default folder locations for the installation. Choose the default, Typical setup, when prompted. When the installation is complete, point to the Finish button.

The JBuilder 3 software installs (Figure A-3).

4 Click the Finish button to close the JBuilder 3 Setup wizard.

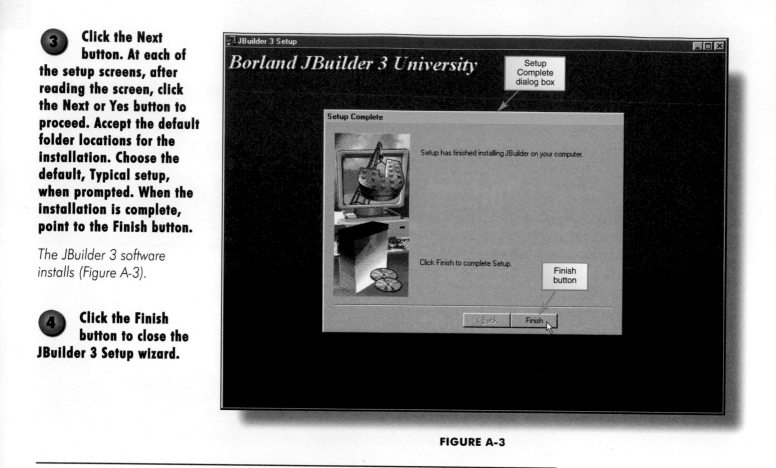

FIGURE A-3

The installation process creates a command on your Programs submenu titled, Borland JBuilder 3 University. You can use this new command to access JBuilder 3. You still can access Java from the command prompt for stand-alone applications.

Other Ways

1. Click Start button on taskbar, click Run on Start menu, click Browse button, look in CD-ROM drive, type Install.exe, click OK button

APPENDIX B
Reserved Keywords

Reserved Keywords

The following table lists the reserved keywords in the Java programming language. Because of their reserved status, these words cannot be used as names for classes and methods or as identifiers for variables.

abstract	else	int	static
boolean	extends	interface	super
break	false	long	switch
byte	final	native	synchronized
byvalue	finally	new	this
case	float	null	throw
cast	for	operator	throws
catch	future	outer	transient
char	generic	package	true
class	goto	private	try
const	if	protected	var
continue	implements	public	void
default	import	rest	volatile
do	inner	return	while
double	instanceof	short	

APPENDIX C
Java Certification

What Is Certification?

Certification is a process where people in the computer industry can prove they have skills in a certain computer or software related area by taking a certified exam. Software and hardware companies, government agencies, and technology consortiums offer the certified exams. For example, for application user certification, Microsoft offers several exams, including the Microsoft Office User Specialist (MOUS) exam. Another example is the A+ Certification exam, sponsored by a consortium of companies that wish to offer hardware knowledge and repair credentials. Java programmers, developers, and architects take a certified exam to demonstrate their programming skills, as well. Certification provides a standard, tangible way of measuring technical skills; it also can offer job advancement opportunities and third party validation of your skills.

Sun, IBM, and other companies offer certification exams for Java programmers. Table C-1 lists several current certification exams and their descriptions. Most of the certification exams have updated the Certified Programmer examination to the Java 2 platform.

A new Certification Initiative sponsored by companies such as Sun Microsystems, IBM, Novell, and Oracle currently is being formed which will attempt to create an industry wide standard. It will contain five exams, which will be recognized by participating companies. The goal of the initiative is to promote industry-wide standards for validating the skill of Java professionals.

Table C-1 lists some of the current certification exams. For more information on these exams and to locate an exam close to you, visit the Java Programming Web site at http://www.scsite.com/java/cert.htm.

Table C-1   Java Certification Exams

CERTIFICATION	SPONSOR	DESCRIPTION
Sun Certified Programmer	Sun Microsystems	Beginning level. Requires the successful completion of a multiple-choice and short-answer exam covering the specifics of the Java language. It has no prerequisites.
Sun Certified Developer	Sun Microsystems	Requires programmer certification with any JDK release as a prerequisite. The test consists of two parts. You must download a programming assignment from the Sun Educational Services Certification Database. There is no specific time limit for the completion of the programming assignment. An essay test then is given that requires short answers regarding design decisions made in connection with the programming assignment.
Sun Certified Architect for Java Technology	Sun Microsystems	Requires successful completion of a multiple-choice and short-answer exam, and has no prerequisites. It is designed to test a broad scope of program design skills and object-oriented methodologies.
IBM Certified Specialist	IBM	Requires successful completion of a closed book, multiple-choice, computerized, knowledge-based test. It contains approximately 60 questions with a 75-minute time limit.
Certified Solution Developer (CSD)	IBM	Requires successful completion of 59 multiple-choice and short-answer questions, and a 120-minute time limit.
Certified Advanced Technical Expert (CATE)	IBM	Requires successful completion of a previous IBM/Java certification and a closed book, multiple-choice, computerized, knowledge-based test. It contains approximately 60 questions with a 120-minute time limit.
Certification Initiative — jCert Initiative, Inc.	Collaborative	A collaborative effort by multiple companies to bring to market a common, standard, cross-vendor, Java technology certification.

Why Should You Get Java Certified?

Being a Java Certified Programmer, Developer, or Architect provides a valuable industry credential – proof that you have the Java skills required by employers. By passing one or more certification exams (usually 71% is a passing grade), you demonstrate to employers your proficiency in programming or application development. Java and Internet-related technologies are among the fastest-growing areas in an ever-expanding technological society. Companies constantly are looking for employees with proven expertise and programming skills. These companies include software houses that need programmers who can get up to speed quickly, temporary employment agencies that want to prove the expertise of their workers, large corporations looking for a way to measure the skill set of potential employees, and training companies and educational institutions seeking Java programmers, teachers, and Webmasters with appropriate credentials.

How Can You Prepare for Java Certification Exams?

Completing the projects in this textbook will give you a good start toward the certification exams. Table C-2 lists the objectives of the beginning level exam for Java Certification. Your own application and practice of Java programming is critical to your successful completion of the exam. Sun Educational Services offers a training course at various centers all over the world, as do many companies and learning centers.

Table C-2   Objectives for Beginning Level Java Certification

OBJECTIVES
Demonstrate knowledge of Java programming language fundamentals by writing correctly structured Java classes for applets and applications and appropriately using all data types.
Determine the result of applying every combination of operators and assignments to any combination of types.
Declare variables and classes with appropriate use of access control, initialization, and scope.
Make correct use of all flow control constructs, including exception handling.
Make correct use of overloading, overriding, and inheritance.
Identify guaranteed garbage collection and finalization behavior.
Make correct use of Threads, Runnable, wait(), notify(), and synchronized.
Use the facility of java.lang, java.awt, java.awt.event, and java.io packages.
Recognize the benefits of encapsulation in the Object Oriented paradigm, and be able to implement tightly encapsulated classes in the Java programming language.
Use the Java Foundation Classes software to build visual applications.
Write applications that are independent of language or location, using the internationalization APIs.
Use the jar command to package together the components of a Java technology-based application.

Shelly Cashman Series Certification Web Page

The Shelly Cashman Series Java Certification page (Figure C-1) has more than 15 Web pages you can visit to obtain additional information on Java and other certification programs. The Java Certification page (www.scsite. com/java/cert.htm) includes links to general information on certification, choosing an application for certification, preparing for the certification exam, and taking and passing the certification exam.

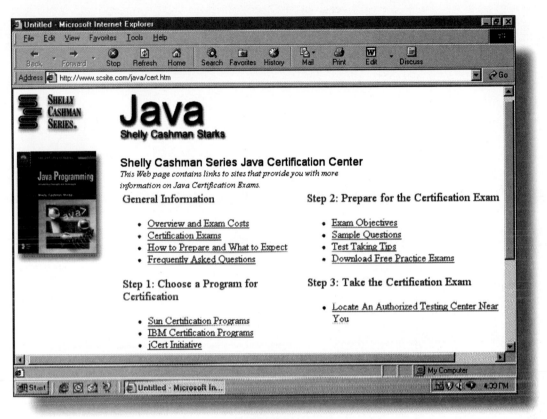

FIGURE C-1

APPENDIX D
Options and Exceptions

Options and Exceptions

This appendix lists the compile and runtime options you may include at the command prompt; options that will help you manage your files, classes, and variables. This appendix also lists exceptions from the java.io package. For a complete list of exceptions from all packages, consult the Java documentation. Appendix A describes how to browse the documentation.

Java Compiler Options

The javac compiler comes with several options to include when you compile a Java program. These options always begin with a hyphen and are typed after the word, javac. For example, if you want the compiler to display the source files that are being compiled and loaded and the total time it takes, you would type `javac -verbose Filename.java` at the command prompt. The javac compiler then would display each class that is loaded in support of the designated Filename, the creation of the new class, and the total time in milliseconds.

Table D-1 lists the options and their descriptions.

Table D-1	javac Options
OPTION	DESCRIPTION
-bootclasspath <path>	Overrides location of bootstrap class files
-cp <path> -classpath <path>	Sets search path for application classes and resources
-d <directory>	Specifies where to place generated class files
-deprecation	Output source locations where deprecated **Application Program Interfaces (APIs)** are used
-encoding <encoding>	Specify character encoding used by source files
-extdirs <dirs>	Override location of installed extensions
-g	Generates all debugging info
-g:{lines,vars,source}	Generates only some kinds of debugging information, specified by a comma-separated list of keywords: line number debugging information, local variable debugging information, or source file debugging information
-g:none	Generates no debugging info
-nowarn	Generates no warnings
-O	Turns on optimization, which may hinder debugging or enlarge class files (you must use an uppercase O)
-sourcepath <path>	Specifies where to find input source files
-target <release>	Generates class files for specific JVM version
-v -verbose	Enables verbose output about what the compiler is doing and displays all the classes as they are loaded

Java Runtime Options

The Java interpreter comes with several options to include when you execute a Java program. After the word java, type a hyphen and then the keyword from Table D-2. For example, if you want the interpreter to display the version of the SDK that is being used, you can type `java -version` at the command prompt. The interpreter then would display the version of the Java virtual machine that is running on your system.

Table D-2 lists the Java runtime options and their descriptions.

Table D-2	Java Runtime Options
OPTION	DESCRIPTION
-? -help	Displays standard usage and help message
-cp \<path> -classpath \<path>	Sets search path for application classes and resources
-cs -checksource	Checks to see if the source code is newer than its class file; if true, a new version is compiled
-D\<name>=\<value>	Sets a system property
-debug	Used with remote Java files that are to be debugged later
-noasyncgc	Turns off asynchronous garbage collection
-noclassgc	Disables class garbage collection
-noverify	Turns off class verification
-v -verbose	Enables verbose output about what the compiler is doing; displays all the classes as they are loaded
-verbosegc	Displays a message each time garbage collection occurs
-verify	Verifies all class are loaded
-verifyremote	Verifies classes are imported or inherited (default setting)
-version	Displays product version
-X	Displays help on non-standard options (you must use an uppercase X)

The java.io Exceptions

The java.io package provides for system input and output through data streams, the file system, and **serialization,** which is the term used to send or receive complex objects through a stream. When you use the java.io package, you must use the words, throws IOException, in the method header to alert the compiler that input/output errors might occur. Although the compiler's thrown error messages are a clue to the encountered problem, documentation about the different exceptions is available on the Sun Microsystems Web site (see Appendix A).

Table D-3 summarizes the possible exceptions thrown by the java.io package.

Table D-3   java.io Exceptions

EXCEPTION	DESCRIPTION
CharConversionException	Throws for character conversion exceptions
EOFException	Throws when an end of file or end of stream has been reached unexpectedly during input
FileNotFoundException	Throws when an attempt to open the file at the specified pathname has failed
InterruptedIOException	Throws when an input/output operation has been interrupted
InvalidClassException	Throws when the serial version of the class does not match the class descriptor, the class contains unknown data types, or the class does not have an accessible no-arg constructor
InvalidObjectException	Throws when one or more deserialized objects failed validation tests
IOException	Throws when an unspecified input/out exception has occurred
NotActiveException	Throws when serialization or deserialization is not active
NotSerializableException	Throws when an instance is required to have a serializable interface
ObjectStreamException	Superclass of all exceptions specific to the object stream classes
OptionalDataException	Throws when unexpected data appeared in an ObjectInputStream trying to read an object
StreamCorruptedException	Throws when control information that was read from an object stream violates internal consistency checks
SyncFailedException	Constructs an SyncFailedException with a detail message
UnsupportedEncodingException	Character encoding is not supported
UTFDataFormatException	Signals that a malformed UTF-8 string, a method of storage using the least amount of space possible, has been read in a data input stream or by any class that implements the data input interface

Index

INTERNATIONAL LICENSE AGREEMENT FOR EVALUATION OF PROGRAMS

Part 1 - General Terms

PLEASE READ THIS AGREEMENT CAREFULLY BEFORE USING THE PROGRAM. IBM WILL LICENSE THE PROGRAM TO YOU ONLY IF YOU FIRST ACCEPT THE TERMS OF THIS AGREEMENT. BY USING THE PROGRAM YOU AGREE TO THESE TERMS. IF YOU DO NOT AGREE TO THE TERMS OF THIS AGREEMENT, PROMPTLY RETURN THE UNUSED PROGRAM TO IBM.

The Program is owned by International Business Machines Corporation or one of its subsidiaries (IBM) or an IBM supplier, and is copyrighted and licensed, not sold.

The term "Program" means the original program and all whole or partial copies of it. A Program consists of machine-readable instructions, its components, data, audio-visual content (such as images, text, recordings, or pictures), and related licensed materials.

This Agreement includes Part 1 - General Terms and Part 2 - Country-unique Terms and is the complete agreement regarding the use of this Program, and replaces any prior oral or written communications between you and IBM. The terms of Part 2 may replace or modify those of Part 1.

1. License

Use of the Program

IBM grants you a nonexclusive, nontransferable license to use the Program.

You may 1) use the Program only for internal evaluation, testing or demonstration purposes, on a trial or "try-and-buy" basis and 2) make and install a reasonable number of copies of the Program in support of such use, unless IBM identifies a specific number of copies in the documentation accompanying the Program. The terms of this license apply to each copy you make. You will reproduce the copyright notice and any other legends of ownership on each copy, or partial copy, of the Program.

You will 1) maintain a record of all copies of the Program and 2) ensure that anyone who uses the Program does so only for your authorized use and in compliance with the terms of this Agreement.

You may not 1) use, copy, modify or distribute the Program except as provided in this Agreement; 2) reverse assemble, reverse compile, or otherwise translate the Program except as specifically permitted by law without the possibility of contractual waiver; or 3) sublicense, rent, or lease the Program.

This license begins with your first use of the Program and ends on the termination of this license in accordance with the terms of this Agreement. You will destroy the Program and all copies made of it within ten days of when this license ends.

2. No Warranty

SUBJECT TO ANY STATUTORY WARRANTIES WHICH CANNOT BE EXCLUDED, IBM MAKES NO WARRANTIES OR CONDITIONS EITHER EXPRESS OR IMPLIED, INCLUDING WITHOUT LIMITATION, THE WARRANTY OF NON-INFRINGEMENT AND THE IMPLIED WARRANTIES OF MERCHANTABILITY AND FITNESS FOR A PARTICULAR PUR-POSE, REGARDING THE PROGRAM OR TECHNICAL SUPPORT, IF ANY. IBM MAKES NO WARRANTY REGARDING THE CAPABILITY OF THE PROGRAM TO CORRECTLY PROCESS, PROVIDE AND/OR RECEIVE DATE DATA WITHIN AND BETWEEN THE 20TH AND 21ST CENTURIES.

This exclusion also applies to any of IBM's subcontractors, suppliers or program developers (collectively called "Suppliers").

Manufacturers, suppliers, or publishers of non-IBM Programs may provide their own warranties.

3. Limitation of Liability

NEITHER IBM NOR ITS SUPPLIERS ARE LIABLE FOR ANY DIRECT OR INDIRECT DAMAGES, INCLUDING WITHOUT LIMITATION, LOST PROFITS, LOST SAVINGS, OR ANY INCIDENTAL, SPECIAL, OR OTHER ECONOMIC CONSE-QUENTIAL DAMAGES, EVEN IF IBM IS INFORMED OF THEIR POSSIBILITY. SOME JURISDICTIONS DO NOT ALLOW THE EXCLUSION OR LIMITATION OF INCIDENTAL OR CONSEQUENTIAL DAMAGES, SO THE ABOVE EXCLUSION OR LIMITATION MAY NOT APPLY TO YOU.

4. General

Nothing in this Agreement affects any statutory rights of consumers that cannot be waived or limited by contract.

IBM may terminate your license if you fail to comply with the terms of this Agreement. If IBM does so, you must immediately destroy the Program and all copies you made of it.

You may not export the Program.

Neither you nor IBM will bring a legal action under this Agreement more than two years after the cause of action arose unless otherwise provided by local law without the possibility of contractual waiver or limitation.

Neither you nor IBM is responsible for failure to fulfill any obligations due to causes beyond its control.

There is no additional charge for use of the Program for the duration of this license.

IBM does not provide program services or technical support, unless IBM specifies otherwise.

The laws of the country in which you acquire the Program govern this Agreement, except 1) in Australia, the laws of the State or Territory in which the transaction is performed govern this Agreement; 2) in Albania, Armenia, Belarus, Bosnia/Herzegovina, Bulgaria, Croatia, Czech Republic, Georgia, Hungary, Kazakhstan, Kirghizia, Former Yugoslav Republic of Macedonia (FYROM), Moldova, Poland, Romania, Russia, Slovak Republic, Slovenia, Ukraine, and Federal Republic of Yugoslavia, the laws of Austria govern this Agreement; 3) in the United Kingdom, all disputes relating to this Agreement will be governed by English Law and will be submitted to the exclusive jurisdiction of the English courts; 4) in Canada, the laws in the Province of Ontario govern this Agreement; and 5) in the United States and Puerto Rico, and People's Republic of China, the laws of the State of New York govern this Agreement.

Part 2 - Country-unique Terms

AUSTRALIA:

No Warranty (Section 2): The following paragraph is added to this Section: Although IBM specifies that there are no warranties, you may have certain rights under the Trade Practices Act 1974 or other legislation and are only limited to the extent permitted by the applicable legislation.

Limitation of Liability (Section 3): The following paragraph is added to this Section: Where IBM is in breach of a condition or warranty implied by the Trade Practices Act 1974, IBM's liability is limited to the repair or replacement of the goods, or the supply of equivalent goods. Where that condition or warranty relates to right to sell, quiet possession or clear title, or the goods are of a kind ordinarily acquired for personal, domestic or household use or consumption, then none of the limitations in this paragraph apply.

GERMANY:

No Warranty (Section 2): The following paragraphs are added to this Section: The minimum warranty period for Programs is six months.

In case a Program is delivered without Specifications, we will only warrant that the Program information correctly describes the Program and that the Program can be used according to the Program information. You have to check the usability according to the Program information within the "money-back guaranty" period. Limitation of Liability (Section 3): The following paragraph is added to this Section: The limitations and exclusions specified in the Agreement will not apply to damages caused by IBM with fraud or gross negligence, and for express warranty.

INDIA:

General (Section 4): The following replaces the fourth paragraph of this Section: If no suit or other legal action is brought, within two years after the cause of action arose, in respect of any claim that either party may have against the other, the rights of the concerned party in respect of such claim will be forfeited and the other party will stand released from its obligations in respect of such claim.

IRELAND:

No Warranty (Section 2): The following paragraph is added to this Section: Except as expressly provided in these terms and conditions, all statutory conditions, including all warranties implied, but without prejudice to the generality of the foregoing, all warranties implied by the Sale of Goods Act 1893 or the Sale of Goods and Supply of Services Act 1980 are hereby excluded.

ITALY:

Limitation of Liability (Section 3): This Section is replaced by the following: Unless otherwise provided by mandatory law, IBM is not liable for any damages which might arise.

NEW ZEALAND:

No Warranty (Section 2): The following paragraph is added to this Section: Although IBM specifies that there are no warranties, you may have certain rights under the Consumer Guarantees Act 1993 or other legislation which cannot be excluded or limited. The Consumer Guarantees Act 1993 will not apply in respect of any goods or services which IBM provides, if you require the goods and services for the purposes of a business as defined in that Act. Limitation of Liability (Section 3): The following paragraph is added to this Section: Where Programs are not acquired for the purposes of a business as defined in the Consumer Guarantees Act 1993, the limitations in this Section are subject to the limitations in that Act.

UNITED KINGDOM:

Limitation of Liability (Section 3): The following paragraph is added to this Section at the end of the first paragraph: The limitation of liability will not apply to any breach of IBM's obligations implied by Section 12 of the Sales of Goods Act 1979 or Section 2 of the Supply of Goods and Services Act 1982.